D1232026

No Prouder Place

CANADIANS AND THE BOMBER COMMAND EXPERIENCE

1939–1945

No Prouder Place

CANADIANS AND THE BOMBER COMMAND EXPERIENCE

1939–1945

DAVID L. BASHOW

Vanwell Publishing Limited

St. Catharines, Ontario

Vanwell Publishing acknowledges the financial support of the Government of Canada through the Book Publishing Industry Development Program for our publishing activities.

Design: Carol Matsuyama
Cover: *Vicky the Vicious Virgin*, painting by Ron Lowry

Vanwell Publishing Limited
1 Northrup Crescent
P.O. Box 2131
St. Catharines, Ontario L2R 7S2
sales@vanwell.com
tel: 905-937-3100
fax: 905-937-1760

Printed in Canada

Library and Archives Canada Cataloguing in Publication
Bashow, David L., 1946–
No prouder place: Canadians and the Bomber Command experience, 1939 to 1945/David L. Bashow.
Includes bibliographical references and index.
ISBN 1-55125-098-5
1. Great Britain. Royal Air Force. Bomber Command—History. 2. World War, 1939–1945—Aerial operations, Canadian. 3. Bombing, Aerial—Germany. I. Title.
D792.C2B373   2005   940.54'4971   C2005-905397-6

Table of Contents

Acknowledgements and Introduction

Like so many books of its kind, *No Prouder Place* has been a collective effort from the outset. It is, first and foremost, a story for and about our aircrew veterans, told in large measure by the veterans themselves. For all those who took the time and the effort to share with us their wartime experiences, I am profoundly grateful.

Many other individuals and organizations provided help along the way. I am grateful to Don Pearsons and his staff at Air Force Heritage and History for their financial assistance, for their moral support, and for their enthusiastic responses to my myriad requests for photographs. The Directorate of History and Heritage at National Defence Headquarters and the Canadian War Museum both generously provided assistance and granted me permission to reproduce some of the key visual elements contained herein. Vic Johnson and his staff at *Airforce* magazine were also exceptionally helpful, and I greatly appreciate their permission to reproduce some key recollections from the veterans gleaned from past *Airforce* articles. At the Royal Military College of Canada (RMC), John Marteinson, Teri Bolton and Monica Muller cheerfully provided invaluable technical assistance and advice when I needed it. Dr. Steve Lukits, Chair of the English Department at RMC, has been a staunch supporter of my efforts and an outstanding sounding board for my ideas on content and structure. His candour and enthusiasm are greatly appreciated.

Thanks also to Major Mike McNorgan for his prompt and thorough photographic research at our National Archives and the Department of National Defence Film Library. And a very special thanks to his brother, Pat McNorgan, for his enthusiastic support, and also for his kind contribution of three original and evocative paintings that I feel really add another dimension of quality to this book. I am extremely grateful to Ron Lowry for the striking cover painting and for his wonderful colour side profiles of representative aircraft from both sides of the bombing campaign. Ron never ceases to amaze me for his exceptional talent and attention to detail, bringing the aircraft to life through the magic of his brushwork.

I am also very grateful to Vanwell Publishing for believing in the book and its merits, and a warm thanks in particular to Angela Dobler. She is a consummately professional editor and this manuscript is far better for having been exposed to her gentle yet thorough touch upon it throughout.

As always, deepest thanks to my dear wife and soul mate Heather, for her tireless support and for her understanding of my far too obsessive behavior, particularly on those three o'clock mornings when most ideas materialized and begged expression.

Readers should note that considerable thought and effort went into the structuring and the formatting of this book. In the end, I decided to present the story in a chronological rather than a thematic manner. However, since the book is first and foremost a story about human behavior under great stresses, and while the human element of the bombing campaign permeates the text from start to finish, I have deliberately devoted an entire chapter to human themes and issues at around the halfway mark. Also, a detailed analysis of the costs and the gains of the bombing campaign has been deliberately relegated to an appendix, in order not to interrupt the flow and the style of the story itself. Having said that, I sincerely hope readers will not overlook this portion of the book, since I feel it is essential to understanding what Bomber Command achieved during the Second World War, and at what cost.

One of the most distinguished Canadians to serve in wartime Bomber Command was Reginald John Lane from Victoria, British Columbia. Commencing operations in the dark, dark days of 1941, Reg Lane would go on to complete three full operational tours, command the elite 405 "City of Vancouver" Squadron within the Pathfinder Force, rise to the rank of group captain at age twenty-four, and win the Distinguished Service Order, two Distinguished Flying Crosses, and a Mention-in-Despatches along the way. He would also meet the love of his life, Barbara Andrews, a Yorkshire lass whose home was very close to the Canadian 6 Group's headquarters. Lane had an equally stellar peacetime career, filling many senior appointments in the postwar Royal Canadian Air Force and the Canadian Forces, rising to the rank of lieutenant-general and serving as Deputy Commander-in-Chief, North American Air Defence Command before his eventual retirement in December 1974. At that time, he was appointed a Commander of the American Legion of Merit for his distinguished contributions to both Canada and the United States in the cause of peace.

A gregarious, effervescent man who lived life to the full, always with his dear wife Barbara at his side, General Lane was a tremendous source of assistance, motivation, and inspiration to me in the preparation of this book. He had reviewed the draft manuscript during the late summer of 2003. I was thrilled when he told me how taken he had been with it, and how he felt it had captured the essence of the Bomber Command experience. I was equally honoured when he agreed to write the book's foreword. Sadly, that was not to be. Reginald John Lane passed away abruptly in October 2003, before he had a chance to put pen to paper. However, Barbara Lane has graciously consented to write the foreword in his stead. This is as it should be, for the story of Reg and Barbara Lane is not only a war story, but also a love story, a love forged in the tumult and uncertainty of wartime, and one that endured and flourished in peacetime. They had been together for sixty years when Reg passed away, and in Barbara's own words to me, theirs was "a perfect marriage." Hers is also a highly significant and unique perspective since, in her way, Barbara Lane speaks for all the loved ones of those gallant crews who waged their relentless battle night after night, day after day, so long ago now. I am deeply honoured and appreciative that Barbara has consented to grace these opening pages with her thoughts.

—David L. Bashow
  Kingston, Ontario
  July 2005

Foreword

Before my husband Reg passed away from a sudden heart attack on the 2nd of October 2003, he had agreed to write the foreword for this book, No Prouder Place, a tribute to the Canadian contribution to Bomber Command's wartime endeavours. After his untimely death, David Bashow suggested that I might write the foreword on Reg's behalf, but from my own perspective.

For me, this book is full of nostalgia, and many of the personal experiences of the aircrews themselves are told in their own words, from their own recollections. The pages also contain a wealth of research. While the book is somewhat detailed and technical in places, I am confident that aircrew such as my husband, historians, and devotees of the period will understand it, perhaps better than my particular vantage point and background permits. Having said that, I also served in the Royal Observer Corps during the war and, as a result, I was able to understand the complexity of many of the situations mentioned herein.

I was born in England and lived there until I met my future husband in 1944, married him in Yorkshire in 1945, and sailed for Canada aboard the S.S. *Aquitania* in June 1946. We were introduced to each other by my pre-war dancing teacher. She joined the Women's Auxiliary Air Force (WAAF) and, after receiving her commission, was attached to the Canadian 6 Group Headquarters at Allerton Hall in Yorkshire. Reg had recently arrived at Allerton as Senior Operations Officer (Air 1), fresh from being commanding officer of 405 Pathfinder Squadron at Great Gransden, Bedfordshire.

My friend thought it would be a good idea for us to meet. When she telephoned me, I was very hesitant—a group captain must be *old*, at least thirty, and I was nineteen! However, I agreed, rather reluctantly, and we all met at the Queen's Hotel in Leeds. After having a drink, my friend left, leaving me with Reg to have dinner. By now, I was pleasantly surprised to find that he was a *young*, 24-year-old group captain! I took him to meet my parents and their friends at their local pub in the country. He seemed to enjoy the evening and he was invited by my parents to stay with us at any time. Reg subsequently became very close to my parents, and although I was their only child, they were quite happy when we became engaged about eight months after our first meeting.

After VE-Day, he was scheduled to go out to the Pacific and to the Japanese war as Chief of Bomber Command Operations in that theatre, and Reg said he did not wish to get married until the war was over. By this time, he was stationed at Bushy Park, preparing to fly to Okinawa. Fortunately for us, as he was about to enter the aircraft to go overseas, an orderly ran to stop him and told him that an atomic bomb had just been dropped on Hiroshima. In short order, VJ-Day was being celebrated and plans were underway for our wedding. Reg was then asked to stay in England after we were married to become the station commander at RAF Odiham in Hampshire. From there, Dakotas were flying to the continent to help with food relief, displaced persons, and so on.

This marked the beginning for me of a wonderful life as an air force wife. We had a perfect marriage, which resulted in four kind and loving children. Without them, I could not have endured my great and recent loss. I did not know Reg during his most hectic and dangerous bombing days, which was fortunate for me, but I do recall him talking about his experiences during the raid on the *Tirpitz*. He had watched his friend Don McIntyre's aircraft ahead of him as it caught fire, but he was in trouble himself. Flak had smashed into his Halifax's main wing spar, narrowly missing a fuel tank. The flight home became a nerve-jangling endurance test, with the crew waiting to see if the spar would fail and send the aircraft spinning into the North Sea.

On another trip, he returned with 120 holes in the fuselage and wings. As the ground crew said the next day, "Sunshine" must have flown with a gentle touch or his wings would have fallen off. "Sunshine" was his nickname in 35 Squadron. He was *my* "Sunshine."

—Barbara Lane
 Victoria, British Columbia

Prologue

*The more darkness in night attacks hinders and impedes the sight,
the more must one supply the place of actual vision by skill and care.*

—Scipio Africanus
236–184 BC

Give me five years and you will not recognize Germany again.

—Adolf Hitler
Circa 1933

In 1346, at the battle of Crécy, King Edward III and the English army were faced with dreadful, near-hopeless combat odds. Knowing this, Edward gave the place of both greatest honour and greatest danger to his eldest son, the sixteen-year-old Black Prince. That place was commanding the vanguard on the right of the line. The ensuing battle was arduous, and Black Prince's division bore the brunt, but the English prevailed. From these origins, the Right of the Line has become synonymous in battle as the vanguard, or place of greatest danger, and in ceremony, as the place of greatest honour.

And so it was for Bomber Command during the Second World War, acting for a very long time as freedom's vanguard when no other significant offensive action by Britain and the Dominions or the enslaved nations of Occupied Europe was possible. Mirroring Canada's Great War efforts, as part of a contribution all out of proportion to the nation's population and economic capacity, Canadian airmen played a proud and distinguished role in the bomber offensive, from the first day of conflict until the last. Indeed, with over 10,000 fatalities from a wartime total of approximately 40,000 Canadian aircrew who served with Bomber Command, Canada was by an enormous margin the second-largest contributor of personnel to the British portion of the bombing campaign. *No Prouder Place* will celebrate the Canadian achievements, but always within the broader context of the bomber offensive itself, and how it evolved and developed, based upon changing needs and circumstances.

In order to appreciate and understand the Allied bomber offensive over Europe, inaccuracies, both unwitting and contrived, that have characterized this campaign must be put right. While it is always proper to seek the truth behind man's actions, one must question somewhat the appropriateness of reviewing history through a lens of present-day sensitivities in an attempt to second-guess the motives of those who acted in good conscience based upon perceived needs and information available at the time. Unfortunately, it has become somewhat fashionable to apply unsubstantiated revisionism with respect to the morals, motives and methods of men of character making difficult decisions in real time during the prosecution of this campaign. By the same token, little effort has been made to tabulate and update the results of the bombing, results that were far more successful than has been generally previously acknowledged. This book shall attempt to redress those shortcomings with respect to the documentation of policy, plans, operations, and results, while paying particular attention to the human side of the effort.

The reader must bear in mind that while the bomber offensive, including the campaign against the German industrial cities, was being waged, the majority of Britons and Canadians alike were in favour of it. The first significant seeds of the moral controversy surrounding the campaign were sown by the immediate postwar US Strategic Bombing Survey and the smaller report of the British Bombing Survey Unit. Both surveys were in part critical of what the bombing had achieved with respect to the curtailment of industrial production, but ignored the fact that even the bomber offensive's most ardent advocates at the time did not feel that bombing alone could shut down German war production completely. One member of the US survey team was the American economist John Kenneth Galbraith, who later contradicted his own findings by declaring that the bombing had been largely a waste of time and effort. He stated, "We were beginning to see that we were encountering one of the greatest, perhaps the greatest, miscalculations of the war."[1] His inconsistent observations laid the foundations for widespread criticism of the campaign during the latter half of the Twentieth Century. However, much more scholarship has since been completed, and it presents a different and more accurate analysis of the results of the bombing.

Skeptics who note that some elements of German war production significantly increased during the later war years do not take into account that the Reich's war production was running well below maximum capacity when hostilities commenced, and would not significantly change until Germany's declaration of Total War after the German defeat at Stalingrad in January 1943. The destabilization and decentralization of the war industries was intensely distracting and inefficient, borne to a great extent on the backs of an enormous slave-labour force dragooned from the Nazi-occupied territories. The mind boggles at what industrial capacity this slave state could have achieved without diversions created by the bombings.

Allied bombing during the Second World War was both tactical and strategic in application. It was, to a great extent, an independent campaign wherein the properties changed from time to time, but which evolved as a prerequisite for a land invasion of the European continent. One of its highlights was the subsidiary Anglo-American Combined Bombing Offensive of 1943 and 1944, tasked among other things with the defeat of the *Luftwaffe* and all its components. This campaign, which included direct attacks on aircraft production, aircraft in transit, and airfields, would deal a catastrophic blow to the overall German war effort and to the Reich's ability to defend itself.

Regarding the bombing of industrial urban centres and the concomitant necessity for the Germans to decentralize or disperse their manufacturing:

> In some cases large resources were tied up in building new factories in bomb-safe areas in a situation where building labour and materials were in desperately short supply. The impact on German morale was equally debilitating. Bombing did not produce the overthrow of the Hitler regime but the effect on those regularly subjected to bombing in the major industrial areas was intensely demoralizing.[2]

German citizens interviewed after the cessation of hostilities were nearly unanimous in their viewpoint that the bombing had been the hardest wartime condition to bear. The campaign distorted and distracted German strategy and forced a massive diversion of resources to counter the bombing threat, shifting vital men and materiel away from the other combat theatres. Due to the overwhelming need for fighter aircraft to counter the bombers, and the concentration of those resources in northwest Europe, the German armies, from 1943 onward, found themselves gradually deprived of air support at a time when Allied production of combat aircraft began dramatically rising.

> Bombing not only diverted German military effort to home defence on a large scale, but also encouraged desperate solutions from Hitler that further undermined economic capacity and postponed the introduction of military technologies that might have had a decisive effect.[3]

With respect to the human element of the bomber offensive, Marshal of the Royal Air Force Sir Michael Beetham, himself a distinguished Bomber Command wartime pilot, had this to say:

"The bomber crews did not enjoy what they had to do. They were very conscious that some innocent civilians unavoidably were being killed in the course of the bombing of industrial cities, but they had a job to do and knew that war was a bloody business."[4]

Geoff Marlow, who flew a distinguished late-war tour of operations as a pilot with 434 Squadron also had thoughts on this subject:

> I looked down from my cockpit at the city below. It seemed that most of the buildings were already roofless and in ruins, and I felt uncomfortable about dropping more bombs on those below who had already suffered such misery. I also admired the fighting spirit of these people who refused to give up, but my admiration was coupled with a deep anger at leaders whose undying fanaticism caused the slaughter to continue long after they knew they would lose the war.
> . . . They (our airmen) met their death in various ways. Some had gone without warning when their bomb load exploded from impact with the ground or another plane. Others went down with their bombers burning from end to end, spinning wildly out of control, unable to bail out because of injury or being trapped within the aircraft. Others had feverishly managed to abandon ship, only to float down into the freezing cold of the wintry sea on into a mob of infuriated civilians seeking revenge for the loss of their homes or loved ones.[5]

However, it should be noted at the outset that the campaign against the industrial cities was but

a fraction of Bomber Command's overall wartime effort, and its other significant contributions shall also be discussed in depth.

The reader should prepare for the reality that the early bombing was not very effective, but it was the only significant offensive weapon available to the western Allies for a protracted period. It served notice to the Axis powers and gave hope to Britons and their allies by visibly demonstrating that they could, and *would*, strike back.

> Even the pyramids will pale against the masses of concrete and stone colossi which I am erecting . . . I am building for eternity—for . . . we are the last Germany.
>
> —Adolf Hitler, 1936

ONE

Prelude to War

There is no prouder place,
none more deserving of honour,
than the right of the line.
—John Terraine

Without doubt, British bombing policy during the Second World War was influenced by the strategic aerial bombardment experiences of the First World War. Over one hundred German *Zeppelin* and giant fixed-wing bomber raids on Britain produced nearly 3500 casualties.[1] Moreover, they generated widespread shock, a sense of vulnerability, and a significant disruption of wartime production out of proportion to the actual damage inflicted. This widespread disruption included lost time due to the suspension of manufacturing, the upheaval of transportation systems, worker consternation and anxiety, and the diversion of limited human and materiel resources to directly combat these threats. To a much lesser extent, the Independent Force of the Royal Air Force conducted a limited strategic bombing campaign against the enemy's core industries towards the end of the war. However, General Sir Hugh Trenchard, the Independent Force's first commander and later the RAF's Chief of the Air Staff from 1919 to 1929, staunchly maintained, throughout the 1920s, that the psychological impact of the bombing significantly overshadowed the material damage, in his view, by a factor of twenty to one.[2] A postwar bombing survey team had concluded that while the material damage had indeed been light, panic had been widely reported in the cities that had been bombed. In attempting to foresee the future utility of aerial bombardment, and based on the bombing results observed in both Britain and Germany, the air staff of Trenchard's day felt that material damage to the enemy would be very secondary compared to the chaos sown by the moral (or morale) collapse of personnel working in the vital public services sectors, such as water supply, food distribution, lighting, power, and transportation.[3] Thus, throughout the 1920s and early 1930s, Hugh Trenchard, later reinforced by British Prime Minister Stanley Baldwin (in relative lockstep with the doctrine espoused by the Italian General Guilio Douhet and the American General "Billy" Mitchell), essentially shaped the RAF's conventional wisdom that "the bomber would always get through," and that determined aerial attacks on the enemy's war economy "would produce such crushing damage to both natural resources and civilian morale that the opponent would have to sue for peace."[4]

There was a strong countering sentiment, however, to establish a strict set of international rules to govern the use of this new weapon. Doctor David Hall of Oxford has noted: "The 1923 Hague Draft Rules of Aerial Warfare was the first authoritative attempt to clarify and formulate a comprehensive code of conduct, but they were never adopted in legally binding terms. Growing awareness of the military potential of aircraft throughout the 1920s and 1930s ultimately proved too serious an obstacle to reaching an agreement."[5] A significant deterrent to reaching consensus was the inability to establish what constituted a legitimate military target under new conditions of total warfare between industrialized nations:

> Factories making armaments and the transport bringing them to the battle fronts naturally were included in the category of legitimate targets once the means of attacking them were available. Consequently those civilians in them or dangerously close to them might just have to be equated with civilians in legitimately attacked places. Moreover, precedent was on the side of the air planners. Naval bombardment of ports and towns was an accepted act of war. It was even codified in Article 2 of the Convention on Naval Bombardment, signed at The Hague in 1907. Article 2 stipulated that a naval commander who used his ship's guns to destroy military objectives in an undefended port or town "[incurred] no responsibility for any unavoidable damage which may be caused by a bombardment under such circumstances." The advent of air power merely increased the opportunity of reaching and destroying such targets.[6]

British historian Richard Holmes has also offered a comment on the ambiguity of international law with respect to aerial bombardment at the time:

> Briefly, an attacker is required to exercise discrimination when this does not increase the risk to his own personnel, *but the ultimate responsibility for the fate of civilians in a siege lies with the defender, who may at any time put an end to their suffering by surrender*, and whose counter measures may reduce the possibility of discrimination, for example by obliging the attacker to bomb from a greater altitude or by night.[7]

Not surprisingly then, when Bomber Command was officially established in 1936, the RAF War Manual of that year clearly stated that "the bomb is the chief weapon of an air force."[8] And the new command was formed within a parent service that had been seamlessly committed to the utility of a strategic bombing policy from that service's inception during the Great War. Furthermore, the perception of the relative invulnerability of the bomber had been erroneously reinforced through acts of indiscriminate aerial bombardment of civilians by various totalitarian nations of the day, including the Japanese on Hankow and other defenceless Chinese coastal settlements, the Italians on native villages in Ethiopia and, perhaps most notably, by the fascists under the Spanish Generalissimo Francisco Franco on Barcelona and then Guernica in April 1937. These bombings served chilling notice to the western democracies of a distinct lack of scruples associated with the use of this weapon by the totalitarian regimes; a realization that would be strongly reinforced during the opening innings of the Second World War. The greatest concern rested with Germany, which was now regarded as being Britain's most likely future enemy.

On 14 July 1936, Bastille Day, Bomber Command formed as part of a broad-brush reorganization of the RAF. Along with the formation of distinct Fighter, Coastal, and Training Commands, this structural change was made in order to encourage greater specialization and to promote greater efficiency. It provided Bomber Command with a more distinct and defined strategic role, based on a growing conviction among air planners that long range air attacks deep into enemy territory could be productive. At issue was the precise role the command would perform in the event of war, and this was initially not clearly defined. It was conceived primarily as a deterrent, to be used only for bombing military targets. Senior military and political leaders only vaguely assumed that RAF bombing policy would re-engage where it had left off in 1918, its *raison d'être* to attack enemy industrial centres to deprive them of war materials and also to demoralize the population.[9]

During the period of rearmament from 1934 onwards, the role of bombing was defined more specifically:

1. To assist in the defence of Britain by attacking enemy airpower assets;
2. To assist the army and the Royal Navy (RN); and
3. To attack an enemy's economy, but only under circumstances where the government felt that an attack on enemy civilians could be justified.[10]

However, late in 1937, the Royal Air Force was given the task of deciding what specific economic and military targets it should attack if it were required to do so. To that end, the Air Ministry penned the Western Air Plans, a list of thirteen specific RAF objectives in the event of war. Contained within these objectives were three which applied directly to Bomber Command:

1. Attacks on the enemy's air striking force;
2. Direct support of military operations by disabling enemy communications behind the battle front; and
3. Attacks on the German war industries, especially those situated within Germany's industrial heartland, the Ruhr.[11]

In September 1937, Bomber Command's second commander-in-chief, Air Marshal Sir Edgar Ludlow-Hewitt, declared himself to be most enthusiastic about the third objective. Ludlow-Hewitt felt that an enemy's air assets, now broadly assumed to be those of Germany, would be too widely dispersed and therefore either too hard to bomb or beyond the effective range of command aircraft. A similar argument was made for enemy road and rail lines of communication. Therefore, the Command's senior staff believed that attacks on German industry were more achievable and had more strategic utility than the other two objectives.

In December, Bomber Command was asked to draw up a prioritized list of targets, which was done jointly by military Air Intelligence and the civilian Targets Sub-Committee, a branch of the Industrial Intelligence Centre. Given a need to target the most critical elements of a complex industrial system, the military planners favoured attacks on the electrical power grid, while the civilian agency promoted attacks on the Ruhr dams, as well as rail and canal transportation lines. In the end, the Air Staff of the RAF felt both these directions and their predicted results were excessively optimistic. Furthermore, the Joint Chiefs of Staff, the ultimate uniformed decision-making body in Britain, was also unconvinced. Therefore, Bomber Command was told to restrict its operations to those against the enemy air force and to the protection of British shipping. Also, for the time being, only clearly identifiable military targets were to be attacked.

However, Ludlow-Hewitt knew that his force had some serious limitations. The conversion from antediluvian First World War vintage aircraft to newer, more modern types was taking longer than anticipated. The light bombers, such as the Fairey Battle and the Bristol Blenheim, were altogether unsuitable for longer-range, heavy bombing missions. Even the newer, heavier twin-engine bombers which were coming on board from 1936 onwards, the Handley-Page Hampden, the Armstrong-Whitworth Whitley, and the Vickers Wellington could not, with a full bomb load, range much further afield than the Ruhr valley. Defensive armament was at best sparse and of mere rifle calibre. Electronic aids to navigation were virtually non-existent and only the Whitleys, the least competent of the new-series bombers, were conducting any night flying training at all. Targets were often virtually impossible to locate, even in broad daylight or bright moonlight in friendly environments. Furthermore, it was 1939 before the Command acknowledged that the pilot could not simultaneously fly and navigate the aircraft. This eventually led to specific training for a crew navigator; a task initially performed by the observer, along with the dropping of bombs.[12] Undoubtedly, the early thinking that pilots could and should essentially do everything had contributed to gross inefficiencies and a ghastly accident record. In the two years immediately prior to the outbreak of hostilities, there had been 478 accidental forced landings in the command simply because pilots lost their way. Furthermore, most of these accidents occurred in fair-weather daylight.[13] Bombing accuracy was a joke. The primitive bombsights of the day introduced gross errors in accuracy if even one of myriad release parameters was conservatively violated. From a relatively high level, such as 10,000 feet, only three out of every 100 bombs dropped landed remotely near the target area.[14]

In 1936 one of the key proponents of a heavy versus a medium bomber force was Group Captain Arthur Harris, Bomber Command's Deputy Director of Plans at the time. An Englishman who spent a number of his formative years in Rhodesia, Harris would win his argument for a longer-range offensive capability. A new specification thus called for a bomber capable of flying 3000 miles while carrying a bomb payload of 8000 pounds at 28,000 feet. The four-engine Short Stirling of 1941 was developed to meet these criteria, and this aircraft proved to be significantly disappointing with respect to the specified service ceiling. In 1938, further specifications were issued for an ideal bomber, which also possessed much better defensive armament so that it could cope with the latest generation of fighter aircraft. It was also to have a top speed of 300 mph and the ability to carry 12,000 pounds of bombs. These capabilities would eventually be achieved by modifying the designs of two-engine bombers into successful four-engine variants. They would evolve into the Lancaster and the Halifax, which would become the mainstay aircraft of the Command from 1942 onwards.

Under a series of pre-war expansion schemes, the Air Staff planned to phase in forty-one medium bomber squadrons and eighty-five heavy bomber squadrons by the spring of 1941. However, the British industrial capacity of the period could not cope with this ambitious plan. A significant amount of the rearmament budget had been required to create the necessary industrial infrastructure. Manpower expansion was much more positive. The RAF Volunteer Reserve was established in 1937, and its mandate was to train 800 pilots per year. But the public response exceeded all expectations. During the next three years, it produced more than 5000 pilots and it drew volunteers from all of the Dominions. On the eve of war, the RAF had a manpower strength of 118,000 regular force members and 68,000 reservists. The Command's most pressing need was for new airfields capable of handling the heavier aircraft coming on line, and this included appropriate runways and maintenance facilities. By 1939, Bomber Command operated 27 airfields in the south and east of Britain, divided among four operational groups and one reserve group. This infrastructure was already 300 percent of 1934 levels. The Command's first headquarters was located at Langley in Buckinghamshire. The better-known High Wycombe facility would not become Bomber Command's nerve centre until 1940.

Just prior to the Munich Crisis of 1938, Ludlow-Hewitt told Prime Minister Neville Chamberlain that Bomber Command was virtually useless in its present state. He offered that his aircraft could only reach the peripheries of northwestern Germany, and that they would incur unacceptably high combat losses against the known German defences. In this extraordinarily frank admission, he maintained that to commit the Command to offensive action in its present state would be courting a major disaster. Even more than eighteen months later, when the German Blitzkrieg rolled through France and the Low Countries, the Command was mainly confined to assisting the land battle on the continent, still having nothing but the most rudimentary attack capabilities. Other than assistance to the land forces, Bomber Command was limited to reconnaissance duties, propaganda (leaflet) raids and sorties against naval targets in the North Sea and on its peripheries. The following full statement of military objectives on the very brink of war is telling. (Public shock and fear of indiscriminate civilian bombardment was by then looming large.) It also acknowledges a joint Anglo-French agreement reached in April 1939 which was intended to avoid the intentional bombing of civilians:

> Our policy in respect of air bombardment at the outset of a war was agreed with the French in the course of the Staff Conversations in London in April this year in the following terms. "The Allies would not initiate air action against any but purely 'military' objectives in the narrowest sense of the term, i.e., Naval, Army and Air Forces and establishments, and as far as possible would confine it to objectives on which attack would not involve loss of civil life."
>
> Action against objectives will be subject to the following general principles:
> (a) The intentional bombardment of civil populations is illegal.
> (b) It must be possible to distinguish and identify the objective in question.
> (c) Bombardment must be carried out in such a way that there is a reasonable expectation that damage will be confined to the objective and that civilian populations in the neighbourhood are not bombarded through negligence.[15]

Policy makers made it quite clear that unrestricted aerial warfare was not considered to be in the best interests of Great Britain. The ban on posing a risk to civilian lives would only be lifted the following May, and even then somewhat tentatively, when Winston Churchill replaced Neville Chamberlain as Prime Minister. Therefore, Bomber Command would be forced, for better or worse, to accept this stringent limitation on its conduct well beyond the outbreak of hostilities.

And where did Canadian airmen factor into these precursors to war? By 1934, the Canadian government was beginning to see the need for a renewed emphasis on national defence spending in general and on military aviation in particular, although it was not imbued with quite the same sense of urgency as were many Britons. As tensions in Europe continued to mount, however, appropriations for the Royal Canadian Air Force increased, albeit modestly. Nonetheless, it took the Munich Crisis of 1938 to really reinforce the lamentable state of the Canadian military. In order to counter the harsh realities of technological obsolescence and diminutive force structure, the January 1939 Parliament approved an unprecedented $60 million appropriation for defence spending, of which $23.5 million would be earmarked for the RCAF. The plan was to build an operational air force of eleven permanent and twelve auxiliary squadrons, although all of them were to be dedicated to home defence, with no provision being made at that time for a Canadian expeditionary force to reinforce the RAF in time of need. By the spring of 1940, the RCAF expected to have 250 aircraft on strength and a further 107 on order.[16] Modernization, however, was going to be a painful and protracted process. Obsolete and underpowered Fairey Battle light bombers and a handful of Hawker Hurricane fighters were the most "cutting-edge" aircraft in the service inventory at the commencement of hostilities.

Many young Canadian men joined the Royal Air Force during the inter-war years, and they did so for myriad reasons. According to Canadian historian Hugh Halliday:

> For many it was a burning wish to fly, coupled with the belief that Britain offered more opportunities than Canada, where the Depression had savaged both the RCAF and com-mercial firms. No doubt there were also political convictions—the sense that Fascism was a growing menace that had to be stopped, and the RAF would be part of that process before the RCAF. A few may have had more personal motives.[17]

Halliday makes it clear, for example, that one eventual Canadian luminary in Fighter Command left medical school in Canada and sailed to Britain after ending a troublesome affair with a woman. Foreign military service apparently provided an expedient solution to his problems.[18]

Known collectively as CAN/RAFs, the earliest of these sons of the Dominion date their RAF service from the end of the Great War. Perhaps the most famous was Raymond Collishaw, Canada's sixty-one-victory ace from Nanaimo, British Columbia. In June 1940, Collishaw commanded all operational RAF units in Egypt as an air commodore. Group Captain Harold Spencer Kirby of Hamilton and Calgary was another distinguished veteran of the First World War. During the Battle of France, he would command a bomber wing of the RAF's Advanced Air Striking Force.[19] Other CAN/RAFs also eventually achieved high rank in RAF service.

During the 1920s and early 1930s, a trickle of worthy Canadian lads joined the RAF through nomination to the RAF Cadet College at Cranwell, and also as recent graduates of Canada's Royal Military College. Once rearmament commenced in earnest during the mid-1930s, an ever-increasing number of "Imperials" applied to join the RAF as both aircrew and ground crew. Hugh Halliday maintains that as many as 950 CAN/RAF aircrew, serving as both commissioned and non-commissioned members, and many additional members in the ground trades may have been in RAF service at the outbreak of the war. However, Halliday feels that there would not have been more than 700 CAN/RAF pilots or observers who had achieved a measure of operational proficiency by that time.[20] Many of them were serving with Bomber Command squadrons when war was declared. Most of them were very eager to take the fight to the enemy. Most would not have long to wait.

TWO

To War: The Early Innings

1939–1941

We had to make war as we must, and not as we should like to do.

—Lord Kitchener
20 August 1915

Whoever lights the torch of war in Europe can wish for nothing but chaos.

—Adolf Hitler
Speech to Reichstag, 21 May 1935

A Force with Limitations

On 31 August 1939, Bomber Command had a paper strength of 55 squadrons and 920 aircraft, but three days later, its effective strength had plummeted to 25 squadrons and 352 aircraft. They were clustered in four groups, each flying a single type: Bristol Blenheims, Armstrong Whitworth Whitleys, Vickers Wellingtons, and Handley Page Hampdens, all twin-engine monoplanes. This extremely rapid force reduction occurred because ten squadrons equipped with 160 obsolete single-engine Fairey Battles were deployed to France as the Advanced Air Striking Force (AASF) on 2 September, only to be decimated in combat the following spring. Also, two Blenheim squadrons from 2 Group were assigned to the British Expeditionary Force (BEF) as part of its air component, and one of the Whitley squadrons was not yet operationally ready. Seventeen of the remaining squadrons could not be mobilized, since they had been saddled with training mandates on the outbreak of hostilities.

While all the RAF's twin-engine bombers were relatively modern, they were certainly primitive compared to the four-engine types that would soon follow them into service. None possessed more than the most basic bomb sights, and all lacked electronic aids for navigation or bombing. Perhaps most important, their defensive armament had been woefully neglected. Their performance capabilities were variable; their limited effective ranges were the most glaring and consistent deficiency.

That ponderous, graceless, "old flying cow," the Whitley, had entered service in March 1937. It was slow, cumbersome, heavy and unresponsive on the controls, but it was the first heavy British bomber to have a retractable undercarriage and turreted defensive armament. Jack Watts, a stalwart Canadian Bomber Command veteran, recalls: "When you saw a Whitley take off, it was really quite amusing. It looked just like a bloodhound going down the track."[1] This "nose down, slab-sided and plank-winged lumbering giant"[2] also had an all-metal stressed skin fuselage, it was immensely strong, and it was stable as a rock. The definitive Mark IV variant, in service from May 1939, was powered by two Rolls-Royce Merlin X engines, but it had a humble top speed of only 245 mph at 16,250 feet. It also maintained a disturbing, characteristic 8.5 degree nose-down attitude in level flight, but had a bomb-carrying payload of 3400 pounds. Reginald Lane, a Canadian Bomber Command legend (from whom much more will be heard in the ensuing pages) sardonically recalls the Whitley as "the dear cow that would take off at 100 miles per hour, climb at 100 miles per hour, and stall at 100 miles per hour, even with its perpetual nose-down attitude."[3] Whitleys were exceptionally unpopular with those who flew in them. Although robust, they were underpowered and drafty in the extreme, and this prompted one Whitley veteran to observe that when one flew through rain in this supposedly enclosed aircraft, one got wet. Charles Patterson, a wartime Whitley pilot, undoubtedly spoke for many when he observed: "I'd never seen such a dreadful boring-looking thing, nose-down, going at what looked like about fifty mph."[4] Nonetheless, the Whitley soldiered on for years.

The Hampden was "terrible to fly in, cramped, no heat, no facilities where you could relieve yourself . . . but a joy to fly."[5] Sleek and manoeuverable, the "Flying Panhandle," "Flying Tadpole," or "Flying Suitcase" had a distinctive, deep fuselage, which gracefully tapered to a slender tail boom. However, this unorthodox construction guaranteed early obsolescence because there was no room in the fuselage for future development. The Hampden entered service in 1938, and although it could carry 4000 pounds of bombs and had defensive guns in dorsal, ventral, and frontal positions, these weapons were very light and limited in their traversing capability. With its two 1000-horsepower Bristol Pegasus engines at full throttle, the Hampden could charge along at a respectable 265 mph. However, it was not without vices, as Canadian Hampden pilot Terry Godwin recalls:

> We learned that the Hampden had a bad habit that if you skidded or slipped, the rudder bar would slam over and a stabilized yaw would result. One member of our course took his Hampden up to 10,000 feet and wilfully put it into a stabilized yaw. He got it out at 4000 feet! Quite often when turning on a final approach to land, if things were not just right, such a yaw would occur with no height to recover.[6]

Another distinguished CAN/RAF Hampden pilot, Wing Commander Cam Weir, who commanded 61 Squadron in 5 Group while they were flying Hampdens, had attempted to seek such a fault in the aircraft, to no avail. He also wrote an official letter to the Air Ministry to that effect. However, his original opinion of an aerodynamically fault-free Hampden was short-lived:

> Some weeks later they were doing an army co-op exercise shooting up an ack-ack post at 50 feet. He (Weir) noted an army major standing there and watching him. The rudder bar

slammed over, he realized he was going to crash, so all in a split second he decided to reduce power, in fact, right off. The plane came out of the yaw and he landed safely back at base. He sent off a much different letter than he had originally . . . The same fault appeared in the Mark I and the Mark II Halifax. It was corrected in the Mark III.[7]

In spite of its shortcomings, the Hampden was in continuous action over the continent for the first two years of the war. Nelles Woods Timmerman, a Canadian from Kingston, Ontario, who joined the RAF in 1936 and enjoyed a distinguished wartime career in Bomber Command, thought highly of the Hampden. "It was a great aircraft to fly, with excellent visibility from the cockpit, and responsive, superior handling characteristics, even at low speeds. I felt, however, that it was poorly armed, with one fixed and one moveable .303 machine gun forward and twin .303 guns in the dorsal and ventral positions."[8] Although Timmerman may have been unimpressed with the Hampden's defensive armament, others were certainly impressed with the way he used it. During the spring of 1940, Timmerman was flying Hampdens with 49 Squadron out of Scampton in Lincolnshire. On the night of 1/2 May, after returning from an abortive mine-laying mission near Norderney in the Frisian Islands, he made Bomber Command history by engaging an enemy Arado 196 floatplane with his front gun and successfully driving it into the sea. Arthur Harris himself, then the 5 Group commander, was instrumental in recommending Timmerman for a Distinguished Flying Cross (DFC) for this singular feat. His recommendation formed part of the official award citation: "[Timmerman] is the first pilot of a Hampden to destroy an enemy aircraft with his front gun. His enthusiasm, zeal, cool determination in the face of the heaviest opposition and the outstanding example he has set, are worthy of the highest award."[9]

Light yet powerful, the Bristol Blenheim was in service from 1938 onwards. It was blisteringly fast for its day with a top speed of 307 mph. However, it lacked range and, like its contemporaries, it was under-armed. Furthermore, it was only able to carry a disappointing maximum of 1000 pounds of bombs in its minuscule internal bomb bay. Nonetheless, because of its speed, its vulnerability and its limited effectiveness as a daylight bomber, it was employed for a short period as a night fighter until more suitable types became available. Air Vice-Marshal Tony Dudgeon, a decorated Blenheim pilot, recalls its vulnerability:

> The Blenheim is a lovely aeroplane to fly, but it is about as damage-resistant as an electric light bulb. It had no self-sealing tanks or anything and if you got hit by something-or-other, frankly speaking, you'd had it.[10]

The most successful of Bomber Command's wartime starting stable was the Vickers Wellington. Affectionately nicknamed the "Wimpy" after J. Wellington Wimpy, Popeye's corpulent hamburger-eating chum, the somewhat portly Wellington was a docile yet lively performer. Initially powered by Pegasus engines, the single engine performance of the earlier Marks was referred to as "a long, controlled dive," but later variants fared much better, powered by either Bristol Hercules or Pratt and Whitney R-1830 radials, both of which were in the 1600 horsepower class. As was the case with Bomber Command's other twins in early 1930, Wellingtons were hacked down in droves during the early, unescorted daylight raids. In spite of this inauspicious start, the doughty Wellington became by far the most important, enduring, and endearing of the twins, serving as the mainstay of the Command until four-engine types appeared in numbers. Although largely obsolete over Europe by mid-1943, the most refined and numerous variant of the type, the Mark

X, could routinely carry nearly as great a bomb load at 4500 pounds as the four-engine American B-17 Flying Fortresses and B-24 Liberators, and it could carry up to 6500 pounds of ordnance on short-haul missions.

The Wellington's fabric-covered geodetic "basket weave" construction was the brainchild of an outstanding engineer named Barnes Neville Wallis. Strong and yet flexible, it allowed both flak and cannon shells to pass through without creating significant structural damage, unless a vital component was hit. The extensive fabric covering merely served to streamline the aircraft and to keep out the elements—something that could not be said for Whitleys. The aircraft's critical weight and stress points were so broadly distributed that enormous portions of it could be shot away and it would still doggedly bring its crews home. When flying alone at night, its requirements for defensive armament and fuel were less than its requirements during formation endeavours, and the "Wimpy" applied these weight savings toward carrying a greater bomb load. Rugged and capable, possessed of shortcomings but no known vices, Wellingtons were held in affectionate esteem by their crews, who even sang about them to the tune of "Waltzing Matilda:"

> Ops in a Wimpy, ops in a Wimpy,
> Who'll come on ops in a Wimpy with me?

Into Action

British bombing policy was deliberately non-provocative for the first six months of the Second World War. Bomber Command's activities were limited to strategic reconnaissance, propaganda leaflet raids, and the destruction of enemy shipping in their home ports and at sea. Crews were repeatedly cautioned that the greatest care was to be taken not to injure enemy civilians, and that, for the present, there were no alternative bombing targets to the German High Seas Fleet.

The first day of Britain's war with Germany, 3 September 1939, dawned clear over the North Sea, and by midday, ceilings were still virtually unlimited. At precisely 12:03 pm, a Blenheim captained by Flying Officer A. McPherson from 139 Squadron lifted off from RAF Wyton on a reconnaissance of German naval ports. Clearly visible from 24,000 feet, three capital ships in the company of four cruisers and seven destroyers were massed in the Schillig Roads, which led into the Wilhelmshaven naval base. But the sightings which McPherson signaled to British authorities were useless because of the failure of his onboard radio transmitter. Therefore, news of the sightings was delayed for hours while the frustrated pilot returned to base as fast as possible. Finally, at approximately 6:15 pm, eighteen Hampdens and nine Wellingtons—a truly "mixed-bag" force drawn from six separate squadrons from both 3 and 5 Groups—launched for the German coast. Flight Lieutenant Thomas C. Weir of Winnipeg (mentioned earlier in this chapter in reference to an event when he was considerably more senior), was piloting a 44 Squadron Hampden on this mission, and thus became the first Canadian airman of the Second World War to participate in an offensive sortie.[11] However, the weather had by then become worse, with severe thunderstorms en route and darkness rapidly approaching. No contact was made with the enemy shipping and the small attack force returned uneventfully to base.

Next morning, Flying Officer McPherson, still undaunted, was off at 8:35 am on another reconnaissance of the Wilhelmshaven area. This time, the weather en route was bad. Solid cloud prevailed from sea level to 17,000 feet, with heavy embedded rain squalls. But McPherson persevered and was able to locate and photograph warships at Brunsbüttel, where the Kiel Canal meets the North Sea, and again at Wilhelmshaven and in the harbour's approaches, the Schillig Roads.

Following McPherson's second reconnaissance report, in the late afternoon fifteen 2 Group Blenheims from 197, 110, and 139 Squadrons sortied against Wilhelmshaven. Concurrently, fourteen 3 Group Wellingtons from 9 and 149 Squadrons were sent out against two battleships that had been seen at Brunsbüttel. Led by 110 Squadron's Squadron Leader, K.C. Doran, and with Pilot Officer Selby Roger Henderson of Winnipeg navigating the lead aircraft, the Blenheim force, through a remarkable combination of skill and luck, found their targets in the Schillig Roads. These turned out to be the pocket battleship *Admiral Scheer* and the cruiser *Emden*. However, faced with a 500-foot overcast ceiling, the attackers were forced to bomb from almost mast height with 500-pound General Purpose bombs, fused for a 11.5 second detonation delay to ensure safe escape from their own fragmentation patterns. Squadron Leader Doran reported on the raid the following day:

> We could see a German warship taking on stores from two tenders at its stern. We could even see some washing hanging on the line. Undaunted by the washing, we proceeded to bomb the battleship. Flying at 100 feet above mast height all three aircraft in the flight converged on her. I flew straight ahead. The pilot of the second aircraft came across from one side, and the third crossed from the other side. When we flew over the top of the battleship we could see the crews running fast to their stations. We dropped our bombs. The second pilot, flying behind, saw two hit. We came around, and the ship's pom-poms began to fire as we headed for home. My navigator saw shells bursting almost on the tail of the aircraft.[12]

Thus it transpired that Henderson, sitting in the scalloped transparent nose of the lead aircraft, was the first Canadian airman to engage the enemy during the war.[13] On their attack, which clearly caught the defenders by surprise, the 110 Squadron Blenheims hit the *Admiral Scheer* with at least four separate bombs. However, none of them exploded, probably as a result of the low altitude of the attack, which would have precluded fuse arming, and also because of the resilient nature of the battleship's thick armour plating. By now however, the German defences were alerted, for which the third 110 Squadron aircraft paid dearly:

> The enemy reacted quickly and the remaining aircraft of 110 Squadron came under fire. Blenheim N6199 was struck by flak and crashed directly into the bow of the cruiser *Emden*, killing all four aboard the aircraft. The pilot, by way of a remarkable coincidence, was Flying Officer H.L. Emden. The impact resulted in the German Navy's first casualties of the war as nine sailors aboard the warship were killed as well.[14]

At this point, the four surviving Blenheims from 110 Squadron headed for home, while the 107 Squadron contingent commenced their attack runs.

Pilot Officer Henderson was not the only Canadian in action over Wilhelmshaven on 4 September 1939. Piloting 107 Squadron's Blenheim N6240 was Sergeant Pilot Albert Stanley Prince, who had been born in Montreal but emigrated to England with his family at an early age. Prince joined the RAF in 1935 and was, by 1939, a relatively experienced pilot:

> There was no element of surprise when Sergeant Prince arrived over the target. The German flak was heavy and well directed. Three of the four bombers which attacked were shot down during their low level bombing runs. A German witness reported the fate of a fourth: *"The crew of one Blenheim attacked at such a low level that the blast of their own bomb on the*

warship destroyed the RAF aircraft." Apparently the delay fuse malfunctioned . . . The aircraft flown by Sergeant Prince was one of three which appear to have been shot down by flak. In an interview with a German journalist, Sergeant G.F. Booth, the observer [navigator] whose position was in the nose of the Blenheim was asked, "if he noticed how the aircraft was brought down." He answered, "we hit something . . . I was looking forward. I just saw the water and heard the crash." It appears that the aircraft went down quickly, but Sergeant Prince must have had some control as the bomber was ditched in the harbour. All three crew members were successful in getting out of the aircraft and were picked up by a pilot boat. But Sergeant Prince had been mortally injured during the landing and died later in hospital.[15]

Thus to Albert Stanley Prince fell the dubious distinction of becoming the first Canadian Second World War casualty from any of the fighting services, a full five days before Canada's declaration of war. Meanwhile, attacks by the Wellington contingent carried out on the battleships at Brunsbüttel were ineffective, which cost that attacking force two aircraft. It was also thought that one of the Wellingtons accidentally bombed the town of Esbjerg, which would have constituted a navigational error of 110 miles! All in all, Bomber Command's first operational sorties were not an auspicious beginning.

Other Canadians were also in action. On the night of 3/4 September, Robert Stevenson of Victoria, British Columbia, and John Sproule of Brandon, Manitoba, had each climbed aboard Whitleys as part of a ten-aircraft leaflet raid on German cities. Collectively, this tiny force dropped 5.4 tons of leaflets and assured their place in history as the first to drop materiel of any nature on Germany during the Second World War. The same night, Pilot Officer George C. Walker of Gleichen, Alberta, flew a reconnaissance mission over the Ruhr valley as a second pilot in a Whitley from 58 Squadron.[16] These three Canadians had actually flown operations before the west coast of Canada realized that Britain was at war with Germany.

And so it began. The bombing was still tentative and non-confrontational, but leaflet raids, known as "Nickels," proliferated throughout the autumn of 1939. William H. Nelson of Montreal and David A. Willis of St. Boniface, Manitoba, flew in separate 10 Squadron Whitleys on propaganda raids the night of 8/9 September.[17] The following night, Flying Officer Allen B. Thompson of Penetanguishene, Ontario, became the first Canadian wartime guest of the Third Reich when his 102 Squadron Whitley was brought down on another leaflet raid. This occurrence was still such a novelty that Thompson was personally greeted by *Reichsmarschall* Hermann Göring before the Canadian was packed off to prison camp. Three weeks later, on the night of 29/30 September, William Isaac Clements of North Devon, New Brunswick, became the first member of the RCAF to fly an operation over Germany. As a Canadian on exchange duties with the RAF, this Royal Military College of Canada graduate piloted a 53 Squadron Blenheim on deep reconnaissance out of Metz, France, to the Hamm-Hannover area.[18]

While fans in North America thrilled to the Green Bay Packers in their domination of the National Football League and the silver-screen sparring of Clark Gable and Vivian Leigh in *Gone With the Wind* that autumn, the bomber crews wrestled with real-world problems. The drafty Whitleys provided the airmen with their own frozen hell:

On 27 October, for example, one crew reported that they "experienced icing conditions at 1000 feet, and ten-tenths cloud with sleet at 2000 feet. Crystalline ice formed over the turrets, leading edges, and cabin windows. At 10,000 feet the temperature was -22° C, the front turret was frozen and the trimming tabs jammed by ice . . . The cockpit heating system was useless, and everyone was frozen with no means of alleviating their distress. Some members of the crew butted their heads on the floor and the navigation table in an endeavour to feel some other form of pain as a relief from the awful feeling of frostbite. . . ." As a result, they "felt incapable of cohesion of thought or action, and the rear gunner could not have resisted fighter attack. In any case his vision was obscured by ice on the turret."[19]

Furthermore, the weather in late autumn of 1939 was a precursor to the coldest European winter in forty-five years, during which frost was reported all the way down to the Italian Riviera. The discomforts which followed would only be magnified at bombing altitudes. The problem of crew comfort certainly left room for improvement

Little comfort was found, however, in the realization that the German defences were not yet formidable. While the anti-aircraft artillery (flak) was occasionally categorized as heavy, it was not particularly effective. In fact, only fourteen Bomber Command aircraft were lost on night operations between the commencement of hostilities in September and the start of the Norwegian campaign in April 1940, and not all of these were a result of enemy action.[20]

Perhaps the most sobering revelation for the Command during this period was that navigation at night was proving considerably more difficult than in daytime. Some early crashes in neutral Danish, Belgian, and Dutch territory caused considerable embarrassment to His Majesty's government, and necessitated routing restrictions to avoid accidental airspace violations. Also, prior to the war, Command planners were confident that once over the target area, the specific objectives were identifiable from bombing altitudes. "In particular, the planners assumed that crews should have little difficulty identifying so-called self-illuminating targets like steel mills and oil refineries or those that lay near prominent geographical features such as rivers or lakes. The experience gained from Nickelling proved otherwise."[21] The reality was that even on clear nights, when viewed from 12,000 feet or higher, only relatively large cities or bodies of water could be positively identified, while smaller features such as small villages and roads could only be distinguished below 6000 feet. Individual buildings such as factories, which were the specific targets of attacks, could only be discerned below 4000 feet, and this was a suicidal altitude band from which to brave the enemy guns.[22] Thus, night target finding even on clear nights was not yet practicable, and fear of retaliation also restrained the British from attacks which might cause civilian casualties. Therefore, some day bombing sorties against German naval forces continued, but only sporadically, and they were largely ineffective. When they *did* occur, the RAF day bomber forces were, for the most part, decimated by the *Luftwaffe*.

The German defensive response to embryonic British night bombing efforts was initially and appropriately low-key. The *Luftwaffe*, like the RAF, believed that strategic day bombing would carry the day and patterned its defences accordingly. Although the threat of night attack had been doctrinally addressed—the intention was to rely heavily on early-warning radar and radar-directed flak, augmented by fighters that were guided by pre-positioned searchlights in rigidly defined zones—priorities were instead given to the rapid buildup of the day fighter arm. As a result, although eleven specialist night fighting wings had been theoretically authorized in June 1939, only seven had been formed when hostilities commenced. At that time, all were re-assigned for daylight operations. In October, Germany's need for a dedicated night fighter arm was re-established, but only three squadrons were formed in one wing, *Nachtjagdgeschwader* 1 (*NFG* 1), flying twin-engine Messerschmitt Bf 110s, augmented by a number of ill-suited single-engine Bf 109s. "There seemed little point in committing more men and machines to the task when the enemy was only dropping paper."[23]

On 22 November, however, Bomber Command's commander-in-chief, Air Marshal Ludlow-Hewitt, was directed by the Cabinet to mount a series of day attacks in strength against the German fleet. On 3 December a force of twenty-four Wellingtons was sent to the Heligoland Bight in clear skies, where they attacked two German cruisers, eight merchantmen, and other smaller ships. They claimed hits on one of the cruisers and one merchantman, and also sank a minesweeper. All this without loss, in spite of attacks by several German fighters. Unfortunately, this was a high-water mark for Bomber Command's daylight operations. A second raid on 14 December against a battleship and a cruiser near Heligoland at the mouth of the Elbe River was not nearly as successful. A solid cloud base at 800 feet precluded bombing by the twelve attacking Wellingtons, but did not deter a spirited defence by the Germans. In all, three Canadians participated in this mission, including the leader, Wing Commander John Griffiths, the skipper of 99 Squadron, and Flying Officer John Dyer from Minnedosa, Manitoba. On this attack, flak and fighters would account for five of the "Wimpys," but all three of the participating Canadians survived. Griffiths became the first Canadian airman of the war to be awarded a DFC, but Dyer was killed in action the following spring.[24]

> Four days after the Heligoland raid, a three-squadron strike was staged against shipping at Wilhelmshaven. Squadron Leader Archibald Guthrie of Reston, Manitoba, led Wellingtons of 9 Squadron which included two more Canadians, Flying Officers John Challes of St. Catharines, Ontario, and William MacRae of Regina.
>
> Dirty weather improved as they flew out, and by the time they swung down the Heligoland Bight the air filled with fighters, the first vectored onto a target by *Freya* radar. When the fighters withdrew, the Wellingtons ran into heavy flak near Bremerhaven, which was empty of ships. They cut back eighteen miles across the bight to Wilhelmshaven where they spotted several ships at quay-side. But, mindful of standing orders, Guthrie was unable to order the attack for fear of killing civilians.
>
> Although the Wellingtons bombed some ships near Wilhelmshaven, once out of flak range they were again attacked by fighters and a long and deadly duel followed. A Wellington in the lead section fell in flames while another broke apart, and a third left its signature in smoke as it spiralled into the water.
>
> In the long flight homeward, Wellingtons claimed twelve enemy aircraft, but ten Wellingtons fell during attacks, two went down at sea, and three crash-landed in England. All remaining seven aircraft had dead or wounded on board. Guthrie's and Challes' crews were among the dead and MacRae was among those who crash-landed on the British coast. He was awarded the DFC but was killed the following March.[25]

Second Thoughts

These discouraging daylight results soon caused the Command to seriously reconsider its prewar daylight bombing policy. The pragmatists concluded that while daylight, precision raids had become prohibitively dangerous, astro-navigation could at best only get crews to within twelve miles of a specific target. Nor were electronic navigational beacons, still relatively new, expected to make much of a difference.

> Looking to the future, but persuaded that Bomber Command required additional time to build up its strength, the air staff now began to argue that the focus of bombing should shift from producing physical damage, which required sustained and intensive operations and demanded more accuracy than Ludlow-Hewitt could guarantee, to lowering enemy morale, which it wishfully thought could be accomplished by as few as two hundred sorties a week. The idea was to despatch small numbers of aircraft (perhaps no more than thirty) to Germany each night, dispersing them in time and space through as many air defence zones as possible and setting off almost continuous alarms over the whole Reich. This would upset the "nerves and digestion" of the German population and might eventually make living conditions so unpleasant that those employed in the war industries would be "loathe to continue at work."[26]

Decisive results were not expected from this psychological approach to bombing in the short haul. To inflict real damage the intelligence staffs felt the target must be the oil industry, the German economy's weakest link. They concluded that the neutralization of twenty-two of the enemy's main facilities, of which fifteen were located less than a hundred and fifty miles from the North Sea (particularly in the Ruhr area), could have a decisive impact on the German war effort.[27] Thus, on 22 February 1940 the Chief of the Air Staff, Air Chief Marshal Sir Cyril Newall, approved the oil plan. At the same time, Bomber Command began its conversion to a night bombing force. While both Newall and the outgoing Bomber Command chief, Ludlow-Hewitt, were optimistic that this plan was feasible, the Command's new helmsman, Air Marshal Charles "Peter" Portal, was not so sanguine. Portal told Newall that for average crews, target identification at night was only possible under the best conditions of visibility, and even then only when the target was on the coast or on an enormous waterway, such as the Rhine River. "Under the latter conditions about 50 percent of the average crews might be expected to find and bomb the right target in good visibility; if the target has no conspicuous aids to its location, very few inexperienced crews would be likely to find it under any condition."[28]

The *Luftwaffe* Responds

Meanwhile, there was a significant amount of planning and forethought associated with improving the embryonic German night fighter arm. In keeping with their aforementioned doctrine, the night fighters were initially vectored toward their targets by primitive *Freya* early-warning radars. Developed in the 1930s with a detection range of 100 kilometres, the *Freyas* provided approach direction information, but no measure of enemy altitude. However, they were augmented by an even more simplistic but effective sound detection system. These sound detectors could actually pick up the sound of the bombers taking off from their bases in Britain. German historian Lothar Simon elaborates:

> Sound detectors like the direction finder C39 provided acoustic aircraft detection. It was operated by two men; one for detection, one for height, and a well-trained crew could pinpoint a target to within one degree . . . This information was then electrically transmitted to the searchlights.[29]

Since the German night fighters were not yet equipped with airborne intercept (AI) radars, their early successes in this developing art lay in radio controlled guidance to the incoming bomber forces, triggered by inputs from the early warning radars and the sound detectors, and close cooperation between the flak, the searchlights, and the night fighter crews. Visual location and the subsequent "coning" of the bombers by the searchlights then permitted attacks by the lurking Messerschmitt Bf 110s in a system known as *Hellnachtjagd*, or "illuminated night fighting." At the core of *Hellnachtjagd* was a grid network devised by *Generalmajor* Josef Kammhuber, the commander of the first German night fighter division (and later the entire arm),[30] who devised a system of night fighter boxes of airspace that were co-located with the fixed searchlight belts. Initially established behind the Zuider Zee and along the Rhine River, the aim of this system was to have an individual night fighter dedicated to each airspace box measuring approximately twenty miles by forty miles. In due course, the Kammhuber Line of defences would stretch fifteen miles deep and unbroken from Holland and the Scheldt Estuary in the south to the island of Sylt abeam the German–Danish border in the north, as well as into Occupied France. This formidable electronic fence blanketed the most probable ingress and egress routes of the bombers. The *Hellnachtjagd* system was used successfully to defend the Ruhr in early 1940, and it proved to be a practical solution, as long as the British bombers were not flying in a concentrated stream, and were not deliberately attempting to avoid the searchlight belt. This belt was capable of illuminating a bomber flying up to twelve kilometers above the earth's surface, well above the operational altitudes of all the Second World War standard bombers. The German night fighters would lay in the darkness near the lights, waiting for them to snare a prey. Hans Joachim Jabs, one of the most successful of the German night fighter pilots explains:

> The searchlight batteries located the incoming bombers with the help of a radar controlled master searchlight. Once they got a bomber, then all the other lights would join in, until it was caught, like a fly in a spider's web, unable to escape.[31]

Being coned by searchlights was an absolute hell for the attacking bomber crews, and would remain so throughout the entire night bombing campaign. The radar-directed master beam was a white light so pure and bright that it actually had a blueish tinge. So brilliant and intense was the master beam that it dazzled and disoriented the bomber crews. Frequently, if the coning procedure occurred away from the target area, the radar-directed flak would cease firing at a coned bomber, an ominous portent that a German night fighter had visual contact with the bomber, was headed inbound for the kill, and was thus to be spared accidental damage from its own defences. Thus, getting coned was not only terrifying and disorienting, it was also a precursor to unwanted attention by a German night fighter.

Bomber Command was relatively quick to respond to the *Hellnachtjagd* threat:

> Once this essential structure was analyzed, patterns could be discerned: losses to fighters were highest on clear nights; lowest on cloudy nights and outside the searchlight zone; and unaccountably rare above 14,000 feet, even though this was well within the range of the grouped searchlights. As a result, High Wycombe began to introduce countermeasures. Routes were planned, when practicable, to skirt Kammhuber's line or to take advantage of gaps identified in it; and pilots were told to bomb from 16,000 feet, a height from which it was felt—optimistically, it turned out—they could still see specific objectives on the ground. When deep penetrations were required, it was also recommended

that pilots make maximum altitude over the North Sea, dive through the defensive flak and fighter belt at best possible speed, and then regain height in the German interior, where defences were weaker.[32]

Winds of Change

Then, reason enough to adopt a more aggressive bombing policy came on 8 and 9 April 1940 when the Germans invaded Norway and Denmark. Ironically, the previous day the Deputy Chief of the Air Staff (DCAS), Air Chief Marshal Sir Richard Peirse, had urged the opening of an air offensive to stymy the Germans before they were able to seize advance bases in the Low Countries.

> "We know the brittleness of German morale," he pointed out with quite unjustified optimism, and so should begin night operations "directed towards the moral (sic) and psychological factor." The three Service chiefs also agreed with Peirse but cautioned that the government might yet be reluctant to unleash an air offensive while Britain had not yet been bombed. They were right: the political restrictions remained in force throughout the Norwegian campaign.[33]

Even the *Blitzkrieg* against the Low Countries, however, did not provoke a significant bombing policy change. While Peirse continued to implore his superiors to give Bomber Command free rein, the War Cabinet did not yet feel that the political climate was suitable to begin bombing German civil targets. There was widespread fear among leading politicians such as then Prime Minister Neville Chamberlain; Lord Halifax, the Foreign Minister; the new Secretary of State for Air, Sir Archibald Sinclair; the Chief of the Air Staff (CAS) Sir Cyril Newall; and, as of 10 May 1940, the new Prime Minister, Winston Churchill—that Bomber Command would be frittered away on these attacks and would no longer serve as a deterrent force against the *Luftwaffe's* bombing arm. But the Germans had at no time been deterred by the threat of aerial bombardment, and early civil bombing opportunities were thus lost. "On 15 May, however, with the Germans pouring west from Sedan (and following the *Luftwaffe's* bombing of Rotterdam the day before), the gloves finally came off and High Wycombe (Bomber Command Headquarters) was authorized to attack oil refineries and railroad targets east of the Rhine."[34]

That night, approximately 100 Command aircraft conducted "pinprick" raids on sixteen separate targets in the Ruhr, with negligible results. On the night of 17/18 May, a force of forty-eight Hampdens bombed Hamburg, twenty-four Whitleys attacked Bremen, and only six Wellingtons attacked Cologne's railway yards. Again, the overall damage was largely insignificant. Sensing that these early, largely piecemeal raids were futile, Churchill now came to believe that because of the dynamic nature of the German advance, the focus of the bombing effort needed to be temporarily shifted from the oil industry and concentrated on the *Wehrmacht's* lines of communication. Sir Charles Portal stridently argued that his Command should continue the longer-term assault on the industrial Ruhr basin, but orders from the Air Ministry (and thus the political elite) dated 19 May were unequivocal. "Although oil remained on the target list, the railway marshalling yards supporting the German advance were the first priority during this 'critical week.' "[35]

Concurrently, Canadian Bomber Command airmen were forward deployed with the RAF in France and were active in tactical bombing against the Germans from the start of the May *Blitzkrieg*:

> As Nazi columns rolled westward, 32 Fairey Battles of the Advanced Air Striking Force hit

(German) troops in Luxembourg, thirteen were lost and all were damaged by intense flak. Flight Lieutenant Eric Parker of Vancouver was killed while Flight Lieutenants Arthur Roberts of Vernon, British Columbia, and Al Matthews of Calgary became Prisoners of War. George Muncy of Calgary flew with a Blenheim squadron which lost four of twelve machines that day . . . One Blenheim squadron was virtually wiped out, losing seven of nine machines bombing the bridges at Maastricht, The Netherlands . . . By Day Three, things were so bad that they were calling for volunteers in the best tradition of the Dawn Patrol. A flight of six Battles from 12 Squadron was wiped out when it went after two bridges. On a strike against the bridges at Sedan in northeastern France, 40 of 71 aircraft were lost, and the following day, 32 of 66 Battles were shot down. Flight Lieutenant Gordon Clancey of Semans, Saskatchewan, led a flight of five Battles from which only one returned. Clancey and his crew were among the missing and became POWs.[36]

Of this period it can be truly said that no other undertaking of the same scale conducted by the RAF suffered a comparable rate of sacrifice. However, this early surge of tactical bombing in support of the French land forces would soon be superceded by new strategic bombardment priorities. It was emphasized that oil was to remain the main strategic objective, with aircraft factories located in the main cities the recommended alternative targets for dark nights. However, the Air Ministry emphasized that these planned raids were not to "degenerate into mere indiscriminate action."[37] But they did so, although this result was not intentional. "Industrial haze over the Ruhr and poor navigation by many crews (who, in a continuing effort to spread the alarm, made their own way to the objective by whatever route they preferred) meant that many targets were never identified. German records reveal that 70 percent of the bombs dropped fell on open countryside."[38]

This was also much a period of bombing experimentation for effect, as an interesting intelligence report of the period to the Prime Minister through his chief scientific advisor, Professor Frederick Lindemann (later Lord Cherwell), reveals:

NOTE ON THE ATTACK OF GERMAN FORESTS

The question of setting fire to German forests has been constantly under review by the Air Staff. The report dated 1.7.1940 was received and carefully considered by them, although by the date of the receipt the long, dry spell was over and the inclement summer months, unsuitable for incendiarism, had set in.

. . . The value of setting fire to German forests has always been fully realized. It is not, however, an easy matter to start a forest fire with incendiary weapons dropped from aircraft and the chances of the fire spreading, once started, are largely a matter of luck.

. . . During the advance of the German Army through the Ardennes, forests were attacked and fires started. The bombing directive issued to Headquarters, Bomber Command, on 20th June 1940, contained the following paragraph:

"11. As you are aware there are extensive areas of coniferous forests in Germany which are believed to be extremely vulnerable to incendiarism at this time of the year. Some of these areas are in the vicinity of important military objectives and aerodromes where a forest fire might have valuable results in dislocating German military and industrial activities, apart from the morale effect. A separate note and map of the suggested areas will be sent to you in the course of the next few days in order that you may examine the possibility of undertaking incendiary attacks during the dark period."

As a result of this the Black Forest (area "a" in paragraph 4 of the attached report) was attacked by 30 Wellingtons on the night of 29/30 June and 23—250-lb. plus 840 25-lb. incendiary bombs dropped. Many fires and explosions were reported but none of the fires developed into a forest blaze.

On the night of 30 June/1 July, 22 Wellingtons attacked forests south east of Frankfurt and again started many fires which failed to spread to any appreciable extent.

. . . The weapons necessary to set fire to forests are unsuitable for the attack of most other targets so there is no question of providing alternative objectives for aircraft detailed for this task. Of recent weeks the main aim of the air striking force has been to counter enemy provisions for the invasion of England and to reduce the scale of air attack which may be launched against this country.

—Colonel Grand
19 July 1940

<u>Prime Minister</u>
This is the Intelligence Report for which you asked.[39]

Once France capitulated on 22 June, Bomber Command's mandate became considerably simplified, since it no longer had to support an Allied army in the field. Shortly thereafter, the Foreign Office began quoting supposedly reliable sources from the continent that the bombing was instilling panic among the German civilian population.[40] At this point, some of the greyer heads in the land's highest councils began to think that an unfettered campaign against the German industrial cities might indeed significantly impact enemy morale and save the United Kingdom from an invasion. Over the next five months, six separate policy directives detailing attack priorities were sent by the Air Ministry to Bomber Command as those in authority struggled to identify and prioritize the greatest threats faced by Britain, whether they were air raids or actual invasion,

and they established the target lists accordingly: aircraft assembly plants; airfield storage facilities; airfields in Holland, Belgium, and northwest France; oil; barges and troopships in the German-held Channel, North Sea, and Baltic ports. Despite their differences, however, these directives had one thing in common: they all provided lists of specific objectives. That issued on 13 July, for example, limited the main effort to fifteen factories and plants, ten of which were related to the aircraft industry and five to oil.[41]

However, Bomber Command was not happy with any of these directives, since Portal and his senior planners were convinced that his crews were simply incapable of finding and destroying precise targets. Therefore, around mid July, Portal requested permission to strike the larger industrial towns instead, in order to undermine enemy morale. That request was summarily denied, with the Air Ministry insisting that *material* destruction still had to be the primary goal.[42] Nonetheless, the stage was set, through these expressed doubts about the Command's capabilities, for future policy shifts which would alter the fates of many German civilians. From 1941 until late 1944 the majority of Bomber Command's sorties consisted of area-bombing by night; and the chief reason for this turn of events was that "the only target on which the night force could inflict effective damage was a whole German town."[43] The RAF's Official History Branch Narrative identifies this linkage directly with Sir Charles Portal and the more pessimistic, yet pragmatic attitude which he would bring to future Air Staff deliberations on bombing policy. Ultimately,

due allowance was made for the inaccuracy of bombing, by ensuring that targets selected were not isolated, but if possible in large centres of population and industry. This was the reason for the initiation of area bombing and the selection of "industrial centres" instead of factories.[44]

And so the raiding continued, although it still lacked focus and continuity, and Canadian airmen continued to distinguish themselves. Flying Officer David Albert Romans of Halifax, Nova Scotia, joined the RAF as a CAN/RAF in March 1939. David Romans was only nineteen when war was declared, but he soon became a seasoned veteran. During the Battle of Britain Romans performed an act of bravery that earned him the respect of colleagues and superiors alike in 44 Squadron. It also brought him Nova Scotia's first Distinguished Flying Cross of the war. A brief excerpt from the official citation elaborates: "On the night of 18/19 July 1940, whilst carrying out a bombing attack on Eschwege aerodrome at approximately 5000 feet in Hampden aircraft P1324 . . . the aircraft was hit by an anti-aircraft shell . . . rendering the pilot, Pilot Officer W. Walker unconscious . . . The navigator/bomb-aimer, Pilot Officer D.A. Romans . . . climbed into the cockpit and sat on the pilot's knees, and flew the aircraft safely back to base."[45]

The *Luftwaffe* Triggers a Policy Shift

During the summer of 1940, the *Luftwaffe* precipitated a distinct change in RAF policy by provoking an attack which had a "domino effect" and in all likelihood cost the Germans the Battle of Britain. On the night of 24/25 August, they accidentally bombed central London, and Prime Minister Churchill demanded immediate retaliation by the RAF. The next night, approximately fifty crews were sent to bomb Berlin. With the target shrouded in dense fog, the results were as inaccurate as ever, the majority of the bombs falling in open farmland to the south of the capital. Six aircraft were lost on the raid, which had included some Canadians. Arthur C.P. Clayton, a CAN/RAF who joined the RAF in 1938, flew one of 83 Squadron's Hampdens that night,[46] while Mervyn Mathew Fleming of Ottawa piloted a 58 Squadron Whitley out of Linton-on-Ouse.[47]

The following night the Germans bombed London again, deliberately this time. Three nights later, on 30 August, it was Berlin's turn again. This time Bomber Command drew blood. Some of the bombs struck the city centre near the Görlitzer railway station. Ten Berliners were killed and three times that number were wounded. Prior to the bombings, the capital had existed in a surrealistic sense of detachment from the war. Throughout the previous winter, the entertainment had still been heavily American-accented. For example, the Marmorhaus Cinema featured Eleanor Powell and Robert Young in *South Sea Nights*, while the Kurbel headlined *Dick und Doof*, which literally translates to "Fatty and Stupid," but actually referred to the slapstick comedy duo, Laurel and Hardy. Throughout the first half of 1940 such diversions could still be found, although since the spring the cinema fare had turned distinctly more martial in flavour, with the *Wochenschau* or weekly news programs trumpeting the battlefield successes in Scandanavia, the Low Countries and then France. However, the Berlin raids provoked widespread German public discontent and disquiet. Hitler, in a retributive rage, ordered an all-out assault on London and other British cities, the start of the so-called Baedeker Raids, throughout September—just in time to spare the RAF's vital airfields and command-and-control facilities from further specific and concentrated attacks.

> Inch by painful inch, both British and German policies were slipping from ones aimed at precise objectives to ones of area bombing with psychological overtones. On 2 September,

for example, Portal observed that although he was not yet involved in attempts to burn down whole towns, "that stage will come." The next day Churchill asked that Bomber Command "pulverize the entire industry and economic structure" of the German war economy; and, three days later, he called for a series of "minor" but "widespread" attacks on smaller German towns intended to destroy the population's faith in their air defences. Portal responded with a list of twenty such places and urged that it be made public in order to provide a clear statement that, "as a reprisal for each night of indiscriminate bombing by the enemy, one of these towns would be selected for indiscriminate bombing by the RAF."[48]

Initially, the incumbent Chief of the Air Staff, Sir Cyril Newall, was not persuaded by either Churchill's vindictiveness or Portal's predictions that the time was ripe for a wholesale bombing policy change. Furthermore, Sir Richard Peirse, who was then Vice Chief of the Air Staff (VCAS), clearly articulated the Air Ministry's bombing priorities in a letter of the period to the Prime Minister:

5th September 1940

Dear Prime Minister

I have been considering the suggestion you made to the C. in C. Bomber Command that we should spread our bombing offensive as widely as possible over the cities and small towns in Germany within our reach.

As Portal told you, we have already drawn up a plan on this basis which has as its object to cause as widespread dislocation and disturbance as possible over all the important industrial areas in Germany.

This plan was conceived, however, at a time when it seemed possible we might have to begin bombing operations in Germany during the winter months when unfavourable weather and bad visibility might prevent us directing our offensive to the more precise targets required by our major plan.

The plan we are working to now has as its object; (i) The reduction of the scale of air attack on this country by the destruction of the aircraft industry, (ii) The destruction of the oil resources which we believe to be the most vulnerable link in Germany's war economy, (iii) Dislocation of transport and communication systems.

Incidentally (iii) is very closely interconnected with (i) and (ii).

To make this plan effective with the small forces at our disposal, we cannot afford to disperse our effort on to other targets (excepting of course those immediately concerned with invasion or profitable naval targets).

Moral (sic) effect is not gained by sporadic harassing, but is proportionate to the material damage done. And if we hope seriously to cripple Germany with our small bomber force we must try to put every bomb on to a target which contributes to our plan. Systematic destruction will paralyse both materially and morally—harassing does neither— but fortunately our planned targets take us widely over the face of Germany.

I do hope therefore you will agree to the importance of sticking to our present plans.

Yours Sincerely,
R.G.C. Peirse[49]

However, when the *Luftwaffe* subsequently dropped thirty-six parachute mines on London, a form of attack which precluded precise aiming, Churchill again demanded retribution, and with mines as well. A new bombing directive issued on 21 September identified specific high-value aim points in the German capital, such as its largest power stations. Newall and his staff however directed that they be attacked with bombs, not mines, since the Air Staff recoiled at Churchill's desire to counter the London attack with "indiscriminate frightfulness."[50] When Berlin was next attacked on 23/24 September, eighteen specific targets were visited by 129 aircraft. At the end of the month a dejected Portal again recommended that since his crews were still unable to locate and bomb precision targets, their efforts should be directed "primarily against the will of the German people to continue the war."[51] Yet the Air Staff still did not agree, nor did Archibald Sinclair, the Secretary of State for Air. However, Sir Charles Portal had a powerful friend and a sympathetic ear in Winston Churchill. On 4 October, Portal was appointed Chief of the Air Staff, displacing Cyril Newall, and Sir Richard Peirse, a staunch advocate of city attacks, replaced Portal at High Wycombe as AOC Bomber Command.

New Officer Commanding, New Mandate

From now on, Portal's desire to attack the industrial centres as frequently as possible would carry significant weight. While oil targets carried top priority on clear, moonlit nights, when it was darker Bomber Command was henceforth to "make a definite attempt . . . to affect the morale of the German people."[52] In an interesting letter of the period, Sir Archibald Sinclair noted that when piecemeal harassment attacks against the German cities were directed at their railway marshalling yards, the results, confirmed by intelligence reports, were promising.[53] Such wartime intelligence snippets, coupled with a certain application to previous British experiences, played a large part in determining broader policies such as bombing priorities.

However, the new counter-city raids were soon under fire from the Prime Minister for a perceived lack of intensity. Peirse then promised, as an example, to pick Berlin targets that were well-spaced, in order to insure broad attack distribution across the city. While this attack policy was certainly grounded in the lack of a precision bombing capability, there was also an emotional component at play. The German attack on Coventry 14/15 November,[54] followed by similar raids on Bristol and Southampton, drove the planning for Operation Abigail, a retaliatory attack on a selected German city. Because of bad weather the raid did not occur until 16/17 December 1940, when 134 Command aircraft were launched against Mannheim. For the first time, a British raid opened with an incendiary laydown and subsequent crews were then instructed to bomb on the ensuing fires; an early and rudimentary form of target marking. While the damage was thought to be widespread at the time, subsequent analysis found it to be much less than had been claimed.

This first campaign against the German cities was short-lived, since on the day of the Mannheim raid an exceptionally over-optimistic report on the damage to date to Germany's synthetic oil plants was released. Although the accuracy of this report was quickly dispelled, Portal conceded its importance. After the Chiefs of Staff concurred with his analysis in early January, Portal ordered a campaign against seventeen of the Reich's largest synthetic oil plants. These attacks on area targets were relegated to nights when weather precluded action against the more demanding, pinpoint refinery targets. Sir Richard Peirse was officially informed on 15 January 1941 that destruction of enemy oil was to be considered the "sole primary aim" of the bomber offensive, until further orders were received.[55] Nonetheless the War Cabinet was not at this time of a mind "to discourage ruthlessness by Bomber Command; the feeling was that the British people were entitled to know that they were giving as good as they were getting."[56] On 13 January 1941 the Defence Committee approved the latest Portal-sponsored bombing proposals. London had just been bombed by 141 raiders the night before, and by 137 of the enemy the night before that. In fact, the 12 January raid was the third attack against London in the new year, adding to three in December, which included a maximum effort by 413 *Luftwaffe* bombers on 8 December.[57]

One interesting result of the bombing to this point was registered concern over the effectiveness of the bombs themselves. There had been numerous complaints about the reliability of the bombs on the Berlin raid, and this ineffectiveness was attributed to their limited explosive weight. The majority of the bombs then used were of the 250-pound variety. The Command soon began experimenting with higher yield 500-pound bombs, which would merely serve as precursors to a much larger range of weapons soon to follow,[58] although the 500-pound General Purpose bomb soon became a standard load for Bomber Command. There were also some concerns about weapon fusing, generated by a number of dud releases, but most of them were traced "to faulty manipulation of the fusing gear by ground or aircrews,"[59] and this problem was soon rectified.

However, bad winter weather and changing war circumstances severely curtailed the embryonic oil campaign. For the first two months of 1941 bombing missions were only possible on thirty-three nights. "Of these only three were devoted exclusively to attacking oil—as compared with 19 on naval targets, six on industrial towns and five on the Channel ports."[60] In the end, only 221 sorties were flown against oil targets during the period from January to March 1941, whereas nearly twice that number had been flown during the last quarter of 1940. Since Sir Charles Portal estimated that 3420 sorties against oil facilities were required to neutralize those seventeen designated oil targets, the actual effort expended was minimal. While these limited oil sorties were partly a result of poor weather, another forced diversion for the Command—a recurring one that would consume a significant amount of Bomber Command's energies and resources over a considerable amount of time—was Germany's intensified U-boat and warship campaign in the North Atlantic. For example, in January 1941, 124 sorties were flown against Wilhelmshaven in an attempt to sink the battleship *Tirpitz*, while a further 116 sorties were flown against the giant warship on 28 February 1941 alone.[61] March brought alarming losses in Allied shipping, and Churchill then directed air strikes on U-Boat harbours and construction facilities. While Portal resented this further distraction for his Command, which he blamed squarely on the Admiralty's inability to control the *Kriegsmarine*, he complied fully with the Prime Minister's wishes. Accordingly: "Coastal cities like Hamburg, Kiel, and Bremen, as well as several French ports, would bear the brunt of bombing until mid-summer, and Bomber Command's contribution to the aerial mining campaign, abandoned just a few months before, was intensified."[62] The French port of Brest, in particular, would find itself the target of Bomber Command's attentions many times in the coming months in repeated attempts to destroy the battleships *Scharnhorst* and *Gneisenau*. The two capital ships entered Brest on 22 March after a successful rampage of North Atlantic waters, during which time they sank twenty-two Allied vessels between them. For the next eleven months, until February 1942, they were the target of many unsuccessful bombing attacks, although *Scharnhorst* was severely damaged by five bombs while temporarily anchored at La Pallice, some 200 miles south of Brest, on 24 July. Furthermore, mass attacks throughout April 1941 had forced the captain of the *Gneisenau* to moor the ship temporarily out in Brest harbour, where it took a direct hit from a torpedo dropped by a Coastal Command Beaufort. The damage inflicted required six months to repair. However, a frustrating lack of decisive results led to innovative and desperate attempts to permanently cripple the two enormous ships. In July, the *Gneisenau* was hit again by multiple bombs while undergoing repairs in drydock at Brest.

Torontonian Bob Dale, a wartime navigator who eventually completed three operational tours and was awarded both the Distinguished Service Order (DSO) and a Distinguished Flying Cross for gallantry, was one of the earliest British Commonwealth Air Training Plan (BCATP) graduates to reach Britain's shores. Flying in Wellingtons with 150 (RAF) Squadron during his first tour, he had been with the squadron for less than two months when in June 1941, and prior to the more successful July raids, they were ordered to attack *Scharnhorst* and *Gneisenau* while they were both in drydock at Brest. On this occasion, Bomber Command elected to send a large force over the port at high altitude to draw the Germans' fire, while a solitary Wellington simultaneously attacked the ships from ultra-low level. Although Dale's crew had only four operations to their credit at this time, they were nonetheless assigned the low-flying role in the mission.

It was, Dale said, "quite obvious to us, that being one of the least experienced crews, we were the most expendable."[63] Their hearts in their mouths, Dale and his crew swept in low over the moonlit harbour, scattering delayed action bombs all over the drydock. Luck rode with them, for although their bombs were ineffective against the two giant warships, not a single round fired from the ground struck their aircraft, and they escaped unscathed.

Coastal Command shared a number of operational duties with Bomber Command, particularly during the early war years. During 1940 and 1941, and frequently flying the same aircraft, such as Blenheims, Coastal Command crews flew many mine-laying and reconnaissance missions. They were also employed in hazardous anti-shipping strikes and attacks on enemy coastal and port facilities. These early strike missions, particularly those conducted against enemy shipping, were made all the more arduous and frustrating because the Blenheims (unlike the Beauforts) were normally only equipped with Bomber Command's general-purpose high explosive bombs of the day. Torpedoes and depth charges were not yet broadly available. From the earliest operations, Canadians shared these dangers. One of the earliest RCAF airmen to fly with Coastal Command out of Britain was Pilot Officer Norman Duncan MacLennan from Toronto. At the time, MacLennan was very much a member of a select group, since "of two hundred and three Canadian pilots who received their wings in 1940, only twenty were posted to the United Kingdom, ten going to RCAF squadrons and ten to the RAF."[64] Norman MacLennan left Canada for the war on 28 February 1941 on a troopship, and was dead less than four months later. A happy, gregarious young man with a zest for life, he truly loved flying, as evidenced by his letters to family while he was a student pilot flying Ansons at Brantford, Ontario. "At first I was rather disappointed at not being made a fighter pilot, but now feel that this is the better job, even though an Anson will neither loop, roll or spin without a wing falling off."[65] Flying Blenheim IV aircraft out of RAF Station St. Eval in Cornwall with 53 Squadron, MacLennan and his crew had participated in a night bombing mission to France on 10/11 June 1941, had sustained battle damage, and crashed while attempting to recover at their home base. All crew members were killed. A particularly poignant wartime postcard home from Norman's brother Jack, who served overseas with the army and visited his brother's grave in late 1942, has survived: "I feel very humble since my visit to that little churchyard and so helpless—He rests where his beloved planes roar above almost continuously. Shall write soon. Jack."[66]

Some New Equipment

Soon, improved bombing performance became a broader issue. As opposed to the old ways of allowing individual aircraft to plot their own courses to a given target, the air staffs had begun to insist on timed, standardized courses for all raid participants, to concentrate forces over the targets at any given time and hopefully saturate the defences. This was the true beginning of the bomber stream, the timings and routings of which would later be honed to perfection. There was also a push by the Air Staff to accelerate the development and introduction of electronic navigational and bombing aids. These initiatives were viewed with skepticism and apathy by both the Air Ministry and the "Union of Navigators," who were frequently either reluctant to embrace new ideas or were intimidated by them. Simultaneously, the Prime Minister complained about the delays in introducing the heavier bomber types into service. The four-engine Short Stirling first flew in May 1939, but it did not fly on operations until February 1941, and even then its performance was disappointing. An enormous aircraft, its cockpit sat nearly twenty-three feet off the ground. The main wheels were as tall as a small adult. Even the massive wing roots were almost as thick as a standing man. However, it was doomed to mediocrity because of its ninety-nine-foot wingspan, which was not long enough to generate sufficient lift for the aircraft's massive fuselage. This limited the operational ceiling of early variants to around 10,000 feet, exacerbated by the initial installation of underpowered Bristol Hercules II radial engines. Although Stirlings would eventually be fitted with uprated Hercules IX powerplants, nothing could be done about the short wingspan, which had been insisted on by an obtuse and incredibly myopic Air Ministry solely in order to fit the 100-foot-wide hangar doors mandated by the RAF's prewar expansion schemes! The uprated engines raised the aircraft's effective ceiling to around 15,000 feet, but this was still dangerously low for offensive operations. Already sluggish at these "higher" altitudes, the Stirlings could not reach the collective security of the bomber stream with the high-flying Lancasters and, eventually, the later variants of Halifaxes. Its lower maximum operating height also made the Stirling more vulnerable than both the Lancasters and Halifaxes to icing, which caused it to become even more unstable. Furthermore, its bomb-carrying capacity was relatively modest over the longer ranges, and structural limitations within the bomb bay restricted the maximum size of bombs being carried to 2000 pounds. Still, it would soldier on as part of the Command's Main Force until late 1943, when it was pulled from operations over Germany, because of its operational ceiling limitations. Thereafter it was relegated to attacks on Occupied France and to special duties, such as electronic countermeasures, glider tow, and transport/re-supply clandestine operations. Many Canadians flew the Stirling, including DFC winner Murray Peden from Winnipeg. The Stirling required a lot of care and attention close to the ground, and its idiosyncracies included an insidious tendency to swing to the right on the take-off roll. To counteract this required some skillful juggling of the throttles, as Peden recalls:

> So pronounced was this starboard swing that a special written acknowledgement was taken from every student pilot and pasted into his log book before he was allowed to go solo in a Stirling . . .
>
> The Stirling had another noteworthy characteristic, one common to most heavy bombers in some measure, but more pronounced in the Stirling than any other heavy I ever flew. When you did your flare-out and check on landing, she dropped onto the runway like a 30-ton boulder; there was no float to speak of at all. If you checked six inches above the runway the result was a beautiful landing. If you checked a foot and a half above the runway you arrived very firmly and definitely; and if you were two feet above the runway when you cut the throttles it felt as though the undercarriage were being driven through the wings. The potential violence of the consequences made for more than normal concentration on the final approach.[67]

A much more successful four-engine mount for Bomber Command, the Handley Page Halifax made its operational debut in March 1941. It was initially planned to be powered by two Rolls-Royce Vulture engines, however the decision was made in 1937 to switch the powerplants to four Rolls-Royce Merlins, and this was fortuitous. While the aircraft had some significant shortcomings, particularly those variants produced during the first two years of operations, and although it would never be as popular as its famous nocturnal partner, the Lancaster, Halifaxes in various models became a mainstay of Bomber Command and 6176 of them were built for the RAF. Again, many Canadians crewed the Halifax throughout its operational life, and their experiences will feature prominently on the following pages.

Another huge, early, four-engine disappointment for Bomber Command was the Boeing Fortress I, the RAF's designation for the B-17C, a much inferior precursor to the formidable B-17E, F, and G models, which later were mainstays of the US Eighth Air Force in England and elsewhere. Twenty Fortress Is had been flown to England in the spring of 1941, and they served in Bomber Command briefly with 90 Squadron in 2 Group. Based on their exceptionally high operating altitude and what was considered to be comparatively heavy defensive armament, they were felt suitable (against the advice of the Americans) to operate with relative impunity in daylight and without fighter escort, succeeding where the Wellingtons had failed in 1940. Their many faults included manually operated versus power turreted machine guns for defence—which did not cover a vulnerable blind cone astern—inadequate armour plating, extreme physiological discomfort for their crews at the higher operating ceilings, shortcomings associated with the early Sperry bomb sights, a limited radius of action, and defective engines exacerbated by operations at rarefied altitudes.[68] Daylight bombing operations with this disappointing aircraft were abandoned by the RAF after September 1941, by which time they had flown only 51 operational sorties. Fewer than half of these had been deemed effective. Operational losses were limited but unsettling, and they included Canadians. That Haligonian early-war DFC winner, David Albert Romans, was only twenty-one during the late summer of 1941, and already he had survived many bombing raids over Germany and the occupied territories. Serving with 90 Squadron on 8 September 1941, Romans and three other Fortress crews were tasked with a bombing mission to Occupied Norway. Shortly before noon, just off the Norwegian coast near the town of Bygland, his formation was jumped by a flight of *Luftwaffe* Bf 109s, which included *Leutnant* Alfred Jakobi and *Feldwebel* Karl-Heinz Woite. This was Jakobi's first contact with the new enemy type, and he was bound and determined to do it right. Rolling in on Romans's aircraft, which also carried as a gunner Sergeant Henri Merrill of Dorion-Vaudreuil Quebec, the German was met by a hail of defensive fire and was hit in his right wing. Meanwhile, Woite successfully engaged another of the Fortresses, which disappeared in heavy cloud and was never heard from again. The Fortress gunners gave as good as they got, and two of the attacking '109s were shot down. However, Jakobi was not yet finished, and he soon re-attacked Romans's Fortress.

> It was 11:27 AM, and this time Jakobi hit his target. Almost immediately the bomber burst into flames, but not before its gunners shot down one of the German fighters.
>
>   Romans's ship plummeted wildly downward. No parachutes were seen escaping from the Flying Fortress. Although no explosion was seen from the air, investigators later confirmed that it crashed in a mountainous region, killing all on board. There were unconfirmed reports suggesting that Sergeant Merrill may have attempted to bail out, only to be killed on hitting

the ground . . . A few days later, occupying German troops in Norway buried Flying Officer Romans and his crew in a collective grave in the Bygland church cemetery.[69]

The surviving Fortresses were soon relegated to patrol duties with Coastal Command.

Yet another disappointing new RAF heavy bomber type was the Avro Manchester. Although it appeared to be a twin-engine aircraft, it was actually placed in the four-engine category, since its 1750 horsepower Rolls-Royce Vulture powerplants were each a pair of Rolls-Royce Kestrels sharing a common crankcase and propeller. The airframe design was exceptionally sound, but the engines proved to be this aircraft's downfall. The coupled engine concept was complex and unreliable; its worst fault was a tendency to bearing failures and subsequent fires while airborne. Interestingly, the Germans had no better luck coupling engines on large bombers. Their comparable failure was Ernst Heinkel's He 177 *Greif*, powered by two enormous Daimler-Benz DB 610 engines, each generating 2950 horsepower. Each DB 610 consisted of a pair of DB 605s, coupled by a clutch and gearbox driving a common, massive propeller. Unlike the German initiative, the coupled power of the Vultures was still not enough to adequately propel a 50,000 pound aircraft. Flying Manchesters so equipped with 207 Squadron, pilot W.J. "Mike" Lewis said: "We really should have had 2500 hp engines. If you felt that you'd lost one, that was it, you weren't coming home. It didn't matter if you feathered the propeller or not, there was only one way you went and that was down."[70] He also recalled just how harrowing even a routine takeoff could be with a full bomb load and full fuel on a typical summer evening out of Waddington. He noted that the longest landing run of the period at Waddington was the landing patch for their *Lorenz* or beam approach system, which was about 4200 feet. There was obviously no margin for error under these circumstances.

> There was a low transmitter building similar to the instrument landing system (ILS) shack at a modern airfield. Three miles away there was a small country church with the usual tower. I would tuck the tail against the hedge along the Sleaford Road at the northeast, hold her on brakes as long as I could at max power, and then let go. If I lifted off and my wing tip was above the *Lorenz* shack light as I crossed the upwind hedge, I felt my take-off had been up to par. I'd have the undercarriage on the way up. After it was up, I would start to bleed the flaps up. If I had wheels and flaps up and I crossed over the church at 100 feet, I felt that I was getting everything that the aircraft could give me on takeoff.[71]

Lewis further recalled a Manchester doing an engine ground run-up with pistons flying out the side of the nacelle.[72] As a wartime economy measure, the bearings had been made without silver and thus did not possess the requisite hardness and strength. The large end-bearings would collapse the connecting rod, the piston would fling itself overboard and that would spell the end of the engine. The Manchester made its operational debut in February 1941, but a substantial number of the aircraft failed to return from raids, and of these, many were attributed lost because of engine failures. Nonetheless, it muddled through until June 1942 with the Main Force. One was used only on a trial basis with 408 (RCAF) Squadron in early 1942. Mike Lewis, who won a DFC as a Bomber Command CAN/RAF earlier in the war, also remembers the gallant nature of his peers on 207 Squadron during this unhappy period of operations, a time when recognition and support did not appear forthcoming from the higher Command echelons:

> My strongest feelings from this period in my life are about my peers: the aircrew who flew these aircraft. Until about June 1941, the captains, navs, w/ops, and tail gunners were all

men doing their second tour of Ops. Only when losses decimated their ranks to the point where the air force was incapable of supplying experienced personnel as replacements, first-tour personnel began to feed in. These determined men went unrewarded for their magnificent efforts. Whether it was right or wrong, it was usual to recognize aircrew with decorations for outstanding performance. In 207 Squadron, the first Manchester unit, from the time we started Ops on 24 February until I was shot down, (7-8 September 1941), the only decoration awarded to the squadron aircrew was a Bar to his DFC for Burton-Giles. During this time, we received no visible support from Bomber Command and little or no morale [sic] support from 5 Group . . . That we were able to keep morale high was due solely to the quality of the men involved.[73]

A number of other Canadians also flew in Manchesters in the three RAF squadrons equipped with them, including the ill-fated David Albert Romans. When the airframe was modified to accommodate four Rolls-Royce Merlin engines, it became the incomparable Lancaster, a mainstay of wartime Bomber Command.

One aircraft type introduced to Bomber Command in 1941 that proved to be a delightful, unexpected bonus was the de Havilland Mosquito. It had been championed in 1939 by the Command's AOC at the time, Ludlow-Hewitt, and Air Chief Marshal Sir Wilfrid Freeman of the Air Council as a panacea solution to the urgent need for a "speed bomber" and a fast, photographic reconnaissance machine. Built largely of non-strategic materials such as plywood, and powered by two Rolls-Royce Merlins, the "Wooden Wonder" or "Freeman's Folly" excelled in these roles and also in night fighting and intruding. In production from July 1941 onwards, the first of many was delivered to Bomber Command just prior to year's end. Making its operational debut in early 1942, this marvelous aircraft could eventually carry a 4000-pound bomb over a range of 1750 miles, or a greater weapons weight for shorter hauls. It could also cruise at 315 mph at 30,000 feet and attain an astonishing top speed of 425 mph at that altitude. It became invaluable to the Command in the years to come, and many Canadian airmen crewed them. Over 1100 of the aircraft were built under license during the war by de Havilland Canada at the Downsview plant in Toronto.

Along with the introduction of new aircraft types to Bomber Command in 1941, forward strides were being made in offensive armament. The 500-pound General Purpose (GP) demolition bomb was refined and became the RAF's wartime "workhorse" in that category. 1000-pound (GP) bombs also made an extensive and sustained appearance, although by 1944 they were no longer in vogue. However, the most dramatic ordnance introduced to the Command in 1941 was undoubtedly the 4000-pound "cookie" blast bomb. On 31 March this new high-capacity weapon was used for the first time on operations, by Wellingtons against Emden. By the end of May, it was in frequent use. Consisting of nearly two tons of high explosive Ammatol wrapped in a thin metal casing, this blast weapon was particularly destructive when used in conjunction with boxes of 30-pound incendiary bombs. The "cookie" was an extremely adaptable weapon, and one of them could even be carried aboard the Mosquito. In 1943 the "cookie" was augmented by the 8000-pound "blockbuster" and in 1944 by an even larger 12,000-pound demolition bomb.

The Germans Bolster Their Defences

Throughout 1941 the Germans made wholesale, responsive changes to their night fighting procedures. Once the British learned to avoid the searchlight belts, the Germans developed the

Dunkelnachtjagd or "dark night fighting" system. At the heart of this system were the giant *Würzburg* detection, height-finding, and gun-laying radars; a quantum leap over the primitive *Freyas*. Introduced in early 1941, 1500 of them were eventually built. The extremely accurate *Würzburgs* were comprised of a huge dish antenna and an evaluation unit, were accurate to within a quarter of a degree, and could detect targets at ranges of between fifty and seventy kilometers. They were used in conjunction with the early-warning *Freyas* and coordinated through the control rooms of regionally responsible air divisions. The resulting radar plots of both enemy and friendly force tracks were maintained by individual plotters. These plots, projected as coloured points of light— red for hostile and blue for friendly—and continuously updated, were then used by individual fighter controllers to provide tailor-made interception guidance to single night fighters. The controller would watch the respective plots of friend and foe, then gradually move his assigned fighter to a kill position astern of and below the enemy bomber. This became known as the *Himmelbett* or "heavenly four-poster bed" method of night fighting, with each bedpost representing an essential part of the system; searchlights, ground control, flak, and night fighters. *Himmelbett* was in full operation by the end of 1941. However, the boundaries of those airspace boxes earlier established were still rigidly enforced, and airspace transgressions were only rarely permitted at this time. In fact, limiting to one the number of night fighters in any *Himmelbett* box at any given time proved to be the system's Achilles Heel. Bomber Command soon recognized this limitation and concentrated its nightly bomber streams into one zone, thus severely limiting the number of countering fighters available for combat in any given location. Eventually, the *Himmelbett* system was modified to redress this procedural inflexibility, but not entirely during *Generalmajor* Kammhuber's tenure as *Inspecteur der Nachtjagd*, or commander of the night fighter force.

A new system known as *Kombinierte Nachtjagd* (combined night fighting) was formally introduced by the Germans during the latter half of 1941 in an attempt to orchestrate the flak and the fighter assets as effectively as possible. These combined forces were to be concentrated around Bremen, Cologne, Darmstadt/Mannheim, Duisburg, Frankfurt, Hamburg and Munich in three sectors, each of which was equipped with a long-range *Freya* radar as well as two *Würzburg-Riese* (Giant Würzburg) units. As with *Hellenachtjagd*, once the bomber was detected by the *Freya*, one of the *Würzburgs* would track it while the other directed a night fighter in an attack. Both *Würzburgs* reported positions to a flak divisional headquarters, where friend-and-foe information was plotted and continuously updated as a series of red and blue dots in the *Himmelbett* manner, on a frosted glass map known as a Seeburg Table. With this continuously evolving tactical information, the *Flakleitoffizier* (anti-aircraft control officer) kept the flak and searchlight batteries informed, while the *Jägerleitoffizier* (fighter control officer) directed the fighter onto a specific quarry. Normally under these conditions of positive control, the flak was limited to a maximum height of 4000 meters, although the divisional commander could authorize higher firing if the attacking fighter was unlikely to be struck.

> However, for various reasons this system did not always work as its inventor had intended. Often the flak division commander, whether from personal ambition or through poorly interpreted data, failed to cease fire at the correct time, or else a fighter on a bomber's tail would not break off before it flew into the flak zone. Thus, it was not rare for fighters to be shot down by their own flak. These losses ultimately led to the abandonment of *Kombinierte Nachtjagd* as a failure.[74]

In March 1941 Air Chief Marshal Sir Wilfrid Freeman, then senior RAF officer in the Ministry of Aircraft Production, noted:

> "Priority of selection should be given to those [targets] in Germany which lie in congested areas where the greatest moral (sic) effect is likely to result." Despite the unfortunate misspelling, it was obvious what Freeman was suggesting, and this, ironically, was taken up by the Deputy Chief of the Air Staff, Air Vice-Marshal Arthur Harris, who, when said of Mannheim and the recently added city of Stuttgart to the U-Boat production targets said: "Both are suitable as area objectives and their attack should have high morale value." These two statements would greatly influence future Bomber Command thinking.[75]

By 1941 the British intelligence community had confirmed German intentions to move part of their garrisoned fighter forces out of France to the Mediterranean theatre and points eastward. In order to tie down as many as possible of these forces by forcing the *Luftwaffe* into defensive operations, the Air Staff approved a limited daylight offensive against targets in northern France, even though the largest part of Bomber Command's operational activity had become nocturnal. These operations were intended to lure the *Luftwaffe* into the air and to reduce its strength through combat, and also to disrupt enemy activity as much as possible in the coastal belt. Some of these offensive sweeps were flown exclusively by fighters, in raids known as "Rhubarbs"—pinprick, nuisance attacks on enemy airfields, docks, and railway facilities. More packaged efforts, however, known as "Circuses," would involve a number of Bomber Command Blenheim IVs escorted by several squadrons of fighters. Because of their limited bomb capacity, the Blenheims were frequently unable to do significant damage. In the spring of 1941, however, the Douglas Boston III, which at 2000 pounds capacity could carry double the internal bomb load of the Blenheim, began to significantly augment Bomber Command's day bomber fleet. It provided an improvement to the admittedly small RAF daylight bombing thrust.

The BCATP Starts to Deliver

By the end of November 1940 the first graduates of the British Commonwealth Air Training Plan (BCATP), possibly Canada's most important wartime contribution, had made their way overseas. The initial thirty-seven observers were joined by the first pilot graduates of the BCATP on 1 March 1941. This early trickle quickly became a steady stream and then a veritable torrent of aircrew, generated for the war against the Axis powers. The Canadian portion of the BCATP graduated 132,000 aircrew of all categories during the war, including 73,000 Canadians.[76] These men of Canada included, in round numbers, 26,000 pilots, 13,000 navigators, 6000 air bombers, 26,000 wireless operators/air gunners and 2000 flight engineers.[77] A majority of these airmen served in Bomber Command. By mid-April 1941 1680 graduates of the Plan were already in England. By year's end nearly 6700 were serving overseas, and yet only 600 of them were serving in RCAF squadrons.[78]

The BCATP was certainly gathering a head of steam. After the pilot trainees were selected at an Initial Training School (ITS), the next step was seven weeks at one of twelve Elementary Flying Training Schools (EFTS) for fifty hours of flying training in Tiger Moths or Cornells, dovetailed to about three times as many hours of classroom instruction. Nearly a quarter of all the pilot trainees "washed out" at this preliminary level, while the successful ones continued on to one of twenty-five Service Flying Training Schools (SFTS), for what was ultimately only ten weeks and an additional seventy-five hours of flying time. Those destined for multi-engine aircraft won their coveted pilot wings at this level in twin-engine Airspeed Oxfords, Avro Ansons, or Cessna Cranes. Bombing and gunnery practice, initially an integral part of "wings" training, was made the responsibility of the RAF operational training units (OTUs) overseas in the summer of 1940.

Air observers of the day completed twelve weeks at an Air Observer School (AOS), which concentrated on the theory and practice of basic aerial navigation. During this period, the observer candidates completed sixty to seventy hours of flight training and also spent many hours in the classroom. This was followed by a month at a bombing and gunnery school, followed by another month at an advanced school studying astro-navigation.

Specialized training for wireless operators/air gunners started with twenty-four weeks at wireless school, followed by a month of bombing and gunnery practice. Air gunners as such were not trained in Canada until 1942.

While a mere trickle of BCATP pilots was sent overseas in 1940, the other aircrew trades were more substantially represented. The first class of Canadian observers, who began their wartime careers at No. 1 Initial Training School in Toronto on 29 April 1940, received their badges on 26 October 1940 and were immediately detailed for overseas service.

> In November and December they were followed by two more classes of observers, seventy-seven pupils in all, one hundred and forty-nine wireless operators/air gunners, and nineteen air gunners, graduates of #1 Bombing and Gunnery School at Jarvis, Ontario, #2 at Mossbank, Saskatchewan, and #4 at Fingal, Ontario. Except for the ten pilots sent to RCAF squadrons overseas (and ten more sent to RAF units) the Canadians were absorbed into the RAF, most of them going to Bomber Command.[79]

Jack Watts of Hamilton, Ontario, was one of the early air observer graduates of the BCATP. Posted overseas in the spring of 1941, he spent three and a half years in Bomber Command. He flew three full operational tours for a total of 104 operations, ended the war with the rank of squadron leader, and won the DSO as well as a DFC and Bar. All his wartime service was in British or Australian squadrons. In fact, of the twenty-three wartime pilots with whom he flew, only one was a Canadian.

Watts entered the BCATP early, and as was to be expected, the organization was not yet functioning like a "well-oiled machine." Processing through No. 1 Manning Depot on the Canadian National Exhibition grounds in Toronto in early 1940, the system could not yet provide Watts and his colleagues with complete uniforms, thus restricting their public freedom of movement by confinement them to the grounds in off-duty hours. However, what happened next appears to be a classic case of wartime over-compensation. When he graduated as a breveted air observer early the following year, and after successful completion of a celestial navigation course at Rivers, Manitoba, Watts and some of his colleagues were ushered before an Eatons tailor, who had been instructed to kit them out as officers, and who also told them not to worry about payment. But these young officer-selectees had received no notification, official or otherwise, of their commissioning. When the finished uniform was delivered to his home while he was on embarkation leave, he still did not have his notification of commissioning, and young Watts returned the tailored masterpiece to Eatons. A short time later, while his charges awaited overseas embarkation at RCAF Station Debert, Nova Scotia,, the station commander tersely announced to all those who had met the tailor in Rivers: "OK, you have 48 hours. You've been commissioned. You're to go to Halifax and get outfitted, then report back."[80] Ironically, many had the tailoring done by Eatons of Halifax.

Commissioning notification and uniform provisioning would become considerably more efficient in the years to follow.

Jack Watts sailed for Britain as one of nearly 400 passengers aboard HMS *Arania*, an armed merchant cruiser, in convoy with thirty-six other ships out of Bedford Basin, Halifax, in the spring of 1941. The *Arania* was placed in the centre of the convoy, surrounded by tankers and cargo vessels, since it carried the bulk of the convoy's most precious commodity—trained manpower for the war effort—and this convoy had no escort. While Watts's three operational tours were fraught with danger, just getting to Europe via the North Atlantic was no picnic, either:

> We stood on the deck, looking out, and while we were there, the lookout called "Sub starboard," and it was as far out as you could see. Just a dot on the ocean, which he identified as a sub on the surface. The next thing was the call "Sub on the port," and again, just as far as you could see out on the horizon, just another dot on the surface. What we did not know was that there was a line of subs submerged, and we were sailing down the middle of them . . . Then, the sudden calls, "Torpedo starboard," and "Torpedo port," and both these tracks were heading directly for our armed merchant-cruiser. The first one crossed in front from one side; the other crossed in front from the other side. Each picked off ships on either side (of us), hitting them square. One was a tanker. It just went up with a tremendous explosion—split in the middle. It went down, but of course as it did, it spread high octane gas on the surface of the ocean, which caught fire. [Even though there were survivors in the water] . . . our skipper's orders were obviously first and foremost to save his passengers, and he immediately turned on full speed. We'd been an eight-knot convoy to that point. He turned on the speed to about eighteen knots and turned the ship into the direction from where the torpedo had come, so as to make the *Arania* the smallest target possible. Everybody was so in awe of what was going on— nobody was panicking, just dumbstruck really—and as we sailed away, ships were being blown up right where we had just been. The convoy that had been so beautiful and orderly was now all over the place. All of a sudden, there was a tremendous impact shock on the *Arania* and we thought, "Oh my God, we've been torpedoed." But there was no call. And what had happened, apparently, was that one of the subs that had fired the initial torpedoes had come up for a periscope sighting and we hit him below our water line, and then sailed right across the top of him. As we sailed over, our crew tossed off depth charges, just to make sure that although we had struck him, we were going to sink him. So these things were going off behind us, and this furor was going on all over the place, and we were heading straight ahead. As it turned out, we escaped. We subsequently learned that nine of the 37 ships had been lost in the engagement.[81]

Increased Canadian Presence

The Canadian contribution to the strategic bombing offensive was quite unique from that of the British, and eventually, that of the Americans as well. In order to fully appreciate the human dimension of this contribution, it is important to understand how the Canadianization process affected the contribution. As we have seen, from the "opening shots," individual Canadian airmen participated in combat operations with RAF units. Eventually, indigenous RCAF units were formed in all the RAF's Commands. However, with the exception of 6 Group in Bomber Command, the largest RCAF unit size was the wing. Indigenous RCAF wings were established in the fighter-bomber, army cooperation/reconnaissance and day fighter disciplines, while night fighter, intruder, transport and maritime patrol squadrons operated as individual RCAF squadrons within RAF wings.

Canadian aircrew permeated Bomber Command as they did the RAF in general, for the entire duration of the war. Indeed, by January 1943 nearly one-third of all Bomber Command squadrons were designated either Allied or Dominion units and Canadians comprised roughly twenty-five percent of the Command's operational aircrew on strength at war's end.[82] They served in virtually every RAF squadron, and did so with great distinction. However, memories of the Great War during which Canadian military formations were for the most part kept subservient to British higher authority were still fresh in 1939. The Canadian Executive felt that, whenever and wherever possible, Canadian servicemen would fight best and be the most contented serving in indigenous Canadian units under Canadian commanders. The Statute of Westminster of 1931 had recognized that the various Dominions were now responsible for their own foreign and defence policies, and provided broad autonomy for Canadian units overseas, but these were sweeping generalities, open to interpretation. The Visiting Forces Act of 1933 amplified on the 1931 legislation and reinforced that wherever and whenever possible, Canadian soldiers, sailors and airmen were to serve in Canadian units under Canadian commanders. Furthermore, when Prime Minister Mackenzie King signed the BCATP into being on 17 December 1939, Article XV of the Agreement declared that graduates of the Plan from the Dominions would be identified with their countries of origin through membership in Dominion units.[83] This was amplified by the bilateral, stage-setting Ralston-Sinclair Agreement of December 1940, which dictated how Canadian airmen would be employed and treated overseas. Specifically, Canada was permitted to establish Canadian units and formations overseas as quickly as possible and man them to the greatest extent possible with Canadian aircrew. This policy initiative would become known as the "Canadianization" process. These RCAF units were governed by RCAF regulations, procedures, and chains of authority. Eventually, there were forty-seven flying squadrons overseas, including fourteen heavy bomber squadrons. Although indigenous RCAF squadrons had been formed within the RAF since 1940 in the fighter and army cooperation disciplines, unit representation within Bomber Command was slower to evolve. The first RCAF heavy bomber squadron to form was 405 Squadron, equipped with Wellingtons, at Driffield in Yorkshire on 23 April 1941, under the umbrella of 4 Group. They flew their first combat missions in mid-June. By 24 June 408 Squadron, flying Hampdens, had been activated at Lindholme, also in Yorkshire, as part of 5 Group. Since the creation of these squadrons occurred within six months of the Ralston-Sinclair Agreement, practicalities demanded that initially, the squadron commander, the flight commanders, and the first cadre of experienced aircrew would have to come from the RAF. At the outset this certainly held true, and when 405 Squadron commenced operations in June, only 16.5 percent of the pilots were Canadian, although that included the commanding officer and both flight commanders. Wing Commander P.A. Gilchrist, a CAN/RAF from Point Pelly, Saskatchewan, who had joined the RAF in 1935 was chosen to lead the unit. He already wore the mauve and white diagonally-striped ribbon of the DFC under his pilot wings, which had been awarded for gallantry in action the previous year. Slightly better overall numbers were posted initially in 408 Squadron, where twenty-five percent of all aircrew positions were occupied by RCAF members.[84] By late fall, however, the Canadianization rate had improved somewhat, although many non-Canadians would continue to serve in RCAF heavy bomber squadrons, as well as Canadians in RAF squadrons, for the duration of the war. Also, by year's end 1941 two more RCAF heavy bomber units, 419 Squadron and 420 Squadron, were activated, again with twin-engine Wellingtons and Hampdens respectively.

Many "firsts" were registered by these new squadrons during their earliest months of operations. Sergeant Jim Kirk of Hamiota, Manitoba, was the first Canadian to be shot down from the first RCAF heavy bomber squadron. He was the first of many. A graduate of only the second wireless air gunners' course in Montreal during November 1940, Kirk received further training in Britain and was then posted on 5 July 1941 to the neophyte 405 Squadron, by then based at Pocklington in Yorkshire. Situated beside an old Roman road, the base, which had been used as a grass strip during the Great War, was a designated mid-1930s RAF Expansion Scheme field. Updating the base did not begin in earnest, however, until the outbreak of war in September 1939. Unlike the relative splendor of the pre-war establishments, accommodation at Pocklington consisted of dreary, prefabricated, corrugated iron Nissen huts mounted on concrete pads, and they were cold and damp for the greatest part of the year. For Jim Kirk, they would never be more than a temporary home:

> Nine days later, Sergeant Jim Kirk was airborne on his first operational sortie with a crew of five RAF airmen aboard a Wellington Mark II. Their target was a rubber factory in Hannover. Shortly after bomb release, the aircraft was hit by flak which disabled the starboard Merlin engine. Unable to maintain altitude, the captain, Sergeant Thrower, ordered the crew to bail out and Kirk was the first to abandon the crippled Wellington.[85]

Finding himself in an open field in bright moonlight, Kirk soon realized he was in Germany, about thirty miles east of the Dutch border. He hooked up with the Dutch Resistance and successfully evaded capture for many weeks. However, in the company of two Dutch Jews and a British army corporal from a highland regiment who had escaped from Dunkirk, his luck ran out in October:

> Not far out of Utrecht they encountered a road block manned by SS troops who ordered them from the car, appearing to know who they were. "I have never been able to discover just what happened, but something had gone terribly wrong and the Germans were waiting for us," Kirk said. He was taken to The Hague and interrogated by the *Gestapo*, who attempted to discover who had aided him during his evasion. He refused to give any information and after four days they gave up . . . For Jim Kirk, the first Canadian on the first RCAF bomber squadron to be shot down, "the rest of the war was a series of prison camps in Germany and Poland. I was in northwestern Germany when our camp was liberated by the British 8th Army in April 1945."[86]

Wing Commander Nelles Woods Timmerman from Kingston, Ontario, a CAN/RAF who had already won the DFC, caught the eye of the RAF's Chief of the Air Staff, Sir John Slessor, in early 1941. Slessor also noticed Timmerman's Canada flashes. Timmerman soon found himself posted to Lindfield on the Hatfield Moors, to become the first wartime commander of 408 Squadron. He was also successful at the outset in persuading 5 Group Headquarters to pry loose two experienced CAN/RAFs from other units to be his flight commanders. However, within a month of its formation, the squadron was moved to Syerston in Nottinghamshire, a new base nestled between main highway A46 and the River Trent: "In June 1941, we had sixteen Hampdens at 408 Squadron, operating from grass strips," [Timmerman] recalled,

> "Bombing targets on the continent was largely ineffective because they were difficult to find and we had no radar to help us. That was why we went out, usually on an individual basis, looking for any enemy targets we could find." . . . Soon after Timmerman's arrival

That ponderous, graceless "old flying cow," the Armstrong Whitworth Whitley. (Author's Collection)

Hampden EQ–H of 408 Squadron doing an engine run-up at Balderton in Nottinghamshire. It was lost in combat over Denmark the night of 8 May 1942. (DND PL4715)

A Bristol Blenheim in a steeply banked turn. (Author's Collection)

An early wartime shot of 405 Squadron Wellingtons at dispersal. (DND PL4501)

Getting ready to go. A Canadian bomber crew suits up. (DND PL15271)

Inside view of a Hampden looking forward. (DND PL4709)

In the face of a Hampden bomb aimer. (DND PL4708)

Ground crew servicing a Bristol Blenheim. (Author's Collection)

Pilot Officer Norman Duncan MacLennan.
(Norma Kelkar)

A Short Stirling on the takeoff roll with a Famous British Person in the foreground. (Shorts 65133)

One of twenty B-17Cs delivered to the RAF as Fortress Is. (Author's Collection)

Early war shot of 405 Squadron's Operations Room. (DND RE 74-385)

Standing in front of their Hampden, from 408 Squadron, l to r: Sergeants Cornwall, Dunn, Manson and Norton. (DND PL7121)

A 408 "Goose" Squadron Hampden on takeoff. (DND PL4700)

Before his meteoric rise in rank, a very youthful Sergeant Reg Lane in 1941. (Lane Family)

A Canadian airman drops leaflets from a Wellington. (DND PL4661)

Interior of the Wellington looking forward. The geodetic "basket weave" construction is apparent.
(DND PL4972)

at 408 Squadron, Handley-Page Limited donated £50 to each Hampden squadron, stating that COs were free to use the money as they saw fit. Timmerman decided to seek approval to create what would be the first badge for any RCAF squadron overseas. "My first choice for the centre of the badge was an autumn-colored, red maple leaf, but for reasons having to do with the rigid rules of heraldry, it was rejected. The Canada goose, which I thought was also native to our country, was quickly approved. As for the squadron motto—*For Freedom*—it was an answer to a simple question, 'Why were we here?'"

"One of our hairiest sorties was the minelaying trip to Brest Harbour when the German battle cruisers *Scharnhorst* and *Gneisenau* were there.[One of many raids against the two moored cruisers] We arrived over the target to find the Germans had laid down a thick layer of smoke, completely covering the harbour area, so that dropping our mine at the normal height of 1000 feet was out of the question. We went down on the deck, barely skimming the water. The mine was released and we quickly turned for home."[87]

Timmerman fails to mention in this account the intense enemy fire they faced going in and coming away from the target. Nelles Timmerman epitomized leadership by example, and he was also characteristically forthright with his crews, giving them no false illusions about the dangers associated with various aspects of operational flying. For example, part of his crew briefing just prior to the Brest raid stated:

> Minelaying is one of our most dangerous operations. It is unspectacular compared with bombing, but to be effective, mines must be laid in places which naturally will be well defended. Mines must be dropped at low altitude. This will put your plane within easy range of all flak, ship and shore, light and heavy, and of course there will be barrage balloons. Your target tonight will be a German harbour. Weather reports of the area to be visited are bad. Low clouds, fog, mist and low icing conditions can be anticipated. I expect further weather reports in an hour or so but frankly I am not hopeful. Furthermore, there is no possibility of the flight being cancelled—it is too important. Those are our orders and they must be carried out.[88]

Nonetheless, in its early months under Timmerman's able command, 408 Squadron seemed to lead a charmed life. In fact, until one of its Hampdens was shot down during a raid on Mannheim during the night of 22 October, 142 sorties had been flown before casualties were sustained or any aircraft went missing in action.[89] This record is particularly commendable, since the squadron was temporarily withdrawn from night operations during the last week in August to serve as additional bait for Fighter Command's new daylight Circus operations over France, which they did with limited success for the next month. They were fortunate to have been provided fighter escort on these missions. "Unescorted operations by daylight—mostly the concern of No. 2 Group—were far more deadly, leading to a loss rate of 7.1 percent between July and November 1941, while that for night raids was only 3.5 percent."[90]

Timmerman added a DSO to his awards in September, and left 408 Squadron in March 1942 after flying a total of fifty combat operations. He completed a distinguished wartime career as the station commander of Bomber Command bases at Odiham, Topcliffe, and Skipton-on-Swale.

Meanwhile, other Canadians were building illustrious wartime careers with Bomber Command. Sergeant Robert Steele Turnbull of Govan, Saskatchewan, enlisted early and had won his pilot wings by January 1941. He was one of three brothers who served on operations with Bomber Command, all of whom were awarded the Distinguished Flying Cross. Bob Turnbull had a meteoric rise through the ranks, progressing from sergeant to wing commander in less than one year. War's end found him promoted yet again to group captain and in command of RCAF Station Croft within 6 Group of Bomber Command. Along the way, he flew more than two operational tours, beginning with seventeen operations in antediluvian Whitleys, and ending with command of 426 Squadron out of Leeming, flying both Halifaxes and Lancasters. Handsomely decorated for his accomplishments, Turnbull returned home with a Distinguished Flying Medal (DFM), a DFC and Bar, the Air Force Cross (AFC), a Mention-in-Despatches (MiD) and the French *Croix de Guerre* with Silver Palm. His wartime letters home to his future wife, Tannis Davidson, during his first operational tour with 78 and 76 Squadrons RAF provide interesting snapshots of life for a young non-commissioned (at the time) aircrew member from the Dominions within the RAF of the period, and the implied disparities between his lot and that of the commissioned officers.

APRIL 29, 1941

'Nother bad crash last night. A very good friend from Rhodesia went into the "deck." Cause unknown/Talking to him not twenty minutes before it happened and saw them take-off and then crash. What a strange world of fortune this can be—things happen so suddenly and leave you with such lost feelings that are impossible to describe. And still we fly on.

MAY 6, 1941 Sergeants' Mess, Abington

Also had an uneventful trip over Paris on a leaflet raid. Great fun but nothing of interest even got close to us. Will save you a leaflet to commemorate our first trip to Europe. Would like to give you the events of the trip but am afraid it wouldn't pass the censor.

[Spent] Sunday evening walking around this village with a couple of fellows who were in our course at Saskatoon, but failed, so had to wait for the next lot. Joke of it is they both got their commissions. Guess you've got to have a wing commander or a group captain for a relative to get anywhere in this outfit—haven't given up hopes yet—'fact I'm working harder and have higher hopes than I ever had.

P.S. Had a long talk with a flight lieutenant today and he said I had a very good chance of getting a commission. He is our armament instructor, was very pleased with my exam results (so am I) and said my recommendation would go in accordingly. Sounds very encouraging—wish I had some pull on that side of the water. We'll just keep up the hard work—believe it's going to pay after all.

MAY 17, 1941 Sergeants' Mess, Middleton St. George

Spent my six days leave in London. Intended to stay at the home of one of my crew. However, in reaching it in the morning there was not very much of what was once a really beautiful home. Fortunately, every one was away at the time but they lost almost everything. Consequently I had to go into London and stay. Got my first taste of what a big bombing raid is like. You more than likely read in the papers about last Saturday nite. It was terrible. Had the pleasure of spending the hours from 11 'till 4 the next morning on a fire hose and at times I'd have given anything to be in (a) nice deep shelter somewhere. London was lit up just like day—you would read in the papers of the terrific damage but to see and hear it all fall is something no one can describe. Managed to stay clear of all the bombs but wasn't very funny at times—will be able to tell you all about it when I see you.

Have already sewn your lock of hair in the scarf you gave me. It will bring me luck as you always have dear and I couldn't ask for a more pleasant reminder that you are thinking of me and pulling for me.

MAY 20/21, 1941 Sergeants' Mess, Middleton St. George

Well dear, it's just about time I got ready for the short trip. Will go and get my thermos filled up with sugarless tea and collect the rest of my food for my "midnight snack" over Germany. Some fun and you certainly do get hungry. From now on you will certainly be able to keep track of me. Keep your eyes open for news of 78 Squadron. We are the crack outfit—so we think.

JULY 9, 1941 Sergeants' Mess, Middleton St. George

Everything is going first rate and am in "A" condition. Just came in from playing golf but it's the first time I've been out for some time. "Happy" and I were in to see a "flick" last nite but to (sic) many in the queue so just had something to eat and came back to camp. Now that the "moon period" is here we are very busy and have spent a couple of good nites over Osnabrook (sic) and Munster . . . Ran across a Me.110 on one of our trips but after the first shot or so he wouldn't come at us at all, thank goodness.

[During this interval, after seventeen operations in Whitleys, Turnbull completed a conversion to Halifaxes.]

AUG 20, 1941 Linton-on-Ouse

Well my dear I've achieved one of my ambitions—am now captain of a four-motor job. Probably noticed the change in address but it is only for this week and then we'll be back again to our home station but in a new squadron—just down here to learn all about these "over-sized kites." They certainly are some "blunderbus" but they are very good and easier to handle than one would expect—here's hoping I can continue to cope with them.

This is quite the country around here and is very much typical England as one always imagines it. We are staying at a lovely old country home. The surrounding landscape is really grand—massive old trees, lovely green lawns, beautiful rose garden with its many little statues—all in all it's quite all right as one wanders through the paths it's very hard to imagine the strife which surrounds this small isolated Utopia of ours here.

Things are going first rate for me. Am feeling fine and am doing quite O.K. Well over half of my trips in now and when we get cracking again on these "new things" (bet you wish you knew what they were called) it shouldn't take long to finish them off. Got word of my commission and [it] is just going through Canadian records—dear knows how long that will be.

P.S. Just been invited out on a apple orchard raid—believe I'll go but bet they're still green.

SEPT 22, 1941 Middleton St. George

Was in to Darlington one night to see a lousy stage show but made that up by treating myself to a grouse supper. Really nice and what a change for my poor stomach—wonder it stood it . . . I've spent the spare time teaching some of the boys baseball and even got them interested in Canadian rugby. . .

See where our "kites" have been officially announced—have you seen a picture of them yet, dear?—"Halifax"—Saw Lady Halifax break the half-bottle of champagne on the nose for the public appearance and later saw it again in one of the news shorts. Also any pictures you see of "L" flying you can think of me 'cause they took photos of it when yours truly was at the controls. Quite a tub and am quite proud of the fact that I was one of the first to fly them on "ops."

OCT 28, 1941 Middleton St. George

You will have received my cable by now giving you the news that I'm finished my Ops.

Yes dear, we're actually done our trips and no longer have to do our night trips over "Jerry land." Must admit that it came as a sort of a surprise—as no doubt it did to you—but it is a rather pleasant one. Certainly is a grand feeling though.

NOV 4, 1941 Middleton St. George

Lost another one of my pals last nite which means out of four of us who always were together there's only myself left—must sound like a small child lamenting the loss of a favourite toy. Makes me sit back and wonder how I ever managed to get through but we shall ever thank our luck that has been with us here.[91]

Bob Turnbull's commission finally came through in November. Just prior to finishing his first tour, he was recommended for the DFM, which he soon received. The correspondence attached to the award recommendation suggests the esteem in which he was held:

A Canadian pilot of outstanding capability and personality. A very sound and well above the average Halifax pilot. An exceptionally thorough, reliable and conscientious captain of aircraft. Altogether a gallant fellow whose courage and never-failing enthusiasm should be rewarded. On his last trip to Nuremburg (12 October), he spent one hour circling round in the target area before he definitely identified, to his satisfaction, the target; then he bombed it and started fires. His crew follow him to a man.[92]

Other Canadians of the period had much shorter and less illustrious, although no less exciting, Bomber Command experiences. Donald A. "Pappy" Elliott of Swift Current, Saskatchewan, completed his observer training in February 1941 and arrived in England in April. He was subsequently posted to 99 Squadron at Waterbeach in June, flying in Wellington 1Cs. Elliott's wartime operational career was short. He was shot down by flak on 8 July 1941, running up on the main railway station in Cologne. Coned by searchlights, the aircraft was disabled by flak, but all crew members parachuted safely. Elliott actually landed beside a flak battery and was picked up immediately. Fortunately, the entire crew survived. Elliott recalls:

My most memorable Op was my last one—during the early hours of July 8, 1941. I was in the nose of our Wellington acting as the bomb aimer, as we approached our target for that night, the main railway station in Cologne. We were flying at 15,000 feet when we were coned by searchlights and hit by flak. Our pilot immediately ordered the crew to bail out. There was a long journey back to the navigator's table (about 15 feet) to get my parachute and then return to the front of the aircraft in order to jump out of the hatch in the nose. Once I tore off my oxygen and intercom tubes and released my foot from a flying boot that flak splinters had jammed under the bottom step of the three which lead down from the cabin—all went well. After briefly considering the alternative—about one millisecond—I did not hesitate to jump. When I left the aircraft, I was clutching the ripcord of the parachute which when pulled, would open it. I now believe that I neglected to do so.

One's terminal velocity in those circumstances reaches 120 miles per hour, so I had about a minute and one-half to think about my situation. My first thought was that there would be a flash of light and then I would be dead. My next thought was that I should get in touch with my mother at Swift Current, Saskatchewan, by ESP and tell her that I was in a bit of trouble. As soon as I finished that, I must have pulled the ripcord because my parachute opened. I believe that I was then up at about 1000 feet, since there was a full moon and I could see the horizon and the ground clearly. The landing was a "piece of cake." As soon as I took off my parachute harness, I felt that I should get in touch with my mother once more and cancel my original message. So I went into my ESP mode again and informed her that I was now safe and sound. Four years later when I came home to Swift Current, my first question to my mother was whether or not she had received my message. I was more than a little disappointed when she said that she had not! Obviously, ESP does not always work when you want it to![93]

Not all problems for the young RCAF flyers overseas were associated with operations. Reg Lane, in the early autumn of 1941, was completing his OTU in Whitleys at Abington in Berkshire. Lane recalls his first night solo, crewed with a student second pilot, when a rapidly-deteriorating flight situation dictated an innovative interpretation of crew cooperation:

The airfield [at Abington] was grass, the lighting nothing but a bunch of flare pots— absolutely no lights anywhere. I took the airplane off, we climbed up to do a circuit and land, and as we were on our final approach at a very low altitude, I got a red light—in other words, a wave-off—and proceeded to open the two engines to full power, asking the second pilot if he would bring the flaps up. There was a routine for this. The second pilot brought the flaps up about fifteen degrees at a time to prevent the aircraft from sinking. This very fine young second pilot thought I had decided to bring the flaps all the way up in one fell swoop, and as a result, the aircraft almost fell out of the sky! I managed to get the throttles really wide open, and we climbed a wee bit, at which time, the second pilot froze on the controls. He was in a state of fright and, I must admit, I wasn't far off that myself. However, he was in *such* a state of fright that he would not let go of the dual controls, and meanwhile here I was, trying to fly this airplane and do another circuit and go in to land. I finally had to hit him across the mouth with the back of my hand, although it was a *gloved* hand, to make him let go of the control column, which he then did. We then proceeded to go around and I did all the cockpit checks, etcetera, and landed the airplane, taxied in, and told the flight commander that I was not going to fly with that second pilot again.[94]

Shortly thereafter, Lane was posted to 35 (RAF) Squadron at Linton-on-Ouse in Yorkshire, where his first operational flight commander was the future Victoria Cross winner and Bomber Command legend, Leonard Cheshire. His squadron commander was Wing Commander Jimmy Marks, also a leader of exceptional character and a Bomber Command household name, even at that early stage of the war. Thus, Reg Lane was strongly influenced early in his operational career by two charismatic air leaders of the highest calibre.

Almost immediately on his arrival, the squadron began converting to the Halifax Mark 1, since no standardized Heavy Conversion Unit (HCU) existed in those early days of operations. There was an apprenticeship program of sorts set up to ease the transition of new pilots into operations. The newcomers flew as second pilots to an experienced aircraft captain for a few operations, known as "second dickie" trips, in order to gain operational experience before taking an aircraft out on their own. For example, Reg Lane flew such trips to Berlin, Hamburg, Cologne and to Brest twice, in unsuccessful bids to sink the *Scharnhorst* and the *Gneisenau*, prior to being assigned his own crew in early 1942.

Other crew members had different forms of apprenticeship. At Leeming flying Whitleys with 10 (RAF) Squadron, Jack Watts was learning what a true "jack of all trades" the observer had to be at this stage of the war. Just three days after his arrival, Watts's crew was one of three detailed to go to Ostend in Belgium. This was commonly known as a "nursery trip," and all the crews were new, with little prior experience. Jack Watts explains:

They were the new crews and they were being given the experience of going into enemy territory, on a night raid, with very limited penetration of enemy defences. So in a sense, it was a sort of soft break-in to see what it was like; to get over the newness of being a bombing crew, to see how you worked together, and whether you actually achieved the objective of hitting the target. But it also meant [in this case] that you had coastlines to work with, which gave you a better chance of being accurate in your navigation. You also got a better opportunity for a good bombing run if you were attacking from the water side, since you were not going to get peppered with flak until you got close to the target. So the whole thing was quite appropriately classified as a nursery target . . .

[With respect to operational focus] the most overpowering aspect was the sheer concern of being able to navigate the aircraft to the target . . . I wasn't concerned about enemy action, not in the slightest, because I was so absorbed in navigating, to get within visible range of the target, and then to be able to take the thing on a bombing run right into the target. Just being challenged by that aspect of it, I never even thought about the fact that we were going into enemy territory. Rather, "Could I find it?" "Could I get there?" When we arrived and I had the pilot on the bombing approach, then it was tremendous. I could give him a straight run at the target, just like doing it in practice.

With respect to flak, I saw these things coming up like hose pipes, colored lights coming up and peeling over, it looked like they were going right over the wing tips. It just didn't mean anything . . . it just looked colorful. And searchlights . . . It just didn't look like an activity that meant anything until I had dropped the bombs . . . But once I had done so, you kinda came to the realization that you had done your job, now what the hell was going on around here? They're shooting at you, there are searchlights on you, and *now* you really came alive. There's a little *danger* here. It got the adrenaline flowing, that's for sure.[95]

More Changes

On 9 July 1941 a new Policy Directive argued that "the weakest points in [the enemy's] armour lie in the morale of the civilian population and in his inland transportation system."[96] This statement would pave the way for further policy changes with respect to bombing policy downstream. Two other tactical changes to the manner in which the bombing was conducted were implemented in July, and again, they portended future, broader policy changes:

> The practice of blind bombing on ETA through heavy cloud was suspended, crews being told to attack instead "any . . . town or built-up area" they could see. The instruction to bomb from 16,000 feet or more, adopted in April but not always followed, was also rescinded once it was realized that, from that height, crews could not "recognize even the target area." Pilots were directed to fly lower, in order to pick out their precise aiming points; and if that proved impossible they were to bomb from a height which would allow them to hit "the particular town in or near which" the aiming point was situated. It was acknowledged that these aiming points might include town squares, churches, or municipal buildings even when, for example, railway marshalling yards or road junctions were the objective of the attack.[97]

Henceforth, Germany would be attacked more frequently, with greater intensity and less target discrimination.

During the first half of 1941, although Bomber Command's operations had continued at a brisk pace when weather and opportunity permitted, it was becoming increasingly obvious that the night attacks were not meeting damage expectations, in spite of the enthusiasm and the dedication of the crews. The General Purpose bombs were too small and unreliable. New weapons, however, were slowly being introduced. Bombing accuracy was still woefully inadequate in spite of rudimentary target-marking techniques which had already been implemented, such as those used on Mannheim in December 1940. These "fire raising" techniques were offset by the convincing use of decoy fires by the Germans, set alight in open fields: "In May 1941 over half the bombs dropped by Bomber Command fell in the country, away from villages, towns and cities."[98] The concern was legitimate, and in August, Lord Cherwell, Churchill's scientific advisor, tasked Mr. D.M. Butt of the War Cabinet to examine existing crew bombing photographs to obtain an accurate picture of the latest results. They were indeed sobering. Of over 4000 photographs taken in June and July, when bombing weather was generally optimum, some 650 were singled out for special attention. These depicted a hundred separate raids on twenty-eight different targets on forty-eight nights in which the crews claimed to have hit their targets.

> During moon periods, only one in four photographs taken on raids to German and French targets showed that the bombs had dropped within five miles of the target. In non-moon periods the proportion within five miles dropped to one in fifteen photographs; over Germany only, the figure was one in twenty, and the results over the important Ruhr industrial area were even worse than that.[99]

The inquiry had defined the target area itself as having a radius of five miles, producing an area of over seventy-five square miles.[100] In late summer 1941 the Butt Report emphasized the need to examine bombing techniques and also to improve navigational procedures, since daylight raids were proving to be too dangerous. Those in authority concurred that it was unthinkable to completely abandon the bomber offensive, since it was at the time the only viable way to strike back at the enemy. The report also included an examination of the effect of bombing on civilian morale, based on the British experience during the Blitz, and concluded that bomb damage to homes, water supply, power sources and the food distribution systems had a greater effect on lowering of morale than did the loss of friends or relatives. Ultimately, these observations would have an enormous impact on future bombing policy.

During October, the bombing focus was clearly aimed at transportation targets in Germany, although the AOC-in-C Bomber Command Sir Richard Peirse's broad directives for the period are also worthy of note:

OFFICE OF THE MINISTER OF DEFENCE
APPENDIX "A"

SECRET

BOMBER COMMAND OPERATIONS AGAINST PRIMARY TARGETS
PERIOD SEPTEMBER 28TH TO OCTOBER 26TH, 1941.

GERMANY

Class of Target	A/C Despatched	% of Total
Transportation	998	39.7
Industrial (Morale)	449	17.9
Shipyards	180	7.2
Aircraft Factories	151	6.0
Land Armaments (Essen)	173	6.9
Public Utilities (Power Stations)	41	1.6
Other Targets	13	0.5
TOTALS	2005	79.8

SECRET

The A.O.C-in-C. Bomber Command's directives for his night bombing effort cover broadly the following operations:—

(i)   Primary offensive against transportation and morale targets in Germany.

(ii) Objectives in Kiel, Hamburg, Bremen and Wilhelmshaven to hamper the German submarine building programme whenever the weather conditions are such that he decides to concentrate his attack on North-West Germany.

(iii) Periodic attacks on the battlecruisers at Brest and with his freshmen crews on the enemy-occupied ports opposite our coasts whenever the weather conditions are favourable.

(iv) Sea-mining with a limited effort by the Manchesters and Hampdens.

(v)   Diversions as ordered e.g. Italy, Land Armaments (Essen) etc.[101]

The Admiralty had previously successfully emphasized its continued concerns about the construction of U-boats. Accordingly, the Chiefs of Staff recommended to the Prime Minister that AOC-in-C Bomber Command's directives be modified to permit higher priority action against enemy shipbuilding yards and operational submarine bases, recommendations that were subsequently approved. This explains the continued higher priority assigned to these tasks in the aforementioned document, and is noteworthy for the amount of influence the Admiralty had with the Prime Minister's Office on the conduct of air operations during the period. Specifically:

Supplementary Directive to Bomber Command

In view of the importance of hampering the German submarine construction programme at the present time, it is necessary to give high priority, as far as weather conditions allow, to the ports of Kiel, Hamburg, Bremen and Wilhelmshaven.

Whenever the weather conditions are such that you decide to concentrate your attack on N.W. Germany you should detail as your objectives such targets in one or more of these ports as you consider most likely to achieve the above object. You will doubtless also maintain your present principle of following up a successful attack with subsequent concentrations as closely spaced as weather conditions permit.[102]

The operational submarine bases at Brest and Lorient are also important, but you will be advised as soon as a diversion of your present scale of effort on Brest seems justified.[103]

Throughout the autumn, inclement weather forced many bombing delays and outright cancellations. However, the forced inactivity led to a certain sense of operational desperation when the weather was, at best, marginal. This was typified by the record number of sorties flown during the night of 7/8 November:

392 aircraft were despatched with the main objectives being Berlin (169 aircraft), Cologne (75) and Mannheim (55). The Berlin raid suffered not only from cloud obscuring the target, but also at the hands of flak and fighters. 21 aircraft (12.4%) were lost (10 Wellingtons, 9 Whitleys and 2 Stirlings). Overall, 37 aircraft failed to return, a rate of 9.4%. These losses were rapidly swinging the balance against Bomber Command. Indeed, no air force could sustain this amount of losses for any length of time and, in an attempt to rebuild the Command's confidence, less well-defended targets were chosen for future attacks. In four months, Bomber Command had lost the equivalent of its entire frontline strength, 526 aircraft, and morale on the squadrons was low.[104]

Berlin had been attacked on the night of 7/8 November, in spite of a weather forecast so atrocious that the 5 Group commander, Sir John Slessor, diverted his forces, which included 408 Squadron, to Cologne. Still, hail, sleet, heavy cloud, electrical storms, and icing played havoc with the crews who made it to the Third Reich's capital, to be met by particularly alert defences. Only half of those that returned claimed to have even seen the city's outskirts. The damage inflicted was inconsequential. Of the ten crews from 405 Squadron that went to Berlin, half attacked the general vicinity of the target area, while four others chose alternate targets at Wilhelmshaven and Kiel. One aircraft was lost, three more were damaged and one crash landed on return to England. Flight Lieutenant John Fauquier recalled that because of the near-uniform overcast, the raiders had to rely solely on dead-reckoning and forecast winds for the long haul up to the target over the North German Plain:

> Finally, we reached the point where we thought, and hoped, Berlin lay . . . dropped our bombs and turned for home. It wasn't long before I realized we were in trouble because the winds had increased greatly in strength and were almost dead ahead. Eventually, I lost height down to a few hundred feet—to avoid icing conditions and to save fuel since the head wind would be less strong. I have seen the North Sea in many moods but never more ferocious than that night. Huge waves of solid green water were lifted from the surface and carried hundreds of feet by the wind. After what seemed like hours in these appalling conditions I realized we were unlikely to make base. I had little or no fuel left and told the crew to take up ditching positions . . . It was then I saw briefly one of those wonderful homing lights and made a bee-line straight for it.[105]

Fauquier and his men landed, half-frozen, utterly disgusted, exhausted, and bitter that they had been sortied against the German capital in such highly unsuitable weather conditions. Something had to change, and soon did:

> On the 13th, the Air Ministry dropped the bombshell to the Command's AOC-in-C, Air Marshal Sir Richard Pierse [sic], that the bomber offensive in its present form was to be stopped whilst the future shape and tactics of Bomber Command was debated. With the exception of a few minor raids in the following months this is exactly what happened and, by early January, Pierse had been posted from his position.[106]

The specific guidance to "go slow" to the AOCs of both Bomber Command and Fighter Command served as a portent for sweeping policy changes early in the new year.

MOST SECRET.

CS.10488/D.C.A.8.   13th November 1941.
8.3553/D.C.A.8.

Conservation of Forces

Sir,

I am directed to inform you that the War Cabinet have had under consideration the intensity of air operations recently undertaken in Bomber and Fighter Command. They have stressed the necessity for conserving our resources in order to build a strong force to be available by the spring of next year. It is requested that you will have this principle in mind in planning operations generally in the future. Whilst it was realized that in vital operations heavy losses must be faced, it was considered undesirable in present circumstances and in the course of normal operations that attacks should be pressed unduly especially if weather conditions were unfavourable or if our aircraft were likely to be exposed to extreme hazards.

> I am, Sir,
> Your obedient Servant,
> (Sgd.) N.H. BOTTOMLEY.
> Air Vice-Marshal,
> Deputy Chief of the Air Staff.

The A.O.C.-in-C., Bomber Command.
The A.O.C.-in-C., Fighter Command.[107]

Operations for the rest of the year continued at a slow pace. They included yet another partially successful daylight raid on *Gneisenau* in Brest on 18 December. The same day, an Associated Press poll of sports writers selected the New York Yankees' Joe DiMaggio as their Athlete of the Year. But, while monumental policy shifts were being debated in the highest councils that grim autumn and winter, the rank and file of Bomber Command struggled gamely in their personal campaign against the enemy, and their lives were punctuated by harrowing experiences. Jack Watts had one such occurrence in October on his fifth operation, something that would almost happen to "Johnnie" Fauquier the following month on the Berlin raid:

> We were returning home from Stuttgart, which was a rather deep penetration, and the winds were far from forecast. Plus I think we'd taken some shrapnel, so all-in-all, we were running short of fuel . . . The options were to bail out over enemy territory or take our chances crossing the sea. We decided to keep going and to try to make the (British) coast . . . Soon, it was quite clear that we were going to have to make a ditching in the sea . . . So we got the crew down in the escape area in the mid-fuselage, and I stayed up with the pilot thinking that he would need some assistance . . . Tom probably made the best landing he had ever made. But when the nose of the aircraft dropped into the sea, it was like hitting a wall of concrete. There was just an absolute shock of a hit on the aircraft nose. The bombing panel was caved in completely and of course the water was a real torrent under pressure. I had been laying on the floor beside the pilot. I got up, already in water, and the pilot was slumped over the controls. I shook him and he came to. His harness had broken on impact and had hit his face on the panel. He was dazed and I was calling at him to get out through the top escape hatch, which we did . . . Eventually, as we walked down the length of the fuselage from outside, it sank below the surface, so we didn't really *enter* the water, we just descended with the ship. As we got back to the rear escape hatch, we could see some of the crew in the water, and our ship just sank.
>
> This is October. After awhile, all five of our crew are established in the aircraft dingy [sic], pitching and bobbing on a rough sea and feeling thoroughly sorry for ourselves, but we soon got picked up by a Royal Navy minesweeper.[108]

The navy crew was even more overjoyed to see Watts's crew than the airmen were to see them. They had apparently never had any previous success rescuing downed aircrew and were already discontinuing this particular search, when an alert crewman caught a fleeting glimpse of something on the water. Watts and his colleagues were subsequently inducted into the Goldfish Club, exclusive to those whose lives were saved at sea thanks to rubber liferafts.

In London that dreary autumn, the staunch inhabitants were still digging out from the heavy enemy raiding that had continued unabated until June. Shortly thereafter, the air attacks ebbed significantly and then trickled away to nothing as the *Luftwaffe* concentrated its attentions elsewhere. Londoners were quietly proud of the overall fortitude they had demonstrated during the previous year, and were fiercely determined to back the war effort and put paid to the evil regime that had brought them so much suffering. Patriotic themes, embodied in various activities, music, and films abounded. Two of the most popular films were *A Yank in the RAF*, starring Tyrone Power and Betty Grable, and *Dangerous Moonlight*, starring Anton Walbrook. The latter epitomized the extreme hardships faced by Bomber Command crews at the time, and it introduced one of the most enduring passages of music to emerge from the Second World War, *The Warsaw Concerto*, composed specifically for the film by Richard Addinsell. When played by Louis Kentner and the London Symphony Orchestra, it was an instant hit that gave its listeners heart and helped make a strong international appeal for assisting Britain and the Dominions in their ongoing struggle against the Axis powers.

THREE

The Long, Dark Night
1942

*I watched him being very badly shot
up and on fire and goodness knows what,
and I thought, well that's it.*

—Reg Lane
Trondheim Fjord, 27 April 1942

Despair and Hope

Early 1942 marked the nadir of Allied war fortunes. The *Wehrmacht* continued to steamroll across the Soviet Union. On the North Atlantic, both merchant and naval shipping from Britain and the United States was being lost to German submarines at unsustainable rates. In North Africa, Germany's favourite new combat commander, Erwin Rommel, drove his forces to within reach of the Suez Canal. In the Far East, Japan was in firm control of Malaya, Burma, the Philippines, and the East Indies. It was also a bittersweet year for Bomber Command. On one hand, the force suffered high casualty rates as it further codified, refined, and bolstered the bombing offensive against Germany and the Axis. On the other, significant new technologies and techniques were introduced, and the Command also acquired a new helmsman of iron will and single-minded determination. Furthermore, from 7 December 1941 onward, Britain, the Dominions, and the Allies—including, since June, the Soviet Union—were no longer alone in the war against the fascists. The Americans soon entered the war, bringing with them their enormous industrial potential and manpower resources. On 2 January 1942 in Washington, twenty-six nations signed the Atlantic Charter, drafted the previous year by Roosevelt and Churchill, which formally codified the war aims of the western democracies. From July onward the Eighth Air Force, flying primarily out of East Anglia in their B-17 Flying Fortresses and B-24 Liberators, hammered the Axis by day while Bomber Command applied relentless pressure by night.

In January the aircraft most frequently associated with wartime Bomber Command was brought into service. An offshoot of the dreadful Manchester, the Avro Lancaster was a magnificent fighting aircraft, and it would serve Bomber Command with distinction for the rest of the war and beyond. Essentially a Manchester with four engines and two vertical fins, the enduring and endearing Lancaster would receive very few major modifications throughout its career, since to do so would have detrimentally affected production rates. However, minor modifications, those which could be done in the field or which did not seriously interrupt production, were made. After a successful first flight on 9 January 1941 and highly successful flight trials, the aircraft was rushed into immediate production and the first mass-produced variants appeared that autumn. At Waddington, 44 Squadron, a Hampden outfit, became the first Bomber Command unit to transition to the new type, followed closely in the new year by a greatly relieved 97 Squadron at Woodhall Spa, whose members could not divest themselves of their hated and feared Manchesters quickly enough. First to employ the aircraft on operations, 44 Squadron conducted mine-laying in the Heligoland Bight on 3 March 1942, and two squadron aircraft bombed Essen a week later. However, public revelation of the new type would not occur until 17 April, when a mixed force of twelve "Lancs" from 44 and 97 Squadrons were foolishly sortied against the *Maschinenfabrik Augsburg-Nuremburg* (MAN) plant, which was engaged in the production of U-boat diesel engines. The mission demanded a long and unescorted daylight raid to Augsburg, since the greyer heads at Bomber Command Headquarters believed the target had to be attacked during the day in order to inflict a sufficient level of damage. Also, the Lancasters were flown at low level throughout the mission in order to maximize the element of surprise. However, they encountered stiff opposition, and only five of them returned to base, although the attacking force seriously damaged the target, "and it was generally conceded that no other type of bomber then in service in Europe could have pressed home the attack. Squadron Leaders Nettleton and Sherwood, the leaders of the attack, were both awarded the Victoria Cross, the latter posthumously, and this highest award for valour was later to be awarded to nine other Lancaster aircrew members."[1] Two of those nine Victoria Crosses were won by Canadians.

From then on, the aircraft was rapidly put into widespread service. Standard production Lancaster Is were fitted with four Rolls-Royce Merlin XX engines, which developed 1480 horsepower at 6000 feet, while later variants were fitted with slightly more powerful Merlins. Although the Lancaster I was the most widely produced variant, the Lancaster III differed solely in having American Packard-built Merlins, with appropriate changes to engine controls and accessories. The only version of the aircraft with significant external differences was the Lancaster II, powered by Bristol Hercules VI or XVI radial engines, a hedge against any potential supply failure of the American-built Packard Merlins. Only 300 of this variant were produced, but their altitude performance, compared to that of their Merlin-engine brothers, was disappointing, and they would eventually be withdrawn from service. Canada's Victory Aircraft Corporation at Toronto would also eventually produce 430 license-built Lancaster IIIs, known as Lancaster Xs, and these aircraft would incorporate enlarged bomb bays, unique defensive armament, and a slightly different variant of Packard Merlin engines. The Lancaster could carry a 14,000 pound bomb load for 1660 miles at a cruising speed of approximately 210 mph, and could cruise significantly faster for the shorter hauls.

Not many serious technical problems dogged the Lancaster in service, particularly in comparison to its inconsistent cousin, the Halifax, although early production variants experienced vertical fin failures during aggressive manoeuvring until the problem was isolated and structural reinforcement was incorporated. Later, a number were lost, likely due to problems with the fabric covering of the elevator, but procedural changes corrected this shortcoming. An enduring cause for concern was the size, location, and limited number of the aircraft's emergency escape hatches, a deficiency that would never be rectified, and about which more shall be mentioned in due course.

As for bombing policy, the Butt Report had significantly undermined confidence at the highest levels in the overall bombing strategy. While the grey heads struggled to clarify the future role of the Command, Churchill had since September become progressively more disillusioned with respect to its potential, and indeed, how significantly strategic bombing could alter the course of the war. He urged his senior airmen to consider only the targets and tactics that the Command, "under current circumstances, could realistically damage."[2] Meanwhile, reports began to surface that morale as well as confidence in Bomber Command's senior leadership was plummeting, and this effectively sealed the fate of Sir Richard Peirse. In January 1942, he was posted to India and Air Vice-Marshal J.E.A. Baldwin, the 3 Group commander, became the *pro tempore* Commander-in-Chief, Bomber Command. Shortly thereafter, new policy guidance strongly reflected the Chief of the Air Staff, Sir Charles Portal's views, as they had repeatedly been expressed over the preceding eighteen months. Air Ministry Policy Directive Number 22, issued on 14 February 1942, stated that henceforth, the primary objective of Bomber Command was "the morale of the enemy civil population and in particular, of the industrial workers."[3] The same day, the American Chairman of the War Production Committee and the Secretary of State jointly announced that no new tires for passenger cars would be sold in the United States for the duration of the war. These attacks were to be manifested as large raids on selected area targets in the major industrial areas of Germany, and while industrial aim points were always to be identified and specified, collateral damage in terms of "dehousing" the civilian population was considered to be an acceptable, indeed desirable, adjunct to the bombing. The Ruhr area, particularly Essen, was designated of primary importance, and Berlin was also highlighted on the desired target list. "To make sure there was no misunderstanding about what was being called for, the next day Portal told his DCAS to remind High Wycombe that 'the aiming points are to be the built-up areas, *not*, for instance, the dockyards or aircraft factories where these are mentioned.' "[3a] Naturally, this would not apply if the dockyards or the factories *were* the specific targets of Bomber Command's attentions for the raid in question.

An Uncompromising New Helmsman

Ten days later, on 24 February 1942, leadership of the Command passed to the man historically most closely identified with the bombing of Germany, an Englishman and a true child of the Empire who spent a measure of his formative years in colonial India and Rhodesia, Air Marshal Sir Arthur Travers Harris. Blunt, tenacious, and single-minded to the point of obsession, Harris had thoroughly absorbed the findings and recommendations of the Butt Report and he was convinced the bombing could only be effective when his forces were concentrated en masse to overwhelm the enemy defences, and also when navigational and bombing techniques had been vastly improved. Fulfilling those two preconditions became his most energetic endeavours during the first half of his tenure.

Above all he carried with him the conviction that no single target on the enemy side held the answer to German defeat. He remained hostile to what he called "panacea" targets, not because they were difficult to hit—and the accuracy of Bomber Command operations increased remarkably over the war—but because he realized that an enemy economy and social structure could not be dislocated by an attack on just one of its many elements with the prospect of forcing a decision. Bombing was a blunt instrument during the Second World War, and Harris pursued a strategy that he believed would use that instrument to best effect.[4]

This strategy was the main objection to Harris's wartime leadership of the Command. While Harris is acknowledged as a bold and tenacious leader, a significant number of learned voices have questioned why he did not pursue some specific target types more repeatedly and conclusively, and why he violated the spirit of those in higher authority by not directing the Command more aggressively at what was deemed higher priority targets during the war's final year. That said, historical hindsight is invariably graced with "twenty-twenty-or-better vision," whereas the very real fog of war frequently intercedes to demand, explain, or justify different paths taken along the way. More on these issues will be tabled later. However, Harris's policy does highlight the reality that, while Bomber Command eventually possessed precision bombing specialists in the form of 617 (Dambuster) Squadron and a few other specialized units, precision attack capabilities never became widespread throughout the Main Force during the war.

The Channel Dash

Until just two days before the implementation of Policy Directive Number 22, flight operations had continued in a desultory manner. On 12 February 1942, in a brilliant effort known as Operation Cerberus, the Germans elected to break their capital ships out of Brest harbour and return them to German waters. At high speed and with generous fighter cover under the able leadership of the young, charismatic ace, *General der Jagdflieger, Generalleutnant* Adolf Galland, the battle cruisers *Scharnhorst* and *Gneisenau*, along with the lighter cruiser *Prinz Eugen*, steamed boldly and defiantly up the English Channel to freedom. Caught totally by surprise on a day when bad weather and low cloud gave the ships maximum concealment, various RAF commands and also units of the Fleet Air Arm struggled to mount a response. An initial attack by naval Swordfish aircraft was as futile as it was gallant. For its part, Bomber Command started attacking in three waves, from 1:30 pm onwards, in what was the Command's largest daylight operation of the war to date. Most of the bombers were unable to locate the elusive ships, and no hits were scored by those who did drop bombs. However, both the *Scharnhorst* and the *Gneisenau* were slowed, but not disabled, after they struck mines that had recently been seeded by 5 Group Manchesters and Hampdens in the Frisian Islands. All the warships reached home waters safely, but the ships were now effectively bottled up in home waters for some time. *Gneisenau* was later severely damaged in an air attack at Kiel, while *Scharnhorst* was sunk by the Royal Navy battleship *HMS Duke of York* enroute to Murmansk on 26 December 1943. The damage done to British prestige and confidence was, however, unmitigated. Strong enemy naval forces had not been seen, much less permitted, in the Channel since Tourville's victory over the combined English-Dutch fleet off the Isle of Wight in 1690. On a positive note, the "Channel Dash" freed Bomber Command from the expensive requirement to bomb the capital ships while they were in Brest harbour. Almost 3500 tons of bombs had been dropped on the giants in recent months, at a cost of 127 aircraft. However, they had on several occasions been damaged, they had been effectively prevented from sailing against Atlantic Allied shipping, and the attacks had persuaded the Germans to return the deadly warships to the relative sanctuary of home waters. Jack Watts remembers the event from the perspective of a "near participant." While many of his colleagues bombed the capital ships, Watts missed the operation because the Halifax in which he was a crew member had a ground collision with the squadron commander's aircraft just prior to take-off.

> The *Scharnhorst* and the *Gneisenau* should never have been able to escape, but the trouble was we had been getting more successful in attacking them in the ports in France, so these ports were no longer a safe haven from the point of view of the Germans, and if they had to keep repairing the ships, then obviously they were not going to get much use out of them. They wanted to get them back into places further out of range, say in Germany, where they could give them more protection. Kiel was one of those places. In 10 Squadron, we were given the role of high level attack and equipped with armour-piercing bombs on the basis that it was the only way we could damage those ships, and they were, of course, targets that were difficult to hit [on the move].[5]

Aside from enemy shipping and other areas of interest, there were forty-three German cities included on the new target list. "Bomber Command, in effect, was to become a force of mass property destruction; the new yardstick of success would be the number of "acres destroyed" in the cities."[6] This was going to be a long-term proposition, and under its new commander, the force would no longer fritter away its resources night-by-night on multiple targets with minuscule attacking forces. For the foreseeable future, the "calling card" of Bomber Command would be one primary target per night.

Eyes in the Night

As was the case on the North Atlantic in the submarine war against the *Kriegsmarine's* wolfpacks, the night air war over Europe soon became a deadly game of technological "cat and mouse" or moves and counter-moves by the opposing sides. New tactics were continuously developed to exploit these technological advances. In both camps, the aircrew became increasingly dependant on the scientists. In general terms, the British scientific community provided increasingly sophisticated equipment to navigate, to bomb accurately, and to mask the bomber's presence, while the Germans proved innovative and resilient in finding different ways to locate and to vanquish Bomber Command aircraft.

A new navigational aid called *Gee* (Ground electronics engineering) had been tested in 1941, began operational service in January 1942, and became widely available through mass production in the spring. A great amount of faith was being placed in this equipment to solve all the Command's technological problems. Not only was *Gee* expected to electronically guide the bombers to their targets, it was expected to serve as a blind bombing device that could accurately deliver ordnance within a specified area in up to 10/10ths cloud conditions. The optimism was founded on the equipment's inherent robustness and simplicity, the fact that it did not emit tell-tale electronic signatures to enemy fighters and radars, and that it could be fitted to an unlimited number of attack aircraft because of the excellent capacity of *Gee's* ground stations.

Gee consisted of three widely spaced transmitters in the United Kingdom sending out synchronized pulse signals and an airborne receiver which, after measuring the difference in time of receipt of these transmissions, provided the basis from which the aircraft's distance from each transmitter could be calculated. Transferring this data to specially prepared lattice-grid maps, a *Gee* operator could then establish his position and pass course corrections to his pilot.[7]

Indeed, the prospect of delivering bombs in cloud and thus, at the time, being impervious to attack from night fighters, was compelling. The only drawback was that sooner or later, probably within six months, the Germans would find a means to electronically jam the equipment, but downstream developments were already being tested. In the meantime, all targets in the Ruhr area were within its range and it took the Germans ten months to develop effective jamming techniques.[8]

Gradually, the component parts of a new bombing strategy, both material and doctrinal, were developed. However, Arthur Harris did not rush headlong into the new policy and instead, devoted late-February operations to attacking the German capital ships in their home ports of Kiel and Wilhelmshaven. However, on the night of 3/4 March, a raid by 235 Bomber Command aircraft on the Renault factory in Boulogne-Billancourt, just to the west of central Paris, involved the greatest number of bombers sent to a single target during the war to that point. Also, record bomb tonnages were dropped, and record concentrations of aircraft over the target area were generated. The Billancourt raid was also unique in that it pioneered an abundant use of target marking flares. Damage inflicted was extensive and losses were minimal, although French civilian casualties were very heavy.

Against the Cities

Five nights later, on 8/9 March, came the first true attack of the so-called First Battle of the Ruhr. The chosen target was the highest-priority city of Essen, and *Gee* was used in support of the Shaker plan of attack, "which involved a first wave of aircraft laying a flare path six miles long upwind of the aiming point to mark the approach, a second wave of fire-raisers, and then the main force, carrying both explosives and incendiaries. This technique of target identification and illumination actually emulated German techniques employed during the Blitz. Many of the 211 aircraft despatched found the general target area, one pilot from No. 420 Squadron reporting he could see the flares over Essen 'when approaching the Dutch coast.' "[9] However, even with the use of *Gee*, the markers were not particularly effective and much of the Main Force missed the target area in dense smog. Poor performances were chalked up to a lack of crew proficiency. Follow-up raids did not yield significantly better results, and *Gee* was not performing to what were perhaps unrealistic expectations. While *Gee* could get the bombers to the Ruhr and within sight of the specific objectives, the precise aiming point had to be determined visually, and that was exceptionally difficult in conditions of heavy smoke, industrial haze, heavy, blanketing flak bursts and an array of bright, distracting searchlights. Pilot Officer Jerrold Morris recalls:

> Long before you reached the target area you would see ahead of you a confusing maze of searchlights quartering the sky, some in small groups, others stacked in cones of twenty or more. These often had a victim transfixed, as if pinned to the sky, their apex filled with red bursts of heavy flak. The ground would soon be lit up with lines of reconnaissance flares like suspended street lights, here and there illuminating water, perhaps a section of

river, that you would frantically try to identify. As the raid developed, sticks of incendiaries criss-crossed the ground sparkling incandescent white, until a red glow would show the start of a fire. The Germans liberally sprayed the ground with dummy incendiaries and imitation fire blocks in the neighbourhood of important targets, hoping to attract a share of the bombs. Gun flashes, photo flashes, bomb bursts, streams of tracer of all colours, and everywhere searchlights—it was all very confusing, especially when the air gunners were directing the pilot to avoid flak and searchlights at the same time.[10]

Confusing, and not only for the attackers. Wilhelm Johnen, an eventual *Hauptmann* (Captain) and *Ritterkreuz* (Knight's Cross) winner with thirty-four accredited aerial victories, was overhead Duisberg at 17,000 feet on the night of 26/27 March, piloting a Messerschmitt Bf 110 night fighter. Johnen was a member of *I Gruppe* of *Nachtjagdgeschwader I*, based at Venlo in Holland. His orders were to attack any enemy aircraft caught in searchlight beams above 15,000 feet, the arbitrary dividing line of shared responsibility between the flak and the night fighters. Johnen eventually spotted a Wellington and closed for the kill:

> Hesitantly the white beams flitted to and fro like the arms of an octopus until at last they had caught a bomber. The British machine was flying at about 14,500 feet and took no avoiding action. The gunners below made him their target but they were shooting too far ahead. I decided to attack. Risop [radio operator] quickly transmitted the code word "*Pauke, Pauke*" to the ground station. I dived from my superior altitude and got the bomber in my sights. The air speed indicator needle rose to 330 mph. The bomber grew ever larger in the sights. Now I could clearly see the tall tail unit and the rear gunner's Perspex turret. My machine came into the searchlight area and a few well-aimed bursts lashed the bomber's fuselage, tearing off huge pieces of the fabric. The Tommy was on fire and turned over on its back.[11]

The fact that Johnen made his attack over Duisberg when the Main Force was supposed to be bombing the Krupp works in Essen again trumpets the shortcomings of Bomber Command at this time. This was yet another failure on this very difficult target, located in a huge, amorphous mass of light and activity which, like Berlin, was extremely confusing. Only twenty-two high explosive bombs fell on Essen that night, destroying two houses and killing six civilians, but inflicting no damage to industrial infrastructure. Furthermore, the attacking force lost nearly 10 percent of its participating aircraft. A raid on the city the night before had produced even worse results, although a much lower aircraft loss rate.[12]

The searchlights generated acute anxiety in the aircrews, not only through their disorienting effect, but also because they telegraphed the bomber's location to the waiting flak and fighters. Jerrold Morris elaborates:

> The most alarming factor of the German defences was undoubtedly the searchlights. They had master beams, radar controlled, during the preliminary search . . . Once caught, every searchlight in range would fix you and, wiggle and squirm as you might, you couldn't shake them off. Then the guns joined in and filled the apex of the cone with bursts; it was a terrifying thing to watch. All too often, the sequel was a small flame, burning bright as the aircraft fell towards the ground, followed by the beams all the way down, as if loath to leave their victim; then darkness, until the beams lifted to begin their search again. Everyone dreaded being coned: if it happened, the only sensible thing to do was to head

GERMAN NIGHT FIGHTER DEFENCES
AND BOMBER COMMAND

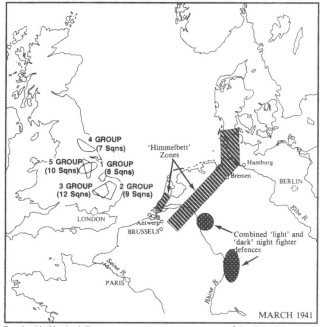

MARCH 1941

Reproduced by Mapping & Charting
Establishment.

© Compiled and drawn by the
Directorate of History.

GERMAN NIGHT FIGHTER DEFENCES
AND BOMBER COMMAND

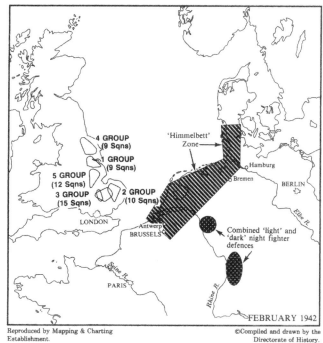

FEBRUARY 1942

Reproduced by Mapping & Charting
Establishment.

©Compiled and drawn by the
Directorate of History.

away from the defended area by the shortest route, but pilots often executed hair-raising manoeuvres, falling into spins or diving almost to ground level. Some got away with it.[13]

Arthur Harris was a man in need of a victory, or better still, a string of victories. The yet-embryonic bombing offensive was very much at risk in a time of myriad needs and limited resources. Tangible proof that area bombing worked was needed to silence the doubters and the "nay-sayers," up to and including those resident in the Prime Minister's Office. Perhaps even more importantly, Harris knew the morale of his crews was flagging. Successes would help convince them that their gallant efforts over the continent, night after dreaded night, were not in vain. A successful *Gee*-led raid, the first assessed as such, had been conducted on Cologne on 13/14 March, and this operation was considered five times more effective than the average of all recent raids on that city. The leading crews accurately marked the target with flares and incendiaries, and they were followed by equally accurate bombing. However, this proved to be an isolated success. The old Hanseatic port city of Lübeck received the Command's attentions on the night of 28/29 March, and since the target was only lightly defended, many attacks were pressed home from low level, at around 2000 feet. Aided to a limited extent by *Gee*, but more so by a full moon and good target visibility, more than 400 tons of bombs were dropped that damaged nearly 62 percent of all the city's buildings. This raid was considered the first major success for Bomber Command against a German target, but because of the weather, the poor defences and the limited requirement for *Gee*, it did not prove the Main Force's abilities. Also, Lübeck's ancient, timbered houses and narrow streets had been extremely susceptible to fire. And even on this lightly defended target, loss rates for the Command were nearly 5 percent.[14]

Essen was re-visited on 12/13 April with 251 aircraft, although not many of their bombs actually hit the Krupp works. "This raid concluded a disappointing series of raids on this target, which was judged to be the heart of the German armaments industry. There had been eight heavy raids since the first *Gee* raid on 8/9 March." These are the actual figures:

> Aircraft dispatched: 1555
> Crews reported bombing Essen: 1006
> Aircraft lost: 64
> Aircraft bombing photographs *within five miles of Essen*: 22

Essen's records show that industrial damage was caused on only two occasions.[15]

Still experimenting with *Gee*, the force bombed Cologne again on 22/23 April, with instructions to bomb only on their *Gee* fix. While some of the sixty-nine attackers hit the city, others bombed as far as ten miles away.[16]

Harris still needed an unqualified success, and Rostock, another ancient and highly flammable port on the Baltic, was visited on four consecutive nights, starting on 23/24 April. While using many of the area attack tactics employed on Lübeck, the force also conducted a separate, precision attack on the Heinkel aircraft factory works on the southern outskirts on all four nights. The last two raids were particularly successful and the series resulted in the destruction of 70 percent of the *Altstadt*, or old town. However, in spite of superficial damage, the Heinkel plant actually returned to 100 percent production within three days. The attack also prompted Propaganda Minister Joseph Goebbels to declare, albeit temporarily, that "community life . . . is practically at an end."[17] Although the damage done was misleading, Bomber Command was holding on, for the moment.

The fire-raising process was by this time becoming a standard characteristic of the area bombing campaign. It had been determined that the best value from the bombing lay in starting a significant number of fires, which would overwhelm the firefighting services and would then continue to spread and create further property damage, even after the last of the raiders had departed the target area. To that end, the initial element of the attacking force normally dropped high explosive weapons intended to crater roads and produce obstructing debris, which would hinder the passage of emergency vehicles. This advance guard was followed by a Main Force carrying a mix of conventional high explosives, high capacity 4000-pound blast bombs and many four-pound incendiaries, each weapon type playing a vital part in the chain of destruction by fire:

> The blast from the 4000-pounders—of which 300 could be soon dropped on a typical raid—would blow away roofing cover and smash windows in blocks of flats over a wide area. The mass of small 4 lb incendiaries—300,000 on a typical raid—would lodge in the exposed attics and upper stories and start fires there.. The heavy 30 lb incendiaries—about 25,000 per raid—would penetrate to lower floors and start fires there. The block warden and his assistants would have to start tackling fires on both upper and lower floors, with air rushing through the broken windows to feed the fires; at the same time, the high explosives which fell throughout the raid were intended to deter the fire fighters.[18]

For those under attack therefore, firefighting entailed the risks of additional bombing and the dangers of the fires themselves, hampered rescue efforts, and guaranteed further property loss. Concentrated bombing could thus cause whole areas to burn out of control. Bombing out significant numbers of workers meant that vast resources, both materiel and manpower, had to be devoted to their care after the attacks, including repair and reconstruction crews, specialized heavy rescue teams and special organizations devoted to evacuation and relocation. "It all added to the strain on resources and the whole process both affected war production and civilian morale."[19]

Sink the *Tirpitz*

Unquestionably, the most dramatic use of Bomber Command during this period was not directed at the enemy's industrial heartland. It was a series of precision versus area attacks against a German capital ship. After the loss of the *Bismark*, the largest remaining Axis battleship was the *Tirpitz*. From the end of March until the end of April the German giant, which was temporarily moored in a Norwegian fjord and was preparing to wreak havoc in the North Atlantic, was subjected to three separate concentrated attacks by Bomber Command. The first occurred on 30/31 March and it was conducted by thirty-four Halifaxes from 10, 35, and 76 Squadrons. Bad weather forced a one-month delay, but the second raid occurred on the night of 27/28 April by thirty Halifaxes from the same three squadrons, augmented by eleven Lancasters from 44 and 97 Squadrons. A final raid the following night by twenty-one Halifaxes and eleven Lancasters from the same units damaged the warship, but it was eventually repaired in place. *Tirpitz* was later back in service and was the recipient of many more British and Soviet aerial attacks before its final demise at the hands of 617 Squadron specialists in November 1944.[20] Along with other Canadians, Jack Watts and Reg Lane both participated in the 1942 *Tirpitz* raids, and their recollections are gripping. Reg Lane had been flying Halifaxes with 35 Squadron out of Linton-on-Ouse since the previous autumn. By early 1942 he had completed his operational checkout phase, had been assigned his own crew, and was by then a relatively experienced operational pilot. However, all his training and preliminary combat experience were soon to be put to the test over the deceptively beautiful Norwegian coast:

> The trips came pretty quickly, and then we got to the 30th of March 1942, when we did the first low-level night attack on the *Tirpitz* up in Norway. The *Tirpitz* was anchored in one of the very narrow fjords just up behind Trondheim. Well, that was an experience. It was a bright, moonlit night and there was snow all over the ground and the hills and as a result, it was just like daylight. The defences were located all over the sides of the hills and the mountains on the lead-in to where the *Tirpitz* was moored, and we were to attack at masthead height, which meant around 200 feet. It was a very, very warm reception that we received. I was carrying a load of incendiaries, believe it or not, the idea being to drop them on the *Tirpitz* to create fires and help light up the whole situation. However, as soon as we got over Trondheim, the Germans started a great big smokescreen in the fjord where the ship was located and as a result, we didn't see the boat at all. All we got was a very warm reception from the light ack-ack . . .
>
> Obviously, the British Navy was very concerned that the *Tirpitz*, which had been moved north from Kiel, was getting close to being operational, and of course the RN was deeply concerned that if that great big battleship ever got out into the North Sea, it would be a disaster and would very likely require more than just the Home Fleet to sink it or make it surrender.
>
> As a result of the operationally-bad first trip against the vessel, the mission was laid on again for the 27th of April. It was a repeat story, basically. A lovely clear night when we arrived over Trondheim to fly up the fjord. We had again a very warm reception from the light ack-ack; mostly 20 mm and 37 mm defences, but the *Tirpitz* was again covered in smoke and we couldn't see a thing. I went in with another chap, a boy by the name of Don McIntyre. We had flown from north Scotland, which we had used as an advanced base. We flew up in formation and had agreed that whoever was leading would go in first. Well, Don was leading when we got over Trondheim, so he went in ahead of me. Again, it was about like daylight. I watched him being very badly shot up and on fire and goodness knows what, and I thought, well that's it. I didn't see what happened to him because by that time I was rather busy myself trying to keep on course to drop the mines we were carrying this time. The idea was to drop the mines between the shore of the fjord and the battleship. This was on a timed run, but it was not the easiest of attacks due to the intense ground fire coming from all directions. When we got back to base I found the airplane had been quite badly damaged and one shell on the starboard side had hit the main spar of the wing and then exploded. It cracked the spar to the point where the aircraft had to have a wing change. If that shell had impacted a few inches either way, it would have hit a fuel tank and we probably would have blown up.
>
> There was another Trondheim trip laid on the night after, but my aircraft was unserviceable due to the wing problem and there were no other airplanes available, so I did two of the three [1942] Trondheim trips. As I recall, the squadron sent about twelve crews up north, and we came back with about five. We'd lost over half of them. It was a *very* nasty operation.[21]

Lane modestly does not mention that his conduct on the two *Tirpitz* special operations he flew was given specific mention (along with other sorties) in the citation for his first Distinguished Flying Cross:

> These attacks were carried out at a height of 150 feet . . . in the face of intense opposition

from the battleship and gun batteries on both sides of the fjord. Flight Lieutenant Lane's tour of operations has proved to be one of steadfast determination to reach the target.[22]

Jack Watts was also a very active 10 Squadron participant in the 1942 campaign against the *Tirpitz*. In fact, he flew on all three operations against the battleship and his recollections are similar to those of Reg Lane:

The crews were told this was extremely hazardous and the trip was to be purely voluntary. We were told that we would have to go in at 250 feet level, which was just about the mast height of the ship, and that we would be provided with a special kind of mine, four of them. The idea was to come in at 250 feet right alongside the cliff wall and then drop the mine at the stern of the *Tirpitz,* and if there was a slight overshoot the mines could roll down the cliff wall so that they would be between the ship and the cliff wall, which would actually increase the impact shock. The planners felt that if we could attack at the stern of the ship where the more delicate components lay, that would maximize the damage. We would go in at 250 feet and around 210-220 knots, then we would have to pull up almost immediately after the attack to clear the cliff at the other end of the fjord. We never thought very much about what the enemy would be doing at the same time. We were thinking merely of the technical aspects of a rather high speed, low level hazardous entry through a very restricted area.

To reach the *Tirpitz* in Norway, we had to launch from Lossiemouth in Scotland . . . In all we did three different raids. We did one which, because of the weather, was useless in a sense. But our leaders felt it did not break the security of the RAF's intentions because it didn't telegraph what was the specific target. We had been attacking airfields and so on in Norway on other instances . . . There was a break until they thought the weather was going to be right—we had to have moonlight, and we had to have clear air to make this low-level night attack—and it was a little while before we had good conditions again [almost a month].

For the second operation, it was a little better than the first time in the sense we had good weather. We actually made a good landfall. We were to fly down the main Trondheim fjord at about 4000 feet. You passed Trondheim over on your right, then went down to the end of the fjord where you reached this small Alten Fjord. The idea was that you got within sight of the Alten Fjord, you dove down from 4000 feet, leveled out at 250 feet, and made your entry to this small fjord right up against the cliff wall, dropped your bombs on the tail of the target and pulled up out of the cliff. This was the *idea* . . . When we went this second time, the weather was fantastic. Coming in at 4000 feet, the view was absolutely marvelous. It was like flying in a cathedral . . . The mountains all around, with snow-capped peaks and the water down below. You could see everything stark and clear . . . However, when we went down to get into the small fjord, we found that somehow they had been alerted, the smoke generators had been turned on all around the fjord, and [as had occurred the month prior] Alten Fjord was full of white smoke. So we had to make a blind approach at 250 feet from the tip of the fjord, time it with a stopwatch until you figured you were over the target, drop your mines, pull up, blind, and hope you cleared the cliff wall. It was frightening in itself, but there was *no resistance* [at that particular moment from the ship itself]. They didn't fire because, obviously, that would have revealed the target . . . We did a blind attack, we dropped our weapons, pulled up, and came out. There were people who didn't make it. When we got back to Lossiemouth, we were kinda heaving a sigh of relief . . . Then the AOC said, "I don't think we have put the *Tirpitz* out of action, and we're going to have to go again tonight."[23]

Watts and his crew did repeat the operation on the 28th of April, flying a similar profile. In his own modest way, Watts failed to mention in his account that on the previous evening they had been caught in a searchlight beam which directed an enemy fighter onto his Halifax while they were coming up the fjord. Furthermore, the ground defences reacted in a totally different manner than he implies in his narrative. A brief excerpt from Watts's DFC citation laconically describes what happened:

> Flight Lieutenant Watts is a courageous and highly skilled navigator who has done much to ensure the success of many of the sorties in which he has participated. One night in April 1942 he was the navigator of an aircraft detailed to attack the naval base at Trondheim. On arrival at the target area the aircraft was intercepted by an enemy fighter but Flight Lieutenant Watts coolly and skillfully directed his captain down through an intense barrage and the fighter was unable to follow. The objective was then attacked from an extremely low level [150 feet]. The following night when attacking the same objective, Flight Lieutenant Watts distinguished himself by his brilliant navigation.[24]

Watts had this to say about the ground defences at Alten Fjord, particularly those encountered on the night of 28 April: "The flak was completely around the perimeter of the fjord, firing down. Flak from one side was hitting the cliff wall, the flak from the other side was hitting the water, and the ship was firing up from the middle, and they had a fair amount of flak on board that ship! We lost a fair number of aircraft on the raid, but even of the aircraft that got back, nobody got through without getting hit."[25]

One of the other Halifax captains from 35 Squadron during the April raids on *Tirpitz* was Glenn Powell Gardiner from Merlin, Ontario. He received a coveted "Immediate DFC" for his gallantry over Norway:

> Pilot Officer Gardiner was captain of an aircraft detailed to attack the German Naval Base at Trondheim on two nights in April 1942 . . . Despite intense opposition, Pilot Officer Gardiner pressed home his attacks and returned to base safely. He displayed outstanding airmanship, courage and devotion to duty which have been an inspiration to other members of the squadron.[26]

However, Gardiner was shot down before he could receive his DFC from the King, as was then the custom whenever possible. On 6 May 1942, on an operation to Stuttgart, his Halifax II was raked "from stem to stern" by cannon shells from a Messerschmitt Bf 110 at 100 yards range, which completely shot away the controls and set the starboard wing alight. Of his crew, three, including Gardiner, escaped to become prisoners of war, but four others perished with the aircraft.[27]

On the 28 April attack, the *Tirpitz* was damaged, although not decisively. It was two long years before the RAF finally put an end to the giant warship.

During the spring of 1942, not all the exciting, exacting flying was being done on operations. By now, Bob Turnbull, newly commissioned and proudly wearing the ribbon of the Distinguished Flying Medal (DFM) beneath his pilot wings, had completed what was at the time a non-standard period of operational flying. Prior to going back on operations Turnbull and others like him were assigned to impart their operational experiences to fledglings at a Halifax conversion unit. His words home underline one of the realities of wartime instructing—that an instructional "rest" from operations, given the training tempo and the urgent and continual requirement to provide new aircrews was most often not restful at all:

March 25, 1942 Marston Moor
Nr Yorks

As I told you in my past letters we are instructing on Halifaxes. What a job it is—give me a single engine aircraft any day to instruct on. At present have two Czechoslovak pilots as pupils who speak about as much English as I do Check [sic], so you can imagine how well we manage . . . However, we shall "cope" and are really getting along first rate.

   Just moved to my new sleeping and living quarters. "Rufforth Manor" is the name of the place. Really a grand old house and at present am sitting in front of an open fire in a grand big room shared by two of us. Only drawback is that we are about four miles from the 'drome so if we miss our bus it makes an uncomfortable walk. It is great to relax after a day's flying and [I] quite enjoy it.

March 30, 1942 Marston Moor
Nr Yorks

You were asking what I did on days off. Well Tannis, so far since coming here to instruct I've had about two days free and on both occasions have slept the clock almost around. Even on "duff" days we are kept busy giving lectures [and] find it is no joke flying these aircraft about with a half-trained pupil, who thinks he knows everything about flying, at the controls. However, must not kick, I guess, as I have run across much worse jobs. Find we are much in the limelight, as there are so few four engine aircraft instructors, a good deal falls with us.[28]

Major changes in the composition and duties of multi-engine operational crews took place in the spring of 1942, shortly after the appointment of Harris to the helm of Bomber Command:

In March 1942 the Air Ministry had decided that only one pilot was necessary in medium and heavy bombers. A new crew member, air bomber, was introduced and the air observer, whose duties previously included bomb dropping as well as navigating, and who was also expected to pinch-hit for the gunners in an emergency, was reclassified as a navigator. The operation of various electronic aids to navigation now coming into service and the higher standards of navigational accuracy demanded meant that navigation was now a full-time job. Only one wireless operator/air gunner was to be carried instead of two, the other being replaced by an air gunner without wireless training. This ruling meant that Vickers Wellingtons, previously manned by two pilots, an observer, and two wireless operator/air gunners, in future would carry one pilot, a navigator, an air bomber, an air gunner, and a wireless operator/air gunner. As the latter was becoming more and more a specialist in radio operating, an additional air gunner was sometimes added to the crew. The standard crew in Avro Lancasters and other heavy bombers consisted of seven members: a pilot, navigator, air bomber, wireless operator/air gunner, two air gunners, and a flight engineer who if necessary could take over from the pilot and land the aircraft.[29]

Gradually, from June 1942 onwards, navigators destined for specialization in bombing had their course expanded from twelve to twenty weeks, allowing for considerably more airborne practice and specialization. Air bombers spent eight weeks, later increased to twelve weeks, at a Bombing and Gunnery School (BGS), followed by six weeks at an Air Observer School (AOS), concentrating on map reading to be able to assist the crew navigator, and also receiving more practice bombing. Specialization was also increasing in the other aircrew trades:

Commencing in 1942 considerable progress continued to be made in the training of air gunners and wireless operator/air gunners. Previously the tuition of these two categories had suffered from inadequately trained instructors and lack of proper equipment. To raise the standard of wireless operator/air gunners who were increasingly becoming specialists in radio work, their course at wireless school was extended from twenty to twenty-eight weeks followed by six weeks of gunnery training. At the same time the air gunners' programme was increased from four to twelve weeks, comprising six weeks of ground training and six weeks of air-firing practice.[30]

The seventh bomber crew member was the flight engineer. They were originally aero-engine technicians who tracked and regulated engine performance in the air, but were also trained, somewhat inconsistently, to take over from a pilot if he were injured or killed. Nearly all flight engineer training was conducted in Britain until July 1944, when a specialist school equipped with Halifaxes was formed at Aylmer, Ontario.

The Canadianization of the RCAF Overseas

By the end of 1941, with only 600 RCAF airmen serving in RCAF squadrons, Canadianization was not going particularly well overall. In fact, nearly 60 percent of all RCAF airmen served in other than RCAF units throughout the course of the war. Therefore, most of them were effectively placed beyond the reach of Canadian authorities, a very embarrassing situation for the Canadian government. However, two new RCAF bomber units, 419 Squadron and 420 Squadron, were formed in mid-December 1941. Initially equipped with Wellington Mark ICs pending availability of the faster and higher-flying Wellington Mark IIIs, 419 Squadron was based at Mildenhall in 3 Group territory and flew its first operational sorties in January 1942. Again, following what had become something of a tradition, the unit's first commanding officer was a CAN/RAF, the highly capable and charismatic Wing Commander J. "Moose" Fulton, DFC, AFC, who had already completed a distinguished tour of thirty operations with 99 Squadron and an equally distinguished tour of duty with the Armament Defence Flight Experimental Section at Farnborough. One of the two initial flight commanders was also a CAN/RAF, Squadron Leader F.W.S. Turner, who had been bombing Germany from the earliest days of the war. Fulton was a tireless, fearless and popular commander, who led from the front and fully shared the risks of his men, in spite of orders at the time to squadron skippers to minimize their operational flying. "This combination of dedication and concern would lead the squadron into taking Fulton's nickname for its own after his death in action, and eventually getting it officially recognized, so it became No 419 (Moose) Squadron, RCAF—the only Canadian squadron to be named after a person."[31] Fulton flew over twenty operations as commanding officer of 419 Squadron, including an attack on Kiel at the end of April, for which he received the DSO for bringing home an aircraft badly crippled from an attack by a German night fighter. However, his luck ran out on the night of 28 July, when he was last seen over the enemy coast being attacked by German fighters.[32]

At Waddington, 420 Squadron began forming in late December 1941 with Hampdens. The unit was declared operationally ready on 21 January 1942, when five of their aircraft bombed Emden, while a sixth seeded mines near Heligoland. However, within 420 Squadron at the end of January, only one of sixty-eight aircrew positions was being filled by a Canadian, in spite of the many RCAF aircrew members now in Britain, and also in spite of British assurances to make a serious effort to post all available RCAF personnel to RCAF units.[33] Sir John Slessor, the 5 Group commander, had strong feelings about the lack of Dominion personnel being posted to the Article XV squadrons at the time:

> "This business of the Article 15 Squadrons is awfully difficult, particularly until we can persuade the Air Ministry to post Dominion crews to the right OTUs serving the proper Dominion squadrons . . . What happens at the moment of course is that we get driblets of crews at odd times and they have to go anywhere where there is a vacancy; subsequently, it is very difficult to move them because it means breaking up crews and usually they are extremely averse to leaving the squadrons with which they have begun their operations." Slessor, who later observed that the implications of Article XV were both "senseless" and "a pity from the broad point of view of Commonwealth unity," was averse to breaking up crews, particularly if it meant taking Canadians "away . . . from, say a Manchester or Lancaster squadron" and posting them to an RCAF Hampden squadron—in which case "we should never get the heavy squadrons operational."[34]

While some senior RAF officials were openly sympathetic to and supportive of the Canadianization process, there is no doubt that it was frequently inconvenient and outright disruptive at times. Training capabilities and capacities and the urgent wartime need for units often did not allow for such tailor-made nationalistic solutions, no matter how great the desire to accommodate the wishes of the Canadian government. Time would prove, however, that while many RCAF airmen strongly resented being placed in RAF units instead of with their countrymen, just as many would swear that the mixed nationality squadrons within the RAF were very rich experiences for them and were the preferred way to serve. Many of the British air leaders, particularly at the unit level, were sympathetic, tolerant and inspirational in their demeanour and performance, and their loss was felt keenly when they were killed in action. Reg Lane from 35 Squadron elaborates:

> (In August) I had just finished my first tour of operations, and so the squadron commander sent me on leave before starting my second tour. After leave, I was staggered and stunned to come home to find that my CO, the finest leader I have ever known or encountered, Wing Commander Jimmy Marks, had gone missing in my airplane. At this point in the war, he already had the DSO and Bar and the DFC and Bar. A *very* experienced bomber pilot and it was a great loss when he went missing.[35]

And yet many, particularly the non-commissioned members, felt they were being treated inequitably and they frequently railed against the heavy hand of British authority and classism. As with so many other events in life, these individual impressions seem to have been very much driven by personality. It is also certainly true that individual airmen greatly resented being torn away from their crews once a tour of operations was underway. Crew bonding was an extremely cohesive force on the bomber squadrons, and it trumped nationalistic bonding most of the time. This was often overlooked by some members of Canada's senior leadership in their enthusiasm to further Canadianization at any cost.

Meanwhile, Canadianization within Bomber Command and elsewhere in the RAF proceeded unabated in 1942. The process was led by the formation of a fifth heavy bomber unit on 25 June, 425 "Alouette" Squadron, a francophone formation equipped with Wellington IIIs. They were based at Dishforth, located near Ripon in Yorkshire and just beside the Great North Road, also known as the A1. Dishforth was one of the early bases that had been built under the pre-war expansion schemes and it was provided with the substantial brick-built accommodation of the period. In

1942, this was 4 Group territory, and in October 425 Squadron was augmented at Dishforth by 426 "Thunderbird" Squadron, also equipped with Wellington IIIs. The Thunderbirds were just one of six more RCAF heavy bomber squadrons formed in the latter half of the year. Air Marshal Harold "Gus" Edwards, the new Canadian Air Officer-in-Chief of the RCAF Overseas, was much more nationalistic than his predecessor, Air Vice-Marshal L.F. Stevenson,[36] and he pushed Canadianization vigorously in an attempt to establish a stronger measure of national control over Canadian airmen in-theatre.[37] Indeed, by June 1942, 70 percent of the overall aircrew in RCAF squadrons were Canadian, although there were fewer in the bomber squadrons.[38]

During the spring, Air Vice-Marshal Edwards thanked the sympathetic British ears at the Air Ministry for doing all they could to ensure that as many crews as possible serving on RCAF squadrons were "one hundred percent Dominion,"[39] and yet the roadblocks to Canadianization continued.

> In fact, the AOC of No 4 Group, a New Zealander in the RAF (Air Vice-Marshal Carr) who at the time had one RCAF squadron under his command, was "very much against the formation of . . . all-Canadian squadrons" and, believing mixed units were happier, he told Edwards so. "I feel that your squadrons miss a lot by being posted to RCAF squadrons. In RAF squadrons they mix and operate with English personnel and personnel from the other Dominions, and all get to train and respect each other. The various personnel gain a great deal from their association and assimilate fresh ideas from many parts of the world which broadens their outlook."[40]

Still, Air Vice-Marshal Carr was instructed to do "everything possible, short of interfering with the operational efficiency of any particular crew,"[41] to expedite complete Canadianization. Five months later, while Canadianization within 419 Squadron stood at a laudable 88 percent, within Carr's RCAF squadron (405), the rate was only 50 percent. Therefore, while told to cooperate with the Canadian political desires, it would appear that Carr did not do so, particularly when his group is compared to the Canadianization rate achieved by the sympathetic Air Vice-Marshal J.E.A. Baldwin in 3 Group.

Fundamentally profound societal differences between the British and men from the Dominions were a considerable source of friction in wartime Britain, and these differences were often manifested in different attitudes to authority. The British military's defence of its small, pre-war regular force with its tradition-bound way of life, replete with public school values and class distinctions, which treated British working class volunteer inductees with some disdain, occasionally resulted in unfair treatment to non-commissioned aircrew. While the new wave of British inductees was more inclined to accept these class distinctions as inevitable, many of the more egalitarian and demonstrative men from the Dominions, particularly from Canada and Australia, found these attitudes at the very least rankling, if not outright undemocratic. Leadership and command were felt to be questions of competence and substance and not a matter of style. Respect had to be earned, not assumed. Conversely, the British upper class view of North Americans and other "New Worlders" was frequently elitist, less than flattering, and resulted in confrontation. An RAF report of the period makes this distinction:

> The new world—American and Canadian alike—is impetuous, enthusiastic, sometimes childish, often self-assured and usually not a little boastful. It likes to seem tough and it likes to show off. One RAF officer, the CO of an RCAF squadron, told us that Canadians

are erratic: they want quick excitement, but cannot settle down to a hard grind. Another RAF officer, the CO of an OTU, said that the Canadians are a pretty unsophisticated lot, who come over with a chip on their shoulder, and put on a tough exterior to cover up a sense of inferiority. A number of RAF officers told us that Canadians do not know how to hold their drinks.[43]

Differences in attitudes to discipline caused rifts as well:

Canadians have no veneration for spit-and-polish. And they dislike discipline when it appears as the arbitrary will of a person in a superior rank. They must feel that discipline makes sense before they accept it wholeheartedly. When it goes flatly against common sense, they despise it.[44]

The British views were manifested in considerably more preferential treatment of commissioned officers within the RAF. By comparison, the United States Army Air Force (USAAF), similar to the Canadian and the Australian forces, was much more egalitarian in its treatment of personnel, exemplified by the sharing of common mess halls and a predilection for all-ranks social functions.

The executive of the RAF in some cases harboured grave concerns about the significant influx of Dominion aircrew, apparently fearing a shift of influence from their own preferred methods, since their own service was unable to take in "enough young men of the British middle and upper classes, the supposed natural leaders and 'backbone' of British society."[45] Some influential and respected British air leaders were noted for their condescending attitudes toward "the Colonials" or "the Imperials,"[46] although many were also exceptionally tolerant and understanding. However, even Sir Arthur Travers Harris feared what he termed an "alienation of the Service"[47] by the men from the Dominions.

While Canada negotiated BCATP agreements with policy offsets to provide the RCAF Overseas with greater freedom from British control, this was obstructed at various levels by the British government in general and the RAF in particular. One of the key issues concerned the commissioning of RCAF aircrew in RAF units. Historian Allan English elaborates:

At higher levels it was perceived as the unwarranted political interference of a junior ally in operational matters where Canada had little influence. Consequently, some senior RAF commanders simply circumvented Canadianization when it suited them. At lower levels, the policy was seen as disruptive to morale, and efforts were made, especially with RCAF NCO aircrew, to "blot out" their Canadian identity by insisting that they belonged to the RAF once they left Canada.[48]

When the BCATP was renegotiated in May and June 1942, solicitations from the irate parents of RCAF airmen serving overseas with the RAF to Canadian Members of Parliament brought the question of aircrew commissioning to a head. Prior to the 1942 renegotiation, the BCATP policy had been to commission 50 percent of pilots and observers and 20 percent of wireless operators and air gunners; half at graduation and the other half based on performance during operations. However, Canadian Air Minister C.G. "Chubby" Power disliked the quota system, which he believed was based on the British concept that only members of a certain social strata were worthy of holding commissions.[49] "The Canadians drew attention to the sense of unfairness, 'damaging to morale,' to inequalities in pay, transportation, travel allowances and messing, and made a telling point by mentioning the effect of these inequalities on those unfortunate enough to become prisoners of war . . . They dwelled on the injury to the team spirit when 'the crew, as an entity, is not able to live and fraternize, the one with the other, during leisure and off-duty hours.' "[50] Therefore, Canada insisted that the revised Agreement should state that all pilots, navigators, air bombers and observers who were considered suitable according to the standards of the Canadian government and had been recommended for commissions were to be commissioned.[51] Power voiced his opinion on the subject to British authorities:

> I gave these young fellows my word . . . but only after you agreed. I realize that Canadian and British ideas on commissions are not identical and that we may upset your officer-NCO balance in RAF squadrons. Nevertheless, I hope to live in Canada after the war, but you fellows will still be in England.[52]

However, the British refused to budge on this issue. Canada then argued a compromise: to commission all its pilots and observers on graduation, 25 percent of all other categories on graduation, and a further 25 percent of this latter category at an unspecified later date.[53] This was still not acceptable to the British authorities, and the two nations eventually agreed to differ. In November 1942, Power learned that only 28.7 percent of RCAF pilots and observers serving operationally with the RAF under the old rules had been commissioned to that point. Since field commissions were subject to British Air Ministry approval, and since the RCAF had been automatically commissioning 25 percent of its total pilots and observers on their graduation from BCATP, that the RAF was only commissioning a paltry additional 3.7 percent of eligible Canadian aircrew. Ironically:

> That reluctance did not extend to its own aircrew, however, as on 1 September 1942, 57 percent of RAF pilots and observers were officers. The discrepancy was even greater in the (specific) case of pilots, as 67 percent of those wearing uniforms held commissions compared with only 29 percent in the RCAF.[54]

In the end, Canada circumvented British intransigence by commissioning a greater number of BCATP graduates. In fact, from 1943 onward, it commissioned all its pilots, observers, navigators and air bombers, although it adhered to existing quotas for commissioning the other air trades, such as air gunners, for the time being.[55] This was similar to American policy. However, this issue and other elements of the Canadianization process would continue to meet stiff resistance at all levels within the RAF, and it would continue after the formation of a distinct RCAF group within Bomber Command in 1943.

By the spring of 1942, the drums were beating loudly in Ottawa and among Canadians overseas, to form the air equivalent of an indigenous operational army. And while new RCAF squadrons continued to form overseas in 1942, Canada never sought operational autonomy from Britain, as did the American Eighth Air Force out of England from 1942 onward. The Canadian government, by earlier agreement, was already funding the vast majority of BCATP operations conducted in Canada, and the additional negotiated costs to the nation for indigenous air formations would include the provision of RCAF groundcrew, as well as the assumption of operating costs and some equipment requirements from the British. In May 1942 at the Air Training Conference held to negotiate an extension to the BCATP the British delegation eventually conceded that a Canadian bomber group[56] should be formed, and that in preparation for doing so, the existing RCAF bomber squadrons should be consolidated in the 4 Group area, partly so that they could benefit from the experience and tutelage of the seasoned 4 Group units. Along with 425 and 426 Squadrons forming at Dishforth in June and October respectively, during August and September, 408, 419 and 420 Squadrons joined 405 Squadron in Yorkshire and County Durham. Also at the May conference, it was agreed that Victory Aircraft in Toronto was to license-build the Avro Lancaster. For this reason the Canadian group was ultimately to be equipped with Lancasters. However, new units, as the junior service formations, would be required to start out equipped with Wellingtons until sufficient four-engine types became available. This was RAF policy for all new units; that the most senior squadrons were the first to upgrade, regardless of national origins. Thus, the six additional RCAF bomber squadrons that formed in late 1942 were initially all equipped with either Wellington IIIs or Wellington Xs. Nonetheless, November 1942 was a banner month for Canadianization in Bomber Command, with 428, 429, 431 and 432 Squadrons all coming on line, and each with an establishment of eighteen Wellingtons.[57] Moreover, 405 Squadron, the first of the Article XV squadrons to form, was also the first to receive four-engine aircraft when they converted to Halifax IIs in April, and 408 and 419 Squadrons were similarly equipped in October. This high-level decision was in all probability a contributing factor in the quest to equip the Canadian group with Lancasters.

Operation Millenium

As the spring of 1942 progressed, while the Coca-Cola and Pepsi-Cola companies announced that their four-year trademark disputes had been settled amicably and the 25th PGA championship was being won by two-time runner-up Sam Snead, Arthur Harris continued to feel that a more spectacular demonstration of what his Command could achieve with area bombing was required for the War Cabinet. The raids on the Ruhr, Rostock and Lübeck, while showing some promise, had been generally ruled indecisive. Furthermore, tactical innovativeness was needed to reduce the punishing losses to the aircrews. To that end, in early May he and his planners began to orchestrate a massive raid that would utilize a thousand bombers on a single target in one night. This was a formidable task, since at the time the Command could normally only field 400-500 operational bombers per night. However, at mid-month, he suggested his plan to Sir Charles Portal and won not only his support, but that of the Prime Minister. Such a plan would call for the temporary assistance of other commands, such as Coastal Command, and would ultimately even require the services of the training and conversion units and only partially trained crews, when the Admiralty refused to release Coastal Command aircraft for the operation.

The fundamental idea was to organize the attacking force into a compact stream, not more than forty miles wide, for a decisive blow against a single target. As many aircraft as possible were to be concentrated over the target in the shortest possible time in an effort to completely saturate the defences and the firefighting services. Thus, this so-called bomber stream was primarily defensive in purpose rather than intended to further bombing effectiveness, although this was very much a desired offshoot. In order to be decisive, Operation Millennium had to be directed against a major industrial centre, one which the enemy was prepared to defend tenaciously. Harris also felt that the raid would provide a significant boost to the sagging morale of his crews and the British public in general, while simultaneously delivering a crushing blow to the morale of the German people.

Cologne was to be the target, and 1047 bombers, the majority of which were Wellingtons, were sortied on the night of 30/31 May, including seventy-one aircraft from the four RCAF bomber squadrons active at the time.[58] Led by *Gee*-equipped aircraft from 1 and 3 Groups in bright moonlight, the force commenced bombing at 12:47 am and started significant fires, which effectively served as beacons for the rest of the Main Force.[59] Nearly 900 of the bombers that were sent out released 1455 tons of bombs, of which two-thirds were incendiaries.

> Property damage on the raid totalled 3330 buildings destroyed, 2090 seriously damaged and 7420 lightly damaged. More than 90 percent of this damage was caused by fire rather than high-explosive bombs. Among the above total of 12,840 buildings were 2560 industrial and commercial buildings, though many of these were small ones. However, 36 large firms suffered complete loss of production, 70 suffered 50-80 percent loss and 222 up to 50 percent.[60]

On top of this damage, sixty-six public utilities were attacked. Also, 469 fatalities were incurred, an additional 5027 were injured, and perhaps more significantly, 45,132 were bombed out of their homes. In all, at least 135,000 souls either temporarily or permanently fled the city. It cost Bomber Command 41 aircraft, or 3.93 percent of the attacking force.[61] While there had been safety concerns associated with saturation of the skies over the target area, only two aircraft were lost to mid-air collisions during the ninety-minute raid. In fact, later raids were safely compressed to within a bombing window of twenty minutes without generally causing serious problems. It is estimated that twenty-two aircraft were lost over the target area, including sixteen to flak and four to night fighters, while most of the other losses were incurred in the night fighter boxes located between the coast and Cologne. A British news communiqué from 31 May makes the success public, and closely mirrors the actual combat losses, considering that two aircraft were also lost on the intruder operations:

> Last night a force of considerably over 1000 bombers attacked targets in the Ruhr and Rhineland. Cologne was the main objective. Full reports are not yet available but preliminary reports of the crews indicate that the attack was an outstanding success. By dawn the fires and smoke were visible from the coastline of Holland and reconnaissance early this morning reported a pall of smoke rising to 15,000 feet over the target. During this operation other aircraft of Bomber Command and aircraft of Fighter, Coastal and Army Co-operation Command attacked enemy aerodromes and enemy fighters attempting to intercept. 44 of our aircraft are missing from all these operations.[62]

Not surprisingly, a German High Command communiqué, also dated 31 May, describes the results from a different perspective, although it actually *understates* the British losses:

> During last night British bombers carried out a terrorist raid on the inner city of Cologne. Great damage was done by the effect of explosions and fires, particularly in residential quarters, to several public buildings among them three churches and two hospitals. In this attack directed exclusively against the civilian population, the British Air Force suffered most severe losses. Night fighters and A.A. artillery shot down 36 of the attacking bombers. In addition, one bomber was shot down in the coastal area by naval artillery.[63]

Participating crews knew they had witnessed a categorical success. The raid was a major morale booster in Britain, but had the opposite effect in the Third Reich. In the words of William L. Shirer: "For the first time the civilian German people, like the German soldiers at Stalingrad and El Alamein, were to experience the horrors which their armed forces had inflicted on others up to now."[64]

No. 419 Squadron's *Gee*-equipped Wellingtons bombed in bright moonlight with very little cloud cover as part of the first wave, and the aim point in the city centre was clearly discernible. Enemy flak and searchlight prediction appeared to be overwhelmed by the sheer numbers of the attacking force, nor were any night fighters observed over the target in the raid's early stages. Squadron Leader J.D. Pattison saw none:

> The moon was full, so we didn't expect much darkness to hide in . . . [but] the enemy defences were completely foxed from the outset. There was no serious flak all the way in. When we first got to the target area, the defences appeared to be trying to pick up the aircraft with searchlights, but by the time we left they had given it up as a bad job.[65]

By the time 405, 408 and 420 Squadron aircraft arrived over the fiercely blazing target as part of the last wave, it was easy to find. Also, as this was the most concentrated portion of the raid, casualties were light.

Wolfgang Falck, one of the most gifted and popular leaders of the fledgling German night fighter arm, recalls the effect of the bomber stream on the German defences:

> At that time we were using the *Himmelbett* system. Only one night fighter at a time was allowed to hunt in one area. That worked against individual bombers. You could pinpoint them and pass them from one *Himmelbett* zone to the next. Suddenly the bombers were coming in a stream and our *Himmelbett* technique didn't work any more . . . The second set-back was that a large number of targets was, strangely enough, harder to detect and harder to fight. And the bomber stream would divide to attack several targets, while previously it had been pretty clear which target they were aiming for.[66]

One other innovation which is not often mentioned was used on the Cologne raid. In all, some fifty-six intruder sorties were carried out against German night fighter bases along the attack route, although no particular success was gained on this occasion.[67]

A Case for Retribution?

On the day before the Cologne raid, the war's most memorable act of retribution by conquered Europeans against their Nazi occupiers took place; the assassination of the diabolical Reinhard Heydrich, chief of the German security police, the SS security service (*Sicherheitsdienst*) and deputy chief of the Gestapo. On 29 May 1942, Heydrich, the Acting Protector of Bohemia and Moravia, was assassinated by two members of the free Czechoslovak army parachuted in from England. The German reaction was swift and incredibly brutal. They took a terrible revenge on the Czech populace and the Jews, culminating in the complete destruction of the village of Lidice near Prague, the execution of all its male inhabitants, and the murder or expulsion of virtually all the village women and children to concentration camps. The sole purpose of this despicable brutality was to serve as a chilling example of the consequences of resistance to Nazi rule.

When Winston Churchill heard about the German reprisals, he was livid. The highly classified flow of documents that ensued is particularly fascinating, for it could well have resulted in the use of Bomber Command strictly for reprisal purposes. The following letter was written by Churchill to his Foreign Secretary, Anthony Eden, and was dated 14 June 1942, five days after the destruction of Lidice:

> I am asking the Chief of the Air Staff and Bomber Command to consider bombing two, or perhaps even three, villages in Germany as a reprisal for the cruel obliteration of the Czech village of Lidice. As you are the keeper of our conscience on these matters, perhaps you will let me know before tomorrow's Cabinet what you think.

The Minute reply to Churchill from Eden is dated the following day:

> I agree and like the plan. No doubt we must be ready for counter action against our villages, but that is an operational matter.[68]

The next day, the President of the Czechoslovak Republic-in-exile, Eduard Benes, wrote the following letter to Churchill:

> My dear Prime Minister,
>
> I was very grateful to you when you mentioned yesterday in Buckingham Palace that the Allies might perhaps be able to check the ferocious German brutalities committed against the Czechoslovak patriots by simply answering these reprisals with counter-reprisals. And I was greatly impressed to learn that you personally were thinking of this procedure and that the War Cabinet would deal with the matter. I thank you warmly for all this. The whole Czech community of Lidice has been obliterated in the most barbarous fashion. And yesterday the Germans gave the Czech people a new ultimatum expiring on Thursday night: unless the attackers on Heydrich are discovered by that time, they threaten to begin with another sequence of the most brutal reprisals. Therefore, if it were really possible to undertake some counter-measures—to attack, as you put the matter, 2-3 German localities, the reason for this attack being at the same time made known—I believe that it would be not only a great encouragement to our people at home, but that it would certainly also compel the Germans to put at least some limits to their murdering. Thanking you once more very warmly for all that you may be able to do in this matter,
>
> I remain, my dear Prime Minister,
> Sincerely yours
> Eduard Benes[69]

In a 15 June "Most Secret" letter to the Prime Minister, Sir Arthur Harris acknowledged that the operation could be done, but only in bright moonlight and "the justification of giving up one of our rare fine moonlight nights to this task can only be judged on political factors. The military-moral effect, though small, would not however be negligible . . . I would prefer to have the objective and 'the reason why' announced after the event. I am looking out suitable targets."[70] As it happened, the assassination team, along with 120 members of the Czech Resistance, were shortly thereafter cornered in the Karl Borromæus Church in Prague, besieged by troops of the SS, and subsequently killed to the last man.[71] Whether or not the perceived urgent need for counter-reprisals was subsequently re-evaluated by Churchill, whether Eden's limited concern about the potential for countering German bombing was considered, or whether those in authority elected under the circumstances to "take the moral high ground" has not been discovered. However, War Cabinet met on the same day of the Harris and Benes letters to the Prime Minister and arrived at the following conclusion: "The main point made in discussion was that such action could only be carried out effectively by a considerable number of aeroplanes, on a clear moonlit night. Action on the lines suggested would therefore mean the use of forces which would otherwise be employed against objectives of greater importance. At any rate, the War Cabinet decided that this suggestion should not be followed up."[72]

More Large Raids and the Singleton Report

The Millennium Forces were assembled twice again in June for raids on Essen and Bremen, but the weather was not as cooperative as it had been for the raid on Cologne. Over Essen on the night of 1/2 June, although many, many flares were dropped by the raid leaders, the crews had great difficulty finding the target in extensive ground haze and low cloud. Bombing was scattered and generally ineffective, and the cost was thirty-one crews lost. On 25/26 June, Bremen was the target. Again, cloud cover played a detrimental role, but the raid was still a qualified success through the good use of *Gee* in setting marking fires by the lead crews. Along with damage to other industrial sites, an assembly shop at the Focke-Wulf fighter factory was obliterated, and total time over target was compressed down to sixty-five minutes. The Command lost forty-eight aircraft, 5 percent of the attacking force. Support intruder operations against the German night fighter airfields, similar to those conducted on the Cologne raid, were used for both Essen and Bremen, with slightly more success.[73] With the Operation Millennium series Sir Arthur Harris had proved that his Command could be effective when his forces were concentrated against worthwhile and appropriate targets. He had provided a reasonable—and timely—success with the Cologne raid, for the other service Chiefs of Staff were clamouring to have the bombing force disbanded and then committed piecemeal to the separate services for tactical use. The earlier Butt Report had so disillusioned the Prime Minister that he tasked his scientific advisor and comptroller, Lord Cherwell, to commission an assessment of the potential value and efficacy of a concentrated area bombing campaign. The result was "The Report on the Bombing of Germany," written by an independent assessor, Mr. Justice John Singleton. It was delivered to Cherwell on 20 May 1942, ten days before the Cologne raid. While the Singleton Report played down the feeling that area bombing could win the war by itself, his findings were significantly more encouraging than those of D.M. Butt. Singleton felt that Germany's war effort could be hampered and limited by attacks on factories engaged in war work, as well as damage to communications grids and public utility services. He also felt there were gains to be made by tying down significant numbers of fighter aircraft, anti-aircraft artillery, searchlights, specialized military personnel, and a very large air raid precautionary and rescue service. The enemy's morale would likely also be affected by the disruptions and dislocations, the destruction of their homes and possessions, and all the inherent dangers themselves.

Some of Singleton's terms of reference from Lord Cherwell were to speculate on what results would most likely be achieved from Bomber Command's continuing attacks, at the greatest possible strength, on Germany for the next six, twelve and eighteen months. His report was also was influenced by an earlier memorandum prepared by Cherwell, which examined the effects of the Blitz on Britain, and arrived at the following conclusions:

> Investigation seems to show that having one's house demolished is most damaging to morale. People seem to mind it more than having friends or even relatives killed. At Hull

signs of strain were evident, though only one-tenth of the houses were demolished. On the above figures [for heavy bomber production] we should be able to do ten times as much harm to each of the fifty-eight principal German towns. There seems to be little doubt that this would break the spirit of the people.[74]

Not only were Cherwell's estimates of bomber production and bomb damage highly inaccurate, Richard Holmes believes that "the extrapolation to 100 percent destruction of fifty-eight cities was an absurdity on its face, all of which was promptly pointed out by Sir Henry Tizard, a scientist of comparable stature and the Ministry of Aircraft Production on the Air Council. His reward was to be buried by attacks on his integrity [there was bad blood between him and Cherwell] and even his patriotism. It was an episode that reflected little credit on the government, and the most likely explanation for it is that Cherwell belatedly realized the political damage the Butt Report [of 1942] had done, and sought to make amends."[75]

Justice Singleton doubted that a sustained bombing policy was by itself sufficient to win the war or even to produce decisive results, but he felt it could certainly impede German action and help the Soviet Union:

> It is impossible to see what this effect will be in twelve-to-eighteen months without considering the position of Russia. If Russia can hold Germany on land I doubt whether Germany will stand twelve or eighteen months of continuous, intensified and increasing bombing, affecting as it must her war production, her power of resistance, her industries and her will to resist (by which I mean morale).[76]

However, while Singleton endorsed the value of T.R.1335 (*Gee*) as a navigation aid, he was not confident about its utility for target identification. Instead, he saw a need for more sophisticated target identification devices, unaffected by atmospheric conditions, and he also recommended the establishment of a specialized target identification force.

> The navigation aid (T.R.1335) now in use should prove of great help to get the crews to the neighbourhood of the target, but it is limited in range and, to some degree, in accuracy. A new target finding device (*H2S*), from which there are great expectations, is in course of production but I am told that it is not likely to be in use before the autumn, and perhaps not this year . . .
>
> The navigation aid ought to take the crews reasonably near the target but thereafter the human element comes in and, however well trained the men are, they may fail to identify the target: they are dependent on conditions of weather and on the nature and position of the target, they may be led astray by decoys or by a fire accidentally caused, and they are hampered by the enemy's defences . . .
>
> Before I concluded the Inquiry I had the advantage of seeing two officers who had recently been using T.R.1335 in night bombing attacks on Germany. They are officers of great experience. They are both completely satisfied with the accuracy of T.R.1335 provided that it is used by a specially trained crew. In such conditions they say it will take you within four miles of the target longitudinally with a possible error of two miles laterally. They regard it as of tremendous help. It is in the last few miles that the real difficulties arise and they can only be overcome by determination and will power. The crews are not by any means all of the same calibre, and the officers to whom I refer are firmly convinced of the desirability of a specially trained Target Finding Force, which, they believe, would lead to greatly increased efficiency in bombing . . .

> If *H2S* comes up to expectations the load of bombs then carried will have a much greater effect than a like load carried today. Until that device, or something similar, is in use the success of the operation is dependent on the identification of the target area. Recent results are not encouraging except in almost ideal weather conditions, and there are few nights in the month on which such conditions can be expected, and few targets on which a night bombing attack can be really successful.[77]

Harris took careful note of Justice Singleton's findings, whose Report, coupled with the success of the Cologne operation, won Bomber Command a reprieve for the moment. Harris knew, however, that mass bombing and concentration of forces over the target area were not enough. Accurate and consistent target identification was also a prerequisite for success. He acknowledged the utility of *Gee* as a navigation aid and indeed, *Gee* were relied on heavily throughout the remainder of the war, especially as a highly reliable tool for returning crews to get fixes on their home bases. But its limitations precluded consistently successful application in the target area by all but the most skilled crews, particularly as the range to targets increased, and there were many qualitative disparities among those crews. Other electronic aids to navigation and target identification were being developed, but they would require some months to bring into service.

A Need for Specialized Target Marking

While the technology evolved, Harris and his group commanders pondered the requirement for specialized target finding and target marking crews. Senior Air Staff planners, particularly Group Captain S.O. Bufton, the Deputy Director of Bomber Operations, felt this responsibility should be given to an elite corps separate from the Main Force. Harris and some of his senior entourage, however, were afraid such a culling of the best aircrew from the existing squadrons would demoralize those who remained with the line. Also, he undoubtedly viewed the creation of any elite unit as detrimental to the public school values of teamwork and collective effort for the common good. Instead, he wished to use the best existing squadrons within each group—a designated roster of Raid Leaders—to locate targets and lead attacks. The disagreement centred around the efficacy of area bombing the industrial cities in the longer term. Harris believed it could, in time, win the war, and that the present marking procedures were adequate for area tasks by average crews. The Air Staff under Bufton believed that area bombing was just a transitory stage of development, and that sooner or later, smaller and primarily strategic targets, the "panacea targets" so hated by Harris, would have to be obliterated. While Harris was undoubtedly correct at the time about the efficacy of area bombing, since no individual type of enemy target, whether it was ball-bearings, oil, aircraft or transportation, could be totally eliminated—and therefore grind the Axis war machine to a complete halt—the Air Staff was taking a longer view. When both camps appeared to be at an impasse, Harris was overruled by Sir Charles Portal, who believed the continued evidence of ineffectual bombing justified the establishment of a special cadre of "Target-Finders." However, Harris would, in the following years, continue to stridently resist his force's "diversion" as he viewed it, to specialty targets and additional taskings, and many more examples of this leadership pattern will be presented in due course. With respect to the creation of an elite force, however,

> Harris reluctantly complied. On August 11th the force was activated under the leadership of the Australian airman D.C. Bennett, recently returned from Sweden after crashing during

an attack on the *Tirpitz*. On August 18th, shortly after the Germans had succeeded in jamming the *Gee* apparatus, the new force undertook its first attack, against Flensburg. Harris could not stomach the Air Ministry title of "Target-Finders" and christened the new group "Pathfinders."[78]

At first, the Pathfinder Force was a true hodgepodge of units and aircraft types. The founding squadrons, which would eventually collectively become 8 Group, were 7 Squadron equipped with Stirlings, 156 Squadron flying Wellingtons, 109 Squadron with their speedy Mosquitos, 35 Squadron, now equipped with Halifax IIs, and 83 Squadron flying Lancasters. An immediate improvement in the concentration of bombs dropped in the general target area resulted, but not an improvement in accuracy. That had to wait for the introduction of the new electronic technologies and also for the inauguration of special-purpose target marking pyrotechnic flares, both of which would begin to appear early in 1943. From then on, the equipment and tactics of the Pathfinder Force would become progressively more accurate, sophisticated and flexible, and by 1944, the Pathfinders were capable of guiding the Main Force against very precise targets, and doing so in almost any weather conditions.

During the autumn of 1942, while Donald Bennett and his embryonic force were experimenting with new marking techniques, the Pathfinders were being used principally to locate and illuminate Main Force targets. "The Pathfinders led 26 attacks on Germany; on six occasions, in very bad weather, they completely failed to find the target; of the remainder, in better conditions, they found and marked three times out of four—and to everyone's surprise their losses, at less than three percent, were considerably less than had been expected."[79] However, the Pathfinders would not be fully implemented until the new year. Therefore, "precision bombing, whether by day or night, continued to be outside the capability of Bomber Command, which left a choice between area bombing or nothing—which in war meant no choice at all."[80]

More New Equipment

Although *Oboe*, like *Gee*, had been successfully tested in 1941, the first operational use of the system was not made until December 1942. It provided much greater accuracy in locating and actually hitting the target. *Oboe*'s strength lay in its accurate measurement of distance with radio waves. It used two transmitting stations, separated by more than a hundred miles, sending out two separate and very accurate signals. Specifically, it could produce an accuracy of 300 yards, although its operational average was roughly doubled, still a highly acceptable result.[81] The controlled aircraft would fly down one signal beam toward the target, and when the second signal intersected the first, the ordnance release point had been reached. Yet it had limitations. Its range was limited by the curvature of the earth. Effectively, the *Oboe* limit line extended only about 300 miles out from England, which meant that although the Ruhr and northern German cities such as Cologne could be bombed with heretofore unavailable accuracy, much of Germany was still beyond the range of *Oboe*. Also, it was only capable of controlling a few aircraft at a time, initially about twelve, which did not make it at all suitable for the Main Force. However, it was ideal for the Pathfinders. In fact, it would come to be used exclusively by the speedy PFF Mosquitos, and so it proved to be relatively immune from enemy airborne interceptions. Furthermore, the Germans were never able to *effectively* jam *Oboe* signals, as they did with *Gee*.

Getting there was half the fun. The ride over to England via troop ship. (DND PL4881)

Time to go. Boarding the crew bus to dispersal. (DND PL10811)

A Canadian Wellington crewman getting ready to go to Axis Europe. (DND PC2475)

Opposite top: Lübeck cathedral in flames, 28/29 March 1942. (Author's Collection)

Opposite bottom: A Halifax B. Mk. I of 405 Squadron banks for the camera. (DND PL10457)

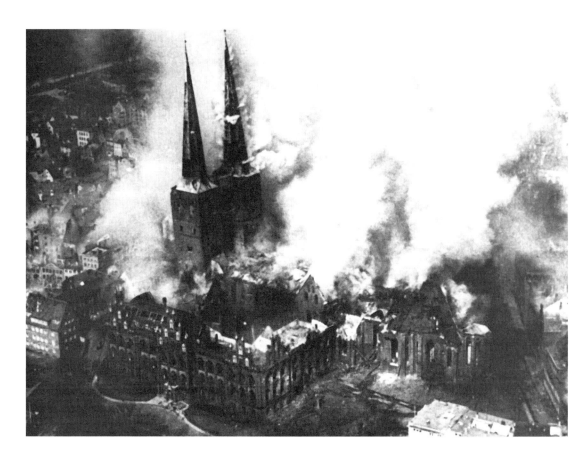

A relatively early war shot of a Canadian bomber navigator at his station. (DND PL4958)

Opposite top: Group Captain Bob Turnbull (centre) later in the war when in command of a 6 Group bomber station at Croft. (DND PL33941)

Opposite bottom: No. 425 "Alouette" Squadron became the fifth Canadian heavy bomber unit to form overseas, on 25 June 1942. This representative picture of a 425 Squadron Halifax III was taken much later in the war. (DND PL43950)

A Canadian Wellington being bombed up. (DND PL7095)

Opposite top: Bombing up an early model
Canadian Halifax. (DND PL19507)

Opposite bottom: A Stirling getting bombed up for
operations. Although rugged, they had many
shortcomings. (DND PL4961)

Wellingtons of 426 "Thunderbird" Squadron, ready to move out. (DND PL15382)

As the bombers ranged further and further into the Reich, the effective signal strengths of both *Gee* and *Oboe* declined, making accurate bombing of the deeper targets more difficult. However, on 30 January 1943, an electronic aid to target location and identification was introduced which very significantly increased Bomber Command's capability, when seven Stirlings from 7 Squadron and six Halifaxes from Reg Lane's 35 Squadron marked Hamburg for the Main Force. This second innovation was the short-wave centimetric *H2S* ground mapping radar, which was being developed in parallel by the Royal Navy as ASV III for the anti-submarine war in the North Atlantic. The system allowed the bombers to operate well beyond the effective ranges of *Gee* and *Oboe*, as well as to bomb without visual reference to the ground. However, while clearly-defined waterways such as coastlines, and some cultural returns such as isolated population centres of a distinctive shape, were relatively easy to interpret, it was very difficult to locate precise aiming points with the earlier *H2S* sets. This applied particularly to specific targets that were lost in ground clutter in the larger cultural returns, such as Berlin, and the sets were often technologically temperamental. Eventually, a new version using the 3-centimetre waveband was fielded, and it provided much sharper images of ground returns, which greatly improved the system's accuracy. *H2S* was installed in ever-increasing numbers throughout the Main Force in 1943 and 1944 as more and more sets became available.[82] However, *H2S* also emitted an electronic footprint by which it could be detected and located, although it could not be jammed. A captured, partially intact system which became available to the Germans soon after its operational debut allowed them to develop the countering *Naxos* apparatus, which was capable of detecting *H2S* from up to sixty miles range. Nonetheless, while blind bombing on *H2S* was never as accurate as blind bombing on *Oboe* at optimum range,[83] nor visual bombing with the improved Mark XIV bombsight that would be available in due course, the radar was an invaluable expedient for marking and bombing in conditions of 10/10ths cloud. "It meant that the German people were not able to sleep peacefully, wherever they were, and whatever the weather conditions over the Reich: respite came only when the weather at bases made it too hazardous to get the Main Force down."[84] *H2S*, particularly in its earlier forms, however, was simply not discriminating enough of ground returns in densely populated areas to be an extremely accurate blind bombing device.

During the autumn of 1942, the purpose-built marking pyrotechnics had not yet been introduced.

> Makeshift markers, 250-pound and 4000-pound cases filled with an incendiary charge of benzole, rubber and phosphorus, were used to distinguish PFF incendiary bombs from the Main Force incendiaries. They were effective only in the early stages of the attack but, like illuminating flares, were intended solely as a guide; Main Force crews were briefed to locate the aiming point for themselves. In the New Year, when Target Indicators specially designed for Pathfinders were introduced, the policy was gradually changed. *H2S* enabled the PFF heavy squadrons to find the target more consistently; TIs to mark the aiming point distinctively; and *Oboe* was a blind bombing aid that was more accurate than visual marking. By the end of February, the Main Force was being instructed to bomb the TIs instead of trying to locate the target itself; PFF had graduated from a target-finding force into a target-marking force.[85]

Back in North America, Ted Williams batted .356 with 36 homers and 137 RBIs for the Boston Red Sox, the 1671 mile Alcan-Alaska highway between Dawson Creek and Fairbanks was completed, an Arrow Harvest Stripes dress shirt could be purchased for $2.50, Humphrey Bogart and Ingrid Bergman premiered in their new Warner Brothers film *Casablanca*, and the Washington Redskins upset the Chicago Bears 14-6 in the 10th NFL Championship game before 36,006 fans. However, throughout that grim summer and autumn, representative raids with their grim loss statistics paint a sombre picture of the altogether different world being experienced by Bomber Command: Saarbrucken and Nuremburg on 28/29 August; 275 sorties, 30 aircraft (10.9 percent) lost . . . Bremen on 4/5 September; 251 aircraft dispatched, 12 aircraft or 4.8 percent of the force lost . . . Düsseldorf 10/11 September; 479 aircraft sortied, 33 or 7.1 percent of the force did not return . . . Essen on 16/17 September; 369 dispatched, 39 (10.6 percent) did not return . . . Munich on 19/20 September; 168 sortied, 12 aircraft (7.1 percent) lost . . . Flensburg on 1/2 October by 27 Halifaxes of 4 Group; good results but nearly half the force (12 aircraft) lost . . . Cologne 15/16 October; 289 aircraft dispatched, 18 (6.2 percent of the force) did not return . . . Milan on 24/25 October; 8.5 percent lost . . . Hamburg 9/10 November; 213 aircraft sortied, 15 (7.0 percent) did not return . . . Stuttgart 22/23 November; 4.5 percent lost . . . Frankfurt 2/3 December; 5.4 percent lost . . . Duisburg 20/21 December; 12 aircraft (5.2 percent) did not return . . . Munich 21/22 December; 8.8 percent lost.

While there were also many relatively successful operations conducted during this period with lesser loss rates, it was obvious to all that being an aircrew member of Bomber Command during 1942 was not conducive to longevity.

A Major Disappointment

Although the Lancaster's introduction into service revealed very few structural shortcomings or deficiencies, the same could not be said of the Halifax. The earlier Merlin-engine models were underpowered, had many hydraulic systems failures, were limited in their top-end cruising speeds and operational ceilings, had bad exhaust flame damping, which increased their chances of being seen by enemy night fighters, and—perhaps the most insidious fault of all—they displayed a particularly nasty rudder-stall vice when being manoeuvred aggressively, especially at lower airspeeds. This was the result of a design deficiency that produced a condition known as rudder overbalance, and it would require a complete re-design and replacement to correct the flaw. However, the insufficient power provided by these Merlin-engine variants had profound operational ramifications. The lowered cruising speeds and especially the significantly lowered operational ceilings made the Halifaxes particularly vulnerable to night fighter attack and more vulnerable to flak. They were also vulnerable to bombs dropping on them from their own high-flying Lancasters above. Furthermore, their bomb carriage capacity was significantly less than in the Lancaster. Kenneth McDonald, a pre-war CAN/RAF pilot of British birth, flew his Bomber Command tour with 78 Squadron during the dark days of 1942 and 1943, winning a DFC in the process. He recalls the operational limitations of the early Halifaxes:

> They had acquired too much operational equipment, so that fully loaded, at operational height, they were slow, flew soggily and were inclined to yaw and drop into a fatal spiral with rudders locked over. Then they added kidney cowls to blanket the exhaust flames from night fighters, and that for [Leonard] Cheshire, was the last straw. He considered it made the aircraft more dangerous than the enemy and asked permission to take the cowls off his squadron's aircraft. Everyone disagreed except his AOC, Air Vice-Marshal Carr,

who let Cheshire do so, with the result that his losses fell. It was the first step to taking off a lot more: front turret, mid-upper turret and armour plate. Freed of the excessive drag and weight, the plane flew more comfortably, and the engines were not overworked and the losses fell further.[86]

However, the tone of various letters written by Sir Arthur Harris from late 1942 until early 1943 on the sorry state of the Halifax and these ad hoc solutions leaves no doubt as to his acute frustration and disappointment on behalf of his aircrews. While Sir Arthur was not an aeronautical engineer, as a pilot, his instincts about aircraft that did not look right certainly held true:

Air Marshal F.J. Linnell, CB, OBE,
Ministry of Aircraft Production,
Millbank, S.W.1

ATH/DO/5C   16th October, 1942.

<u>SECRET & PERSONAL</u>

Our friend the Halifax which, as you rightly say, stinks.

I have little faith in the gains to be expected from the carrying out of minor modifications, even if they come up individually to expectations, will be additive in effect where additional miles per hour are concerned.

I find the greatest difficulty in distinguishing between a Halifax and a Lancaster on the ground and, although I am a child in such matters, it consequentlyseems to me that most of the Halifax troubles are to be found in the wing shape and section and the engine positions. If that is so, I wonder if it would not be possible virtually to convert the Halifax into a Lancaster by re-designing the whole Halifax wing to a more or less exact proportion of the Lancaster wing provided that it could be done without interfering with the wing roots and inboard construction.

It may be that if such an alteration were possible we should get virtually another Lancaster without having to go anything like as far in a general change-over. We should at least get simultaneously whatever improvements may be apprehended from the dropped engine nacelles and acquire a wing which would take the complete power egg as in the Lancaster, which makes so much towards ease of engine changing and maintenance.

I know that you are fully aware of the vital urgency of doing something and doing it quickly to get the Halifax right. The morale of the Halifax units is definitely cracking. This is not as yet ascribable to the squadrons themselves, but we are getting to the usual stage with suspect aircraft where the young intake from the OTUs arrive under a sense of injury that they have been selected for Halifax flying, and old lags coming back on their second tour and hoping for Lancasters become despondent at their prospects of survival on the Halifax.

(Sgd.) A.T. HARRIS[87]

Air Vice-Marshal R.S. Sorley, OBE, DSC, DFC,
Air Ministry A.C.A.S. (TR),
King Charles Street, Whitehall, S.W. 1.

ATH/DO/4D   18th March 1943

<u>SECRET</u>

I am not in any way impressed by your letter, dated 16th March 1943 Ref. A.C.A.S. (TR) DO/588.

You may have increased the <u>top</u> speed of the Halifax by 30 miles an hour. This might have been satisfactory in September 1942, when you held your Conference, but today it still leaves the Halifax far behind the Lancaster in every way. Furthermore, this improvement has been achieved by the sacrifice of the front turret, jettison pipes, and many minor items, all of which the Lancaster has, and is still some 15 m.p.h. faster at <u>cruising speed</u>, which is the speed which matters.

You say that the Series 1A for which you submit figures, was selected at random from the production line. My information is that only two to date have so far been made, and very nearly hand made at that, and they certainly have not reached my Command. Not much random selection about that, and definitely not a production aircraft!

The comparison of the maximum weak cruising figures you give for the Series 1A with those given by Boscombe Down, for Lancaster I R.5546 selected at random (Figures taken from the 31st Part of Report No. A. & A. E. E./766 dated 12th January 1943, Table II) is:

Series 1A	H.R.679	18000/20000 ft.	210/215 M.P.H.
Lanc. I	R.5546	19000/21000 ft.	231/234 M.P.H.

You will note that the Lancaster is 12/19 M.P.H. faster at 1000 ft. higher, and has a better air miles per gallon figure.

There really isn't any comparison—the Lancaster is an aeroplane and the Halifax a failure.

Having so far shown your Series 1A up so badly, I have still not said anything about the many other defects in the Halifax. The rudder tail trouble with its vicious characteristics, the excessive vibration in the engine mountings, causing an enormous number of engine and radiator failures.

Regarding this latter defect, I know you will come back and say you have produced modifications to overcome this failure. This may be true, it has yet to be proved, but the vibration is still there, and until the modifications which have not yet reached the Command are proved, the failures will persist and cause high unserviceability and unnecessary maintenance.

Your para. 7 shows you are misinformed, as we have not yet received any Series 1A. We therefore cannot be pleased with them. We have received the faired-in front nose type, from which we remove the mid-upper turret, and this gives a performance much the same <u>as an almost unarmed bomber</u>.

It is of some slight advantage to regain the lost performance but this so-called performance is still far below what is required today, and in six months time will be completely unacceptable.

Why we go on producing such an aircraft I cannot understand. If my suggestion made last August, that all production of the Halifax should be stopped and turned over to Lancaster, had been followed and the effect which has been put into the Series 1A, put into the turn-over we should by now be much nearer having good Lancasters in place of the bad Halifax.

In spite of what has and is being done to the Halifax, I am unmoved by your letter and still consider that the sooner we are rid of the Halifax the better.

(Sgd.) A.T. HARRIS[88]

Many of the earlier shortcomings of the Halifax, except the recurring hydraulic system problems, were rectified by the Mark III and MarkVII series,[89] which were powered by uprated sleeve-valve radial engines and flown operationally from November 1943 onward. However, Harris's comment about dissatisfaction with and trepidation of the aircraft beginning at the Heavy Conversion Units is telling, since these units were frequently equipped with the early, war-weary models that had been retired from operational service. Heavy combat losses of the Merlin-engine variants during the bitter winter of 1943/1944 resulted in their withdrawal from the seven Bomber Command squadrons so equipped, including four Canadian units. They were relegated from the deep penetrations over Germany to Gardening operations and raids over northwest Europe. Since this policy change occurred right after a disastrous raid on Leipzig on 19/20 February 1944, at the height of the Berlin raids, it undoubtedly prevented many Canadian casualties. Eventually these squadrons were re-equipped with superior Mark III/VII Halifaxes or Lancasters, and once again became fully operational within the Command.

Jim Northrup from Saint John, New Brunswick, had a distinguished tour with 415 Squadron, completing thirty-three operations and winning the DFC in the process. While he only flew the Halifax III model operationally, he has vivid recollections of some of the shortcomings of the earlier models flown during his type conversion training:

> All Halifaxes had exceptionally strong airframes. The Mark I was powered with Rolls Royce Merlin XX engines which simply did not have enough power. The Mark II and V had Merlin XXII engines and these were rated at 1450 horsepower, but the maximum you could obtain was 1390 "through the gate." Basically, the Marks I, II and V were the same aircraft except that the Mark V was a Mark II that had been retro-fitted with the Mark III rectangular rudders, this job being done at a repair depot or right on the squadron. This overcame the problem of the Marks I and II where at any degree of bank over 60 degrees, you could encounter rudder reversal and suffer complete loss of control. These aircraft were sluggish on takeoff and climb, and if loaded and you lost an engine on takeoff, you were going down. Now all these aircraft I flew were well-worn and were subject to engine fires from glycol leaks or broken oil lines. During the month I spent at Heavy Conversion Unit there were six crashes from fire and I nearly contributed another one. The airdrome [sic] was fogged in solid and I was making a beam [instrument] approach. At 100 feet I could just make out the runway and throttled right off when a red Very [flare] shot went right past my nose. I went to full throttle and immediately knew I had trouble on the starboard side. I looked out and saw smoke and figured it was the starboard outer, but asked my mid-upper gunner to confirm this before I pressed the feathering button and fire extinguisher. He confirmed this so I went through the procedure and then went "through the gate" on the remaining three engines. I was at very low airspeed, the aircraft was shaking badly, and I was having trouble keeping her straight. I finally got a hand on the "undercarriage up" handle and got the wheels up. I had full flap on and bled this off a few degrees at a time as I figured I would stall if I did it too fast. By the time I got the flaps up and nursed the aircraft up to 1000 feet, which was the minimum at which I could let my crew bail out, we were 70 miles from base and my navigator had to navigate us back. I made another approach on the beam and told Control I was landing, regardless of any conditions.
>
> Another chronic problem was runaway propellers, and you have not lived until you have heard the scream of a propeller out of control. The pressure on the prop is so great that it will not feather and within a few seconds, the prop tears loose from the reduction gear and if you are lucky, it hurtles off into space instead of coming through the cockpit. On a positive side however, I knew these were good engines as I had run three of them "through the gate" on that instrument overshoot for an hour when the maximum allowed

time was five minutes. I later learned that the way the engines were attached to the wing caused an airflow problem that contributed to engine failures. By the end of the course I did not think there were too many chances of surviving a tour on these aircraft, but we were told the Mark III was a much better machine.[90]

And yet, the dissatisfaction with the Halifax I and II series was far from uniform. For example, Reg Lane flew two of his three operational tours in these early models, the third tour in Lancasters. While Lane was admittedly a pilot of exceptional calibre and the Halifax Is and IIs that he flew would have been relatively new at the time, his resounding endorsement of the aircraft provides an interesting counterbalance to the issue:

> Now the Halifax . . . I found the Halifax a very satisfactory airplane. We had a lot of damage . . . One time we were beaten up by a night fighter very badly and the only way I could escape was by literally standing the airplane on its nose. It was a (Messerschmitt) '110 that came in and my tail gunner, Jimmy Scannell, gave me the usual warning, "Prepare to go starboard," or whatever . . . The fighter opened up, but all the shells missed us, but then it was only a matter of a minute or so before Jimmy said, "He's coming in again, skipper." This time, he did hit us and put a few shells into the airplane. Fortunately, no engines were hit and there was no fire. A few minutes later, Jimmy said, "He's coming in again, skipper. I'm sorry, but all my guns have been frozen since we reached altitude and I cannot fire a shot in anger." This was not uncommon. There would be a little condensation at lower level, then as you climbed, the breech blocks would freeze and there was nothing you could do. When Jimmy told me that, I realized we were not long for this world and I stood the airplane on its nose. We were on a trip to Hamburg. Down we went, literally, and I had to trim the aircraft out of the dive—I couldn't just use the control column to pull out. Eventually we got back to base and when we landed, the ground crew and engineering officer took a look at the airplane and said we had been very lucky to get home. The wings—all the metal on the wings had rippled. In other words, everything was about to come apart. I mention that to show that the Halifax was capable of taking an awful lot of punishment and not once did I ever have a problem with its controls. I've heard stories about troubles with the tail assembly but I never did have that problem.[91]

When six additional RCAF heavy bomber squadrons formed in the latter half of 1942, Sir Arthur Harris balked. Allan English elaborates:

> Harris worried that if the operational squadrons were manned by "coloured troops," as he disparagingly referred to Dominion aircrew, he would lose operational control of his force, because the Dominions insisted on being consulted on personnel issues such as aircrew disposal and tour length. To hold on to what he saw as his operational prerogatives, Harris sometimes acted independently of Air Ministry policies. This and other RAF actions that undermined Canadian authority eventually forced the RCAF to take measures to ensure that its wishes were respected.[92]

A significant number of writers of the period and Canadian historians have taken offense to this particular Harris remark, labeling it not only deprecating but racist. However, both the remark and the speaker need to be placed in context, and not measured against modern social sensitivities. Was Arthur Travers Harris a racist? Probably no more so than others of his ilk. In fact, Harris would have been a product of his class, his times and his upbringing. As a follow-on to a British public school education, by spending some of his formative years as a member of the British upper middle class in India and Rhodesia, he would almost certainly have been imbued with, not so much a sense of disdain for others, but of the apparent superiority of the British way of life, social structure and manner of conduct. These would have been impressions he carried with him throughout his lifetime. They would produce a certain rigidity of thought and would undoubtedly limit the flexibility of his thinking in terms of what could be expected from non-Britons. As to the remark itself, while it would be considered reprehensible today, the term "coloured troops," as it was applied to men from the Dominions, has a distinct historical linkage dating back to at least the Great War. In the wartime Royal Flying Corps and later the Royal Air Force, the term was in widespread use, even by Dominion troops in reference to themselves, and no derogatory stigma was attached to it.[93] Arthur Harris had been a front line combat pilot during the Great War and would have been familiar with the term and its accepted usage. If anything, Arthur Harris was a British elitist rather than a racist, and he behaved in lockstep with that certain arrogance of his class. However, his wartime correspondence and briefings, up to and including those to the Prime Minister, were liberally salted with racial slurs and crude exhortations to punish the enemy. Excerpts from a letter to Prime Minister Churchill, in response to comments solicited by the Prime Minister on an intercepted Japanese *Ultra* signal, suggest that he was comfortable speaking in such terms to the Prime Minister, which also suggests a shared value structure and point of view for Winston Churchill.

TOP SECRET

STRICTLY PERSONAL   30th September, 1944.

ATH/DO

Prime Minister,

You ask for my comment on the Ultra paper sent me today.

   Of our past experience the Jap diplomats are usually stuffed with Boche propaganda and inclined to swallow it hook, line and sinker . . .

   I have always maintained that no matter how well the Boche has fought outside his own frontiers, we should see him for the first time really fight his damnedest when driven back onto his own frontiers . . . His last ditch is indeed his last ditch—and well does the Boche know it . . .

   I agree therefore with the views expressed by the Jap on . . . (etc)

                                               (Signed)
                                               Arthur T. Harris[94]

   Harris did not believe that Canada would be able to produce enough Lancasters to equip a squadron conducting sustained operations, much less a group. In fact, as early as 20 June 1942, Harris decided to make 6 Group a Halifax formation. However, his reasons for doing so bear close scrutiny. For one, his prognostications with respect to Canadian industrial capability would prove correct. While the prototype Canadian-built Lancaster X, *The Ruhr Express*, was delivered overseas in August 1943, "this had been an outright publicity stunt. The machine was far from being operationally ready. Only thirteen more Lancaster Xs were built before the end of the year, and the first squadron was not equipped with the type until No. 419 Squadron received them in March 1944."[95] Perhaps more pragmatically, during the operational disappointments of 1942/1943, Harris was under extreme pressure from both the Air Ministry and, indirectly, the Canadian government to equip RCAF squadrons with four-engine types as soon as possible. Canadian authorities strenuously objected to the number of RCAF twin-engine Wellington squadrons being formed, and were somewhat concerned that 6 Group would become an exclusively Wellington-equipped group. Since 4 Group, with whom 6 Group had been twinned, was essentially a Halifax formation, and given the equipment pressures being placed on the RAF by the Canadian government (in spite of the initial agreement to equip 6 Group with Lancasters), it made eminent sense to designate 6 Group a Halifax unit, for contiguous training, logistical support, commonality of equipment, and so on. Furthermore, Harris was eventually better than his word at providing Lancasters to 6 Group. While designated Canadian Lancaster squadrons were initially equipped with the decidedly inferior Lancaster II powered by Bristol Hercules radial engines,[96] No. 6 Group finished the war equipped predominately with Lancasters. Eleven out of fourteen squadrons were so equipped, in addition to 405 Squadron of 8 Group, the Pathfinder Force.[97]

Arthur Harris, to his credit, never relented in the continuous pressure he brought to bear on the Air Ministry and Sir Frederick Handley-Page to make the Halifax an acceptable operational aircraft, and therefore, accusations that he was saddling the Canadian group with a decidedly inferior aircraft are unwarranted.

Some Feedback Registers at Whitehall

During late 1942 there was a growing body of evidence that, in spite of the direct damage to German industry caused by the early raids, "the most serious problem confronting the German authorities is that of re-housing the bombed out population and providing them with clothing and other necessities of life."[98] This appeared to be compelling proof of the validity of the area bombing campaign. Specifically:

SECRET
Copy No. 16   No. 346, dated 22.9.42
Central Department
                              The R.A.F. heavy raids.

The following, <u>dated early August</u>, is from a <u>new</u> source on trial, who is, however, well placed and in close touch with the German Air Ministry—*Reichluftfahrtministerium*, referred to below as R.L.M . . . At the moment the fear of the R.A.F. giant raids is far greater than any anxiety about an "invasion".

Unrest in the bombed areas is great and in those districts to which the homeless and children from "air threatened regions" have been evacuated a certain nervousness is already noticeable, because the evacuees naturally talk about their experiences.

These big raids cause mass destruction. In spite of the statements in the *Wehrmacht* reports, the destruction of war production factories is fairly considerable. The loss caused by the destruction of food stores and depots is extraordinarily great, as the food cannot be replaced.

The effect on the civil population of such raids is not to be underestimated. For instance, in Köln [Cologne] there were between 3000 and 4000 dead [officially only just over 100 were reported], which of course the population of Köln know very well. They spread the information and this undermines confidence in the reports of the *Wehrmacht*. In Köln there were at least 200,000 persons rendered homeless, who for the most part have been evacuated, as in the city itself no new buildings or temporary premises could be erected quickly enough.

The problem of the homeless people is the most difficult. There is a shortage of houses and accommodation everywhere, in the country as well as in the towns. As a result, wooden hutments have to be erected everywhere . . .

In the R.L.M. there are officers of high rank and influence who seriously fear that the winter will see unrest and demonstrations, unless these mass raids are successfully dealt with. But if the S.S. has to be used against the civil population, a deplorable situation will arise. According to these officers the great danger is not an "invasion", but the systematic destruction of German towns by the R.A.F.[99]

In late 1942 significant overall Allied bombing policy changes were planned. The Americans, flying primarily out of bases in East Anglia in their B-17s and B-24s, had been taking the war to the Axis through daylight operations since the summer. Their doctrine was diametrically opposed to that of the RAF. They were utterly convinced that massed formations with extremely heavy defensive armament flying in daylight would prevail, and no amount of countervailing RAF strategies or experiences would deter them. Excerpts from the Prime Minister's year-end policy guidance to his War Cabinet highlight British concerns for the future, given the heavy out-of-country commitments that were by now being made for Operation Torch, the British and American landings in Algeria and Morocco. Furthermore, Churchill's words leave little doubt that he and his staff felt that the "American experiment" would ultimately fail, and even the Americans were making their bombers suitable for night operations, should the need arise:

MOST SECRET   Copy No. 2
W.P. (42) 580
December 16, 1942.

TO BE KEPT UNDER LOCK AND KEY
WAR CABINET

AIR POLICY

Note by the Prime Minister and Minister of Defence

The bombing offensive over Germany and Italy must be regarded as our prime effort in the Air. It is of utmost importance that this should not fall away during these winter months, when the strain of the Russian and Anglo-American offensives will be heavy on the German and Italian peoples . . . Arrangements have been set on foot for raising Bomber Command to 50 Squadrons by the end of the year, and all the necessary action has been taken to ensure that this target is in fact reached. The United States are persevering with the idea of the daylight bombing of Germany by means of Flying Fortresses and Liberators in formation without escort. This policy and our official attitude towards the United States Air Force and Government about it require examination . . .

The brute fact remains that the American bombers so far have rarely gone beyond the limits of strong British fighter escort. Their bombing of the U-Boat bases in the Biscay ports has been ineffectual or at the most has yielded very small results . . . They have not so far dropped a single bomb on Germany. The effect of the American bombing effort in Europe and Africa, judged by the number of sorties, the number of bombs and the results observed, compared with the very large quantities of men and material involved, has been very small indeed. . . .

On the other hand, it should not be overlooked that the American bombing force in Great Britain has been continually depleted in the interests of "Torch"; that they make large claims of killing enemy fighters, which, even if reduced to one-third, are still appreciable; that they have sometimes been attacked without fighter escort and have given a good account of themselves without disproportionate loss; and finally, that the accuracy of their high-level bombing is remarkable, especially if they are not interfered with at the moment of discharge.

Listening to all that I hear from every source, I have, during the two months of writing this paper, become increasingly doubtful of the daylight bombing of Germany by the American method. The danger of their having all their ammunition teased out of them by minor attacks by enemy fighters increases with every mile of penetration. . . .

If the American plan proves a failure, the consequences will be grievous. In the first place, it will be a heavy shock to public opinion in America. In the second place, American industry is already largely committed, and becoming increasingly committed on a vast scale, to the production of heavy bombers which are not fitted for night bombing. Thirdly, we shall have brought over and maintained in this country large numbers of personnel on our best airfields, thus adding to the length of our own attacking journeys without being able to count on any corresponding return in their assistance in our Air offensive on Germany. . . .

We should, of course, continue to give the Americans every encouragement and help in the experiment which they ardently and obstinately wish to make, but we ought to try to persuade them to give as much aid as possible (a) to sea work, and (b) to night bombing, and to revise their production, including instruments, and training for the sake of these objects. . . .

There is, of course, the alternative to which I have called attention in my note to the Chiefs of the Staff on plans and operations in the Mediterranean, Middle East and Near East (W.P. {42} 543), that "The United States form of daylight attack would have its best chance in the better weather of the Mediterranean."

All these matters require earnest attention . . . since it would clearly be disastrous to undertake the gigantic commitment involved in building up an Anglo-American Bomber force of 5000 to 6000 heavy bombers without being absolutely sure that the American bombers were capable of sustained attack, without disproportionate loss, on Germany. The United States have affirmed their decision to produce 82,000 combat planes in 1943, and the Minister of Production has returned with firm agreements regarding the distribution of these aircraft. It will be seen from paragraph 12 of Appendix B of his report (W.P. {42} 568) that "every effort is being made to make the United States heavy bombers suitable for night bombing. A comparatively simple modification has been evolved which gives reasonable hope of success. Modification sets are now being tried out both in this country and in America." This work should be given highest priority and progress reports made at short intervals. . . .

[Furthermore], the Wellingtons must not be prematurely discarded until it can be shown that concentration upon the Lancasters, which is evidently in itself most desirable, causes no falling-off in bomb deliveries on Germany. W.S.C.

10 Downing Street, S.W. 1,
December 16, 1942.[100]

In the end, the British and the Americans would agree to differ, and their differences would forge the mighty Combined Bomber Offensive of 1943 and beyond.

FOUR

Battering The Reich: The Road to Hamburg

Early 1943

The damage is colossal and indeed ghastly . . . Nobody can tell how Krupps is to go on . . . It drives one mad to think that some Canadian boor, who probably can't even find Europe on the globe, flies here from a country glutted with natural resources which his people don't know how to exploit, to bombard a continent with a crowded population.

—Joseph Goebbels, Diary

February–March 1943

In 1943 Bomber Command's overall size and ordnance-lifting capability—made possible by a new preponderance of heavy bombers, especially the Lancaster—enabled the Command to carry out widespread industrial area attacks envisaged in 1940.[1] The growth rate in both the numbers of bombers available and their carrying capacity was phenomenal.

> In December 1942, there were 262 heavy bombers available on average over the month; by December 1943 the figure was 776, and a year later the average was 1381. The bomb lift of the force rose even faster: in December 1942 it was a mere 667 tons; a year later 2,930 tons; by the winter of 1944 an average of more than 6,300 tons.[2]

These figures were considerably lower than Bomber Command's portion of the 4000 to 6000-aircraft joint Anglo-American bomber fleet[3] on which Arthur Harris, Sir Charles Portal, the Air Staff, and the American authorities wanted to base their strategic bombing strategy. From 1943 onwards, however, Bomber Command worked closely with the Americans in an all-out assault against the Reich's fundamental war fighting capabilities. The bombing policy being followed by the Command on the eve of 6 Group's operational debut was one of night area bombing, using or straddling the centre of built-up industrial areas, industrial complexes, or a distinctive landmark, usually slightly long of the specific target as the primary aiming point. This aiming policy was partially a hedge against the bombing phenomenon known as "creep back," where successive bomb impact points throughout the duration of a raid tended to develop progressively short of the actual target or aim point. It frequently resulted in damage to residential dwellings and non-industrial infrastructure in the vicinity of the industrial targets. However, the War Cabinet deemed this result of the bombing entirely legitimate, indeed desirable. Furthermore, these results placed additional burdens on the Reich's war economy in order to repair this damage. To effect these ends, at the dawn of 1943, Harris had at his disposal sixty-two squadrons or 1200 aircraft, of which thirty-six were heavy bomber squadrons consisting of eighteen squadrons of Lancasters, eleven of Halifaxes, and, for the time being, seven squadrons of Stirlings.[4]

For Germany, 1943 would be the worst year of the war to date, epitomized by the debacle at Stalingrad; defeats in North Africa and Sicily; the tide turning against them in the U-boat war on the North Atlantic; the capitulation of fascist Italy and its re-emergence, at least in part, on the Allied side; and the failure at Kursk of the last great German offensive in the east. And although the cost was heavy, the incessant Anglo-American battering of the Reich from the air scored telling blows.

The Formation of 6 Group

In contrast, 1943 was a pivotal year for both Bomber Command and the RCAF Overseas.

In the spring of 1942, as part of the re-negotiation of the BCATP, Canada had agreed to pay the salaries and benefits of all RCAF personnel overseas. On 23 January 1943 Canada also agreed to pay for the maintenance and equipment of all RCAF squadrons overseas, a further step in the Canadianization process.[5] For Canada, the year was ushered in by the inauguration of its own indigenous bombing group, the largest Canadian air formation ever to be fielded in battle. The Allied bombing offensive then evolved into a massive, highly coordinated effort, with the Americans pounding the Axis by day and the "heavies" of Bomber Command attacking by night. It became a continuous, twenty-four-hour strategy that would penetrate to all corners of the Greater German Reich and the other European Axis nations, providing no respite for the inhabitants.

The 1943 offensive for Bomber Command generally consisted of two drawn-out campaigns: the so-called Second Battle of the Ruhr, which commenced on 5/6 March and ended indefinitely in July; the Battle of Berlin, sixteen dedicated raids which began on 18/19 November and ended on 31 March/1 April the following year; and the Battle of Hamburg, a shorter, self-contained series of operations that spanned the period from 24/25 July to 2/3 August.

On 25 October 1942, 6 Group started operations from its temporary headquarters at Linton-on-Ouse. Air Marshal "Gus" Edwards's choice for initial command of the group was Air Vice-Marshal George E. Brookes, the AOC of No. 1 Training Command, an officer who had briefly served overseas with the Royal Flying Corps during the Great War, but whose acknowledged strength lay in his extensive experience with flying training. And 6 Group needed a lot of training before it would be effective on operations. Brookes was also considered a capable officer, British born, who could provide a tactful, diplomatic bridge in relations between RAF senior officers and the Canadian airmen. Furthermore, Air Marshal Edwards warned Brookes that there would not initially be enough senior RCAF officers available to fill the senior planning and operations staff billets at the new Command, and thus 6 Group Headquarters was liberally peppered with RAF officers loaned to the embryonic Canadian group.[6] Brookes did not possess a great breadth of operational experience or credibility, however this was offset early on by some stellar Canadian officers. Squadron Leader Bill Swetman, for one, had already won a DFC while completing a distinguished operational tour with 405 Squadron and later added the DSO to his awards as the gallant, highly respected skipper of 426 "Thunderbird" Squadron. Other notables included Group Captain C. Roy Slemon, who proved to be an unqualified success as the group's Senior Air Staff Officer (SASO), and Wing Commander J.E. "Johnnie" Fauquier, Slemon's right hand man who had relinquished command of 405 Squadron and was well on his way to becoming a Bomber Command legend in his own right.

One of Brookes's first tasks was to find a permanent site for his headquarters. In September 1942 an agreement had been reached with the Air Ministry to requisition from Lord Mowbray a rambling old seventy-five-room Victorian castle located at Allerton Park near Knaresborough. Lord Mowbray turned out to be a very resentful landlord, who complained loudly and vociferously about the many inevitable alterations to his property. According to Brookes, he was " the worst pessimist I have ever met for a man of forty-seven, no patriotism and full of himself and his troubles."[7] The remodeling of Allerton Park, sardonically known throughout its Canadian tenancy as "Castle Dismal," took considerable time, and was not actually completed until late spring 1943. Brookes appears to have remained quite detached from the operational realities of his command, frequently visiting Bomber Command Headquarters at High Wycombe as well as 4 Group Headquarters and 5 Group Headquarters, but also concentrating excessively, it would appear, on the progress of the renovations to his headquarters. This may have furthered an impression of aloofness and lack of attention to operational priorities among his aircrew and staff. "What Harris thought of the Canadian AOC when he arrived at High Wycombe we do not know, but by early December he was 'alarmed at the prospects' of No. 6 Group under Brookes's command."[8] However, Bill Swetman felt that Brookes and his contributions have generally become maligned over time. Swetman characterized Brookes as a fussy person, inclined to dwell excessively on trivial matters, and he felt that many of Brookes's shortcomings were probably attributable to a lack of intermediate command experience. However, Swetman also found him to be an honest man, true to his word, although his leadership was hardly as inspirational as that of his eventual successor. Bill Swetman also gives a great amount of credit to the SASO, Roy Slemon, for the relatively efficient running of 6 Group Headquarters during the group's early days.[9]

Canada's indigenous bombing group began its operational career at one minute past midnight on the first day of 1943. By March it was comprised of nine operational squadrons flying out of six separate bases, and more squadrons and bases would later join the group. When 405 Squadron, the most senior RCAF heavy bomber squadron, brought its twenty-one Halifax IIs to Topcliffe in March after it was temporarily seconded to Coastal Command, the unit joined 408 Squadron at Leeming and 419 Squadron at Middleton St. George, each with eighteen Halifax IIs, to form the Halifax minority within the group. All the other initial 6 Group squadrons were flying Wellingtons in different models, and the units usually had a mix of the older and newer variants on establishment.

Unit	Base	Equipment
405 Squadron	Topcliffe	21 Halifax IIs
408 Squadron	Leeming	18 Halifax IIs
419 Squadron	Middleton St. George	18 Halifax IIs
420 Squadron	Middleton St. George	10 Wellington IIIs, 8 Wellington Xs
424 Squadron	Topcliffe	10 Wellington IIIs, 8 Wellington Xs
425 Squadron	Dishforth	17 Wellington IIIs
426 Squadron	Dishforth	7 Wellington IIIs, 2 Wellington Xs
427 Squadron	Croft	11 Wellington IIIs, 4 Wellington Xs
428 Squadron	Dalton	12 Wellington IIIs, 6 Wellington Xs

For some months to come, the already-formed 429 and 431 Squadrons would remain with 6 Group's neighbouring 4 Group, based at East Moor and Burn respectively. However, Canadian government and British Air Ministry pressures to convert the existing RCAF heavy bomber squadrons to four-engine aircraft as they became available, coupled with new squadron establishments, the despatch of existing squadrons overseas, their secondment elsewhere and the creation or assignment of new 6 Group airfields, all combined to make 1943 a chaotic and destabilizing year for the fledgling group. These factors would rip many of the Group's most experienced crews from its grasp, at a time of sweeping, fast-paced changes and a high-pitched operational tempo for Bomber Command. In retrospect, it is small wonder that this degree of disruption found expression in high initial operational losses for the Canadians in their new organization.

A Canadian Home in the North Country

The stations were located between the Pennines to the west and the Cleveland Hills to the east, in an area of rolling hills and quiet vales in the East Riding of Yorkshire, which placed the 6 Group airfields the furthest in Bomber Command from the European continent. This meant thirty to sixty minutes more flying time on average were required to reach continental targets than for most members of the more southerly based groups. Additionally, since there was limited manoeuvring space between the bordering hills, many of the airfields had dangerously overlapping traffic patterns. For example, nine Bomber Command airfields were situated within a ten nautical mile radius of Linton-on-Ouse, including Marston Moor, Dishforth, Tholthorpe, Dalton, Rufforth, Topcliffe, and York, and while the danger of aerial collisions was great during the day, it was even greater at night because of the high number of aircraft engaged in operations. Also, northerly winds brought smog from industrial Middlesbrough, while southerly winds carried factory smoke from the Leeds-Bradford area. And the elevated terrain in the east meant that returning aircrew could not descend to break cloud out over the North Sea, as was often an option for their southern cousins in Lincolnshire and East Anglia. Living conditions at the bases also varied considerably.

The pre-war Expansion Scheme stations such as Linton, Leeming, and Dishforth were all well constructed, mostly of brick, and they had comfortable living and dining facilities as well as established and varied recreational facilities. However, all of the bases were located near population centres. And, since thirsty young men will be thirsty young men, they all adopted favourite "watering holes" in the neighbouring towns and hamlets. In Leeming Village, for example, the three village pubs prospered mightily during the war years, none more so than The Black Bull. Other popular stops included The Wensleydale Heifer in West Witton, The Birch Hall Inn in Goathland, The Punch Bowl and The Victoria Arms in Swaledale, the Fox & Hounds in West Burton, the Thwaite Arms in Coverdale, and the White Bear in Masham.

There were many diversions for the Canadians in Durham and Yorkshire, and many men from the Dominion fell under the spell of their wartime home in northern England and the earthy hospitality of its inhabitants. York had its medieval four-gated walls, as the city had been occupied successively by Romans, Anglo-Saxons, Vikings, and Normans. However, it was medieval York that provided the most enduring treasures, including the walls and the breathtaking Minster Cathedral, the largest Gothic cathedral in England, which took more than 300 years to construct. Many a Canadian explored the meandering lanes and old foot passages with their quaint overhanging thatched, half-timbered houses, and they oriented themselves, on sightseeing tours or pub crawls, by the three major ancient towers of the Minster. The red-roofed grey-stone market town of Helmsley near the ruins of the Rievalux Abbey was tucked within a hollow on the North York Moors. Many wartime pints were downed by the Canadians at Helmsley's Black Swan. And they visited Castle Howard, northeast of York, the baroque ancestral home of the earls of Carlisle, with its splendid 10,000 acres of surrounding parkland. At the thriving market town of Thirsk Canadians consumed pints at The Royal Oak free house, whose sign recollected the tree that sheltered Charles II after the Battle of Worcester. On the north coast Scarborough boasted a fashionable night-life, and its massive Victorian Grand Hotel could and *did* host several hundred boisterous airmen simultaneously.

Living and messing conditions varied considerably within 6 Group. Flight Lieutenant James T. Sheridan, a pilot and DFC winner with the 426 Squadron "Thunderbirds," recalled that on the established bases with permanent quarters, such as Linton, officers were normally quartered two to three to a room, with individual rooms, when available, reserved mostly for the squadron commanding officers. However, again depending on availability, all field grade officers, that is, squadron leaders (majors) and above, were provided with individual rooms as often as possible. While the pre-war stations offered many amenities, the war-built facilities featured the ubiquitous and hated Nissen huts. On the new stations, personnel were given bunks in separate huts for officers and men.[10] The quarters were identically Spartan, however, with the rows of bunks interspersed with the dreadfully inefficient coke stoves down the centre:

> built of curved corrugated sheets with brick or wood ends, and often, like Dalton, plagued by a "lack of heating in living quarters . . . and also absence of running water" as well as unsatisfactory sewage systems. It is impossible to know precisely how the environment of a particular station affected the officers and men posted to it, but one keen observer certainly noticed such things. Flying Officer F.H.C. Reinke (a journalist commissioned into the RCAF and sent overseas to record his impressions of air force life) had no doubt whatsoever that a squadron's morale depended, at least in part, on where it happened to be. Linton-on-Ouse, a prewar station and home at times to Nos. 408 and 426 Squadrons, was aesthetically pleasing despite its "utilitarian . . . almost grim" camouflaged headquarters buildings. Wherever possible "lush grass, shrubs, and countless young trees" and rose beds had been planted "to soften the general effect." Messes, bars and dining rooms were all attractively decorated in warm colours, and there were ample recreational facilities—two

softball diamonds, along with a lacrosse field and horseshoe pitching sites. In addition, vegetable gardens were being harvested to supplement normal rations. For those who wished to go off station, there were a dozen or so pubs within easy cycling distance, while the city of York was a bus-ride away.[11]

Conversely, Skipton-on-Swale, which eventually became a satellite station of Leeming in 6 Group's central geographical area, was barren and dingy in the extreme. Nor were the facilities convenient for the personnel assigned there. For example, at one time, the airmen's showers were located a full mile from their lodgings, an unhappy situation not conducive to the maintenance of personal hygiene. And what of those Nissen huts?

> The only heat you could get from the coke stoves was in trying to light the bloody things. It was just bloody marvellous to come back off a hairy op to those freezing huts and go to bed in your flying suit . . . And those fucking straw pillows and straw-filled pieces of mattress. I think they called them biscuits. You couldn't keep them on the springs, what-ever they were called. I got so mad at the pillows I went out and bought a regular one at each station![12]

Tholthorpe, although it was a new station, had attractive lawns surrounding its Nissen huts and also boasted well-decorated messes. "The differences . . . were probably attributable to the personalities of the base, station and squadron commanding officers."[13]

Early 6 Group Operations

From its earliest operations 6 Group found itself in the thick of a regenerated anti-submarine cam-paign. In fact, 6 Group's first combat operation of the war was a Gardening mission flown by six Wellingtons of 427 "Lion" Squadron. On the night of 3/4 January 1943, its ZL-coded aircraft, manned by crews who had only been operational for about two weeks, dropped mines off the Frisian Islands as part of a larger Bomber Command minelaying effort off the French and Dutch coasts. Furthermore, of the 316 sorties laid on in January, 195 were executed against the U-boat pens at Lorient, and nearly a hundred more were Gardening operations conducted in the North Sea and the Bay of Biscay. The first actual bombing mission of the war for 6 Group occurred on the night of 14/15 January, when nine Group Wellingtons and six Halifaxes bombed Lorient as part of a larger composite force of 122 aircraft. Wing Commander Blanchard, the CO of 426 Squadron, was airborne on a weather check in Wellington X1599, coded OW-M, at 2218 hours, several minutes ahead of the other eight squadron aircraft detailed for the raid from their advanced staging base at Moreton in Warwickshire. Blanchard soon reported favourable conditions, which allayed concerns about icing, and the rest of the Wellingtons then launched, each with their war load of two 1000-pound bombs, as well as incendiaries.

> Heading south, the No. 426 Squadron aircraft crossed the English coast at 12,000 feet; by the time they reached France, Blanchard was flying at 16,000 feet. As they approached the French coast, the rear gunner, Sergeant J.H. Eveline, reported an enemy aircraft at 1000 yards on the port quarter down. He then announced that a Ju 88 had flown right by, apparently having failed to spot the Wellington.
>
> Over France, Blanchard manoeuvred around the towering cumulonimbus cloud in bright moonlight. Sergeant Riles spotted another Ju 88 on the starboard quarter at about 800 yards, and Eveline called for evasive action to starboard and opened fire. Blanchard

had turned the Wellington through about 270 degrees before the rear gunner reported that the enemy aircraft had broken off the attack after closing to 400 yards. Blanchard got back on course for the target, and arrived just as the Pathfinders began laying flares. After orbiting the target area for about twenty minutes to observe the action, Blanchard dove to 12,000 feet and the bomb load was released at 0122 hours. Following the attack, they remained in the target area for another twenty minutes before setting course for England.[14]

Blanchard, while manoeuvring around a thunderhead on the return flight, managed to overfly Guernsey, where he encountered heavy flak. Now low on fuel, he diverted into Stanton-Harcourt in Oxfordshire, and then proceeded back to Moreton the following day. There, he found the rest of the 426 Squadron force from the night before, except for Pilot Officer Milne and his crew, who had not returned from Lorient. Thus, Pilot Officer G. Milne of Calgary, Alberta, and his crew of four other Canadians and one Englishman became the first of 6 Group's operational fatalities. There would be many more in the months to follow.

In February, the group flew 1005 sorties, including 312 to Lorient, 193 to Wilhelmshaven and 84 to St. Nazaire. Gardening sorties were flown on nine separate nights, and 200 additional sorties were generated against Cologne and Hamburg.[15] More significant and prolonged ordeals were waiting in the wings for the neophyte group in 1943.

Throughout the bitter winter of 1942–1943 Arthur Harris was writing more letters. While many were penned to anyone of influence who would listen in a dogged attempt to make the Halifax an acceptable bomber, Harris also wrote at length to the Chief of the Air Staff, Sir Charles Portal. In a January 1943 continuance of themes he had articulated the year before, Sir Arthur expressed his grave concern with respect to the Canadianization process, its recent manifestation in the form of 6 Group and the precedence this established, as well as a number of related issues, all of which appeared to him to challenge British hegemony within his Command. Portal's February 1943 reply is worth presenting in its entirety, since it addresses virtually all of Harris's concerns.

SECRET

Air Marshal Sir Arthur T. Harris, KCB, OBE, AFC,
Headquarters Bomber Command,
Royal Air Force,
c/o G.P.O. High Wycombe,
BUCKS.

7th February, 1943.

My dear Harris,

The question of the number of Dominion and Allied squadrons in Bomber Command, which you raised in your letter of 10th January has now been fully considered in the Air Ministry.

In Bomber Command about 30% of the squadrons are Allied or Dominion and about 35% of all the crews. On both counts they are less "A. and D." than Fighter Command who have 43% Allied and Dominion squadrons and 41% of crews. The proportion of Allied and Dominion crews in Bomber Command is likely to increase somewhat since by the end of 1943 some 43% of our crew intakes will come from Dominion and Allied sources. This should not, however, be reflected in the proportion of squadrons. There are 6 more Canadian squadrons to form under present commitment but these are not likely to form until fairly late in 1943 and when Target Force "H" is completed less than 25%

of the squadrons in Bomber Command should be Dominion or Allied.

We have always been fully aware that dominionisation (sic) produces difficulties and causes friction particularly when, as in Canada, the whole question is given wide publicity. I do not, however, think that these figures for Bomber Command give undue cause for alarm. I am afraid it is simply not practical politics to cut down the flow of Dominion and Allied personnel, both because we are committed to train a certain proportion of Dominion entrants and because with the great manpower shortage it would be impossible greatly to increase the flow of British personnel to take their place. I realize that your troubles have been increased recently because of the large number of new Canadian squadrons we had to form at the end of last year, and of the difficulties created unnecessarily by the Canadian Headquarters in this country. We have, however, just got (the RCAF Chief of the Air Staff) Breadner to visit this country (he arrived yesterday) and I very much hope that in consequence we shall be able to smooth over, at least to some extent, the Canadian difficulties. I certainly hope that the situation will deteriorate no further.

You raised certain specific questions where dominionisation (sic) creates difficulty.

The first is the possibility of the Australians demanding an Australian Bomber Group. It is true that they are asking that their squadrons should be concentrated at selected stations within a single Group. Negotiation on this matter are in progress and it is likely that we may have to accede to their wishes. I agree that the next step is likely to be a proposal that an all-Australian Group should be formed. I am at one with you in disliking this but it may be very difficult to prevent it. It is after all a natural aspiration and the gratification of it need not seriously increase our difficulties if the Australians play their part properly.

You mentioned the poor quality of some of the Dominion Commanding Officers.[16] This is most unfortunate but I hope that the Dominion authorities would not object to making changes if the reasons were explained to them. Perhaps you would let me know if you have tried to make any changes and if so what difficulties you have had.

When you wrote to the Secretary of State you suggested that we should encourage the despatch overseas of some of the Dominion and Allied squadrons. I agree that these should bear at least their share in overseas despatches; the Poles, for instance, might well be prepared for some of their squadrons to go overseas if we have to send any more out. We will certainly look into this possibility. It is also hoped that it will be possible to improve the machinery for securing the consent of the Government concerned for the move of Dominion squadrons from one theatre to another, by going through Service channels instead of through political ones. We will let you know if we succeed.

Finally, you commented in your letter to me on the effect the whole question was likely to have on our relations with the Americans. I do not think your anxiety on this score is justified. Many of these organisation questions were considered at Casablanca and the Americans proved most amenable to our views. You may already have heard that they have agreed to put the 8th Bomber Command under my strategic direction until they are quite prepared for American units to work under a British Commander-in-Chief in the Mediterranean.

You will see from what I have said that the whole question has been thoroughly considered, that the difficulties are not minimised but that we do not feel exaggerated alarm at the future position. I trust that your fears will prove unfounded and that the general position will get better rather than worse. If there are any ways in which it can be improved in matters of detail I hope you will let the Air Ministry know.

Yours ever,
C. Portal[17]

Another Policy Change

The establishment of 6 Group coincided with a major bombing policy change mandated by the Casablanca Conference held in Morocco in late January. At Casablanca, Churchill, Roosevelt, their advisers, and their military commanders decided it was time to take a fresh look at their combined war fighting policy. After they reaffirmed their overall "Germany first" plan, a strategic compromise was struck to carry the war next to Sicily and Italy, thereby postponing a cross-Channel invasion for the moment. Part of the rationale for this decision was that the U-boat menace on the North Atlantic had to be contained, if not removed, before an American army could be assembled in strength in Britain. This would pave the way for a cross-Channel invasion into northwest Europe, either in the spring or summer of 1944. Meanwhile, the combined air forces of Britain and the United States would mount a mighty Combined Bomber Offensive (CBO) against targets in the Greater German Reich, the European Axis powers and Occupied Europe. This campaign would have as its mandate

> the progressive destruction and dislocation of the German military, industrial and economic system, and the undermining of the morale of the German people to a point where their capacity for armed resistance is fatally weakened.
>
> Within that general concept, your primary objectives, subject to the exigencies of weather and tactical feasibility, will for the present be in the following order of priority:
>
> > (a) German submarine construction yards
> > (b) The German aircraft industry
> > (c) Transportation
> > (d) Oil plants
> > (e) Other targets in enemy war industry
>
> You should take every opportunity to attack Germany by day, to destroy objectives that are not suitable for night attack, to sustain continuous pressure on German morale, to impose heavy losses on the German day fighter force and to contain German fighter strength away from the Russian and Mediterranean theatres of war.
>
> Whenever Allied armies re-enter the Continent, you will afford all possible support in the manner most effective.[18]

At Casablanca, the commander of the American Eighth Air Force, General Ira C. Eaker, won qualified British support for the daylight strategic bombing campaign he had been advocating for his forces. Based on highly disciplined, tight formations and a concomitant massing of defensive firepower, Eaker had long argued that mass daylight bombing attacks were not only strategically feasible, but were also the most economical and effective use of his bomber resources. In diametric opposition, the British favoured their much larger, looser bomber stream employing individual attacks by night. Prime Minister Churchill in particular was highly dubious of the American direction, based on the bitter experiences of the Royal Air Force in daylight bombing during the early war years. In the end, it may well have been Eaker's utterance of a chance phrase, assessed by Churchill for its dramatic impact and public relations value, that "made the case" for daylight bombing. According to American historian Edward Jablonski:

> "If the RAF bombs by night," Eaker said, "and we bomb by day—bombing around the clock—the German defenses will get no rest." Churchill withdrew his objections to the AAF's tactics and shortly after his return to England used Eaker's phrase, "bombing

around the clock," in a speech to Parliament. It was the germ of the Combined Bomber Offensive of both day and night raids that soon became official policy and would wreak havoc on Germany in the months ahead.[19]

Bombing around the clock became an enormous Anglo-American cooperative effort which lasted—with this particular mandate unbroken—for the following sixteen months until the spring of 1944. It ranks as one of the most demanding and intense prolonged campaigns in modern military history. Even the most conservative of historians concur that, although it may have been doctrinally flawed, there can be no doubt that the Combined Bomber Offensive (CBO) and follow-on bombing initiatives decisively influenced the course of the Second World War.[20] Indirectly, it provided the beleaguered Soviets with some measure of relief in a kind of second front by tying down substantial numbers of enemy personnel, artillery and aircraft in the West, long before a land invasion through northwest Europe was feasible. Directly, the various United States Army Air Forces, working in concert with Bomber Command, destroyed most of Germany's coke and ferroal-loy industries and most of its fuel, hard coal, rubber and steel manufacturing capability, as well as much of its tank, truck and tire production capacity.[21] Furthermore, when the CBO mandate was modified some months later, it dealt mortal blows to the German day fighter arm.
Additional guidance was forwarded to Sir Arthur Harris with respect to the aforementioned policy priority list as follows:

> The above order of priority may be varied from time to time according to developments in the strategical situation. Moreover, other objectives of great importance either from the political or military point of view must be attacked. Examples of these are: (i) Submarine operating bases on the Biscay coast . . . (ii) Berlin, which should be attacked when conditions are suitable for attainment of specially valuable results unfavorable to the morale of the enemy or favorable to that of Russia.[22]

The point was also made that some Bomber Command assets were required to assist in the upcoming Allied campaigns in Sicily and Italy. Once Harris had received his marching orders from the Casablanca decisions, it became patently obvious to him that he had not been granted unrestricted operations against the German industrial cities, as he had wished. He stewed over his new mandate for a number of weeks and then replied with comments to the Air Staff that re-worded his Command's role as follows (my italics): "The primary objective of Bomber Command will be *the progressive destruction and dislocation of the German military, industrial and economic system aimed at undermining the morale of the German people to the point where their capacity for armed resistance is fatally weakened*" . . . This version implies that Bomber Command was to concentrate on undermining German morale *by attacking industry*; meanwhile the USAAF would concentrate on specific targets—which, as everyone knew, was the USAAF's intention anyway."[23]

Neither Sir Charles Portal nor any of his Air Staff either corrected or amended Sir Arthur Harris's subtle interpretation of the Casablanca decisions, and it was clear from the outset of this campaign that both the American and the British air forces would effectively go their own ways with respect to specific areas of concentration.

Six months later, the Casablanca Directive was modified to acknowledge the growing strength of the German air defences and to specifically target the German day fighter arm in a range of bombing options. " The German fighter force was given the status of 'intermediate target," and its destruction was made the primary goal. The campaign was given the unambiguous codename *Pointblank*."[24] Specifically, it directed Bomber Command toward:

> (i) the destruction of German air-frame, engine and component factories and the ball-bearing industry on which the strength of the German fighter force depend
> (ii) the general disorganization of those industrial areas associated with the above industries
> (iii) the destruction of those aircraft repair depots and storage parks within range, and on which the enemy fighter force is largely dependent (iv) the destruction of enemy fighters in the air and on the ground.[25]

While Bomber Command also felt the stinging power of the German fighter arm, Harris tended to view the German aircraft industry as "panacea" targets, and while he would not ignore them, he tended to apply his priorities elsewhere, leaving the bulk of the specific Pointblank targets to the Americans.

More Sophisticated Target Marking

The Pathfinder Force made great evolutionary strides in 1943, with increasingly accurate navigational aids, an efficient bombsight, specialty-trained crews, assignment of the most capable aircraft available, and the marking of targets in a distinctive and continuous manner. *Gee* and *Oboe* have already been mentioned, including the exclusive use of the latter by PFF Mosquitos. However, it is worth emphasizing that by 1943, *Gee* was proving to be of widespread value as an electronic homing signal to guide the bombers back to their stations in England. With *H2S*, improved Mark III sets in the 3-centimetre band would help discriminate aiming points from background clutter on some targets, although for optimum navigational use, "twenty towns and five different groups of islands had been pinpointed and coastlines stood out clearly: the rivers Rhine and Elbe had been identified, Hamburg docks, the Zuider Zee and the lakes near Lyons, too."[26] A few of the 3-centimetre sets were available to PFF Blind Marker crews for the start of the Berlin raids in mid-November.[27] The Air Position Indicator (API), linked to the bomber's compass, had already been introduced, and it displayed the aircraft's latitude, longitude, and true course at any given moment, although only in conditions of no wind or when winds had been accurately programmed. The Group Position Indicator (GPI), an attachment to the API, took the navigator's latest wind calculations into account and traced the track of the aircraft to the target. Thus, it eliminated errors on a dead reckoning (DR) run to the target "caused by pilots having to take evasive action, and they could be redirected on to the aiming point if a change of course was necessary."[28] Naturally, the system's success depended on the application of an accurate wind, as well as a good starting fix for the DR run. Later in the war, the PFF used this method to good effect for bombing and marking particularly well-defended targets, supplementing *Oboe* skymarkers, and for laying down accurate, concentrated markers for targets that rested beyond the range of *Oboe* and did not break out well on the *H2S* radar.[29]

Most promising of all was *G-H*, which was essentially *Oboe* in reverse. In this case, a signal was transmitted by the bomber to two ground stations, which could simultaneously serve up to eighty different aircraft. Accurate to within 200 to 400 yards, it did suffer *Oboe's* range limitations, however, and its transmissions could also be homed in on by enemy night fighters. Therefore, it was not employed for the Berlin raids, being used instead for some time only by bombers making shallower penetrations into enemy territory.[30]

While the Main Force eventually had access to most of this equipment, it became increasingly clear that these journeyman campaigners of the Command needed some accurately placed, consistent and standardized pyrotechnics to serve as primary aiming references. Thus, the PFF, from its inception, was at the vanguard with its specialist crews, and was eventually equipped with just Lancasters and Mosquitos for maximum effectiveness, flexibility and reliability.[31]

Naturally, once the aiming points had been precisely located, they had to be precisely marked, and from the summer of 1943 onwards, the Mark XIV bombsight gradually replaced the very-limited Mark VII Course Setting Bombsight. Unlike its predecessor, the Mark XIV could indicate the ground point where the bombs would impact at any given moment, irrespective of whatever manoeuver the host aircraft was conducting at the time. This automated, gyro-stabilized instrument even permitted evasive action on the final run-in to target, as long as the last eight to ten seconds prior to release were in steady coordinated flight, although not necessarily level or straight flight.[32] The instrument's computer measured true airspeed and altitude automatically, then calculated the indicated airspeed and factored in sea-level pressure and target elevation to give the true altitude above the target. Course updates were provided by the DR compass, and as long as the navigator's wind inputs were accurate, the release parameters were very accurate. The Mark XIV bombsight was also designed for use with H2S for blind bombing runs, a significant key to Bomber Command's phenomenal accuracy for specialist units in virtually all weather conditions later in the war.

Needless to say, distinctive, highly visible Target Indicators (TIs) were also a key factor in the successful bombing equation. Furthermore, the Germans had become increasingly adept at creating false target complexes in open areas, surrounded by various searchlights and guns. They would ignite dummy incendiaries within these areas, which matched those of the RAF in appearance and gave the very realistic impression of a town being both attacked and defended. So convincing were these decoy fires that many crews were deceived into thinking they were the real target areas.

During the early days of the PFF, while purpose-built TIs were being put into production, the Main Force had to make do with more primitive target markers. Two of the earliest were called the Red Blob and the Pink Pansy. "Red Blob fires were 250-pound incendiaries filled with a mixture of benzol, rubber and phosphorus which burnt with a red glow. Pink Pansies were 4000-pound bomb casings filled with the same ingredients and coloured so that the initial flash was of a distinctively brilliant pink."[33] However, while these early markers frequently helped identify a target, they were not able to accurately mark a specific aim point. In order to assure bombing concentration in the correct location, TIs needed to have excellent ballistic properties to ensure their accuracy, as well as distinctive and enduring colours and properties which would attract the Main Force bombers, and yet be very difficult for the enemy to imitate. Two fundamental methods for marking a target emerged—skymarking and groundmarking—although the process was divided into three overall categories. These consisted of blind groundmarking, code-named *Parramatta*, visual groundmarking, code-named *Newhaven*, and skymarking, code-named *Wanganui*. When utilizing *Parramatta*, the Pathfinders would drop TIs via *H2S*. Then, designated "Back-Ups" would drop TIs of a contrasting colour on the averaged impact point of the first markers dropped. The Main Force would then be instructed to bomb the average or Mean Point of Impact of these latter TIs, using the primaries only if the secondaries were no longer burning or visible. *Musical Parramatta* were groundmarkers dropped by *Oboe*-equipped Mosquitos, and when they were used, Back-Ups continuously refreshed these primary markers, on which the Main Force would in this case be instructed to concentrate its efforts. *Controlled Oboe* emerged later in the war, when a need for exact precision on attacks became much more prevalent. This included targets located either close to Allied land forces in the field, or specific targets, such as railway marshalling yards within urban areas in the occupied territories. On these operations, target marking was placed in the hands of a PFF Master Bomber or airborne controller, who would assess the accuracy of the *Oboe* TIs and then advise the Main Force which markers were closest to the Aiming Point and therefore to be used. When visual groundmarking was employed (*Newhaven*), hooded flares for illumination were frequently used, and markers were often withheld. *Controlled Newhaven* emerged in the last year of the war, again when precision bombing was required or when targets were located in circumstances similar to those required for *Controlled Oboe*. In this instance, specific proximity markers were dropped and illuminated by flares, and a Master Bomber then relayed precise and updated instructions to the Main Force.

The skymarking or *Wanganui* technique was employed when the target was obscured by cloud and the Main Force dropped their bombs on selected flares. Later in the war, when daylight raids again became the norm, coloured Smoke Puffs in yellow, green, red and blue that burned for eight minutes replaced the flares, as they were easier to see. Although *Oboe*-controlled *Musical Wanganui* was initially the only successful skymarking method, once use of the Group Position Indicator (GPI) became widespread, this form of marking achieved an accuracy that would rival even that achieved with *Oboe*.[34]

For groundmarking, the first challenge was to find a type of ordnance suitable for delivery by both the PFF Mosquitos and the heavy bombers. It was soon determined that 250-pound bomb casings, available in quantity, would work when filled with sixty twelve-inch red, green and yellow pyrotechnic candles. Used with a barometric fuse, they would ignite and cascade to the ground where they would burn for approximately three minutes. If fused to function at 3000 feet, a TI ground pattern of approximately 100 yards was produced, but functioning lowered to 1500 feet yielded a tighter TI pattern of 60 yards. Later in the bombing campaign, the functioning altitude was lowered further, yielding even greater accuracy. This new line of TIs made its debut over Berlin on 16/17 January 1943. Since *Oboe* marking always occurred at intervals, the challenge was to increase the burn time of the markers to avoid gaps. This was done by placing time delay fuses on some of the TIs, and eventually, by varying the number of candles burning at any given time, as well as the delay times. Through these innovations, the life of the TI was quadrupled to twelve minutes. Ground markers were released in salvo, and again, Main Force bomb aimers were briefed to release on the centre of a salvo, since the peripheral TIs were frequently either strays or enemy decoys. In order to minimize the number of crews that bombed on decoys, from the Peenemünde raid of 17/18 August 1943 onward, specialty 250-pound Red Spot flares were employed, and they burned a deep red for up to twenty minutes. Later, a Green Spot flare was also introduced, but by their very nature, these spot flares were often obliterated by the smoke and fire of bombing, and were thus often more effectively used on pinpoint precision targets or as route markers for the bomber stream.

Throughout the bombing campaign, other innovative ideas to counter German decoy effectiveness were introduced, with varying degrees of success. They included TIs which emitted two Morse letters for a period of approximately twenty-two minutes, candles strapped in bundles of three, which changed colour on a regular basis, and even a 1000-pound bomb casing filled with 200 candles, which could burn with very high intensity for up to twenty minutes.

For skymarking, either flares or candle TIs, complete with parachutes, were employed. The flares were either green or red, but an innovative variant ejected seven stars of contrasting colours at intervals of twenty seconds, with each star burning for eight seconds. Another popular sky-marker was the thirty-pound White Drip, a molten magnesium flare that produced a distinctive tail up to 1000 feet long. During the last fifteen months of the campaign, even more creative flares and smoke markers came into use.[35]

Air Vice-Marshal Donald Bennett, the brilliant, innovative, and demanding wartime commander of the PFF, offered the following thoughts on the effectiveness of his Target Indicators:

> The intensity of the target indicators . . . was very great, and indeed right to the end of the war the enemy never really produced a very good copy. As we expected trouble, we arranged for all sorts of combinations and variations of colours and the like. We were prepared to use different colours for different purposes, and indeed to change colours if necessary during a raid so as to ensure the correct aiming point even if the enemy were sufficiently alert to watch and copy . . . Each TI consisted of a large number of these pyrotechnic candles, ignited by the initial bursts, which meant that the fire-fighters on the ground would take a considerable time to get around to the job of putting them all out. Moreover, their burning period was relatively short anyway, and so there was no question of their being dealt with in that manner. Continuity of marking was achieved by replenishing from above.[36]

However, while the PFF would evolve into a highly versatile, effective and efficient fighting force, the challenges were many, and the force effectiveness was limited during the early months of 1943.

Sir Arthur Harris Takes the Initiative

Harris inaugurated his interpretation of the Combined Bomber Offensive directive with a strike in force by 442 aircraft at the Krupp works in Essen on the night of 5/6 March 1943. This operation initiated the so-called Second Battle of the Ruhr, which lasted throughout most of July and consisted of forty-three major attacks on Axis targets, including more than 18,000 sorties against the various industrial cities of the Ruhr and the Rhineland. It cost Bomber Command 872 aircraft destroyed.[37] Although the period was collectively known as the Battle of the Ruhr, just under half of the forty-three operations were conducted against targets located elsewhere. Some industrial centres were singled out for repeated attention. For example, Essen and Duisburg were each attacked five times while Cologne was targeted on four separate occasions. Sometimes the losses were particularly costly. Of 317 aircraft sent to Pilsen, Czechoslovakia, on 16/17 April, thirty-six did not return, a loss rate of 11 percent, and against Oberhausen on 14/15 June, seventeen of the 203 bombers sortied were shot down, a loss rate of 8.37 percent. As a participant with 35 Squadron of 8 Group, Reg Lane recalls the Pilsen raid and the still-rudimentary Pathfinder operations associated with it:

> Pathfinder ops in those days were pretty grim. It was tricky . . . It was very tricky. We were finally screened (end of second operational tour) on 16 April 1943—an attack on the

Skoda Works in Pilsen, Czechoslovakia—a very, very long haul . . . eight-and-a-half hours . . . I remember the trip well. There was a bit of cloud over the Works. We let down, trying to get a visual on the manufacturing plant, without any success. There were no defences, curiously enough, and finally, we dropped our bombs on what we thought was the target and headed for home. Then we decided to have a look at another concurrent raid that was going on in the Ruhr, but we got a little too close and were coned by search-lights. I thought, "You bloody fool . . . What are you doing getting this close to another target when you know full well there is an attack on?" Well, I ended up crossing the Rhine at about a thousand feet just to escape the defences.[38]

Sometimes the losses were very light. Against Nuremburg on 8/9 March, only seven of 355 (2.08 percent) failed to return. Over Kiel on 4/5 April, only twelve of 577 (2.07 percent) were lost. And an attack on Duisburg on March 26/27 had been even more successful in this respect. On that particular operation, only six of the 455 sent out failed to return, for a loss rate of 1.31 per-cent.[39] Furthermore, in the words of John Terraine, what became clear during this period "was that a big force, tightly concentrated behind its Pathfinders, could saturate and penetrate the Kammhuber defences with far less loss than large numbers of bombers making their straggling way towards a target on a wide front."[40] However, Bomber Command, in spite of its recent growth, was also coming uncomfortably close to an unsupportable sustained casualty rate during the Second Battle of the Ruhr.

Nevertheless, the raids were certainly scoring telling blows, and the Germans were feeling an increased sense of vulnerability to attacks from the air, witnessed by the diary entry of Joseph Goebbels on the havoc levied on Dortmund on the night of 23/24 May 1943. The 826 aircraft despatched, the largest raid during the Second Battle of the Ruhr, bombed in clear weather and hit the city hard, especially the Hoesch steelworks, which ceased production.

> The night raid of the English on Dortmund was extraordinarily heavy, probably the worst ever directed against a German city . . . Reports from Dortmund are pretty horrible . . . Industrial and munition plants have been hit very hard . . . Some eighty to one hundred thousand inhabitants without shelter . . . The people in the West are gradually beginning to lose courage. Hell like that is hard to bear . . . In the evening I received a [further] report on Dortmund. Destruction is virtually total. Hardly a house is habitable.[41]

An interesting story concerned a Canadian Wellington from 431 Squadron, still a part of 4 Group, which took part in this particular raid (my italics).

> Just after leaving the target, the Wellington was coned by searchlights and hit several times by fragments of flak. The rear gunner reported that he thought the aircraft was on fire. The pilot twice put the aircraft into a steep dive to evade the searchlights but was not able to do so. There was some confusion over whether an order to bail out was given by the pilot and the pilot actually did leave the aircraft. The bomb aimer, Sergeant SN Sloan, an Englishman, took over the controls and eventually was able to shake off the search-lights. The navigator and wireless operator were still aboard and Sergeant Sloan flew the aircraft to England and made a perfect landing at Cranwell. He was immediately awarded the Conspicuous Gallantry Medal, commissioned, and posted to a *pilot training course.* The wireless operator, Flying Officer JBG Bailey, and the navigator, Sergeant GCW Parslow, received immediate awards of the DFC and the DFM respectively.[42]

By this point of the war, Bomber Command four-engine aircraft were crewed with only one pilot and also a flight engineer who had usually received only the most rudimentary flight training, and it is astonishing how many Command aircraft handicapped by a missing or incapacitated pilot were successfully returned to base by aircrew other than the pilot. Three months after the Dortmund raid the hero of the night was a Canadian bomb-aimer serving with 622 Squadron of the RAF. What follows is the citation for a rare Conspicuous Gallantry Medal awarded to Sergeant John Calder Bailey of Saskatoon:

> This airman was the bomb aimer of an aircraft which attacked Berlin one night in August 1943. When leaving the target area a fighter was encountered and in the subsequent action the bomber sustained much damage and its pilot was seriously wounded. He endeavoured to regain control but slumped over the control column and had to be assisted from his seat. The aircraft lost considerable height and one of the engines was out of action. Displaying rare coolness, Sergeant Bailey took over the controls and flew the aircraft to an airfield in this country. Although he had never attempted to land a heavy bomber before, he succeeded in making a masterly landing. This airman displayed great skill and resource and was undoubtedly responsible for the safe return of the aircraft and his crew.[43]

Ironically, Bailey had failed out of pilot training at an early stage in March 1942, prior to becoming a bomb-aimer, and would do so yet again after his award-winning Berlin raid, when he was commissioned and returned to Canada for pilot training in January 1944![44]

A Game of Cat and Mouse

The electronic countermeasures war was becoming progressively more sophisticated. In December 1942 the use of airborne jammers through the broadcasting of engine noises on *Himmelbett's* fighter control wavebands was attempted. Code-named *Tinsel*, its output power was so limited however that it was easily countered by the Germans, who increased the strength of their ground signals. Another system known as *Mandrel* was also fielded in December to jam the *Freya* early-warning radars, but it too was only partially successful. It was yet another innovation, *Corona* and *Airborne Corona,* that proved for the moment to be the most effective. This equipment could jam enemy fighter controllers by superimposing a knowledgeable German-language commentary on their transmissions. When it made its operational debut in the autumn of 1943, it was very effective. Later still, *Cigar* and *Grocer* were used to good measure against enemy VHF radio and *Lichtenstein* Airborne Intercept (AI) radars respectively. *Airborne Cigar* was a mobile derivative of the earlier innovations. Reg Patterson, a Regina native who flew as a pilot with 101 Squadron later in the war and won the DFC in the process, recalls some of these innovations, termed "special duties."

> It was known as *Airborne Cigar*, or *ABC*, and 101 Squadron was the only *ABC* squadron in Bomber Command that I knew of, but then, the people that knew the least about things were usually the people that were doing them! Each aircraft carried an eighth crewman known as the Special Duties Operator. We flew with all groups that might be flying on any given raid, so quite often, 101 Squadron would be on a raid from which the rest of 1 Group, the parent formation, was stood down. As 101 Squadron was large and able to put up 45-or-so aircraft on a raid, every aircraft was not necessarily carrying a Special Duties Operator. There was a second wireless position right behind the main spar,

just aft of the regular radio operator's position, which was where the SDO sat. All these SDOs were people who spoke and understood German fluently. The aircraft were so dispatched that they were evenly dispersed amongst the entire bomber stream. Each SDO was constantly monitoring the known German fighter control frequencies and as soon as one of them picked up a ground station vectoring the fighters, they would clamp down their transmitter key and there was a microphone out in one of the engine cowlings that would transmit nothing but engine noise. Of course, the ground station would immediately change to another predetermined frequency with the fighters, but with twenty-or-so SDOs "covering the dial," they were soon caught and jammed again. After a bit of this nonsense, one of the SDOs would tune in to one of the command frequencies and transmit, in perfect German, instructions for the fighters to go somewhere else. It sounds a bit like kids' games, but apparently it was quite effective. A very good thing from our point of view in 101 was that we always knew when enemy fighters were near us because our man could hear them talking. The interesting Canadian aspect to all this was that over two-thirds of all the Special Duties Operators were Canadian from around the Kitchener area. Their ancestors were German but they were Canadian through and through. And one of the operators that flew with me quite a few times was a Dutchman. These Special Duties Operators did not form a part of any particular crew. They were just assigned out of a pool for each particular trip.[45]

However, the early jamming of German radars and communications equipment with *Airborne Mandrel* and *Tinsel* proved largely indecisive. And a tail-warning radar named *Monica*, introduced in the spring of 1943, could not differentiate between friendly bombers and enemy night fighters. Furthermore, the Germans soon developed their own *Flensburg* receiver to home on *Monica*. A more discriminating follow-on system known as *Boozer* ended up responding to both *Lichtenstein* and *Würzburg* radars and was thus found to be no better at specifying a direct attack on any particular aircraft. And the game of electronic cat-and-mouse continued, as the Germans developed the *Naxos* passive tracking device to home in on *H2S* emissions, and also those of *Fishpond*, "an extension of *H2S* intended to detect the night fighters which it was unknowingly attracting."[46]

The Ruhr campaign also highlighted increasing performance and design deficiencies in both the Wellington and the Halifax fleets. Those associated with the Halifax were particularly disappointing, since the expectations had been high and the manufacturer's promises seductive, to say the least. Throughout 1943, Sir Arthur Harris continued his relentless campaign against Handley-Page to make the Halifax Mark IIs and Vs at least marginally suitable for operations, until they could be replaced with Lancasters and the new Halifax Mark III. In fact, at the dawn of 1943 Harris still held out a glimmer of hope for the Mark III, although Handley Page

was always weeping crocodile tears in my house and office, smarming his unconvincing assurances all over me and leaving me with a mounting certainty that nothing . . . is being done to make this deplorable product ready for war or fit to meet those jeopardies which confront our gallant crews. Nothing will be done until H-P and his gang are kicked out, lock, stock and barrel. Trivialities are all that they are attempting at present, with the deliberate attempt at postponing the main issue until we are irretrievably committed . . . In Russia it would long ago have been arranged with a gun, and to that extent I am a fervid Communist! If I write strongly it is because I feel strongly, as I know you do, for the jeopardy . . . my gallant crews (face) and the compromising of our only method of winning this war.[47]

The Halifax's defensive armament was particularly inadequate, including the limited view and protection afforded from behind and below, and the exceptionally poor view from the tail turret.[48] These deficiencies yielded extremely strong admonitions from Harris to both the manufacturers and the Air Staff to provide viable remedies in the shortest possible time, and they also fostered Harris-sanctioned stopgap initiatives to temporarily improve the situation at the squadron level. These included jury-rigged perspex downward observation blisters and vision ports, and eventually, a .5-inch "mid under" gun installation on some units. Insufficient damping of the engine exhaust flames was also cited by crews as being excellent visual homing aids to the German night fighters, but this problem would not be properly remedied until the introduction of the Halifax Mark III into combat in November.

The Wellington fleet was mostly relegated to Gardening operations during the summer and early autumn, because of its vulnerability and limited utility on Main Force German targets. The last Main Force Wellington Bomber Command operation was flown on 8 October 1943. The Wellingtons were augmented in Gardening duties and in attacks on French targets in November by the Stirlings, when the latter aircraft were also withdrawn from Main Force attacks on German industrial targets. A similar fate befell the Halifax II/V fleets from February 1944 onward, but by then, the new Halifax IIIs were becoming available in substantial numbers.[49]

These and other changes were needed if the majority of Command operations were to be mounted on clear nights when Pathfinder marking could be fully exploited, since loss rates would otherwise continue to be prohibitive. The only foreseeable alternative was to rely more extensively on *Oboe, Gee,* and *H2S* in instrument conditions, with all the limitations they presented. Accordingly,

> Harris declared that while he was willing to concentrate on "the most valuable target" on clear nights when ground-marking was practical, he did not want to attempt deep penetrations in summer, preferring to use the shorter nights to attack precise targets in France or German objectives east of Emden-Dortmund-Munster. Larger areas would have to suffice when visibility was marginal or winds were high, but because of recent experience over the Ruhr he was convinced that Bomber Command could not return to the same area night after night without risking heavy losses. The focus of attack would be shifted frequently . . . In the poorest weather, however, he promised the CAS no more than that he would make for the largest possible area where "even a very scattered raid is likely to do worthwhile damage."[50]

Once More Against the German Industrial Heartland

Canadian aircrew, both in 6 Group and scattered throughout the Command, participated extensively in the Ruhr raids, an area they sardonically referred to as "Happy Valley." This huge amorphous mass of light and smoke was in fact defended by the most concentrated flak and searchlight batteries in the Reich, as well as the best and best-equipped of the German night fighter units. For its part, 6 Group contributed nearly 2100 sorties and a concomitant loss of 161 crews, a 7.6 percent loss rate overall, and the highest in Bomber Command during the period.[51]

At Essen, five *Oboe*-equipped Pathfinder Mosquitos marked the centre of the city perfectly, and the Main Force then bombed in three waves over a period of forty minutes; Halifaxes were in the first wave, followed by Stirlings and Wellingtons in the second wave, with high-flying Lancasters bringing up the rear. A full two-thirds of the bombs were incendiaries, and a third of the remaining high explosive bombs were fused for a long delay, which netted a great amount of additional disruption. Post-strike reconnaissance attributed 160 acres of destruction to the attack, and hits were registered on fifty-three separate buildings within the Krupp complex,[52] which was extensively damaged for the first time during the war. At least 153 of the attacking aircraft planted their bombs within three miles of the target. Fourteen aircraft were lost, representing 3.2 percent of the attack force. This raid was a blueprint for the rest of the Ruhr campaign, during which Bomber Command's overall effectiveness demonstrated significant improvement to that of previous years.

For this raid 6 Group provided 78 aircraft, three of which did not return, one 419 Squadron Halifax and a Wellington each from 420 Squadron and 426 Squadron. Laurence Motiuk, a wartime bomb-aimer with 426 Squadron, summarizes the Dishforth portion of the effort for the night:

> The 5 March raid on Essen was the first trip to Happy Valley for No. 426 Squadron. Dishforth contributed twenty-three crews: eleven from No. 425 Squadron and twelve from No. 426. The dusk departure of the two squadrons was a very impressive sight. The bomber stream flew first to the coastal town of Egmond, Holland, then just north of Amsterdam, then to a turning point at Dorsten, fifteen miles north of Essen, which the Pathfinders had marked with yellow flares. Flight Sergeant S. Pennington's aircraft had just reached the coast of Holland when an unserviceable port engine forced a return to base. They were carrying a 4,000-pounder that was fused live, and then dropped into the sea.
> The No. 426 Squadron crews attacked the target from an average altitude of 16,000 feet, aiming for the red and green target indicators laid by the Pathfinders. Ten crews dropped mixed loads of 500-pound bombs and incendiaries and one dropped a blockbuster. The defences of the target area included heavy flak and searchlights, confirmed by Flight Lieutenant Millward's special reconnaissance. As the crews departed, they saw many huge fires, which were still visible from the Dutch coast 130 miles away.[53]

The second raid of the Ruhr campaign was carried out, again against Essen, on 12/13 March, when 457 aircraft were sortied. Among them was the pilot Sergeant J. Gilles Lamontagne and his 425 Squadron crew in Wellington BK340, "T-Tare." Lamontagne successfully bombed the target and was on the return trip, heading flat-out for Dishforth, when he was badly mauled by a German night fighter over the German-Dutch border. Fire immediately broke out in the cockpit and the bomb-aimer's compartment, but Sergeant Lamontagne remained resolutely in control while other crew members attempted to extinguish the flames. However, the German attacked again before they could complete their work, and started another fire amidships. Although they had run out of extinguisher fluid, the bomb-aimer, Flight Sergeant J.A.V. Gauthier, managed to beat this new conflagration out with his hands. Eager to administer the *coup de grâce*, the German night fighter attacked a third time, leaving the Wellington blazing furiously, with the elevator controls catastrophically crippled.

This time, Lamontagne grasped the utter futility of the situation and ordered his crew to bail out, while he struggled with his dying bomber in an attempt to provide a steady egress platform for them.

> As all too often happened, the escape hatch jammed with the heat and Flight Sergeant A.W. Brown, the navigator, had to hack it open with an axe. The bomber struck the ground 20 miles north-east of Altmark near Spaabruck, Holland, and the crew landed safely on Dutch soil. However, all but Lamontagne were apprehended the next morning by the

Gestapo. Once on the ground Lamontagne found himself separated from his crew for he had been the last one to leave the aircraft. He tried to hide as best he could, but after a couple of days he too was apprehended by the *Gestapo* and taken to a concentration camp. What a world away Dishforth seemed now.[54]

Early Doubts and Concerns

Lamontagne, Brown and Gauthier remained prisoners for the next two years, and the gunner and the wireless operator, both severely wounded, were repatriated prior to the cessation of hostilities. When the RCAF eventually learned of Lamontagne's actions that terrifying March night in 1943, he was awarded a Mention-in-Despatches in the King's New Year's Honours List for 1945.

The combat record of 6 Group during the majority of its first year of operations proved to be not only disappointing, but also disturbing. Loss rates for the Wellingtons climbed to 9 percent in June, which was well above the 5 percent figure that Bomber Command had earlier speculated was the maximum long-term sustainable loss rate that would not be cataclysmic for aircrew morale.[55] From February to November 1943, and especially from May through July, during the latter part of the Battle of the Ruhr, 6 Group's losses were frequently greater than those of its geographical neighbour, 4 Group, similarly equipped with Halifaxes and Wellingtons. Naturally, this unhappy fact provoked extensive comparisons. For the period May to July, 6 Group's losses averaged just over 6 percent per operation, a debilitating rate over the long haul.[56] Furthermore, within this period there were two occasions when the loss rate rose to 11.5 percent (11–13 May, 21–25 June), and on 12/13 May, eight of sixty sorties, or 13.3 percent, did not return from Duisburg.[57] (See Appendix for a fuller discussion of loss rates.) Losses for 6 and 4 Group peaked in January–February 1944, and from that point onward their losses were similar until the end of the European war. While at the time the losses were particularly alarming, in retrospect, it would appear that 6 Group's early problems were dominated by widespread aircrew inexperience. This is not to imply that other important issues did not weigh heavily, including additional new unit formations, type-conversions, relocations, transfers, and deployments, somewhat poor flying discipline, occasionally questionable senior leadership, and the failure of the broader Halifax community to share germane operational information with the neophyte Halifax-users of 6 Group.

In March, 405 Squadron joined 6 Group after temporary secondment to Coastal Command For the rest of the year, the group prevailed through the inauguration of four new squadrons, the loss of 405 Squadron to the Pathfinder Force,[58] the transfer of 429 and 431 Squadrons from 4 Group, the acquisition of two new bases at Linton-on-Ouse and Tholthorpe, and the re-organization of the group into geographic sub-groupings for administrative streamlining.[59]

Part of the turbulence was undoubtedly generated by the Canadianization process itself—the perceived need to stand up indigenous RCAF heavy bomber squadrons within 6 Group as rapidly as possible. A related problem was the Canadian desire to shed the Wellingtons and convert the group to four-engine aircraft as expeditiously as circumstances would allow. During the spring and summer of 1943, the conversion process unfolded at a hectic pace as the Halifaxes became available in greater numbers. Furthermore, Arthur Harris was better than his promise to provide the group with a Lancaster squadron in 1943 in preparation for 6 Group's eventual transition to the aircraft. He decided that the 300 less capable radial-engine Lancaster Mark IIs should be equally distributed between 3 and 6 Groups. To that end, three 6 Group squadrons received Lancaster IIs in 1943, commencing with 426 Squadron in June.[60]

Also in June, 6 Group was deemed large enough to start to be organized into distinct geographical area sub-groupings. The first to be so designated was 62 (Beaver) Base, with its main facility at Linton and sub-stations at East Moor and Tholthorpe. Later the following year, it was joined by 63 Base in the central geographical area, with its main base at Leeming and a sub-station at Skipton, and by 64 Base in the north, consisting of its main base at Middleton St. George and a sub-station at Croft, known to the locals as Neasham. In 1944, these operational bases were complemented by 61 Base, which became a consolidated home for the training or Heavy Conversion Units (HCUs). Its main base became Topcliffe, which supported 1659 HCU, while sub-stations were established at Dishforth and Wombleton, supporting 1664 HCU and 1666 HCU.[61]

Geoff Marlow, a pilot and DFC winner with 434 Squadron, recalls life at Croft when the base had reached a mature wartime state in 1944:

> Our squadron shared Croft with 431 Squadron. About 400 of the approximately 2000 men based on the station were aircrew. There were two crossing runways and a perimeter track for taxiing around the field. Each of the 36 planes was allotted one of the circular concrete parking pads, called dispersal points, that were spaced around the track to reduce the risk of damage from strafing attacks. Near the track were large hangars that were used only when the planes needed major maintenance or when they were damaged in combat. Usually several planes from each squadron were out of service at one time, leaving only 13 to 16 aircraft per squadron available for operations. The remaining buildings around the field housed the Armoury, with its supply of bombs and other munitions; Flying Control, with its control tower; the Operations Room, where the crews were briefed before a raid; and the Meteorological, Parachute and Photographic Sections. Another building called "Flights" had rooms assigned for the special needs of pilots, bomb-aimers, navigators, gunners, wireless operators and flight engineers. All of these buildings were prefabricated and very basic.
>
> About half a mile from the immediate airfield area was the Officers Mess, the Sergeants Mess, canteens, combined dance hall and cinema, hospital and stores. Further away were the sleeping quarters . . .
>
> Obviously, the best spot in the [Nissen] hut was next to the stove, and I was fortunate in being only a few feet away from it. On one side of me was my navigator, Al Mackie, and on the other side were two crew members from 431 Squadron. Across from me was another pilot, Warry Rothenbush, and other members of his crew.
>
> There were, however, some disadvantages to being close to the stove, because the rest of the inhabitants tended to use my bed as a sofa or kitchen table on the occasions when someone received a parcel from home containing Spam or corned beef and was willing to fry it up on the stove and share it with the others. We also used the stove to heat up buckets of cold water drawn from a common tap shared by several huts. This was our "bathing" water. We applied it to our bodies by scooping it out and splashing it onto the exposed areas and then applied a little soap and a wash towel. There was a latrine building nearby that we used in dire emergencies, but we preferred the toilets at the Mess or at "Flights." There was also a communal bathhouse about 1000 yards away, but I only used it once during my stay on the squadron as it was a very draughty building with poor facilities where one risked getting pneumonia and other undesirable diseases. My solution to the bathing problem was to use the splash and sprinkle system during our six-week on-duty period and then take one or two showers a day during the next one-week leave. Oddly, I

have no recollection that any of us smelled, but I suppose we all did and took it for granted since no self-respecting male would be caught dead in those days using deodorants, even if they had been available. Our uniforms were never dry-cleaned, and I would press my pants by sprinkling them with water and placing them under my mattress. They would turn out razor-sharp by the next morning. But, on the whole, we were a scruffy lot.[62]

Mediterranean Adventures

Throughout early 1943, Harris continued to lobby for permission to deploy a fair share of Dominion and Allied squadrons on duties outside Britain. Given the chaotic nature of 6 Group's activities in the spring of 1943, it might have been prudent to exempt the formation from these taskings for the time being, but that was not to be. On 3 April 1943 the Air Ministry asked the Canadian government to approve the deployment of three experienced Wellington squadrons for a two-month tour of operations to North Africa to support Operation Husky, the invasion of Sicily. Air Marshal Edwards at Headquarters RCAF Overseas recommended the plan to Ottawa, but also insisted on a high Canadianization rate for the squadrons to be deployed. Also, he stipulated that the formation had to be under the command of an RCAF officer, and the overseas tour of duty for the crews was not to exceed three months. Edwards also wanted three new Canadian heavy bomber squadrons formed within 6 Group to replace the deployed forces.[63] Ottawa concurred with Edward's recommendations and informed the Air Ministry of this decision on 10 April. However, the demand for a high level of Canadianization resulted in the existing 6 Group squadrons being culled of experienced airmen as well as experienced ground crew, and this left the novice group even more short of personnel with operational know-how at a critical juncture.

Nos. 420, 424 and 425 Squadrons were the units selected to become 331 Wing, which would fall under Sir Arthur Tedder's parent Mediterranean Air Command, as part of 205 (RAF) Group. For this desert deployment, the squadrons exchanged their older series Wellingtons for new Mark Xs, suitably tropicalized to protect them from sand and dust storms, or siroccos, characteristic of the semi-arid climate in central Tunisia. The unit establishment sizes were increased from a Bomber Command standard of sixteen to twenty aircraft. In deference to the isolated nature of the posting, coupled with the proven increased incidence of personnel ailments in the region, each squadron was authorized to carry five extra aircrews, although no additional support personnel were assigned. The Air Ministry, while not prepared to sacrifice experience for national identity, tried hard to achieve a high Canadianization rate for the wing at the outset. However, "only eighteen of the thirty Wellington crews to be sent to North Africa each month would come from RCAF sources. Accordingly, if the three Canadian squadrons suffered heavy casualties early on, before a pool of RCAF replacements had been built up, they would inevitably find themselves with a higher proportion of British and other Commonwealth crews."[64] On 7 May 1943, 331 Wing officially formed at West Kirby, Cheshire, under the command of a future RCAF Chief of the Air Staff, Group Captain Larry Dunlap, a prewar regular force officer. Dunlap flew out to North Africa on 21 May in order to establish landing grounds for his embryonic wing. On arrival in theatre, he was informed by Tedder's staff that it would be impossible for him to operate 331 Wing out of the plains of Tunisia because it was deemed impossible to supply them there and, at any rate, all the useable space on the plains had already been claimed. Instead, the Canadian wing would be required to operate out of the mountainous regions further to the south and west in an area between Algeria and Tunisia.

However, Dunlap was determined that his night operations would not take place from those second-rate lodgement conditions. He went forth to reconnoitre, and in a classic emulation of the native barter system, he was able to persuade a major in the U.S. Army Corps of Engineers to rough out two dirt airfields for him in two days near the town of Kairouan, halfway between Tunis and Sfax, approximately thirty miles inland from the Mediterranean coast. Larry Dunlap recalls:

> There were three RAF Wellington wings down there already, and mine was to be the fourth . . . Group Captain "Speedy" Powell, the commander of 330 (RAF) Wing, told me that "if you treat that major right, he might build you a couple of fields . . . If you produce some scotch, it'll help . . . and if you're also prepared to lose a little money at the poker table, that'll increase your chances." Sure enough, he built one of those fields in 48 hours, and he built the other field in *less* than two days.[65]

Dunlap then convinced Mediterranean Air Forces Headquarters that he had found suitable lodgings on the Tunisian plains, and that the RAF should now find the means of supplying him with food, fuel, and ammunition. They reluctantly agreed, and the wing was in place and ready to go three or four weeks prior to Operation Husky. However, the wing's deployment to Africa was not totally uneventful, as recalled by Dunlap:

> The Wellington really wasn't terribly suitable for operations over Germany. It didn't get high enough and it didn't fly fast enough, but it was all there was available for us at the time . . . When I was posted out to North Africa, I took three squadrons of the latest Wellington Mark X, and this proved to be quite a useful and satisfactory aircraft for the desert operations. It could operate in all the dust and the dirt without suffering too much, and it took off with a pretty good load from those dirt fields.
>   We had a little trouble getting through the Bay of Biscay. I think the Germans were expecting Churchill to fly out to one of his conferences and they had laid on some long-range patrols out over the Bay. Two of my aircraft got intercepted. One of them got shot down but the other managed to get back in to Portugal and make a landing. That wasn't a very auspicious beginning to our operations in North Africa, but we were flying sixty aircraft out there, so although it was a sad loss, the bulk of them did get through safely.[66]

Unlike the area bombing campaign being conducted against the Axis by Bomber Command out of Britain, the Sicilian campaign was a strategic compromise in keeping with Britain's peripheral strategy, to strike, in Churchill's words, at the "soft underbelly of Europe," to help secure the sea lanes of the Mediterranean for the safe passage of Allied shipping, and to dissuade the Americans from a premature, all-out cross-Channel assault against western Europe, which they had code-named Operation Sledgehammer. The main targets for Operation Husky were enemy airfields on Sicily and the Italian mainland, bombed in order to prevent the *Luftwaffe* and the Italian *Regia Aeronautica* from striking the landing forces. Supply routes to the island were also to be attacked, in order to prevent the Axis forces on Sicily from reinforcing and re-provisioning their garrisons.

Operations for the wing commenced on the night of 26/27 June, when aircraft from 420 and 425 Squadrons attacked an air base on the southern Sicilian coast at Sciacca. Although the defending flak was significant and there was also spirited aerial opposition, only one combat loss was recorded, and even this was offset by the claimed destruction of a German night fighter by 425 Squadron.

When almost directly over the town, Wellington R-for-Roger, (captained by Flight Lieutenant

C.M. Blakeney, a Texan in the RAF) was attacked by a Junkers 88, whose presence was realized only when it opened fire. Gunner Flight Sergeant J.P. Goyette was so startled that his thumbs automatically hit the firing buttons and froze there for fully six seconds. The range throughout most of the long burst was practically point blank. He couldn't miss. The German fell away and moments later, an aircraft was seen blazing on the Mediterranean.[67]

However, 424 Squadron had substantially more problems in its operational debut in-theatre the following night. The difficulties included a crash on takeoff, the loss by another aircraft of a 4000-pound "cookie" on takeoff, and the ground abort of four other aircraft that were not bombed up in time to participate in the raid. Two nights later, targeted against Messina, 424 Squadron lost two more crews to enemy action. Other losses initially befell the wing, resulting in a 5.3 percent loss rate for June. In July, however, the loss rate dropped to just .5 percent and the missions became much more varied. Along with very successful attacks on Catania, Villacidrio, Olbia, and especially Gerbini, the main *Luftwaffe* fighter base on Sicily, the wing sortied against barracks and railroad yards at Cagliari on Sardinia, as well as other mainland Italian and Sicilian targets. Still, while the direct operational loss rate was low, other problems were encountered. There were six forced landings in July, and the ground explosion on 6 July of a bombed-up and fueled 424 Squadron Wellington on the ground killed three and wounded others. Also, dietary shortcomings and regional illnesses were leaving their mark, including cases of infectious hepatitis, jaundice, malaria, dysentery and diarrhoea. Even though the ubiquitous and terminally boring issue rations were eventually supplemented by the local purchase of chickens and other regional delicacies and amenities, such as fresh water and straw matting for beds, the living conditions remained Spartan and were a source of constant irritation throughout the deployment. Dust storms were frequent, flies were everywhere, and scorpions and 125° F heat made life in the desert intolerable for Canadians, who were used to much more temperate conditions. And yet, wing personnel were very proud of the work they were doing in support of the invasion, a lot of friendly rivalry existed among the three squadrons, and most of the airmen took their living conditions in good-natured stride. However, the lacklustre rations caused dreams of food to replace those of women, as Sergeant L. MacLauchlan, one of the ground crew stalwarts from 424 Squadron explained in a letter home to his old Bombing and Gunnery BCATP station at Fingal on Lake Erie:

> Life out here is certainly different to say the least, but we have become accustomed to the sun and sweat, sand and flies. Takes more than that to stop a Fingalite. No wet canteen to go to when work is done, though. We get a half bottle of beer per week sometimes . . .
>
> Our "48s" [two days of leave] are spent at a rest camp on the Mediterranean, where we live the life of Riley. Not quite like Port Stanley, (a well-known resort on Lake Erie) perhaps, no music or pretty figures but lovely water and cool breezes. And if you care to, you can bargain with the countless Arabs for grapes, melons and almonds, and if you are lucky, a bottle of "Vino Rouge." Altogether not a bad life . . .
>
> The ever-present "Y" man also provides us with pictures and sports equipment. The shows, of course, are shown under the stars which literally fill the sky out here. The nights are magnificent, cool and clear; quite a contrast to the days.
>
> The usual topic of conversation, believe it or not, is not women, but food. Beef steak and ice cream lead the list by a good margin. Also I believe a nice cool ale is a favourite subject.[68]

NO 331 WING OPERATIONS IN THE MEDITERRANEAN
26 JUNE - 6 OCTOBER 1943

ITALY

YUGOSLAVIA

LIGURIAN SEA

Pisa 1(26)
Leghorn 1(27)

Elba

Bastia 1(31)

CORSICA

Grosseto 1(20)

Viterbo 3(69)

Civitavecchia 1 (22)
Cerveteri 1(21)

○ROME

Lido di Roma 1(3)
Cisterna 1(24)
Frosinone 1(30)

Castelnuovo 1(23)

Formia 6(129) **Foggia 1**(29)
Gaeta 1(4) **Aversa 1**(14)
Grazzanise 1(23) **Benevento 1**(23)
Villa Literno 1(27) **Capodichini 6**(145)
Naples 4 (112)
Bagnoli 1(27) **Battipaglia 4**(124)
Torre Annunziate 2 (41) **Taranto 2**(4)
Pompei 1(32)
Salerno 3(77)
Montecorvino 3(61)

○Sapri

Oblia 1(18)

SARDINIA

TYRRHENIAN
SEA

Villacidro 1(18)
Cagliari 3(41)

IONIAN
SEA

Paola 1(26)

NOTE: Bold figures indicate number of raids. Figures in brackets record sorties flown. Sorties do not include early returns, leaflet raids and electronic jamming missions.

Evacuation of Sicily
Total 6 (137)

Pizzo 2(48)

Messina 10(228)

San Giovanni 2 (43)

Reggio di Calabria 1 (8)

Trapani 1(16)

Randazzo 1(24)
Enna 1 (25)

Sciacca 1(15)

Catania 2 (14)
Catania 1 (27)

Caltagirone 1 (6)

Syracuse 1(15)

Gerbini 3(53)

TUNIS○

Pantelleria
(Italy)

TUNISIA

No 331 Wing

○Sousse
○Monastir
Kairouan

MALTA
(Gt. Br.)

Airfields . . . .
Transportation centres . . .
German Evacuation
August 11-17 1943 . . . .

Sfax○

MEDITERRANEAN   SEA

Operation Husky commenced on 10 July, and for the next five days the wing was attacking a wide variety of targets throughout Sicily in support of the landings. Also, and perhaps most importantly, six wing crews flew screening missions with *Mandrel* electronic jammers, which were considerably more useful than they had been over northwest Europe, effectively masking the invasion fleet.[69]

From 15 July onward, 331 Wing attacked mainland Italian targets in earnest. Naples became a focus of attention, since the railway yards, ports and airfields in the area were major embarkation points for Axis war materiel destined for Sicily. Although the flak was often intense and accurate over Naples, and the searchlights vigorously active, especially around Capodichino airfield and a cluster near Mount Vesuvius, no combat losses were incurred during this period. Later in the month, 331 Wing was given a brief respite from operations. Early losses had required Larry Dunlap to integrate into his command a significant number of RAF personnel as replacements, and while this temporarily brought his wing's Canadianization rate down to around 74 percent—much to the chagrin of Air Marshal Edwards back at RCAF Headquarters Overseas—the imbalance was short-lived. As Canadian replacements began to pour in, the overall Canadianization rate had quickly been restored to a much more acceptable 80 percent.

By early August, the wing had returned to operations, and the task at hand was to prevent as many German and Italian combatants as possible from retreating to the Italian mainland. Accordingly, the Canadians were kept busy attacking the withdrawal beaches, barges, and other transportation vessels on the Straits of Messina at the northeastern tip of Sicily. The Germans deployed a lot of mobile flak into the area to defend their withdrawal, and it proved costly to the Allied aviators. More than a thousand sorties were flown by Allied aircraft during this phase of operations, which included 350 made by 331 Wing, and the gun defences at times rivaled those encountered over the Ruhr valley. The wing lost five aircraft and twenty-five airmen during these operations, and still some 40,000 German and 62,000 Italian troops successfully escaped to mainland Italy.[70] Another crew of 424 Squadron had a very close brush with death. Pilot Officer Alan Carrick Grout, a twenty-one-year-old pilot from Vancouver, was among those tasked to bomb beaches at Cape Bardi in the early morning hours of 13 August 1943. Grout and his crew experienced significant port engine problems some fifteen minutes short of the target, but they elected to continue the bomb run anyway. Approximately ten minutes after the bombing they were headed for home when the cantankerous engine failed, then caught fire, and the fire soon appeared to be raging out of control. Grout decided to make an emergency landing back in liberated Sicily, rather than risk a long return to his North African base. However, extensive cloud cover obscured the Sicilian coastline, and their power loss had driven them down to 2000 feet from their bombing altitude of 7500 feet. At this altitude, they were below some of the coastal hilltops which protruded above the cloud deck. Still not able to hold altitude and with the starboard engine now overheating, Grout cautioned his crew for an imminent bailout.

> The fire on the port engine by this time was very fierce and protruded underneath the wing. The fabric caught fire and I could see the leading part of the wing blazing. I ordered the crew to bail out . . . As the wireless operator left the aircraft a large mountain loomed up, I had to bank very steeply to the left and I opened up the starboard engine to its fullest power. As I missed the wall, I dived out of the aircraft . . . (which), a few seconds later, exploded against a ravine wall. When I landed in my parachute, I found I had bailed

out in a valley . . . by 0600 hours I had climbed out of the ravine and I then started to look for the rest of the crew . . . At approximately 0830 to 0900 hours I ran across some American Army men who accompanied me in my search for the rest of the crew . . . In the meantime the bomb aimer and rear gunner had found each other and together they located the wireless operator, who had either broken or badly sprained his ankle . . . Helped by Italians they carried the wireless operator to the coast.[71]

Once there, the Americans gave the wireless operator more first aid. Grout eventually joined up with the other crew members, and together they were placed aboard an American transport aircraft bound for Tunis. But their ordeal was not yet over, as Grout explains:

We were on course for approximately thirty minutes when the aircraft ran into a (barrage) balloon cable. The bomb charge on the cable blew approximately two square yards out of the wing of the C-47 Dakota. Losing control of the aircraft, the pilot finally picked up the stalled wing and landed at a fighter 'drome called Lacata. During the bomb charge explosion, shrapnel pierced the fuselage and struck the bomb aimer . . . in the arm, behind the ear, and cut the ear itself.[72]

While the bomb-aimer and the wireless operator both ended up in hospital, Grout and his tail gunner eventually made it back to Kairouan, where they were reunited with their navigator, who had arrived separately the day before.[73] Alan Grout never looked back. The following spring, his sustained, superior, operational performance was recognized with the award of a DFC, and the harrowing night over Sicily was singled out for special mention:

Flying Officer Grout has completed a lengthy tour of operations against a wide variety of targets in Germany and Italy. He has displayed a great coolness in the face of danger and on one occasion he skillfully piloted his seriously damaged aircraft back to friendly territory, staying at the controls until all his crew had left by parachute, following them himself with seconds to spare. Shortly afterwards, this officer renewed operations with undiminished enthusiasm, courage and determination.[74]

Held in Theatre by Popular Request

The capture of Sicily was not intended to be a precursor to the invasion of Italy, but rather as a limited operation to secure Allied dominance of the Mediterranean for its shipping. However, the pull to invade the Italian mainland became irresistible in the spring of 1943, although in order to obtain American acquiescence, the British had to commit to a cross-Channel invasion of northwest Europe in May or June of 1944. Goals for the Italian campaign were limited to the capture of Naples and the strategically important airfields around Foggia—which were also key to the defence of southern Italy—and the possible liberation of Rome, which would make it the first Axis capital to fall under Allied control. For 331 Wing, bombing support for the invasion meant an extension of the Canadian mandate in-theatre. The wing was originally to have returned to Britain at the end of July, but the departure was moved to 15 September 1943 so that the Canadians could participate in bombing operations for the first two weeks of the new campaign. Just prior to the early September landings at Reggio di Calabria in southern Italy by the British and Canadians, and by the Americans further up the Tyrrhenian coast at Salerno, 331 Wing was kept busy bombing the Foggia airfields, the railway yards around Naples, rail and road targets in the vicinity of Salerno, and also the steel works at Bagnoli and at Torre Annunziata, which was close to Naples. These raids effectively paralysed the Axis capability to reinforce the landing areas, and once the Allied armies were safely ashore, the wing's mission changed to tactical support behind the Salerno beachhead, in order to thwart any German counter-attack in the region. However, in spite of intense bombing of enemy roads, communication lines and supply depots, the Germans mounted a spirited defence, so that for a time, the success of the landing appeared in doubt. Therefore, a request was made by Desert Air Force to retain 331 Wing until the Allied bridgeheads had been secured and the advance north had commenced.[75] Again, Air Marshal "Gus" Edwards agreed, and the wing was informed that the potential existed for an eventual move to mainland Italian bases in November.

In the meantime, bombing operations continued. In fact, a highly successful raid by 126 Wellingtons on the Battipaglia-Eboli road resulted in the delivery of 237 tons of ordnance and the effective blunting of a strong German counter-attack spearheaded by crack enemy armoured formations. It also served as the justification for both the Chief of the Air Staff, Sir Charles Portal, and RCAF Headquarters Overseas, embodied in Air Marshal Edwards, to retain the Canadian wing in-theatre.

> "I have recently seen some account of the exceptionally good work done by the Canadian Wellington wing in the Mediterranean," Sir Charles Portal commented to Edwards when he learned of these efforts, "I am told that the scale of effort in relation to the size of the force has probably been higher than has ever been achieved anywhere in the past and included operations on 78 of 80 successive nights, with a nightly average of 69 sorties . . . Tedder has signalled in very warm terms about this outstanding achievement. I have already asked him to convey my appreciation to all concerned but I should like to let you know personally how greatly I am impressed by this splendid record of No. 331 Wing. We are all greatly looking forward to the time when, with newer and better equipment, they will resume their operations against Germany."[76]

Throughout September and for the first week of October, 331 Wing pounded the Axis relentlessly. The Official History of 424 Squadron captures the spirit and diversity of this high-pitched operational tempo:

> Throughout September the squadron had been detailed for 167 operational sorties. Of that total, 164 were successful, with two early returns and one aircraft missing. Bombs were dropped on Gatta, Aversa, Bottipaglia, Castelunova, Viterbo, Benevenuto, Formia, Frosinone, Pompeii, Cisterna, Cerveteri, Pisa, San Guisto, Bostia, Leghorn and Torre Annuziato. Leaflets were dropped on Corsica, Rome, Bologna, Ravenna, Madena, Arrezo Perugia, and over the Sardinia East coast. There was one exceptionally successful attack on the airfield at Cisterna. The raid caught the aerodrome by surprise. Sticks of bombs were observed straddling aircraft lined up on the aerodrome. The aircraft caught fire and the flames quickly spread from aircraft to aircraft. Bombs burst on the runway, on the buildings and on the hangars. All the hangars appeared totally wrecked and fires could be seen many miles away from the target . . . The squadron continued with daily bombing attacks and during the first week of October, Grasseto, Civitavecchia and Formia were hit, and Nickelling [dropping propaganda leaflets] was completed over Sezia, Leghorn and Pisa. Two aircraft were missing.[77]

War may indeed be hell, but it is not without its share of amusing ironies, and the 331 Wing deployment was no exception. On one particular night, 425 Squadron was tasked to bomb an airfield just north of Rome. Armed with a 4000-pound "cookie"—which habitually caused the

Wellington to bolt upwards a few hundred feet when it was released, thereby confirming to the crew that it had been successfully dropped from the aircraft—this particular crew bombed a perfectly clear target under flares in heavy flak at 8000 feet and felt the characteristic upwards lurch at bomb release. The automatic camera photo flash functioned, revealing a perfect drop with bombs exploding all over the airfield. However, the crew's elation proved short-lived. Five minutes later, after starting their homeward leg, they did their routine after-bombing check, which consisted of opening the bomb bay doors and sliding an item called the jettison bar across. At that point, there was a sudden thump while the "Wimpy" did its dramatic post-release levitation. Shortly thereafter, this crew was rocked by an enormous explosion as their "cookie" exploded beneath them in an olive grove.

> The lurching sensation over the target had obviously been caused by the heavy flak bursts. Our bomb hadn't fallen on the target after all. It was a quiet crew that flew across the "Med" for Africa.
>
> At debriefing none of the crew mentioned the incident—but we were fascinated by the descriptions given by the other crews of what they had seen. They reported seeing a huge munitions dump explode south of the target. Just where we had dropped our 4000-pounder. The next morning, when the target films were developed and the aiming points posted on the target maps, our photo was credited with a direct hit.[78]

This period of intense operations successfully thwarted German attempts to counter-attack and repel the Allied invaders. By early October the enemy had retreated further north, the front had become sufficiently stabilized, and 331 Wing had bombed itself out of work. Leaving their trusty Wellingtons behind, the wing boarded troop ships in Algiers on 27 October 1943 and disembarked in Liverpool ten days later in rain and snow. They then proceeded back to their British bases at Dalton, Dishforth and Skipton and, after a brief period of leave, began to re-equip with new Halifax IIIs, just in time to participate in the Berlin raids. The wing had compiled a formidable operational record during the North African deployment, and at relatively low cost. A total of 2182 sorties had been launched against the enemy on a full 82 of the 102 nights spent in-theatre, weather conditions permitting a much more predictable and sustained campaign than that conducted out of England. Only eighteen aircraft were lost on operations, for an overall loss rate of just 0.8 percent. A further eighteen aircraft were written off in accidents, mostly during the critical takeoff and landing phases.[79] However, the cost in blood for renewing the fight against the Reich out of Britain was about to become much harder to bear.

Others Leave Their Mark

While the Bomber Command story from the Second World War tends to focus primarily on its operations out of Britain, by the end of 1943 Bomber Command operations were truly global in nature. Canadians served in significant numbers in every theatre to which the Command was deployed. By January 1944, there were sixteen Bomber Command squadrons in the Mediterranean theatre alone, along with a further ten in India and Ceylon.[80] A full 60 percent of all Second World War RCAF airmen served in RAF units, and many did so with great distinction. The Bomber Command story was no exception. One of the most outstanding acts of courage and determination under great duress was attributed to Flying Officer Alan William Jessup Larden, a bomb-aimer from North Bay, Ontario. Larden arrived in England in June 1942, and by the following spring he had been assigned to 218 (RAF) Squadron, which was then equipped with the operationally limited Stirling. A flight sergeant at the time, Larden took part in a number of bombing raids on industrial cities in the Ruhr valley. The Stirling's limited combat ceiling made it vulnerable to ordnance and other objects dropped from above by "friendly" aircraft—a significant risk to Stirling crews in 1943, and Larden's crew was no exception.

> During a raid on Hamburg on 29 July 1943 while the Stirlings were labouring along at a modest altitude, the high-flying Lancasters and Halifaxes were dropping their bombs. The plexiglass from Larden's aircraft was shattered by a drop bar from some aircraft above. The next night a much more serious incident occurred over Remscheid when more than 20 three-pound incendiaries spiked their way through the wings of Larden's Stirling and a 50-pound incendiary burned its way through the centre of the fuselage, narrowly missing the main spar.[81]

However, Larden and his crew seemed to be leading a charmed existence, and by August 1943, they were eagerly approaching the end of their first operational tour and a well-deserved respite from combat. It all ended prematurely on the night of 12 August 1943. Larden's crew, along with twelve others from 218 Squadron alone, had been briefed earlier that day for a raid on Turin, one of the last Italian cities to be bombed prior to Italy's surrender. What transpired that night won for Flight Sergeant Larden the Conspicuous Gallantry Medal (CGM); for Flight Lieutenant A.L. Aaron, the pilot, the Victoria Cross; and for both the wireless operator and the flight engineer, the Distinguished Flying Medal.

> The raid started off in routine manner and nothing went amiss until the final run on the target. Then everything happened at once. The bomber received devastating bursts of fire from an enemy fighter. Three engines were hit, the windscreen shattered, the front and rear gun turrets were put out of action and the elevator control damaged. The navigator, Flying Officer W. Brennan, the other Canadian member of the crew, was instantly killed and others were wounded. The pilot, badly injured, slumped over the controls, causing the aircraft to go into a dive. As the Stirling plunged toward the ice-capped Alps, the flight engineer managed to regain control and at 3000 feet he had the bomber levelled out.[82]

What happened next is succinctly described in the citation to the CGM later awarded to Larden. The Conspicuous Gallantry Medal is an extremely rare and prestigious award. Only twelve have been presented to Canadian airmen, and it is considered second only to the Victoria Cross as a valour decoration for non-commissioned officers. It was intended to bridge the gulf between the DFM and the VC for them, and eventually, it became referred to as "the Other Ranks" DSO.[83]

> He (the pilot) was removed from his position and Flight Sergeant Larden coolly took over the controls. The aircraft was down to three thousand feet and Flight Sergeant Larden realized that he would be unable to gain height sufficiently to cross the Alps so (he) decided to make for North Africa without (a) navigator and flying a crippled bomber. The situation was serious, but displaying outstanding skill and determination, this airman succeeded in reaching an airfield in Algeria; although he had never previously landed an aircraft, Flight Sergeant Larden came down perfectly with the undercarriage retracted. In the face of extreme peril this airman displayed courage, coolness and resource of a high order.[84]

The pilot had been assisted to the rear of the aircraft and given morphine to ease his pain, but

Flight Lieutenant Aaron insisted on helping Larden in every way he could, including writing directions with his left hand. At the controls, out over the Mediterranean, and with no way to navigate, Larden could not be sure of his location and his fuel was soon running dangerously low.

> As the situation became critical he spotted the flare path of the (RAF) Airport at Bone, Algeria. Flight Lieutenant Aaron summoned his last reserves of strength to direct Larden in the hazardous task of landing the damaged aircraft in the darkness with undercarriage retracted. Larden had never landed an aircraft before. He made four practice approaches, then started down. It was a perfect landing. Nine hours later, Flight Lieutenant Aaron died of exhaustion caused by his exertions in his wounded condition to save his aircraft and crew.[85]

The surviving members of this crew were soon returned to Britain, but they were all posted to non-operational units. Presumably, higher authority had decided they had done quite enough in combat for the war effort. Larden was later commissioned and in September 1944 was repatriated to Canada.

German Defences Improve Once Again

Bomber Command's operations were becoming more effective in 1943, and the same held true for the countering German defences. However, German technological and tactical agility tended to be more reactive and passive than that of the Allies, partly because of a certain rigidity of thinking by the night fighter arm's first commander, General Kammhuber, and also because of the many conflicting demands and priorities of the German war effort.

And yet, several significant technological innovations had already been introduced to the night war by the Germans. *Spanner*, a primitive infra-red sight designed to home on an adversary's hot exhaust plumes and engine stacks, turning them into visible light, was tested as early as 1941. However, *Spanner* had difficulty discriminating the exhaust gases and flames from other IR and bright light sources (such as the moon), but more importantly from ground fires, which were frequent in the Reich during the period, and thus it found very little practical application. Later variants of the system would fare better. Nevertheless, the next technological innovation constituted a significant breakthrough, when the *Lichtenstein B/C* airborne interception (AI) radar produced by AG Telefunken became available in significant numbers during the early summer of 1942. Plagued by many early design and production problems, *Lichtenstein* garnered a reputation for unreliability, and its cumbersome multiple antennae, resembling those of a giant insect—while theoretically providing more flexibility to the attacking fighter—brought a twenty-five mph performance penalty to the aircraft's top speed. When the system worked, it was limited to 140 degrees of horizontal search and 60 degrees of vertical search in an effective range band of two miles down to two hundred yards.[86] And while in time modifications to the set produced a useful and reliable piece of equipment, Kammhuber did not envision it being used by crews to any great extent. Instead, he saw it as a limited tool tied to his sacrosanct *Himmelbett* ground controlled interception (GCI) system, merely replacing searchlights for the final attack phase by "illuminating" the target aircraft. But *Himmelbett*, although structured and simple, was inflexible because the fighters were limited to a particular "box" of airspace built around a specific homing beacon. And Kammhuber felt that, rather than providing more freelancing authority to the night fighters—

which he saw as being potentially chaotic—the answer lay in expanding his GCI system until the orderly *Himmelbett* boxes covered all of the Reich, as well as its northern and western approaches. As the RCAF Official History notes:

> This emphasis on inflexible, centralized control was in sharp contrast to the decentralization and flexibility of German army doctrine as expressed in the mission-oriented orders of *Auftragstaktik*, with which Kammhuber would have been familiar before his transfer to the *Luftwaffe*.[87]

In the spring of 1942, Kammhuber had asked for just such an expansion, but the associated costs would have been enormous, since at the time the Reich was not considered to be under serious, sustained attack from the air, and the *Luftwaffe* was massively committed in other theatres, particularly the east. Expansion of *Himmelbett* would have required 600 additional *Würzburg* radar sets, 270 additional night fighters, (three entire *Geschwader*, or wings) along with an equal number of *Lichtenstein* AI radar sets and an extra 150,000 ground personnel. He also asked for the development of a panoramic radar, which would provide 360 degree coverage, and the design of purpose-built night fighters.[88] However, "the design of specialized night fighters was put off. Most Junkers 88s and Dornier 217s continued to be allocated to the *Ostfront* as bombers, radar development did not receive a higher priority, and at the political level at least, flak remained the air defence weapon of choice."[89]

Some growth to *Himmelbett* was realized, but it was much slower than Kammhuber wished, and it left great blocks of German airspace, especially the eastern and southern areas, without adequate coverage. The expansion was concentrated around the original belt, from Denmark to Paris, with emphasis on the Ruhr and the industrial areas bracketed by Stuttgart, Frankfurt, and Mannheim. Until another purpose-built night fighter from the Heinkel works emerged, however, Kammhuber had to make do with dreadfully unsuitable Dornier Do 217s and the somewhat better Messerschmitt Bf 110s and Junkers Ju 88s, which were to become the backbone of the force. And, the drag penalty imposed by the *Lichtenstein* antennae meant that even the Bf 110s and Ju 88s, but particularly the Messerschmitt, were not much faster than their quarry, especially the Lancaster.[90]

Yet, by the spring of 1943 the night fighter force had doubled from its March 1942 figures to 400 aircraft, the majority of which now carried AI radar. Also, the crews were now better trained, and mobile *Würzburgs* were used to fill the gaps in the defensive belt. Furthermore, a fighter control and radar picket ship named *Togo* was stationed in the Baltic to cover the northern approaches and to provide early warning of Gardening operations.[91]

By 1943 nearly 20,000 anti-aircraft guns of all calibres were dedicated to the air defence of the Reich, a commitment which, Albert Speer later maintained "could almost have doubled the anti-tank defences on the Eastern Front."[92] Still later, the total rose to approximately 15,000 heavy guns so committed, with a further 42,000 lighter weapons in support.[93]

After the Millennium raid on Cologne, coordination of the entire night fighter system was streamlined. *Jagddivision* headquarters were established at Deelen, Döberitz, Metz, Schleissheim, and Stade, linked by communications to each other and to a central headquarters, *Luftwaffenbefehlshaber Mitte*, in Berlin. This new administrative arrangement facilitated the hand-off of night fighters from one *Himmelbett* box to adjacent ones, allowing the fighters more time to stalk prey and to effect an intercept. Furthermore, the individual boxes were now frequently grouped in clusters of three, with triple the number of fighters available to engage a concentrated enemy force.

Yet, this heavy investment in personnel and materiel was bound to cause dissatisfaction among the other fighting forces. While the night fighters were shooting down more bombers, they were not accounting for 10 percent of the enemy raiders, the arbitrary figure, based on *Luftwaffe* experience in the Battle of Britain, that the Germans predicted the RAF would consider an intolerable loss rate. This period also marked the emergence of the great aces, household names such as Lent, Streib, Schnaufer, Radusch, Vinke, Jabs, Meurer, zu Sayn-Wittgenstein and their crews. Ultimately, there were hundreds of night fighter aces, including twenty-four with fifty or more victories.[94] Major Wolfgang Schnaufer would outscore them all with 121 confirmed victories, winning the Knight's Cross with Oak Leaves, Swords and Diamonds along the way. Respectfully labeled "The Phantom of St. Trond" by Bomber Command crews, his wartime successes were widely reported. Schnaufer survived the hostilities and many harrowing combat experiences, only to perish in a collision with a logging truck on the Bordeaux-Biarritz highway during the summer of 1950.[95]

While the great night fighter crews were emerging, their losses were also mounting, from 31 in February 1943 to 107 in July, many caused by landing accidents. These losses did not bode well for a force with limited expansion capabilities, which could at best hope for the replacement of its combat casualties.[96]

Discontentment with the rigidity of the *Himmelbett* system had been building throughout 1942. During the autumn, experimentation with free ranging tactics within the bomber stream had taken place, but they had not been particularly successful. Kammhuber rejected the experiments at the time, for although he approved of the tactics in principle, along with not wanting to weaken his *Himmelbett* system, he did not feel that the present iterations of AI radars could reliably find the individual bombers. However, the freelance concept, which became known as *Zahme Sau* (Tame Boar), was reviewed again in the spring of 1943, following the Hamburg raids.

Hectic Times in 6 Group

When the three squadrons which had deployed as 331 Wing returned to 6 Group from their term in North Africa, they found the Command fraught with problems. Some became continuous themes throughout the year. During this period of brisk, unrelenting operational tempo, the establishment of new Article XV Canadian bomber squadrons and aircraft type conversions for other squadrons continued. Both these initiatives were intensely destabilizing and robbed established squadrons of experienced crews at a time when the Second Battle of the Ruhr and then the later Berlin raids were in full force. Stability and experience were desperately needed on the operational squadrons then reaching forward into the Third Reich. Air operations in early 1943, coincidental with the Battle of the Ruhr and when so much else was going on within Bomber Command, were almost too much for the neophyte 6 Group to bear. However, while equipment changes and intense operational activity continued until the cessation of hostilities, 6 Group adapted to these changes and challenges much more readily than it had at the outset.

In March, at the beginning of the Second Battle of the Ruhr, 6 Group was comprised of nine operational squadrons located on six separate bases. While 420, 424 and 425 Squadrons were lost to the parent unit for six months commencing in May, 432 Squadron joined the group that month, equipped with Wellington Xs. The following month, 434 Squadron came on board, flying Halifax Vs from the outset. During the summer of 1943, the pace of conversions to four-engine types quickened, largely at the insistence of the Canadian government, as Halifaxes became broadly available. To that end, in May 427 Squadron was moved to Leeming from Croft for conversion to Halifax Vs, followed by 428 Squadron from Dalton in June. Also in June, 429 Squadron was transferred from 4 Group to 6 Group, bringing with it its airfields at East Moor and Wombleton. In July 431 Squadron joined 429 as the last of the 4 Group transfers. Earlier in June 426 Squadron had moved to East Moor under the tutelage of 1679 Heavy Conversion Unit, when they became the first of three 6 Group squadrons to receive the radial-engine-powered Lancaster Mark IIs. Similar fates befell 408 and 432 Squadrons in August and October. Of the 300 Lancaster II variants produced, 125 were eventually distributed to these Canadian squadrons. So equipped, they would play prominent roles in the upcoming Berlin raids. After training, 408 and 426 Squadrons moved to Linton-on-Ouse for operational duties, while 432 Squadron flew its combat sorties out of East Moor. There they converted to Halifax IIIs in February 1944, and were joined in operations in July by the last of the 6 Group formations, 415 Squadron, which transferred from Coastal Command and was also equipped with Halifax IIIs. Previously, on 25 September 1943, the newly formed 433 Squadron had been the first of the 6 Group units to be equipped with the new Halifax III. Their initial complement of aircraft arrived in early November, and after a short period of operational training under the 427 Squadron "Lions," they flew their first combat missions on 2 January 1944.

By late 1943 the Halifax had become the predominant operational mount for 6 Group, and when 420, 424, and 425 Squadrons returned from the desert in November they were equipped with the Mark III variant. Then, in sequence, 427, 432, 429, 431, and 434 Squadrons traded in their earlier series Halifaxes for Halifax IIIs from January through May 1944 and 431 Squadron received some of the still newer Mark VII variants. The Mark VII was essentially a Mark III with a more capacious bomb bay and permanent fuel cells in the inner wings, in place of the wing bomb bays. In March 1944, 419 Squadron became the first 6 Group unit to equip with Canadian-built Lancaster Xs, although 405 Squadron, by now a well-established part of the Pathfinder Force, had received a few of the earliest of these variants to augment their Lancaster Is and IIIs the previous year.

Table 4.1 6 Group Squadron Particulars

Squadron	Familiar Name	Identification Code	Joins 6 Group
405	Vancouver	LQ	1 March 1943
408	Goose	EQ	1 January 1943
415	Swordfish	6U	12 July 1944
419	Moose	VR	1 January 1943
420	Snowy Owl	PT	1 January 1943
424	Tiger	QB	1 January 1943
425	Alouette	KW	1 January 1943
426	Thunderbird	OW	1 January 1943
427	Lion	ZL	1 January 1943
428	Ghost	NA	1 January 1943
429	Buffalo	AL	15 June 1943
431	Iroquois	SE	15 July 1943
432	Leaside	QO	1 May 1943
433	Porcupine	BM	25 September 1943
434	Bluenose	WL	13 June 1943

The Group Falters, Then Recovers

Not all of 6 Group's early troubles were attributable to the headlong rush towards Canadianization, overseas deployments, type conversions, new station allocations, or even directly to the brisk operational tempo of the period. Combat losses were a serious concern, and not all were occurring during action over the industrial cities. For example, Gardening or mining operations were frequently used to initiate freshman crews and neophyte squadrons to combat operations, and for seasoned, battle weary crews who were considered to be at higher risk on the deeper penetration raids. The Wellington fleet was rapidly becoming one of these high-risk units. On the night of 27/28 April, on what should have been a routine Gardening operation to the Heligoland Bight in the western Baltic, crews strayed too close to the extensive flak batteries located at the mouth of the Elbe River and over Heligoland itself, which resulted in the destruction of twenty-two of the 226 aircraft sortied. Three 6 Group aircraft, 8 percent of the Canadian representation for the night, failed to return.[97] While this unhappy operation was not particularly indicative of the loss rates generated on other Gardening sorties, it was demoralizing and unexpected. Bomber Command could ill afford such losses on the relatively low-risk missions. Moreover, 6 Group loss rates for the overall period of February through July 1943 were the worst in the Command, especially in May, June and July, when the failed-to-return rates for sorties despatched averaged 6.8 percent, 7.1 percent and 4.3 percent respectively.[98] Other elements heralded 6 Group performance as the worst in the Command. Aircraft serviceability was a lacklustre 60 percent, and serviceability for some electronic components, such as the *Gee* sets, was also the poorest in Bomber Command. A significant number of aircrew psychological problems were also manifest, and the rate of those considered Lacking in Moral Fibre (LMF) and declared to be "waverers" or "fringe merchants"— in other words, those unwilling to press on to the target area with resolve—was, although still low, the second highest in the Command.[99] Collectively, these results suggested that something beyond the anticipated growing pains was seriously wrong with 6 Group.

> There are also indications that early in the life of 6 Group, Brookes and his staff, like ambitious schoolboys eager to impress, tried to compensate for their lack of professional standing by doing more than they were asked to do. In January and February 1943, for example, the Canadian AOC boasted to his diary that he had committed more, and sometimes many more, crews to individual operations than High Wycombe had asked for. The same desire to please and impress—and to get results when others could not or chose not to—may explain why, during the same period, operations were cancelled (because of weather) much later in the day by Brookes's headquarters than they were by other groups further to the south, where flying was almost always less risky in good or bad conditions. The medical officer from No. 420 Squadron was certainly aware of this tendency and complained that, by holding squadrons at readiness until the last moment, hoping they might fly despite already bad or deteriorating weather, the AOC was placing the glory of his group first rather than concerning himself with flying safety or the additional strain he was causing his crews on an almost daily basis.[100]

While the foregoing practices soon ceased, other problems surfaced. A pervasive sentiment was that Canadian bomber units were becoming saddled with second-rate equipment, and this adversely affected both morale and unit pride. It also inhibited RCAF personnel elsewhere in the Command from requesting service in or transfer to Canadian bomber squadrons. Also, the group accident rate remained high, although this was undoubtedly partially attributable to the Yorkshire location and operating conditions. Overall, Brookes and his deputy, Air Commodore Roy Slemon, became convinced early on that one of the root causes of 6 Group's problems was a lack of flying discipline being practiced by the crews.

> That also seemed to explain 6 Group's higher losses: ignoring the routes laid down by command, too many pilots were straying from the protective cover afforded by the bomber stream. At the same time, however, one of the OTUs backing the Canadian group was complaining that navigators recently graduated from the BCATP and arriving from Canada were not only slow in chart work, astro-navigation, and map-reading, but that the pilots they teamed up with had little sympathy for navigational burdens—an endemic problem, it seems, since the same criticism had been voiced for some time. Harris's suggestion that, in addition to all this, some Canadian crews had "unjustifiably failed to press home their attack" was undoubtedly the most damning and worrying comment on No. 6 Group's operations. Admitting that squadron and station commanders had doubts about the "keenness" of some of their crews, the AOC replied they would be more vigilant in identifying those who were failing to pull their weight. Greater attention would be paid to the tactics of bombing and evading enemy defences, something Brookes agreed had been neglected.[101]

Brookes and his staff concluded that a significant overall contributor to 6 Group's travails was the lack of combat experience of his crews. The 331 Wing deployment was syphoning off many of the experienced personnel, and the rapid formation of new squadrons resulted in widespread inexperience within the group. Since it was generally acknowledged that most aircrew did not reach peak efficiency until approximately halfway through their first combat tour, Brookes felt this widespread inexperience was bound to affect performance, and to become even more pronounced during a period of intense operational campaigning.[102]

Sir Arthur Harris was not mollified by these explanations when they were advanced from the Allerton Park headquarters, and he tasked his Operational Research Section to do an independent review of 6 Group's performance. At the same time, they were to review 4 Group, 6 Group's geographical neighbour, for comparison, which was similarly equipped with a mix of Wellingtons and Halifaxes, and which had been assigned some training responsibilities for the neophyte Canadian group. The draft ORS report released on 10 July 1943 contained a lot of unflattering speculation with respect to the Canadian shortcomings, including the suggestions that 6 Group crews were employing inferior tactics, had not judiciously assimilated the maintenance practices of 4 Group, and that the significant number of early sortie returns might also reflect "lowered morale." However, the report also observed that the Canadian crews were being more frequently engaged by German night fighters and speculated that this was probably attributable to its geographical location. When attacking targets in the Ruhr, 6 Group aircraft entered the bomber stream closest to the enemy coast and thus benefitted the least from the stream's collective security. It also agreed with Brookes that many of the Wellington losses were no doubt attributable to the syphoning off of experienced crews for 331 Wing, although it could not explain the high Halifax loss rate.[103]

The uncompromising language and excessive speculation of this draft was too strong for Harris's deputy, Air Vice-Marshal Robert Saundby, and for Harris himself, to present to Brookes and his staff. A kinder, gentler version softened the blows, although not the general thrust of the conclusions, but Harris and his staff did significantly underplay the importance of the experienced crew deployments to North Africa, with its potential diplomatic ramifications. The OAS report also acknowledged that there were many similarities in the operational tactics recommended by headquarters staffs to the member squadrons within the two groups (my italics):

> Both told their crews to strive for height, a natural thing for them to do anyway in order to avoid flak and hide from fighters among the Lancasters. *But once No 4 Group determined that fully loaded Halifaxes had little tactical freedom because they were bound to an "excessively" narrow height band, it quickly reduced their bombload by as much as a ton. Introduced at a time when 6 Group losses were soaring, information about this change in procedure seems not to have been passed on to the Canadians by either No 4 Group or High Wycombe.* Instead, echoing the old formula about bad flying discipline in the RCAF, the only specific advice given to Brookes was that there was too much "straying from the main bomber route" in his group and that the "greatest improvement may well be obtained by giving close attention to this point and thus improving the concentration."[104]

Neither RCAF Overseas Headquarters nor Air Vice-Marshal Brookes took the ORS findings lightly and Brookes even admitted that shortcomings in navigation and flak avoidance procedures had probably contributed to some of the losses. Air Marshal Edwards speculated that it might be prudent to stand the group down from operations until more definitive causes and solutions could be determined. However, on the closest examination Brookes became convinced, and convinced others, that his first conclusions had been correct: that the primary cause for most of the losses had been the relative inexperience of his flyers, and that this unhappy state of affairs would correct itself in relatively short order. In another positive sign, the "waverer" rate dropped to a mere 0.13 percent in August, the lowest in the Command. Two further ORS studies, the last completed in October 1943, bolstered the conclusions of Brookes, the last report citing the negative impact of all the Halifax conversions during the period and allowing that many of the Wellington losses could be attributed to the massive influx of new, inexperienced crews. A concurrent inquiry by the Operational Research Branch at RCAF Overseas Headquarters agreed with these findings overall, and also blamed the formation's northerly location, the frequent changes of unit locations precipitated by the conversion and base allocation processes, and the influx of many "relatively untrained" ground crew. As contributing factors, this parallel investigation also concluded that all these issues, except the northerly location of the group, would mend over time.[105] In fact, a performance turnaround was certainly apparent by January 1944.

> No. 6 Group's Halifax loss rate was now lower than No. 4 Group's, and its Lancaster II loss rate was lower than No. 3 Group's. Indeed, the Canadians compared unfavourably with other groups only when operating against targets in the Ruhr and southern Germany, in which case the fact that their bases were "at the extreme north of all the bomber groups" was assumed to have had "an adverse effect." It had taken a number of months, but now at least there were satisfactory answers for what had happened during 1943's Battle of the Ruhr. Of them all, inexperience had been the most important.[106]

In February 1944 command of the group passed to a new AOC, Air Vice-Marshal Clifford Mackay McEwen, a twenty-seven-victory ace from the Great War and an inspirational warrior chieftain in every sense of the word.

Against the Ruhr Dams

While Bomber Command pummelled Germany's industrial heartland in an unrelenting area bombing campaign during the spring of 1943, other forces were marshalling to prepare a graphic demonstration of the Command's evolving precision attack capabilities. On the night of 16/17 May 1943 this became the now-legendary Dams Raid by Bomber Command's new precision attack specialists, 617 Squadron. Canadian airmen made up a significant portion of the attacking force. In fact, of the 133 aircrew who participated aboard nineteen specially-modified Lancasters, twenty-nine were Canadians, and another was an American serving in the RCAF.

Operation Chastise had originated in the fertile mind of British scientist and engineer Barnes Neville Wallis, who had earlier helped design the R 100 airship, then the Vickers Wellesley, which was the first aircraft fashioned around his unique, geodetic "basket weave" construction This structural breakthrough was followed by his enormously successful Wellington. However, his energies were increasingly directed at creating much more effective aerial ordnance. Before the war started Wallis had envisaged the concept of attacking six critical Ruhr dams with the intention to deny the Germans power to produce steel for weapons. The plan called for the construction of a 6000-pound skipping bomb,[107] a spherical mine which was delivered against the faces of the appropriate dams, creating a breach and allowing the escaping water to exacerbate the destruction. Through experimentation, Wallis determined that a dimpled sphere, resembling a giant golf ball, was the most aerodynamically efficient shape for his skipping weapon. The dimples generated lift and allowed the weapon to travel further. A backspin motion was generated on the weapon by a special delivery cradle on the host aircraft. This would keep the bomb close to the dam face after impact for optimum explosive effect at detonation. He penned a research paper on the subject for various government agencies, which caught the eye of Sir Henry Tizard, then scientific advisor to the Air Ministry.

> It's really quite a simple idea, you know, using the principle of the back-spin to deliver the weapon tight against the dam face with the resultant shock waves from the underwater explosion breaking the dam itself . . . It's the direct opposite of what happens if you put back-spin on a tennis ball—that jumps up—if you put it on water it jumps forward. That was the secret of the whole blessed thing. Simple.[108]

However, it was the Admiralty that was initially interested in his skipping bomb concept as an application against enemy surface vessels. Initial tests validated this idea. Arthur Harris first heard about Wallis's proposed application against the Ruhr dams in February, and rejected it as being nonsensical. An interview with the inventor in March won him over, however, and at mid-month he charged Air Vice-Marshal Ralph Cochrane, the AOC of 5 Group, with the formation of a special squadron to handle the task. Since Harris was about to commence his main spring offensive, and disapproved of the formation of elite units, he was reluctant to remove an existing squadron from the line for one specialized operation. Therefore, his mandate to Cochrane was to call on his beloved "old lags," the veteran tour-expired volunteers, who were prepared to fly just one more combat mission. Cochrane chose a short, doughty, twenty-five-year-old wing commander as their leader, the commanding officer of 106 Squadron, Guy Penrose Gibson, DSO and Bar, DFC and Bar. Gibson had flown in combat from the commencement of hostilities and was already completing his third operational bomber tour. He had also done a brief tour on night fighters, accounting for at least four enemy aircraft.[109] Gibson officially formed 617 Squadron at Scampton on 21 March 1943. While some members of his new unit felt he was somewhat self-absorbed,[110] to Arthur Harris and to Ralph Cochrane he epitomized all the public school values they held so dear. To most he was a jolly extrovert. "Not a cerebral man, he represented the apogee of the pre-war English public schoolboy, the perpetual team captain, of unshakable courage and dedication to duty, impatient of those who could not meet his exceptional standards." To Ralph Cochrane "He was the boy who would have been head prefect in any school."[111] Although he was a demanding man, Gibson constantly fretted about the welfare of his crews.

Negative impressions of him appear to have been minimal. On the eve of 617 Squadron's formation Joe McCarthy, a distinguished American serving in the RCAF and a pivotal player on the ensuing raid, was a flight lieutenant wearing the first of his two DFCs. The tall, husky, redheaded youth from Long Island vividly recalls the springtime telephone call from Gibson:

> "Gibby gave me a call at Woodhall Spa in March 1943. Anyway, he asked me if I'd like to join a special squadron for one mission. He also asked if I could bring my own crew along knowing that I'd just finished my first tour with 97 Squadron. I said 'Sure' and the next thing we knew we were at Scampton. Gibby didn't fool around" . . . Navigator Danny Walker from Blairmore, Alberta, had just completed his first tour with Gibson's 106 Squadron and was enjoying a well-earned rest at an OTU when the call came: "Guy got in touch with me and asked if I'd like to rejoin my old 106 crew, which was skippered by Dave Shannon (an Australian) and come on up and be part of this new squadron he was forming. I said I would and left immediately. Guy was a terrific air leader."
>
> Joe McCarthy, who became a Canadian citizen and served 28 years with the RCAF, added a thought: "Guy was one of the finest gentlemen I met in the war. As far as operations went, well, he was the King."
>
> Air gunner Fred "Doc" Sutherland of Rocky Mountain House Alberta offered this opinion on the 'King of Operations': "Gibson was a born leader. He was a short, cocky, very confident person. He was the leader and he let you know it. There was no monkey business. It was wartime and when he said, 'I want this done,' you did it and that was that."[112]

The twenty-one crews Gibson had assembled six weeks prior to the raid were Bomber Command's cream of the crop. All had done at least one operational tour and a number had done two or more. The DFC was virtually the unit badge, and they were all well known in a Command where there was no shortage of outstanding, colourful personalities. While Gibson did not reveal their target, he shared the basic attack parameters with them, and they were daunting. Their weapons would have to be delivered at night, in level flight at 150 feet and 240 miles per hour, over water, at a range of 400–450 yards from the face of the target, and probably under enemy fire. Practice low-level deliveries began immediately, as did further trials with the weapon. The spherical bomb later became a steel canister containing 6000 pounds of high explosive, although the casing, the special mount and the spin drive added a further 3000 pounds of weight. To accommodate the weapon's seven-foot circumference, the bomb bay doors had to be removed, and to lighten the aircraft the front gun turrets were also removed. Nighttime deliveries were practiced relentlessly, and simulated during the day by covering the cockpits with blue plexiglass and then flying with amber goggles. The pace of flying training was intense, and shortly before the operation was to be flown, in early May, Barnes Wallis laid an even greater challenge on Gibson and his crews. Under trials, the spherical weapon casing was consistently breaking up when released from a 150-foot altitude. In order to guarantee its structural integrity, it would now have to become cylindrical in shape, and would now have to be released from just 60 feet! However, a significant problem remained in those days prior to the advent of radar altimeters: namely, how to accurately and consistently judge an exact low elevation at night over water. There have been several speculations as to how the problem was solved, but the most enduring and certainly the most charming involved Gibson's navigator, Flying Officer Harlo "Terry" Taerum, a Norwegian-Canadian farm boy from Milo, Alberta, and Gibson's bomb-aimer, Pilot Officer "Spam" Spafford. Clifford "Capable" Caple, the squadron engineering officer and his team of brilliant technicians had used triangulation to devise a crude "penny bomb sight" which, when portions of the target were viewed through a peep-hole and appeared superimposed in the sight's frame, provided a cue for the correct mathematical range to release the bomb. On the attack, this distance assessment was provided by the bomb-aimer. To solve the release altitude problem, also done through a form of triangulation, white spotlights were mounted on the fore and aft belly of the aircraft, and rigged to have their beams form a predetermined pattern, initially at 150 feet, then later at 60 feet. It was the navigator's responsibility on the bomb run to provide correction cues to the pilot. However, when Gibson was briefing his men on the proposed solution, his fun-loving crew was quick to claim authorship of the spotlight idea, and under very un-scientific circumstances:

> Pilot Officer "Spam" Spafford interrupted, "I could have told you that. Last night, Terry and I went to see the show at the Theatre Royal (AKA The Old Windmill), and when the girl there was doing her strip-tease act there were two spotlights shining on her. The idea crossed my mind then." Some versions of the story claim that Spam and Terry came to the squadron with the idea after the show but the idea of using spotlights was nothing new. After some experimentation, lights were placed so that the beams would form a fig-ure eight just forward of the starboard wing. This allowed the navigator to see them through the Perspex blister on the starboard side of the cockpit.[113]

Perhaps the final, and the most pragmatic comment on the subject belongs to one of the raid survivors when he was interviewed for *Airforce* magazine in 1985: "Who the hell watched spot-lights at The Old Windmill?"[114]

As April became May and the practice flying hours continued to mount, the flyers became increasingly restive about the nature of the mission.

> By now the crews were getting edgy. Many had been due for a rest before this mission came up. They'd been flying night and day for several weeks, had dropped hundreds of practise bombs, had logged between 150 and 200 hours flying time per man and still they didn't know the target. Speculation was rife. Joe McCarthy remembers:
>
> "I guess we thought of every possible target from the submarine pens at Le Havre, the old 'S' and 'G'—*Scharnhorst* and *Gneisenau*—the Kiel Canal and of course, the *Tirpitz*. But I don't think anybody thought about the dams. I don't think anybody knew of them."
>
> Fred Sutherland said: "We were all guessing and the only thing we were sure of was that it was going to be tough. We'd all had quite a bit of experience and after a while you get a feeling for a tough target. We had a feeling—I know I did—that this was going to be real tough."[115]

On 15 May 1943, Gibson was authorized by Sir Arthur Harris to brief the pilots, navigators, bomb-aimers, and the flight engineers on the targets. The others would have to wait awhile longer, as strict secrecy and compartmentalized information release were the watchwords and would remain so until the day of the raid. Meanwhile, "Capable" Caple reported that only nineteen aircraft could be made ready for the mission, since the others had been too badly knocked about during training to participate.

> The crews were shown exact, scaled down models of the dams and surrounding countryside. Now they knew what they had to deal with and while the general reaction was "Thank God it isn't the Tirpitz," no one had any illusions about it being a "piece of cake." Known flak positions were pointed out and noted with great care, as were power grids and high ground, but in everybody's mind was a nagging thought. As Danny Walker recalled to me:
> "None of us were all that sure that we could knock those huge things down with the weapons we had. Sir Barnes said we could and we sure hoped he was right."[116]

As if the release parameters were not enough of a constraint, the bomb, code-named Upkeep, had to be delivered at the height of the spring runoff, when the water level in each of the dams was only four to five feet below the surface of the reservoir. Furthermore, the water surface itself had to be as smooth as possible for the ordnance to function properly. On top of all the other variables, the crews would be flying through difficult and dangerous terrain, they were committed to a very predictable attack path up the lakes to the face of the dams, and they would probably have to run a gauntlet of enemy defensive fire and barrage balloons. Even the most optimistic of their number knew this was going to be profoundly challenging.

On the morning of 16 May, Guy Gibson was told that the operation was on for the following night. The attack plans were now released in detail. The vertical reference points to determine the release distance for the "penny bomb sight" were the sluice towers on the flanks of the dam superstructures. The nineteen crews participating in the attack were subdivided into three sections. Gibson would lead the main force of nine aircraft, flying in three "vics" of three via a southern route against the Möhne and Eder dams. Their in-bound route would take them out over the North Sea, threading the islands at the mouth of the Scheldt estuary, past Bergen-op-Zoom and Eindhoven to the Rhine River at a point north of the heaviest flak concentrations associated with the Ruhr. Then at Wesel they were to turn east for a short distance, then sharply south between the heavily-defended cities of Soest and Hamm. This, in theory, would place the Möhne dam right below them. Meanwhile, Joe McCarthy would lead a diversionary force of five aircraft on a northern route in an attempt to confuse the enemy defenders and to split the night fighter forces. They would cross the Dutch coast near Texel, then head out south over the Zuider Zee, then alter course southeast at Harderwijk until past Apeldoorn, and finally, press on to the Sorpe dam. Because his route was longer, McCarthy's force would take off first. The remaining five aircraft would constitute the airborne reserve element. As losses mounted or other needs surfaced, they were diverted to the appropriate targets. If not required for the primary targets, a number of important secondary dams had been designated for their attention.

As it transpired, Joe McCarthy ground aborted his primary aircraft, was forced to use a spare, and then ended up seventy-five miles behind the other four members of his flight when they crossed the Dutch coast. Almost immediately, the third Lancaster in his force, piloted by Les Munro, was shot up so badly that it was forced to return to Scampton, leaving eighteen remaining.

Meanwhile, Geoff Rice, Munro's wingman, hit the water while taking violent evasive action and his Upkeep was actually torn from the aircraft. He was also forced to air abort and return to Scampton, and the force was down to seventeen aircraft. The problems were only beginning for this ill-fated flight. In the lead, the crews of Vernon Byers of Star City Saskatchewan and Richard Barlow, an Australian, encountered devastating ground fire between Harderwijk and Apeldoorn. Both their Lancasters slammed into the ground, taking all fourteen crew members to their deaths. Three of them were Canadians. Perishing with Byers was his rear gunner, Jimmy McDowell of Geraldton, Ontario, and Barlow's front gunner was Harvey Glinz from Winnipeg. The costs of the raid were mounting and as yet, there had been no bombs dropped on target.

Meanwhile, Gibson and the main force were well into their southerly route. But near Wesel, Flight Lieutenant Bill Astell, a veteran of over two tours, was ripped from the night sky. Three more Canadians died with him; Pilot Officer Floyd Wile, the navigator, from Scotch Cove Nova Scotia; the wireless operator, Warrant Officer Abram Garshowitz; and the front gunner, Flight Sergeant Frank Garbas, both from Hamilton, Ontario.

Soon, Gibson and his seven other crews were circling the Möhne. While the others dispersed to predetermined orbit points, the young Englishman started his run across the lake. With flak bursting all around them, and with young "Terry" Taerum feeding course and target information to his pilot, they thundered closer to the dam face. Taerum's duty as the aircraft approached the dam was to make sure the aircraft was at the required 60 feet and he took his position at the per-spex blister on the starboard side of the cockpit. As they approached the dam he switched on the lights at 12:25 A.M. and began giving directions to Gibson, "Down—down—down," and then after the lights converged on the water, "Steady—steady." Gibson's bomb exploded just short of the wall. Then John Hopgood and his crew of "M-Mother," which included two Canadians, was shot down at the target,[117] while the bomb of the third Lancaster, piloted by the Australian "Micky" Martin, veered slightly off course but still appeared to achieve a direct hit. Meanwhile, Guy Gibson was everywhere in the target area, providing encouragement and directions to his attacking crews. For Martin's bomb run, he deliberately positioned himself abeam of the Australian's Lancaster in order to draw the enemy guns away. Then, Squadron Leader Melvin "Dinghy" Young (so named because he had rowed for Cambridge) took "A-Apple" down to the lake surface, this time flanked by both Gibson and Martin providing firing cover. Yet another apparent direct hit, and still the ugly concrete monster defied all the airmen's attempts to destroy it. The fifth Lancaster across the lake was that of the burly Englishman, David Maltby, in "J-Johnny." And this time it worked. Undoubtedly weakened by the earlier close calls, the Möhne was breached at 12:50 A.M., sending millions of tons of water cascading through the ragged tear in the wall just twenty-two minutes after Gibson dropped the first Upkeep. After ordering Maltby and Martin back to Scampton, and taking "Dinghy" Young along as a back-up lead, Gibson herded the remaining three aircraft with bombs off to the Edersee, fifty miles eastward, wondering if they would be able to fell the Eder with just the three bombs. David Shannon, another Australian, made the first run. His Canadian navigator, Danny Walker, recalled what happened:

> "There was no flak at the Eder. The big problem here was the shape of the valley which held the lake. Like a deep bowl surrounded by hills about 1000 feet high, I guess. So it took a really skillful pilot to get us down to the required 60 feet off the water at the exact speed. It was also a major headache for the bomb-aimer, who had to make the assessment

as to whether to drop the bomb or go around again—he had only split seconds to make that decision—before the pilot had to shove on full power to get up and over those hills. It was very difficult and we made several dummy runs but couldn't quite get it right, so Guy called us out and sent in Hank Maudslay."

Squadron Leader Maudslay, one of Bomber Command's most experienced pilots, had been a tower of strength during the training period. Now, on the attack, he too had some difficulty but on his third run appeared to have everything under control when something went terribly wrong. Sergeant Fred Sutherland, the front gunner with Les Knight's crew, which was circling about watching the action below, saw what happened and remembers it this way:

"I think they were having trouble with the height and dropped the weapon either a little late or a hair early. Anyway, it hit the top of the dam and exploded. We figured he'd blown himself up—there was this huge ball of fire. Gibson kept calling him on the intercom, 'Hank, are you alright Hank? Can you hear me? Come in Hank!' Finally a faint shaky voice came back and said something like 'returning to base'—I heard it and so did a lot of the other boys. But that was the last we saw or heard of them, the explosion and the faint voice. Whatever happened they didn't make it home."[118]

There were just two bombs left now. David Shannon in "L-Love" then scored a direct hit on the dam face, but still the behemoth held. One left. It fell to yet another Australian, twenty-two-year-old Les Knight in "N-Nancy," to get the job done. Two Canadians were part of Knight's crew; "Doc" Sutherland at the front guns and Harry O'Brien of Winnipeg "riding shotgun" in the rear turret.

"As the tail gunner I was looking straight down at the dam. With the bomb gone Les had the aircraft practically standing on its tail as he reached for more height. I imagine the rest of the crew were looking forward to see if we were going to clear this hill ahead of us because it was on my mind too. But when the explosion came this enormous column of water seemed to be coming straight up at me—right at my turret. I couldn't move—it was awesome and scary . . .

By this time we'd created quite a stir over Germany and I personally was very concerned about night fighters. I couldn't understand why we didn't see any. And why they didn't protect those dams better than they did is still a mystery to me."[119]

Meanwhile, big Joe McCarthy and his crew in "T-Tommy" had arrived over the Sorpe all alone. Although there were no defending guns to contend with, the valley floor was partially blanketed in ground fog, which almost totally obscured the huge dam. Also, high hills at either end of the target required numerous dry runs to get the attack parameters right. In the end, McCarthy's Upkeep scored a direct hit on the Sorpe, but the dam, of a different stone and earth construction, held fast.

The airborne reserve flight also had their hands full. As the early results of the main force's efforts became known, two Lancasters, those of Bill Townsend in "O-Orange" and Charlie Anderson in "Y-Yorker," were tasked by 5 Group Headquarters in Grantham against secondary targets. While Anderson was not able to locate his dam, the Schwelme, in extensive ground fog and ended up bringing his Upkeep home, Townsend found and accurately bombed the Ennerpe dam, damaging it significantly. The remaining three Lancasters of the reserve flight, Pilot Officer Bill Ottley, an Englishman piloting "C-Charlie," Pilot Officer Lewis Burpee from Ottawa at the helm of "S-Sugar," and Flight Sergeant Ken Brown from Moose Jaw, Saskatchewan, flying "F-Freddie," were sent to the Möhne to support the main force, if ultimately needed. Abeam of Hamm, Burpee and Ottley were both shot down by flak. Sergeant Steve Oancia of Stonehenge, Saskatchewan, Ken Brown's bomb-aimer, witnessed their demise:

> They were only seconds ahead of us, less than a mile, I suppose. I saw the tracers coming up, saw them hit the aircraft, saw the tanks explode into balls of fire which climbed a bit before the machines hit the ground. Then the bombs blew up, throwing out a lot of light, which gave us enough time to fly around this flak position near Hamm airport. It all happened in just seconds.[120]

Ken Brown and his crew later maintained, tongue in cheek, that it was around this time they changed their call sign from "F-Freddie" to "F-Frightened." When they arrived at the Möhne and found it breached, they were further diverted to the Sorpe. The different construction and location of this dam required different approach tactics.

> Stretched out in the glass nose of the aircraft, Sergeant Oancia had a front row seat to the hair-raising sequence of events that preceded his dropping of the weapon. He recalls:
>
> "We must have run across that lake a dozen times before Ken was sure he'd got everything right. The movement of the aircraft and the props moved the mist around so that in the end we had a pretty clear view of the target. Even so, it was a little dicey for a while and I was mighty glad when we got rid of the thing."
>
> Ken Brown recalls how he put everything together for the drop: "After we nearly hit the hill the second time, we pulled up and stooged around for a while and had a general pow-wow on how we should handle this attack. We decided we'd have to lay a trail of incendiaries on to the thing. There was a church spire right in line with the dam and we used this as an aiming point for our run-in. We went ahead and laid our incendiaries, burned down an awful lot of trees, but we got a clear run. As we came in over the church spire I had to cut the power back almost to a stall, then shove the stick forward and come screaming down the side of the hill with the power right off. When we hit the level where I thought it was 60 feet, I shoved on the power and ran along the sloping side of the dam, an extremely short run I might add, to the point of release. There was no time for lights before we had to climb like mad to clear this hill. It was necessary to make ten runs before we got it right. There was an interesting effect when the bomb went off. A tremendous percussion ring rose very quickly and in seconds the fog was gone. A remarkable sight. We didn't break the Sorpe but along with Joe McCarthy's attack we did considerable damage, so considering all the problems encountered, we were reasonably satisfied with the effort. I understand the Germans had to drain the lake, which put it out of action for the rest of the year."[121]

The determined efforts of the crew of "F-Freddie" that night resulted in the award of a Conspicuous Gallantry Medal for Ken Brown and a Distinguished Flying Medal for Steve Oancia. But first, they had to get home. Steve Oancia and Ken Brown recall:

> "Night fighters didn't bother us because we were too low but after crossing the Zuider Zee with dawn beginning to break behind us, all hell broke loose near the Den Helder area. Suddenly I saw tracers coming at us from *above*—searchlights began to shine *down* on us from a bank of flak towers. We were right on the deck and I felt I could reach out and touch the water. Fortunately, our front gunner made the lights waver just enough for Ken to see a huge sea-wall staring us in the face. He managed to lift the aeroplane over this wall just in time and then we flattened out on the North Sea side and we were going home."

Number 6 Group's first Air Officer Commanding, Air Vice-Marshal George E. Brookes. (DND PL142657)

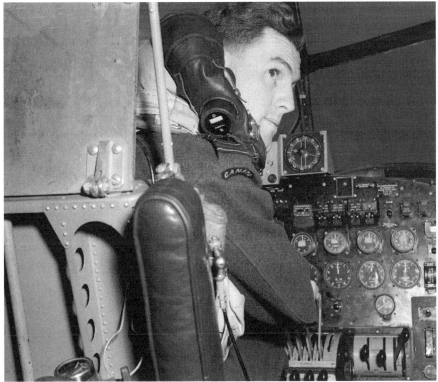

Wing Commander Bill Swetman, a gallant and popular airman, at the controls of his Lancaster while in command of 426 Squadron in 1943. (DND PL28449)

Serious business, cigarette rationing in 6 Group. Note the enforcer on the table. (DND PL30786)

Opposite top: Proud ground crew of O-Orange, a Halifax II of 419 "Moose" Squadron at Middleton St. George, early 1943. Corporal Girard Skip Power is on top of the heap. (Doug Delaney)

Opposite bottom: Aircrew en route to their waiting Halifax on the ubiquitous bicycles of Bomber Command. (DND PL20000)

An obviously enthusiastic Halifax rear gunner. (DND PL22001)

Some 4000-pound "cookies" heading off to war from the bomb dump. (DND PL 26964)

Crew of *Per Flak ad Nausium*, a 419 Squadron Halifax B. Mk. II. The event is obvious and the recipient was Düsseldorf on 7 June 1943. Anne was a Dutch refugee who personally raised $500 and sent it to Canada's Chief of the Air Staff for a bomb to be dropped on Germany. (DND PL19060)

A Canadian bomb aimer in front of his early-model Halifax. (DND PL19336)

Many hands at work on a 408 Squadron Halifax II at Leeming during the summer of 1943. (DND PL19509)

A 426 Squadron Lancaster II gets a multiple tune-up prior to a raid. Q for Queenie sports a queen of hearts card aft of the nose turret. (DND PL22236)

The Stirlings were nearing the end of their deep penetration career early in 1943. The relatively short wingspan is evident. (Shorts ST535)

Sergeant George Oliver, the rear gunner of *Zombie*, puts finishing touches to the artwork on his 408 Squadron Lancaster II. (DND PL29071)

Another view of *Zombie*, with someone at the bomb aimer's station and a thoughtful birthday greeting on a General Purpose bomb designated for *der Führer*. (DND PL29072)

A 331 Wing Wellington taking off from its Tunisian base in a typical cloud of dust and sand, late-summer 1943. (DND PL 18308)

The Upkeep weapon as mounted on a 617 Squadron Lancaster, "G-George."
(Author's Collection)

425 Squadron was among the earlier 6 Group units to be re-equipped with superior Halifax IIIs upon their return from the Mediterranean theatre of operations. (DND PL40185)

Opposite top: The Möhne Dam after its breaching. (Author's Collection)

Opposite bottom: The city of Hamburg after the raids. However, the extent of the damage seen here is deceiving. (Author's Collection)

Ken Brown recalls this flying moment:

> "Those Jerry gunners did a first class job on us. They must have thought the roundel on the side was a target because they blew it completely off. We were badly damaged and it was a miracle nobody was wounded. It was a relief to have the North Sea below us as I got a new heading taking us back to Scampton and bacon and eggs."[122]

For most of the night's raiders, their perilous odyssey was nearing an end. However, "Dinghy" Young's luck ran out somewhere near the Dutch coast, when he and his crew of "A-Apple" fell victim to either flak or a night fighter. The frigid, grey waters of the North Sea became the final resting place for Young and his brave colleagues, including Flying Officer Vincent S. MacCausland of Tyne Valley, Prince Edward Island. MacCausland was the thirteenth and last Canadian to give his life on the Dams Raid.

As the survivors straggled back to Scampton, Clifford "Capable" Caple marveled how many of the Lancasters had made it back at all:

> The damage was enormous. There were holes big enough for me to crawl through. Parts of some of the aircraft were torn completely off. Instruments and equipment in some had been so badly shot up that the crews had to fly back by guess and instinct rather than by any other method. I still find it difficult to understand how so many of those fellows ever got home and why they were able to survive what must have been terribly heavy flak."[123]

There was no doubt that the raid had extorted a substantial cost in Bomber Command blood. Harris had lost eight of his best crews, 42 percent of the nineteen dispatched. Of the thirty Canadians or members of the RCAF that went out that night, only seventeen survived. However, it was initially felt that great damage had been done. "The floods spilled out across the Ruhr valley for over 50 miles, extinguishing blast furnaces, flooding coal mines and swamping homes and over 100 factories. Over 1200 people drowned."[124] Both the Möhne and the Eder had been successfully breached. The Sorpe had been extensively damaged by the direct hits, and the Ennerpe had been damaged as well. The achievements of 617 Squadron were greeted with the utmost enthusiasm and the survivors became instant heroes. "Terry" Taerum recalled the immediate aftermath in a letter to his mother. He said very little about the operation

> because you've probably heard more about it in the papers than I can say . . . It was by far the most thrilling trip I have ever been on and I wouldn't have missed it for anything. We all got back in the Mess about 5:30 in the morning and then we really did relax . . . A couple of days later five of us went to the factory where they made Lancasters and gave the workers a pep-talk. Can you imagine me giving a speech? We were just about mobbed for autographs afterward. The next thing was five days of leave in London, and all the boys were down there, so we really had a time. At the end of five days, we were ordered back to our station to meet the King and Queen. They had lunch with us in the Officers' Mess and afterwards came out and inspected us. I was very lucky because I was introduced to both of them. The Queen is most charming and gracious. It really was quite a day . . . One morning they woke me up and told me that I had been awarded the DFC. Later I had the ribbon sewn on my tunic. Can you imagine me strutting around town with it afterward.[125]

But just how much significant damage had actually been inflicted on the Germans? During the planning stages, the Ministry of Economic Warfare, consulted as to which dams were the most essential to the German war effort, was convinced that the Sorpe rather than the Möhne was the dam to breach in order to achieve a critical shortage of water to the Ruhr, but felt that the best option would be to destroy both dams. Between them, they controlled about two-thirds of the Ruhr's water supply.[126] But the Wallis skipping bomb was optimized for use against the ferro-concrete Möhne and Eder dams, not the stone-and-earth construction of Sorpe. The Sorpe's differences were acknowledged by the planners and both McCarthy's and Brown's Upkeeps were released without spinning, and both crews achieved direct hits, but in the words of Albert Speer, "Fortunately the bomb hole was slightly higher than the water level. Just a few inches lower—and a small brook would have been transformed into a raging river which would have swept away the stone and earthen dam."[127] While the Möhne and the Eder were successfully breached, and the Germans themselves reported "a dark picture of destruction,"[128] Speer was extremely puzzled as to why Bomber Command's resources had been fragmented to attack the Eder dam, whose function was largely agricultural, and which had nothing whatsoever to do with supplying water to the Ruhr valley.[129] Within days, the Reich's Minister for Armaments and War Production had diverted more than 7000 men from fortifying the Atlantic Wall to rebuilding the Möhne and Eder and repairing the other dams. Speer and Hitler were deathly afraid Bomber Command would re-visit the dams before the September rains fell. On 23 September 1943, they just barely finished closing the breach of the Möhne before the autumn rains commenced. In Speer's words, "While we were engaged in rebuilding, the British air force missed its second chance. A few bombs would have produced cave-ins at the exposed building sites, and a few fire bombs would have set the wooden scaffolding blazing."[130] To the amazement of the Germans, the remaining Ruhr dams had been relatively spared, which allowed water to be diverted to essential industries in relatively short order. Joachim Fest, a recent biographer of Albert Speer, blames Arthur Harris for a golden opportunity lost at this juncture:

> Not only did he fail to attack the neighbouring barrages, he never carried out the expected incendiary raids in the Ruhr, which would have wreaked havoc in the area because the fire brigades had no water. With his improvisational skill Speer had restored the barrages and arranged for two hundred batteries of heavy flak to be posted between Dortmund and Düsseldorf by the second half of September. But there were no further attacks on the dams. Speer spoke ironically of the powerful ally he had in the enemy's general staff.[131]

But Arthur Harris had other reasons for not re-attacking the dams. For one thing, he was led to believe, partially through the fog of war, that the damage was significantly more devastating than had been the case. For another, his crew losses had been significant, and even three weeks after the raid, Sir Ralph Cochrane was having problems getting 617 Squadron back up to strength. Harris was also well aware that the Germans had greatly bolstered the defences at the dams, effectively tying down still more manpower and materiel that could have been utilized against the Allies elsewhere. This was also a victory of sorts.

The Dams Raid heralded a new precision capability for Bomber Command and it proved to be a bridge between the way the Command had been used to date and the way it would be employed in the future. The very fact that a precision raid was conducted at very low altitudes, at night, by limited numbers using highly specialized ordnance made it unique. Also, VHF radios had been fitted to all the participating Lancasters so that Guy Gibson, acting as an on-site commander, could exercise direct and highly flexible control of his force in the target area under dynamic, changing circumstances. "This idea was taken up, and soon all Bomber Command aircraft had VHF, and the Pathfinder Force was using a 'Master of Ceremonies,' or 'Master Bomber,' to direct the activities of Main Force bombers over the target, as Gibson had done over the Möhne, with a resulting improvement in accuracy and a definite reduction in 'creep back.' "[132]

Sir Arthur Harris, although saddened by the losses was absolutely delighted with the outcome and mandated Air Vice-Marshal Cochrane to retain 617 Squadron as a specialist unit, man it with experienced crews, and train it for precision deliveries of increasingly more sophisticated specialized ordnance. In the months and years to come, 617 Squadron, later augmented by 9 Squadron, successfully attacked and pulverized such targets as the Michelin tire factory in Clermont-Ferrand, France, as well as the Bielefeld viaduct, the Saumur railway tunnel, the Antheor viaduct in Italy, the submarine pens at Bremen and Hamburg, the pocket battleship *Lützow*, and perhaps most dramatically, the battleship *Tirpitz*. Direct hits with the specialist 12,000 pound Tallboy and, much later, the 22,000 pound Grand Slam "earthquake" bombs were needed to destroy most of these targets. The use of these weapons in conjunction with new Mark XIV gyro-stabilized automatic bombsights (SABS) eventually brought the average 617 Squadron bombing error, the Circular Error of Probability (CEP), down to a remarkable less-than-100 yards. Along with increased bombing accuracy and much more efficient target destruction, the precision squadrons also pioneered innovative and effective marking techniques.[133]

The impact of the Dams Raid on morale was enormous. Just as the scout aces during the Great War had provided inspiration and a catalyst for service beyond the abattoir that the Western Front had become, the daring exploits of Gibson and his raiders fueled the imagination and adulation of both Bomber Command and the general public at a very trying time during the bomber offensive. Its very audacity and innovativeness gave hope for the future and a sense of purpose to many.

The recognition was soon forthcoming. On 25 May 1943, the *London Gazette* announced the award of thirty-four decorations to the surviving participants of the Dams Raid, including seven to members of the RCAF. Highlighted by a Victoria Cross for Gibson, Distinguished Service Orders were also awarded to Joe McCarthy and David Shannon, Ken Brown received the Conspicuous Gallantry Medal, Danny Walker got a Bar to his Distinguished Flying Cross, and Terry Taerum was awarded a Distinguished Flying Cross. Three other Canadians received awards, including a well-deserved Distinguished Flying Medal for Steve Oancia.

But there were still many bitter battles to be fought, and within the Command at this time, the individual odds against survival were hard to beat. Before the books had closed on 1943, twenty of the fifty-six survivors of the raid were dead. Terry Taerum was killed during the first operational use of a new 12,000 pound bomb, directed against the Dortmund-Ems Canal. He and his crew perished near Ladbergen on the night of 15 September 1943. Guy Gibson lasted substantially longer, but ultimately, his concern for his crews proved to be his undoing. Arthur Harris later recalled:

> To enforce a second rest on him I had to make a personal appeal to another warrior of similar calibre—Winston Spencer Churchill—who there and then ordered Gibson down to Chequers and took him with him to the United States. There he arranged for Gibson a short period of traveling around air bases to talk to American airmen. In a third and final effort to force him to rest from operations, he was put on his Group's staff. A few days later he was found in his office with—literally—tears in his eyes at being separated from his beloved crews and unable to go on operations. It was in fact breaking his heart.

He always had direct access to me, and upon further pressure from him and his AOC I quite wrongly allowed him to return to operations. He appointed himself "Master Bomber'—the most vital task of all—on his last operation, which was, of course, a complete success. He was heard to give his crews a pat on the back over the radio and then start them homeward. He never returned.[134]

Hamburg in the Spotlight

Without a doubt, the keystone event in Bomber Command's summer offensive against the Reich was Operation Gomorrah, the bombing of Hamburg by both the RAF and the USAAF for ten days around the end of July. Its essential elements were really adding to the misery of the German people in 1943, first by water during the Dams Raid, and now by fire with the razing of Germany's "Gateway to the World," home to Johannes Brahms and the notorious Reeperbahn.

At the time, Hamburg was the second largest city in Germany with a population of close to two million people. It was singled out by the Ministry of Economic Warfare as being the fourth most valuable city in Germany in its contribution to the war effort, the first three being Berlin, Duisburg and Bochum/Gelsenkirchen. This Ministry assigned Hamburg the following specific, categorical industrial assets:

(a) <u>Priority 1+</u> (highest possible)
One liquid fuel (or substitute) target
Two shipbuilding targets

(b) <u>Priority 1</u>
Four transportation targets
One public utility target
Two liquid fuel targets
Two non-ferrous metal targets
One shipbuilding target
One engineering and armament target
One textile target, and
One rubber target

(c) <u>Priority 2</u>
Four public utility targets
One solid fuel target
One liquid fuel target
Four non-ferrous metal targets
Five aircraft and aero-engine targets
Two shipbuilding targets
Six engineering and armament targets
Four chemical and explosive targets
Four foodstuffs targets

(d) <u>Priority 3</u>
Numerous fuel, engineering, chemical and foodstuffs targets.[135]

Hamburg was particularly singled out for destruction because its shipbuilding facilities churned out half of the U-boat fleet, and also because, unlike Berlin, it provided a very distinctive and clear *H2S* radar return for navigation and target marking, situated as it was on the North Sea coast at the mouth of the Elbe River. Harris stated in his memoirs that he had wanted to "have a crack" at Hamburg for a long time. Fundamentally, his greatest hope for the bomber offensive was that it would force Germany to capitulate without the requirement for a land invasion of the continent and the concomitant horrendous loss of life for both combatants, associated with massive land engagements. The Second Battle of the Ruhr had ended, and overall, Harris was pleased with the results. His intention was now "to shatter a large but more concentrated target—one ideal for Bomber Command tactics and equipment."[136] His plan called for not a series of raids, conducted by his Command at night in coordination with the Americans who were laying waste to the city by day. Bomber Command's contribution consisted of four major strikes on Hamburg, interspersed with major efforts on other targets.

Not all those in the British corridors of power were enamoured with the plan. Sir Henry Tizard, as a prominent but now unofficial scientific advisor to the Executive was often at loggerheads with Churchill's official scientific advisor, Lord Cherwell. Just three days prior to the first raid of the series, he implored the Prime Minister, stating,

> We look forward to an occupation of Germany in the not very distant future. Doubtless the Russians have the same hope. From what town are we to administer the occupied territories? If Germany were to surrender with Berlin practically intact, while all the leading cities South and West of it were reduced to the condition of Cologne and Düsseldorf, it would be impossible to base the administration of Germany anywhere except in Berlin.
>
> Hamburg is anti-Russian, anti-Prussian and anti-Nazi. It may well be soon, if not already, anti-war. Apart from submarine construction and shipping generally it is not industrially important. It is a centre of commerce rather than production. It is a very important port and might therefore be much more useful to us alive than dead . . . The provisional conclusion therefore is that Hamburg should be left alone, and that it is much more important to attack Hannover, Magdeburg, Brunswick, and especially Berlin.[137]

While Tizard did concede that Hamburg was "a much easier target than Berlin and probably easier than such places as Hannover and Brunswick,"[138] Churchill appears to have been quite taken with this line of reasoning, and repeated Tizard's arguments, including his conclusions and recommendations to General Ismay and the Chiefs of Staff Committee, asking for an immediate review of the attack plan.[139] In short order, Sir Charles Portal, Chief of the Air Staff, trotted out the aforementioned priority target list for Hamburg to Churchill via the Secretary of State, also concluding,

> it seems abundantly clear that Hamburg is much more than a dormant centre of peacetime commerce and if so I certainly do not think we should refrain from bombing it.
>
> It is a moot point whether bombing produces a more desirable effect when directed upon anti-Nazis than upon the faithful, but it can at least be argued that anti-Prussian and anti-Nazi tendencies may be more rapidly translated into action under the stimulus of bombing . . . To sum up, as at present advised, the Air Staff regard Hamburg as a very important objective, the destruction of which would hasten the end of the war. They are therefore not in favour of sparing it for the reasons given by Sir Henry Tizard.[140]

This reply appears to have mollified Churchill, and it no doubt reflected the view of Lord Cherwell, who had the Prime Minister's ear. Churchill placed a lot of faith, often erroneously, in Cherwell's opinions. At any rate, the first raid of the series was launched that very night, on 24

July. Also, a new technological innovation was inaugurated by Bomber Command on this raid, to telling effect. It was called *Window* or *Chaff*, and would become known to the Germans as *Düppel*. It consisted of strips of paper-backed aluminum foil cut to half the wavelengths of the German radars, and when dropped in clusters by the approaching bombers, it effectively jammed the *Würzburg* and *Lichtenstein* sets by flooding their cathode ray tubes with false echoes. Initially, it threw the defences into disarray, but the British operational planners knew that its element of surprise would be short-lived, and it would only be a matter of time before the Germans fielded countering technologies and tactics. Still, the early uses of *Window* caused a great amount of consternation until the Germans learned to home on the Chaff clouds themselves, then concentrate on finding specific targets within them. The Germans were also handicapped at this stage by excessive reliance on their rigid *Himmelbett* system, which allowed very little tactical flexibility. Soon however, they countered with the new free-ranging *Wilde Sau* or Wild Boar single-seat fighter tactics, which had been tentatively introduced earlier that summer, and with the freelancing *Zahme Sau* (Tame Boar) concept mentioned earlier.

The first raid occurred on the night of 24/25 June. It consisted of 791 aircraft, including 347 Lancasters, 246 Halifaxes, 125 Stirlings and 73 Wellingtons. Only twelve of the total force were lost, an exceptionally low loss rate of just 1.5 percent for the period, attributable in no small measure to the effective use of *Window*. Canadians from 6 Group participated extensively, contributing seventy-two crews, all of whom returned home this night.

Over the target the weather was clear, the winds light. While a concentrated raid developed after adequate if somewhat scattered marking by the Pathfinders, only half the force bombed within three miles of the centre of Hamburg. A "creepback" of six miles in length developed, but since this was a very large, spread-out city, severe damage resulted, particularly in the northwestern districts. The time over target of the attacking force was exceptionally concentrated, and the entire raid lasted only forty-six minutes. The city centre was also extensively damaged; specifically, the ancient *Rathaus* or city hall, the main telephone exchange, the main police station, and the *Nikolaikirche,* a very old and treasured landmark. Regrettably, the destruction did not extend much into the dockyards and the submarine building facilities on this occasion. However, the concentration of force applied, coupled with the use of *Window*, threw the rigid *Himmelbett* system into complete chaos, as the crews were vectored towards hundreds of false target echos. The radar-directed guns and searchlights were also effectively stymied. One RCAF bomber captain participating that night later commented in his flying log-book on the view of the city from above, as he witnessed it on leaving the target area: "The general impression was of a volcano belching fire and smoke."[141] Eventually during the Hamburg raids, the ground controllers would throw up their arms in frustration and authorize freelance operations by the night fighter crews over the city, but only after urgent entreaties from these crews, and not during the earliest attacks. The German night fighter ace Peter Spoden recalls:

> I was at the Hamburg raid and I remember the terrible fires, but at that time we had tactics that were completely wrong. We were given boxes, areas of sky 150 km by say 200 km, and there we had to stay. I was over Greichswald and I could see, because the fires were so terrible, the silhouettes of the four-engined aircraft over Hamburg, but I was not allowed to leave my box. We were shouting, "We must go to Hamburg, we can see them, we can see them!" but we were not allowed.[142]

On 25 July, the city was attacked in daylight by a force of Eighth Air Force B-17s, and again by a small diversionary force of Mosquitos that night, while the Main Force payed a visit to Essen. The intention at Essen was to capitalize on the limited period of surprise offered by *Window*, and the result was probably the worst damage inflicted on the Krupp works during the entire war. (Doctor Gustav Krupp had a stroke the following morning from which he never recovered, undoubtedly saving the Allies from bringing him to trial as a war criminal on the cessation of hostilities.) Bomber Command lost 3.7 percent of its force during this Essen raid, most of it from the heavy barrage flak, since the radar-directed variety and the night fighters were rendered virtually useless by *Window*. The Canadians fared slightly better than the average, losing just two of the sixty-six crews that participated.[143] The following morning, martial law was declared throughout Italy as Marshal Pietro Badoglio formed a new government purged of all fascist leaders, and future rocker Mick Jagger entered the world in Dartford, Kent.

During the daylight hours of 27 July, Hamburg was punished yet again by the Americans, who completely destroyed the Neuhof power plant and also inflicted considerable damage on the Blohm und Voss U-Boat shipbuilding facilities. However, the bombing activities of that night proved to be the most memorable, when 787 Bomber Command aircraft visited the port city again. The marking, all carried out by *H2S*, was particularly well concentrated and there was very little "creepback." What followed truly lived up to the code name Operation Gomorrah. In the words of the Bomber Command Campaign Diary:

> This was the night of the firestorm, which started through an unusual and unexpected chain of events. The temperature was particularly high (30 degrees Centigrade at 6 o'clock in the evening) and the humidity was only 30 percent, compared with an average of 40–50 percent for this time of the year. There had been no rain for some time and everything was very dry. The concentrated bombing caused a large number of fires in the densely built-up working-class districts of Hammerbrook, Hamm and Borgfeld. Most of Hamburg's fire vehicles had been in the western part of the city, damping down the fires still smouldering there from the raid of 3 nights earlier, and only a few units were able to pass through roads which were blocked by the rubble of buildings destroyed by high-explosive bombs early in this raid. About half-way through the raid, the fires in Hammerbrook started joining together and competing with each other for oxygen in the surrounding air. Suddenly, the whole area became one big fire with air being drawn into it with the force of the storm. The bombing continued for another half-hour, spreading the firestorm area gradually eastwards. It was estimated that 550–600 bomb loads fell into an area measuring only 2 miles by 1 mile. The firestorm raged for about 3 hours and only subsided when all burnable material was consumed. The burnt-out area was almost entirely residential. Approximately 16,000 multi-storied apartment buildings were destroyed. There were few survivors from the firestorm area and approximately 40,000 people died, most of them by carbon monoxide poisoning when all the air was drawn out of their basement shelters. In the period immediately following this raid, approximately 1,200,000 people—two-thirds of Hamburg's population—fled the city in fear of further raids.[144]

Seventy-eight 6 Group crews participated in the raid, the most successful of the ten-day campaign against the city. The returning airmen were "all emphatic that Hamburg was blazing more furiously than on Saturday night . . . The smoke from the fires was so thick that it penetrated into the cabins of the bombers, almost choking the crews. Hamburg was blazing like a paper box."[145]

On this memorable operation, 6 Group lost just one aircraft. "So great was the number of bombers in the air that Wing Commander M.M. Fleming, DFC, reported when he came home to Yorkshire that 'the greatest danger was the risk of collision with other aircraft over the target.' and that he himself had participated in four 'near misses.' "[146] Another participant, Flight Lieutenant A. Forsdike, described the inferno he had witnessed that night:

> Set in the darkness was a turbulent dome of bright red fire, lighted and ignited like the glowing heart of a vast brazier. I saw no streets, no outlines of buildings, only brighter fires which flared like yellow torches against a background of bright red ash. Above the city was a misty red haze. I looked down, fascinated but aghast, satisfied yet horrified. I had never seen a fire like that and was never to see its like again.[147]

The scale of suffering at Hamburg was so enormous that the Germans labeled the event *Die Katastrophie*. The words of propaganda chief Joseph Goebbels in his diary for 29 July reflect a measure of this concern:

> During the night we had the heaviest raid yet on Hamburg . . . with 800 to 1,000 bombers . . . Kaufmann [the local *Gauleiter*] gave me a first report . . . He spoke of a catastrophe the extent of which simply staggers the imagination. A city of a million inhabitants has been destroyed in a manner unparalleled in history. We are faced with problems that are almost impossible of solution. Food must be found for this population of a million. Shelter must be secured. The people must be evacuated as far as possible. They must be given clothing. In short, we are facing problems there of which we had no conception even a few weeks ago . . . Kaufmann spoke of some 800,000 homeless people who are wandering up and down the streets not knowing what to do.[148]

The third major raid of the Hamburg series took place on the night of 29/30 July, with 777 aircraft despatched. This time the marking was less accurate and most of the damage was done in the residential areas again, with widespread fires but no resulting firestorm. There were also considerably more night fighter engagements, as the defenders started to effectively counter the earlier effects of *Window*. In all, twenty-eight raiders were lost during the operation, a loss of 3.6 percent of the attacking force.

The final round of the siege against Hamburg took place on the night of 2/3 August, when electrical storms and heavy icing enroute played havoc with the bomber stream:

> A peculiar example, which occurred in 6 Group, was the sudden attack of two kinds of weather on one aircraft, captained by Sergeant M.M. Humphreys, which was forced to pull out and turn back to base before reaching the target, as it was then losing altitude at a rate of 400 feet a minute, due to heavy icing. Just as the decision to return was taken, all four engines were simultaneously struck by lightning and momentarily cut out. The aircraft went out of control temporarily. Minutes passed before the instrument panel behaved normally. Humphries and his crew returned safely, however.
>
> Young Vanderkerckhove [Pilot Officer G.P. Vanderkerckhove] had his troubles again that night . . . Heavy icing and starboard drag, from engine trouble, caused constant loss of altitude, hauling the aircraft down to 4000 feet over the Kiel Canal before Hamburg was reached. The crew decided to keep on to the target, even though they might be forced to bail out over enemy territory. The bombs were dropped, and somehow they limped home to Yorkshire.[149]

The Nazi hierarchy was profoundly shaken by the bombing of Hamburg, as the operation had been intended. In his memoirs, Albert Speer stated:

> Hamburg had put the fear of God in me. At the meeting of Central Planning on July 29 I pointed out: "If the air raids continue on the present scale, within three months we shall be relieved of a number of questions we are at present discussing. We shall simply be coasting downhill, smoothly and relatively swiftly . . . We might as well hold the final meeting of Central Planning in that case." Three days later I informed Hitler that armaments production was collapsing and threw in the further warning that a series of attacks of this sort, extended to six more major cities, would bring Germany's armaments production to a total halt . . . Fortunately for us, a series of Hamburg-type raids was not repeated on such a scale against other cities. Thus the enemy once again allowed us to adjust ourselves to his strategy.[150]

Indeed, the industrial damage, on top of all the residential and infrastructure damage, appeared spectacular, and "Production at several chemical works, engineering firms and shipyards was halted altogether . . . Josef Kammhuber was profoundly disturbed by the thought that his crews would have to stand by 'helplessly' and 'watch the great cities of their country go up in flames one after the other' if the results of this raid could be repeated elsewhere."[151]

This intensity and concentration of operations could not be sustained, however, nor could firestorms, which were made possible by the combination of peculiar weather and atmospheric conditions, be generated at will. Furthermore, excessive concentration on any particular target worked against Harris's belief that destruction of any form of target could win the war. Also, the damage created was not as bad as first thought. Yet it cost the city about two months of war production, even though "within five months, total output had recovered to about 80 percent of the pre-raid levels."[152] But the burden placed on all sectors of German society—including construction, transportation, and agriculture—to rectify the damage required an enormous diversion of industrial resources, which could have been otherwise directed at the war effort. It significantly curtailed U-boat construction and development at a critical juncture in the *Kriegsmarine*'s North Atlantic campaign. In the city, the entire tram and subway system had been brought to a standstill, gas and electrical supplies had been massively disrupted, and 250,000 of the city's 450,000 apartments and flats had been completely destroyed. All this damage required the concerted attention of many people and services to repair, as well as vast amounts of strategic materials.

The German night fighter arm now started incorporating considerably more flexible tactics, and the "cat and mouse" game of move and counter-move continued to evolve and change in the dangerous night skies over the Reich in response to initiatives fielded by both sides. Still, the raids served as a chilling portent of things to come, and the biblical prophecy paraphrased by Sir Arthur Harris the year before was certainly coming true.

> They have sown the wind,
> And they shall reap the whirlwind.
> —Sir Arthur Harris, 1942

FIVE

A Time For Fortitude
The Human Element of the Bombing Campaign

Bearing enormous loads of bombs and petrol, these heavy aircraft, both because of their weight and on account of the need to conserve fuel for the long hours of endurance, travelled, by comparison with the German night fighters, very slowly, making an airspeed of perhaps 180 knots on the way out and 210 knots on the way home. Though they could perform the famous "corkscrew" manoeuvre by which they sought to evade or at least to present a more difficult target to the fighters, their manoeuvrability was, nevertheless, far inferior to that of their smaller and more speedy opponents.

Restricted to .303-calibre machine-guns, they were substantially outshot and completely outranged by their cannon-equipped enemies. Their armour-plating was progressively removed, until little remained, to increase their bomb-lifting capacity. Belching flame from their exhausts as well as radar transmissions from their navigational and fighter warning apparatus made them all too apparent to those who hunted them. Once engaged in combat, they had little chance of victory and not much of escape, while the large quantities of petrol, incendiary bombs, high explosives and oxygen with which they were filled often gave spectacular evidence of their destruction. Outpaced, outmanoeuvred and outgunned by the German night fighters and in a generally highly inflammable and explosive condition, these black monsters presented an ideal target to any fighter pilot who could find them, and it was the night fighters which caused the overwhelming majority of the losses sustained by Bomber Command.

—Sir Charles Webster and Noble Frankland[1]

By the summer of 1943, Bomber Command had matured into a technologically and tactically sophisticated weapon, engaged in an all-out, relentless campaign, night after night, against the European Axis countries. The mighty, cooperative effort known as the Combined Bomber Offensive would become one of the most focused and demanding prolonged campaigns in modern military history. As punishing as this massive air offensive was to the Germans and, to a lesser extent, the Italians, its cost for the Allies was great. Throughout the entire European air war more than 18,000 Allied bomber aircraft were lost and 81,000 British, Commonwealth, American and Allied airmen forfeited their lives,[2] including a significant number of aircrew, particularly those from Britain and the Dominions, who perished on operations prior to the commencement of the Combined Bomber Offensive. Bomber Command's fatalities constituted the largest portion, with 56,000 of its aircrew making the supreme sacrifice. Between 1942 and 1945, the Command flew more than 300,000 operational sorties. At peak periods of the bomber offensive, such as the Second Battle of the Ruhr and the Berlin raids of 1943/1944, for every 100 airmen who joined an operational training unit, fifty-one were killed on combat operations, nine more were killed in non-operational accidents and twelve became prisoners of war. Three were wounded or injured badly enough to be removed from operations, and one successfully evaded capture in enemy territory. Only twenty-four of the original 100 emerged unscathed from these arduous periods of combat.[3] But while Bomber Command's morale faltered on occasion, it never entirely failed. No other component of the western Allied combatants suffered the same enormous casualty rates over a sustained, long-term campaign, nor did they face "the mathematical certainty of their own deaths so routinely and so unflinchingly."[4] Specifically, fewer than 1 percent of the participants suffered debilitating combat stress that rendered them unable to carry on operations against the enemy, and significantly fewer were categorized with a shortage of moral fibre or resolve.[5] Since the number of combat casualties related to stress was considered by most in the organizational hierarchy to be surprisingly small, given the highly detrimental conditions involved, it is certainly as important to highlight the reasons for this vast demonstration of psychological resolve as it is to mention the reasons for the relatively infrequent failures.

What enabled the crews to prevail so steadfastly overall? Bomber Command aircrew, like their American counterparts, were motivated to join the war effort by a wide range of emotions, including patriotism, righteousness and a sense of duty. All of them were volunteers. For the British, who had witnessed the ravaging of their island from the air earlier in the war, that patriotic sense of duty was probably more pronounced than it was for the men from the Dominions, who "were far from their homes, and many did not feel the personal sense of commitment to the war that was possible for Englishmen."[6] Other compelling draws were the lure of flight itself and the thrill of service in a dimension considered glamourous by aviation-minded citizens of the day. On the whole, these were fit, rigorously selected, well-trained young men who at least commenced their operational tours secure in the belief that they were vital cogs in the war effort, that their contributions were both necessary and meaningful, and their cause, just. The RAF and the Dominion air forces fostered the elite status of the crews through distinctive brevets or flying badges, decorations and achievement awards, such as the operational tour wing and the Pathfinder badge, and the flyers were fiercely proud of these marks of distinction. However, the grim realities of air combat, especially the random nature of the bomber casualties, eventually dispelled the more glamourous notions. As the unrelenting, bloody and depressingly random casualties incurred during the bombing campaign unfolded, crew motivations for continued engagement of the enemy had much less to do with patriotism and much more to do with pragmatic issues, ranging from self-esteem to simple survival. "Like the airmen of all nations, they were concerned about pay, privilege, rank and prestige to some extent. But ultimately their morale . . . depended to a great degree on the quality of their equipment, the length of time they were kept in combat, the results they obtained and the rate of attrition."[7] Douglas Harvey, a distinguished Canadian Lancaster II pilot and DFC winner with 408 Squadron, has argued that while the military elite were preoccupied by lofty goals, such as the strategic war aims, the goals of the aircrew flying the missions were generally more narrowly focused, exemplified by the following comment in reference to Sir Arthur Harris:

> At the time I knew nothing of Harris's grand design or of the horrible ordeal that lay ahead of me. His goal was the total aerial destruction of Germany. My goal, like that of other kids in Bomber Command, was quite simple: to carry out thirty raids, the magic number that constituted a tour of operations.[8]

In his book, *Tanks Advance*, Ken Tout has made an evocative analogy between musical instruments, patriotism, and the realities of combat and battle fatigue. While the specific references apply to armoured operations, the emotions generated were certainly applicable to bomber aircrew as well:

> I marched away
> to the glorious trumpets of war,
> the haunting horns of ambition, the pounding tubas of discipline.
>
> I limped back home
> to the shivering violins of fear,
> the moaning violas of pain,
> the sombre cellos of self-knowledge,
> the stumbling basses of self-doubt.
>
> Only later
> did I discover
> that I was my own composer
> and my own conductor.[9]

However, crew solidarity, a sense of shared danger, and an exceptionally strong motivation not to do anything to jeopardize the other members of their aircrew team or family helped to mitigate the effects of combat stress. Many aircrew prevailed in the face of formidable obstacles simply because they would rather perish than let their buddies down. Bomber crews, in many ways, became classic examples of small-unit cohesiveness. Loyalty, and the strength they derived from these loyalties, is a major reason why most of them were able to prevail in the face of such daunting adversity.

> We were intensely preoccupied with our own crew and very strongly motivated not to let it down. Apart from our commanders and three or four other crews that were close contemporaries, we knew few other aircrew on the station as more than passing acquaintances.[10]

The Dangerous Sky

In order to understand the extent of the human contribution, we must first grasp the environment and the challenges that were presented to the crews. In essence, flight itself is conducted in what is a potentially hostile environment, and combat airmen are sustained in this environment by artificial means. In the words of American historian Mark Wells, "Thus, airmen, more than any other wartime combatants, had to deal not only with the direct challenges of combat, but also faced the life-threatening hazards of their surroundings." And those hazards constituted a very real element of friction in the airman's world, from take-off until landing: "the sky itself magnified what arguably might be considered the 'normal' physical and mental stresses placed on any combatant."[11] Many day-to-day hazards of air operations combined to take a vast toll on the Main Force and also the American daylight raiders. While many veterans, particularly over a cool ale or two, will become nostalgic about the flying characteristics of their Lancasters, Halifaxes, Stirlings, Fortresses, and Liberators, these aircraft were all exceptionally difficult to fly at times, especially when overburdened by volatile fuel loads and high explosives on take-off from chronically short runways, or when returning from difficult raids with extensive battle damage and/or wounded crew members. Systems failures were commonplace, and routine operations at maximum permissible settings left little room for error. For example, a single engine failure on take-off, even with four engines available, normally constituted a death sentence for the hapless crew. Also, the gruesome pyrotechnic effects of 2000 gallons of high octane fuel and 10,000 pounds of high explosive ordnance igniting were both spectacular and unnerving to other crews awaiting departure, adding further to the psychological stresses.

> Pilot skill was the difference between life and death for a crew at all times, not only when attacked, [but] never more so than on takeoff when loaded with tons of explosives. It was an inescapable moment of dry-mouthed tension for all on board and, unlike enemy action, it was experienced on every sortie. One pilot recalled the drill: "Right hand on the throttles, thumb advancing port outer to stop her swinging, stick forward to get the tail up, deft use of rudder to keep her straight, the needle creeps up to 90 knots marking the point of no return." The flight engineer acted as co-pilot and a mistake on his part could be no less fatal.[12]

Not all the mechanical failures experienced on take-off were associated with an aircraft's primary systems, such as engines or flight controls. Douglas Harvey recalls one such event which, while amusing in retrospect, was anything but amusing at the time.

> The Lancaster had a pilot's seat that could be raised or lowered by means of a long handle, much like the parking brake on old cars. Pulling up on the lever would ratchet the seat to a higher position. Unfortunately, the ratchet had a habit of slipping.
>   Taking off in total darkness one night, I reached the end of the runway and pulled the control column back to lift off when my seat crashed to the floor. This put me below the windscreen and the swiftness of disappearing scared the hell out of me. I managed to fly with my hands over my head as we thundered into the blackness, while scrambling to find the lever and jack the seat back into position.[13]

When Harvey mentioned the problem to one of his ground crew on return, he was told that he worried too much! He got the same reply when it happened again . . . and again! After the third failure, a considerably more forceful demand for repair, which contained an implied threat, finally got the misbehaving seat fixed.[14]

Weather is notoriously unreliable over Britain and northwest Europe. Structural damage, including catastrophic airframe failures caused by turbulence and icing, were common. As late in the war as 5 March 1945 twenty 6 Group aircrew were killed in take-off accidents in one night aboard seven crashed aircraft. The raid, an operation to Chemnitz, started disastrously when crews later reported that, "during the climb, they encountered varying degrees of icing near Linton. The icing was particularly bad in one area where cumulus cloud had apparently developed within the stratocumulus layers. During their climb from Tholthorpe, three Halifax crews encountered icing so severe that the pilots could not maintain control of their aircraft and ordered their crews to bail out."[15] Pilot Officer Jimmy Waugh of 420 Squadron, an intrepid gunner who was awarded both a DFM and later a DFC for his wartime exploits, was one of the lucky survivors that night:

> On the 5th of March 1945 I was involved in what I believe to be one of the worst aircraft accidents that had ever happened in England to that date. While flying as a spare mid-upper gunner, with our aircraft loaded with petrol and high explosives, we climbed to 10,000 feet where we encountered severe icing and the pilot was unable to control the aircraft. At 7000 feet we were ordered by our pilot to "JUMP, JUMP" but due to difficulties with the engineer, I did not get out until [the] base of cloud, which was [at] approximately 1200 feet. At approximately 800 feet the explosion of [the] aircraft on impact caused me to become severely tangled with my parachute. Finally at about 300 feet I managed to untangle [the] shroud lines, etc., from my parachute harness and alight with slightly more than normal impact. The remaining six members of the crew did not jump and were all killed in the explosion. No trace of the bodies could be found. The largest piece of the aircraft that could be found was no larger than a normal sized wash basin.[16]

Other hazards to flight abounded. Major performance limitations or design flaws handicapped some of the bomber fleets, such as the Stirlings and the earlier models of the Halifax, and those shortcomings have already been discussed. However, engines generally were often notoriously unreliable and instruments and control surfaces frequently froze or otherwise failed. Murray Peden recalls his early operations piloting Main Force Stirlings:

> Even when most equipment was working well, it was almost a given that on every operation something would malfunction. Between the "routine" action of dodging flak at our modest level, it was not uncommon, for example, to have one engine start to run hot, which posed an unpleasant problem in a Stirling, already well below the height of the bulk of Main Force.
>
> Or an intercom point would start acting up, very serious if it was a gunner's; or someone would start having difficulty with his oxygen supply, and even in a Stirling, this could be serious if it were protracted. Compasses were prone to be affected by well-charged clouds, and their verification and the re-setting of the gyro directional indicator was a near-constant chore.[17]

Supplemental oxygen systems failed and fatally incapacitated crew members, usually without warning, and life-sustaining oxygen was a vital requirement at the altitudes most raids were conducted. During the Second World War, these systems, especially the regulators and the connectors, were unreliable, and the effects of hypoxia or oxygen starvation were generally not well known. An alert crew could occasionally make a life-or-death difference, while many others were probably not so lucky. In late 1943, a Halifax crew from 429 Squadron flying out of Leeming were the fortunate ones:

> It was on one of these high-level daylight exercises across Scotland that the pilot, Flying Officer Les Thompson, called up the flight engineer, Flight Sergeant Stan Fisher, on the intercom and asked him if he could see the black cat walking across the wing between the two engines. The crew all woke up on hearing this and Flight Sergeant Budgen, the wireless operator, found the pilot's oxygen line was disconnected. He quickly coupled it up before [the pilot] could pass out.[18]

Air traffic control was primitive at best, and air traffic congestion incessant. For example, the overlapping traffic patterns at the 6 Group stations have already been mentioned, and with only the most rudimentary navigational aids, mid-air collisions and ground impacts caused by spatial disorientation were commonplace. Also, "with thousands of young, relatively inexperienced airmen at the controls of complex, multi-engine aircraft, there were a huge number of crashes very likely due simply to pilot error."[19] RAF Bomber Command had nearly 6000 airmen killed in training accidents alone during 1943 and 1944. For the entire war period, accidents killed nearly 12 percent of the combatant force.[20]

Airfield control was generally procedural rather than technological at the time. Individual aircraft were channeled into a landing sequence, assigned a numerical priority, and provided with a time separation from a preceding aircraft. Control was normally done visually, and in poor visibility it frequently broke down. Murray Peden recalls:

> The problem, more often than not, was not finding your way back to base, but finding the visibility there safe for what you had in mind, namely getting down and climbing into the crew bus. When the weather clamped, and you were diverted to another drome, it was usually along with the aircraft from half a dozen other dromes that had also been taken off the board by fog or morning mist. Even with reasonable visibility at the new stopping place, the circuit was over-filled with tired crews, often running short of juice, and anxious to get down PDQ. They often produced some of the more hair-raising incidents of the night just by bad flying and a touch of irresponsibility.
>
> Air traffic control separation, at these times, was as good as one could expect under such abnormal circumstances. I cannot quote with any great assurance the time interval between landings, but to the best of my recollection, I would say it was about a minute between touchdowns. On our own base's circuit, we had, by experience, learned to position ourselves when we were Number Two to pancake, fairly well along the downwind leg as the guy ahead of us called "Funnels" to show that he was in the funnel and just a few degrees off his final approach heading.
>
> We, in turn, would try to give our "Funnels" call the minute we heard his "Clear of the runway," sometimes deferring it a whisker or three so as to avoid getting an Overshoot order from Control. On nights when things were tight, the man in the Airfield Control Post (ACP) hut at the end of the runway tended to turn a Nelsonian blind eye to someone in the funnel who had modestly not yet announced his presence for the foregoing reason, shutting his gaze to the nav lights on the guy at the far end of the runway and willing him to turn off right about now, but with the Very pistol and red cartridge ready to go, even at the last minute if necessary.[21]

Aircraft returning with unserviceable or malfunctioning radios, and there were many, were equipped with recognition flares and briefed on specific "colours of the day," to ensure that the airfield controllers and ground defences did not mistakenly consider them as German intruders, who were a routine threat. The use of *Gee* as a vectoring device to home stations was a widespread and preferred recovery option, and many Bomber Command navigators became particularly adept at getting their crews home to within a fraction of a mile through skilled use of this valuable equipment. Navigators, like all crew members, were not infallible however, as Halifax pilot and DFC winner Bob Pratt from Toronto (who flew his operational tour with 434 Squadron), later recalled. On one occasion when he was low on fuel, Pratt was informed by his navigator, Willie, that they had successfully completed their return trip and were now over British soil. After acknowledging this, Pratt let down through clouds, spotted an airfield and started an approach; thinking that he would land, get fuel and his bearings, then continue on to his home base. However, on final approach, the airfield defences opened up on the hapless Halifax. The same thing happened after an orbit and a second approach, when Pratt fired the flare colours of the day. After Pratt fired a second round of identification flares, the airfield defences ceased firing. Bob Pratt then asked his navigator to re-confirm that they were, in fact, over Britain. His navigator then asked him to head generally north while he took an astro-navigation shot for verification. Pratt, flying in pouring rain, sardonically observed that in that weather they would not even be able to see a single star, let alone get an accurate positional plot. He then asked his wireless operator to try to get an electronic vector from Britain. This was immediately successful, and they were then informed by anxious British controllers that they had been attempting to land on a German airfield! Pratt urgently retracted his landing gear, headed north to England, and eventually landed at a coastal fighter base without further incident. His reaction to his navigator's performance and to that of the posting authorities is priceless:

> We got home, and I said to Willie, "That's your last trip with me." So they gave him his commission and sent him home, as a navigation instructor.[22]

The SCS 51 system, initially developed in the USA, was one of the new approach aids being introduced to service late in the war. Introduced to Britain early in 1944, it provided azimuth direction, the localizer, and glide path information to the user through a system of tone modulation discriminations. This was a great advance over the earlier beam approaches, as it provided a continuous indication of deviations from course. The civilian version of this equipment became famous as the Instrument Landing System (ILS). Also developed late in the war was the Ground Controlled Approach (GCA), which consisted of an extremely high precision microwave radar, which provided the position of a "target" aircraft in azimuth, range and elevation. By this means the position of a landing aircraft relative to a predetermined approach path was displayed on a ground scope, whereby a skilled operator could provide directions to "talk the aircraft down." This equipment however, was still in a developmental stage during the war years. Similarly, the use of short-range microwave Airfield Control Radar (ACR) for directing the flow of aircraft in the vicinity of airports was pioneered at several Bomber Command stations during the war years, and much valuable experience was gained for future applications.

The most common means of positioning for landing in bad weather was the Standard Beam Approach (SBA)—when it was used. Although widely introduced in 1939, it did not achieve widespread popularity. This was partially because of the unreliability of the equipment, but also because considerable practice was required to become skilled in its use. Its inherent weaknesses were that it was slow and time-consuming, there were vagaries in radio reception on the dedicated frequencies, and it lacked glide path and continuous range information to touchdown. During the latter years of the bomber offensive, when the Main Force was broadly equipped with VHF radios (as pioneered by Guy Gibson and 617 Squadron on the Dams Raid), a standby Direction Finding (DF) or homing service was provided to aircraft whose normal aids to navigation had been put out of action.

However, the RAF knew it needed an approach option for returning aircrew that would permit them to penetrate the last few hundred feet of fog and low cloud in conditions that totally obscured the ground. To that end, an innovative chain of emergency landing fields with long, wide runways was constructed, primarily along the coastal approaches, to provide sanctuary to the returning bombers. The airfields were also equipped with a system designed by the Fog Investigation Dispersal Operation (FIDO), consisting of elevated pipes paralleling the length of the runway, which warmed the air and burned off the fog with a double row of burners that were fed with gasoline under pressure and distributed by a pipeline. Fearsome in appearance, they were very effective and saved many lives, although they were extremely costly to construct and to operate. One such base in the chain, equipped with a 9000 by 700-foot runway, was opened at Carnaby on the east Yorkshire coast in March 1944, and it saved many aircraft and crews, particularly from 6 Group. At Carnaby alone, over 1500 operational landings utilizing FIDO were recorded during the European war.[23]

The aerial battlefield over northwest Europe was replete with dangers. American tactics in daylight dictated tight formations for optimum use of massed defensive firepower and offensive bombing accuracy. However, many hours of close formation and vigilant visual scanning of the aerial battle-field, exacerbated by vibration, noise, extreme cold, and the forces of gravity, were physically debilitating in the extreme. At night, Bomber Command did not face as great a fatigue factor from flying extremely close formation in the bomber stream, but "the gloomy conditions of cloud cover and darkness increased the chances for mid-air collisions or navigation errors."[24] In fact, mid-upper gunners undoubtedly saved more lives by warning their pilots of impending collisions than they did by firing their guns, especially on the climb-out to the altitude prescribed for joining the bomber stream on any given night.

A Matter of Luck

In spite of generally excellent flight training received by the crews, chance played a major role in determining their fate. Although experience was a useful tool in isolation for extending aircrew survival, casualties were often depressingly random, and various system malfunctions often claimed many crews who were at the peak of their experience, confidence and productivity. Also, it was frequently just a matter of luck if a particular aircraft was singled out for attack by an enemy fighter, or if a shell from an anti-aircraft barrage exploded lethally close.

> The raw crew who arrived one morning only to be posted missing a few days later were not always victims of their own lack of experience: our casualties were evenly distributed. The old hands, now few in number, would react quicker to a situation but in the thickly concentrated bomber stream chance played a big part. The will to fight on when attacked, to use every trick and turn to defeat the enemy fighter, to stay with the aircraft when there was the least possibility of getting the crew home was strong in all the young captains and it often paid dividends.[25]

However, the crews strongly held to some beliefs beyond randomness that could hasten their fates. For Bomber Command airmen, aircraft illuminated by fires, bright moonlight, or the dreaded radar-controlled searchlights often became fatal statistics. As the crews became increasingly aware of this random nature of aerial death and the critical role of luck, many responded with a form of fatalism, often glumly calculating their odds against survival. Others did everything they could to improve their chances, including the cultivation of teamwork, diligent training, and painstaking attention to even the smallest details. Superstitions abounded, and Murray Peden has recalled that some refused to buy a new service cap while engaged in operations, and that good luck charms and mascots were everywhere, with Saint Christopher medals, rosaries and rabbits feet being seen as frequently as sextants, flashlights, parachutes and escape kits. "Jock Wilson carried a little yellow duck with 'Berlin or Bust' written on it. In addition he packed a small towel and soap 'to wash my feet with in the dinghy.' One of our pilots, a short chap named Jackson, used to carry a large panda and tuck it behind his seat."[26] Others took "lucky" girls' stockings very seriously. "One captain of an aircraft forbade his crew to take out a WAAF [Womens' Auxiliary Air Force] who had lost two man friends in quick succession. There was no point in adding to the risks, he said."[27] John Lewis, a distinguished Canadian navigator who flew a total of forty-six operations with 426 Squadron and then later with 405 Squadron as a Pathfinder, winning a DFC and Bar along the way, also recalls some of the ritualistic behavior:

> Believing it would help stave off disaster, some would don their flying gear only in a specific order; some would urinate on the tail wheel of the aircraft; others would carry talismans of various shapes and sizes. Some would insist on boarding the aircraft first, second, third, etc.; others pledged they would not launder their white-wool submarine sweaters until they were through with ops. As we were rolling down the runway on take-off, I would silently repeat the Lord's Prayer.[28]

Others showed somewhat contemptuous disdain for such beliefs. Leonard Cheshire, the Bomber Command legend who won virtually every high British decoration for officers for gallantry, including the Victoria Cross, is typical of this camp. "He had no sense of carrying a mascot. Didn't have much faith in mascots . . . You needed luck, not mascots. You either had luck or you hadn't."[29] Still others dealt with the mathematical odds in a rather lighthearted manner. Bert Houle was a distinguished Canadian veteran, and although his war service was with the fighter community, the sentiments and the logic could certainly be applied to bomber operations:

> Many pilots built up their courage with a philosophy that went something like this. "There is only a 25 percent chance that I'll get shot at, and if I am there is only a 25 percent chance that my aircraft will be hit. If the aircraft is hit there is only a 25 percent chance that the hit will be serious. If it hits a vulnerable spot there is only a 25 percent chance that I will be hit. If I am hit there is only a 25 percent chance that it will be fatal. With odds like that, why should I worry?"[30]

At any rate, sometimes you just had to have luck to survive, and that applied to both the aircraft and their crews. Several Lancasters could be singled out for their combat longevity, including "Able Mabel," a 100 Squadron Lancaster flown operationally by Canadian pilots Jack Playford and Lloyd C. "Mo" Morrison.[31] Of the Canadian-built Lancaster Xs, KB 732, coded VR-X from 419 Squadron, was arguably the greatest of them all. KB 732 was the thirty-third of 430 Mark Xs to roll off Malton's Victory Aircraft assembly line. Christened "X-Terminator" by 419 Squadron, it became the first Canadian-built "Lanc" to shoot down an enemy fighter, when gunners Bill Mann and Paul Burton blasted down a Ju 88 over Achères, France, on the night of 7/8 June 1944. Both of these gunners eventually received DFMs for this action. Prior to war's end, "X-Terminator" amassed eighty-four combat operations, the last being a raid on Wangerooge, 6 Group's final combat operation of the war. It never failed to bring its crews home safe and sound.[32]

In contrast, some aircraft proved to be unlucky when associated with the assignment of the three-letter squadron and individual identification codes. Perhaps the most notorious of these was 425 Squadron's KW-G, "G-George." However, "G" for Ginx," as this cursed series of aircraft became known far and wide throughout 6 Group, applied only to Wellingtons and Halifaxes. The European war ended before this coding could be applied to any of the unit's Lancasters which came into service late in the war.

> Eight bombers, two Wellingtons and six Halifaxes, had carried squadron code KW-G during the *Alouette's* 30-plus months in action. Two were lost on their first mission. Five prior to the seventh. Six had been destroyed in fatal crashes. All had been subject to what, in retrospect, can only be considered a bizarre gremlin. But the toll in aircrew, all young and eager to help the cause of peace, had been even greater.
>
> In May 1945, when the squadron started receiving its new Lancaster bombers for use with Tiger Force, likely no-one thought about the one carrying KW-G. Fortunately for some aircrew, however, the war in the Far East ended before the jinx was tested again there.[33]

Once a bomber was mortally hit, the crew usually only had seconds to react in order to save their lives. If they survived the crippling attack and had the opportunity to bail out of a disabled bomber, the crew faced exposure to fire, the structural failure of aircraft components, the inability to reach escape hatches, especially in the Lancaster, the less-than-perfect reliability of parachutes, and subsequent exposure to oxygen deprivation, frostbite, and perilous landing conditions. Sadly, moving more than a few feet in a wildly-gyrating stricken bomber was often impossible. This condition particularly applied to those Bomber Command aircrew obliged to negotiate the notorious main wing spar of the Lancaster, which was imbedded deep in the fuselage. While the following comments are American in origin, they are also certainly applicable to Bomber Command operations:

> That horrible plunge to earth; this is what unnerved even the bravest. The parachute did not always promise succor. There were ships that were torn in half, or had a wing blown loose to flip-flop crazily through space, while the bomber whirled in a tight spin, and centrifugal forces pinned the men inside helplessly, like flies smashed against a wall. How long does it take to fall 25,000 feet inside the blasted wreck of a Flying Fortress? Whom is there to ask?[34]

Individuals, like aircraft, were also blessed or cursed with good or bad luck. A very few survived four operational tours, while many more were felled on their first combat mission. For others, even in the most seemingly hopeless situations, it was simply not meant to be their time. There is the often-repeated story of one Lancaster rear gunner, blown out of his turret at 18,000 feet over Germany in winter, without his parachute. He landed in a snow-covered bed of pine boughs and suffered little more than superficial cuts and abrasions. Another bizarre incident, as mentioned earlier, occurred on 5 March 1945, when 426 Squadron despatched fourteen Halifax Mark VIIs on a raid. However, freezing fog in the Vale of York claimed LW 219 "Y-Yoke", piloted under the hands of Flight Lieutenant T. Emerson. Under its full bomb and fuel load for the long trip across Germany, it struggled to gain height but, as the flying surfaces iced up, the added weight was just too much and at 15:00 hours, just twenty-one minutes after take-off, "Y-Yoke" fell out of the sky, partially disintegrating in the process. The fuselage fell into Nunthorpe Grove, York, and an engine plummeted into the kitchen of the Nunthorpe Secondary School. The wireless operator/air gunner, Pilot Officer J. Low, bailed out of the disintegrating aircraft, only he was too low and his parachute did not open properly. However, the resulting explosion from the crashing bomber blew him up into the air sufficiently to allow his parachute to deploy, decelerating his fall. He landed heavily on the shed roof, seriously injured. All other crew members were killed. Also five civilians were killed and a further eighteen injured.[35]

At least one aircrew member survived the experience of being pinned inside his spinning bomber by gravitational forces, only to be blown clear to safety when it exploded. Wireless operator Harry Lomas described his emotions at the time: "Having accepted it was physically impossible to escape, I felt no urgent need for despairing frenzied effort. The end would be sudden and painless, and the fear was suddenly expunged. There came no flashbacks of my past life. All I was conscious of was a feeling of resignation and intense sadness that all was going to end like this."[36]

Tail-End Charlie

Of all the bomber crew stations, the most dangerous, the least survivable was held by the man in the rear turret. His was the coldest and most detached position of all. Often the perspex panels on his turret had been removed, the so-called Granston Lodge modification, adopted to facilitate the early spotting of German night fighters. Bundled in extra garments, including electrically-heated suits to ward off the -40° C outside air temperatures, his lot was a miserable one. Since space was extremely limited in the turret, the rear gunner's parachute had to be stored in the aft fuselage. Thus, the gunner had to exit the turret, don the parachute, then rotate the turret door to the stern of the aircraft in order to bail out. In reality, the turret frequently jammed, trapping the gunner inside. At any rate, this method of escape was not recommended in the Lancaster, since all crew members, including the rear gunner, were advised to exit through the emergency hatch in the nose of the aircraft. An egress during flight via the rear fuselage crew entry door on the Lancaster was also fraught with risk during many flight conditions. However, for the rear gunner, encumbered with extra garments and with the greatest distance to travel to safety, exit through the front door hatch was extremely difficult.[37] The odds against this gunner surviving were certainly lengthened by the manufacturer's rather callous disregard for his emergency egress route. Few Lancaster rear gunners survived a mortal hit on their bomber, and they were occasionally seen to be defiantly firing their weapons right up to the instant of ground impact, rather than attempting escape.[38] While the other crew members were huddled together in the nose section in relative security, comfort and mutual support, "Tail-End Charlie" lived, and frequently died, in an isolated and lonely world of his own. Kenneth McDonald was a Canadian born in Bristol, England, who served as a pilot with 78 Squadron in 4 Group, and won the DFC. His is a touching tribute to the rear gunners in general and his own in particular.

> It is the rear gunner who is alone, aft of the tail surfaces, in the slipstream of the four Merlins, from the take-off, when he is first off the ground as the tail lifts with the Halifax's gathering speed, until six or seven or eight hours later he sees the ground coming closer, the approach lights flash by, and the tail wheel hits the runway. All that time, the equivalent of a normal day's work that he has put in at the end of a normal day, he has been on his own in the dark, cold, poised at the levered end of a 71-foot fuselage, his head never still, searching, searching, for the moment when one of the shapes he has learned to recognize appears below, or above, or to one side, and he alone must decide whether its pilot has seen the glow of the Halifax's eight stub exhausts, or is tracking another Halifax, or

a Lancaster, that the gunner can't see. He has already alerted the pilot. If the shape turns, or climbs, or noses down, toward his own aircraft, he does two things at once: he calls "Corkscrew left (or right), go," the moment he fires his four Brownings at the shape, and keeps firing as the turret is dragged down and twisted and pulled up in the stomach-wrenching attitudes of the corkscrew.

It took a special kind of courage to fly as a rear gunner, the "two o'clock in the morning courage" that Napoleon said he had very rarely met. Mac McCoy was like that. He didn't say much. In fact, no-one spoke except to deliver a message, such as change of course, a wireless transmission from base, the bomb-aimer's instructions, or an aircraft sighting. He never complained. On the Turin trip, when he was in cloud most of the way, bumped about and half-frozen, I doubt it occurred to him that he might have left his turret for the less-cold fuselage while we were in cloud. But the cloud might have broken, or a fighter might have found its way to us by radar, so he kept his post . . .

The next time we saw each other after Linton was in 1947, when I drove up to the gate at Trenton and there was Mac, raising the barrier. He had left at the end of the war, didn't care for civilian life, and re-enlisted as the Leading Aircraftman he then was, grinning at me, with his air gunner's brevet and his DFM. We lost touch after that but I still feel closer to him than even the others.[39]

Defensive Capabilities and Tactics

American bombers were generally much more heavily armed, although heavier guns were fitted to some Bomber Command aircraft later in the war. Relying on their massed firepower, most B-17 Fortresses and B-24 Liberators had at least ten .50 calibre flexible machine guns, and when arranged in group formations of multiple combat boxes, they produced a truly formidable volume of protective fire. By contrast, Bomber Command emphasized stealth by night for self-defence, trading speed and increased bomb load for defensive armament. Woefully under-armed, the Command's standard machine gun was the Browning .303 calibre which, although it dispensed significant volumes of lead, lacked the range and destructive power of the heavier guns. Furthermore, ventral turrets were generally removed on Bomber Command aircraft from 1943 onward to make room for the *H2S* radar dome. This lack of defensive coverage from below made Sir Arthur Harris uneasy in the extreme, and he encouraged both formal and localized initiatives to redress this shortcoming. Harris had legitimate cause for concern, since the elimination of the ventral guns allowed the Germans to field a formidable, innovative and deadly weapons system known as *Schräge Musik*, which shall be discussed later.

In order to foil the attacking night fighter's gun tracking solution, Bomber Command crews developed the "corkscrew" manoeuvre. The corkscrew was taught as a last ditch defensive tactic, either to force an attacking enemy night fighter to overshoot the bomber's flight path, or to deny him a stable tracking solution for his guns. This manoeuvre was assiduously practiced by the bomber crews on routine affiliation exercises with Fighter Command aircraft, and it was also extensively and repeatedly briefed prior to operations. If performed correctly, it allowed a bomber to continue on a course while presenting the attacking fighter with an extremely difficult target. When he was warned about a threat from astern, the pilot "firewalled" his throttles while simultaneously banking at forty-five degrees in a diving turn to port or to starboard, depending on the exact location of the threat and guidance from the gunners, losing 1000 feet of altitude in just six seconds. During the manoeuvre, the bomber would normally accelerate to approximately 300 mph. After 1000 feet of descent, and still in the banked turn, the pilot pulled his bomber up into a climb. Then he reversed the turn, bleeding off his airspeed sharply and hopefully forcing a flight path overshoot of the attacking enemy fighter. Regaining his original altitude, and with the airspeed now down to around 185 mph, and still in his turn, the bomber pilot pushed the aircraft down in another dive. Again picking up speed, he descended through 500 feet before commencing another turn reversal. If the enemy night fighter had been particularly tenacious, and had remained "camped at 6 o'clock" to the bomber throughout the evasive action, the bomber pilot was forced to repeat all or a portion of the manoeuvre. The physical effort required to wrestle a heavy bomber around in these extreme conditions was debilitating, and has been compared by some to the labour required from a skilled oarsman pulling hard during a boat race.

Anti-aircraft fire was either barrage flak, which attempted to saturate a given patch of airspace with lead, or it was directed by radar, as were the master searchlights. Barrage flak was extremely difficult to counter, unless areas of known concentrations could be seen and avoided. From 1943 onward, the Pathfinders and later, elements of the Main Force, were actively using avoidance tactics against the radar-directed guns from known sites. The rough rule of thumb, as worked out by the 8 Group Tactics Officer, was to change headings randomly by at least fifteen degrees in either direction every twenty seconds, or vary the altitude by 500 feet every twenty seconds. This would usually cause the radar-directed flak to "lag" the bomber's flight path, although it did nothing to mitigate the possibility of a hit on following aircraft. Once on the final bomb run, and once the aim point had been positively identified, the aircraft had to be held straight and level for the bomb-aimer, no matter how intense the gun defences were over the target. This interval, which undoubtedly felt like an eternity, normally lasted about two minutes.[40] However, once the Mark XIV gyro-stabilized bombsight was in extensive service, more manoeuvring in the target area could be routinely permitted, even, in a limited manner, to the moment of bomb release. After that final run-in, however, the aircraft still had to be held steady for the photoflash, the photographic proof of the accuracy of a bomb drop on target.[41] This vulnerable period, when the bomb-aimer was still in control of the aircraft, was an extremely tense time, since it was during this stage of operations that most aircraft were lost to the radar-directed flak and searchlights. The searchlights were terrifying, as their intense brightness was extremely disorienting. Being thus "coned" by searchlights was both dramatic and unnerving, and often caused pilots to make fatal flying errors, or to lose their nerve and attempt to dive out of the light . . . and into the range of the massed lighter guns clustered below. Many crews did not survive the experience, as described by one who did:

> Turning back was quite out of the question, we therefore flew steadily onward and, as we did do, we found that we were skillfully handed over from one group of searchlights to another. There was nothing we could do in that nightmare situation; it was impossible to see outside our aircraft to any worthwhile degree because of the dazzle, and all sensation of speed seemed to vanish. The world had disappeared and we felt as if we were hanging motionless in space.[42]

Jimmy Sheridan, a 426 Squadron pilot who later won a DFC flying Halifaxes, recalls getting coned and how he got the searchlights to break their deadly lock on him:

> The Ruhr valley was one of the most heavily defended areas in Europe, with hundreds of

flak guns, searchlights and fighters. As one highly-decorated, experienced wing commander put it, "A target in the Ruhr strikes fear into the heart of *any* pilot." It had been stated that if one was coned over the target area, it was impossible to get out of it. Hundreds of searchlights and flak guns would converge on the hapless bomber, creating a cone miles wide. However, fighters *also* converged. Then, all the flak guns would fill the cone with shells, or a fighter would swoop in for the kill.

I was coned one night on a run into target in the Ruhr. I started corkscrewing at full throttle in a shallow dive. In doing so, I noticed that a cloud had formed over the burning target thousands of feet below. I thought that if I could position myself over the cloud, it might break those searchlight beams. By the grace of God, I got there and it did so. I then dropped my bombs and flew home without further incident.[43]

Pilot Bob Pratt summed up the psychological impact of flak: " It scared the hell out of you, to be exact. And anyone who wasn't scared of it is not here with us today."[44]

Thus, the bomber offensive was fraught with risk both from the inherent dangers of flight and from enemy combat. Murray Peden provides an excellent analogy for the effect the repeated confrontation with these risks could have on the crews, knowing as they did that killers were lurking in the darkness, poised to strike them at any time during their bomber's long journey in harm's way:

Compared with the armament they are carrying, you are virtually defenceless. Moreover, you must carry a pail of gasoline and a shopping bag full of dynamite in one hand. If someone rushes at you and begins firing, about all you can do is fire a small calibre pistol in his direction and try to elude him in the dark. But these killers can run twice as fast as you, and if one stalks and catches you, the odds are that he will wound and then incinerate you, or blow you to eternity.

You are acutely aware of these possibilities for every second of the five or six hours you walk in the darkness, braced always, consciously or subconsciously, for a murderous burst of fire, and reminded of the stakes of the game periodically by the sight of guns flashing in the dark and great volcanic eruptions of flaming gasoline.[45]

Unwilling Guests of the Reich

While the odds were stacked against Bomber Command's crews surviving a mortal wound to their aircraft over enemy territory, especially in the Lancaster, many men did successfully exit their stricken aircraft. In all, 9784 Bomber Command aircrew and 54 groundcrew became prisoners of war of the Axis nations, and 138 of them perished in captivity.[46] During the course of the entire war, 2276 RCAF aircrew and fourteen groundcrew members of the RCAF Overseas became prisoners of war.[47] The vast majority, 1849, were members of Bomber Command and thirty-one of them died in Axis hands.[48]

Although most were treated quite fairly as prisoners of the Third Reich, as mandated by the rules of the Geneva Conventions (particularly when compared to prisoner treatment at the hands of the Japanese and in the concentration camps), some prisoners found themselves outside of this generalized protection. In Germany, the *Luftwaffe* was responsible for the incarceration of air force prisoners and their care was generally fair and humane, in spite of erratic and inconsistent supplies of food and basic needs, particularly towards the end of hostilities. During that time, even the parcels from the International Red Cross, which bolstered the rations supplied by the Germans, were no longer being systematically distributed.

Barbara and Reg Lane tie the knot, 3 December 1945, St. John's Church, Moortown, Leeds, Yorkshire.
(Lane Family)

Men with a Purpose. (Author's Collection)

Battle of Germany. The bombing enjoyed wide spread wartime support at home. (Author's Collection)

Canadian ground crew service one of the disappointing and short-serving Avro Manchesters.
(Author's Collection)

Fine study of a Canadian Wellington at dispersal. (DND PC2473)

A 419 Squadron Wellington in flight. (Author's Collection)

Several new aircraft were introduced to operations during the early war years. This Lancaster Mk. I flew with 50 Squadron, one of the first Bomber Command units to be equipped with the aircraft. (Author's Collection)

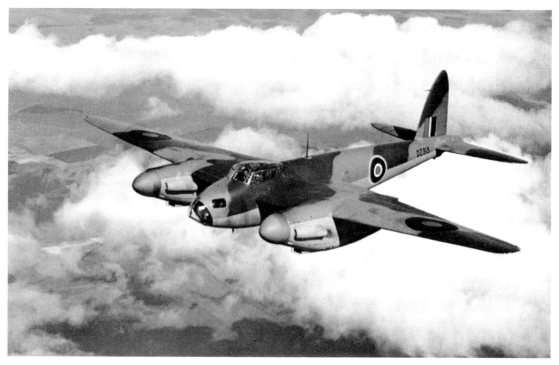

The de Havilland Mosquito was a very capable and flexible aircraft, and it contributed a rich and varied operational life. (DND PMRC 75-346)

NO 6 GROUP BASES IN THE VALE OF YORK

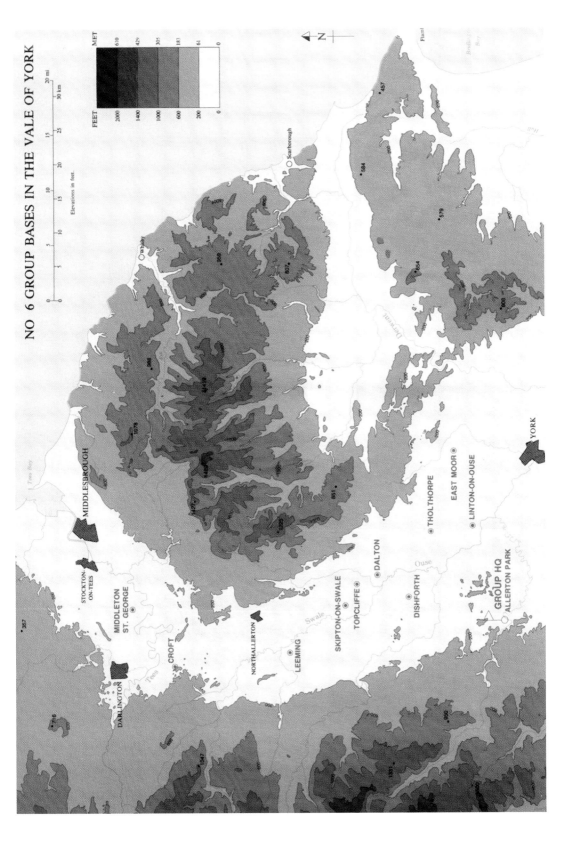

Night Target, 1943 by Miller Brittain. (CWM 10889)

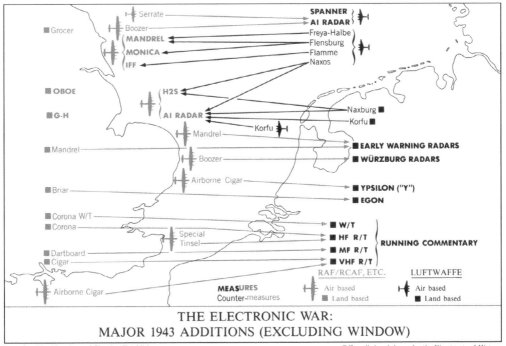

THE ELECTRONIC WAR:
MAJOR 1943 ADDITIONS (EXCLUDING WINDOW)

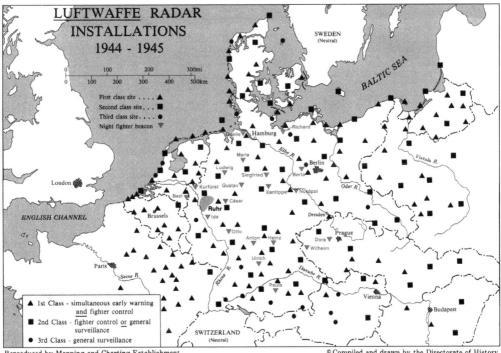

War in the Mediterranean theatre of operations. *Air Raid on San Guisto, Pisa* by Paul Goranson
(CWM 11435)

Disembarkation point for many 6 Group crews proceeding on leave in "The Big Smoke." *King's Cross Station* by Carl Schaefer (CWM 11828)

Marshalling of the Hallies by Paul Goranson (CWM 11402)

Opposite top: "Big Joe" McCarthy (centre) and his distinguished crew of Dambusters. On his immediate right is Pilot Officer Donald Arthur MacLean from Toronto, McCarthy's talented navigator. MacLean, a flight sergeant at the time, was awarded a DFM for his part in the raid. (Author's Collection)

Opposite bottom: Bomber variant Mosquitos on the ground. (Author's Collection)

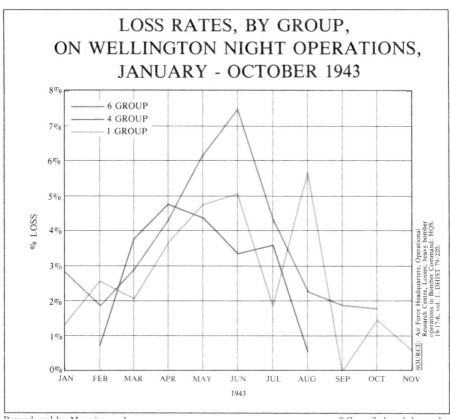

LOSS RATES, BY GROUP,
ON WELLINGTON NIGHT OPERATIONS,
JANUARY - OCTOBER 1943

6 GROUP
4 GROUP
1 GROUP

% LOSS

8%
7%
6%
5%
4%
3%
2%
1%
0%

JAN   FEB   MAR   APR   MAY   JUN   JUL   AUG   SEP   OCT   NOV

1943

SOURCE: Air Force Headquarters, Operational Research Centre, Losses; heavy bomber operations in Bomber Command: HQS. 19-17-6, vol. 1. DHIST 79/220.

Reproduced by Mapping and
Charting Establishment.

© Compiled and drawn by
the Directorate of History.

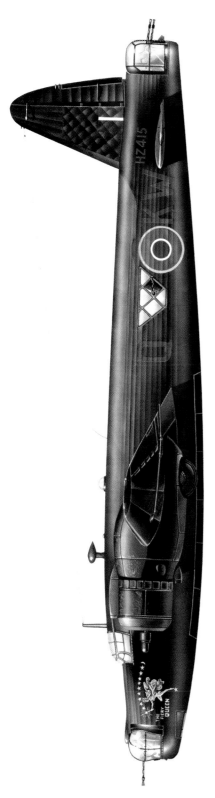

Vickers Wellington Mk.X, *The Fiery Queen*, in service with 425 "Alouette" Squadron as part of 331 Wing in North Africa. The name and nose art later adorned a Halifax B Mk. III when 425 Squadron converted to the new type on its return to England from the Mediterranean theatre. Painting by Ron Lowry. (Not to scale)

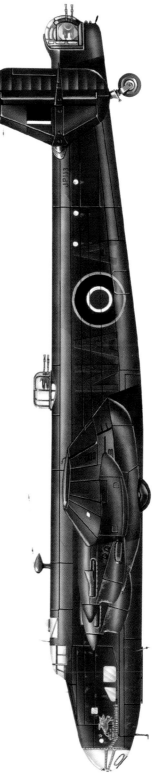

Handley Page Halifax Mk. II, *Git Up Them Stairs*, from 428 "Ghost" Squadron. The name was actually a sardonic reference to the aircraft type's limited ability to climb to higher (and safer) bombing altitudes. This aircraft was attacked by a German night fighter on a sortie to Lens on 21 April 1944 and subsequently made a crash landing at Attlebridge in Norfolk. Painting by Ron Lowry. (Not to scale)

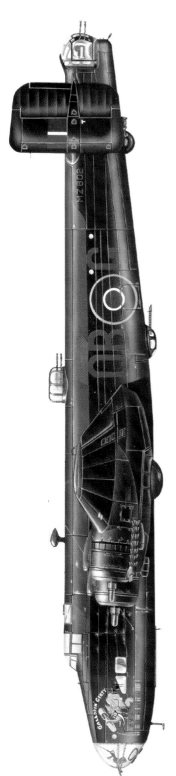

Handley Page Halifax Mk. III, *Gallopin' Gerty*, from 424 "Tiger" Squadron. The elephant's name is *Fi-Fi*, and this is the aircraft in which Conspicuous Gallantry Medal winner Peter Engbrecht scored the majority of his air-to-air gunnery victories. Painting by Ron Lowry. (Not to scale)

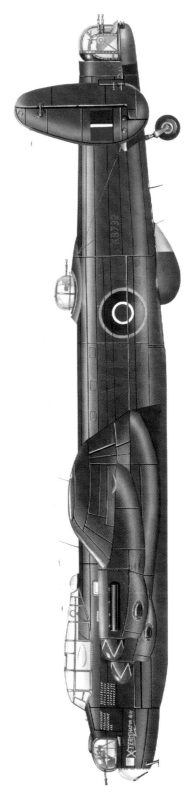

Lancaster Mk.X, *X-Terminator*, an eventual eighty-four operations veteran from 419 "Moose" Squadron, whose gunners also managed to shoot down two German fighters. Unfortunately, although it survived the war, the aircraft was not preserved for posterity. Painting by Ron Lowry. (Not to scale)

As the war waged on into late 1944 and 1945, however, and the bombing became even more widespread, Joseph Goebbels whipped up resentment against the *Terrorfliegers* among an increasingly frightened, disenchanted, and embittered civilian populace, much as Ilya Ehrenburg did for the Soviets. Day-to-day life in Germany was becoming increasingly chaotic; the breakdown of order and restraint became progressively more routine. In this atmosphere the search for escaping prisoners of war placed an additional manpower burden on a system now stretched to the breaking point. Accordingly, new laws and policies were promulgated with respect to escaping prisoners. Airmen parachuting into Germany were often assaulted and beaten, and occasionally lynched on landing. The fury of their captors was largely dependant on when and where the capture occurred. In the immediate wake of the February 1945 Dresden raid, Goebbels suggested to Hitler that several thousand Allied prisoners should be executed in reprisal. This suggestion was welcomed by Hitler, Jodl, Keitel and other members of the Nazi ruling elite, but it was totally opposed by Hermann Göring.[49]

These initiatives had official, albeit secret, sanction under the terms of the *Kugel Erlass*—the Bullet Decree—of 1944. This directive called for captured aircrew, particularly those who were re-captured after attempting escape, to be transported to the Maulthausen concentration camp near Vienna, where they were either to be immediately executed or worked to death by hauling rocks up the staircase to the quarry located there. "More than 40 American, British and Dutch officers were so treated within a few months—the latest in a long series of German actions against captured soldiers, ranging from the notorious Commando Order of 1942, which led to the murder of many British Commando soldiers, to the execution of 50 RAF [and Allied] officers captured after the 'Great Escape' from *Stalag Luft III* in March 1944."[50] Other aircrew were murdered by fanatics or by the *Gestapo* in the course of escape attempts or on re-capture. It is worth emphasizing that, while he was guilty of many other crimes against humanity, Hermann Göring, along with many other soldiers and German civilians, was totally opposed to these atrocities: "Göring offered Allied aircrew his personal protection, and the *Luftwaffe* and *Wehrmacht* soldiers generally took no part in reprisals against Allied flyers, frequently rescuing them from beatings or murder at the hands of Nazi Party members or the mob."[51]

However, the new official direction for the treatment of POWs came as the result of the escape of many air force prisoners from *Stalag Luft III* at Sagan, some 160 kilometres southeast of Berlin in Upper Silesia, on the night of 24/25 March 1944. This mass break-out from two of the original three tunnels superbly engineered by the prisoners yielded seventy-six escapees before the stampede was detected and curtailed. Hitler, incensed, ordered all those recaptured to be executed. However, he eventually calmed down, and on the advice of Heinrich Himmler—that the execution of all of the escapees could pose a credibility problem in future, agreed that more than half of those recaptured were to be shot and cremated. The subsequent directive was teleprinted to *Gestapo* headquarters under Himmler's order, and a list of fifty was culled from the seventy-six escapees by General Nebe and Dr. Hans Merton. These men were taken away singly or in small groups by representative agents from various *Gestapo* field districts or regional headquarters. "The *Gestapo* groups submitted almost identical reports that 'the prisoners, whilst relieving themselves, bolted for freedom and were shot whilst trying to escape.' This famous expression has now passed into history as a euphemism for cold-blooded murder."[52]

Of the seventy-six escapees, fifty were murdered, twenty-three were eventually returned to prison camps, and three escaped to freedom via either neutral Sweden or Gibraltar. Among the fifty slain were five members of the RCAF, including four aircrew members of Bomber Command.[53] Postwar trials conducted by the Allies in 1947 and 1948 resulted in the execution or imprisonment of many of the perpetrators, while the Soviets disposed of others. Still more committed suicide rather than face legal accounting for their crimes, while others were killed accidentally or in combat during the Reich's final hours.[54]

While the mass escape from *Stalag Luft III* is the best-known atrocity committed against Allied airmen, there were others. "Between 1 February and 30 April 1945 as many as seven RCAF airmen may have been murdered, including Flying Officer T.D. Scott of No. 432 Squadron, shot down after the 15/16 March raid on Hagen and executed by the *Gestapo* the next day. Two more were shot after bailing out near Opladen on 30 March."[55] Even earlier Squadron Leader Edward Weyman Blenkinsop of Victoria, British Columbia, the Deputy Master Bomber for the raid over Montzen, France, on the night of 27/28 April 1944, was the sole survivor from his Lancaster. Blenkinsop was piloting one of the ten Canadian bombers felled from fifty-five RCAF sorties generated that night.

> Succoured by the Belgian "underground" Resistance, Blenkinsop elected to continue the fight with them rather than attempt a return to England. He was finally captured by the *Gestapo* in December 1944 while participating in an attempt to blow up a house used by the Germans. Never identified as a downed airman, he was eventually sent to Neuengamme concentration camp where he died of heart failure on 23 January 1945, it has been suggested, as the result of a lethal injection.[56]

Perhaps Blenkinsop, whose name is inscribed on the Runnymede Memorial, ventured beyond the pale and forfeited his rights as a captured airman by working with the Resistance and engaging in acts of sabotage while in civilian clothing. On the same night, it would appear that Flight Lieutenant G.J. Smith from 405 Squadron, who was shot down over Belgium was deliberately allowed to bleed to death from serious head wounds in a German hospital at Dienst. As a result of postwar investigation, charges of "gross negligence" were filed with the United Nations War Crimes Commission against the German attending physician, but by then, the Commission's stale leads had evaporated.[57]

Sometimes there were fewer doubts. It was almost certain, for example, that Flying Officer W.S. Sewell of 434 Squadron, shot down over Kassel on 22/23 October 1943 "had been . . . hanged by the civilians in Kassel on landing." And it was even clearer that Flying Officers H.W. Birnie and D.S. Jamieson of No. 426 Squadron, who were shot down over France on 28/29 June 1944 and who tried to return to the Allied lines in civilian clothes, had been executed by the *Gestapo*.[58]

Yet another casualty was Flying Officer Roy E. Carter of 431 Squadron, a navigator shot down in a Halifax on the Sterkrade raid of 16/17 June 1944.

> Roy Carter bailed out successfully, but while he was being hidden by Dutch civilians in a house at Tilburg, he was discovered by the Germans on 8 July and shot, together with a Pathfinder pilot from 83 Squadron and an Australian airman. The bloodstained Dutch flag which covered the bodies after their death was brought to England in 1983 and placed in the No. 83 Squadron Memorial Chapel in Coningsby Parish Church.[59]

An American serviceman named G.B. Lloyd from Exchange, West Virginia, wrote the following in a letter to Roy Carter's mother on 16 April 1946:

I met Roy at a little village called Dinther in North Brabant, Holland, about the 28th or 29th of June 1944. He had only been shot down a little over ten days then. We travelled together to Schÿndel and then to Tilburg, where we arrived Tuesday, July 4th, [and] we had to go to separate houses. [In] one house there were two other boys (RAF) and the folk spoke English (Mrs. Koba's). At the other place [there] was only room for one and no-one spoke English, so since I had been down since March 6th and spoke some Dutch, I was taken there. Saturday evening, one of the organization came and told me that Roy and I would be taken to Belgium the next day. [On] Sunday, July 9th, I was waiting for the organization to come for me when one of them came and very excitedly told me that three of the *Gestapo* (Dutch working with the Germans) had broken into the Koba home and with no offer to let them surrender or anything, shot the three flyers who were there. [He also said] that they had captured several of the Underground and would be looking for me shortly. This boy and I left immediately and hid in the woods until Thursday when we went to Antwerp, Belgium. Sunday, I was turned over to the *Gestapo* by some false organization people.

After a period of about three weeks in a dungeon, I landed in a prison camp and stayed there until liberated by the Russians on April 30, 1945 . . .

Now, while I have no actual proof by seeing, I am sure in my own mind that Roy was one of the boys murdered by the *Gestapo* at Mevrouw Koba's. She was shot at a camp that same week. During the few days I spent near Tilburg, I did all the investigating that my faculties would allow. I saw in a Dutch paper that the *Gestapo* had "liquidated three terrorists in the home of Mevrouw Koba on Diepstraat." I learned that the name of the *Gestapo* leader was Piet Gerrits, which I reported when I was liberated and [I subsequently] heard he was captured.[60]

After the executions, the bodies were taken to nearby Vught concentration camp and then cremated. Roy Carter's name is also inscribed on the Runnymede Memorial. He was posthumously awarded a Mention-in-Despatches.[61]

Association with Resistance forces in the Occupied territories, either by contrivance or by happenstance, could generate dreadful repercussions for Allied airmen, as Ed Carter-Edwards, a wartime member of 427 "Lion" Squadron, flying Halifaxes out of Leeming, recalls. Carter-Edwards had dreadful experiences, and his words are all the more chilling when written in his spare style:

Completed 21 ops. Shot down on #22—8 June 1944 at 1:30 AM, west of Paris. Target—Acheres but we never reached it—bailed out from our burning Halifax. Assisted by French Underground but betrated to the *Gestapo* by a collaborator. I was classified as a spy and saboteur and threatened with execution. Then, I was horribly beaten and thrown into Fresnes, a civilian prison run by the *Gestapo* and those sadistic SS (Death's Head) forces. Eventually, I was taken by French cattle cars (80-90 per car) to the Buchenwald concentration camp to be executed. Here, we witnessed and also experienced sadistic, barbaric acts of inhuman indecency inflicted on innocent prisoners. After 3 months in Buchenwald, we were taken to *Stalag Luft III* on a death march in January '45. Then, by box car to Marlag-Milag. Then, another march in April '45, and eventual liberation near Lübeck on the 5th of May, 1945.[62]

In spite of the daunting odds, some airmen successfully evaded capture and made good their flight to freedom. Escape was seldom straightforward, exemplified by the case of Sergeant Jean Louis Nazaire Warren from 434 Squadron. Warren, a native of Pointe-au-Pic and Murray Bay,

Quebec, had been shot down over Cologne in November 1943. Injured during the crash of his aircraft, he gave himself up for treatment and was subsequently imprisoned at *Stalag IVB* at Mühlburg. After making a successful "trial" escape attempt on 17 March 1944, he made a further successful break on 1 May and eventually made contact with the Dutch Underground at Borne. Later, he and a companion moved to Nijverdal, away from increased activity and attention from the Germans in the area.

> Early in August 1944, Sergeant Warren moved [again] to Zwolle and hid in a boat until the end of the month when he was given shelter in a castle near Hattem. The German search parties were very active, but he successfully evaded them and eventually reached Gorssel, where he remained for eight weeks. Six of the weeks were spent hiding in a cave under a pigsty with two Poles and a Dutchman. The Germans made a surprise search and the members of the party were ultimately arrested. After brutal treatment they were taken to the Landwacht prison. Although Sergeant Warren produced his identity discs, he was treated as a terrorist and badly manhandled during interrogation. Later, he was put in a cell measuring 6 feet X 12 feet with thirteen others.
>
> For three weeks they remained in the cell with no one being allowed out for any purpose. Later, he was taken to an empty house for interrogation and further brutal treatment was carried out. Eventually, Sergeant Warren was moved to Oxelhoft where conditions were even worse. On 1 February 1945, he and 93 others were put into two boxcars and sent to Germany.
>
> During the journey, some of the party pried open a window of the boxcar and made an attempt to escape, but the guards saw them and opened fire. Sergeant Warren succeeded in getting away and evading capture by wading through waist-high water all night. The next evening, he made contact with the Underground organization and was taken to Lobith. The next night, an attempt to cross the Rhine River was made, but those who tried had to return to the starting point, owing to strong enemy opposition. The party was then taken to a farm to be evacuated. Sergeant Warren and some others posed as members of the farmer's family and moved with them. Later, he posed as a Dutch policeman in order to prevent being taken again. He continued to evade capture until liberated by British forces in April 1945.[63]

This amazing odyssey, worthy of a Hollywood movie, ended in Sergeant Warren receiving a very well-deserved British Empire Medal for his prolonged gallantry and resolve.[64]

A Happy Exception

Not all experiences of Allied airmen shot down over Axis territory were unpleasant in the extreme, aside from the pain of losing friends in combat. In fact, those experiences were occasionally as bizarre as they were unique. Witness the late-war adventures of Sergeant A.D. Dennis, the flight engineer of Flying Officer H.R. Sproule's all-RCAF Halifax VII crew, flying with 408 Squadron out of Linton-on-Ouse:

> On the morning of 2 March 1945, we were assigned to take-off in "F-Freddie" for a close-cooperation raid on Cologne. Due to difficulties with this aircraft on the previous mission and the fact that we were carrying a 2800 pound overload, we expressed concerns about taking it. We were then assigned to fly "R-Roger." In the dark we loaded aboard and as everyone got settled, the pilot, Herbie Sproule and I, proceeded to start engines. In spite of all I and the groundcrew did, we were not able to get the first engine started. So after

a brief exchange of "Oh-dear-me's," we were reluctantly given airframe EQ 715, "T-Tear." I say "reluctantly" because "T-Tear" was a brand-new Halifax Mark VIIA with only fifteen flying hours on it, and the first new aircraft the squadron had seen in some time. I can imagine that there was some reluctance to entrust this prize to a junior crew.

We stumbled in the dark out of "R-Roger," across to the next dispersal and climbed aboard "T-Tear." By this time everyone else was ready to go. Our start-up was done in record time and before everyone was quite settled, we were rolling. I had made a brief mental note as I walked up to the aircraft that the call numbers added up to thirteen . . .

We were stacked at the bottom and the end of the second wave, so as we approached the target, there was plenty of flak. Overhead the target, there were several hits on aircraft around us. We dropped our load right on target at 10:15 hours, turned south out of the target area, then west again for home. This whole time, we were experiencing a great amount of flak. The German army was then bottled up in the Cologne area and all along the Rhine, trying to get across the river in front of the American advance. All their firpower was brought to bear on this raid. As we turned west, Herbie Sproule asked for more power to climb a bit out of this mess. I stepped out of the astrodome, moved up to the throttles, and for no reason that now makes sense, noted that it was 10:18 hours. The next recollection I have was that of viewing the back of the pilot's head as I extracted myself from a pile of junk back in the rest-bed area, while I simultaneously unhooked the nose pieces of my dark glasses from up my nostrils.

There was no roof, windshield, sides, instruments, or radio equipment between the mid-upper turret and the pilot's seat, except for the door to the engineer's compartment, which contained my parachute in the pocket of the door. As I crawled up the floor to the front of the aircraft, I saw that the oxygen bottles had all exploded, and where I had been standing seconds before was a large hole. I took my 'chute out of the door and clipped it on, then the door promptly blew away. I then saw movement forward in the nose, and Jim and Moose (navigator and bomb-aimer) did a quick exit out the front hatch. I remember thinking that they never even waved good-bye. In all fairness, Jim had been blown on top of Moose's back in the nose of the aircraft, and by the time he got back to check, he found the wireless operator dead, the area where I was standing was blue sky, and the pilot was kneeling on his seat trying to assess the situation. So Jim felt that they were all alone, and thus the hasty exit. It appears that an 88mm shell hit the plate under the pilot's seat, exploding the oxygen bottles, killing the wireless operator. And wounding the mid-upper gunner and myself. Johnny Street, the mid-upper, managed to get back and tell Vern Hunt, the tail gunner, to bail out, but he was unable to get out of the aircraft himself.

Herbie and I did a short appraisal of our situation by sign language. It is difficult to do much conversing with a 160 mph -10° C wind in your face. We decided to leave the aircraft, even though we were still flying, as we had no engine controls, and try as we might, we could not decide in which direction we were heading.

I made sure Herbie was all clear to get out of his seat, waved good-bye, then went down and rolled out of the front hatch. My 'chute came out in a stringer and in spite of the fact that I felt my left arm was broken, I wasted no time in pulling shroud lines to get it to take air. When the 'chute finally opened, it was a mixed blessing, as flak had torn through the pack in the aircraft and it looked more like a lace curtain. The skirt was cut, along with a shroud line, and that whole gore was ripped to nearly the top of the 'chute. So along with all the holes, there were two complete gores open. I recall looking at the mess above me and remembered an article in "TE-EM," a wartime flight safety magazine, about a Spitfire pilot who had landed safely with 300 bullet holes in his 'chute. I thought to myself that if he could do it with 300 holes, I could do it with this mess. Perhaps my

Caterpillar Club pin, subsequently awarded for a life-saving parachute descent, should have only been two-thirds the length of everyone else's . . .

As I enjoyed the quiet weightlessness of the fall, I did an assessment of my situation. My left arm felt as though it was broken, but was by now only bleeding slightly from all the holes I could see from the wrist to the elbow. I tucked it into my harness so that it would not flop around on landing. At this point, I was resigned to breaking both legs because of the speed of my descent. The top of my head felt rather mushy and wet, but there was no pain, so I assumed that my thick skull had survived. The fact that I could see only gray haze from my right eye bothered me the most. The right side of my back felt like I had been kicked by a horse, but apart from all that, I seemed to be in good shape. During this whole descent, I felt as though I was a third person watching the whole scene. The 80 mph winds over the target area were still with us and I was making a fair ground speed on my descent. It was evident that my landing was going to be into a treed area, so I tried to hang limp with my face covered and my legs together, just sneaking an occasional peek until I saw the ground start to rush up. Someone had told me that this period of the descent took eleven to twelve seconds, so I waited and waited. I counted out fifteen seconds, and tried to reason why my senses were not responding. "If I were dead, then the brain must still be able to think, and I could still feel some sensations. If I was alive, then I should have a look around and see where I was." I finally took a good look from under my arm, and there I was, just two feet from the ground in a huge Alder tree. I turned the harness buckle and dropped to the ground. There was no way I was going to attempt to dispose of my 'chute, as there was a branch through every one of the holes, and the 'chute literally belonged to the tree. I later heard it took a crew two days to cut down the tree and remove the 'chute.

No-one came to the landing site, so, seeing a farm house about a half-mile away, I made my way along some fences up to the house. At this point, I knew that I was not going to remain conscious for very long, and the head wound was slowing me up a little. Nothing in our training had prepared me for the next turn of events. We were well inside Germany, just south of Bonn, outside the little town of Bad Godesberg. I rang the door-bell and then stepped back from the door, because I realized I was not too presentable a sight. The door was opened by a twelve-year-old girl who ran calling for her mother. I stood there trying to prepare a sentence in my high school German to explain my situation. When the lady of the house arrived, she calmly asked me, "What do you want me to do?" It took me a second or two to realize that I was hearing perfect English. I assured her that I was not armed, and would she please notify the authorities that I was there and needed medical help, and could I please have somewhere to sit down out of the cold until they arrived. She took me by the arm into the house, calling directions to someone else as she led me to the most elegant master bedroom I ever expected to see in a farm house. They spread a huge towel on the bed and me on top of it. After a quick look to make sure that there were no wounds still bleeding, they covered me up to keep me warm until the medical team arrived from the village. The team consisted of the local doctor and the priest. They made jokes about how they had all the eventualities covered between them, such as, if the doctor wasn't needed, then the priest was. The clergyman took my Rolex off my left arm, washed the blood off, wound the watch and put it back on my right wrist. As soon as this team left, I was told it would be at least two days before the army could get through to pick me up as things were badly disrupted because of our raid. The lady of the house removed all my blood-soaked clothes for washing and gave me a sponge bath to lessen the danger of shock. I then phased in and out of consciousness for the next day or so, but each time I woke up, my "little nurse," the daughter, was sitting by the bed ready with a drink of tea or juice or something to eat. Then, her brother would come in to relay some further information, such as, where and how the wireless operator and the mid-upper gunner were buried, or how they were coming along with recovering my 'chute, or, most interestingly, how the pilot and tail gunner were doing locked up in the town jail, singing with the local children through the cell window.

The area around Bonn was occupied by Canadians after the First World War, and it seemed that everyone around there had either a whole family or at least one member of the family living in Canada, so I was presented with a steady stream of visitors coming to see that this Canadian was being well looked after. Even the gun crew that claimed the hit came in to see how I was and offered me their cigarettes. So you see, up to this point, things were not as we had been briefed.

On the third evening, an army doctor and driver arrived in an ambulance to take me to the hospital at Remagen . . . My stay in hospital there was punctuated with a very lively artillery battle over the Ludendorff railway bridge over the Rhine at that point. I was witness to General Patton's troops taking that bridge. I was then liberated around 10 March and removed to an American hospital at Reims. I then had to remain in the MASH hospital in France for over a month until I was well enough to travel on my own to Brussels for identification. Being the only permanent patient in the hospital, I received a great deal of care, resulting in my gaining some thirty pounds, which caused some embarrassment on my return to Bournemouth . . .

My pilot used to berate me for not wanting to take part in escape drills, and so on. It was my theory that, in life, you rode with fate and any respectable return would be by taxi . . .

After some sick leave I was back in Bournemouth, screening returning aircrew POWs for about six weeks, when one morning, I met Herbie Sproule, my pilot, going to breakfast. He looked awful. He was wearing exactly what he had been shot down in, and he had been marched 500 miles by the Germans near the end. After a truly warm greeting, we went in to breakfast together. It was halfway through breakfast before he realized that I had been true to my philosophy after the bail-out, and all the time and sympathy he had expended in the past on my welfare had been wasted. And to top it off, I had ridden all the way back from the war while he was walking! This, I think, ruined his breakfast, if not his whole day. After breakfast, we hooked up with our navigator, bomb-aimer and tail gunner.

Over the years, they have softened their reproach, and we are on very close terms, but do not ask Herbie Sproule, our pilot, to walk anywhere.[65]

The Electronic War

Bomber Command deliberately purchased stealth, speed and increased bomb carriage capacity at the expense of reduced self-defence capabilities and placed a great amount of faith in electronic deception, warning and jamming equipment, and associated techniques. *Window*, so enormously successful at Hamburg, was supplemented by *Mandrel*, which was an electronic method of jamming the early warning radars. However, the Germans eventually countered with *Freya-Halbe*, *Mammut*, and *Wassermann* radars, all with various anti-jamming properties. And the Germans also had their own jammers. *Heinrich* and *Bumerang*, to deal with *Gee* and *Oboe* respectively, and *Naxos* and *Naxburg* to home on *H2S*. As a counter to the AI *Lichtenstein* radar and the infrared detection device known as *Spanner*, which homed on a bomber's hot engine exhausts, the Command fielded *Monica*, a warning radar designed specifically to cover the bomber's vulnerable stern area. German countermeasures to *Monica* followed, notably the *FuG 22 Flensburg*, which homed on the British innovation. Naturally, the Command soon introduced counter-countermeasures. However, one lesson that was only slowly and painfully learned by both sides was that most of this sophisticated new technology left an electronic signature, thus providing an unintentional marker as to a particular transmitter's whereabouts. Many aircraft were lost from both fighting camps due to this new phenomenon. Bomber Command's myopia about electronic signatures started as early as the spring of 1942. At that time, there was a widespread yet irrational belief, fostered by a few incredible coincidences, that the electronic cycling of the Identification Friend or Foe (IFF) equipment prevented enemy radar-directed searchlights and flak from locating the bombers. So widespread was this misguided belief that the Air Ministry actually for a time approved a modification to the IFF called the "J-Switch," which allowed the aircraft to emit an electronic footprint for one-half second every twelve seconds in a highly predictable manner. In effect, this misguided procedure was providing an excellent homing beacon to the Germans.[66]

Bogus radio transmissions from England to German night fighters, code-named *Drumstick*, *Fidget* and *Jostle*, later supplemented by the airborne *Tinsel* transmissions, further served to confuse and deceive. "All these exotic tools and techniques came into play incrementally, spread over the length and breadth of the bomber offensive, each with its own grotesque identifier—*Cigar* and *Airborne Cigar*, *Corona*, *Dartboard*, *Grocer*, *Piperack*, *Perfectos* and *Shiver* on one side, *Donnerkell*, *Dudelsack*, *Erstling*, *Flamme*, *Laubfrosch*, *Lux* and *Sagebock* on the other."[67]

Yet, while most of these innovations lent progressively more accuracy, efficiency, and sophistication to the bomber war, it was the undisputed, sustained courage of the crews—volunteers all, who brought these new technologies to the combat arena, night after night—that made the campaign a distinct if costly success. In the words of Canadian historians Brereton Greenhous and Hugh Halliday: "The bomber offensive of 1942–43 and the first months of 1944 was the Second World War's equivalent of the First World War's Somme and Passchendaele."[68]

Training for Combat

By 1943 the RCAF presence in Britain was enormous,[69] and postings there now followed established patterns. After negotiating the Atlantic on a troop ship, first stop for most Canadian aircrew was the RCAF Reception Depot in the coastal resort town of Bournemouth. Usually, in relatively short order, bomber aircrew were shipped out for follow-on training at an Advanced Flying Unit (AFU), an Operational Training Unit (OTU) and a Heavy Conversion Unit (HCU). Jack Bower-Binns of Aylmer, Quebec, served a distinguished tour as a navigator in 4 Group with 578 Squadron. He won the DFC in the course of thirty-seven operations and was cited for his enthusiasm, fine offensive spirit, fearlessness, and the consistently high standard of his work.[70] However, that was all in the future. Here, he comments on his good fortune in obtaining essential transport early, and on his advanced training, including the seemingly casual nature of crew pairings, which resembled the selection of partners at a Saturday night dance.

> The ship (the *Queen Elizabeth,* which sailed from New York) was crammed with American soldiers, who seemed to pass the whole crossing playing craps. The crossing took less than five days to Greenoch in Scotland. The train ride to the RCAF Reception Depot in Bournemouth took a whole day!
>
> Time in Bournemouth was taken up with dances at the *Pavilion,* but also refresher courses and parades. I recall one parade when my best friend Jimmy Hatchwell and I were

in the rear rank when we spotted a couple of Raleigh bikes in a shop window. Nothing was said but we both broke off and raced into the shop and we purchased them—one each! And for only £ 6.0.0. each. I kept mine the whole of my stay in the UK and gave it to my young brother-in-law when I returned to Canada.

From Bournemouth I was posted to a battle course in Sidmouth in Devon, and then on to #10 (Observer) AFU at Dumfries in Scotland. It was noteworthy mainly because the staff on this station had their own private Mess, which was kept quite separate from us students. This didn't stop us from having a bang-up party at the end of the course in which many of the less-aloof staff joined in. The flying highlight on this course was probably almost ditching in the Irish Sea when the pilot took some little time to find the reason for the starboard engine cutting out and getting it restarted!

The OTU was noteworthy for the crewing-up exercise. My pilot and I met on the platform at the railway station in Kinloss—quite by accident. We hit it off immediately. I found our bomb aimer (a Canadian, Dave Robertson) in the Mess and the Skipper found the gunners and wireless operator in the NCO's Mess. Flying was exciting in the old Whitley bombers. Circuits and bumps—and long cross-country navigation exercises, mostly over the sea—lots of cloud and not many navigation aids. Got excitingly lost once over the North Sea, and another time, we ground-looped the kite on landing back at base. There were no injuries, only a bruised ego . . .

Our conversion to Halifaxes was quite uneventful. We picked up our flight engineer there and proceeded to 51 Squadron, from which we were in on the formation of 578 Squadron from the very beginning. We completed 37 operational sorties, which included Berlin, Stuttgart, Schweinfurt, Frankfurt, Düsseldorf, Karlsruhe, Essen, Gelsenkirchen, Kiel, some rail yards, "V" weapons sites, ports, aerodromes, and so on. After the invasion, we helped the army at Caen and other places. Of course, we had much excitement with flak, searchlights, fighters, engines shot out, and landings away from base at fighter and American aerodromes in fog and other bad weather, and with disabled aircraft. Perhaps the greatest of all events was the great joy and relief of seeing daybreak, back safely at base, after long, hard trips to Germany.

Later, I spent about six months instructing navigators on Halifaxes and Lancasters at Conversion Units. During this time, the war in Europe ended, and I shall never forget the huge gathering in the city of York. All at once, the vast crowd stilled. The band struck up *Land of Hope and Glory*, and all joined in singing the verses. Without any doubt, this was the most moving expression of relief, joy and pent-up feelings of thanksgiving I have ever experienced.[71]

Merrill Burnett, a gunner and eventual DFM winner with 426 "Thunderbird" Squadron, also recalls the suprisingly unsophisticated crew allocation process, as it was practiced at the Operational Training Units:

At #22 OTU, the method used was to assemble all the new aircrew in a large room or hanger. Each aircrew trade was grouped together; for example, bomb-aimers, navigators, wireless operators and air gunners. Then, pilot would approach each group and ask if someone wanted to fly with him. Any uncrewed personnel were then either held over or transferred to another Operational Training Unit.[72]

The New World Meets the Old World

Crew structuring was significantly different between the American and British bomber forces, and the formality of rank was often much more blurred in the American military. Bomber Command essentially consisted of two air forces; the pre-war, largely commissioned, upper-middle class, public school Regular force, and the vast augmentation of largely non-commissioned volunteers from the lower-middle and working classes. Class structure was still very much an element of British military society during the Second World War, and its hierarchy harboured grave concerns about the dilution through battle casualties of their public school, upper-class core element. Regular force officers and senior NCOs were often exasperated by the appearance and conduct of many of the temporary officers and NCOs. This mind set is important, since it helps explain the relatively Draconian approach the RAF would later adopt in dealing with those who could no longer face combat, particularly the NCOs. Roger Coulombe, a pilot with 426 Squadron, became famous as "The Berlin Kid," flying in a record twelve of the nineteen major attacks on the city during August 1943 to March 1944. He was also commissioned and won a coveted "Immediate DFC" along the way. Coulombe recalls the early days of his tour at Linton, conducted initially as a sergeant pilot:

> I got along fine with the three British "blokes" in my crew, but I didn't like the British administration officers all that much. We sure had to march stiff and straight in what they called the "attention area," that is, near the administration buildings, especially so if you were a non-commissioned officer. Otherwise, some English administration officer would open his office window and order you to get close so that he could get your name and reprimand you right on the spot. I never found them very sympathetic, except for Wing Commander Crooks, who was a wonderful and very sympathetic person, and he was British. We were blessed with good leadership in 426 Squadron during my tour of operations. Wing Commander Leslie Crooks, DSO, DFC, was the commanding officer when I arrived on squadron. He had done a first tour on Wellingtons but unfortunately, was shot down and killed during the raid on Peenemünde: the very first raid of his second tour while flying a Lancaster Mark II.[73]

In the American system, the pilot, co-pilot, bombardier and navigator were almost always commissioned officers, while the flight engineer and the five gunners were almost always sergeants in various grades. Under the British system, while the gunners and the flight engineer were generally not commissioned, the pilot, navigator and the bomb-aimer may or may not have been officers. Since both the American and the British hierarchies felt that the pilot was the logical aircraft captain and crew commander, the British inconsistency of rank with respect to crew positions often led to awkward situations and additional stress if a junior pilot was attempting to discipline or coordinate senior crew members. Under the American system, although officers and NCOs slept in separate quarters, they usually ate and frequently socialized in All Ranks Messes, and their hierarchy actively encouraged mixed-rank activities. In the British system, NCOs and officers, echoing the class system, were messed in strict segregation, although mixed crews often socialized in off-station venues. However, the British Executive frowned on this somewhat and especially on any formally organized mixed-rank functions. A 1943 report on personnel issues attacked the practice of holding All Ranks dances at bomber stations. This reinforcement of social claims was frequently frustrating to the more egalitarian aircrew from the Dominions who were under RAF control, since their shared social values were much more akin to those of the Americans than those of the British:

> The Commonwealth aircrew, especially, believed that it was their very intimacy with their

crews, their indifference to rank, that often made them such strong teams in the air. An Australian from 50 Squadron cited the example of a distinguished young English ex-public school pilot who was killed in 1943.

> This boy, he said, was a classic example of an officer who never achieved complete cohesion with his crew, who won obedience only by the rings on his sleeves and not by force of personality. "He simply wouldn't have known how to go out screwing with his gunners in Lincoln on a Saturday night." In his memoirs, Harris argues that the English made the best aircrew, because they had the strongest sense of discipline. It was a difference of tradition.[74]

Whether the sentiment was widespread or sustained throughout the RAF that the "Colonials" lacked discipline is a matter of debate, but the observations of historian Max Hastings on this subject are interesting, and may help explain why men from the Dominions were not frequently given command positions in Bomber Command outside their national formations, even though, given their proportional representation it would seem obvious to do so. Thus, one is led to suspect that there was some cultural and social bias by the British Executive coming into play:

> To survive, brilliant flying was less important than an immense capacity for taking pains, avoiding unnecessary risks, and maintaining rigid discipline in the air. Canadians were highly regarded as individual aircrews, but incurred intense criticism as complete crews, as squadrons, as (eventually) their own No. 6 Group, because they were thought to lack the vital sense of discipline. A 50 Squadron gunner who was sent one night as a replacement with an all-Canadian crew came home terrified after circling the target while they sang "Happy Birthday to You" down the intercom to their 21-year-old pilot. Later in the war, 6 Group became notorious for indifference to radio telephone instructions from the Master Bomber over the target.[75]

In addition to these dissatisfactions, the British occasionally exacerbated problems by infringing on the jealously guarded free time of the aircrew temporaries, saddling them with extraneous disciplinary responsibilities which they were neither trained for nor inclined to accept.

> Aircrew are becoming more and more divorced from their legitimate leaders, and their officers are forgetting, if they ever learnt them, their responsibilities to their men. Aircrew personnel must be disabused of the idea that their sole responsibility is to fly . . . and to do this, their leisure hours must be more freely devoted to training and hard work.[76]

The problem here was that the old, Regular force pre-war RAF, just like the Regular force echelons of the other services, was applying its professional expectations to these "citizen airmen," who were, by and large, only planning to serve "for the duration." Those same unrealistic expectations certainly also held true within the Canadian and American services, between the Regular force cadres and the militia types, the reservists, and those only in for wartime service. Douglas Harvey's experience as an NCO pilot of the rank inconsistencies within bomber crews on the Bomber Command template was typical. Also typical was his reaction when chastened by higher authority for a crew member's minor infraction:

> The next morning I was called into the CO's office for an explanation of why one of my crew was improperly dressed. I remember saying, "I'm not his mother, for Christ's sake!" How should I know why he was dressed like that? I then received some news. As the pilot

and captain of the aircraft I was supposed to be in charge of my crew at all times. I could understand my responsibilities when we were flying but I couldn't see how this could work on the ground. Keeping track of a crew, according to the CO, should be the captain's responsibility, even though I had a mixed crew; sergeants and officers. I was a sergeant. On the ground, regulations dictated that I must salute my crew officers, do their bidding, and call them sir. In the air, they were to jump when I gave an order. How insane![77]

However, there are many specific examples of British fairness and many generous acts of compassion and kindness to Canadians. Many of the Canadians felt that the multinational RAF squadrons were absolutely the best way to serve, while others yearned to be exclusively with their own kind, governed by Canadian national regulations and policies. It appears, like so many of life's experiences, to have been very much an individual perception, driven in no small measure by the personality and the character of the officers under whom they served.[78] Murray Peden, who did all his operational flying with the RAF, offered the following comments:

> I never wanted to fly in 6 Group—not because I didn't have the highest regard for my fellow Canadians, but because I had started out with 214 Squadron, RAF, purely by the luck of the draw, and quickly made a lot of good friends there. When The Great Gus (Air Marshal Harold Edwards, Air Officer Commanding-in-Chief, RCAF Overseas) began beating the bushes and trying to round up Canadians in RAF squadrons looking to get back in with their fellow Canadians, our reaction was to let him know, very quickly and very bluntly, that we did not want any such posting. The Great Gus, when he learned of the reaction of most Canadians in our situation said that we were chumps. We in turn thought that he was—well, a word that sounds like manhole. If the Canadian government . . . had gone into this program right from the outset, things might have been quite different.[79]

A 1947 report by British psychologists Charles P. Symonds and Denis J. Williams on wartime psychological disorders in flying personnel extensively discussed the importance of leadership in helping airmen to accept and to carry the load of operational flying. Symonds and Williams found "no exception to the opinion that good leadership was vital, and many thought it was the most important factor of all."[80] Canadian airmen, serving with both their national squadrons and with RAF formations, have emphasized that the wartime leadership was generally of a particularly high calibre, and that having the backing of the British citizenry was a formidable boost to aircrew spirits. Lloyd C. "Mo" Morrison, a late-war Canadian Lancaster pilot who flew his combat operations with 100 Squadron, had the following comments on the subject:

> On leadership I can only say that I believe we Canadians in RAF units were fortunate to have been led by vastly experienced RAF officers. My personal wartime experience, played against 35 years of post-war service and involved observation since, suggests that wartime leadership was, in the main, of higher quality. This may be due to a well defined purpose—a "cause" which has been present in most occasions when indifferently trained and equipped forces have prevailed . . .
>
> The conduct of Bomber Command operations on "home ice" as it were, was of tremendous value. We had continuous, unobtrusive support from the people of the towns and villages surrounding our bases. We were, in almost every case, still in or just out of our teen years. To come "home" night after night to a "family" who shared our culture and history and went to incredible lengths to make us welcome was a morale booster of incalculable value.[81]

Life in Wartime Britain

Living conditions in wartime England also had an impact on aircrew morale. The RAF, as part of the host nation, and its Canadian members generally operated from at least somewhat established facilities, such as those in Yorkshire and Lincolnshire. However, the accommodation on the expansion bases, as already mentioned, was frequently dingy and barren in the extreme. This state of affairs certainly also applied to most of the American bases, located largely in East Anglia. Jimmy Sheridan recalls his wartime quarters in Britain:

> I had a mixture of quarters. On some bases we lived in pre-war buildings that were like hotels—solid buildings. Others were Nissen huts which were adequate but usually uncomfortable—hot in summer—cold and damp in the winter. They were heated by stoves burning coke, which nobody seemed to know how to light or to keep going. The occupants of the hut had to look after the stoves themselves, and with different flying hours, there was no one there to keep them properly stoked. This meant that coming in from night flying during the winter there was no heat in the hut, which resulted in damp sheets for the bed. I got chilblains in both heels at this camp. Went to the Doc and he more-or-less said, "Tough. Walk on your toes." I just toughed it out without losing any flying. It was at this camp we had a cement block building for a bath house—unheated in winter—snow on the ground—bath tub with wood pallet for a floor but hot and cold water. On a day off I would get to the nearest town and rent a hotel room to have a decent warm bath and bedroom.
>
> As for food, it was adequate but of poor quality, but it was the best they could do, no doubt. It was then I learned beef could be cut paper thin. As for mutton, it came to be abhorred by all. But we survived. When listed to fly an operation, we were allowed one whole egg cooked any way we wished—the only time we saw an egg—otherwise it was powdered egg all the way.
>
> Once I got on Squadron, we got a pre-war building, which was great. Three officers to a room with shared bath facilities—good lounge rooms and dining room, too. We even had batman and laundry services.[82]

Jim Northrup of 415 Squadron recalls life at East Moor, from where he flew his tour of operations:

> Life on the Squadron was pleasant. You were out of the petty crap of Training Command and things were much more relaxed. We trained continuously on abandoning an aircraft, dingy drill in the pool, fighter affiliation and cross-country trips for the newer crews. The food was not the greatest but you could survive on it and we could always get a decent meal in York. However, to this day, I don't eat liver, lamb or Brussels sprouts. Aircrew on ops always had bacon and eggs before and after a trip.
>
> They would only serve powdered milk as the local milk was unpasteurized.
>
> When I was on OTU in the Midlands, a very pretty girl of about sixteen had a little stand set up beside the farm house where she sold glasses of fresh milk for a shilling. We had to walk by her on the way to the airdrome and everybody would have a glass. She must have done very well as most of us gave her two shillings, one for the milk and one for the smile.
>
> Our barracks were about a mile from the Mess, dispersed in the trees. and the amount of heat generated depended on your ability to burn the "clinkers" they called coke. Power was turned off at 10:00 PM, and if you were up at 3:00 AM for a daylight op, it was quite an art to be able to shave in the dark. On a normal day, you got up at 7:00 AM and reported to the Flight Commander by 9:00 AM as to the status of your crew. This was then given

to the CO, so he knew how many crews were available for operations. If ops were on that night, the crews selected would know by 9:30 AM so that they could check their aircraft and then rest until briefing time. Those not flying would have some training laid on. The station was then closed to anyone leaving the station, which in some ways was silly, as often when we were in York whooping it up, the taxi drivers would come into the pubs and the dance hall and loudly announce that all aircrew were to return to their stations as ops were on.

Your laundry was something you had to look after yourself, and I found a lovely lady in Sutton-on-the-Forest to do mine. I thought of her as being quite old, but she probably was only forty or so . . .

Our transport on the Squadron was limited to a canvas-covered stake truck and one old bus. In 1986, I started to organize a function to put up a marker at East Moor, and a ground crew type wrote me from Quebec, asking me if I remembered the beautiful red-haired girl who drove the bus. He then went on to say he had married this girl and could never understand why none of the aircrew had made a play for her. I wrote and congratulated him on his good fortune and explained that on the way out to our aircraft our minds were fully occupied on the operation, and on returning, we were initially too tired to do much thinking about girls. Actually, I remembered her very well as she was not only very pretty, she was very pleasant. Our ground crews worked very hard and a Yorkshire winter is not a pleasant thing. They built a small shelter by the dispersal pens so they could get out of the weather and warm up. I had the same ground crew all during my tour of operations. They were a hard working bunch and my aircraft was always ready to go. They kept it clean and there were never any oil streaks around the engine cowlings. To them, it was their aircraft and their crew that was flying it. Once a month I took them to *The Blacksmith's Arms* for beer and lunch. The pub always put up a splendid spread for us and the boys really appreciated it.[83]

The aircrew were not always housed on base, and although billeting on the economy could be somewhat charming, it also brought its own problems, as Roger Coulombe recollects from his time at Linton:

As sergeant pilots with 426 Squadron I was billeted in an old peacetime manor, a couple of miles from the station, that had been requisitioned for the aircrew. We were quartered two to a very small room with very narrow bunks that had three separate "cookies" for a mattress, and a sort of a round pillow that looked like part of the trunk of a tree, and was as hard. On getting up in the morning, we had stiff necks and would often find we were lying on only one of the cookies, the other two having shifted about. We also had no sheets; just a gray wool blanket.

Apart from the uncomfortable sleeping accommodation, the worst threat to our night's sleep and health was the enormous quantity of rats. During the time I resided in Aldwark Manor, I slept every night holding a fire poker in one of my hands to fight the rats in case of attacks. I even saw a big rat eating one of my chocolate bars, which was lying in a chair just inches from my face. My presence in bed did not seem to disturb him one bit. The rats were running up and down the stairs as you entered the main entrance at night. They could be in the bathroom eating soap where you went to shave in the morning. You had to chase them away if you wanted to be able to shave. I know of at least one gunner of a crew who was bitten on a foot by a rat who had gotten under the blanket in his bunk.

There were so many rats in the basement that, if you ever had to go there, you could see them running all over the water pipes, even in twos. I had nightmares about being attacked by rats for several years after the war, and they only eventually stopped after six or seven years.[84]

The austere quarters were for the most part just a place to "crash" between operations, wartime leave policy was as generous as possible to the combat crews, the local distractions were plentiful, and the host citizens were generally warm and generous. Howard Ripstein, a wireless air gunner on 426 Squadron, recalls:

> Operational aircrew were granted one week of leave out of every six and Lord Nuffield paid for rail travel anywhere in the UK. Generally we went to London. Personally, I went to visit a Canadian family in Minchinhampton, Gloucestershire, for R and R after about three days of the hectic life in the Big City . . . Locally, York was a fun place and the ladies one met in *Betty's Bar* and the *De Grey Rooms*, a dance hall, were delightful and frequently easy lays! While in London, while I was and always have been a great believer in interservice cooperation, I was never interested in any liaison with *The Piccadilly Commandos*, who, for about two pounds, would do the naughty deed and likely give one a dose of the clap.[85]

Jim Northrup also remembers the generosity of the British, both during his formal leaves and also the day-to-day living among them:

> We worked 42 days and then got nine days leave. Lord Nuffield (of Morris Automobiles) owned hotels all over England and Scotland, and if you were Canadian aircrew on operations, he would put you up at any one of his hotels for free. You just decided where you wanted to go and requested it a couple of weeks ahead of time. The hotels were first class; great breakfasts and a well-stocked bar where you could get onion sandwiches until 3:00 AM.
>
> The people in Yorkshire also treated us very well and Canadian airmen still get a warm welcome there.[86]

Similar sentiments were expressed by Ron Cassels, a wartime navigator on 428 "Ghost" Squadron, and they echo the feelings of the vast majority of Canadians who served in Britain:

> The war gave many of us the opportunity to see the beautiful British Isles and see many places with historic significance. We had the opportunity to meet the local people, many of whom invited us into their homes. The ordinary folk had the habit of going to their pub at night and having one or two beers, playing some darts and having a restful sociable evening.
>
> We were young and taking part in a bitter conflict. On our nights off we went out to the local pubs. There is no doubt that we took them over and in the course of doing so we drank too much. The regulars never complained.
>
> They sat back in the corner with their pint and kept quiet while we used their dart board, and sang our dirty and boisterous songs. Our noisy behavior must have been most annoying but I never heard them complain.
>
> When we went on leave we crowded on the trains and didn't care what compartment we were in. Tourist tickets were as good as first class until the conductor made you move, which was very seldom. The British made us welcome and used their limited rations to give us tea. I often think of the poor farmer whose farm yard was just behind our dispersal. Every time old "Z" for Zombie started, he had a hurricane across his yard. We did our flying at all hours and it must have been next to impossible for him and his family to get

a good night's sleep. The British people treated us very well.

(But) There were a few that regarded us as colonials. We were not from the upper class or the right school and therefore should not be officers or leaders.[87]

Important Respites

Along with regular leave, special leave of several days was given as frequently as was operationally possible. Headquartered in London, the excellent Lady Ryder Leave Organization placed Commonwealth aircrew as honoured guests in many stately British homes, as well as with other Britons from all walks of life and social standings. These wartime acts of generosity and hospitality are still remembered by many veterans with great affection, and numerous long-term friendships were founded in this way. Many Canadian airmen took war brides in Britain during the war.[88] Sid Philp, a navigator with 426 Squadron, recalls some of his off-duty experiences while at Dalton and Linton, as well as another significant problem for the Canadians in wartime Britain, that of rationalizing British English with Canadian English.

> Dalton provided me with two firsts. It was the NAAFI mobile canteen there that served me my first Mars bar; for the rest of my stay in England I looked forward to getting my weekly Mars bar ration—and it is to this day my favourite chocolate bar. It was at the same canteen that I was first addressed as "Luv." When the young NAAFI lass first asked me "Wot'll you 'av luv?" I thought she was being inordinately forward. But I soon found out it was a very common Yorkshire expression.
>
> Which reminds me of another piece of vernacular that floored me . . . On an early leave I paid a visit to one of my maternal aunts in Glasgow. Apparently a cousin had an apartment just around the corner from my aunt's and they insisted that I make use of the apartment overnight. The very feminine cousin, who was about my own age (19), showed me to the quarters and, on leaving, she said, "I'll be around to knock you up in the morning." She must have wondered about the surprised look on my face. To her a knock up was a morning wake up call. To me it was a pregnant remark.
>
> Yet another bit of the language misunderstanding. I well remember the first time I met the gentleman who was to become my father-in-law. It was a Sunday afternoon and he was standing in the parlor after having had a few pints at his club. On being introduced, he said, "Ee, he's a fine lad. Aye, you're a fine lad." I thought he was giving me his seal of approval. Actually, by "fine" he meant that I was long and skinny!
>
> York . . . where a street is called a gate, a gate is called a bar, and a bar is called a pub! Many is the time I got on or off the Linton bus at Exhibition Square across from *Bootham Bar* and from the *De Grey Rooms*. Initially, the main attractions were the watering holes, the principal one being the many hours there ordering and consuming bitter beer by the trayful. The skipper couldn't join us in these plebeian activities since he was the squadron commander.
>
> Later, after meeting the lady who was to become my wife, I was content to spend more time in such places as cafes, for Welsh rarebit on toast, the cinemas and the *Theatre Royal*.
>
> There are two places in York that are, for quite different reasons, very memorable for me; one is St. Olave church and the other is Lendal Bridge. The Church of St. Olave, which backs onto the grounds of St. Mary's Abbey, was dedicated in the year 1050 to Olaf, the patron saint of Norway. In June 1644, during the Civil War, the church tower— which had been used as a cannon emplacement—was blown up. Almost exactly 300

years later, on 11th November 1944, another momentous occasion took place there; the former Mary Marshall and Sid Philp were married.

Lendall Bridge spans the River Ouse not far from the railway station. The southern end of the bridge extends out from a little circular tower with a parapet wall. Before the construction of the bridge, the tower had been used by the men who operated the ferry across the river at that point. The tower, which is sometimes known as the Dead House because it had been used as a mortuary for bodies pulled out of the river, has a flight of narrow winding stairs leading to a tiny room at the top. In 1944, the room was roofed and was entered through a heavy wooden door which had a small barred see-through aperture. One bright summer afternoon that year, Mary and I were walking across the bridge when I decided to have a look at what was in the tower. To this day, I don't know whether or not what I saw was an apparition. As I climbed the steps, I noticed that the door was padlocked. I looked through the aperture and saw an old man standing in a darkened room. He had greying dishevelled hair and a beard, he was dressed in sackcloth and was manacled and in chains. When Mary looked, she said that she could see nobody. I just turned on my heels and said to her, "Let's get out of here." That vision was, and still is, vivid.[89]

Food, Glorious Food

While quartering was largely a matter of luck for all airmen, the Americans were much better off in provisioning matters than their British and Commonwealth counterparts. It must be emphasized that there were many, many food shortages in wartime Britain, and the aircrew, particularly those on operations, were better off than the average citizens, who generally accepted their austere wartime conditions with stoicism, grace, and good humour. Although the British were providing as best they could for their Commonwealth and Allied wartime guests, there is no doubt that British wartime food was particularly galling to the men from the Dominions, who, like the Americans, were conditioned to generally much better fare. The Americans provided their troops with foodstuffs imported directly from North America, whereas the Canadians were mostly provisioned from British stocks, through the British messing system. For the Canadians, the dissatisfaction started early, usually on the troop ship crossings to Britain, and it maintained a generally predictable level thereafter. Sometimes, however, the Atlantic crossing was particularly unpleasant, as the following excerpts demonstrate:

It was the most distasteful messing ever encountered in my Service life. One could taste sand grit in all the greens served which, to top it all, were boiled to a "glop" soup in a large open kettle from which the contents were ladled by an enormous cook who refused to wear anything but a singlet. The weather was warm and at each bend of his bountiful body, sweat droplets would fall in the soup making ringlets on the greasy surface. Finally, this reached all proportion of decency and I therefore contacted our medical officer, one Dr. Rankin, who applied his authority. Conditions improved, but not totally.[90]

We now eat with the RAF. The technical name for this unseasoned pig-swill we're fed is "plain wholesome food." The lunches are edible but uninteresting. The other meals aren't big enough to keep a canary in good voice. And the Mess stinks to high heaven, a greasy lavatory smell that is enough to kill the finest appetite, mother. You may think I'm joking, still, this is the plain, simple truth—*we're hungry all the time*. I'm speaking for myself and Rusty and for every other Canadian on this accursed station.[91]

At one training station in England, the Orderly Officer was a real "pukka" type, complete with handle-bar moustache. One day, we were served tripe, and when the Orderly Officer asked for complaints, my buddy stood up. Over marched the Orderly Officer and the Orderly Sergeant. "Yes? What is it?" the officer demanded. Pointing at the tripe, my friend asked, " Is this to be eaten or has it already been eaten?" He got twenty-one days Confined to Barracks.[92]

The food was bloody awful on the station. I haven't eaten a Brussels sprout since 1945. The coffee was weak so we drank tea, of some unidentified blend. The sausages were 80 percent bread, and the eggs powdered. Decent steaks were not available. Were it not for the Black Market and parcels from home I would have starved on the RAF rations. After an operation we got real fried eggs and good bacon with rum-laced coffee, which I can still taste. Once, a dietician decided that we should be served poached eggs, which almost caused a riot.[93]

Most airmen soldiered on with resignation and a sense of being in it together, the grumbling about food being, at any rate, the serviceman's universal prerogative. Roger Coulombe remembers the food at Linton, but puts the situation in perspective:

The food in the Sergeants Mess was minimal. Of course, many supply ships were sunk by U-boats coming across the Atlantic Ocean. Therefore, a lot of the food destined for us went to the bottom of the sea. However, the English civilian population was no better off. They made great sacrifices and they were very brave and cheerful in spite of their miseries. I think the civilian population was admirable. And the civilians we met at the pubs were always very pleasant and sympathetic. They seemed to like us Canadians.[94]

However, occasionally, Canadian airmen caught a glimpse of how their American counterparts were faring, and it certainly provoked a certain amount of nostalgic envy. Sid Philp recalls:

Most of 6 Group's airfields were located in the Vale of York where, during the winter months, it was not uncommon for fog to descend during the early morning hours and obscure the whole countryside. If that occurred, as it frequently did, when bombers were returning from a night mission, they had to be diverted to other airfields in the south. One such night (or morning) we had to land at Bury St. Edmonds, an American bomber station. What an eye-opener! What generosity! I had been in England for about a year-and-a-half and had become accustomed to good, but not great, RAF food with its rationed amount of rabbit stew or sawdust sausages and Brussels sprouts or powdered eggs. The first thing I noticed when I entered their dining hall was a sign saying "take all you want but eat all you take." Then the first meal served up was frankfurters and sauerkraut. For me, at that time, that was a veritable delicacy! But the best was yet to come; for dessert we had real fresh fruit salad with, if we wanted, ice cream. Wow! Later, we were sitting around the officers' mess just shooting the breeze; the Americans thought we were strange because we stayed away from the bar. Then they discovered that we were not supposed to take cash with us on our operations and we were virtually penniless. At that, they told us that the bar was open to us and we could have whatever we wanted for as long as we wanted. We didn't over-partake of their hospitality, but we weren't terribly annoyed that the weather kept us there for three days.[95]

Others had positive recollections of the wartime British food which appeared to depend on specific circumstances. Reg Patterson, a late-war pilot flying with 101 Squadron, recalls his situation, and also some convenient denial exercises on the part of his navigator:

The food in general in our Officers' Mess was very good. Our sergeant-cook had been a chef at the Trocadero in London before the war. He certainly did his best with what he had. We always had what was called an operational meal last thing before we went down to briefing and thence off to the aircraft. It usually consisted of an egg and some sandwiches. Aircrew were the only people that got eggs. It almost seemed like a bribe. The sandwiches were quite often large ham sandwiches. My navigator was a Jewish boy from Windsor, Ontario, Flying Officer Morley Ornstein. He was a big fellow with an even bigger appetite. He would dig into those sandwiches and grin all around, saying, "I don't know where they get their chickens from around here, but they sure are good." As a navigator, he was superb.[96]

That 50–50 Chance

For the crews of Bomber Command, the full risks associated with combat flying were generally not evident until operations commenced. As previously mentioned, relatively early in the bombing campaign, the RAF determined that "an average casualty rate of five percent per mission was considered to be the most that the bomber crews could bear without faltering over any prolonged length of time."[97] Also, experience gained from the Western Front during the Great War had shown the value of front-line rotations, followed by periods of rest from combat. "If men were going to be able to sustain themselves during night after night of arduous and extraordinarily dangerous flying, some sort of rotation policy was necessary."[98]

Prior to the spring of 1943, the generally accepted length of the first operational tour was approximately 200 cumulative flying hours on combat operations, normally followed by a minimum of six months service in a training or related staff billet, followed by a second and roughly equal operational tour. The 200 hours of combat flying time roughly equated to thirty operational trips.[99] Aircrew were removed from combat operations by death or severe injury, through capture by the enemy, at the request of higher authority, or at the discretion of the member's commanding officer. This latter, highly subjective category was meant to determine when an individual had done enough—one who did not fit within the earlier boundaries but needed a respite from combat. However, this practice was frequently held hostage by Service needs and occasionally lacked the application of even-handed common sense, a quality that was not uniformly demonstrated throughout Bomber Command, especially during the early years. There is also little doubt that there was occasionally an element of favourable bias, particularly when applied to commissioned or pre-war Regular force aircrew. It was decided therefore that operational flying needed to be broken up into manageable portions of time, from which there must be a reasonable chance of survival. "It was generally accepted that it should be drawn at a point which offered a '50-50 chance.' "[100] It should be noted, however, that the actual odds against survival were held somewhat in confidence by the Executive of the RAF during the war years.[101] Those odds varied considerably at various times throughout the bombing campaign. Some individuals have maintained that losses and loss rates were deliberately withheld from the public during the war, while countering claims have been made that the Executive was totally transparent about the losses. While the RAF did not go out of its way to routinely report losses and loss rates to its aircrew, there is no evidence of a deliberate attempt by authority to deceive the crews that the odds of survival were actually better than perceptions or reality dictated. For one thing, in a reflection of the usual transparency of

RELATION BETWEEN LOSS RATE
AND PERCENTAGE OF CREWS
SURVIVING 10, 20 AND 30 OPERATIONS

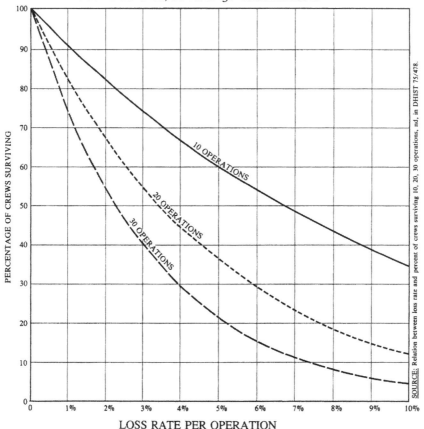

LOSS RATE PER OPERATION

This graph depicts air crews' chances of survival given a constant loss rate
(which never happened) or the average loss rate for the period in which they
flew. No. 6 Group's loss rate of 5.5 per cent from March–June 1943, which suggested that only 18 per cent of crews would survive thirty operations, was cause
for considerable concern at Bomber Command Headquarters and in Ottawa.

British war policy, the BBC Home Service accurately broadcast individual raid losses on a routine
basis, and the crews would have known roughly how many aircraft had participated in any given
operation. Also, the overall strength and compositions of various raids were made public, at least
on occasion, and they would have been routinely briefed to participating crews.[102] Loss rates,
although not dwelt on, would have been easy to calculate. Kenneth McDonald elaborates:

> We knew what the chances were from personal experience on squadrons, from the num-
> bers reported missing each day by the BBC, from word of mouth accounts of casualties
> elsewhere within 4 Group, and obviously from passage through HCUs of course after
> course of aircrew to squadrons. What we knew instinctively was confirmed many years
> afterwards when the "Diaries" published the mathematical chances of a crew surviving
> fifty operational flights at various rates of loss. At the highest rate shown, four percent,

out of 100 crews, thirteen would survive. Also cited is that "The casualty rate during the coming period, that of the opening operations of the Pathfinder Force (which was when we started operating), would be 4.6 percent." We didn't know this at the time, but the average loss rate on the trips we did in that same period was 5.7 percent.[103]

Harris and his staff had grave concerns over the possible perception that a contractual agreement codifying a tour length was being entered into with the airmen under his command, and these concerns were not without substance. However, on 8 May 1943, Bomber Command codified operational bomber service into two combat tours of thirty and a maximum of twenty sorties respectively for the Main Force, with an intervening staff or instructional tour of duty of normally not less than six months. Other operational tour lengths were established in the other commands at the same time. Concurrently, Sir Arthur Harris also reduced another significant source of anxiety to his crews by curtailing operational flying in clearly unsuitable weather, a policy turnaround which undoubtedly saved many lives and aircraft from needless accidents. "The tour of operations, with its definite promise of relief, was a sheet anchor of morale in Bomber Command. It made the unbelievable endurable."[104] However, the vision of the average aircrew member was extremely short, and few grasped at the time that their operational flying would not be completed after the first tour. This frame of mind was undoubtedly a psychological defence mechanism.[105]

Some Would Falter

Inevitably there were some, not many overall, who could not face the continued stress, and these occurrences were usually associated with periods of extensive operations and high combat losses. The spring of 1943 and the winter of 1943/1944, which corresponded with the battles for the Ruhr and Berlin, were particularly challenging.[106] It is fair to say that the unique characteristics of the strategic bombing campaign placed extraordinary strains on the airmen who participated in it. The challenges often appeared overwhelming and the pressure to prevail was relentless. For many, the only meaningful goal was survival, and personal experience coupled with the grim mathematical statistics often compounded to warn that survival was doubtful at best. Small wonder that aircrew were rendered highly vulnerable to both the physical and the mental symptoms of stress.

In their initial report on RAF psychological disorders, Charles Symonds and Denis Williams particularly noted the impact of physical fatigue when added to heightened levels of anxiety. The combat mission itself imposed many stresses on the crews. Operational conditions, such as weather, duration of the operation, the nature and the intensity of the defences and the frequently hazardous return trip certainly contributed to the stress. However, most aircrew found " the anticipation of a raid as great a load as the raid itself, unless it happened to be unusually hazardous."[107] Other qualified observers echoed these findings, and both the American and the British camps cited briefings, cancellations, and especially late cancellations as having pivotal, even disastrous effects on morale.

> No one who saw the mask of age which mantled the faces of these young men after a period of continued standing by, punctuated by inevitably false alarms, is likely to forget it. Their pallor, the hollows in their cheeks, and beneath their eyes, and the utter fatigue with which they lolled listlessly in chairs about their Mess, were eloquent of the exhaustion and frustration which they felt. In ten hours they seemed to have aged as many years.[108]

Other factors were cited as contributing to stress, including the alternating nature of the air war, and crews recall the unreal contrast of returning to a peaceful, pastoral England after spending agonizing hours over Germany in the most horrific conditions:

> Life on the squadron was seldom far from fantasy. We might, at eight, be in a chair beside a fire, but at ten, in an empty world above a floor of cloud. Or at eight, walking in Barnetby with a girl whose nearness denied all possibility of sudden death at twelve.[109]

One common denominator of stress to the airmen was the recurring jolt brought about by suddenly empty living quarters and dining facilities; mute testaments to the sudden and violent passing of friends:

> Their attitude to losses and the deaths of friends was particularly striking. It was one of supreme realism, of matter-of-fact acceptance of what everyone knew perfectly well was inevitable. They did not plunge into outspoken expression of their feelings, nor did they display any compromise with conventional reticence about the fact of violent death. They said, "Too bad . . . sorry about old so-and-so . . . Rotten luck." Their regret was deep and sincere, but not much displayed or long endured. They were apt and able to talk of dead and missing friends, before mentioning their fate, just as they talked of anyone else or themselves. It took the loss of particular friends or leaders, flight commanders or squadron commanders, to produce a marked reaction among a squadron. Then they might feel collectively distressed, have a few drinks because of that, go on to a party and feel better.[110]

Even the process of joining an operational unit could be unnerving for some aircrew.

> During the late evening on December 3 1943, a new crew arrived from nearby Topcliffe having just been posted to 429 Squadron. Duly reporting to the Orderly Room for "billets," they were informed the NCOs' aircrew billets were all filled and they would have to bunk in the Airmans' Quarters for the night. They were then cheerfully informed that an "Operation" was in progress that night and that there would be plenty of space for them in the morning. This shook them up, especially when they saw all the NCO aircrew queued up to get their "operational supper" that night at the Sergeants' Mess, all looking very serious and grim, with no horseplay or joking.[111]

Perhaps one of the most profound stressors of the bombing campaign, both to aircrew and to ground crew, was the psychological impact of battle-damaged aircraft returning with dead or wounded on board. At RAF Station Woodbridge, which was only one of the RAF's master emergency airfields, 516 killed or wounded airmen were returned in 1720 aircraft in a one-year period from January 1943 to January 1944.[112] The following excerpt, although from an American airman's diary, typifies the carnage involved in these occurrences:

> B-17 *Tinkertoy* ground-looped just off the runway. *Tinkertoy* had her nose shot out and the pilot had his head blown off by a 20mm cannon shell. There was hardly a square inch of the entire cockpit that was not covered with blood and brain tissue. One half of his face and a portion of his cervical vertebra were found just in front of the bomb bay. The decapitation was complete.[113]

Symonds and Williams also concluded that there were "three critical periods in which men are likely to show the effects of stress, as well as a critical period after exceptional strain has been experienced." These were identified as being after the first few trips, when the enormity of what an individual was up against had been digested, around the twelfth-to-fourteenth mission, when the individual felt he had used up his quota of luck, the tour-end was still far off, and he could not go on, and within a few operations of tour completion, when men generally acquired a renewed sense of hope that they might actually survive.[114] Many surviving aircrew members have said they experienced some variation of this pattern, although many denied having been through Symonds and Williams "mid-tour slump" and there were also many exceptions to their generalized findings:

> That increasing of tension generally did exist only for the first few (five or six) trips. After that, particularly if the initial trips had been "hairy," a feeling of invincibility developed and a little complacency set in. I suspect that complacency may have led to more than a few mishaps. That attitude continued and grew until the end of a crew's tour was in sight. At that point there was a complete reversal and a numbing tension took over and intensified until the final flight was completed.[115]

Sid Philp's comment on a feeling of invincibility following from difficult initial combat operations is interesting, particularly as his own first mission was far from uneventful:

> The first bombing raid that I took part in was on the 21st of January 1944; the target, Magdeburg. It occurred during the period that has come to be known as the Battle of Berlin. Our planned route took us east across the North Sea, then a feint towards Berlin before turning south to the target. The return trip was to be a beeline west over a heavily defended piece of real estate, across the Frisian Islands, then the safety of the North Sea and back to base. There was to be very little moon, but also very little cloud cover to hide in. The low murmurs from the veteran crews at briefing implied that this was not going to be a "piece of cake."
> Our skipper that night was fairly new to the rest of us. Our first pilot had not returned from his initial "second dicky" trip and we had flown only a few hours with this guy. This lack of joint training was to lead to some problems. It was only later that I discovered that I had been giving him "True" courses to set on the D.R. compass and he had been setting them on the magnetic compass and was flying magnetic courses. The result was that we were constantly heading north of our planned route and our final leg south towards the target seemed to take forever. We were, of course, late in arriving over the target which was well lit up by then . . .
> Shortly after we left the target area, we had our first fighter attack and the pilot attempted his first "corkscrew." This was a violent manoeuvre that was designed to make shooting deflection impossible and to lose the stalker. Well, his attempt was so extreme that he put the aircraft into a spin. I can recall my navigation instruments floating around in front of me while I was suspended between my seat and my desk. Now, you weren't supposed to be able to pull a Halifax out of a spin, but somehow, our guy accomplished it. While we shook that first fighter, two others found us later and we again had to take evasive action, but now our skipper was more circumspect and the action was somewhat less violent. Before crossing the coast, we were coned by searchlights and were lit up like stage performers; at the same time we were hit fairly badly by ack-ack. One piece went right through the rear turret without touching the gunner; another piece ripped out some wiring next to the engineer; a third piece tore a ridge in the outside of the wireless operator's boot; and yet another spent piece landed on my desk. More evasive action let us out of that predicament and the crew got nary a scratch! However, our tanks received minor holes and we made a landing at an emergency 'drome on the southeast coast. Just as we levelled off before touchdown, our engines cut due to lack of petrol. We rolled to the end of the runway and had to be hauled by a tractor from there.

I do not recall being frightened at any time while in the air and was able, I believe, to carry out my duties efficiently. However, once out of the kite and into a bus, I started to shake as though I had a severe chill. The shaking kept up until I arrived in the debriefing room and some clever soul, seeing my condition, handed me a mug of coffee with a very stiff shot of rum in it. I don't think any of the rest of the crew experienced the shakes then and I never did again. The next day we went out to the aircraft and counted 85 holes in it.[116]

It was perhaps understandable that surviving these early perils could have led to some form of crew over-confidence. However, for Murray Peden, the initial reaction to operations was quite different:

I cannot subscribe, from my own recollected experience, to the theory of three main phases in the level of stress from operational flying. I do recall that on our very first op, which was a "Nickel" dropping leaflets at Montargis in France, I was very conscious that this was my first time over enemy territory, and I wondered anxiously how I would react to hostile action directed my way, most concerned that I should not panic and do something that would stamp me or my crew as less than press-on types. At age 19, it was the highest tension I'd ever had to endure. And it was acute.

Fortunately, the flak we saw that night was quite distant for the most part so that we by-passed that anticipated strain. It was still a new and tremendous strain to be flying at night in the enemy's ball park, knowing that at any moment a Ju 88 could sweep in on us and pound us with cannon and machine gun fire. The tension stemming from that knowledge one struggled to keep concealed in the background. Nevertheless it was there, as it was throughout one's whole tour . . .

Next we converted onto Stirlings and joined the squadron for the balance of our tour. First off, a new Skipper had to fly two operations as second dickie with an experienced crew, from which he was supposed to derive the benefit of seeing how veteran pilots coped when Main Force hit a major German target. My first such flight came the same day we got to the squadron. I was hustled to briefing before I even had a chance to park my luggage in a hut. The target was Hannover, and I was to do the trip, my first operational flight in a Stirling, with a crew that had chalked up about 23 ops.

They turned out to be a highly nervous and voluble lot, and their skipper, in my eyes, did not keep them under proper control. From a tension point of view, the trip started inauspiciously as far as I was concerned, first with the sight of a nearby Stirling on fire in the air, slowly sinking before our eyes to its doom on the ground, then, only moments later, with a near-collision between our own Stirling and one on a converging course my experienced Skipper failed to see. It left me, the man under instruction, to seize the controls myself at the very last second and dive sharply, averting by the narrowest of margins the demise of two more Stirling crews. After a long and poorly carried out trip, highlighted by a glaring navigational error, we landed back at Chedburgh base, only to be vigorously strafed, seconds after we reached our dispersal, by an intruding Ju 88. It abruptly shot up a landing Stirling, then veered and whipped the terrain in front of it with long and shattering bursts of cannon and machine gun fire, all the while dropping a small flood of butterfly bombs, many of which exploded viciously as the German pilot swept by. I got up from pressing myself into the concrete during this frightening display with my heart racing and feeling not at all sanguine about how easy it was going to be to soldier through a tour of 30 such operations.[117]

Murray Peden followed this inauspicious start with a more positive experience on his second familiarization trip, which, although far from uneventful, went a long way to restoring his confidence, largely because of the professionalism of the crew. This, in spite of the fact that "we were subjected to all the usual strains of bursting flak, searchlights and fighters—I even saw a Ju 88 very clearly over the target, close to us, stark black crosses plainly visible—but through it all, particularly on the excruciatingly slow and vulnerable bomb-run, with the aircraft lumbering clumsily with open bomb-doors toward the Target Indicators, Sellar (the aircraft captain) remained imperturbable. His commands and responses with the bombardier were crisp and cool, and he seemed almost oblivious to the hellish scene we were flying through . . . Flight Sergeant Sellar was he, the coolest and best skipper I saw for a long time. Briefly it appeared that it might just be possible to last through a full tour."[118] Then, it was time to commence operations with his own crew. As was often the case, an attempt was made to "blood" them on relatively benign missions, and thus the first two operations were to be mining or Gardening trips, sorties which, although supposed to be of relatively low risk, were often fraught with danger.

> The first was to a relatively close area, in the Frisian Islands, and it ran off with nothing untoward happening. Even on this "milk run" type of target, however, one was aware as one skimmed over the water with open bomb doors at 600 feet, that if a flak ship suddenly appeared in the murk, it could easily be game over.
>
> The second mining trip was quite different, a long and much more dangerous journey, far up in the Kattegat, in an area where the German night fighters were much more vigilant. We not only had the misfortune to encounter a skillful and aggressive night fighter, who burst on us twice with impressive determination in a storm of incandescent shellfire, we nearly buried ourselves in the waters of the Kattegat thereafter through an error on my part, and then, while still in the aftershock phase, flew through the most hair-raising exhibition of St. Elmo's Fire I ever saw. It was an electric display that terrified me. After eight hours of gut-knotting tension, we finally landed and taxied to our dispersal back at base. I switched everything off and fitted the control locks in place, then sat slumped in my seat for a minute before heading for the crew bus, wondering again how I could ever sustain myself through another two dozen or more endurance contests like this . . .
>
> Our crew's tour was not really typical, however, because we were briefly taken away from Main Force work on two or three occasions and sent to Tempsford where we went on low-level flights over France dropping supplies to the Maquis. Flying low-level at night imports its own kind of strain. Back with Main Force again later, now flying to the targets with them in B-17 Fortresses, operating radar counter-measures equipment in the charge of a German-speaking Special Wireless Operator, we traded the 12,000 and 13,000 foot trips of the Stirling for an altitude, typically, of 22,000 or 23,000 feet. A few trips like these made us happier with our lot, but never complacent.
>
> In the spring of 1944, participating in the pre-Overlord Transportation Plan bombing program, we got a pointed reminder one night that German fighters were still plentiful, and lethal. Bomber Command despatched a small force on May 8th, 1944, to bomb, at relatively low altitude and in bright moonlight, rail and other transportation targets at Haine St. Pierre in Belgium. Expecting a fairly easy trip, we got a rude shock with the sight of combats breaking out all around us. From a small force of only 123 bombers, the Germans shot down nine, and doubtless damaged others. On a Bomber Command attack on oil plants at Gelsenkirchen, Wesseling and Scholven-Buer on the night of 21/22 June, we once again flew into a beehive of night fighter activity. We ourselves were twice attacked and heavily damaged, and finally struggled home, with one engine on fire and sporadically over-speeding, all the way to a crash-landing at the emergency aerodrome at Woodbridge, where we had a violent collision on landing, cutting a parked Lancaster in

half, just behind its still-loaded bomb-bay. We fled from our own aircraft assisting two wounded crew members. On the Wesseling strike, in close proximity to our own, the 133 Lancasters despatched lost 37 of their number, a loss rate of 27.8 percent that was all too easy for us to believe from our own experience. At the same time, eight more Lancasters were lost hitting the oil plant at Scholven-Buer. A month later, the night of July 28th, 1944, Bomber Command launched a two-pronged attack, our wing bound for Stuttgart, the other for Hamburg. That night we lost 62 bombers, 39 or 40 of them from our group. I saw a high proportion of those stricken bombers go down, several in combats frighteningly close to our own aircraft. Needless to say, the strain of operational flying had not lessened the slightest in this period, and I have to say that if I had thought about it, which I was careful not to do, I would have wondered just how long I could take this sort of grinding strain. We were officially screened early in September, 1944, shortly after a nine-hour trip to Stettin on Aug 29th, 1944. On that last operation, again a joint strike against Stettin and Koenigsberg, we lost 38 bombers, 23 of them on Stettin, our target. The feeling of relief when our C.O. called me in a week later and told me we had been screened was extremely high—and that is gross understatement. Because of the near-continuous experience of highly frightening events, I did not settle down, at any stage of the tour, to a relatively secure belief in the likelihood of a long future.[119]

By late 1943, the sky over whatever portion of the Reich was hosting a visit from Bomber Command on any given night was witness to a pyrotechnic display of great intensity and variety. Along with all the ground fires, the bomb bursts, the flak, the searchlights, the Target Indicators and other markers, in 1943, the Pathfinders were temporarily using route marking flares to aid the Main Force's journey to the target. The procedure did more harm than good, however, as it telegraphed the operation's primary flight path to the waiting German night fighters and flak. While the route illumination practice was soon temporarily discontinued,[120] the lesson was not lost on the Germans. Soon, flare shells fired from below and parachute flares dropped from above helped visually cue the German night fighters to their prey. The pilots could not avoid the seeing this frightening firework display in the target area, since they had to be constantly aware of their surroundings to respond to directions from other crew members, and to scan the night skies at all times for threats. Murray Peden recalls the bomb run from a pilot's perspective:

> Part of the standard grist on most trips was that air-to-air combats would break out from time to time, all too often with the tell-tale flaring finish that marked the deaths of another bomber crew. All this was but the lead-up to each trip's main event, the bombing run itself. At this point, close to the target, the bomber emerged from the precarious shelter of darkness and for five or more minutes flew toward and over the target in what was euphemistically called "the area of illumination" centred over the city. Tom Paine, could he have looked ahead, might have thought his expression about these being the times that tried men's souls very apt. Heading straight and level with the bomb-doors open toward the best concentration of Target Indicators, one flew across a vast panorama studded with bursting flak in the air and bomb-bursts and raging fires on the ground. This progression through a nightmarish scene one made in the glare of a host of chandelier flares dropped by German fighters far above. On each occasion, I strove mightily to ignore these fearsome surroundings for what seemed an endless period, and to concentrate single-mindedly on controlling the aircraft and responding delicately to the bomb aimer's directions for minor course corrections. Provided that one was not attacked by fighters, the bomb run was the supreme ordeal of the operation. A fighter attack, bringing

you face to face with death, up real close, was worse. Even when the bombing run was uneventful—a classification we applied to it even when, on one occasion, we received some minor flak damage in the course of it—the welcome "Bombs gone!" from the bomb aimer was more than welcome. These bombing runs were not experiences I could look forward to without a trace of fear . . . not at any stage.[121]

While the pilot had no choice but to remain in constant contact with what was going on outside the aircraft, not all crew members were so burdened. Donald Sutherland, a Canadian wireless operator, recalls his first time over enemy territory:

I remember my first trip . . . In the Halifax, the wireless operator sat just below the pilot, just slightly in front of him and below him, in the nose, and there was a little window on my left. I can remember going over the coast of Germany, and I remember seeing the flak, and I don't think I ever looked out again. I saw all the flak and the tracers and figured that was enough for me.[122]

Sid Philp also remembers arriving at a similar conclusion during the course of his first operation:

The only time the navigator was not busy was over the target area, since the bomb aimer was then in charge. That night I took the opportunity to take a peek at the target. My first sight was of the line of fighter flares along both sides of our track to the target. These were very bright flares, suspended on parachutes, that were designed to illuminate the bombers for the fighters. They gave the same appearance as when heading into a flare path for a night landing. Among the flares were puffs of bursting flak. Down below were the twinkling lights of bomb bursts and of myriad fires. Shooting up through it all were lines of flak tracer bullets. It was a beautiful and, at the same time, a frightening sight. I decided I had had enough beauty for one night and I crawled back down to my enclosed "office." I never again looked out at the target area.[123]

Dr. D. Stafford-Clark commented on the stressful ordeal that constituted a wartime operational tour in Bomber Command:

There *was* no single moment of security from take-off to touchdown, but often the sight of other aircraft hit by flak and exploding in the air, or plummeting down blazing to strike the ground in an incandescent wreck. The chances of any particular individual surviving his thirty trips alive, unwounded, and without having been forced down over enemy territory were generally accepted by the aircrew themselves as being one-in-five.[124]

In the Royal Air Force, considerable emphasis was placed on preventative treatment for combat stress whenever possible. Returning crews were met with amenities not normally available to the rank-and-file, including hot drinks, cigarettes, doughnuts, bacon-and-egg meals and post-operation spirits. Crews were encouraged to relax and to relate their experiences, in order to vent some of the most immediate reactions to combat. Liberal leave policies have already been mentioned. However, for some of those in need of a respite, and for whom leave did not solve their anxieties, stronger measures were often required. These men were taken off flying duties for short periods, then given additional food, warmth, drink and sedatives. The British strongly emphasized the value of uninterrupted sleep, and so, the administration of "great whacking doses" of sodium barbital was not uncommon. In a large number of cases, this form of treatment was effective since irrational fears and horrifying mental images were often quickly diffused.[125] Cursory review suggests that nearly two-thirds of all Bomber Command's stress casualties were effectively treated by employing these methods at a local level.[126] For those who required more formal treatment, this was carried out at several major neuropsychiatric centres, although RAF psychiatric specialists were always in short supply at the time, and extensive periods devoted to psychotherapy or psychoanalysis were impossible burdens on an unprepared system. Their fundamental goal was, obviously, to return as many airmen as possible to flying operations.

Lack of Moral Fibre

Yet, there was still a very small minority of aircrew who could not prevail. Within the RAF during the Second World War, the Lack of Moral Fibre (LMF) designation was employed "as a means of handling aircrew who would not or could not fly for reasons that were considered unjustifiable."[127] The LMF Memorandum, issued first in 1941 and then revised and clarified in 1943 and again in 1945, targeted "members of aircrews who forfeit the confidence of their commanding officers in their determination and reliability in the face of danger in the air, owing either to their conduct or to their admission that they feel unable to face up to their duties."[128] Aircrew who could not face the strain of operations were classified first as those who were medically fit, but who had forfeited their CO's confidence without being subjected to exceptional operational stresses. A second category was reserved for those who were medically unfit solely on account of displaying nervous symptoms, but again, without having been subjected to exceptional stresses, while a third category covered anyone who was medically unfit and did not qualify for the first two categories.

Mild neurosis cases could be sent to the RAF Convalescent Depot Blackpool or to the Officers Hospital Torquay, but the more severe cases were sent to a Not Yet Diagnosed Nervous/Neuropsychiatric (NYDN) Centre for treatment by specialists. However, Bomber Command generally advocated a harsh approach toward the treatment of neuropsychiatric (NP) casualties. Although some doctors favoured immediate release from the flying service if the problem appeared to be constitutional, or due to a faulty upbringing, and psychotherapy would not likely be successful, their Principal Medical Officer expressed the opinion that "temperamentally unsuitable members of aircrews . . . those lacking confidence . . . should be given no sympathy and should be dealt with by the Executive as early as possible."[129] Thus, the consequences of being branded LMF could be cataclysmic. And there is ample evidence to suggest that officers were treated more humanely than non-commissioned aircrew; again, a by-product of the British class system and the presumption, in some cases, that the lack of public school values would predispose NCOs to failure. John Lewis was asked if he had ever seen evidence of an LMF case during his long and distinguished operational service:

> We were all aware of the consequences of being convicted of LMF. We knew that punishment would be swift and severe; that you would be grounded immediately, stripped of your wings and rank badges, usually in a parade square ceremony before your entire squadron or wing. You might be allowed to remain in the air force on ground duties, but more than likely you would be sent home to Canada, dishonourably discharged and in disgrace. Once, on another station, I witnessed this punishment and the scene stays with me still. After it was all over and the parade had been dismissed, the young man continued to stand there, alone in the middle of the square, head bowed, eyes averted, absently picking at the strands of thread where his NCO stripes used to be. No one approached to offer him comfort.[130]

The *Flying Buzz Saw*, a Lancaster II of 426 Squadron flying out of Linton-on-Ouse, gets a double prop change in preparation for operations. (DND PL26009)

Waiting to go. (DND PL22672)

Opposite top: The ubiquitous rounded Nissen huts and other temporary rectangular huts, housing staples of a wartime bomber base. This is Skipton-on-Swale. (DND PL45597)

Opposite bottom: Life goes on. Baseball on the flight line in front of a taxiing Halifax III. (DND PL28521)

The loneliest job. Lancaster rear gunner Pilot Officer Nuncie "Nick" Leone from Toronto while serving with 405 Squadron. Killed in action over Brunswick, 14 January 1944. Note the Granston Lodge modification, the removal of vision-obstructing Perspex panels. It was drafty but effective. (DND PL26157)

Opposite bottom: Graffiti on the ordnance was also common, and again, it boosted morale. Here, "cookies" from Canada to Germany via a Lancaster II. (DND PL29625)

Nose art was widespread and it fostered esprit de corps. Here, Sergeant AC Shierlaw, a former worker in advertising and display with the *Ottawa Journal*, then a mid-upper gunner with 429 "Bison" Squadron, grins from the cockpit of *Easy Does It Too*. (DND PL26853)

The faces of the enemy. *Oberst* Helmut Lent amassed a hundred and two night fighting victories and eight daytime victories before being killed in a landing accident in 1944.
(Author's Collection)

Major Prinz zu Sayn-Wittgenstein, aristocratic and driven, in a somber inspection of one of his eighty-three confirmed night victories.
(Author's Collection)

The longest-serving aircraft in the German night fighter arm. A Messerschmitt Bf 110G in flight.
(Author's Collection)

A much more capable aircraft in its later variants. A Junkers Ju 88 during an engine run-up.
(Author's Collection).

Whatever it took to get through a tour of operations. Note the panda good luck charm on this Halifax navigator's shoulder. That shoulder belongs to Flight Lieutenant PK Deane, who did survive the war. (DND PL43740)

Opposite: Many survived an operational tour and even excelled while doing so. Pilot Officer Jack Ryan of Toronto, in front of his 425 Squadron Halifax, *Nobody's Baby*, after his last war sortie. Note the DFC ribbon under his pilot wings. (DND PL33337)

Air Vice-Marshal Clifford Mackay "Black Mike" McEwen, a born and inspirational leader if ever one existed. (DND PL 44375)

A father figure to aircrew and ground crew alike, Black Mike McEwen (centre rear) with his airmen. (DND PL28446)

Opposite bottom: Roger Coulombe, "The Berlin Kid" and winner of an Immediate DFC, in the cockpit of his Lancaster. (DND PL26100)

So many lives depended on her handiwork. A WAAF rigger packing a parachute. (DND PL4915)

A technician adjusts the elevator balance bars of a Halifax, while leaning over the ammunition feed tracks of the rear gun turret. (DND PL22921)

"It's going to take a lot of sheet metal, sir." A corporal inspects a battle-damaged Halifax wing. (DND PL7166)

Ground crew clearing snow off a Lancaster's wing at Middleton St. George. (DND PL41650)

Howard Ripstein has offered the following comments on the LMF issue:

> We were all afraid but were afraid to admit it. Had we had Psychology and Psychiatry as we do today it would have been another story and to quit operational flying on account of fear would have been no disgrace. Having said this it was very necessary to have the LMF policy given the context of the times. We had a job to do and would only want to fly with committed comrades.[131]

It is interesting to note that aircrew veterans generally held a compassionate attitude towards those who failed to prevail, but were ruthless with those who failed to *attempt*, or those who deliberately avoided the difficult missions. A former navigator with 408 Squadron, Jim McInerney, wrote of the LMF categorization, "Surely some other terminology could have been applied. I have always violently objected to its use and have expressed sympathy for those to whom it was applied."[132]

Other distinguished veterans have offered thoughts about the LMF process that have been perhaps tempered by time, and also about how fear could gnaw away at a crew's self-confidence:

> As for the LMF cases, I don't have the same attitude as I had during the war. Now I know about the great stress under which operational crews were living before and during raids flying over enemy territory, often aboard aircraft without any operable defences. I am not personally aware of any case of LMF in my own 426 Squadron during the time of my tour of operations. It is possible, however, that some crew members refused to carry on with operational flying.
>
> Nevertheless, I now know enough to be able to understand that flying on German targets during the Second World War could induce enough fear in a crew member to drive him out of his mind and make him mentally sick. I have seen crews on board the bus that was taking us out to the who looked absolutely terrified. Their faces were as white as sheets! They seemed to be in a state of shock. I never did see crews that were petrified prior to taking off for a raid on Berlin come back from those raids. They were always reported missing.[133]

The stigma of being classified LMF had ramifications beyond services in an operational theatre, as noted by Jimmy Sheridan:

> I came across a sad case of LMF during the war. A pilot I'll call "Billy" told me he felt he couldn't bring himself to take the bomber off with a full load. He thought he wasn't strong enough to pull it up off the runway. I tried to convince him it was just like any other time he flew off, that they were very good aircraft, and that he was a strong young man. It was all to no avail. How he got through the conversion unit flying those poor old aircraft, I don't know. He also must have done his two "second dickie" trips. He said he had been lined up twice for an op when both times the trip was aborted for some reason, so he didn't have to go or to make any decisions. I forget what squadron he was with, or what happened when he went back to base after our talk, but after the war, I met a pal of his who told me Billy had been sent home LMF. One day, Billy went out hunting, and in climbing a fence, his rifle discharged, killing him. His pal didn't believe it was an accident, and neither do I. There were probably other factors involved, but since all kinds of young men were thrown into the service from all walks of life, glamorized at home, then traumatized when faced with combat, some compassion should have been shown. It might have been more productive if he had been reassigned to other duties, such as drogue pilot, or to Transport Command on an aircraft he thought he could handle. What a waste of a lot of training.[134]

Unquestionably, the threat of being categorized LMF was a powerful incentive to continue operations. Jim Northrup, a distinguished and decorated Canadian pilot, recalled for historians Spencer Dunmore and William Carter, in *Reap the Whirlwind*:

"I once made an early return and was more worried about being classed as LMF than the fact that my crew and I were very close to 'buying it.'" It is significant that he should have even considered such an eventuality, for he had a very real emergency on his hands. He recalls suffering from a very violent headache as the aircraft climbed. At nineteen thousand feet he passed out. The oxygen system had failed. He regained consciousness to find his bomb-laden Halifax in a power-on spin at seven thousand feet. Fortunately, Northrup was more experienced than the majority of 6 Group pilots, having been an instructor before going overseas. He was able to wrestle the big bomber out of the spin while there was still some air left below.[135]

Northrup later elaborated on this particular event, and on LMF in general:

I had climbing power set at 2400 revolutions and +6 pounds of boost and the last thing I noticed was the altimeter passing through 19,500 feet, enroute to 23,000 feet. Now I never flew on "George" (the autopilot) over enemy territory as it took a few seconds to release the controls after it was switched off, so I was hand-flying the aircraft. The next thing I see is the altimeter reading 7000 feet and I am in a power-on spin. Now, all my time spent instructing comes to the rescue. I go into spin recovery without thinking and pull her level at 1000 feet. I tell Dave to give me a course for home, as we are finished for the night. We land at East Moor with all our bombs on and I can hardly stay awake as I taxi to our dispersal spot. We cannot stay awake at debriefing, and finally, the M.O. sends us to bed. A tough night and no points . . . I sleep all that day and the next night. The following morning, the adjutant wakes me and says the C.O. would like to see me. Right away, I think I will be up for LMF as my aircraft was working perfectly. I go to the C.O.'s office and he seems quite friendly. He asks me how I am feeling and I reply that I am a little tired. He then tells me he has had my oxygen system tested and there was only compressed air in the bottles. He congratulates me on getting out of a sticky situation and tells me and my crew to take the day off. After a crew meeting, we decided that a good meal in York and a visit to *Betty's Bar* would not be out of the way. To the best of my knowledge, it was never determined how my oxygen bottles got filled with compressed air instead of oxygen . . .

I am sure LMF was dreamed up by people who had never been at the sharp end of the stick. Or maybe they were the same people who would not give the First World War airmen parachutes. The strange thing was that it was seldom mentioned, but it was always in the back of your mind. An airman had to declare that he would fly no more before the procedure started. He would be ordered into an aircraft three times, and if he refused, that was that. We only had one chap do this while I was on the Squadron, a sergeant bomb aimer. The sad thing about LMF was that you were totally destroyed in the Service and it must have had a substantial effect subsequently on the man as a civilian. To think of this as cowardice was wrong, as you got a feeling in your body as if you were recovering from a long illness, and you had no control over your body. The movie "Twelve O'clock High" got it just about right when Gregory Peck could not pull himself into the aircraft. I would say that everyone on operations experienced this at some point but were lucky enough to have a few days off, or a couple of nights sleep, and the feeling would go away . . .

The threat of LMF hanging over your head led you to do stupid things. A good friend of mine was on a daylight op and as he crossed the coast of Belgium, he was hit by 88 mm flak in the front of his aircraft and the navigator was badly wounded. All his flight instruments were knocked out and wind was blowing through the holes in the nose of the aircraft. At this point, the crash base at Manston was only twenty minutes away, and he could have dumped his bombs in the Channel and landed, but instead, he elected to continue the trip. When he finally landed at Manston, a tire blew and the aircraft swung and hit the FIDO pipes and was totally destroyed. Three more of the crew were injured and the navigator died from loss of blood.

I also made a stupid decision one night. The op was Cologne and I had a hydraulic failure on take-off, which left me with the starboard wheel and the tail wheel not retracted. I decided to continue the trip and by cutting every corner, we arrived over the target twenty minutes after the raid was over. I could not get above 11,000 feet altitude and was only able to obtain 140 miles per hour airspeed. As we started our bombing run, I saw what I thought was an aircraft on fire, but all of a sudden, two rockets passed in front of me, and right behind them, a Me 163 rocket aircraft going like a bat out of hell. He turned and fired two more rockets, closer this time but "no banana." The flame went out and he was gone. I thought the only reason he missed was because of our low speed. We landed at Manston very low on fuel and I made up my mind I would do no more stupid things, as there were seven other airmen whose lives depended on me. I said to hell with this "press on regardless" baloney, and if I was charged with LMF, so be it.

I was once ordered to organize a station parade with all members of both squadrons attending, drawn up in a U-shape facing inwards. In time a car drew up and an officer and a sergeant pilot got out and walked to the centre of the parade. The officer produced a paper and read something from it, then proceeded to pull off the sergeant's rank badges, buttons, wings, and even tore one shoulder of the uniform. They then marched back to the car and drove away. Now, the officer and the sergeant were not from our station and none of us knew them. I dismissed the parade and some of the chaps wanted to know what the hell was going on, but I was as much in the dark as they were. Now, the strange thing about this was, neither the group captain nor the two flying wing commanders were on parade, which left me, as a lowly squadron leader, the senior officer present. I always felt that this was a staged event, to keep our noses to the grindstone. We also always had a suspicion that NCO aircrew were not given as much leeway as officers.[136]

The New World Begs to Differ

As was the case in other situations where RCAF personnel overseas experienced the occasionally Draconian and class-conscious RAF administrative policies, "difficulties with the British LMF process became evident in Canada when the label of Waverer was applied to some RCAF airmen who clearly did not deserve it."[137] In a countering initiative, the RCAF, relying heavily on its air force legal officers, drafted its own LMF policy in 1944, which emphasized the protection of individual rights and due process of law. "In adopting the creation of *clear and willful evasion of operational responsibility* as a basis for judging the behavior of aircrew, the RCAF regulations moved the LMF procedure away from the bureaucratic, operational and medical realms toward the political and legal arenas."[138] (My italics.) Although it was not promulgated until relatively late in the European air war and affected very few RCAF aircrew, this distinctly Canadian policy signalled yet another victory for Canadian national pride and independence from British control.

Squadron Leader Noel "Buzz" Ogilvie, a native of Ottawa, flew wartime operational tours as a fighter pilot out of Britain and Malta. Late in the war, he was seconded to staff duties, serving on the Special Cases Committee at RAF Warrington, just east of Liverpool and south of 6 Group territory. His task was to help administer the new Canadian LMF policy to RCAF aircrew whose performance had been called into question. Ogilvie explains:

"Chubby" Power, the Minister of Air at the time, had written this Memorandum on LMF, air inefficiency and medical cases. When I got to Warrington, I got hold of the Memorandum and read it very carefully. We had three classifications available. One was "Medically Unfit," one was "Inefficient," and the third was "Lack of Moral Fibre." Only the English could think up a term as treacherous as Lack of Moral Fibre. The individuals being investigated, whether they were air gunners, made up from every aircrew trade we had; navigators, pilots, gunners, everything . . . And the person who was posted to us would be interviewed by a member of his trade, so I would interview the pilots.

We didn't have any trouble with the Medical cases, and Inefficiency cases were also usually straightforward because someone, usually the man's station commander or squadron commander, would say that he was incapable of operating his particular aircraft. Now with the Lack of Moral Fibre cases, according to the "Chubby" Power Memorandum, you had to ask the question, "Has this man carried on to the best of his ability?" And that was the thing that stuck in my craw. We had cases where you'd have, say, a navigator, who, immediately the wheels were pulled up on his aircraft, his writing arm would become useless, he couldn't write, and he would be sent to us under Lack of Moral Fibre . . . We had two psychiatrists on our Board who had interviewed the individual, and obviously there was something psychiatrically wrong with him if this was happening to him. There were also other fellas that had completed maybe ten trips, and as soon as the wheels were pulled up, they couldn't do anything with their right arms either. In these cases, the psychiatrists would come down with a recommendation that the man needed treatment and he should be sent home. OK, no problem . . . The *big* problems were the ones where there was not a *thing* wrong, according to the medical and psychiatric staff, and the man was also being sent to us under Lack of Moral Fibre, *and* it had also been indicated to us that he refused to fly. Those were the tough ones . . . So we would have to make a decision on whether this man had done his best under the circumstances. In a lot of the LMF cases, we ended up classifying them as "Inefficient" and sent them home. For instance, we had a case of a young sergeant pilot whom I interviewed, and I took his whole past history . . . He should never have been selected for aircrew in the first place. And his station commander went on to say that he was "yellow," and all that sort of stuff, so I flew down and met this station commander. At the time I was a squadron leader, and the Special Committee had a lot of wallop. I mean, you could walk into just about any place and ask for files; that sort of thing . . . So I interviewed the station commander, and after talking to him for awhile, I realized that he hated Canadians. Oh, he just hated them terribly . . . So after listening to him, I went back to Warrington, wrote up my report, and said that this individual was not LMF; he was Inefficient, and (we needed) to send him home.

And that was what we would do in a number of cases. We leaned more towards an Inefficiency assessment, even though the psychiatrists would say there was nothing mentally wrong with the man. They would say, "He has no extended tremors, he has no twitching of the eyelid. He's not pulling on an ear," or whatever . . . And I'd say to the psychiatrist, "Well, when was the last time *you* were over the Ruhr on a bombing raid?" So, psychiatry was not an exact science, by any means, and we would "fly by the seat of our pants," even though we had the psychiatrist's story that there was nothing mentally wrong with an individual, and we would try to be as fair as possible. In fact, I thought the system could have been much fairer than it was, because the individual was not represented by counsel, although we had a senior member of a law firm from Montreal with us who wrote all our reports; a very capable guy . . . But as we more often than not gave the break to the individual and designated him as Inefficient rather than LMF, very few airmen were actually classified as LMF, and I'm glad we did it that way . . . We only pursued, in an LMF sense, the most flagrant cases; the most outrageous and clear-cut in terms of their efforts to get out of meeting the enemy, and they were *very* few in number, of all the people who came before us.[139]

Perhaps the last philosophical words on this subject from a veteran should fall to Murray Peden, whose distinguished wartime career and articulate reflections tend to put balance on the LMF policy:

Remembering those who had carefully refrained from risking their precious hides, who had carefully refrained from bearing arms for their country, in any capacity, I always felt that LMF was a dirty label to fasten on someone who had volunteered for dangerous duty and had tried to carry out his commitment. The harsh treatment was necessary simply because the strain was so great. If there had been an easy and graceful way to abandon operational flying, many crews would have found the temptation hard to resist as their tours went on and the bloodshed continued.[140]

However, it would be misleading to place too much emphasis on the overall importance of the LMF policies and their impact . During the entire war, fewer than .2 percent of all Commonwealth aircrew were categorized as Lacking Moral Fibre, and even during some of the most arduous days of Bomber Command's operations, between July 1943 and June 1944, fewer than .4 percent of aircrew members were even identified as being possible LMF cases.[141] This was by any measure a highly enviable record under extremely daunting conditions.

The Balm of Inspirational Leadership

If the LMF policy was a hammer that helped generate the will to persevere during the bomber offensive, inspirational leadership was the velvet glove. Fortunately for Britain and the Dominions, there was no shortage of marvellous leaders in Bomber Command. The home islands produced Guy Penrose Gibson, VC, and Leonard Cheshire, VC, who led his men night after night over the most dangerous targets in inspirational example. By 1943, he had already completed two brilliant operational tours. His men would have followed him to hell and back, and frequently did just that. The Dominions produced, as we have seen, "Mick" Martin, Donald Bennett and Dave Shannon from Australia, while Canada could point with pride to Bob Turnbull, Reg Lane, Johnnie Fauquier, Nelles Timmerman, Bill Swetman and Joe Lecompte. We shall meet even more of them in the pages that follow. Turnbull ended the war as a group captain and a 6 Group station commander, who had already commanded flights and squadrons in distinguished overseas service covering nearly four years. Reg Lane flew three full tours of operations, one of only twenty-four RCAF members of Bomber Command to do so,[142] and he flew against almost every vital enemy target in Europe. Johnnie Fauquier won, among other Commonwealth and foreign awards, the DSO three times during three tours of operations. He served as the commanding officer of 405 Squadron, and a highly successful tour as commanding officer of 617 "Dambuster" Squadron late in the war, for which he voluntarily dropped rank from air commodore to lead the unit. Many people thought Fauquier was absolutely fearless. Instead, his bravery was reflected in the outstanding record he accumulated while he coped with fear. He once told a colleague: "A fellow who isn't afraid lacks imagination. And a guy who has no imagination can't be much of a combat pilot, and certainly never a leader."[143] Bill Swetman and Joe Lecompte were cut from the same cloth, as Roger Coulombe and Jim Northrup recall:

> When Wing Commander Crooks was killed over Peenemünde, he was replaced by a 23 year-old squadron leader who was then promoted to wing commander. His name was William "Bill" Herbert Swetman, DSO, DFC, and he had already done one tour of operations flying Wellington and Halifax aircraft with 405 Squadron. He then completed a second tour of operations flying Lancaster Mark II aircraft with us as commanding officer of 426 Squadron. He was a very good, brave and inspirational leader, and he didn't pick the easiest targets for himself, either. In fact, he participated in the Peenemünde raid the night his predecessor was killed in action. Actually, there were no easy targets in Germany during 1943 and 1944. Swetman flew many raids on Berlin, although I don't know precisely how many, but he came on quite a few of them. So, I can certainly say Bill Swetman was an example of leadership and an inspiration for the pilots of his squadron. He was also a very trusted pilot. Air Vice-Marshal McEwen, the AOC of 6 Group, even flew with him as a "second dickie" on a raid over a German city.[144]

Joe Lecomte commanded both 425 and 415 Squadrons, and later as a group captain, Tholthorpe, a 6 Group bomber station. Along with winning the DFC he was Mentioned in Despatches twice and also awarded the French *Croix de Guerre*. Jim Northrup has fond recollections of this gallant and charismatic leader:

> Wing Commander (later Group Captain) Joseph Hector Lucien Lecompte, DFC, was the most dynamic and outstanding squadron and station commander in 6 Group. He took over 415 Squadron when his predecessor was killed in a mid-air collision, and at the time, the Squadron was not performing well. In the short time he was in command, he whipped it into a top operational unit. Joe was a French Canadian and he had a slight accent. You seldom found him in his office as he was all over the place, checking out training, aircraft, ground crew and barracks. When Joe arrived, he also got a new adjutant, Flight Lieutenant Arthur Caveth, a Permanent Force type who had worked his way up from Aircraftsman Second Class. Joe went into Art's office to meet his new adjutant and found him with a desk stacked high with papers. Joe asked what all that mess was. Art told him it was reports that had not been filed with Group by the former adjutant, and he was trying to process them and send them along. Joe gathered them all up and dumped the whole mess into the stove. Then, turning to Art, he said, "All filed. Nobody at Group will ever miss them." It was my good fortune to arrive at the Squadron just a few days after Joe took command, and I was able to learn a lot about operations from him. He was amazed that I had an all French Canadian crew, and asked how I had got them. When I told him my problems in that respect , he said, "Northrup, you must be a determined type, and we will get along well." We did. After one trip, word came from Group that the raid was not a success, and there would be no points awarded for the operation which, at this time, were required, along with a specific number of sorties, to complete an operational tour. I immediately went to Joe and said this was B.S. . I had hit the Aiming Point and if anybody was off, it was Pathfinder Force. Joe said he would personally plot my target photos and later that day, he told me I was right and that I had hit the aiming

point. Now I did not care about not getting credit for the trip, which nobody did, but the skill of myself and my crew had been questioned and I was not prepared to accept that. Joe was also a hell of a good man at a party, always right in the thick of it. Unfortunately for 415 Squadron, Joe was made station commander of Tholthorpe where 425 "Alouette" Squadron was based. He was a hard man if you sluffed off, but he was very well liked. Joe was Permanent Force, but he did not do well after the war, because he was not a "paper pusher," and people who were not fit to carry his parachute became air vice-marshals. Joe was killed in Montreal while helping people who were involved in an automobile accident.

He was a hell of a fine officer.[145]

One of the greatest examples of inspirational leadership within the RCAF Overseas came from a very high level. In its first year of operations, 6 Group lost 340 aircraft and the death toll would continue to rise until a total of 814 group aircraft had been felled by war's end.[146] It is safe to say that 6 Group, like the rest of Bomber Command, experienced significant morale problems in 1943. Nonetheless, in February 1944 Air Vice-Marshal Clifford M. "Black Mike" McEwen succeeded Air Vice-Marshal George Brookes as air officer commanding, and the fortunes of the group changed dramatically from that time. A dynamic, capable leader who had proved his mettle in the Great War as a distinguished fighter pilot, downing twenty-seven enemy aircraft, McEwen was an unrepentant advocate of arduous, realistic and demanding training, as well as stern discipline. No armchair commander, McEwen led fearlessly from the front, accompanying his crews on their toughest missions and against the explicit orders of Sir Arthur Harris. Knowing that their commander fully appreciated and shared their dangers, 6 Group crews' performance soon became as good as any in Bomber Command, and better than most. "McEwen's presence was soon taken for granted—he even became a good luck symbol. As the men saw it, when the man with the moustache was along, things were going to be fine. They felt drawn to this colourful airman who wanted to share their danger, and when ordered not to, could not sleep while his men were on a raid."[147] Howard Ripstein recalls McEwen's leadership style from wartime service under his command:

He was Air Vice-Marshal Clifford Mackay "Black Mike" McEwen, CB, MC, DFC and Bar, Commander of the Legion of Honour (France), and the Legion of Merit (United States), holder of the Italian *Medal Valoria* and *Croca de Guerra*. In the First World War, he was a contemporary of Bishop and Collishaw, and in Italy, a wing mate of Barker . . .

As Air Officer Commanding 6 Group, Black Mike's credo was leadership by example, albeit, in his case, *illegal* when he flew on operations, usually dressed in a sergeant's uniform. Despite an almost total ban by the highest of authorities, "Bomber" Harris winked at McEwen's actions . . . However, what he was doing soon became known throughout 6 Group and beyond. Group Captain (Retired) Bill Swetman, DSO, DFC, CD, a wartime commanding officer of 426 "Thunderbird" Squadron, vividly recalls such a flight when flying on the last trip of his second tour of operations. At the last possible moment, Sergeant-Pilot McEwen was driven up to Swetman's Lancaster Mark II on the Linton-on-Ouse tarmac, and the AOC climbed aboard.

This trip was particularly interesting, as many bombers were flying raggedly with their navigation lights on. Black Mike soon put a stop to this. How? He threatened to send up Mustang fighters under his control to shoot offenders down, and this threat was confirmed to the writer by Bill Swetman. On the ground as well as in the air, he was a stickler for discipline, standards and training—and more training. Still, he was fully aware of the stress endured by his air and ground crews. Within reason, his office door at Allerton Hall, the group's headquarters, was always open to any of the group's men and women who wanted to see him.

Black Mike never slept when 6 Group was operational. He attended as many debriefings, then known as "interrogations," as he could, informally chatting with the returned, tired crews, many of whom became his close friends after the war.[148]

Along with demonstrating a willingness to share their men's hardships and to provide sufficient rest and relaxation for them, the best combat leaders were able to provide some meaningful philosophy of life to their charges. It would appear that imbuing a sense of fatalism, short of defeatism, worked to a certain extent during the bomber offensive. Philip Ardery, a pilot, expressed it this way:

It helped me to say to myself with complete calm: "You can't live forever. You have had a great deal in your life-span already, much more than many people ever have. You would not shirk the duty of tomorrow if you could. Go into it calmly, don't try too hard to live. Don't ever give up hope: never let the fear of death strike panic in your mind and paralyze your reason. Death will find you sometime, if not tomorrow. Give yourself a chance." And then I would remember that very appropriate sentence of Shakespeare: "Cowards die many times more before their deaths; the valiant never taste of death but once."[149]

Thus, the aircrew who appeared to fare best were those who did not dwell excessively on their fate. "Many crews argued that emotional entanglements were madness, whether inside or outside marriage. They diverted a man from the absolute single-mindedness he needed to survive over Germany. When a pilot was seen brooding over a girl in the Mess, he was widely regarded as a candidate for the 'chop list.' "[150] Inspirational leadership during the bombing campaign involved more than selfless example in combat and the provision of philosophical guidance to subordinates. It also occasionally entailed taking a liberal interpretation of when an aircrew member had "done enough," as codified in the open-ended phrasing of the RAF's operational tour length policy. Jake Walters, a Canadian pilot and colleague of Murray Peden, had experienced a particularly stressful operational tour, fraught with "near misses." By the summer of 1944, he had the bulk of his required sorties behind him, but the cumulative effect of his harrowing experiences had made a deep impact. Peden recalls that while it was not in Jake Walters's character to ask for any relief, squadron crews were getting progressively more concerned about him, fearing that his condition would worsen and cause him and his crew to be killed before they could be taken off operations. Walters would habitually but discreetly throw up during the post-operation interrogations, testimony to the extreme stress with which he was steadfastly attempting to cope. Murray Peden remembers one such incident, after Walters had flown a daylight raid against the railway yards at Chalons sur Marne on 22 July 1944:

After his return, while he sat sipping his coffee and answering the questions of the Intelligence Officer at interrogation, he felt the unmistakable symptoms again, and hurried outdoors. As he stood heaving, one arm bent forward against the corner of the building, he felt someone move behind him, and an arm slipped firmly around his waist to support him until he finished straining.

Then he heard McGlinn's [the squadron commander] voice in his ear: "I think you've had enough, Jake." Thus came the end of Jake's tour, after his twenty-fifth operation. The rest of us on the station were almost as happy as Jake and his crew to see that they had made it, and the Wingco went up another notch in my estimation.[151]

The Need for Recognition

Awards and decorations, bestowed equitably, fairly, and in a timely manner for acts of heroism and exceptional merit, were highly conducive to bettering wartime morale. In recent years, there have been suggestions that the wartime British authorities under-subscribed deserving Canadian service personnel within their honours system. Is this a fair assessment? Hugh Halliday, the acknowledged expert in the field of historical honours and awards granted to members of the Canadian flying services, has observed that there was some confusion in the early months of the war as to the type and quantities of honours that were awarded to Canadian personnel. In time, the confusion gave way to a series of orders specifying which awards were available to Canadians, and which were to be granted under a quota system. Initially, there was some suspicion and antagonism on both sides. There had been a dearth of British awards granted to Canadian citizens in the inter-war years, and some senior Canadians were expecting awards to be made "on a generous scale" in order to compensate for their paucity during the previous twenty years. "If British officers were worried that Canadians would somehow swamp the awards lists, Canadians seemed fearful that British authorities would be niggardly in granting awards."[152] We have already seen in Chapter 2 that gallantry awards were frequently inconsistently awarded or overlooked within the RAF, and specifically noted the unhappy state of affairs in late 1941 on 207 Squadron in 5 Group reported by Mike Lewis, who was flying Manchesters at the time. However, what generally was the ratio of wartime aircrew gallantry awards between the RAF and the RCAF? While some statistics are surprisingly difficult to pin down, others are broadly available. For example, it is widely accepted that approximately 125,000 Allied airmen served operationally in Bomber Command throughout the war years, of which roughly 70,000 were British and 40,000 were Canadian. It is also known that approximately 50,000 Canadian graduates of the BCATP served in operational theatres during the war, which made them eligible for gallantry awards. Thus, Bomber Command was, by an enormous margin, the majority employer of Canadian combat aircrew members during the Second World War. Throughout the war years, the RCAF awarded 4017 DFCs and 515 DFMs to members of the Service for gallantry in the air, the majority going to Canadians in Bomber Command.[153] The RAF awarded 20,000 DFCs and 6600 DFMs during the war, although those numbers presumably include Commonwealth and Allied aircrew in RAF service. Of these, a substantial number, if not a majority, would have gone to members of Bomber Command.[154] Therefore, a rough extrapolation suggests that Canadians were under-subscribed with respect to British honours, particularly regarding the DFM for non-commissioned officers. The Canadian number seems inordinately low in comparison, for in spite of the fact that the Canadian government had adopted a liberal and generous commissioning policy for aircrew during the later war years, there still was a significant number of NCO aircrew engaged in operations. Furthermore, of the twenty-three VCs awarded to Bomber Command aircrew during the Second World War,[155] only two went to Canadians. One was a member of the RCAF and another was a Canadian expatriate in RAF service. However, there was no shortage of worthy candidates, as ten Canadian airmen were formally recommended for the award.[156] For the Dams Raid of May 1943, thirty-four decorations were awarded to the raid's fifty-six survivors, but only seven of the surviving seventeen Canadians were honoured. But, this specific case may constitute too small a sampling base to merit any real conclusions. Still, it indicates a disturbing trend in the recognition and acknowledgement of operational merit from the British, or lack of it.

One possible reason for a reduced proportion of wartime British honours to Canadian airmen was that the first AOC of 6 Group, Air Vice-Marshal George Brookes, does not appear to have assigned any great priority to obtaining decorations for the personnel under his command. However, the same could not be said for Black Mike McEwen. He was very much attuned to the value and necessity of recognition for his people, both the warriors and the supporting crews, and in July 1944, he forcefully instructed his base commanders to increase the number of award submissions. The thrust of his initiatives were reflected in the following letter from Group Captain Johnnie Fauquier, then the commanding officer of 62 "Beaver" Base at Linton, to the commanding officers of 408, 415, 420, 425, 426 and 432 Squadrons:

> Headquarters No. 6 (RCAF) Group has expressed a desire that the numbers of recommendations submitted from this Base for Non-Immediate awards be increased, pointing out that the recommendations submitted by other Groups in Bomber Command are greatly in excess of this Group, regardless of the fact that this Group is reputed to be one of the most efficient from an operational standpoint. In view of this it is considered that the Group is not receiving an equitable share of honours and awards, due largely to the small number of recommendations submitted . . . In order that this situation may be improved it is requested that each squadron submit a minimum of ten recommendations for Non-Immediate awards monthly. This is in no way to change existing instructions relative to recommendations for Immediate awards.[157]

This call for action from Black Mike McEwen had the desired effect, and from the summer of 1944 onward, honours for the personnel of 6 Group were much more forthcoming.[158] This resulted in better group morale, and in the outstanding performance record of 6 Group during the last year of the war.

While this book focuses on the bomber aircrew experience, no such tribute would be complete without acknowledging the tremendous contributions made by the groundcrews. Indeed, when the total number of RCAF personnel overseas was at its peak on 31 December 1944, the numbers of groundcrew were greater than those of the aircrew.[159] Although they did not share the operational dangers the flyers faced night after night, and later day after day, their situation had its own risks. Enemy raids, although infrequent, did occur, and the dangers associated with preparing and maintaining the bombers for duty were numerous. Workplace safety was not a high priority at the time, and the riggers, fitters, and armourers had to work long hours with minimal rest under frequently primitive conditions, particularly during periods of peak operational tempo. Emergency situations abounded, and crash recoveries as well as battle damaged aircraft were seldom routine, and were frequently dangerous. Weapons safety technology was still evolving, and the sheer numbers of operations meant that accidents were bound to happen.

The groundcrew developed fierce loyalties to their squadrons and bases, and most particularly, to the aircrews and aircraft to which they were assigned. They were intensely proud of their flyers, and that pride manifested itself in the prodigious efforts they made to ensure the aircraft committed to their care were in the best shape possible for the flyers to take on operations. And when their aircrews were killed or lost on operations or in accidents, they felt as though a part of them had died as well. Furthermore, since they normally represented the continuum with respect to personnel, the pain of loss through identification with and attachment to *multiple aircrew teams* often fell heavy on their shoulders.

At the end of the war, Sir Arthur Harris acknowledged his Command's many non-combat casualties and paid tribute to the groundcrew and their many contributions and sacrifices.

> Few people realize that, whereas some 50,000 aircrew . . . were killed in action . . . some 8000 men and women were killed at home in training, in handling vast quantities of bombs under the most dangerous conditions, in driving and dispatch riding in the blackout on urgent duty . . . natural causes . . . included the death of many fit young people who . . . died from the effects of extraordinary exposure, since many contracted illnesses by working all hours of the day and night in a state of exhaustion in the bitter wet, cold and miseries of six war winters. It may be ignored what it is like to work in the open . . . 20 feet up in the air on the aircraft . . . this was on wartime aerodromes, where such accommodation as could be provided offered every kind of discomfort.[160]

Groundcrews were also greatly appreciated by the operational aircrews. Russ Hubley, a star wartime gunner and DFC winner on 405 Squadron, recalls:

> The groundcrew were always there. They had their little quirks, but they kept the aircraft in the air, no matter what. They told us in no uncertain terms that the aircraft belonged to them and we could only borrow it. We were to return it in the condition they gave it to us. They'd be there when you took off and they were there when you returned. If there were any problems they'd work all night to fix them. In my opinion, the groundcrew were our unsung heroes and never got the credit they deserved. Without them, we'd have been "up the creek." They performed miracles on a daily basis.[161]

In 1944, Johnnie Fauquier sang their praises to Air Marshal Lloyd S. Breadner, then AOC-in-C at RCAF Overseas Headquarters, when he said, "Canadian groundcrew have been showing themselves to be unquestionably the best in the world."[162]

Because of their limited combat exposure, groundcrew personnel received very few gallantry awards, but quite a few were decorated for acts of heroism under dangerous conditions associated with ground duties. And many more were recognized for acts of extraordinary achievement or particular merit in the performance of their duties by various chivalry awards and/or Mentions-in-Despatches.

Some, like Flight Sergeant S.A. McKenzie, No. 408 Squadron, were rewarded for their efforts—in his case, with the British Empire Medal. "This non-commissioned officer," commented the chief technical officer at Linton-on-Ouse, "has built A Flight up into the best organized and smoothly functioning section on the station. Their record of serviceability and operational failures is second to none."

> A very hard working and conscientious man with a thorough knowledge of his trade, he above all has a vast amount of initiative which he does not hesitate to display . . . While other flights have complained loudly, and called for help . . . whenever they had more than eight aircraft to look after, Flight Sergeant McKenzie has cheerfully prepared as many

as twelve for operations quickly and efficiently without a murmur of complaint. This was not an isolated case either, but occurred daily throughout the period that "B" Flight was converting to Halifax aircraft and "A" Flight was looking after all the Lancasters."

Some lost their lives, and others took extreme risks in trying to save doomed comrades.

> Corporal [P.W.] Butler [No. 433 Squadron], on the morning of December 19th, 1943, was running the engines of "Q" Queenie in conjunction with Leading Aircraftman O'Connor and Leading Aircraftman McEvoy when aircraft "C" Charlie crashed while taking off and landed on top of the aircraft in which Corporal Butler was working. Both aircraft immediately burst into flame. [LAC] O'Connor was rendered unconscious by the crash and Corporal Butler, despite the intense flames, attempted to remove him through the pilot's escape hatch, but was unable to do so. In his attempt to remove his comrade, he stayed in the cockpit of the aircraft despite intense smoke and flames until almost overcome. It was only then that he thought of self-preservation and . . . crawled out of the pilot's escape hatch and jumped from the nose of the aircraft into a pile of flaming debris, thereby breaking both his heels. He proceeded to crawl on his hands and knees through the flaming mass. Corporal Butler showed outstanding courage and determination in his effort to save his fellow worker."

Corporal Butler was Mentioned in Despatches.[163] The bomber offensive was a magnificent effort in the face of continued adversity, a true triumph of the human spirit. The prolonged, sustained fortitude of the crews that flew the operations was that rare form of bravery that Napoleon Bonaparte referred to as the Courage of the Early Morning.

SIX

A Town Called Whitebait
On to Berlin
1943–1944

The battering we received over the North German Plain cost us more than a thousand aircraft and between seven and eight thousand lives. Berlin wasn't worth it.
—Group Captain John Searby, DSO, DFC[1]

It was in 1943—or, to be more accurate, in the span of time contained within the period March 1943 to March 1944—that "independent" strategic air power reached its peak in the Second World War.

—John Terraine

By August 1943, Sir Arthur Harris believed the siege of Hamburg had been successfully brought to a close. Losses had been lower than anticipated, at 87 aircraft from the 2592 that had sortied against the port city. This constituted an acceptable 2.8 percent loss rate, significantly less than the recently concluded Ruhr campaign. Also, in the wake of the Hamburg raids, Albert Speer made a statement which certainly got the attention of Harris: namely, that if six more German cities were pummelled as badly as Hamburg, Germany might not be able to continue the war.[2] This appeared to validate the strategy of area bombing the German industrial cities. Harris now felt the next major focus for Bomber Command should be the complete destruction of Berlin, the Nazi "holy city." There are two separate interpretations of the dates of the Battle of Berlin, because there were actually two clusters of raids launched during this period. A three-raid exploratory series in August and September was essentially a feasibility study, and the "main event" series of sixteen operations took place between 18 November 1943 and 31 March 1944. It was Harris's fervent hope that the obliteration of the capital city would paralyze the enemy's command structure and destroy the

German will to wage war, thus making a blood-costly invasion of northwest Europe unnecessary. He also deeply hoped the Americans would join Bomber Command in a coordinated around the clock effort, as they had done at Hamburg.

The stage was being set for an all-out assault against the capital, and the lengthening late summer and autumn nights made the raids more practicable. Furthermore, there was a seven-month period available before the Command would be seconded to Supreme Headquarters Allied Expeditionary Forces (SHAEF) for use against pre-invasion targets. The zeal with which Harris intended to pursue the obliteration of the German capital was embodied in a frequently quoted letter to Winston Churchill that has since found favour with his detractors for its undue optimism, in light of the actual costs and the results obtained: "We can wreck Berlin from end to end if the USAAF will come in on it. It will cost us between 400-500 aircraft. It will cost Germany the war."[3]

However, a series of very costly raids, starting with Regensburg and Schweinfurt on 17 August 1943 and finishing with another assault on Schweinfurt on 14 October 1943, effectively gutted the American VIII Bomber Command. Without long-range day fighter escorts, the deep penetrations were too dangerous and costly until the magnificent P-51 Mustang became available in large numbers in 1944. While the Americans eventually did go against Berlin in force, it was after Bomber Command's main effort. Thus, Harris's dream of a combined Anglo-American siege on Berlin was not to be. Nevertheless, Bomber Command was prepared to act alone, and during this period Harris also launched thirty-six major raids against other targets, many of which were successful. They will also be covered in the ensuing pages.

Why Berlin?

But how legitimate and important a target was Berlin, this epicentre of the Third Reich? Not only was it Germany's administrative capital, it was also the nerve centre of the Nazi military-industrial complex. Along with housing the headquarters of all branches of the military services, there were nearly one hundred separate military barracks and depots in the area. And with all its rail lines, airports and its sophisticated canal system, Berlin was also a hub of the national transportation network. The city's huge Siemens complex was a cornerstone of the national electrical industry, as were Daimler-Benz, the ten AEG factories and the Bosch, Lorenz, Blauplunkt and Telefunken plants, all of which produced essential electrical components for the *Wehrmacht*. Furthermore, an ultra-secret facility in the suburb of Dahlem, the Kaiser Wilhelm Institute for Physics Research, housed the primary German atomic weapons development program. Additionally,

> The sprawling Alkett factory in Spandau produced self-propelled guns and half the Wehrmacht's field artillery. Borsig, one of Berlin's pioneer industrial firms, made rolling stock, locomotives, and heavy artillery. A DWM (German Weapons and Munitions) factory in the northern district of Wittenau produced small arms, ammunition, and mortars. Tank chassis rolled off the assembly lines at the Auto-Union factories at Spandau and Halensee. BMW's Berlin branch produced a variety of military vehicles, while Heinkel, Henschel, and Dornier made bombers, attack aircraft, and airplane components.[4]

In fact, the city was considered to be of such vital industrial importance that it was singled out as one of the twenty-two German cities most worthy of bombing attention in the Pointblank directive.[5] Berlin was also the main administrative headquarters for nearly every major bureaucratic entity in the Third Reich, including the Propaganda Ministry, the *Gestapo*, the People's Court, the Foreign Ministry and the Armaments Ministry. Other important targets included all the major hierarchy of the National Socialist Party, including the *Führer* himself.

However, there were various factors which made effective bombing of the city a complex problem. Perhaps the greatest disadvantage of its location was that it lay beyond the effective ranges of *Oboe*, *Gee* and *G-H*, which made locating specific targets electronically extremely difficult. Also, unlike the coastal port of Hamburg or the distinctive shapes and clear returns of Düsseldorf and Wuppertal, the *H2S* radar could not break out various elements of the city accurately.[6] The distinctiveness of Berlin's many lakes on radar was not dependable, and the great indeterminate mass of the cosmopolitan build-up tended to change shape on radar, depending on the system's gain or power setting. The capital was also enormously spread out, encompassing more than 900 square miles, and boasted many open spaces, so that "the bombers had difficulty hitting specific targets or wiping out large contiguous areas. In fact, the early raids had achieved so little by the end of 1941 that the British suspended attacks on Berlin for about a year to concentrate on easier targets and to develop technical improvements that would, they hoped, make it easier to hit the German capital."[7] However, the drawback for bombing associated with the city's sprawl was partially offset by the extensive imbedding of industrial works and firms within the residential areas, thus augmenting the legitimacy of these broad districts as targets. Even so, Berlin's largely modern infrastructure meant that the comparatively wide streets tended to limit the spread of fire.

While the city's targets proved electronically elusive, most of the "main event" raids were conducted during the dead of winter when the skies over the city were predominately overcast. This made visual reference target marking for the most part impossible. The Pathfinders thus had to rely on the relatively inefficient skymarker flares dropped on *H2S* returns, and they were seldom dropped in a tight cluster on which the Main Force could bomb accurately.

Since the Nazis considered the city their ideological epicentre, they went to great lengths to protect it. Roger Coulombe recalls the raids in general, then specifically remembers the flak, the fighters and the searchlights:

> Most of our raids over Berlin were done during the late fall and winter when the period of darkness was the longest. And of course, the ground temperatures were also at the lowest. Therefore, at operational height, that is, above 20,000 feet, the temperature could be well below -40° F. If you add to that the velocity of the winds at altitude, plus the airspeed of the aircraft, those temperatures could easily get in the neighbourhood of -50° F and perhaps even lower, with the result that the rear gunner was unable to fire his guns. There was no adequate lubricant at the time that could be used on the breech blocks of the guns to prevent them from freezing at such low temperatures. Knowing that the rear gunner's guns were unserviceable was reason enough for panic in the crew. That happened after we took off for a raid on Leipzig on the night of 20 October 1943, which would have been the eighth raid of my tour. Even though we had been airborne for three hours and 45 minutes and had been flying over enemy territory, it never counted as a sortie for the crew. We took all that risk for nothing. Four of my crew members panicked, making a chorus, and begging me to turn back. Since I could not carry on without the cooperation of those four crew members, I resigned myself to turning back after dropping my bombs over the German territory where we were flying at the time. Back on the ground, I warned my rear gunner to take better care of his guns in the future because I would never turn back again, even if not a single gun was firing. I told my gunners that they had the

responsibility to see that their guns were properly maintained in firing condition in any circumstances.

The Berlin raids were all a sort of an ordeal for a bomber crew because of the great distance we had to fly over enemy territory. There was also always great night fighter activity all the way to and from the target, as well as over the target. I remember a couple of raids when the bomber stream had taken the short, direct route to Berlin, between Hannover and Bremen. The German fighters had marked the route with white flares on each side of the bomber stream. We were flying in between flares and I had the impression of being on a runway doing a landing . . .

The Big City was protected by a tremendous quantity of anti-aircraft guns (both heavy and light flak guns) several miles across. Martin Middlebrook claims in his book *The Berlin Raids* that "the flak area around Berlin measured forty miles across and the searchlight belt around it was sixty miles wide!" Indeed, there was a terrific quantity of searchlights trying to cone and isolate a bomber if the sky was not completely overcast. This combination of searchlights and always-intense flak was terrifying enough.

In addition there was the great amount of night fighters, both single-engine and twin-engine fighters, always ready to engage the bombers in air combat. Our Lancasters had very little firepower, even when our .303 inch machine guns were not frozen. We were no match for the German fighters, who had at least 20 mm cannons, and who could fire from a range that our returning bullets could not reach.

Each raid over Berlin was a "shaky do" for a bomber crew. It was a very long time to be under an acute state of stress. Many of the Berlin raids took over eight hours of flying time to complete because the Big City was so far east. The shortest route, straight in and straight out, was by no means the safest. And there was only one single pilot at the controls at all times. There was no use of automatic pilot over enemy territory, and the aircraft did not have hydraulically-boosted controls. Every manoeuvre was done using human muscles. And you had to react quickly if you wanted to survive a night fighter attack. The gunners were not always able to detect the enemy fighters before they opened fire on us. They attacked from the rear and from below where they could not be seen in pitch darkness, while they could easily see us silhouetted against the lighter sky.

I participated in the Nuremburg raid of 30/31 March 1944 and on five raids against Happy Valley, the Ruhr. I can tell you that none of those raids was as hard on the nerves as a raid on Berlin. Going against Berlin, you felt overwhelmed by the immensity of the defended area. You had the feeling of the impossibility of getting through the collective opposition of so many defences. You felt that your aircraft was inadequate, both in speed and manoeuvrability. And to make things worse, you were freezing in the cockpit because of the inadequate heating systems in the Lancasters, coupled with the extremely low outside air temperatures. Those warplanes had no insulation whatever, and they were not pressurized, either.

During every raid you could observe bombers being coned, surrounded by flak puffs, exploding, disintegrating in mid-air, then going down in flames. Or, engaged in aerial combat, being fired on by Ju 88s, FW 190s or Me 109s, and, in many instances, being shot down as well. It was a scary sight. You felt very insecure during those moments. Even if your own aircraft was not being directly attacked at any given time, some of the flak exploded so close during blanket firing that you could smell the cordite inside your aircraft. And you could have a secondary searchlight beam on you without necessarily being coned. It was best not to look down along the beam because you could easily get dizzy.[8]

Berlin was ringed by defensive fighter stations, and they were always ordered to spare no effort to intercept the incoming raiders before they arrived overhead the city. Early in the war, Berlin's flak defences were deemed insufficient to cope with large-scale raids, and more formidable installations were built. Throughout 1941 and 1942, Albert Speer and his Ministry constructed batteries of flak and searchlights, arranged in a concentric pattern around the metropolis. The innermost ring consisted of three of the largest flak bunkers ever built, and similar installations were developed for Hamburg and Vienna. In Berlin one was erected near the Zoological Gardens, another was placed in northern Humboldthain Park, while the third was situated in Friedrichshain Park, to the east of the Alexanderplatz. These massive, paired bunkers were laid out in a triangular pattern to protect the area contained within. Two paired bunkers were completed for Hamburg in October 1942, while a trio of paired towers was eventually completed for Vienna in 1943 and 1944.[9] They looked like the old Crusader castles,

> with concrete walls 2.5 metres thick, window slits sheathed in steel, and towers bristling with 128-millimeter anti-aircraft guns mounted in pairs. Beneath the roof level were smaller gun turrets housing multi-barreled quick firing "pompom guns" and 37-millimeter cannons for cutting down low-flying aircraft. No wonder British fliers came to regard attacks on Berlin as a nerve-wracking experience. As one Lancaster bombardier put it: "The run-up seemed endless, the minutes of flying 'straight and level' seemed like hours and every second I expected to be blown to pieces. I sweated with fear, and the perspiration seemed to freeze on my body."[10]

While the Berlin raids constituted a major focus for Bomber Command during the winter of 1943/1944, the city was far from being its sole preoccupation. Other targets presented their own challenges, and the Germans were determined not to make it easy for the bombers.

The Hamburg raids, embodied by the electronic jamming of the German early warning and tracking radars, but most especially, through the use of *Window*, had thrown the night defensive system into total disarray. In the words of John Terraine and a related Air Historical Branch monograph: "*Window* meant that the Kammhuber Line, 'on which untold industrial and military effort had been spent, became an expensive and useless luxury overnight; and it became necessary to reorganize the whole system of night fighter defence.'"[11]

German Tactical Innovations and Allied Countermoves

After the Second Battle of the Ruhr, the German night fighter boxes were at least partially abandoned, and free-ranging tactics by the *Luftwaffe* to acquire visual contacts on the bomber targets came back into vogue. Even prior to Hamburg, in April, *Major* Hajo Herrmann, a former bomber pilot and a fervent advocate of *Wilde Sau* (Wild Boar) tactics, had advocated the use of day fighters in the target area, which would take advantage of the illumination provided by the searchlights, ground fires, and the target markers dropped by enemy raiders. Herrmann felt this form of illumination, viewed by the Wild Boars from above and looking down, would result in a significant number of aerial victories. He was proved right, and towards the end of June 1943, he was permitted to form a specialist *Wilde Sau* wing, *Jagdgeschwader* 300. Kammhuber felt, however, that the free-ranging, uncontrolled tactics employed would ultimately sow more chaos among the defenders than the attackers, and he was also proven correct.. "Soon, no-one in the operations rooms knew who was friend or foe. Furthermore, the single-engined aircraft were not well suited to blind flying, and their pilots, most of whom had no experience of flying on instruments, succumbed in large numbers to take-off and landing accidents."[12] *Wilde Sau*, employed piecemeal earlier in 1943, was used for the first time on a concentrated basis during the Berlin raids. However, the problems this initiative created tended to outweigh the gains. Eventually, in March 1944, the Wild Boars were returned to day operations, although not before they enjoyed their moment of glory in the night skies over the Reich. Some of the fighters were experimentally fitted with small, compact *Neptun* radar receivers, but this equipment did little to enhance their success rates at night.

In September 1943, after the initial Berlin raids, *Generalleutnant* Josef Schmid succeeded an out-of-favour Kammhuber at *XII Fliegerkorps* as head of the night fighter arm. Kammhuber had remained rigidly loyal to the inflexible *Himmelbett* system, and had also been completely unrealistic in his demands for new and more equipment.[13] Schmid was no fan of *Himmelbett*, but he was also pragmatic enough to view the Wild Boars objectively. *Zahme Sau* or Tame Boar tactics were altogether different. In a manifestation of the earlier Tame Boar philosophy, he promoted en route interception tactics of the bomber stream and loosened his crews from their strict shackling to GCI controllers, partially sparing them from that system's increasing vulnerability to jamming. Schmid was optimistic that technology would help accomplish this. Quantity production of the improved *Lichtenstein SN2* AI radar would soon be a reality, and this substantially refined system had improved reliability, range, search angles, and most importantly, it was immune to the effects of *Window*. Numerous innovative techniques were used to attempt to illuminate the bombers and highlight them for the defending night fighters. In conjunction with the *Helle Nachtjagd* (Bright Night Fighting) tactics, as mentioned earlier, the route of the bomber stream would soon be illuminated, whenever and wherever possible, by flare shells fired from the ground and by parachute flares dropped by high-altitude aircraft.[14] Along with the flares being strewn regularly along the length of the bomber stream,[15] on overcast nights, searchlight batteries were focussed on the cloud bases, allowing the bombers to be occasionally silhouetted from above, as if being viewed through frosted glass. This latter tactic was first utilized by Herrmann's Wild Boars in the target area when Wild Boar tactics were still in vogue.[16]

By this time, German scientists had also successfully developed two electronic devices which were to be fitted to all the twin-engine night fighters—*Flensburg*, which homed on the British *Monica* tail warning radar receiver from ranges of up to sixty miles, and *Naxos*, which could home on *H2S* transmissions from distances as great as thirty miles. Once these electronic innovations were available in quantity, it was Schmid's intention to completely cease the old point-defence variant of night combat, so susceptible to deception, and concentrate on ranging pursuit operations on a very large scale.[17] Furthermore, a very promising, purpose-built night fighter was being developed to host the new electronic equipment. The Heinkel He 219 *Uhu* (Owl) was manoeuvrable, fast, and with six 20 mm cannons, heavily armed and capable of meeting the de Havilland Mosquito on equal terms. Furthermore, it carried IFF equipment compatible with the *Würzburg* radars, and it was hoped to ultimately insert this potent weapon all along the bomber stream's length. Fortunately for the Allies, it never reached mass production. The March 1943 raid on Heinkel's Rostock facility destroyed many of the construction blueprints, which significantly slowed its development. Then, some relatively trivial development problems predisposed the *Reichluftministerium* (the RLM or Air Ministry) to delay its quantity production. This was a grave error in judgment, since the aircraft's advantages far outweighed its modest growing pains. Indeed, the RLM's shortsightedness on the He 219 was common with this organization, and it virtually guaranteed that the older combat types, such as the Bf 110, the Do 217 and the Ju 88, would continue in production well past their prime.

> Plotting and scheming among the interested aircraft firms, an unfathomable evaluation policy at the RLM, and a lack of technical foresight all did more than their share to hinder the urgently needed re-equipment of the night fighter units, while Germany's towns were bombed into ashes and rubble and many hundreds of thousands were killed. In this way the newly-raised hopes of the night fighter crews were dashed once more.[18]

Of the three older fighter types, the longest-serving in the night fighter arm was the Messerschmitt Bf 110, produced in many variants with an enormous number of modifications. Along with the Junkers Ju 88, it formed the backbone of the *Luftwaffe's* night fighter defence capability. Ace pilot Rudolf Thun recalls the Messerschmitt's performance characteristics:

> How did the Bf 110 fly? I started with an "E," which was badly rigged and a total dog. The "F" without radar was probably the best-flying '110, fully aerobatic and in some respects smoother than the Bf 109, where the slats made some racket when wringing the plane out fully . . . The 110G-4 was sort of a mixed bag. The aerials, exhaust flame dampers, drop tanks, other paraphernalia and, of course, the excessive weight when compared to the original design, resulted in a very limited performance and handling envelope. Single engine flight was barely possible with full rudder, and in this case, the rudder force was extremely heavy and led to rapid fatigue. On the other hand, visibility was excellent, and the control forces pleasant and well balanced when flying reasonably within the performance envelope. This made the Bf 110G-4 an excellent gun platform, and since speed was of no great importance against bombers, the Bf 110G-4 was quite a good night fighter.[19]

In spite of the relatively antiquated equipment, tactical innovation was in no short supply in the night fighter arm. Initially, *Luftwaffe* crews attacked as a matter of course from dead astern, opening fire at ranges from 200 to 400 yards. This tactic tended to make the fighter highly vulnerable and predictable. The more experienced crews eventually began approaching from well below, effectively standing their aircraft on their tails and then raking the vulnerable belly of the bomber as it passed through the fighter's gunsight. This method of attack often caught the bomber crew completely off guard, since the gunners focused their search patterns aft, and not below the bomber, a sector in which their field of view was greatly impeded by the bomber's structure. Also, the tactic reduced the visible profile of the attacking aircraft, frequently masking it in background clutter, and maintained a minimum exposure attack profile in a rapid closure to firing parameters. Once Bomber Command caught on to this tactic, discovering as they did that two-thirds of their aircraft returning damaged had been attacked from below, significant consideration was given to bolstering ventral defences. Also, it led to the development of two further electronic jamming devices: *Shiver*, which modified the bomber's IFF to help jam the *Würzburg* radars, and *Mandrel*, an airborne and ground-based jammer targeted at the *Freya* radars. These jammers augmented the two passive radar warning receivers, *Monica* and *Boozer*. *Monica* was the earliest simple, mass-produced tail-warning radar, while *Boozer* triggered yellow and red warning lights, depending on the type of the threat, when the bomber was being illuminated by either an AI or a ground tracking radar respectively.

While the German night fighters were fielding some interesting and effective innovations,

British night fighters were also becoming increasingly sophisticated and capable. In the summer of 1943, the RAF began sending radar-equipped Beaufighters, then Mosquitos, to infiltrate the bomber stream and attack the German night fighters. But along with their AI radars, these fast intruders had a new technological tool in the form of *Serrate*, an electronic component that could home on the *Lichtenstein* AI radars. Used in conjunction with the British AI radars, and in the hands of a skilled operator, the *Serrate*/AI radar combination proved to be very effective. Bob Braham, a distinguished night fighter ace, flew the first operational missions with this new equipment in a series of experimental bomber support operations during the summer of 1943. He later recalled its first trial in a Beaufighter on the night of 14/15 June, during an attack on Oberhausen. Paired with his extremely able radar operator, "Sticks" Gregory, Braham remembered it being an eerie feeling, stalking the night skies and playing what was assuredly a deadly game of hide-and-seek with invisible foes. Several inconclusive electronic contacts were made that night while the skilled AI operator rationalized his various pieces of sophisticated equipment, until this exchange:

> "Bob, I've AI contact 2000 yards behind. Hard as possible port."
>
> "Are you sure it isn't one of our bombers?"
>
> "Yes. It isn't. The Serrate and AI signals match up. Keep turning, he's only about 1000 yards and 20 degrees on your port and a little above. Now ease the turn a little, and watch it. You're closing fast, you should see him in a second. He's only 600 yards and still well over to port."
>
> "I've got him, I've got him," [Braham] yelled excitedly.
>
> In the moonlight I caught a glimpse of an aircraft on my port beam. At that moment he straightened out, heading south at 10,000 feet. An Me 110. Perhaps he had lost me on his AI. At 400 yards range I opened fire, gradually easing off the deflection so that as I rolled in astern of him, the dot of my electric gunsight was centred on his fuselage. Explosions appeared all over the Messerschmitt. Burning brightly, he dived steeply towards the earth.[20]

By the end of September, the Braham/Gregory team had claimed six Bf 110s shot down with this new equipment, at least three of which are now known to have been flown by some leading *Luftwaffe Experten* or aces, all of whom were killed.[21] From now on, the German hunters frequently became the hunted in their own killing grounds.

For Bomber Command's defensive armament, Sir Arthur Harris fought long and hard to have the Halifax's exceptionally disappointing Fraser Nash FN 20 tail turret replaced, a system which had earned the AOC's extreme frustration and disdain.[22] Harris also instructed his Halifax squadrons to cut holes in the floors of their aircraft, then install Perspex observation blisters and hand-held .5 inch guns. By mid-1943, "he was asking the turret designers and aircraft manufacturers to meet his essentially conflicting demands for more guns, heavier guns, and better vision, all without adding significantly to the aircraft's gross weight or altering its centre of gravity."[23] His determined efforts to ameliorate the defensive armament of the Halifax, and, to a lesser extent, the Lancaster, would eventually pay dividends, although the improvements would not be fielded in haste, and they tended to be piecemeal. Later-model Halifaxes all had a decent Boulton Paul Type "A" Mk. III lower profile dorsal turret equipped with four .303-inch Browning machine guns, each armed with 1160 rounds. All Halifax Mark IIIs and Mark VIIs also got improved "stingers" in the tail. This was either in the form of the Type "E" turret with four .303-inch guns, each with 1700 rounds and a further 4800 rounds reserve for the turret, or the Type "D" turret, armed with two

.5-inch Browning machine guns, the USAAF's preferred defensive weapon. The Type "D" turret was mounted only on the Halifax Mark VII and used operationally in the closing months of the war. It was the embodiment of four years of indecision by the Air Staff to arm the bombers with heavy-calibre guns. This Boulton Paul turret, with 1515 rounds of ammunition per gun, had a field of fire of ninety degrees either side of dead aft, and could both elevate and depress forty-five degrees above and below the horizontal. It was also the first defensive weapons system to be fitted with the airborne gun-laying turret (AGLT) blind tracking radar system, which was code-named *Village Inn*. It required its own IFF system, and so it incorporated an infra-red detector, which would identify and discriminate against any friendly aircraft approaching from the rear that had a special infra-red emitter lamp mounted in its nose.[24] This system was fielded too late in the war to see widespread service, but the Type "E" turret was used extensively, with over 8000 of them being produced, the majority by the Lucas Company. It proved to be a dependable weapons system, popular with the gunners, and many German fighters fell to its guns.[25]

Ventral protection was another matter. While the need, based on known German tactics, was acknowledged, fitment of the *H2S* radome to the bellies of the bombers effectively challenged the installation of a robust turret in that location. Informal solutions were encouraged, and early pioneers included the engineering staff of 419 Squadron, before the unit became the first 6 Group squadron to receive Canadian-built Lancaster Mark Xs in March 1944.[26] The most successful formalized arrangement was the so-called Preston Green Mark II under-defence mounting. Trialled on a Halifax III flying out of Boscombe Down in February 1944, it consisted of a single .5-inch Browning protruding through the rear of the *H2S* radar blister. While the radar was considered essential, bomber production was significantly outstripping that of the radar sets, and therefore it was decided to install Preston Green mountings in a formal mid-under position in all Halifax IIIs not *H2S*-equipped, and this would eventually include quite a few 6 Group aircraft:

> The adapter was fixed across the base of a bowl-shaped enclosure immediately behind the bomb bay. The gunner had an aft-facing bucket seat within the blister, with a tilting back rest. The gun could be swung clear of its aperture when searching, but could be rapidly locked in the firing position if needed.
>
> Had more Bomber Command aircraft been fitted with the Preston Green turret, this previously non-existent protection from attack from below would have cut down the toll taken by Luftwaffe fighters using upwards firing cannon. Unfortunately, when *H2S* production increased, the turrets were taken out, much to the annoyance of the bomber crews.[27]

The Lancaster's defensive armament was also inadequate, although the problem was not as acute as it was for the Halifax. In most cases, the Lancaster's original FN 64 ventral turret was eliminated to accommodate *H2S*, which again created a dangerous blind spot that the *Luftwaffe* would in time exploit. While the wartime supply of the Colt-Browning .5-inch guns was never sufficient, eventually some Lancaster Is, IIIs and Xs were fitted with Frazer-Nash FN 82 or Rose Brothers tail turrets with .5-inch guns, and the Rose turret also had a clear, cutaway panel that offered exceptional visibility. These improved turrets replaced the earlier FN 20 models, which had been armed with four .303-inch Brownings. Additionally, a late war Mark VII variant of the aircraft incorporated the heavier guns in the tail, as well as two .5-inch guns mounted in a new dorsal turret. Late model Lancasters also received the *Village Inn* equipment, identifiable by two small circular flat glass panels in the Perspex nose of the aircraft.[28] Interestingly, of the 430 Canadian-built Lancaster X variants, from the 83rd production aircraft onwards, Lancaster Xs were uniformly fitted with two .5-inch guns in a Martin turret for their dorsal armament, considerably pre-dating the British-built variants.[29]

For ventral armament, and "also used in small numbers, especially by 6 Group, were simpler ventral defence positions fitted with single manually operated .5-inch (12.7mm) or .303-inch (7.7mm) machine guns."[30] Dick Bell, a wartime gunner on 434 Squadron, recalls this lash-up installation as it pertained to Halifaxes:

> The mid-under was in a blister under the Halifax that consisted of using the main spar of the wing as a seat and a .5 inch machine gun that just faced back towards the tail of the aircraft.[31]

Merrill R. Burnett, a gunner with 426 Squadron also notes:

> The mid-under non-rotating turret was a metal blister containing a seat and a safety belt with a 50 cal. Browning machine gun, which was positioned between the gunner's knees. An opening at the rear of the blister allowed visibility to the rear and a bit to each side. A fighter approaching from directly behind and below would have been a good target, but not if he approached from the beam.[32]

The shortcomings of Bomber Command's defensive armament are highlighted by the introduction of a particularly effective, sinister and painfully-long-undetected weapon fielded by the Germans in the summer of 1943. Known as *Schräge Musik* (Jazz Music), it consisted of a battery—usually a pair, but in groups of four or even six of either 20mm or 30mm cannon—obliquely mounted in a night fighter's fuselage to fire forward and upward at an angle of approximately fifteen degrees from the vertical. In an extension of the earlier low stern approach tactic, the idea was to close from the bomber's vulnerable blind cone and then, remaining directly beneath the bomber but flying parallel to it, rake it with fire aimed through a special reflector sight mounted on the roof of the fighter's canopy. Widespread confirmation of this weapon was not released to the crews until early 1944, by which time *Schräge Musik* had claimed many victims.[33] Even when the weapon's existence was confirmed, there was no real counteraction to it, except for the mid-upper and tail gunners, and the mid-*under* gunner (if the aircraft was so configured) to be extra vigilant in scanning this particular attack approach path. Lloyd Morrison echoed the point and said that his 100 Squadron did nothing more to protect the ventral position than harp on the need for increased awareness. However, he offered that, compared to the Halifax, the Lancaster's fuselage at the mid-upper gunner's position was quite slim, the dorsal turret was relatively large, and the mid-upper gunner's visibility downwards, when coupled with that of the rear gunner, was relatively good.[34] The most disadvantaged Bomber Command airmen in this respect, therefore, continued to be the Halifax crews.

Peter Spoden, a distinguished night fighter ace from Essen with twenty-four confirmed victories, and a long-time postwar *Lufthansa* pilot, has suggested: "We were shooting between the two engine nacelles (on either wing), primarily because the fuel tanks were there, but also to give those fellows a chance to parachute."[35] Spoden's gallant comment on his utilization of *Schräge Musik* is interesting, and it was echoed by fellow night fighter ace Rudolf Thun.[36] However, it is difficult to believe that the majority of night fighter aircrew simply did not fire at whatever vulnerable area of the bomber their gun sights were aimed at, and there were many vulnerable components. Fuel cells also occupied the wing spaces between the inner engine nacelles and the fuselage, and five of the seven or eight crew members were clustered in close proximity in the forward portion of the fuselage. Spoden, as well as all the other night fighter crews, would certainly have been made aware of these other vulnerable areas.

A Trip to the "Big City"

The following "generic" raid on Berlin exemplifies what a typical Bomber Command operation in the winter of 1943/1944 entailed in preparation and planning. Rolland St. Jacques, a navigator on 426 Squadron, recalls the start of the routine: "After breakfast, I wonder what the day will bring us; operations, training, or the day off. Early on, around 9 o'clock or so, the news is out. Operations tonight! A look at the crew board confirms the services of 'U-Uncle' are required."[37]

The crews flying that night were normally required to take their aircraft for a brief air test to ensure all its systems were serviceable. However, "normal" procedures could be far from normal, as Roger Coulombe explains:

> All I can remember is that no one was allowed out of the station that day, and that the bar was closed in the Mess. No one was allowed to drink alcoholic beverages that day, at least, not until all the bombers on the raid had left the ground. The pilots were supposed to air test their bombers the day of a raid, but I never could air test the Lancaster I flew on ops because, for my first twenty raids, I never flew the same bomber. And the ground crews working on those different bombers never had them ready in time for me to air test them before a raid. When the ground crews had done the maintenance on my aircraft, it was simply loaded with bombs, and that was the bomber that I was to fly over Germany that night. I didn't have much to say about it. I just took it up for ops, hoping for the best!
>
> Instead of doing an air test, I often worked on general navigation with my navigator, just in case something went wrong with him during the flight. And I'm certainly glad I did for the raid on Munich on 6/7 September 1943 . . . On that night, my navigator, Gerard Tremblay, was taken ill, and I had to accept a "sprog" navigator to replace him. That sprog navigator was . . . flying with an entire crew of sergeants, including myself as a sergeant-pilot and captain of the aircraft. [The navigator] was doing his first operation over Germany, while I was on my seventh, and the rest of the crew were on their fifth. Since [he] had no experience on ops, he made some basic mistakes, like forgetting some very important maps of southern Germany, where we had to fly on our return trip home. Because of that, he couldn't navigate the aircraft back to England. Fortunately, I had worked out the entire navigation with him before the raid, knowing that he was on his maiden trip over Germany, and I didn't trust him all that much, not knowing him at all. Because of his oversight, we had to fly longer than planned, and we were running short on petrol. I had to do an emergency landing at the first landing field we could find on the southern coast of England. And it was high time we landed when we did, because all four engines cut right out immediately after landing. There was not a drop of petrol left in the aircraft's fuel tanks. I could not even taxi the Lancaster to the dispersal area on its own power. It had to be pulled by a tractor from the end of the runway![38]

For many, however, the morning following raid notification meant a short air test prior to lunch, and then a free afternoon for most of them. Some tried to sleep it away, but many never succeeded. This was certainly a stressful period for them. "It was these long hours of preparation and expectation that ate into men's courage and nerves as much as anything that was done to them in the air. Many felt that it was the contrast between the rural peace of afternoon England and the fiery horror of early morning Germany that imposed much greater strain on bomber crews than the even tenor of discomfort and fear on a warship or in a tank."[39] This was the time when dark thoughts and doubts came easily, as they recalled earlier harrowing experiences and imagined others. And they were required to be at their most alert at a time when most human endeavours were at their lowest ebb of enterprise and productivity, the dead of night.

The next step was the mass briefing, either followed or preceded by the traditional meal of bacon and eggs in the Mess, which depended on the take-off time and the station custom. By lorry and by the ubiquitous bicycles, so essential on a spread-out wartime bomber station, the fliers made their way to the Main Briefing Room. Here, the old informality of the Wellington and Hampden days when all and sundry casually gathered around a central table in the Operations Room had disappeared. Now, the term "briefing" was somewhat of a misnomer, as much complex and specialized information had to be imparted to all the participating airmen. After a brief introduction by the station commander, a series of mission specialists, starting with the intelligence officer, elaborated on each critical aspect of the operation. This information was liberally sprinkled with code words. The Bomber Command crews were Ravens, the target (Berlin) was Whitebait. The night's attack would be prosecuted by approximately 650 aircraft flying in six waves, and Zero Hour (Z), the time for first bomb impact, was set for 11:50 pm. Fifteen minutes prior to Zero Hour, ten Skylark Mosquitos would shower *Window* on the attack axis to help protect the initial Pathfinders mark the target with bright red Target Indicator (TI) flares. These markers were periodically refreshed with green TIs by the officially designated Pathfinder "Back-ups," known as Old Crows, available as required from Zero Hour plus one minute until Z + 40. Other support players were Pathfinder specialists known as Recenterers, who were tasked to ensure the green TIs did not drift off the required aim point. All the bombing was continuously orchestrated by a designated Pathfinder Master of Ceremonies who, in this case flying in a speedy Mosquito, would flit about the target area, continuously advising, directing, encouraging and, if necessary, badgering the Main Force members as to where to place their weapons. Accuracy and concentration of effort were the keys, and it was intended to put all Main Force aircraft on this particular raid over the target within forty-three minutes in an attempt to saturate the defences. Aircraft equipped with *H2S* were provided with radar ground references, such as a distinctive rise of land in the vicinity, which would hopefully show up well on the scopes. The crews were then given bearings and distances from these specified reference points to the target area.

Once the intelligence officer had finished his briefing, the meteorological officer was next. Weather forecasting was a much more inexact science in 1944 than it is today. Flying conditions over the British Isles and northwest Europe were frequently dreadful and fickle, particularly during the winter months. And Bomber Command crews were subject to the vagaries of weather. As we have seen, the available approach aids were relatively primitive, and the aircraft were particularly sensitive to the elements, especially icing. As well, the vital tactical focus on mass and concentration of forces by huge numbers of aircraft over the target in a very short period of time meant that all these aircraft were seeking a safe haven for landing back in England at approximately the same time. By this recovery phase of the raid, they were almost always critically low on fuel and they were also normally exhausted from combat and battling the elements, and were thus prone to making errors. Frequently, they had also suffered some form of battle damage or systems failure, and they often had dead or wounded on board. Small wonder the meteorological officer's briefing warranted the rapt attention of all the fliers. Based on forecasts, observations and aerial reconnaissance, his briefing focused on the expected en route and target weather, the predicted winds and temperatures aloft, the forecast barometric pressure in the target area, the potential icing levels, which were a frequent danger, and the anticipated weather conditions in Britain on return.

Next up was the navigation officer, and while the navigators would receive their own specialized briefing later, all crewmen listened attentively to a general description of the night's routing, as well as the known flak and night fighter concentrations and where enemy jamming could most likely be anticipated. Then, the bombing leader spoke of the night's ordnance loads, target markers and procedures, the likely distractions of dummy targets and bogus flares being initiated by the Germans, and the ever-important caution to avoid bombing creepback. The signals officer next provided the force with a number of codes for use in various circumstances at certain times, as well as the radio frequencies needed for emergencies, for recoveries, and for obtaining accurate wind conditions for navigation and bombing. He also refreshed the memories of the crews in the use of *Tinsel*, that particularly disruptive form of noise jamming that keyed a microphone installed at one of the bomber's engines back into the headsets of the German night fighter crews. The engineering leader then briefed such things as power settings, fuel loads, and fuel reserves required for recovery and for diversion, should the need arise. The last of the specialists was normally the gunnery officer, with his unnecessary pleas for vigilance, along with more pragmatic cautions to keep the turrets mobile and weapons ready in the sub-zero conditions. Then, the station commander or base commander would usually close with a short summary of the salient points, remind all assembled that this was a maximum effort vital to the prosecution of the war, and wish them good luck as he and his entourage took their leave. Finally, the airmen shuffled to their feet, chatting among themselves as they gathered up the paraphernalia of their trade.

> They were a queer conglomeration, these men—some educated and sensitive, some rough-haired and burly, and drawn from all parts of the Empire, Great Britain, Canada, New Zealand and Australia . . . Some of them were humming, some were singing, some were laughing, and others were standing serious and thoughtful. It looks like the dressing room where the jockeys sit waiting before a great steeplechase.[40]

Eventually, they proceeded to Flights, where, at a set time they began the ritualistic removal of all personal identification and effects except dog tags. These were given to administrative staff for the duration of the operation. In a poem of the period entitled simply *Security*, John Pudney has evocatively frozen this moment in time:

> Empty your pockets, Tom, Dick and Harry,
> Strip your identity; leave it behind.
> Lawyer, garage-hand, grocer, don't tarry
> With your own country, your own kind.
> Leave all your letters, suburb and township,
> Green fen and grocery, slip-way and bay,
> Hot-spring and prairie, smoke-stack and coal tip,
> Leave in our keeping while you're away.
> Tom, Dick and Harry, plain names and numbers,
> Pilot, observer and gunner depart,
> Their personal litter only encumbers
> Somebody's head, somebody's heart.

The airmen were then issued with keys to their personal lockers, where they dressed with great care and attention in their specialized flying clothing, then waited for their transport to Dispersal, which was another one of the worst periods of anxiety. In due course, it was off to their aircraft to await the moment for start and departure. Here, even more ritualistic behavior abounded, none being willing to do anything to provoke fate into laying claim against them that night. While the moments were often punctuated by an occasional attempt at brittle humour, the tension for each of them could only be mitigated by concentration on the drills and procedures that had been ingrained as their individual responsibilities within the aircrew team. Rolland St. Jacques recalls the moments from the end of the Main Briefing until the aircraft was en route:

> Once these briefings are over, we go over to the Mess for a pre-flight meal, which includes a fresh egg. There was always talk about Canadian bacon and eggs being sent to England for the armed forces . . . I personally never saw a slice of bacon the whole time I was in England. After the meal, I receive Holy Communion from the RC padre. We had a special dispensation, for in those years you would normally have had to fast since midnight before receiving this Sacrament.
>
> By then take-off time, around 4:00 PM, is fast approaching, this being winter with darkness coming early. The crew vans pick up the crews and drive them to their respective "Lanc" on its dispersal pad. The pilot, engineer, wireless operator, bomb-aimer and gunners go through their check-up drills and I take my equipment from my flight bag and set it up on the navigator's table, check my *Gee* box and position my parachute chest pack on the floor at my feet, under the table. I take care of it, for it is my only way out, if need be, at 20,000 feet or so.
>
> We taxi to the main runway, await the green Aldis lamp signal from the control van, the engines roar and we are off. As we climb I am already busy checking course and distance, getting ready to signal a course alteration to the skipper as per the operational briefing. It is still light outside, but darkness is rapidly hiding us from view. We cross the North Sea . . . I never liked that part of the trips; I remembered being told that ditching in the North Sea in winter meant freezing to death if you were not picked up within a very few minutes. And we were flying at night.[41]

The words of pilot Geoff Marlow pertaining to his first operational flight with his own crew provide an interesting counterpoint to those of Rolland St. Jacques. They carry the generic scenario through to bomb release. To make it even more sporting, his raid was done in daylight, a portent of many more daylight raids to follow for the Command:

> [At the Main Briefing] there was a roll call of captains, and each of us answered for our crews. Then the curtain was pulled aside from the front wall to reveal a large map of north-western Europe. The target was to be Gelsenkirchen in the Ruhr. We were to be routed straight into the target across the Dutch coast, each of us carrying 11,000 pounds of bombs and incendiaries. We were told where the main concentrations of enemy fighters and flak were expected to be and were briefed on the weather conditions, start-up times, take-off times and codes for the day. The navigators and bomb-aimers moved to their specialized briefing tables to determine flight plans and bomb settings, and then we all went to put our flying clothes on over our battle dress. The flying boots consisted of wool-lined black shoes, laced in the normal way, with suede leggings sewn into the top of the shoe to cover the calves. They were designed this way not only to prevent the boots from being blown off in the slipstream in case we bailed out, but also to allow crewmen to easily

convert them into shoes once they were on the ground by ripping off the upper legging, thereby facilitating escape and evasion. As we picked up our parachutes, someone made a rather stupid comment about whether his chute had been properly packed and would open if needed.

Then it was time to be taken out to our respective dispersals in lorries. Here our ground crew waited to talk to us about anything related to the plane's maintenance. We all tried unsuccessfully to pretend that this was just another flight no different than many before. We smoked our last cigarette, knowing our next one would not be lit until we returned from the trip. I made a point of walking around the plane to see if it looked in order and stopped at the tail wheel to "spend a penny." It would be my last chance until we were back on the ground again. When start-up time approached we climbed into the plane and made our way through the narrow interior to our respective seats. We all checked our equipment, and I started the port inner engine, using power from a large external portable battery supplied by the ground crew. The powerful Hercules radial engine coughed a bit, but finally exploded into life. Then came the starboard inner, followed by the two outer engines. When they were warm, I revved them up to check their performance. All was in order. The battery was disconnected, I gave the thumbs-up sign, the chocks were removed and away we went taxiing to the take-off point. We maintained strict radio silence during our whole trip, so there was no talking between the control tower and our planes, only visual light signals. The planes took off close behind one another. I noticed that we used up a lot more runway than usual because of the heavy bomb load, and it was a relief to get up into the air. We circled upwards above the clouds and, at a predetermined time, set course over the North Sea. Planes from other airfields met us enroute during the next half hour, until a total of 550 bombers were lumbering toward their target.

As we approached the Dutch coast at 215 mph, we could see the planes ahead flying through a hail of flak from the German gunners. Flak appears as sharp bright orange explosions changing to dark smoke puffs that hang in the air for half a minute or so until dissipated by the wind. There was no way around it, so we also flew through it, hoping that the fragments of bursting shells would not hit us. Half an hour ahead of us lay the Ruhr Valley where our target was situated. As the cloud thinned out around us, we could see in the distance the mist-covered industrial heart of Germany spreading like a cancer across the countryside for miles in all directions. The built-up area around each urban centre made it extremely difficult to distinguish one city from another. But the Pathfinders had done their job and dropped their identifying coloured flares over today's target, enabling us to adjust course in plenty of time. The air was full of planes and bursting flak. My gunners kept an eye on the yawning bomb bays of the planes above us as they juggled into position to drop their bombs over the target. We prayed that their bomb aimers would not panic and let their load go on top of us. From his compartment below me, Doc relayed me instructions to align us with the aiming point. "Right, right—steady—left—OK—hold it—bombs gone."

We kept on this same steady course for 30 seconds until the delayed action of the plane's camera had taken its pictures of the scene below, which was already partly obscured by smoke and dust. These pictures not only served to tell our intelligence people where our bombs had landed, but also told them whether we had shied away from our attack or, perhaps, taken a peaceful flight around the North Sea to fill in the time before our scheduled return! When we returned, we found out that one of our squadron aircraft captains had indeed decided that the flak at the coast was too heavy, so he had turned for home. This was called Lack of Moral Fibre (LMF) and the matter was taken very seriously. The individual who exhibited LMF would first be stripped of his rank and wings and would then be sent off to do some unpleasant ground duties, never to be heard of again by his buddies. I think most of us had long ago made up our minds to accept whatever the enemy might do to us rather than face the lifetime disgrace of being categorized as LMF.

With the first trip as a full crew now completed, we felt we had become experienced and wanted to demonstrate it to the outside world. We did this by pouring beer into each other's hats and then consuming the contents. The hats then immediately lost their newish appearance and became "operational." It would probably be more accurate to say they looked like greasy taxi drivers' hats. By becoming operational we had passed a milestone in our flying careers as important as one's first solo or getting one's pilot's wings. Now our sights were set on surviving 30 operational trips over Germany.[42]

Peenemünde and the Rocket Threat

Extensive Gardening operations accounted for the majority of 6 Group operations in early August, although Mannheim was attacked through cloud on 9/10 August, and Nuremburg the following night. The results in both cases were scattered and inconclusive, but *Window* proved effective and it largely shackled the German defenders, restricting losses for both nights to a respectable 2 percent of those despatched.[43] The Canadians in 6 Group did even better, losing just one of the eighty participating aircraft. However, as the summer of 1943 lengthened, surviving that recently codified thirty-operations tour was becoming more and more difficult. The whole Berlin series lay yet ahead, but even before Berlin, on the night of 17/18 August, Bomber Command conducted a highly significant raid on a small peninsula on the Baltic coast north of Berlin and northeast of Rostock in an area renowned for its beach resorts. Code-named Operation Hydra, as the name implies, the intent was to conduct a decapitating strike on the secret research and development facility for the V 2 rockets at Peenemünde, where Hitler had recently started focusing a tremendous portion of the Reich's industrial output on his so-called vengeance weapons. The raid was unique for a number of reasons. Since it was being directed at a specific facility, it demanded precision, and for that reason, the attack took place in bright moonlight and in a relatively low altitude attacking band, between 6000 and 10,000 feet. *Window* was again used to stymy the German defences, and a diversionary or "spoof" raid was conducted in advance on Berlin in an effort to draw the night fighters away from the intended target. Also, the PFF were using a greatly improved target marker for the first time, and they formally inaugurated the position of a Master Bomber, Master of Ceremonies, or on-scene commander on this raid. As did Guy Gibson at work over the Ruhr dams months earlier, and operating on a discrete VHF frequency, this designated soul, who in this case was the distinguished Group Captain J.H. Searby, commanding officer of 83 Squadron, was to:

> provide the bomber force with minute to minute information regarding the progress of a raid . . . issue warnings of misplaced markers, give the position of dummies and generally assist the bomber force in successfully attacking the correct aiming point. It is further hoped that such commentaries will serve to strengthen the determination of less experienced crews.[44]

One of Searby's deputies at Peenemünde was Wing Commander Johnnie Fauquier, now in command of 405 Squadron for the second time, who would also soon be both a Master Bomber and a group captain.

In all, 596 Halifaxes, Lancasters and Stirlings were tasked against the target in three waves, and the nine diversionary Mosquitos that headed for Berlin at first successfully drew off the bulk of the night fighters. *Window* again proved very effective during the early warning stages. However, some of the initial Pathfinder marking went awry when the *H2S* return, which the experts in 8 Group had confidently predicted would be distinctive and easy to identify, proved to be far less helpful than was hoped. (This was, perhaps, a portent of the upcoming Berlin raids.) Because of the inaccuracy of the early marking, parts of the Main Force first wave dropped their bombs on a camp of slave labourers until the markers were quickly corrected by Searby himself. Thereafter, substantial damage was done to the research facility, and many sources have echoed that the V 2 program was forced to disperse as a result of the raid, and its progress was scaled down and delayed by at least two critical months.[45]

After the initial correction by Searby, the raid went well enough in the bright moonlight and very thin cloud for some time, and although there were early indications to the Germans that something was happening at Peenemünde, the reports were discounted until later in the raid. Peter Spoden, who that night shot down his first of many Lancasters, recalls: "We were told by our ground control people, ' *Alles Kakadus nach Berlin!* All cockatoos to Berlin! All night fighters to Berlin!' [After climbing to acquire a better view] I saw something to the north, a lot of fire, and that was the real attack on Peenemünde, which was about 150 kilometres from Berlin."[46] By the time the German defenders had fully grasped Bomber Command's real intentions, only thirty-five night fighters were available to proceed to Peenemünde, the rest had to land and refuel. Still, those few defenders took a dreadful toll on the later attackers. The exceptional clearness of the night nullified some of the tactical advantages of *Window*, since the night fighters were primarily acquiring their targets visually, and were not significantly depending on airborne radar. *Oberleutnant* Friedrich-Karl "Tutti" Müller, a FW 190 *Wilde Sau* pilot who scored 140 victories in total and won the Knight's Cross with Oak Leaves,[47] recalled that the visibility made it very easy for the defenders. He quickly despatched one Lancaster, which was forced to land in a great plume of spray in the breakers of the Baltic a few yards offshore. The rear gunner of this Lancaster had put up a spirited defence, knocking chunks out of Müller's Focke-Wulf, but in the end it was to no avail.

> I flew back to the target area and found another Lancaster, easily visible against the smoke. I attacked again but this tail gunner was not so well trained or else he was very nervous. His first shots went past me on the left. He swung his turret and fired again, but I had moved to the left and I easily avoided his fire, which passed to my right. The right wing caught fire and then, about a minute later, the wing fell off and he spiralled down . . . I never saw a raid at such low level and in such clear visibility.[48]

Other German night fighter crews were also having exceptional nights. *Oberleutnant* Paul Zörner, who became a major with fifty-nine night victories and was decorated with the Knight's Cross with Oak Leaves prior to war's end, scored his eleventh and twelfth victories over Peenemünde. Flying out of Kastrup airfield near Copenhagen, this crew shot one Lancaster out of the sky from a mere 120 metres range. It caught fire and crashed into the sea. Zörner then returned to the target area and did a quick attack on another from above and behind.

> I think I was a little further back than the first time and my hits were all over him. The combination of moon and that ground mist or cloud made it very easy. It was almost like

a daylight attack. The bomber started burning and, soon after, exploded in the air. As before, there was no return fire and no evasive action. I don't think he ever saw me."[49]

Leutnant Dieter Musset and his radar operator, *Obergefreiter* Helmut Hafner, flying with *II Gruppe* of *Nachtjagdgeschwader 1* in a Messerschmitt Bf 110, shot down at least three of the raiders and engaged three more, probably shooting down at least one of these, before a 619 Squadron Lancaster started a fire in their port engine and also put an incendiary round through Hafner's shoulder. To compound their miseries, they were later fired on by their own light flak. When the engine fire could no longer be contained they were forced to bail out, and Musset broke both his legs when he hit the tailplane on the jump. This was Hafner's first operation, and the same probably held true for Musset.[50] A more dramatic combat initiation is difficult to imagine.

The majority of the casualties Bomber Command suffered at Peenemünde were to aircraft of the last wave, the point at which the German night fighters arrived in force. Bomber Command was not alone in fielding innovations that night. Peenemünde marked the first operational use of *Schräge Musik*. Two fighters so equipped entered the bomber stream as it returned to England and are believed to have gunned down six victims with the new weapon. Bomber Command's losses were an even forty aircraft; twenty-three Lancasters, fifteen Halifaxes and two Stirlings, representing 6.7 percent of those despatched.[51] Although this was felt to be an acceptable blood cost, given the low attack altitude and the bright, moonlit conditions (which were believed necessary for such an important target), it also meant that 6 Group, flying in the last wave, was particularly hard hit. In fact, the Canadian group suffered the highest casualty rate of all when twelve of the sixty-two crews sortied failed to return, a soul-destroying 20 percent of those who went in harm's way that night. Numbers 419, 428 and 434 Squadrons each lost three crews, while 426 Squadron lost two, and 427 Squadron also lost one. Moreover, six of the crews were considered veterans, the lifeblood of their units.[52] Pilot Officer R.W. Charman, who was a navigator in a No. 427 Squadron Halifax remarked, "I had never seen such a night before . . . All over the sky, RAF planes were going down."[53] For 426 Squadron, it was a particularly bittersweet operation. Sweet in that it marked the inaugural use of new equipment; they had just converted from Wellingtons to Lancaster IIs. Bitter because one of the two missing squadron crews at Peenemünde was their popular and respected commanding officer's, Wing Commander Leslie Crooks, DSO, DFC. Laurence Motiuk, a wartime bomb-aimer with the squadron, elaborates:

> In the bright moonlight, the crews found the visibility very good. They were in the third wave so, when they reached the target area, they could see many tremendous fires. Seven crews bombed the target. Six dropped their bomb loads from 7500 to 9000 feet and one from 15,000 feet, the bomb aimers sighting on the Pathfinders' green target indicators. Three aircraft were each carrying a 4000 pound blockbuster and 2760 pounds of incendiaries, and four were each carrying a 500-pound bomb and six 1000-pound bombs. Squadron Leader Swetman and his crew arrived in the target area early, and orbited to the north for about twenty minutes before turning in to make their bombing run at the designated time. As they approached the target, the flying parts of a bomber that blew up nearby narrowly missed Swetman's aircraft. Six of these aircraft made it back to England, where they received diversion orders, but three missed the instructions and landed at Linton. Two squadron aircraft failed to return.
>
> The first missing aircraft was Lancaster DS681/OW "V," with Wing Commander Crooks and crew. The sole survivor was the bomb aimer, Sergeant K.W. Reading, who

bailed out and was taken prisoner. On his release in May 1945, he told what happened that fateful night.

Crooks and his crew reached the target, encountering no flak and very few search-lights. They released their bomb load at 0040 hours and, just after they left the target, a night fighter attacked from behind, without warning. The engines caught fire immediately and the aircraft began to lose altitude. As Crooks circled the Lancaster over the land, the night fighter attacked again, this time across the bows, riddling the nose and setting fires in the wireless compartment and under the pilot's position. These fires were extinguished. Nothing was heard from either of the gunners. At this point, Crooks told the crew to pre-pare to bail out but, even as he spoke, the port wing began to come off. Reading jumped first, at low altitude, followed closely by the navigator, Flight Sergeant A.J. Howes, who was killed because his parachute failed to open in time. The rest of the crew perished in the crash.[54]

In August 405 Squadron in 8 Group began its conversion to Lancaster Is and IIIs, and Canadians in Bomber Command could take pride in the delivery of the first of what ultimately became 430 Canadian-built Lancaster Xs produced for the war effort. The aircraft, coded KB 700 but soon to become known by its nickname, *The Ruhr Express*, was flown to Britain in a well-organized public relations effort by Squadron Leader Reginald Lane, DSO, DFC. Both Lane and *The Ruhr Express* had many exciting wartime experiences still in store for them, but the aircraft, ceremonially presented to 405 Squadron at Gransden Lodge in October, was far from being combat ready. In fact, only thirteen more of the variant were completed before year's end, and on average they required around 1000 man-hours of modifications to bring them up to operational standards once they arrived in England. This was because modifications developed in the United Kingdom could not be incorporated quickly into the production line at Victory Aircraft in Downsview, and changes in Canadian specifications played a delaying role as well. Thus, when *The Ruhr Express* bombed Berlin as part of 405 Squadron on 27/28 November 1943 on its first operational sortie,[55] no other Lancaster Xs were used operationally until 419 Squadron became the first unit to con-vert to the type in March/April 1944.[56]

The Exploratory Raids

Within a week of Peenemünde, Bomber Command felt ready to take on Berlin. On the night of 23/24 August, 727 aircraft, nearly half of which were Lancasters, were sent to the Reich's capital. The designated Master Bomber for the night was John Fauquier, at the helm of 405 Squadron. The night was clear, the visibility excellent with no moon. However, PFF was unable to identify the aiming point in the northwest part of the city on *H2S* alone among the great mass of featureless radar returns emanating from Berlin. Furthermore, the network of waterways which lay along the western edge of the city either did not stand out as well as anticipated or they caused confusion. As a result, the Pathfinders marked an area considerably south and west of the intended aiming point, in spite of Fauquier's determined efforts to bring the markers back on target. Only five of the 468 bombing photos plotted after the raid were later assessed as hitting within three miles of the aiming point.[57] In the skies overhead, the carnage was significant. Although *Window* deflected the flak defences somewhat, still the night fighters were active and successful. Hajo Herrmann's *Wilde Sau* forces employed their free-ranging tactics for the first time to maximum effect and also elicited certain trepidation from the *Himmelbett* crews, who missed the procedural order of the positive control methods they had been taught. *Unteroffizier* Rudolf Frank was the pilot of an experienced all-NCO crew from *II/NJG3* flying the Junkers 88. His radar operator was *Unteroffizier* Hans-Georg Schierholz, and they had flown nearly 250 miles south from their base at Wittmundhafen to fight over Berlin that night. While this was their 118th war sortie, it was their first brush with *Wilde Sau* tactics. They destroyed both a Stirling and a Halifax that night, but their uneasiness over the lack of control was apparent, as Schierholz later recalled :

> Radar had nothing to do with our success that night, only the Wild Boar in the Berlin area. Our crew was somewhat reluctant to try this new method; a new crew, not so set in their ways, would probably have been more willing . . . It was early the next day that we talked to the other crews about their experiences. There were also a lot of questions from senior officers about that first Wild Boar night. My own crew agreed that it had been a success, but we were really *Einzelkampfer*—lone operators—and we still did not like being mixed up with this mass of other aircraft.[58]

In all, Bomber Command lost fifty-six of their number on the night—7.9 percent—which at the time constituted the highest percentage loss on a single raid. The Stirlings suffered the worst, restricted as they were to the lower altitudes. Sixteen of their number—13.2 percent—were felled, while the twenty-three Halifax losses equated to 8.5 percent. The days of both the Stirling and the earlier-series Halifax fleets as part of Main Force were certainly numbered. Their loss rates were becoming both an unacceptable burden and an unsustainable liability. Soon, they would join their Wellington cousins in relatively more benign operations such as Gardening, limited penetration attacks on Occupied France, and Special Duties missions, such as supply drops to the Resistance.[59] Number 6 Group had despatched sixty-eight crews and had lost five—7.3 percent—but eleven returned early for various reasons. Six of the early returnees were from the recently formed 434 Squadron, which had already lost four of its initial crews in combat. This squadron lost one more crew on the night.[60]

While the losses were high and both the marking and the bombing were inconsistent and inaccurate in this first attack of the opening phase of the Berlin offensive, the damage inflicted was actually quite significant. The 1706 tons of high explosives and incendiaries dropped on the city at least partially damaged every government office building on the Wilhelmstrasse. Also hit hard was an officer cadet school at Köpenick, as well as the barracks of Hitler's elite SS guard, the *Leibstandarte Adolf Hitler*, at Lichterfelde.[61] Furthermore, thirteen industrial facilities were totally destroyed, as were 2115 homes and a number of significant buildings at Tempelhof airfield. The Steiglitz, Friedenau, Marienfelde and Lichterfelde districts of the city were particularly hard hit, and the destruction created an element of fear and tension among the populace, along with placing further unplanned and onerous diversions on the German war economy. A Swiss observer's report soon surfaced in London that emphasized many inhabitants' pronounced desire to flee the city, abandoning their jobs in the process. This was music to the ears of Sir Arthur Harris, for it appeared yet again to validate the bomber offensive and to support the bomber campaign against the cities.[62]

After major raids against Nuremburg and Mönchengladbach/Rheydt later in the month, it was Berlin's turn again on the night of 31 August/1 September. This time there was cloud in the target vicinity, and the vague *H2S* returns again confused and frustrated the Pathfinders. Consequently, their markers were dropped well to the south of the intended target. The inaccurate marking was exacerbated by the crash of one of the Pathfinder aircraft, which left its full cascade of marker bombs burning in the wreckage some twenty kilometers to the south of the target area. This resulted in a bombing creepback that extended some thirty miles back along the Main Force approach path. The 622 participating bombers were again throttled by the night fighters, especially those who fell outside the protective cover of *Window*, and the defenders were ably assisted in visual acquisitions of their targets by the first use of brilliant white phosphorous parachute flares dropped from above on the bomber stream. Only one factory was destroyed, but the raid cost Bomber Command forty-seven aircraft, a loss rate of 7.6 percent. The low-flying Stirlings suffered seventeen losses, 16 percent of the 106 aircraft that participated.[63] The Canadian group contributed fifty-eight aircraft, from which seven—12 percent—did not return. Also, the overall early return rate for Main Force on this operation was 14 percent, which implied a certain lack of enthusiasm for facing the capital yet again. The good news was that the raid led Goebbels to order the evacuation of young children and the elderly, as well as adults not engaged in war work, to towns in eastern Germany or to rural areas not expected to experience bombing attacks. This initiative undoubtedly placed additional burdens on the transportation and supply networks, and diverted essential resources from the war effort.[64]

The final raid of the exploratory series took place on 3/4 September, and as a result of the loss rates sustained by the Stirlings and the Halifaxes on the two preceding operations, this visit was conducted by 316 Lancasters and four Mosquitos. The Mosquitos were used to drop spoof flares well away from the intended aim point in another wily attempt to draw off the night fighters. Unfortunately, the marking and the bombing on this raid were also mostly short of the intended targets. However:

> That part of the bombing which did reach Berlin's built-up area fell in residential parts of Charlottenburg and Moabit and in the industrial area called Siemensstadt. Several factories were hit and suffered serious loss of production, and among "utilities" put out of action were major water and electricity works and one of Berlin's largest breweries.[65]

This time, although more damage was caused than on the previous raid, and the overall costs fell slightly to 7.0 percent of the Lancasters—twenty-two in all—this was considered still too high a loss rate for a sustained campaign. With regret, Harris now decided to delay prosecution of the Berlin raids until the longer nights of winter, when more Lancasters, as well as the new Halifax III, would become available. Furthermore, the new 3 centimetre Mark III *H2S* was about to equip the Pathfinders and eventually, most of the Main Force. With its shorter wavelength and narrower, more discriminating beam, it promised clearer definition and better highlighting of ground reference points in the large, built-up areas of metropolitan Berlin.[66]

Meanwhile, throughout the latter part of 1943, Canadians continued to make their presence felt in Bomber Command outside 6 Group. For example, on 77 Squadron RAF at Elvington in Yorkshire, Flight Lieutenant David S. Smart of Gloucester, Ontario, was completing his fifty-sixth operation to close out a second full and highly eventful tour. His first tour of operations had been punctuated by many raids in Wellingtons during extensive early war service in the Middle East. He even later managed to participate in the first three 1000 bomber raids from 21 OTU, Morton-in-Marsh, Gloucestershire, in 1942, where he served as a "screened" instructor for most of that year. Back on operations in Halifax II/Vs the following year, his summation of his overall war experiences is certainly remarkable for its panache:

While with 77 Squadron in the spring, summer and fall of 1943, operations completed included Essen, Cologne, Berlin, plus many others, including Peenemünde, which many consider one of the key raids of the war . . . During the time above, including the first tour, I've had the guns almost blown out of the turret, my Mae West sheared off at the neck by shrapnel and the outline of my head and shoulders cut out by cannon shells, all at different times—not a scratch. Also survived a major crash.[67]

Sometimes one just had to have luck, and David Smart had plenty of that. However, it took more than luck to amass an outstanding wartime record such as his, and it is succinctly captured in an excerpt from the citation for his Distinguished Flying Cross awarded in October 1943, just before his repatriation to Canada:

He has completed a large number of sorties both in the Mediterranean theatre of war and from this country, and in the face of intense enemy action, has frequently proved his tenacity of purpose, courage and devotion to duty.[68]

Other Diversions

Not all Bomber Command's wartime taskings involved yeoman service with the Main Force. As we have already seen, there were many diversions. Perhaps some of the most colourful and challenging were Special Operations duties in support of Resistance fighters in the occupied territories. In late 1943, this was frequently the lot of the Stirling squadrons, since it was becoming increasingly suicidal to commit them to Main Force operations over Germany. Flight Lieutenant Robert E. Mackett from Windsor, Ontario, was a mid-war Stirling pilot with 214 Squadron at Chedburgh, later with 149 Squadron at Lakenheath, and on Special Duties detachments from time to time with 161 Squadron at Tempsford throughout both the other postings. His wartime experiences were rich and varied:

On the night of September 27th, 1943, during a raid on Hannover, we encountered very strong searchlight activity at 18,000 feet coupled with heavy and accurate flak. With outstanding navigation we were able to drop a load of incendiaries over the target within seconds of the "drop time," and still faced such a strength of enemy searchlights that it took violent evasive action to avoid. Gunners and engineer kept up a running patter of groping searchlights, but we were caught with the odd "Blue Master Beam" that would immediately snap on to us. We dropped down to 8000 feet before outrunning the searchlight belt. During these manoeuvres, flak tore a hole through the windscreen, and glass and wind temporarily blinded me. Returning over the Zuider Zee, the rear gunner reported seeing the glow of the Hannover fires 90 miles to the rear . . .

In early October, 1943, after a number of bombing and mining sorties, I was posted on detachment to 161 Squadron at Tempsford to engage in supply dropping to the Maquis and other underground troops operating in France and Belgium. These operations only took place during the moon period. While other clandestine activities were flown from Tempsford, we were charged to fly singly and to deliver three-to-six containers, each weighing about 300 pounds, packed with arms, ammunition, explosives, wireless equipment, food, etc., and anything to hamper the enemy. These containers had to be delivered to a small reception committee waiting in a farmer's field or woods, somewhere in France or Belgium, and dropped by parachute from a height of 450–1000 feet. The major challenge was to locate this small group of patriots who identified themselves on the ground with three red hand torches and one white torch flashing a coded signal. My navigator and I selected our route to the drop area and to avoid detection and plotting by the enemy, we flew at about 500 feet above the ground over the continent at 180 miles per hour. The principal navigation was by map reading from a small scale map handled by the bomb aimer in the front turret giving a running patter to the navigator. On foggy or hazy nights flying "up moon," the pinpoint lights were spotted by the rear gunner looking "down moon." Locating the reception committee was sometimes very difficult since they were attempting to conceal themselves from searching Germans. Often they placed themselves on the side of a hill or in a small clearing in a forest. The drop itself was done at 400–500 feet and 125 miles per hour. For the safety of the reception committee, it was important to discover the drop area, place the load on the site, and leave quickly to avoid drawing any attention to the operation. Such operations took alert flying and very accurate navigation. During the dark period when 161 Squadron stood down, we went back to 214 Squadron at Chedburgh, resuming conventional bombing and mining trips.

Early January 1944 saw us on our way for a "drop" in northern France. It was a clear night with some ground haze, and on locating the "reception committee," we circled for a normal run. It was only when we saw the furrows in the field that we discovered the people on the ground were posted on the side of a hill, and we were flying head-on into the hill. I climbed to 450–500 feet and the load was dropped. However, the last couple of containers hit some power lines that short-circuited and set up some unexpected pyrotechnics.

Returning across France towards the Channel, our route took us on a path between the town of Frevent on the north and some woods two miles to the south of Frevent. At a height of 500 feet, a searchlight came up from the woods on the port side with a barrage of flak. It appeared that red tennis balls were passing between the port inner engine and the cockpit. I moved the aircraft down to where we could clearly see fence posts. Both mid-upper and rear gunners immediately opened fire on the searchlights and they went out. The rear gunner reported the turret on fire but quickly discovered it to be the reflection on the turret perspex of four red-hot Browning gun barrels! We learned from underground reports within 48 hours that in spite of the "high tension fireworks," the underground had received the shipment intact.

As for the Stirling, I flew it on operations and there is no doubt that this aircraft was somewhat of a challenge to get airborne and great numbers were written off during take-off, since its principal characteristic was a violent swing to starboard.

The Stirling took care, gentle persuasion, coaxing and stroking to lift it off the runway, but of all the heavy aircraft, once airborne, it was most sensitive and responsive, smooth and graceful on the controls, and it was an absolute delight to fly. I am indebted to my crew for their bravery and dedication, and of them, Alan H. Deadman, DFC (RAF), Wing Commander (Ret'd) W. "Bill" Wilkinson (RAF), and Bert Waugh (RAAF) have remained close friends to this day.[69]

In the Stirling, there was a chemical toilet, called the Elsan, located at the rear of the aircraft, just in front of the tail turret. Normally, it was polar cold in that part of the aircraft, and thus the toilet tended to be used only in the direst emergencies. Returning from a successful drop to the *Maquis* one night, Bob Mackett felt the unavoidable call of nature. Soon huddled miserably over the Elsan with his clothing lowered, his internal piping was instantaneously frozen solid when he heard a prolonged burst of fire from the mid-upper turret. Horror-stricken, frantically clutching his flying clothing at half-mast over his frozen nether regions, the pilot made a mad dash for the cockpit. Murray Peden, who flew Stirlings at the same time and on the same squadron, recalls:

> Hurling himself into his cold metal seat, with yards of clothing trailing behind him, he seized the controls and put the Stirling through all kinds of wonderful evolutions until a moment came when he dared pause to plug in his own intercom. "What the hell's the matter Tag?" he shouted urgently, addressing himself to the mid-upper, "What're you shooting at?"
>
> "Aw, it's okay, Skipper," Tag replied with carefully affected calm—he had been treacherously briefed and timed by the rear gunner, who had seen Mackett perch on the Elsan—"don't get your shirt in a knot. I was feeling sleepy; just fired a burst to keep myself awake."[70]

Gastro-intestinal shortcomings notwithstanding, the authorities thought highly of Robert Mackett, summarized in the following excerpt from his DFC citation, which was awarded in June 1944:

> His tour of operations is remarkable for the consistent number of successes he has achieved. He has proved himself a daring and skillful pilot whose devotion to duty has always been of the highest order in the face of enemy opposition.[71]

Meanwhile, the Main Force continued to strike at Germany wherever and whenever possible. At this point in the campaign, Bomber Command has been compared to "a heavyweight boxer fighting in the dark, sometimes striking a heavy blow."[72] One such "heavy blow" was dealt to Kassel on the night of 22/23 October 1943. Of the 569 aircraft despatched, a force consisting of 322 Lancasters and 247 Halifaxes, 43 aircraft were lost, representing 7.6 percent of the force. Initial *H2S* marking overshot the target area, which contained, among other elements of industry, a plant for the manufacture of V 1 flying bombs. However, eight of nine following visual markers correctly identified the aim point and placed their TIs accurately. Although the loss rate was heavy, what resulted was the most devastating attack on a German city since the Hamburg firestorm in July, and a similar degree of damage would not be attained again until well into the following year. The bombing was so concentrated that it totally stopped the manufacture of the flying bombs for several weeks, a delay which later provided some valuable breathing space for the Allies. It also created a firestorm at its epicentre, although this one was not as extensive as the Hamburg experience. Furthermore:

> It was on this night that an RAF ground radio station in England, probably the one at Kingsdown in Kent, started its broadcasts with the intention of interrupting and confusing the German controllers' orders to the night fighters. The Bomber Command Official History describes how, at one stage, the German controller broke into vigorous swearing, whereon the RAF voice remarked, "The Englishman is now swearing." To this, the German retorted, "It is not the Englishman who is swearing, it is me."[73]

Nearly three weeks earlier, on the night of 3/4 October, Flight Lieutenant George Laird from Toronto and his crew from 427 "Lion" Squadron were halfway to Kassel, over the Dutch coast, when their ZL-coded Halifax was raked from stem to stern from below by a German night fighter. What happened subsequently won an Immediate DFC for Laird, and the prestigious Conspicuous Gallantry Medal for the flight engineer, Sergeant William Henry Cardy from Port Credit, Ontario.

> Flight Lieutenant Laird and Sergeant Cardy were pilot and flight engineer respectively of an aircraft detailed to attack Kassel one night in October 1943. During the operation the

bomber was hit by a hail of bullets from an enemy fighter. Nevertheless, Flight Lieutenant Laird coolly and skillfully outmanoeuvred the enemy aircraft and set course for [England]. Two of his crew had been killed, however, and Sergeant Cardy was wounded in the arm and in the eye. In spite of intense suffering, this gallant airman refused to leave his post and executed his normal duties until he finally fainted through loss of blood. Later, when he again recovered consciousness, he attempted to do as much as he could to assist his captain in the homeward flight. By a superb effort Flight Lieutenant Laird succeeded in reaching base where he effected a safe landing in difficult circumstances. This officer displayed outstanding skill, courage and tenacity, while Sergeant Cardy's exemplary conduct and great fortitude were beyond praise.[74]

The Main Event

By the middle of November, Bomber Command was relatively rested and ready for its all-out assault on the German capital. Significant forces had been marshalled, and the Pathfinders now also possessed the improved Mark III *H2S* sets, with which they hoped to make a difference in terms of the precision of their target marking.

The first raid of this "main event" series took place on the night of 18/19 November, when 440 Lancasters and four Mosquitos were despatched. A major diversionary raid on Mannheim and Ludwigshafen was conducted simultaneously by a force of 395 aircraft, which included 248 Halifaxes and 114 Stirlings. The diversionary raid bore the brunt of the night fighter attacks, when twenty-three aircraft (5.8 percent) were downed. The bombing, done over cloud cover, was scattered and ineffective.[75]

The primary attack on Berlin was almost anti-climactic. Again, cloud blanketed the capital, marking and bombing were carried out blind, and no assessment could be obtained of the results. Number 426 Squadron sent fourteen Lancaster IIs to the Big City,[76] but four became early air-aborts, returning to base with technical problems. A fifth squadron aircraft was hit hard by heavy flak north of Hannover. They jettisoned their bombs live and diverted to an emergency landing at a base in Norfolk, just as they were running out of fuel, caused by battle damage in their port wing cells. Nine of the fourteen squadron aircraft reached and bombed the target.

> On the way to and from Berlin, the crews encountered icing conditions and, at the target area, they found a complete cloud cover with tops estimated at 10,000 feet, with fair-to-good forward visibility. Eight crews bombed the target from between 18,000 and 23,000 feet, aiming for the Pathfinders' cascading red and green target indicators. The ninth crew bombed on ETA. As they left the target area, crews could see scattered fires and flashes of bomb bursts reflected on the clouds. They encountered several active searchlights and heavy flak in barrage form; four squadron aircraft took flak damage. All nine aircraft returned safely to England, four of them landing at southern airfields as they were running low on fuel.[77]

The damage inflicted on this raid to Berlin was minimal. According to German records, only seventy-five high explosive bombs fell on city territory and no industrial facilities were destroyed. The good news was that the Berlin portion of the night's activities only cost Bomber Command nine aircraft, 2 percent of the force despatched. Ludwigshafen/Mannheim was another matter. Again, only widely scattered results were recorded, but this time it cost twenty-three bombers, of which seven were Halifaxes from 6 Group, a 7.4 percent loss rate.[78]

The en route weather at altitude was exceptionally cold that night. At Middleton St. George on the return, several airmen were hospitalized with frostbite from reported in-flight temperatures as low as -40° Celsius. Two were navigators who incurred excessive exposure at their extremely drafty photo-flash camera hatches, and another was a rear gunner who had cut out a clear vision panel on his turret to facilitate better visibility.[79] The polar temperatures were also playing havoc with the guns again, making the crews exceptionally nervous, as Roger Coulombe later recorded:

> All the guns of the rear turret became unserviceable again, due to frozen breech blocks. My rear gunner became extremely panicky . . . and was begging me to turn back, threatening to jump from the aircraft if I didn't. I told him: "You go right ahead! We're over the North Sea. You might find the water a little cold though, this time of year. As for myself, I am going right on to Berlin with or without you!" After that, he kept his mouth shut and didn't argue.[80]

The chemical plants at Leverkusen were bombed by a mixed force of Halifaxes, Stirlings and Mosquitos the following night, which included Halifaxes from 428 and 434 Squadrons. Overall losses were light, only 2 percent, but two of the nine lost were from 434 Squadron, which had also lost two the night before at Ludwigshafen.[81] The "Bluenosers" were rapidly becoming known as a hard luck squadron, an image they dearly wanted to shed. The attack was another flop, since the Pathfinders were unable to accurately mark the target, and the weather on recovery back in England was atrocious. However, this was the first night the new FIDO fog dispersal was used operationally. Successful recoveries were made at Graveley, and other installations would soon follow.

After a three-day stand-down caused by poor weather, Berlin was attacked in strength again on 22/23 November by the greatest force sent to the capital so far: 469 Lancasters, 234 Halifaxes, 50 Stirlings and 11 Mosquitos. Number 6 Group contributed 110 crews to the operation. Again, the city was completely obscured by cloud, and weather grounded many of the night fighters, which allowed the force to make a relatively straight-in, straight-out route to the target without incurring many casualties. A total of twenty-six bombers were lost, most from flak, and 434 Squadron lost two more crews, its eleventh and twelfth in a month.[82] Ten percent of the participating Stirlings were downed, and these losses represented the proverbial "last straw" for the aircraft. Since August, 109 of them had been felled on raids to Germany, for an average loss rate of 6.4 percent. Along with their other liabilities, their bomb load was simply not as good as the Lancasters or even the Halifaxes, and this was the last night Stirlings were used by the Main Force to bomb Germany.[83]

The night of 22/232 November was the most effective raid on Berlin during the war. "A vast area of destruction stretched from the central district westwards across the mainly residential areas of Tiergarten and Charlottenburg to the separate city of Spandau. Because of the dry weather conditions, several 'firestorm' areas were reported."[84] An estimated 175,000 people were bombed out of their dwellings. The 2501 tons of bombs dropped destroyed or severely damaged the Kaiser Wilhelm Memorial Church,[85] the Charlottenburg Castle, the university, including the *Zeughaus*, the *Hedwigskirche*, the National Library, the headquarters of IG Farben, parts of the Berlin Zoo, much of the fashionable Unter den Linden, the embassies of Britain, France, Italy and Japan, the Ministry of Weapons and Munitions, the Administrative College of the *Waffen SS* and the barracks of the Imperial Guard in Spandau. Hitler's private train received a direct hit, as did the Foreign Office. Best of all, many industrial premises were hit hard, including five factories of the Siemens electrical group, and the Alkett tank works, which had recently relocated to Berlin from the Ruhr.

The Telefunken, Blaupiunkt, and Daimler-Benz factories were also all severely damaged, causing Joseph Goebbels to be appalled by what he saw the morning after the raid.[86]

The following night the city was attacked again, although in smaller numbers, and much further destruction was caused. The flak was deliberately restrained over the target, allowing the night fighters, especially the *Wilde Sau*, to do their work. Twenty of the 383 bombers despatched were lost, in spite of heavy jamming, the dropping of decoy fighter flares, and "the imaginative use of *Corona* to order the night fighters to land [by a German-speaking woman who had been standing by in case the enemy employed a female voice to give the running commentary]." The damage done was again considerable, and included the destruction of the Felsch aero-engine works and the BMW and Siemens plants in Charlottenburg. An additional 300,000 Berliners were left homeless.[87]

On 26/27 November the capital was hit yet again, this time by a force of 265 Lancasters and seven Mosquitos, while a significant diversion of 178 Lancs were sent to Stuttgart, a city considered second only to Schweinfurt in importance for its ball bearing industry. Although the Stuttgart force lost just six of its number, the bombing was quite scattered, and the only industrial damage was the destruction of a Daimler-Benz factory that produced speedboats. Still, the attack split the German night fighter defences, taking some heat off the Berlin force. This segment of the attacking force lost twenty-eight Lancasters (6.2 percent), with an additional fourteen crashing on recovery in England when fog blanketed most of the southern bases. There was a certain bitter irony associated with these recovery losses, coming as they did at a time when FIDO was just becoming available, but was not yet widely available. Although the marking was not particularly accurate, the city was so massive that most of the bombs fell within its boundaries, "and particularly on the semi-industrial suburb of Reinickendorf; smaller amounts of bombing fell in the centre of the Siemenstadt (with many electrical factories) and Tegel districts. The Berlin Zoo was heavily bombed on that night. Many of the animals had been evacuated to zoos in other parts of Germany but the bombing killed most of the remainder. Several large and dangerous animals—leopards, panthers, jaguars, apes—escaped and had to be hunted and shot in the streets."[88]

Number 6 Group was reasonably satisfied with November's statistics, and its overall loss rate was only slightly higher than that of Bomber Command as a whole. Also, as its airmen matured operationally, "the number of Canadian crews credited with bombing the primary target was now higher on average than in Nos. 3 and 4 Groups."[89]

On 2/3 December, 458 aircraft, mostly Lancasters, hit Berlin one more time. No diversions were planned that night, the bombers took a very direct route, and the defending night fighters correctly identified the intended target and were ready and waiting when the Lancasters arrived overhead. Roger Coulombe and his 426 Squadron crew had a particularly harrowing time of it:

> We were coned for five minutes over the target by more than seventy searchlights. We were coned after we had been flying straight and level for a few minutes during our bomb run, and immediately after we had dropped our bombs on the markers. While coned over the target area, we were attacked five times by a Ju 88 and once by a FW 190. My Lancaster was heavily damaged by flak from the ground gun batteries, as well as by the bullets and cannon shells of the enemy fighters. The FW 190 flew in formation with me on my port wing for a few seconds, then peeled off, diving away on his port wing tip to avoid being in the line of fire of the Ju 88. I had seen the face of that German pilot so well during those few seconds, I would have been able to recognize him had I seen him on the ground the next morning.[90]

While Coulombe has modestly downplayed the intensity of the action for him and his colleagues over Berlin that night, Laurence Motiuk's excellent 426 Squadron history fortunately goes into considerably more detail:

> As the flak began to rise, Coulombe tried to escape the cone with a series of violent evasive manoeuvres. As the Lancaster dove and climbed about the sky, mid-upper gunner Sergeant S.G. MacKenzie sighted a Ju 88 on the port quarter down at 400 yards. MacKenzie called for a corkscrew to port, and the fighter immediately broke off without opening fire, then attacked again from the starboard quarter down. MacKenzie gave the order to corkscrew starboard, and the fighter again broke off with no exchange of fire.
>
> The third attack came from the port quarter down at a range of 400 yards; the Lancaster corkscrewed port and the Ju 88 broke off to the starboard beam down. It attacked yet again from the starboard quarter at 400 yards again, Sergeant MacKenzie called for a corkscrew to starboard, and again, the Ju 88 broke away, this time on the port beam down. The enemy pilot launched his fifth and last attack from the port quarter down at 200 yards, and MacKenzie opened fire as he called for evasive action to port. The Ju 88 opened fire and came to within sixty yards, then broke away on the port beam above, offering MacKenzie a perfect target. Tracer was seen both piercing and ricocheting off the fuselage of the Ju 88, and the fighter dove steeply and vanished. During the last attack, the Lancaster sustained damage to its port inner engine, port outer tank, port tire and hydraulics, and its radios.
>
> Throughout the battle with the Ju 88, [the] rear gunner . . . was blinded by the cone of searchlights. During the Ju 88's last attack on the Lancaster, an Me 109 was seen circling about 1000 yards away, dropping white flares. When the Ju 88 pilot opened fire, Coulombe and flight engineer Sergeant E.H. Titheridge spotted a FW 190 boring in from 400 yards off the port bow. The cannon fire from the Ju 88 caused the pilot of the FW 190 to break off his attack, and he dropped out of sight 100 yards off the port beam. MacKenzie, who had fired about 200 rounds during the battle, claimed the Ju 88 as a probable.
>
> As soon as the tussle with the fighters was over, Coulombe shut down the damaged port inner engine and set course for England. Halfway home, the starboard outer engine failed and, over the North Sea, the starboard inner began to act up and lose power. At this point, the situation got a trifle sticky; Coulombe could coax only 1700 rpm out of the starboard inner, but he needed it to put out at least 2400 rpm if the aircraft was to maintain height with that and the port outer, which was still reasonably healthy. They transmitted a distress call, and the USAAF station at Snetterton Heath, Norfolk, lit up its runways and gave Coulombe permission to land. Without a port tire the landing was tricky, and Coulombe got to duplicate the one-wheel landing he made months earlier at the Conversion Flight.
>
> In the morning, Coulombe and his crew went out to survey the damage to their Lancaster. The fuselage and wings were extensively holed by cannon shells and flak. The main spar of the starboard wing was so badly damaged between the engines that the wing tip drooped to the ground. OW "P" Peter went through two months of repair before it could return to service.[91]

Roger Coulombe was awarded an Immediate DFC for his actions that night, although he was still a sergeant-pilot at the time. However, his warrant officer's rank was due, which justified the award of the DFC as opposed to the DFM. This was his fourteenth war sortie and six of them had been to Berlin. And he was only at the halfway mark in his exceptional personal crusade against the Big City.

This was the last raid on Berlin for twelve nights. Bomber operations tended to ebb and flow with the lunar cycle, largely in order to make the force as stealthy as possible. Sir Arthur Harris therefore decided to give his exhausted crews a well-deserved break and he stood them down from operations in the main during the December moon period. Besides, his staff needed a respite to assess what had been accomplished at Berlin to date. In fact, the ORS troops at High Wycombe were pleased and upbeat: the Mark III (3 centimetre) *H2S* was proving good enough for area work. Although the winter weather had precluded aerial reconnaissance, intelligence reports, particularly from the neutral Swiss *Gazette de Lausanne* and Stockholm's *Svenska Dag-Bladet,* indicated the city was being hit hard—sometimes extremely hard—and that the bombing was perhaps intense enough to seriously erode the morale of the citizens. Members of the foreign diplomatic corps also asserted that large portions of Berlin's downtown core had ceased to exist. More technological and specialty crew improvements for the Main Force were also brewing. From the outset, Harris had maintained it would take twenty to twenty-five raids to bring Berlin to its knees, and there had been only five raids in this "main event" series of attacks. "The electronics industry in Berlin had been so severely disrupted (tube and consumer production already fallen by 20 percent and the manufacture of AI radars significantly delayed) that plans were being considered to disperse production, notwithstanding the additional inconvenience that such a major stratagem would entail."[92] Although costly, the Berlin campaign seemed to be working effectively.

During the winter of 1943/1944, the fifth winter of the war, back in the relative sanity and security of North America, the Mills Brothers were topping the charts with their hit song "Paper Doll," and Leonard Bernstein replaced Bruno Walter as the conductor of the New York Philharmonic Orchestra. Spam, a combination protein source of shoulder pork and ham first developed in 1937, was by now being frequently included in a soldier's meal. In November, the Royal Canadian Navy made public the development of a little pink pill called Gravol that could prevent both seasickness and airsickness in 75 percent of the cases tested. That same month, future folk singer/songwriter Joni Mitchell was born in Fort Macleod, Alberta. The top five box office stars for the year were Betty Grable, Bob Hope, Abbott and Costello, Bing Crosby and Gary Cooper. And the average annual wage for a person working in Canada or the United States was around two thousand dollars.

During the winter of 1943/44 rationing was a way of life in the Dominion. Meat, sugar and other commodities all had quotas, and if meal planning had become something of an art form for the average homemaker, nobody was starving, and nobody was afraid of bombs dropping on their heads. Money was plentiful in wartime Canada as there was full employment. However, there was little to spend it on. Savings and investments were encouraged, even mandated by the government, but this was not difficult for a populace with still-vivid memories of the privations suffered during the Great Depression of the 1930s. It was considered one's patriotic duty to buy war bonds, to recycle religiously, and generally make things last and not complain. Gas was strictly rationed, as was rubber, and so travel for recreational purposes was limited. Perhaps the only rubber commodity available in quantity was condoms, a contrived and prudent move on the part of the economic planners, given the rather urgent nature of wartime emotions. Alcohol was rationed and thus, the bootleggers thrived on the sale of home-made hooch, whenever they could hoard enough sugar to produce it.[93]

Wartime Britain, as we have seen, was somewhere between North America and Occupied

Europe and the Third Reich in the extent of wartime privations. Throughout that bitter winter, the bomber crews enjoyed the same songs and movies, if somewhat belatedly, as the folks back home. Rationing was far more pervasive in Britain, and the risk from aerial attack was still a factor, but most took it in stride and counted their blessings. The sense of industry and purpose was both unifying and pervasive. The airmen took their respites from combat when and where they could throughout the British Isles, secure in the knowledge that their civilian extended family was supportive and appreciative of their efforts. However, this was still a period of intense operational strain as night after night, the bloodletting continued.

Life Under the Bombs in the Third Reich

By late 1943, life in wartime Germany was a much different situation. In the wake of the Soviet victory at Stalingrad in February, Joseph Goebbels's Total War edict had fostered fear of the Russians and also extracted every morsel of obedience and augmented production out of an increasingly war-weary populace. For example, every luxury restaurant in Berlin was eventually closed during the year. Soon, the cabarets and theatres that had not been bombed out, such as the Wintergarden, the Scala and the Ka-De-Ko, were forced to close, and the bars and clubs would also be progressively shuttered. In a city so fond and so proud of its night life, only two bars were allowed to remain open within the entire metropolis, and those were dedicated exclusively for the entertainment of members of the *Wehrmacht* transiting through Berlin. Even the city's famous prostitutes were frequently shipped *en masse* to the Eastern Front to provide comfort to the Reich's soldiers. Had the Berlin Philharmonic Orchestra and the State Opera not enjoyed the powerful patronage and support of *Reichminister* Albert Speer, they would also undoubtedly have been shut down. With their indefatigable sense of humour, Berliners would soon joke that the bombing might end one's life, but Joseph Goebbels would keep one from living.

Poor food and coal shortages became pressing issues for the German people. As early as 1941, food and beverage shortfalls had begun to appear, and became progressively worse. First, beer was only available at limited times, a sacrilege to the average working German. Establishments such as the Adlon Hotel began watering down their lager to make it last longer. Then, as vintage wines disappeared, the exclusive restaurants, such as Kempinski's on the Kurfurstendamm, began selling their *Auslese, Spätlese* and *Trockenbeerenauslese* wines to only their regular and exclusive customers. Soon, ersatz commodities began to proliferate.

> Berliners now ate stuff made from purée of pine needles, powdered chestnut, and ground-up ivy leaves. A new cocktail called the "Razzle-dazzle" consisted of wood alcohol and grenadine. Tobacco was not yet replaced by any vile substitute, although a popular brand called "Johnnies" tasted so bad it was said to contain camel dung, courtesy of General Rommel's Afrika Korps.[94]

Perhaps the most despised of the ersatz products was the coffee substitute made from chicory, since it daily affected so many people. By 1943, the real coffee was virtually impossible to find, except for the privileged and the Nazi elite. The drain on livestock soon forced meat reductions, and the number of meatless days proliferated. On these days, the restaurants would substitute a red-hued paste known as *Lachs Galantine*, or ersatz salmon, which tasted to some citizens like soggy sawdust.

As hard liquor disappeared, a faux vodka that "took the roof off one's mouth" or a tasteless raspberry liqueur known as *Himbeergeist* surfaced, but not for long. Soon, again except for the privileged, alcohol disappeared entirely within the capital. "Against its will, Germany had become, perhaps, the most temperate nation on earth."[95] Even before the most intense periods of the bombing, the city's world-renowned public transportation system had fallen into disrepair, through a lack of spare parts and professional neglect, as line after line of the buses and trams shut down. The city's taxi fleet was slashed by 80 percent, its fuel was strictly rationed, and its clients were held hostage to whatever fares the drivers wished to charge. Worthwhile goods all but disappeared from the stores, and even the famous Ka-De-We department store held nothing to tempt buyers. At any rate, by December it was a smoking ruin. Soon enough, the Adlon Hotel and Horchner's would also be bombed-out ruins, the beautiful linden trees that bordered the Tiergarten reduced to charred stumps.

By late 1943 and early 1944, air raid warning and protection services had become well developed within the Third Reich. The vast majority of households were equipped with a *Drahtfunk* (Wired Radio) apparatus, a specialized attachment to home receivers that emitted a monotonous ticking on a specific frequency when there were no enemy bomber fleets reported over Germany. However, when inbound raiders crossed the Reich's frontiers, the constant tock-tock sound changed to an insistent pinging, and the system, transmitting on the *Flaksender* network, would broadcast coded warnings from the combined flak and fighter divisional headquarters mentioned earlier when enemy bombers were detected. The airspace over Germany was divided into coded thirty-five-kilometre by thirty-five-kilometre grid squares with major cities forming reference points, which were also given code names. The direction, altitude, strength and speculated destination of the bomber stream were also presented as update bulletins while the bombers were being tracked, so the average citizen could monitor the progress of the enemy raiders and judge when and if it was necessary to take cover.[96]

The shelters in Berlin were extensive and varied, although for a population approaching three million inhabitants, there were never enough of them and they were usually overcrowded.[97] They ranged from a reinforced, earthen shelter in the cellar beneath one's block of flats, to larger regional facilities, such as the basement of a neighbourhood church. Some of Berlin's *U-Bahn* (Underground) stations also served as shelters, but much of the system, the *S-Bahn* stations, was located above ground or near the surface, and unlike London, many stations offered little protection. A notable exception was a complex of shelters under the *Gesundbrunnen U-Bahn* station. It had been designed to accommodate 1500 people, but more frequently, three times that number were jammed in like sardines during attacks on the city. The air was foul from over-use, and the shelters were fertile breeding grounds for infections. Historian Antony Beevor elaborates:

> Candles were used to measure the diminishing levels of oxygen. When a candle placed on the floor went out, children were picked up and held at shoulder height. When a candle on a chair went out, then the evacuation of the level began. And if a third candle, positioned at about chin level, began to sputter, then the whole bunker was evacuated, however heavy the attack above.[98]

Even more robust facilities were located in Berlin's massive flak towers, which also served as aid stations and raid shelters. Each of the city's three facilities had its own hospital, generating plant, air conditioning and filtration system and indigenous water supply, as well as stored food to (supposedly) last a full occupancy for a year. "Lit with blue lights (they) could indeed provide a foretaste of claustrophobic hell, as people pushed and bundled in their warmest clothes and carrying small cardboard suitcases containing sandwiches and thermos."[99] However, there was even a *Sanitätsraum* staffed by a nurse, where women frequently went into labour. The ceilings, normally dripping condensation, were coated with luminous paint, a prudent precaution for the numerous times during raids when the lights failed. When the main water lines were hit, the flow of water would cease and the *Aborte* or washrooms would soon become disgustingly filthy. This was particularly troublesome to citizens of a nation traditionally obsessed with cleanliness. "Often the lavatories were sealed off by the authorities because there were so many cases of depressed people who, having locked the door, committed suicide."[100]

In a cruel and callous policy characteristic of the Third Reich, shelters were not made available to all inhabitants. Alien workers, of which there were an estimated 300,000 in Berlin, bore the brunt of the discrimination, and the longer the war progressed, the more they were sent in to replace Germans posted to the fighting fronts. While the western European workers, such as the Belgians, Dutch, French, Danes and Norwegians, received German food ration cards and were at least permitted access to shelters during raids, the eastern slave labourers, considered *untermensch* (sub-humans), were accorded no such privileges. During air raids, they were herded into their flimsy barracks, to survive or to die. Forced to wear deliberately humiliating insignia on their prison garments—the blue and white word "Ost" for Ukranians, a yellow and violet "P" for Poles—they were fed practically nothing and were considered expendable. Even more deplorable treatment was afforded Russian prisoners of war, who were given the most onerous, difficult and dangerous labour tasks. They were often worked to death in the rubble-strewn streets of the cities, a policy which, viewed through the lens of Nazi logic, was felt to be good for public morale.

Deception also played a significant role in the air defence of Berlin. Prime targets were extensively camouflaged and dummy targets were erected in the city's outskirts. The unique, highly visible Ost-West Axis was shrouded with a sophisticated camouflage netting complete with painted lawns and trees. The distinctive *Deutschlandhalle*, used for grain storage during the war, was covered with a giant tent, painted to resemble a park. The striking Victory Column was also draped with camouflage. Even Berlin's lakes, so remarkably different in their shapes and sizes, were altered by anchoring giant rafts that floated fake housing projects. Well-known government buildings were duplicated in canvas and wood on vacant lots while the real ones were camouflaged. A major decoy site was built at Staaken on the western approaches to the metropolis from movie sets that belonged to a pre-war film studio. Many of these initiatives were deviously clever and highly effective.[101]

More Innovations

While the period from late 1943 to early 1944 was particularly arduous for the crews of Bomber Command, the authorities were not insensitive to their trials and tribulations. Many initiatives were being implemented to ameliorate their operational conditions. Most of the electronic improvements for navigation, bombing accuracy and better self-defence have already been discussed. Along that vein, *G-H* was first used in a large-scale trial on the Mannesmannröher Werke tubular steel works in Düsseldorf on the night of 3/4 November 1943. This specialty attack was the sub-set of a larger raid on the city by 589 aircraft, and 6 Group provided ninety Halifaxes for this main portion of the operation. The *G-H* trial against this factory complex was conducted by thirty-eight Lancasters, including twenty-seven from 408 and 426 Squadrons,[102] and it demonstrated considerable promise for the future. However, like *Gee* and *Oboe*, it suffered range limitations, and thus it would not factor significantly into the upcoming Berlin raids.

Improvements to defensive armament were a major concern, and as we have seen, progress was slowly being made. Also, the bombers no longer had to go alone on their night forays over enemy territory. The *Serrate*-equipped Beaufighters and Mosquitos infiltrated the bomber stream, wreaking havoc among the defending German night fighters. They were assigned to a new and larger umbrella organization known as 100 (Bomber Support) Group, which officially formed in November 1943. A significant component after February 1944 was two squadrons of specialist-equipped Fortress IIIs, which were essentially B 17G airframes. Also, 100 Group possessed specialist Halifaxes and Stirlings. Infiltrating the bomber stream as well as flying diversionary flight paths and other sophisticated special duties, they were the host platforms for the latest jammers and deception equipment, including *Airborne Cigar, Corona, Window, Dartboard*, and ultimately, an improved version of *Mandrel*. Murray Peden remembers the Fortress III, so different from the Stirling:

> My love affair with the Fortress started with the first takeoff. (The difference in weight was most noticeable—an empty Mark I Stirling weighed 13,000 pounds more than an empty Fortress.) There was no tendency to swing on takeoff, none whatever. The Fortress soared into the air like a carefree gull, and kept on climbing effortlessly. To an old Stirling pilot, her rate of climb was enough to gladden the heart. Furthermore,, she was as stable as a basic trainer in the air, and at the end of the approach, when I flared out to land, I found that she floated as lightly as an Anson. In short, she was a beautiful aeroplane to fly: graceful, responsive, stable, forgiving, and as reliable as the sunrise. After the Stirling, a most demanding aircraft on takeoff and landing, the Fortress was a pilot's dream.[103]

Improved Lancasters in greater numbers were rolling off the assembly lines, and the Command also started re-equipping its squadrons with the vastly improved Halifax III/VII series commencing in November 1943. For the rest of the European war these aircraft were an equipment mainstay, particularly within 6 Group. Eleven of the fifteen 6 Group squadrons flew these variants of the Halifax operationally, although only 415, 426 and 432 Squadrons were still flying them at the end of the European war. All the other group squadrons had converted, in one variant or another, to Lancasters, particularly after the Lancaster X production line in Malton reached maturity.[104]

The Halifax has frequently been labelled a poor cousin in performance capabilities when compared to the Lancaster, although much of this criticism is unwarranted. The Halifax Mark III/VII and the even more powerful Mark VI variants were completely different aircraft from the troublesome and seriously limited Mark II/V models. In fact, the only significant drawbacks of the late model Halifaxes compared to the Lancaster rested with their more limited bomb-bay capacity and range/bomb-load capability, and the previously mentioned downward visibility limitations. Effectively, the largest weapons the Halifaxes could carry were the 8000-pound "blockbuster," while the Lancasters, with special-use modifications, were capable of carrying and delivering the 12,000-pound Tallboy and the 22,000-pound Grand Slam bombs. A simple strengthening scheme was put forward by Handley Page which would have enabled the Halifax to carry Grand Slam, but it was never adopted. There may have been a concern that even a modest structural modification would have disrupted the production lines when there were enough Lancasters available to carry the specialist ordnance. By early 1944 a typical war load for both the Halifax and the Lancaster averaged between 10,000 and 12,000 pounds of ordnance, although the Halifax B. Mark III and later Marks could carry up to 13,000 pounds of bombs. Perhaps most importantly, there was little to differentiate between their service or operational ceilings at around 22,000 feet, although the earlier Mark IIIs without the extended wings did suffer an altitude penalty which became readily apparent during the longer-haul raids conducted during the Berlin campaign. However, the later variants of Halifax tended to be more sprightly than the Lancaster over most altitude bands, although the Lancaster unquestionably had better range.[105] This is not to suggest that the later Halifaxes were flawless. Aside from their early service ceiling limitations, with their air-cooled engines, the rear turrets were even cooler than in the earlier series aircraft, and they seemed to suffer chronic shortcomings in the hydraulic system. However, they garnered a reputation as a sturdy aircraft, one that would do its best to get its crews safely home. And in one critical respect, the Halifax was far superior to the Lancaster: crew survivability in the event of categorical destruction in combat. At issue was the Lancaster's relatively confined fuselage, crew movement over that notorious main wing spar, and the size and location of the emergency escape hatches. For the period from January to June 1943, the overall emergency egress to survivability rate was 10.9 percent for the Lancaster and 29.0 percent for the Halifax.[106] A broader-based statistic, which included the later Halifax variants, showed that 18.8 percent of Lancaster aircrew survived being shot down to become POWs, whereas 34.7 percent of Halifax aircrew survived. The Halifax was popular with those who flew in it, it could absorb a lot of battle damage and still get its crews home, and it floated well when ditched. And when crash landings occurred, the way it tended to break up at its various construction joints occasionally saved the occupants.[107] By January 1944, a full nine Bomber Command squadrons were operational with the Halifax III, including several from 6 Group, and others would rapidly follow.[108] Jim Northrup has fond recollections of the Mark III Halifax, particularly after his experiences with the earlier models:

> When I was checked out on the Mark III on the squadron I knew we had a much better aircraft. The Mark XVI Bristol Hercules radial engines had power, and when you opened up the throttles, you were forced back into your seat. The aircraft did have a vicious swing to starboard that you had to be careful with until you got some airflow over the rudders, which did not take long. You could get 1740 horsepower "through the gate," but it flew well on three engines without using the gate. The second time I flew the Mark III, I climbed to 10,000 feet and rolled into a 90-degree bank and pulled back until I started to grey out, and still the aircraft did not have any tendency to stall. Now we had been taught the standard corkscrew was to be nose down and not more than 60 degrees of bank. I told my gunners we were going to change this to nose down as hard as I could push and roll into 80 degrees of bank. A couple of days later, I had a Hurricane from the Fighter Affiliation Unit do some attacks on us, and he said he was unable to get us in his gunsight, so we used this tactic until the end of my tour. Outside of the engines, the only significant difference between the Mark III and the Mark VII was that the wingspan had been increased to 105 feet 6 inches from 99 feet. There were other small changes but they really meant very little to the pilot. The hydraulic system was changed from Dowty to Lockheed-Messier but all the Marks were plagued with hydraulic problems. The main

difference [from earlier Marks] was the Hercules engine. It was a 14-cylinder, 38-litre air-cooled radial made up from two banks of seven cylinders. Like all engines, they had to be handled with the proper procedures. When taxiing, you had to stop every two minutes and run them up to full throttle to make sure oil was not collecting in the bottom cylinders. Also, after the engines had been shut down, they had to be hand-pulled through two complete revolutions to make sure there was not enough oil in the bottom cylinders to cause "hydraulicing" [sic]. If there was too much oil, you could not pull through, but the starter motor could, and this would bend a slave con rod, and you would have an engine failure. Whenever we landed at a base other than our own, me and my crew always did the hand pull-through. It was hard work, but I was always wary of ground crews other than my own.

They were sleeve-valve engines and burned a little oil, but we had sixty gallons, so this was not a problem. As for fuel, they burned sixty gallons on take-off and then gave between .84 and 1.1 miles per gallon. On long trips, there were two 230 gallon tanks and one 250 gallon tank placed in the fuselage. The fuel from these was pumped into the wing tanks. Now you had a dangerous situation as, unlike the wing tanks, fire retardant nitrogen was not pumped into these three auxiliary tanks when they were empty. If you got a shell in them, they blew the aircraft to hell.

I once saw a Hercules engine stripped down and was very impressed with the quality of workmanship. The supercharger gave 240 horsepower in "S" gear and never gave us any trouble. Up to 20,000 feet, we could pass a Lancaster like it was standing still, but above that, the "Lanc" was a better performer. I once nursed 6-U I (NA124) up to 29,800 feet to get over a storm, but she was pretty touchy at that height. The heating system gave little or no heat and I nearly froze to death until I got one of the gunner's electrically-heated coveralls. The "Hally" was a much better aircraft to land in bad weather than the "Lanc" because you could make a steeper, shorter approach, and once you chopped the throttles, you were on the ground. I only flew the Mark VII on check-outs and locally, but I could see no difference. Outside of the fact that I had wanted to fly single-engine fighters, I was well-satisfied with the "Hally" and I could make it perform. No *Luftwaffe* pilot was ever able to lob a shell into us.[109]

By the middle of December 1943, after the two-week layoff, it was time to visit Berlin yet again. On the night of 16/17 December, 483 Lancasters and ten Mosquitos took a very direct route to the city across Holland and northern Germany, and there were no major diversions planned. As a result, the German controllers plotted the progress of the bomber stream very accurately, and combats were recorded all the way in to the target from the Dutch coast. Heavy fog kept a lot of the defenders on the ground, however, and 100 Group was really flexing its electronic muscles that night, with extensive jamming in the form of Goethe poetry readings and Hitler's older speeches being blasted back to the night fighter controllers on their operational frequencies. Still, the attackers lost twenty-five aircraft, 5.2 percent of those despatched, of which four (10 percent) were 6 Group aircraft. Worse was yet to come. Heavy fog blanketed much of Britain on the recovery, and thirty-four more crews, including three from 425 Squadron, crashed while attempting to land. This brought the night's cost up to fifty-nine aircraft and crews, 12 percent of those who set out. While the skymarking was reasonably accurate, the bombing was quite diffused over a broad area, and little concentrated industrial damage was achieved. However, in the city centre, the National Theatre and the military and political archives were both destroyed and extensive damage was done to the Berlin railway system. More than a hundred large fires were started, taxing the emergency response teams to the limit. The plan was to concentrate the force over the target in a fourteen-minute period, but that degree of concentration was not achieved, and bombers were in the target area for approximately ninety minutes.[110] Roger Coulombe and his crew were very much the late arrivals, after surviving yet another harrowing experience on the way.

We were attacked by a Ju 88 again between Hannover and our target, Berlin. We lost our port outer engine during the attack. The entire right side of the aircraft, starboard wing, nose and fuselage were riddled by cannon shells. We lost our entrance door, which was knocked right off the aircraft, and the dinghy was knocked out of its storage and kept floating in the air, trailing behind the starboard wing and along the fuselage. I kept flying my crippled Lancaster to Berlin just the same, although losing height and also airspeed. Of course, we bombed Berlin late, a few minutes after the bulk of the raid had taken place. Fortunately, we had taken off with the first wave of bombers. So, the delay caused by the air combat and by the loss of an engine put us back some time after the third and last wave of bombers. We were trailing after everybody. We were *solus cum solo* over the target area when we did our bombing run. Fortunately, we didn't encounter any resistance when we bombed, since the Germans were busy fighting the fires that had been started earlier during the raid.

To this day, I have never been able to figure out how and why my crew and I managed to get through those two raids alive and unscathed. How is it possible to be so lucky? Or did we get some help from an invisible power? Even now, I get the shivers every time I think of those two raids.[111]

In the wake of these raids there was a break in the weather over Berlin. Photo reconnaissance sorties were finally able to verify the extent of damage to the city up to this point in the campaign. The results tended to vindicate the efforts extended thus far, and they added considerably to the credibility of Bomber Command's helmsman, Sir Arthur Harris:

Damage is widespread and severe. The area in which the greatest havoc is seen . . . stretches from the east side of the central district of Berlin to Charlottenburg in the northwest and Wilmersdorf in the southwest . . . There is also severe damage in the important industrial districts of Reinickendorf and Spandau . . .

Most important of the industrial works damaged are those situated in Tegel . . . Here the great armaments factory of the Rheinmettal Borsig A.G. (priority 1+) producing guns, torpedoes, mines, bombs, fuses, tanks, and armoured fighting vehicles has had many of its buildings severely damaged by fire and high explosive. The Alkett motor transport assembly works is one-third gutted and four large engineering works, manufacturing small arms and other weapons and together covering 129 acres, have had no less than 25 buildings destroyed or damaged. The great Siemens electrical engineering works (priority 1+) in West Spandau, severely hit in the August and September raids, shows damage to six more departments, while the Siemens cable works (priority 1+) has also been affected, but less seriously. The iron foundry and turbine assembly works of the A.E.G. (priority 1) and the radio valve works of the Osram G.m.b.H. (priority 2), both previously damaged, show further extensive damage. Fire has destroyed buildings in the important chemical works of Schering A.G. (priority 1) at Wedding, also part of a block shared by Pallas Apparate G.m.b.H. and A.E.G. (priority 1) producing aero-engine carburetors, motors and calibrating machines.

A considerable number of factories engaged in manufacturing aero-engines and aircraft components have been damaged, some severely. Included among these must be mentioned

B.M.W., Argus, Dornier and Heinkel, priority firms, all of which have important works in Berlin. Of the damaged factories producing electrical and wireless equipment, Bergemann Electricstaats Werke A.G. (priority 1) and Dr. Cassirer A.G. (priority 3) are probably the most vital.

In addition to the priority firms some eighty identified and numerous unidentified or small works, laboratories, storage and repair depots have been damaged, a few being almost completely destroyed. These industries cover a wide range and their products include vehicles of all types, engines, engine components, armaments, machine tools, electrical equipment, precision tools, various metals, chemicals, dyes, plastics, ceramics, fabrics and foodstuffs. Commercial premises listed in the damage summary number over forty but many more have been omitted as being of small importance . . .

Four gas works (all priority 2) and two gas storage depots have been damaged, two gas holders . . . being burned out. The gas works at Tegel is the largest in the city and here the coal and coke storage depot, a retort house, and two screening houses have been damaged. Other damaged public utilities, where services must have been considerably affected as a result of the raids, include seven water works and pumping stations, five tramway depots and the main postal depots in the central area. Damage to military property includes, besides the War Ministry buildings, five or six barracks and several military stores and motor transport depots . . .

An examination of the statistical analysis of damage shows that over 1250 net acres of business and residential property has been affected in the fully built-up and 50 percent to 70 percent built-up areas covered by these sorties and that over 60 percent of the buildings in the Tiergarten district alone have been destroyed. Very substantial figures are also given for Charlottenburg, Mitte, Schoneberg, Wedding, Wilmersdorf and Reichendorf.[112]

Based on these observations and analyses, the planners sincerely believed that the city had been struck a mortal blow, that the costs were justifiable, and that further hammering of the German capital was warranted.

There would only be two more attacks on the city prior to year's end, however, and while the losses incurred on both raids were not substantial, neither was the additional damage inflicted. When the Germans did their sums at year's end, they noted that the November/December raids had killed more than 8000 people, rendered nearly a quarter-million citizens homeless, and destroyed over 68,000 buildings. Added to the major buildings already mentioned as destroyed or extensively damaged were the Naval Construction Headquarters, the Charlottenburg Palace, the Technical University and the Romanisches Café.[113]

January 1944 brought with it a renewed resolve to finish off Berlin. Interspersed with major raids on Brunswick and Stettin, the capital was attacked in strength on the nights of 2/3 January and 20/21 January. On the latter raid, 4.6 percent (35) of the 759 Halifaxes and Lancasters sortied were lost. No. 6 Group forfeited nine crews, or 6.25 percent of those sent out, but five additional industrial plants were destroyed, and twice that number were severely damaged.[114]

A Toll on the Defences

While the Berlin campaign, including other concurrent major raids, was certainly eviscerating Bomber Command of many of its crews and aircraft, the same held true for the German night fighter arm. The losses incurred to Bomber Command during this period almost brought the force to its knees, but it was also a highly significant and successful war of attrition against the German night fighter arm. *Generalleutnant* Josef Schmid, Kammhuber's heir, lost the best of his fighter crews during the winter of 1943/1944. Among the notables, all of whom fell between late January and the middle of March, were Prinz zu Sayn-Wittgenstein (with 83 victories to his credit), Manfred Meurer (65), Heinz Vinke (54), Egmont Prinz zur Lippe-Weissenfeld (51) and Alois Leuchner (45).[115] These were highly skilled crews who had, among them, accounted for a disproportionately large number of the bombers downed. When these *Experten* fell, they could not be easily replaced, certainly not by the inexperienced and undertrained novice crews then emerging from the *Luftwaffe's* limited training system. Unlike aircrew members in the Allied camp, who had structured operational tours and eventual secondment to non-operational duties, German flyers received no similar respite from combat. They flew until they were killed, or wounded too badly to return to combat. Occasional relief was granted through leave or visits to special recreation and recuperation centres, but otherwise the only alternative to near-continuous combat was promotion out of operational billets, and that was extremely rare. And yet, the top aces were extremely competitive, a characteristic they shared with the best airmen of all nationalities. Perhaps none was more driven than Prinz zu Sayn-Wittgenstein. His former commander, Wolfgang Falck, recalled his impressions while accompanying the young ace early in his career on a train to Berlin to receive a decoration:

> Wittgenstein was a most capable pilot and extremely ambitious, as well as an individualist. He was definitely *not* the type to be the leader of a unit. He was not a teacher, educator or instructor. But he was an outstanding personality, a magnificent fighter, and a great operational pilot. He had an astonishing sixth-sense—an intuition that permitted him to see and even to feel where other aircraft were. It was like a personal radar system. He was also an excellent air-to-air shot.
>
> I was happy to discuss problems with him free from distractions and interruptions and I was determined to make the most of our lucky encounter. I was keen to know his opinion on several operational problems. He was very nervous, with fidgeting hands and an obvious air of anxiety about him. He was anxious because the other night aces might be successful while he was "sitting in a train doing nothing"—as he put it.[116]

By the beginning of 1944 the near-constant nocturnal battles over the Reich were taxing the energies of the night fighter crews to the limit. The whippet-thin Danish-born aristocrat, Major Wittgenstein was by now a distinguished night fighter pilot, who, through tenacity, skill and self-reliance, had amassed a formidable run of aerial victories and won the Knight's Cross with Oak Leaves and Swords in the process. He had been driving himself relentlessly for twenty-eight months of nearly continuous combat and had recently survived a crash landing at Venlo in his Messerschmitt Bf 110.[117] Foreign Ministry worker Georg von Studnitz, a Berlin acquaintance who met the young prince at the Adlon Hotel on New Year's Day, found zu Sayn-Wittgenstein, like so many of his fighter pilot colleagues, haggard, pale and demonstrating a lot of nervous strain. The unquestionably gallant prince apparently needed "strong sleeping pills to get any sleep at all, and even then he wakes up every half-hour."[118]

As with all pitched defensive battles, the perils faced by the defenders were not always of the enemy's making, as Rudolf Thun recalls:

> This was my first day of annual leave, and my bride-to-be had already left by train. But as a "Berliner," I scrambled for this British night raid on Berlin. And here I was, flying at

4800 meters altitude over Berlin, dodging German flak, when the little puffs of smoke came too close to the tail, and waiting for the British bombers, which are still ten minutes away. Suddenly, I am engulfed by the brilliant brightness of five German searchlights. They don't react to our coded signal flares, and suddenly, 20 mm shells impact my cockpit and the left wing—a German night fighter is attacking! With auxiliary tanks under the wings, a Bf 110 could be mistaken at night by an inexperienced crew for a four-engined bomber. The plane is on fire and we parachute into the darkness. On the ground, the Flak commander is very apologetic, and my Division commander lends me his liaison plane to get a change of clothing and to start my vacation. Never work overtime in combat!![119]

After Berlin on 20/21 January, Bomber Command experienced a particularly arduous visit to Magdeburg the following night. Although the city had been the subjects of a few feints and diversions, it had never suffered a major attack, and it was a significant target, because of its steel, synthetic oil, and aircraft engine plants. The Bomber Command Official Diary for the night succinctly captures the highlights of this raid:

648 aircraft—421 Lancasters, 224 Halifaxes, 3 Mosquitos—on the first major raid to Magdeburg. The German controller again followed the progress of the bomber stream across the North Sea and many night fighters were in the stream before it crossed the German coast. The controller was very slow to identify Magdeburg as the target but this did not matter too much because most of the night fighters were able to get in the bomber stream, a good example of the way the Tame Boar tactics were developing. 57 aircraft—35 Halifaxes, 22 Lancasters—were lost, 8.8 percent of the force. It is probable that three-quarters of the losses were caused by German night fighters. The Halifax loss rate was 15.6 percent! The heavy bomber casualties were not rewarded with a successful attack. Some of the Main Force aircraft now had H2S and winds which were stronger than forecast brought some of these into the target area before the Pathfinders' Zero Hour. The crews of 27 Main Force aircraft were anxious to bomb and did so before Zero Hour. The Pathfinders blamed the fires started by this early bombing, together with some very effective German decoy markers, for their failure to concentrate the marking.[120]

During the Magdeburg raid a returning, battle-damaged Lancaster provided the first actual confirmation of the existence of *Schräge Musik*. Although an intelligence report on the system was quickly disseminated, essentially all that could be done was to increase crew awareness of the threat and pursue the ventral protection initiatives.

One of the many fatalities of Magdeburg was Prinz Heinrich zu Sayn-Wittgenstein, himself falling victim after having despatched five more bombers single-handedly during the night's bitter combats. Like the Stirling's earlier operational record, this raid was particularly punishing on the low-flying Halifax II/V fleet. Within a month, units flying this type of equipment did not fly with the Main Force against targets in Germany. They were relegated to the shorter penetrations over Occupied Europe and to Gardening and Special Duties. "Sir Arthur Harris felt he could not ask the crews of these aircraft to face the German defences again and ten more squadrons (including representation from 6 Group) disappeared from Bomber Command's front line, although a few Halifax IIs continued to fly with one of the Pathfinder squadrons."[121]

For Jack Edwin Dickenson from Huntsville, Ontario, a Halifax pilot on 427 Squadron flying out of Leeming, this operational restriction arrived a month too late:

During the night of January 21/22 1944, we failed to return to England following a feint

Oberst Hajo Hermann, founder and enthusiastic practitioner of the *Wilde Sau* or Wild Boar method of night fighting. (Author's Collection)

A *Wilde Sau* scramble. The particular aircraft is a Messerschmitt Bf 109. (Author's Collection)

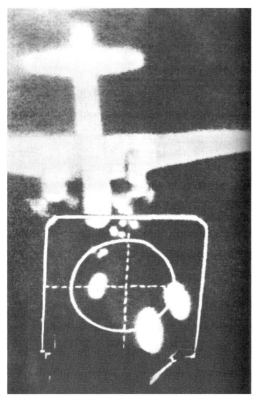

This is a rare, if rather poor, nighttime shot of *Schräge Musik* in action, here against a Wellington. (Author's Collection)

Flight Lieutenant David S. Smart while in service with 77 Squadron, astride the guns of the mid-upper turret on his Halifax. (Halifax Restoration Project, Trenton)

In August 1943 Squadron Leader Reg Lane ferried *The Ruhr Express*, the first Canadian-produced Lancaster X, from Toronto to Britain. (Lane family)

Night bombing attack on Nuremburg, 27/28 August 1943. (DND PL144305)

A very gallant sergeant. William Henry Cardy, a flight engineer on 427 "Lion" Squadron, was awarded an extremely rare Conspicuous Gallantry Medal for his "exemplary conduct and great fortitude" over Kassel, Germany, in October 1943. (DND PL23988)

Opposite top: Roger Coulombe (centre) and his crew of Berlin veterans. (DND PL 29267)

Opposite bottom: Intolerable losses forced removal of the Stirlings from the Main Force against German targets after the disastrous Berlin raid of 22/23 November. However, they soldiered on in a variety of specialized duties. (Shorts ST510)

Early in 1944, Air Vice-Marshal McEwen (left) replaced Air Vice-Marshal Brookes as Air Officer Commanding 6 (RCAF) Group. (DND PL 28361)

Opposite top: Flight Sergeant F.S. Stuart's battle-damaged 426 Squadron Lancaster II, 29 October 1943. The mid-upper turret has taken a major hit. (DND PL22172)

Opposite bottom: 426 "Thunderbird" Squadron personnel pose for a Christmas 1943 propaganda shot around a seasonally adorned 8000-pound present for the Third Reich. (DND PL19911)

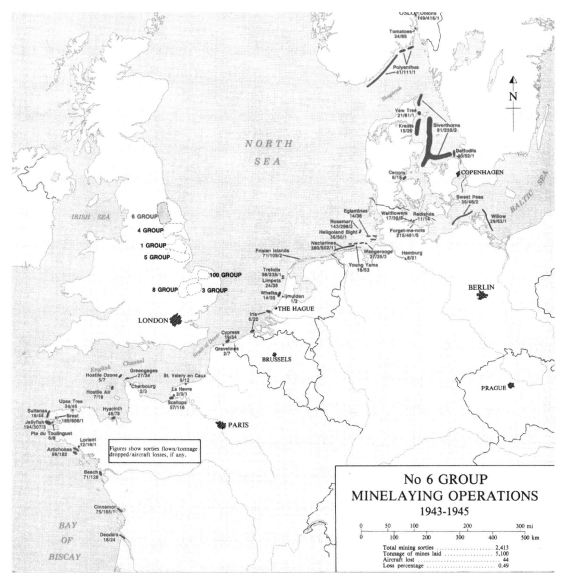

Oslo-Onions
149/416/1

Tomatoes
24/85

Polyanthus
41/111/1

NORTH
SEA

Yew Tree
21/61/1

Krauts
15/20

Silverthorns
81/235/2

Daffodils
40/52/1

Carrots
6/15

COPENHAGEN

BALTIC SEA

Sweet Peas
35/46/2

Eglantines
14/38

Wallflowers
17/39/3

Radishes
11/14

Willow
29/63/1

6 GROUP

4 GROUP

1 GROUP

5 GROUP

IRISH SEA

Rosemary
143/298/2

Heligoland Bight
36/50/1

Forget-me-nots
215/461/5

Nectarines
380/502/1

Wangerooge
27/35/3

Hamburg
8/21

Frisian Islands
71/109/2

Young Yams
18/53

100 GROUP

8 GROUP   3 GROUP

BERLIN

Trefoils
98/235/1

Limpets
24/36

Whelks
14/39

Ijmuiden
1/2

Iris
6/20

THE HAGUE

LONDON

Cypress
19/54

Gravelines
2/7

Strait of Dover

BRUSSELS

PRAGUE

English Channel

Hostile Ozone
5/7

Greengages
27/34

St. Valery en Caux
9/12

Hostile Air
7/19

Cherbourg
2/3

La Havre
2/3/1

Upas Tree
34/46

Hyacinth
46/78

Scallops
57/116

Sultanes
19/44

Brest
186/606/1

Jellyfish
194/307/3

Pte du Toulinguet
6/8

Lorient
12/16/1

PARIS

Artichokes
98/182

Figures show sorties flown/tonnage
dropped/aircraft losses, if any.

Beech
71/126

Cinnamon
75/155/1

BAY
OF
BISCAY

Deodars
18/24

No 6 GROUP
MINELAYING OPERATIONS
1943-1945

| 0 | 50 | 100 | | 200 | | 300 mi |
| 0 | 100 | 200 | 300 | 400 | | 500 km |

Total mining sorties 2,413
Tonnage of mines laid 5,100
Aircraft lost 44
Loss percentage 0.49

Mine laying or Gardening operations remained a viable mission for Bomber Command throughout the main years of the bomber offensive. It was also relatively cheap in blood cost to the Command.

Opposite bottom: One of the very few nocturnal aerial combats captured on film. The blow-up at right clearly shows a Junkers 88 closing to firing range on a Halifax. Photo taken over Hamburg very late in the war. (DND Pl144293)

Two stellar aces, *Major* Heinz-Wolfgang Schnaufer and *Oberstleutnant* Hans-Joachim Jabs in front of a Messerschmitt Bf 110G. Schnaufer ended the war as the highest scoring German night fighter ace with a hundred and twenty-one confirmed victories. Jabs eventually scored fifty victories. At the time this photo was taken, Jabs was *Kommodore* of NJG 1, and the aircraft in the background was his personal mount. (Author's Collection)

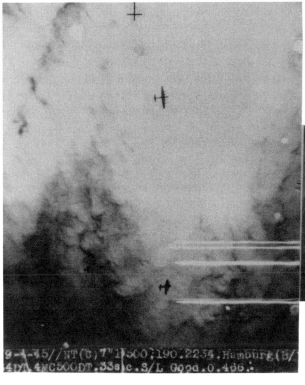

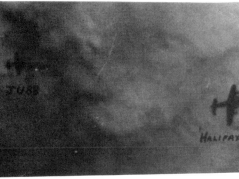

Jack Dickenson (second from right, standing) and his Halifax V crew were felled over Magdeburg 21/22 January 1944, the same night Prinz zu Sayn-Wittgenstein perished after running up a last torrid scoring spree against Bomber Command.
(Halifax Restoration Team, Trenton)

Rolland St. Jacques after his return from a sojourn as an unwilling guest of the Third Reich, 1945.
(Rolland St. Jacques)

Pilot Officer Richard Jack Meek from Vancouver, who was anything but meek, had a stellar wartime career as a navigator with an RAF bomber squadron. (DND PL34811)

Pilot Officer Donald A. Berry (right), a pilot and DFC winner on 426 Squadron, in animated discussion with one of his gunners, Pilot Officer PCR Sambrook, in the Linton interrogation room during the winter of 1943–1944. This crew had a rough go of it during the Berlin raids but survived to complete their operational tour the following spring. (DND PL26617)

attack on Berlin and the bombing of Magdeburg. Although Neil Martin, our mid-upper gunner, destroyed or crippled the Messerschmitt 110 which attacked us, we could not extinguish the fire started by the fighter. After bombing the target, we all bailed out safely, northwest of Magdeburg. Following sixteen months as prisoners, we returned to England. Historians Dunmore and Carter, in their *Reap the Whirlwind*, note that the Battle of Berlin became a fearful test of resolve for the crews of the Merlin-powered Halifax IIs and Vs because they became the lowest flying bomber in the stream following the removal of the Stirling from German targets after the Berlin raid of 22/23 November 1943. They wrote that to be a member of an operational Halifax crew during this period was to be a condemned man. They advised that the performance of the new Hercules-powered Halifax III was a splendid boost for the morale of operational crews.[122]

This is true to an extent, and one reason the decision to curtail operations of the Halifax II/V fleet was easier for Harris to make was because Halifax III squadrons were rapidly coming on strength at the time. However, even with their new equipment, initial loss rates in the Halifax community would continue to be high, as they also were within the Lancaster-equipped squadrons, and thus, aircrew morale and confidence would remain at a low ebb for some time.

Still More Diversions

Meanwhile, there was considerable friction developing between Sir Charles Portal and his Air Staff and Sir Arthur Harris and his Bomber Command Headquarters at High Wycombe. American and British air planners were increasingly at loggerheads as to how best to fulfill the Pointblank mandate, and specifically, Operation Argument, that portion of the offensive directed against the German aircraft industry. Part of the controversy swirled around Schweinfurt and the ball-bearing industry, and roughly half the Reich's total production of this essential product came from that city. On 17 August 1943, the same day as the Peenemünde raid, the Americans had attacked the factories at Schweinfurt and, at a single blow, temporarily reduced its bearing output by 40 percent. A second serious blow did not come until 14 October 1943, by which time the Germans had significantly bolstered their defences. While the damage to the bearing plants was even greater than that inflicted in August, American losses were staggering. Harris resisted attempts to send Bomber Command there at night, having repeatedly asserted that the city was too small, too difficult to find, and too difficult to discriminate from the air at night for application of his area attack doctrine. Also, when senior Americans asserted that they had successfully curtailed bearing production after the October attack and that it would not have to be repeated for a considerable amount of time, Harris felt Bomber Command's services were not required against Schweinfurt. He was also convinced that the Germans had long ago dispersed their bearing production.[123] Furthermore, when the late year analysis of the Berlin raids was completed—coupled with the fact that the Pointblank campaign did not appear to be yielding huge dividends—Harris felt he had all the justification he needed to continue dedicating the bulk of his resources against Berlin and the other industrial cities, many of which were on the Pointblank list at any rate. Still, by January 1944, viewpoints were hardening, and Harris's single-minded determination, coupled with his intransigence towards the so-called panacea targets, was approaching defiance from a subordinate headquarters. The Air Staff and the Ministry of Economic Warfare (MEW) had agreed that a night attack on Schweinfurt was necessary, but Harris did not believe this, and bluntly said so. He was also resisting what he viewed as the diversion of his Command to Overlord targets in preparation for the upcoming invasion. So much so, that Portal genially reminded him on 3 January that not only did Bomber Command have a significant and direct role to play in Overlord, but " ' the criterion by which bombing [operations] are judged' would soon 'be the extent to which they assist Overlord and not as present the extent to which they weaken Germany's . . . power to make war.' "[124] Still, Harris's obstinacy and resistance continued, and on 14 January Portal instructed him in a more forceful manner to "adhere to the spirit of the Pointblank directive."[125] Again, Harris deflected these policy directives with major attacks on Brunswick, Berlin and Magdeburg, forcing an increasingly frustrated Charles Portal to issue an even firmer directive.[126] On 27 January 1944 Harris was told that "Schweinfurt, Leipzig, Brunswick, Regensburg, Augsburg and Gotha were to be Bomber Command's next objectives, and they were to be attacked in that order."[127] Protesting that the weather in southern Germany was not yet right for this operation, and also arguing that he needed more planning time, Harris yet again ignored the Schweinfurt directive, and instead, although undoubtedly acting in good conscience, he sent his force to Berlin three times between 27 January and month's end. As it happened, this block of attacks on the capital was quite destructive, damaging some of the facilities owned by Siemens, Askania, Telefunken, Agfa, Kodak, Zeiss-Ikon, Daimler-Benz and Rheinmettal-Borsig. A further 200,000 inhabitants were left homeless, and widespread damage was reported by the Swedish press Berlin correspondents of *Dagens Nyhter* and *Alexandria*, suggesting that the damage inflicted during the November 1943 attacks paled in comparison to these latest undertakings. Collectively, 1710 bomber sorties were involved in this series, of which 112 (6.5 percent) failed to return. Of that number, 219 sorties were contributed by 6 Group, which also endured a loss rate of 8.2 percent.[128] On the night of 27/28 January, Rolland St. Jacques and his Lancaster II crew from 426 Squadron became part of the overall 6.4 percent, including four crews from the "Thunderbirds," who did not return from Berlin that night. The experiences of St. Jacques are interesting, and he graphically describes these moments of stark terror which were experienced by far too many Bomber Command airmen:

> Having dropped our bombs, we turned southwest on a track between Berlin and Leipzig for home. At about 2100 hours or so, in the vicinity of Leipzig, the rear gunner reported a night fighter some 1000 yards out and behind us. The skipper warned the crew not to all watch him, but to look out for a second one below; a known German tactic at the time. No sooner had he spoken than a loud "bang" was heard and the aircraft was heavily shaken. Said the skipper, "No panic. If he doesn't attack a second time, I can fly us home, even if some of the flying controls have been damaged." Unfortunately, we were not left alone and a second attack followed. Two engines now on fire, as well as part of the fuselage. The rear gunner reported his turret jammed and the skipper said for someone to go help him. Simultaneously, a third attack transforms the fire into a blazing inferno. It is clear that the plane could not survive long, so the skipper gave the order to bail out. As I was clipping my 'chute on, I saw the mid-upper gunner getting down from his turret, and he appeared wounded. And the wireless operator, standing up, was obviously dazed and seemed to be asking what was going on. I couldn't hear a thing, having taken my helmet with its built-in earphones off, so that the Y-wires from it would not choke me as I moved away from my post. So I motioned to him that we were bailing out and proceeded to go down to the bomb-aimer's position and the escape hatch. I found the engineer already there, half-in and half-out, seemingly panicking and yelling that he was jammed in and couldn't get out. So I told him to get back in and try again. The minute he was in

was when I made my move to get out, in case he again panicked and got jammed in once more. The bomb-aimer must have been there also, but I can't remember ever seeing him! He (the bomb-aimer) later stated that when he went to help the pilot with his 'chute, the nose compartment was clear of people. We were lucky that during all that time, the skipper managed to keep the plane on an even keel while it was losing altitude.

Being a non-swimmer, I had no inclination to jump out the front hatch in a dive! So I sat on the edge of said hatch and slid out, with the result that I lost one boot in the slipstream. I lost the other one when the 'chute opened, so I landed in a watery field on a rainy January night in stocking feet. I have absolutely no recollection of counting and pulling the ring! I assume the slipstream pressure pulled my arms away and in so doing got me to pull the ring.

Once on the ground, I noticed a touch of blood on my hand when I ran it through my hair. I surmised that part of the aircraft, possibly the tail wheel, had grazed my head when I jumped. On a humourous note, as I floated down and noticed I still clutched the parachute ring in my hand, I was about to drop it when I thought this could be dangerous as it could hit and hurt someone on the ground, so I put it in my pocket. This after having dropped some 7500 pounds of bombs on Berlin! Once on the ground, I hid my 'chute under some bushes and looked for a place to hide, as I could see flashlight beams in the distance, with dogs barking and their handlers shouting. I found a barn where I hid all night, not daring to light a match to look at my surroundings, for any light in the pitch-blackness of that night would be seen hundreds of yards away. Alternately freezing and sweating, wondering whether I was getting the flu or pneumonia, I saw the night through, only to find out by the morning's light that I had been attempting to sleep on the bare floor, under a hay wagon full of the soft and warm stuff![129]

Only St. Jacques, the pilot, Flight Lieutenant M.C. Wilson from Petrolia, Ontario, and the bomb-aimer, Flying Officer L.H. Power from Sydney, Nova Scotia, survived the bail-out. All spent the rest of the war in a prison camp. Eventually, some civilians captured St. Jacques.[130] "When they asked for his rank, St. Jacques struggled to remember the intelligence officer's lectures but, instead of *Oberleutnant*, the word *Oberstleutnant* came out. His captors advised the *Luftwaffe* they were holding a wing commander and the *Luftwaffe* sent a real *Oberstleutnant* to pick up St. Jacques. The *Luftwaffe* officer took one look at the single stripe on St. Jacque's shoulder and blew up, berated everyone in sight, stomped back to his staff car, leaving a *Feldwebel* (Sergeant) to take St. Jacques to the interrogation centre."[131]

For those crews lucky enough to survive a telling blow from fighters or flak, the trip back to England could be long and arduous, particularly if a crew member was seriously wounded. Clint Seeley of Kingston, Ontario, was a mid-upper gunner with 102 Squadron of 4 Group, flying in Halifaxes out of Pocklington in Yorkshire. His direct wartime contribution to the demise of the Third Reich ended the night after that of Rolland St. Jacques, although unlike St. Jacques, he made it home from this, his twenty-fifth operation:

The date was 29 January 1944 and the target was Berlin. That was the Command's 13th mission of the series to the German capital and our second as a crew. We took off at 00:01 hours as part of a 677 bomber force comprised of 241 Halifaxes, 432 Lancasters, and four Mosquitos. The temperature was -40° F, cold, but that was not the coldest we had been. On our trip to Leipzig on 3 December 1943, the outside air temperature was -65° F, and that was *damn* cold. The course to target was out over the North Sea, across Denmark, then south to Berlin. The trip was normal, with only many friendly aircraft around, no searchlights, no fighters, until we got to Berlin. Then, things sure changed, and not for the better, either. We did our bombing run and were leaving the city when a Me 110 attacked us at approximately 19,000 feet. He did considerable damage to our Halifax "G-George." Our starboard tail section was destroyed, the gyro compass was hit and rendered unserviceable, the starboard outer engine was put out of action, three gas tanks were hit, and the flight engineer noticed the fuel gauges were going down, even though we were not using those tanks at the time. So he pumped the fuel to some empty tanks in hopes that they had not been hit as well, and he turned out to be correct. By the time the pilot, Flight Lieutenant A.E. Kilsby, got the aircraft under control, we had lost several thousand feet of altitude. We then set course for England away from the main bomber stream, as we did not have enough fuel for the longer, more roundabout route home. Kilsby only had a small, standby compass to guide him, but our wireless operator sent out our signal to the three *Gee* stations in England, and we received our position back from them. Thank God for those stations . . . When the fighter attacked us, not only did we receive damage to the aircraft, but I was also wounded. A 20 mm cannon shell came through the ammunition racks in my turret and then exploded beside my leg. This did a lot of damage, all the way from my knee to my ankle. However, I stayed at my position in the mid-upper turret over the next two hours while we got out of German fighter range. We were expecting them at any time because we were alone and far from the rest of the Main Force on the return trip. At times like this you start praying, and on many trips I would say, "Though I am flying through the skies in the shadow of death, I fear no evil, for thou art with me, thy rod and staff they comfort me . . ." After two hours, when we felt we were clear of enemy fighter coverage, I finally got out of my turret and went to the rest position between the two wing spars. It was a *long* trip. Normally, a trip to Berlin took about 7 hours, 40 minutes, but this one took us 9 hours, due to the extensive damage to the aircraft. My leg was hurting quite a bit by then, and I was praying we would get home okay, because I really did not want to bail out over the North Sea, or even over the land. Morning came and we were still flying, but getting nearer to our base. Then I heard our pilot say that he could see land ahead. At that time, we were flying at about 6000 feet. Finally, we could see Pocklington. Kilsby contacted the control tower and asked them to have a fire truck standing by, as we had considerable damage, and he did not know if the undercarriage would work or if our tires were punctured. He also requested that an ambulance be standing by at the control tower, as the mid-upper gunner was wounded.

We finally landed and got about 300 feet down the runway on the roll-out when an engine quit, due to fuel starvation. At the end of the runway, *another* engine ran out of fuel. Although all fuel gauges were now reading empty, the last engine was still running as we taxied to the control tower to get me out so I could go to the hospital. When the medical people entered the aircraft to take me off, I took off my parachute harness and crawled past the base of the turret to the crew door, then on to the stretcher. I had *boarded* "G-George" under my own steam and I was darn well going to *exit* "G-George" under my own steam. I think nearly everyone on the station met our aircraft, as I was the first airman to return to the station wounded, and we were the first aircraft to return to Pocklington with this much battle damage.[132]

On the last raid of the three in the end of January series, another Canadian greatly distinguished himself and was awarded the Conspicuous Gallantry Medal for his actions that night. His name was Warrant Officer Richard Jack Meek from Vancouver, the navigator aboard a 626

Squadron Lancaster. A collective account of the action names two other aircrew members as well:

> Flying Officer Breckenridge, Pilot Officer Baker and Warrant Officer Meek were pilot, mid-upper gunner and navigator respectively of an aircraft detailed to attack Berlin one night in January 1944. Whilst over the target area, the aircraft was hit by bullets from a fighter. Much damage was sustained, the wireless operator was killed and the rear gunner was wounded. Pilot Officer Baker was also wounded, being hit in the face and rendered unconscious. Nevertheless, Flying Officer Breckenridge evaded the attacker and, displaying great determination, resumed his bombing run and successfully attacked the target. Almost immediately, the bomber was again hit by machine gun fire from the enemy aircraft, which had closed in. This time, Warrant Officer Meek was severely wounded, a bullet penetrated his breast bone close to the heart and another one hit him in the shoulder. Coolly and skillfully Flying Officer Breckenridge manoeuvred his badly damaged aircraft, however, and finally evaded the attacker. By now, Pilot Officer Baker had recovered consciousness and, realizing that the aircraft was unprotected, immediately made his way to the rear turret and manned it in spite of his physical suffering, the intense cold, and lack of oxygen. Pilot Officer Baker remained in the turret throughout the homeward flight, except for a short time when he left it to extinguish a fire which had commenced. Meanwhile Warrant Officer Meek, though desperately wounded and suffering intensely, refused to leave his post. Although deprived of practically all his navigational equipment, he plotted the route home with great skill. Eventually Flying Officer Breckenridge reached base where he effected a successful crash landing. His skill, courage and coolness in the face of heavy odds were worthy of the highest praise. Pilot Officer Baker and Warrant Officer Meek proved themselves to be valiant members of aircraft crew, displaying great courage, fortitude and devotion to duty. In spite of their injuries and much suffering they did all that was possible to assist in the safe return of the aircraft.[133]

Richard Meek remained undaunted by his end of January ordeal. After hospitalization and a period of convalescence, he returned to his squadron and to operations. Commissioned in April 1944, by 6 July he had flown many additional sorties to add to the six he had earlier amassed, helping bomb many further targets, including flying-bomb launch sites and other D-Day invasion objectives. In August, he was recommended for and was subsequently decorated with the DFC.

> Pilot Officer Meek has at all times carried out his duties in a most exemplary manner, his work being of the highest order under the strongest opposition the enemy could muster. His cool, quiet disregard of personal safety and the efficiency with which he navigated inspired his crew to the highest standard of morale they achieved, and ensured a maximum safety for his aircraft and crew.[134]

Arthur Harris's campaign against Berlin continued on the night of 15/16 February when, after a respite of more than two weeks for the heavy bombers of Main Force, the capital was again attacked by a force of 891 aircraft, including 561 Lancasters and 314 Halifaxes. The Canadian group contributed 152 crews, of which 136 bombed the target, one crashed during recovery, and four went missing in action: one each from 419, 424, 426 and 434 Squadrons.[135] This was the largest force that had been sent to Berlin, and also the largest non-Millennium bomber force sent by the Command to any target. Cloud cover obscured the city for most of the raid, but some of the Big City's most important war industries were hit, including the enormous Siemenstadt industrial complex. Although the German controllers had instructed night fighter crews not to overfly the city, leaving it free for the flak, many ignored these instructions and attacked the bombers there anyway. In all, forty-three bombers were lost: twenty-six Lancasters and seventeen Halifaxes, or 4.8 percent of the attacking force. "This was really the end of the true 'Battle of Berlin.' Only one more raid took place on the city during this period and that was not for more than a month."[136]

Other Priorities Emerge

The main reason this signalled the end of the Berlin campaign was a Most Secret policy directive from the Air Ministry in Whitehall sent jointly to AOC-in-C Bomber Command and the Commanding General Strategic Air Forces in Europe on 17 February 1944.

(1) <u>MISSION</u>. Your overall mission remains "the progressive destruction and dislocation of German military industrial and economic system, the disruption of vital elements of lines of communication and material reduction of German air combat strength by successful prosecution of Combined Bomber Offensive from all convenient bases."

(2) <u>OBJECTIVE</u>. Under this general mission, objectives of Bomber Command RAF and USSAFE are:-

(A) Primary objective, the German Air Force. Depletion of German Air Force with primary importance on German fighter forces by all means available including attacks against following precision targets and industrial areas and facilities supporting them:

(I) <u>EQUAL FIRST PRIORITY</u>. German single engine (S/E) fighter airframe and airframe component production. German twin engine (T/E) airframe and airframe component construction. Axis-controlled ball-bearing production.

(II) <u>SECOND PRIORITY</u>. Installations supporting German fighter forces.

(B) Other objectives:

(I) <u>"CROSSBOW"</u>. (V-weapons counter-attacks)—Operations by all means available will be taken to neutralize threats developing under "Crossbow".

(II) <u>BERLIN AND OTHER INDUSTRIAL AREAS</u>. Attacks should be delivered on Berlin or other important industrial areas by both Bomber Command, RAF and USSAFE, . . .whenever weather or tactical conditions are suitable for such operations and unsuitable for operations against the primary objective. Targets should be selected so as to cause maximum assistance in achieving primary aim of reducing strength of German Air Force.

(3) <u>CONCEPT</u>. Overall reduction of German air combat strength in its factories, on the ground and in the air through mutually supporting attacks by both strategic air forces pursued with relentless determination against same target areas or systems so far as tactical conditions allow, in order to create the air situation most propitious for "OVERLORD" is immediate purpose of bomber offensive.

(4) <u>COORDINATION</u>.

(A) Chief of the Air Staff, RAF, as agent for Combined Chiefs of Staff is charged with co-ordination of Bomber Command, RAF and USSAFE operations.

(5) <u>"OVERLORD" and "RANKIN"</u>. Preparation and readiness for the direct support of "OVERLORD" and "RANKIN" (invasion in the event of German disintegration) should be maintained without detriment to the Combined Bomber Offensive. Ends.

Time of origin: 171135A[137]

It had earlier been agreed that the Operation Argument portion of Pointblank, that is, devastating and concentrated offensives against the German aircraft industry, was to be completed by 1 March

1944, in order to free the Anglo-American bombing fleets for other operations in support of Operation Overlord. However, adverse weather conditions had largely precluded this, and yet by mid-February, Overlord was little more than three months away.[138] Finally, on 19 February 1944, the weather over the German aircraft factories began to open up, and the portion of Argument known as "Big Week" was about to begin. The Americans were to kick it off with attacks against the Focke-Wulf, Junkers and Messerschmitt factories in the Brunswick-Leipzig area on 19 February, while Bomber Command was to follow up with a vigorous attack against Leipzig on the night of 19/20 February. Although Harris had systematically stonewalled the Air Staff and Sir Charles Portal about beginning Argument earlier and independently of the Americans, the 17 February directive was a clearly mandated order, and Bomber Command's chieftain could no longer refuse the tasking. And so, Leipzig it would be.

In all, 823 aircraft, including 561 Lancasters and 255 Halifaxes, were despatched on this operation. The planning was innovative and included diversionary minelaying operations in Kiel Bay, a "spoof" raid on Berlin and bombing of German night fighter airfields in Holland, but this was a devastating night for Bomber Command. Cloud cover over the target necessitated the use of sky marking, and while the bombing was concentrated in its early stages, it later scattered significantly. Stronger-than-forecast winds meant that some of the bombers beat the Pathfinders to the target area, requiring delaying orbits and exposure to flak and collision. Twenty aircraft were thus felled by flak and a further four lost in mid-air collisions. Many night fighter attacks also occurred, as few had been diverted against the other Bomber Command efforts. In all, and for limited gain, Bomber Command lost seventy-eight aircraft—forty-four Lancasters and thirty-four Halifaxes—9.5 percent of the designated force. "The Halifax loss rate was 13.3 percent of those despatched and 14.9 percent of those Halifaxes which reached the enemy coast after 'early returns' had turned back."[139] Number 6 Group's losses were 14 percent, and another fifteen RCAF crews (nearly 12 percent) returned early. "Heaviest hit once again was No. 434 Squadron, in the fourth wave, with a third of its nine crews missing, but 408 (in the first wave) and No. 429 (in the fifth) were not far behind, losing four (of eighteen) and three (of sixteen) respectively."[140] Many of the night fighter successes were a result of Schmid's increasingly free-ranging en route interceptions of the bomber stream, and these tactics appeared to be paying dividends. Based on the Leipzig losses to the Halifax community, this was the last occasion when Sir Arthur Harris sent the Mark II/V-equipped squadrons on the deep penetrations into Germany. Five Canadian squadrons, Numbers 419, 428, 429, 431, and 434, along with a similar number of RAF squadrons in other groups, were operationally limited to Gardening and shallow raids by this decision, but undoubtedly, it saved lives.[141]

After a successful major attack on Stuttgart (another Pointblank target) the following night with uncharacteristically few losses (1.5 percent of 598 aircraft, with a further five crashes in Britain on the return), Harris was finally drawn to attack Schweinfurt on the night of 24/25 February. The Pathfinders actually had little difficulty finding Schweinfurt this time, although they had some trouble accurately marking it, and the bombing results were somewhat mixed. Still, the attack complemented an American daylight raid made on the factories the previous day, and the losses, although significant at thirty-three aircraft and 4.5 percent of the force,[142] were relatively modest, considering Harris' earlier contention that a Schweinfurt raid would be too costly. Reg Lane was one of the Pathfinders that night:

Target was identified visually. Many details of town and adjacent country positively identified. Load released at 2303 from 17,000 feet on the aiming-point. Ran up river from southwest. Six cans of flares white (first can 2259 hours) and TI [Target Indicator] green over woods two to three miles south of target. Target not sufficiently illuminated. Aiming point not seen until over it. Circled to starboard and made second run from southeast along railway. Found one visual marker T.I. red on aiming-point, another on east end of marshalling yard, and another in the new town. Own T.I. red undershot 6 to 700 yards to southeast. Saw one large bomb burst on island immediately south of aiming-point. By 2310 hours, whole town area well covered with incendiaries with three very good fires, but many incendiaries and several red T.I.s were spreading up to five miles west of the town. Route marking good.[143]

What Might Have Been

After this raid, the weather changed for the worse again, preventing follow-up action against the Schweinfurt complex, although there was certainly no determined push from the High Wycombe camp to re-visit this target or the other bearing plants in the Nazi production constellation. Albert Speer thought this was an incredible oversight, and he felt that, had the Allied counter-bearing campaign been prosecuted with vigour and determination, it could have forced Germany to sue for peace much earlier in the war:

> We were able to avoid total disaster by substituting slide bearings for ball bearings whenever possible. But what really saved us was the fact that from this time on, (the October 1943 raid) the enemy to our astonishment once again ceased his attacks on the ball-bearing industry. Then, (in February 1944) within four days, Schweinfurt, Steyr, and Cannstatt were each subjected to two successive heavy attacks. Then followed raids on Erkner, Schweinfurt and again Steyr. [Here, Speer notes that after only six weeks their production of bearings which were greater than 6.3 centimeters had been reduced to just 29 percent of bearing output prior to the raids.] At the beginning of April 1944, however, the attacks on the ball-bearing industry ceased abruptly. Thus, the Allies threw away success when it was already in their hands. Had they continued the attacks of March and April with the same energy, we would quickly have been at our last gasp.[144]

Albert Speer remained loyal to his belief in this failed opportunity on the Allied side well after the publication of his autobiographical book *Inside the Third Reich*. In the 1999 publication *Speer–The Final Verdict*, his biographer, Joachim Fest, comments on the 1943 attacks and later raids on bearing plants:

> Had the attacks been maintained and included the remaining ball-bearing plants, Speer believed that it would have taken only four months to bring armaments production "to a complete standstill" and the war would have been over . . . it was only in February 1944 that the Schweinfurt factories, along with ball-bearing plants in Erkner, Bad Cannstadt and Steyr, were bombed twice within a span of four days and largely destroyed. After that the Combined Command went back to random attacks, and at the beginning of April bombing of the ball-bearing industry, which had been partially relocated, ceased altogether. The chance of ending the war then was wasted once and for all. As a result of the inconsistent Allied strategy, not a single tank, aircraft, submarine or motor vehicle was lost because of a shortage of ball-bearings.[145]

The Halifax, Warts and All

As the winter of 1944 progressed, evidence continued to mount against the new Halifax III. In spite of its many improvements, the aircraft was exceptionally cold, and the ceiling limitations of the early variants on the longer trips was causing some disquiet. Thus, as early as January 1944, the Cabinet Defence Committee for Supply decreed that once Bomber Command was operating in support of the army after Normandy, Halifaxes should be used only "in conditions of shallow penetration and against lightly defended targets," supposedly leaving the truly strategic bombing tasks to the Lancaster squadrons.[146] As it turned out, this restriction did not come to pass. Performance improvements, coupled with the decline of the German day and night fighter arms, would allow the Halifax III and its derivatives to soldier on with Main Force until the end of hostilities.

However, even the earliest Halifax IIIs were still a significant step forward from the older variants. As Jim Northrup has mentioned, it was actually agile and manoeuvrable, particularly at the lower levels. Sometimes aggressive defensive manoeuvring and an innovative start to a tour of operations paid dividends, as bomb-aimer Malcom Smith, who flew his operational tour with 425 Squadron, recalls. It also speaks highly of the aerodynamic qualities of the Halifax III.

> After a successful raid on Frankfurt, 22/23 March '44, Sergeant Vern Irvine of Toronto was forced to throw Halifax "K-King" into a loop to evade a German fighter. The Nazi fired at the Halifax from 800 yards, and the rear gunner, Mac Smith of Star City, was tossed around so violently he could not fire back. The navigator, Flying Officer Art Mauger of Victoria, British Columbia, found himself and his instruments floating up to the roof. The mid-upper gunner, Sergeant Mesmore "Sonny" Rainville of Montreal, stayed in his turret, although he was afraid he might drop out of the "bubble." When the Halifax came out of the loop, we found the night fighter had disappeared after missing all its shots. It was our first operational flight as a crew together on the Alouette Squadron.[147]

Other Pointblank Targets

Along with the closing raid of the main event series on Berlin on the night of 24/25 March, there were significant attacks on the Paris environs (2/3 March), Le Mans (7/8 March and 13/14 March), Stuttgart (15/16 March), Amiens (16/17 March), Frankfurt (18/19 March and 22/23 March), Laon (23/24 March), Essen (26/27 March), and Nuremburg (30/31 March). Many of these major raids were successful, and they were augmented by quite a few of lesser strengths. A significant number were on the Pointblank targeting list. Canadian airmen continued to excel in the face of danger during the period, both within and outside 6 Group. When the Command visited Stuttgart with 863 aircraft on the night of 15/16 March, a long, southerly ingress route over France and almost to the Swiss border generally delayed the attacks of the night fighters. While most of their interceptions were late, fierce air combats ensued just prior to Main Force reaching the target. However, for Flight Sergeant George Eric Hexter from London, Ontario, a bomb-aimer with 619 Squadron, heated action took place considerably earlier. Both he and his pilot, Flight Sergeant Schofield of the RAF, received immediate DFMs for their night's work, when they early on became members of the unfortunate minority to be singled out for attention by enemy fighters:

> Flight Sergeant Hexter and Flight Sergeant Schofield were bomb-aimer and pilot respectively of an aircraft detailed to attack Stuttgart one night in March 1944. When about 150

miles from the target, the aircraft was attacked by a fighter. Before the enemy aircraft could be evaded the bomber had sustained much damage, while Flight Sergeant Hexter had been wounded in the hand and foot. Undeterred, Flight Sergeant Schofield continued his mission and eventually reached the target, over which he was ably guided by Flight Sergeant Hexter who, though in considerable pain, insisted on remaining at his post. Shortly afterwards the oxygen supply failed but Flight Sergeant Schofield came down to a lower altitude and afterwards flew the damaged aircraft to this country (England), where he effected a safe landing at an airfield near the coast. This airman displayed skill, courage and determination of a high order. Flight Sergeant Hexter also set a fine example of courage and fortitude, and his conduct in trying circumstances was worthy of great praise.[148]

Frankfurt, a Pointblank target, was visited twice during March. The first raid by 846 aircraft on 18/19 March did significant damage, particularly the early waves, but the second attack on the night of 22/23 March by 816 raiders was even more successful:

> The marking and bombing were accurate and Frankfurt suffered another heavy blow; the city's records show that the damage was even more severe than the raid carried out 4 nights earlier. Half of the city was without gas, water and electricity "for a long period." All parts of the city were hit but the greatest weight of the attack fell in the western districts. The report particularly mentions severe damage to the industrial area along the main road to Mainz. 162 B-17s of the Eighth Air Force used Frankfurt as a secondary target when they could not reach Schweinfurt 36 hours after this RAF raid and caused further damage. The Frankfurt diary has this entry: "The three air raids of 18th, 22nd and 24th March were carried out by a combined plan of the British and American air forces and their combined effect was to deal the worst and most fateful blow of the war to Frankfurt, a blow which simply ended the existence of the Frankfurt which had been built up since the Middle Ages."[149]

Two nights later, Bomber Command conducted its last major raid on Berlin of the war, even though the city was later repeatedly attacked by small, highly effective forces of Mosquitos, not to mention many damaging daylight attacks by the Americans in the ensuing months. Of the 811 aircraft despatched, 72 were lost—44 Lancasters and 28 Halifaxes—8.9 percent of the force.

> This night became known in Bomber Command as "the night of the strong winds." A powerful wind from the north carried the bombers south at every stage of the flight. Not only was this wind not forecast accurately, but it was so strong that the various methods available to warn crews of wind changes during the flight failed to detect the full strength of it. The bomber stream became very scattered, particularly on the homeward flight, and radar-predicted flak batteries at many places were able to score successes. Part of the bomber force even strayed over the Ruhr defences on the return flight. It is believed that approximately 50 of the 72 aircraft lost were destroyed by flak; most of the remainder were victims of night fighters. Needless to say, strong winds severely affected the marking with, unusually, markers being carried beyond the target and out to the south-west of the city.[150]

Laurence Motiuk elaborates from the 6 Group perspective:

> The Pathfinders were having trouble with the high winds, which blew their pyrotechnics about. The Master Bomber helped some crews, but others could not hear him, or could not understand his instructions. Most crews sighted on red skymarkers with yellow stars

and cascading red and green target indicators, and released their bombs at 20,000 to 23,000 feet. One crew orbited the target for five minutes, then sighted on a fire seen through breaks in the cloud. Another crew aimed for a large fire, and had just released their bombs when red and green target indicators appeared behind them. No. 6 Group detailed 115 aircraft, of which two failed to take-off, thirteen returned early, eighty-five bombed the primary target, two bombed secondary targets, and thirteen went missing, including one each from No. 420, No. 424 and No. 432 Squadrons; two each from No. 425 and No. 433 Squadrons; and three each from No. 427 and No. 429 Squadrons.[151]

Black Mike Assumes Command

By this time, 6 Group had a new helmsman in Air Vice-Marshal Clifford M. "Black Mike" McEwen. In fact, McEwen, moving up from base commander at Linton, had been appointed AOC just in time for the Augsburg raid on the night of 25/26 February. A hard-charging operational commander who led from the front and cared enormously about his crews, he was also a stickler for discipline and training. The need for better navigation and for more fighter affiliation exercises topped his emphasis list, and his unrelenting influence was soon felt far and wide throughout the group. His forceful leadership would pay dividends in reduced combat losses, although broad conversions to the Halifax III, the start of conversions to Merlin-engine Lancasters, and an impending switch to pre-invasion targets in support of Overlord were also contributing factors to the decline in blood costs. "On the five raids flown between 25 February and 23 March—just after McEwen took over but before he could have had any appreciable impact—the loss rate of 5.6 percent seemed explicable entirely in terms of poor flying discipline and, in particular, because of poor time-and-track-keeping, faults the extra training he instituted was designed to correct."[152]

On 26/27 March it was Essen's turn, and while it was not a Pointblank target, its industrial production was highly important. This time, the German controllers, expecting a deeper penetration, were largely hoodwinked. As it turned out, only nine of the 705 participating bombers were lost— just 1.3 percent of the force. Oboe-equipped Mosquitos marked the target well and accurately, and this was considered a successful attack all around.[153] While the losses were minimal, Roger Coulombe had a chilling observation about the fate of the only missing aircraft of the 106 detailed from 6 Group that night:

> Intense flak and numerous searchlights for activity. I saw a squadron mate of mine, Pilot Officer Olsson and his entire crew, bail out from their Lancaster OW-A. I counted seven parachutes that came out of the aircraft. They had been flying just a few yards below and ahead of me. The searchlight activity was intense, so I could easily read the markings on their Lancaster. Two weeks later, the Red Cross reported that all seven crew members had been killed in action.[154]

Nuremburg, the Worst Night of All

Nuremburg was targeted on the night of 30/31 March 1944. Although the fortunes of Bomber Command were about to change, that was certainly not embodied in this particular raid. Roger Coulombe recollects:

> Ninety-five of our heavy bombers were shot down over Germany on that raid. It was a full moon . . . no clouds . . . and very clear skies! The bombers were leaving vapour trails behind

them. All the German fighters had to do was follow those trails like on a highway to catch up with the bombers and shoot them down. And the German skies were swarming with night fighters of all kinds: Ju 88 . . . Me 109 . . . FW 190 . . . Me 110 . . . etc . . . etc. Indeed, the bombers were being shot down like flies out of the sky all around us. Once, I had tracer bullets flying just a few feet right over my cabin and directed at a bomber flying on my left a few feet above and ahead of me. Unfortunately, the bomber was shot down. I don't need to add that I started violent corkscrewing manoeuvres at that moment.[155]

Since this was in a bright-moon period, the Main Force would normally have been stood-down. However, the planners were relying on an optimistic weather forecast, which called for a high cloud cover on the outbound leg, then clear skies over the target area. As it happened, a Meteorological Flight Mosquito doing a precursor route and target area reconnaissance reported that the high cloud cover was unlikely to be present as a protective cloak for the bomber stream. In fact, given the results of the Meteorological Flight reconnaissance, Harris's trusted deputy, Air Marshal Sir Robert Saundby, recalls that "everyone, including myself, expected the C-in-C to cancel the raid."[156] However, Harris did not do so. The Germans ignored the several diversions incorporated into the attack plan—they were getting very adept at sizing up Bomber Command's intentions— and rallied the vast majority of their night fighters at two radio beacons, which turned out to be astride the inbound approach path of the bombers, since winds had pushed the raiders off their intended course. The first attacks started at the Belgian frontier and were continuously prosecuted over the next hour, all the way to the target and beyond. *Unteroffizier* Erich Handle of *III/NJG I*, flying out of Lyon, recalls the conditions from the German perspective: "Weather was marvellous—clear sky, half-moon, little cloud and no mist—it was simply ideal, almost too bright."[157] Of the ninety-five aircraft—11.9 percent of the force—that were felled that night, eighty-two were lost in fierce battles all along the ingress route and in the vicinity of the target. The blood cost to 6 Group was thirteen of the 120 assigned to the raid, which even at that rate was slightly less than the Command average. For once, given the exceptionally early arrival of the early waves thanks to the extremely strong, unforeseen tail winds (shades of the Berlin trip a week earlier), relative security appeared to rest in arriving late to bomb, which is what happened to most of the 6 Group aircraft.[158] In a bitter irony, the lack of cloud cover at altitude to cloak the bombers inbound thickly obscured the target in the lower levels, and coupled with the exceptionally strong crosswinds on the final approach path, the Pathfinders were unable to accurately and consistently mark the target. A ten-mile-long creepback developed in the countryside to the north of the city, and other markers were placed too far to the east. The only good news was that the fierce winds actually caused about 120 crews to bomb Schweinfurt, located about fifty miles northwest of the city, when it was accidently marked by two Pathfinder crews, but this did little significant damage. The Nuremburg raid marked Bomber Command's highest absolute total for losses on a major raid during the war, and in the end, there was little damage meted out to show for it.[159] J. Douglas Harvey recalled the operation, seen from the cockpit of his 408 Squadron Lancaster II.[160] He felt real apprehension, as all along the approach route, Lancasters were rearing up and exploding in mid-air, while others fell, in flames and out of control:

> I had never before experienced the fear that was gripping me. It was totally irrational; our aircraft wasn't under attack despite the butchery going on all around us. I told myself to calm down, that this was no different from previous raids. But it was different. I could

smell the danger. We, like all the others, were sitting ducks, silhouetted against the solid cloud layer below, lit by the diffused light of the moon, and leaving large, white vapour trails to mark our exact positions. We had never before been able to see the bomber stream over Germany.

Pressing on towards Nuremburg through this man-made Dante's Inferno, Harvey called out to his rear gunner, sighting a German night fighter low, behind and to the right of their Lancaster. The gunner acknowledged the threat, then appeared flabbergasted that Harvey, sitting up front and facing forward, could see it as well. Harvey quipped that the sky was so bright, he could see all the way to Russia, and exhorted his gunners to an even higher level of vigilance.

> My feet actually chattered on the rudder bars as my fear continued. God, will this trip never end? There was nothing to take my mind off the horrors of the night and I felt completely helpless. I continued to roll the Lanc back and forth, searching, searching. The fighter attacks continued as we swept along in the 120 mile an hour wind towards the target. Dim shapes suddenly erupted into balls of fire as bomber after bomber blew up, their explosions lighting the sky and then slowly fading as they disintegrated, the pieces falling to earth. The crew were silent, frozen with fear, awaiting the attack we were sure would come. It never came. With the moon flooding the sky, we were being swept through the bloodiest night Bomber Command ever faced, without a scratch. No time to wonder why.

Inbound, they passed the accidental bombing of Schweinfurt, and correctly deduced that Nuremburg lay further south. After what seemed like an eternity, they had completed their bomb run and were headed for home—into the teeth of what was now a raging headwind. By the time they reached the English coast, they, like many others, were running on fumes, and many of the British bases, particularly the northern ones, were already fogged in. After a stellar performance by their navigator, Harvey was able to recover the Lancaster safely at an Operational Training Base in the south of England called Morton-in-Marsh, just before the weather clamped in there as well.

> We were down. Too exhausted to move I slumped there in my seat. It was six o'clock in the morning. We had flown for seven and a half hours and still had another hour to fly to get back to base. We had been out of bed for twenty-two hours. The King, I thought, had really got his shilling's worth.

This disastrous raid formally, in a pre-arranged manner, closed out the Battle of Berlin campaign. It also became the high-water mark for operational blood losses. From this point onward, although there would still be significant casualties and rough operations on occasion, the casualty rate would significantly abate. This was the result in no small measure of the gradual command transfer of attention to targets in support of Overlord, a policy shift that commenced the very day after Nuremburg, 1 April 1944.

The Berlin Raids in Perspective

The gallant Group Captain John Searby's words at the beginning of this chapter tend to imply that the entire campaign was directed against the German capital, and we know that simply was not the case. From late August 1943 until the end of March 1944, nineteen raids were staged against Berlin, in two distinct series. During the same period, thirty-six additional maximum effort operations were conducted against other major German industrial targets, and while a number of them were either outright failures or fell well below expectations, others were remarkably successful, notably the attacks on Augsburg, Kassel, Leipzig, and Frankfurt. During the main event Berlin series of sixteen raids extending from 23 November 1943 to 31 March 1944, when over 20,000 Bomber Command sorties were flown on major efforts, nineteen "non-Berlin" operations generated 11,113 sorties and resulted in the loss of 555 aircraft. The Berlin raids of the period, which produced a significant amount of damage in their own right, generated 9111 sorties, from which 492 aircraft did not return. Additionally, nearly twice that number were damaged flying against the capital, of which a further ninety-five were ultimately written off as beyond practical repair.[161] However, along with the damage directly inflicted, the forced diversions of men and materiel and the relocation and evacuation of industrial concerns and significant numbers of the populace certainly placed great additional burdens on many sectors of the German war economy. And Berlin, it must be remembered, was a legitimate Pointblank target.

A great amount of technical, technological and tactical innovation was demonstrated by both sides during this campaign. Deliberate diversions and distractions by Bomber Command abounded, and increasingly indirect routes were employed. Concentration of force over the target was developed to an art form, until a force of 800 aircraft could be placed on the target within just a twenty-minute window. Collaterally, the length of the bomber stream, considered to be exceptionally vulnerable when it grew to 300 miles in length, was tightened up to a mere 70 miles, less than a quarter of its 1942 length. A specialist support organization in the form of 100 Group had been added, and their contributions were highly significant. Older equipment, such as the Stirling and the Halifax II/V series, were retired from the Main Force, while new equipment in the form of the early series Halifax III was introduced. However, the initial results with this new aircraft did fall somewhat short of expectations, and these crews had a harder time of it, since "when the fighters struck and bomber pilots made for altitude, whatever their orders, the Halifax IIIs were now left at the lower altitudes (than the Lancasters) and the Germans found them first."[162] The later variants with greater wingspans and improved service ceilings fared much better.

For those who would take Arthur Harris to task for not pursuing the Pointblank mandate as tenaciously as possible during the period, there is some justification, particularly in the case of Schweinfurt and the bearing industry. However, eight of the twenty-two designated Pointblank targets—Berlin, Frankfurt, Schweinfurt, Leipzig, Stuttgart, Paris, Augsburg and Brunswick—were all hit during the main event stage from November 1943 to March 1944. During the broader period, which commenced in August 1943, even more targets on the Pointblank/Argument list were attacked by Bomber Command, including Kassel, Hannover and Bremen. Others were bombed before and after the broader period of the Berlin raids, while other non-Pointblank targets selected for attention at the time, such as Essen, certainly had industrial significance.

As Martin Middlebrook and Chris Everett have stated, "The story of the Battle of Berlin is of a steady deterioration of effectiveness by the bomber force at increasing cost . . . Some of the raids caused serious damage on Berlin; the local reports . . . show that more destruction was caused than Bomber Command suspected at the time . . . But the overwhelming success sought by Harris proved to be elusive."[163] While the morale of the crews undoubtedly faltered during this period, it did not fail. There was, however, a significant deterioration in effectiveness caused by the rotten winter weather, the longer routes which were required, forcing larger fuel loads at the expense of bombs carried, and the increasing number of casualties, which demanded an ever-greater reliance on inexperienced replacement aircrews.

> All these factors applied to the Pathfinders as well as the Main Force squadrons. There was also a steady dilution of effort. In the closing phases of the battle, up to 20 percent of the aircraft despatched by Bomber Command were employed on diversionary or supporting raids and, although it must be said that some of those aircraft were not suitable for Main Force raids, the German defences had forced a departure from the principle of concentration. Finally, the electronic aids which had ensured victory in the Battle of the Ruhr were not available over Berlin. The limiting range at which *Oboe* could be used was the supremely vital factor in the Battle of Berlin.[164]

While many Canadians became casualties in RAF units during the Berlin attacks, the 6 Group record is easier to quantify. The following statistics apply just to raids against Berlin, and not the concurrent maximum efforts. All told, 6 Group despatched 688 Halifax (all variants) sorties on nine of the Berlin raids, and 532 Lancaster II sorties on eighteen of the nineteen total raids. Of these, 55 Halifaxes—8.0 percent—and 25 Lancasters—4.7 percent—did not return. A further 6 Halifaxes and 5 Lancasters were destroyed in crashes. With respect to casualties, 437 men were killed, 127 were taken prisoners of war, 9 successfully evaded capture and 9 more were interned in neutral countries. Of the 12 participating 6 Group squadrons, to 434 Squadron fell the dubious distinction of suffering the highest missing rate in the group—15.6 percent of the 77 Halifax Vs despatched on seven raids. Indeed, this was the highest loss rate for *all* Bomber Command squadrons during the Berlin campaign. The blood cost was 59 squadron members killed in action while 21 became prisoners of war. One determined and lucky soul successfully evaded captivity.[165]

The Berlin raids were arguably the most arduous and taxing period in the operational histories of Bomber Command and 6 Group. However, brighter moments were just over the horizon. Given his participation in twelve of the nineteen operations against the German capital, it is only fitting that the words of Roger Coulombe, "The Berlin Kid," should close this chapter.

> The Big City was recognized as the toughest and most heavily-defended target in Germany because of its distance far inland, as well as for its extremely heavy air defences in the form of thousands of guns, searchlights and hundreds of night fighters. A raid on Berlin was considered a major event in the life of any aircrew member. I did it twelve times.[166]

SEVEN

Operation Overlord
and
Other Diversions

To be a Master Bomber was intensely dangerous. It required circling the target throughout an attack, often descending to a very low level to check the position of the markers and giving radio instructions to both the Pathfinder Force and the Main Force respectively on where to drop their markers or bombs. The success or failure of the raid was heavily dependent upon this brave man who usually was a very experienced and capable pilot. His survival span was very short.

—Geoff Marlow

434 Squadron

By the spring of 1944 the war was going poorly for the Axis forces on all fronts and in all theatres. In the Mediterranean, North Africa was entirely in Allied hands, Sicily had been vanquished, and on the Italian mainland, Anglo-American coalition forces, which included the 1st Canadian Corps, were making steady progress northward in the face of determined German resistance. Although many bloody battles lay ahead and the 1943–44 winter rains and mud had temporarily slowed the advance, great gains were in the offing. Rome and points beyond were squarely in the Allied coalition's sights.

On the North Atlantic, Very Long Range (VLR) Liberators, used in conjunction with other surface and airborne technological innovations, had effectively closed the "Black Hole," the air patrol coverage gap in the middle of the Atlantic. Now, *Grossadmiral* Karl Dönitz's "grey wolves" of the *Kriegsmarine*'s U-boat arm had reversed roles, from being the hunters to being the hunted. This happier state of affairs for the Allies was now engendering a massive build-up of men and materiel at a frenzied pace within the United Kingdom in preparation for the upcoming cross-Channel onslaught in Normandy.

In the east, the Soviets were exerting relentless pressure on the Germans. The end of January marked deliverance for the city of Leningrad from its 900-day siege, the longest in modern history. A series of rolling offensives in the Ukraine, skilfully conducted under the able if brutal leadership of Marshal Georgi Zhukov, soon resulted in the liberation of the region. Onslaughts west of Kiev then pushed the Germans back to the old Polish border, and in the extreme south, across the Dnestr River and the Carpathian Mountains into Romania and Poland. The Russians were soon at the gates of Hungary as well as Romania, and there were indications that both those nations, who were formally allied with Germany, were beginning to implode. In the extreme north, the Russians had been attacking on a 120-mile front extending from Lake Ilmen to Leningrad. Consequently, in April the Finns had sent a negotiating team to Moscow in search of an armistice. Also in April Russian advances captured Odessa and forced the German army to retreat to the fortress at Sevastopol on the shore of the Black Sea.

In the Pacific, the United States Navy held such massive superiority in aircraft carriers and amphibious capabilities that they were able to sustain a dual, simultaneous offensive across the region, forcing the Japanese to engage in battle, first in the Marianas and then in the Philippines. General McArthur's island-hopping campaign was doggedly pushing the Japanese back towards the Home Islands, while Allied command of the waters in the region was almost absolute. In Burma and China, losses incurred by the Japanese in 1944 could not be replaced, and in effect, "the whole of the Japanese effort throughout central and southern China after April 1944 was effort wasted."[1]

Back home, the concern over a potential Japanese invasion on the Pacific coast and in Alaska had completely evaporated. The movie *Going My Way* ruled the box offices for the year, and brought Bing Crosby a Best Actor Oscar. Ingrid Bergman won for the ladies in *Gaslight*. *Sentimental Journey*, *Swingin' on a Star* and *Don't Fence Me In* all dominated the pop charts, and the Saint Louis Cardinals triumphed in the World Series. In April, Guy Lombardo and His Royal Canadians were at the top of the music charts, and Toe Blake scored the winner at the Montreal Forum in sudden-death overtime to bring the "Habs" their fourth NHL Stanley Cup.

Helping in Normandy

During the last year of the European war, from April 1944 until May 1945, Bomber Command achieved its productive/destructive apex. The punishing losses experienced during the winter of 1943–44, particularly those associated with the Berlin raids, almost destroyed the fighting spirit and resolve of the Command. However, with the spring Sir Arthur Harris, somewhat against his will, tasked his forces for the most part against less-distant targets, which helped bring the loss rates back down to less damaging proportions. Longer-term relief would be acquired in April when the Command was seconded to Supreme Headquarters Allied Expeditionary Forces (SHAEF) under General Dwight D. Eisenhower, in support of the impending June invasion of northwest Europe through the Normandy beaches. For the following five months, Bomber Command devoted the bulk of its resources to nearer transportation targets, and to a lesser extent, to attacking the enemy's oil production and storage resources. Specifically, Harris tasked the majority of his crews with hitting bridges over the Rhine River and various French rivers, as well as essential rail yards

Messerschmitt Bf 110G-4, the personal mount of Major Heinz-Wolfgang Schnaufer, the highest scoring German night fighter ace of the Second World War. Note the 121 victory markings on the vertical tail fin. This was Schnaufer's last wartime mount. Although he was at the time *Kommodore* of NJG 4, the aircraft does not carry the usual distinctive chevron markings of his appointment. Painting by Ron Lowry. (Not to scale)

Junkers Ju 88G-6 flown by Oberleutnant Walter Briegleb of NJG 2. The Ju 88G series, which used the angular tail unit of the Ju 188, first made its operational appearance in the spring of 1944. Equipped with an improved *Lichtenstein* AI radar, it was a highly effective night fighter. Walter Briegleb ended the war with twenty-five confirmed victories. Painting by Ron Lowry. (Not to scale)

The Heinkel He 219 was a formidable night fighter and it possessed a lot of cutting edge technology at the time of its service debut, including ejection seats. *Major* Werner Streib of 1/NJG 1 ably demonstrated this pre-production model, finished in non-standard dull aluminum, on the night of 11/12 June 1943, when he shot down five Lancasters with it in half an hour. However, his flaps failed on landing in *Venlo*, and the aircraft broke into three pieces. Streib and his observer escaped uninjured. Painting by Ron Lowry. (Not to scale)

Messerschmitt Me 262B-1a/U1, flown by *Leutnant* Herbert Altner, who served with 10/NJG 11 during the closing weeks of the war. Altner ended hostilities as an ace with twenty-one victories. This aircraft is equipped with a FuG 218 AI radar and state of the art radio and communications equipment. Painting by Ron Lowry. (Not to scale)

Black Mike McEwen (right) appears to be heading somewhere out of country in this Canadian Lancaster II. (DND PC 2479)

A 434 "Bluenose" Squadron Lancaster X photographed later in the war. Note the dark blue propeller spinners. (DND PC2513)

Bomb Aimer, Battle of the Ruhr 1944 by Carl Schaefer (CWM 11786)

Squadron Leader Ian Willoughby Bazalgette, VC, DFC, a very gallant gentleman. Painting by Pat McNorgan.

Stained Glass Window. A tribute to the air gunners of 6 Group. Painting by Pat McNorgan. Here, the artist has taken inspiration from the great film director, Alfred Hitchcock, who was renowned for showing his audience the aftermath of violence, but not the action itself.

Girl from the North Country. A Lancaster Mk. X from 431 "Iroquois" Squadron unloads a graffiti-rich "cookie" on Germany while a German night fighter overshoots. The nose art on *She's Truly Terrific*, Lancaster KB 811, coded SE-T, was inspired by the popular pin-up artist, Alberto Varga. Painting by Pat McNorgan.

A Target Token awarded to the crew of Flying Officer R. W. Juppe after a particularly accurate attack on Leipzig late in the war. It has been signed by Black Mike McEwen. (Author's Collection)

Marshalling Lancasters Against Stuttgart, by Carl Schaefer. Discerning viewers will note that Mr. Schaefer has depicted Lancaster Mk. IIs in this painting, but the potential energy and the moodiness of the scene certainly also applied to later-war operations. (CWM 11836)

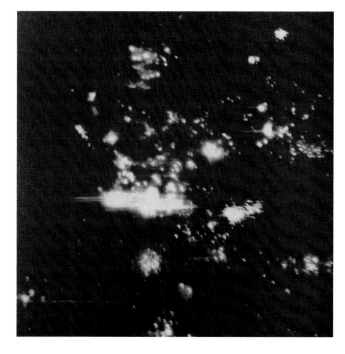

On target. A rare color photograph of an actual late-war attack on a German city. (Author's Collection)

Vicky the Vicious Virgin, a 408 Squadron Halifax III, was flown by Flight Lieutenant Ron Craven and his crew. *Vicky* flew her last flight on the night of 8-9 April 1945 when, as part of a 4, 6 and 8 Group force, it attacked Hamburg and was in turn attacked by a Junkers 88 night fighter. After a fierce bout of defensive manoeuvring, the aircraft and crew made it home safely to England. Craven's crew, along with the rest of 408 Squadron, then converted to new Lancaster Mk. Xs, finishing the war in one also marked *Vicky*. Painting by Ron Lowry

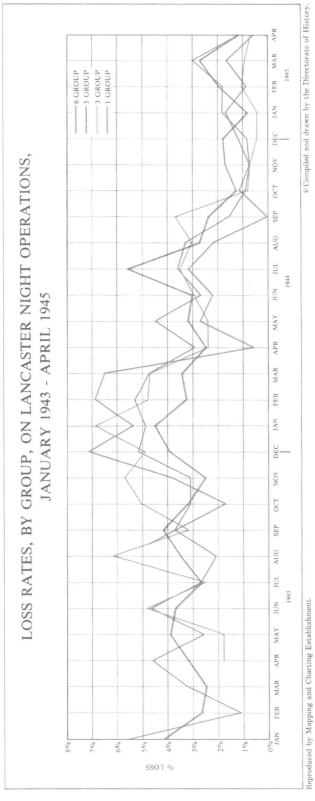

LOSS RATES, BY GROUP, ON LANCASTER NIGHT OPERATIONS, JANUARY 1943 - APRIL 1945

6 GROUP
5 GROUP
3 GROUP
1 GROUP

% LOSS

8% 7% 6% 5% 4% 3% 2% 1% 0%

JAN FEB MAR APR MAY JUN JUL AUG SEP OCT NOV DEC JAN FEB MAR APR MAY JUN JUL AUG SEP OCT NOV DEC JAN FEB MAR APR

1943   1944   1945

© Compiled and drawn by the Directorate of History.

Reproduced by Mapping and Charting Establishment.

LOSS RATES, BY GROUP, ON HALIFAX NIGHT OPERATIONS, JANUARY 1943 - APRIL 1945

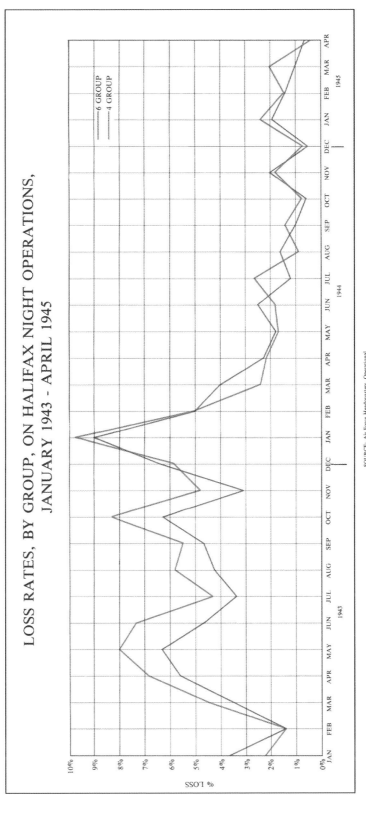

SOURCE: Air Force Headquarters, Operational
Research Centre, Losses, heavy bomber
operations in Bomber Command: HQS.
19-17-6, vol. 1, DHIST 79/220.

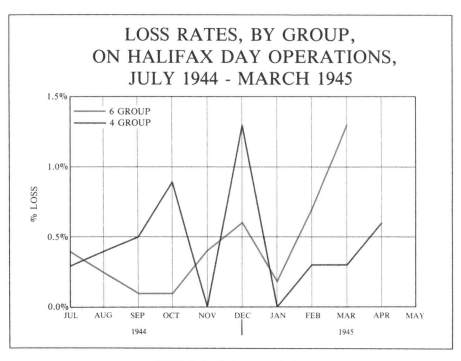

LOSS RATES, BY GROUP, ON HALIFAX DAY OPERATIONS, JULY 1944 - MARCH 1945

SOURCE: Air Force Headquarters, Operational
Research Centre, Losses; heavy bomber
operations in Bomber Command: HQS.
19-17-6, vol. 1. DHIST 79/220.

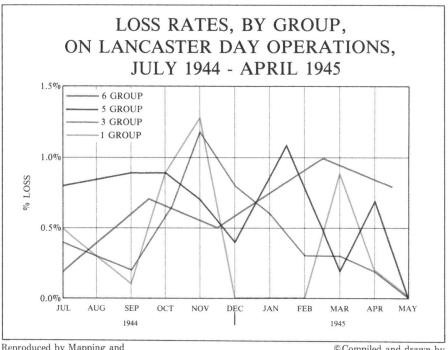

LOSS RATES, BY GROUP, ON LANCASTER DAY OPERATIONS, JULY 1944 - APRIL 1945

Some of the Canadian Lancasters enjoyed useful service lives in the post-war RCAF. KN868, with the yellow propeller hubs, served in Maritime Air Command. (DND RNC 168)

KN851 served as a flying test bed for the Ryan Firebee target drone. (DND PCN 1963)

Barbara and Reg Lane during the mid-1960s. They would enjoy many more happy years together. (Lane family)

Opposite top: The Canadian Warplane Heritage Museum's flagship in flight, the magnificent tribute Mynarski Lancaster. (Canadian Warplane Heritage Museum Hamilton)

Opposite bottom: The Handley Page Halifax Mk. VII restoration, which graces the Air Force Museum in Trenton, will be available for public viewing during the autumn of 2005. (Author's Collection)

And still going strong. Stan Miller celebrates the sixtieth anniversary of his first solo flight in a Tiger Moth—in a Tiger Moth. Oshawa airport, 17 August 2003.

and junctions located throughout northern France and Belgium—key installations, the loss of which would make it exceptionally difficult for the enemy to reinforce his troops once the invasion began. By the time Bomber Command was under the control of the Air Staff in September 1944, and its priority was redirected against other industrialized targets in Germany, the bulk of the German air resistance would have dissipated considerably. Since the Overlord period was characterized by an end to the sustained high casualty rates of the previous months, this proved to be a tremendous morale booster to the crews. Specifically, for 6 Group:

> This shift to much closer objectives, combined with the intensive training imposed on even operational units by its new commander, Air Vice-Marshal McEwen, made a particularly dramatic impact on 6 Group's loss rates. By April, the rate for Halifaxes was down to two percent, never again to rise above 2.5 percent; and for Lancasters it was down to under one percent and would only fractionally exceed three percent in July. Indeed, during the last year of the European war, 6 Group's loss rates would be the lowest in all of Bomber Command.[2]

Heavy losses were still sustained on occasion, however, occurring up until the last days of the war. But from April 1944 onwards, they would progressively punctuate Command operations, rather than dominate them. Therefore, except for a number of isolated cases, losses were relatively light,[3] particularly during the last nine months of the war in Europe—when the majority of total wartime tonnage was dropped. Over two-thirds of the wartime bomb tonnage was dropped on the Greater German Reich from 1 July 1944 onward.[4]

Also, the monthly average number of sorties increased from 5400 in 1943 to 14,000 in 1944, and the average payload-per-sortie nearly doubled.[5] Furthermore, unlike the manpower shortages that were experienced by the land forces during the period, both aircrews and aircraft continued to pour into the bomber groups. In the words of Martin Middlebrook:

> Harris could now regularly dispatch up to 1500 aircraft at any one time, in three or more major raids, dropping 6-7000 tons of bombs. It had taken nearly a year to drop that number of bombs in 1939-40! The introduction of the P-51 Mustang as a long-range escort for the American heavies and the need for the *Luftwaffe* to come up into action and attempt to stem the invasion had drawn the night fighter force into daylight action during the summer and reduced its strength. Bomber casualties now fell yet again, to just 1.0% in this period.[6]

German Defensive Capabilities Decline

By the summer of 1944, "green" German night fighter pilots were joining their operational units with an average total flying time of 110-115 hours, while their British and Dominion counterparts had accumulated nearly twice that amount of flight experience.[7] Not only was the night fighter force culled of its most experienced crews through combat attrition and accidents during the period, but once the invasion foothold on northwest Europe was secured, it lost the benefit of the early warning radar sites on the Belgian and French coasts. And since the bomber stream was progressively routed over the recently liberated territories, many of the earlier long and dangerous approach paths to the heart of the Reich were eliminated.[8]

The success rates for the German night fighter arm plummeted steadily from June until December 1944, not only because of the loss of the western early warning stations, but also from an increasingly acute shortage of fuel and a concomitant reduction in the amount of training experience made available to the replacement crews. Although the night fighter arm was numerically stronger than ever during 1944, the western Allies enjoyed a measure of overall air superiority from 6 June 1944 until the end of hostilities. Tactically for Bomber Command, this was in no small measure a result of the overwhelming use of effective jamming. When on 14 July 1944 an intact Junkers Ju 88G-1, complete with serviceable *Flensburg* and *Naxos* homing devices was captured, Bomber Command immediately responded by ordering only fleeting activation of tail-warning radars and *H2S* ground mapping radars, thus substantially reducing their formerly indiscriminate use. The Command also re-instituted the widespread use of *Window* after September 1944, which, in conjunction with other tactical measures taken, rendered the *Lichtenstein SN2* AI radars largely ineffective. These improvements were later ameliorated by the greatly increased numbers of Lancasters and the vastly improved Halifax IIIs and VIIs now being routinely delivered to Bomber Command. There were still a few occasions, however, when significant casualties were incurred, once the Command returned to the German targets in earnest in September 1944. However, with a few exceptions in February/March 1945, those occasionally high losses meted out to Bomber Command during the autumn of 1944 turned out to be the *Luftwaffe's* last gasp. By December *Generalleutnant* Adolf Galland, the highly respected and charismatic General of the Fighter Arm, admitted that the overall capability of the Reich's night fighter forces in the face of so much Allied superiority had become "insignificant."[9]

Jimmy Sheridan of 426 Squadron put the late war calibre of the German night fighter pilots then being encountered in perspective, and both provide further endorsements of the significantly improved performance characteristics of the new Halifax IIIs:

> It was said there were two kinds of German fighter pilots—New and Old. The New, when fired on by the gunners, would break off and seek another target. The Old would stay right with you, even though the gunners were firing like mad, keeping with you even through the target area, through their own flak and searchlights, until they got you. I had one such experience with a member of this latter group. On a run into target, my gunners called for evasive action via corkscrewing. They began firing. I asked if they were sure it was a fighter, because it was not unknown for two bombers to get into a gunfight in the dark. After several minutes of hammering away at the fighter, we were nearing the point where I had to open the bomb doors. This was the most vulnerable time, and the fighter was still with us. Anyway, I opened the bomb doors, still corkscrewing, levelled out fast, jettisoned the load with my cockpit switch, and peeled off into the darkness beyond. The fighter was *still* with us, and I knew I had to do something drastic or he would get us. Therefore, I did a sudden vertical half-spiral dive into the blackness below. We ended up going from 15,000 feet to 5000 feet in seconds, but we lost the guy and came home without further incident. The next day, a fellow pilot said he saw a bomber going straight down after he left the target. He kept watching for the crash but didn't see it. I enlightened him.[10]

Jim Northrup of 415 Squadron adds:

> We were in the final few seconds of our bomb run when my rear gunner informs me that he has spotted a Focke-Wulf 190 closing fast, and he figures we are the target. He kept calling off the yards, and my French Canadian bomb-aimer is saying, "Steady, Skeeper . . . Steady . . . " I am urging him to drop the damn bombs but he just keeps on with his "Steady, Skeeper . . . Steady." I actually have my hand on the jettison toggle when I feel

the aircraft lift and I knew the bombs were gone. At this moment, the rear gunner gives me a "Starboard, go!" Now, it takes both hands to corkscrew properly so I can't get a hand free to close the bomb bay doors. When I roll to port and pull up as hard as I can, I can feel the aircraft "sweat' from the high-G pull and I think she may come apart, but I dare not slacken off. My rear gunner reports we have lost the '190, so I level out and we get the bomb doors closed. When we get back to base, I tell the Engineering Officer that I have badly strained my aircraft and ask him to please check it over. The next day, he informs me that I have bent the fuselage two inches out of alignment, but he felt the aircraft had no structural damage and was safe to fly. He must have been right as I flew quite a few more trips in this aircraft before she was declared unfit for further operations.

We had bombed Hamburg and were having a good trip; no fighter attacks and we had steered clear of the searchlights and the 88 mm flak. We crossed the Kiel Canal and turned west to fly over southern Denmark and hit the North Sea at the Isle of Sylt. I was flying my own aircraft, 6U-I-NA124, which was performing well, and all systems were "A-OK." I then started a fairly fast let-down from 24,000 feet, as I wanted to cross the coast at around a thousand feet to avoid the fighters at Heligoland. I ended up hitting the Isle of Sylt at 6000 feet and I was holding the control column with my knees as I simultaneously unwrapped my chocolate bar. Now, these were particularly nice bars made by Neilsons . . . thick, dark chocolate filled with a nice cream that did not run all over you. It had been ten hours since our last meal and I was beginning to feel a little gaunt. Just as I crossed the west coast of Sylt, a flak ship anchored there fired at us with everything they had. I dropped my bar and rolled to port as hard as I could. An aircraft flying a little above me ran into this concentrated burst of fire and blew all to hell. My rear gunner then tells me there is a Me 109 closing on us, so I put the aircraft right down on top of the water. Now, another aircraft starts laying chandelier flares right along our track, and it is suddenly nearly as light as day. The '109 is still trailing us but I am hugging the water so close that he cannot get down to our height and declines to attack. At one point, my rear gunner shouts, "Get up Skipper, get up. The *fish* are above us!" This continued for what seemed like an hour and finally, the fighter broke off without ever really closing on us. I then climbed to 1000 feet for the rest of the trip and finally landed at East Moor. I told my ground crew there was a chocolate bar somewhere in the cockpit, but that bar was never found. I was peed off about losing my bar but I harboured no disrespect towards the '109 pilot for not pressing in on us, as I had put him in an extremely bad attack situation. The Me 109 was a poor night fighter, and it took a brave man to do that job in it.[11]

Although encounters between the German night fighter force and Canadian airmen in Bomber Command dropped off significantly after the Berlin raids of 1943–44, they still occurred from time to time. One such encounter, typical for the period, took place on the night of 12/13 May 1944 during an attack on the railway marshalling yards in Louvain, Belgium, just to the east of Brussels. This particular raid, a total 6 Group effort in conjunction with marking provided by the Pathfinders, was a success, although three Halifaxes and two of the PFF Lancasters were lost from the entire force of 120 aircraft. Among the casualties was the 426 "Thunderbird" Squadron crew of Flight Sergeant (posthumous Pilot Officer) William Boyd Bentz, a twenty-three-year-old from southeastern British Columbia. Unfortunately for Bentz, flying Halifax III LW682 and coded "M–Mike," his sparring partner that night was the highly-experienced Martin Drewes, an eventual fifty-two-victory ace, holder of the Knight's Cross with Oak Leaves, and one of the stellar performers of the night fighter arm. Conversely, the Bentz crew members were rookies, flying just their third war operation:

German night fighter ace Martin Drewes was on a roll. On the night of 12/13 May 1944, *Hauptmann* Drewes, his radar operator, *Unteroffizier* Erich Handke, and gunner *Unteroffizier* George Petz had already shot down two Canadian bombers and were all keyed-up to score a hat trick. Cruising through the night skies over Belgium in a Bf 110 twin-engine night fighter, Handke was in the centre seat concentrated on the ghostly blips and squiggles on his primitive radar scope, straining to discern another possible target amid the electronic clutter. Petz was in the back seat, facing backwards . . .

Suddenly, Erich Handke called out a radar contact and gave Martin Drewes a vector to a possible target. Drewes soon spotted the shadowy outline of a bomber through the gloom and climbed toward it. Overshooting the bomber because of his speed, Drewes cursed and yanked the fighter around hard for another try. Bentz and his crew were most likely aware of the threat because the bomber was taking evasive action when Drewes again spotted it and slid his Bf 110 underneath, a favorite tactic for night fighters equipped with *Schräge Musik*, upward firing twin 20 mm cannons.

Bentz and his crew were probably expecting it when Martin Drewes opened fire and raked the Halifax's fuel tanks in the port wing with explosive and incendiary cartridges. Eye-witnesses in the tiny Belgian village of Schendelbeke reported seeing the bomber with its port wing on fire slowly turn east, then stall at low-level, plunge in a near-vertical dive, and hit the ground with a tremendous explosion. All of the crew were killed instantly. Their night's work accomplished, Drewes and his crew returned to their home base at Leeuwarden in Holland.[12]

Postwar the remains of five crew members were exhumed by the RAF's Missing Research Unit in 1947. The Halifax had impacted with such force that it was buried up to ten metres deep in the earth. The wreckage and the remaining three crew members, including "Wib" Bentz, remained undisturbed for the next fifty years until they were recovered and buried in 1997 with full military honours at the Geraardsbergen Communal Cemetery, next to the graves of their five fellow crewmen. Among those gathered to pay a final tribute to the fallen Canadians was Martin Drewes.

During late 1943 and much of 1944, while Bob Turnbull was continuing to make his distinguished presence felt as commanding officer of 427 Squadron, then later as station commander at Croft, his brothers John, another pilot, and Walter, a navigator, were also carving out commendable records within Bomber Command. Both eventually received DFCs for their superior performance under difficult operational circumstances. The trio hailed from the tiny prairie town of Govan, Saskatchewan. Between them the three brothers, collectively known as "The Flying Turnbulls" completed four tours and 118 operations. On five separate occasions, brothers Bob and John flew to the same target unbeknownst to each other. John Turnbull, a Halifax II/V pilot with 419 Squadron, and then later a Halifax III deputy flight commander on 424 Squadron, always managed to keep a sense of humor about his wartime experiences. His recollections of the period illustrate the point.

21 April 1944

I recall being hit by predicted flak while "Gardening" in Brest harbour; one engine knocked out, a sharp pain in my left elbow. "Finally," I told myself, "You've got it!" With my flight engineer Mike holding the control column, I checked for blood and/or torn clothing. Nothing. The hit had banged my "funny bone" against the oxygen tube holder. I was almost too embarrassed to announce my "frightening wound" to my crew!

26 April 1944

Over Essen. You could read a newspaper by its thousands of searchlights. The gunners said they were reading their bibles!

17 June 1944

As a crew we celebrated in a Ripon pub with draught beer plus fish 'n' chips that evening when my DFC was announced. I think it was our jovial rear gunner Joe Malec who commented, "What the hell for? We do all the work!" A truism! A most memorable day was that of the parade square investiture for the medal on August 11 when accompanied by the Royal Family, King George VI visited 6 Group bases. A gusty wind caused his small carpet to curl just as I presented my snappy salute and stepped forward to him. I've often wondered what one would do if one was to trip and stumble into the arms of one's monarch![13]

The risk of mid-air collisions was always present during Bomber Command's wartime operations. Given the high concentration of the bomber stream, it is a miracle that collisions did not occur more frequently. When they did occur, the hapless crews involved rarely escaped unscathed. Merrill Burnett of 426 Squadron describes one such harrowing experience, which occurred just prior to Operation Overlord.

May 22/44

On our third operation as a crew, the target was the railway yards at Le Mans, France. Shortly after bombing and heading for home base, we collided with another aircraft which came from underneath on the starboard side. Our aircraft dropped from 4700 to 3000 feet. Our pilot, Pilot Officer L.A. Mann, had great difficulty controlling the aircraft and when he levelled off, the flight engineer, Sergeant S. Gilder, discovered the port inner engine on fire, which he then extinguished by shutting off the fuel to it. At this time, he discovered the propeller was also missing. The port outer engine was then found vibrating and thus it was feathered. The mid-under turret was damaged and the gunner was hurt. Both his knees were damaged when they got jammed against the .50 calibre machine gun, and he also had a cut on his forehead and was in a dazed condition. Pilot Officer Mann continued to have great difficulty controlling the aircraft, and we actually turned back three times towards France while over the Channel before we made it to England. Eventually, we landed at RAF Station Ford on the Channel coast in Sussex where our injured gunner, Sergeant H. Murphy, was taken to hospital. More damage was found after landing. The port outer engine prop tips were bent back towards the wing, the bomb bay doors were damaged and partly missing, and the port fin and elevator were damaged, which I had previously reported to the pilot. For bringing the crew and aircraft back to England, Pilot Officer Mann received the Distinguished Flying Cross.

The breech of a gun was found jammed into the side of our fuselage, which was traced by our Gunnery Leader and found to be from the mid-upper turret of a 425 "Alouette" Squadron aircraft which had crashed.[14]

By 1944, Bomber Command's nightly sojourns had become complex, highly integrated and synergistic team efforts consisting of multiple Main Force attacks in strength, numerous feinting raids, and all manner of electronic deception and jamming. The support elements worked hand-in-glove with the journeymen campaigners of the Main Force, and actually penetrated the bomber stream in order to provide optimum masking and protection when deploying *Window* or employing other jamming and deception measures. Still, given the stealthy nature of nocturnal operations within the stream, it was most unusual for the Main Force elements to actually see their support brethren on the job. Yet, war breeds bizarre circumstances, and the fog of war could further confuse matters. Dick Bell, a gunner on 434 Squadron, had a very unusual experience on a night raid just prior to D-Day:

> On the next trip, we went to the Kiel Canal to bomb. With all the incendiaries falling all over the target, it was like daylight. As I was checking for enemy fighters, I noticed a large aircraft off the starboard side, door open, and a number of men moving boxes around inside. The aircraft was so close I could have shot it down but it was a Stirling bomber and should not have been there, or so I thought at the time. When I reported what I was seeing to the skipper, he said Intelligence had reported to the pilots that the Jerries were using captured aircraft for propaganda purposes and this was probably one of them. Normally, I would have shot it down, and it looked like they were dropping out propaganda pamphlets, but I didn't want to take a chance on shooting down one of ours. Unfortunately, we gunners had not been properly briefed on this eventuality before going out on raids.[15]

It was fortuitous for all concerned that Dick Bell stayed his hand. In fact, the *Luftwaffe* had acquired and later flew a captured, airworthy Mark I Stirling that had crash landed in Holland relatively early in the bombing campaign. The Germans patched it up, albeit rather crudely, and then used it for test purposes and operational evaluation for a time, but it is thought to have been retired from service well before Dick Bell's incident. This was probably either a 218 Squadron or a 199 Squadron electronic countermeasures specialist aircraft dropping *Window*, not propaganda leaflets, for the Main Force. Or it may have been a Special Operations Stirling from 620 Squadron engaged in clandestine operations, although this is less likely, given the location and the circumstances of the encounter. At any rate, Dick Bell's measured decision not to fire undoubtedly saved a friendly crew and aircraft.[16]

Harris and Portal Square Off

Even after the secondment of Bomber Command to Eisenhower's command had occurred in April, Harris continued his campaign unabated in the highest corridors of power for area bombing. He had long held the sympathetic ear of Winston Churchill, to which the following mid-May 1944 letter to the Prime Minister attests. Harris certainly played his hand with a flair for the dramatic, and the letter is worth presenting in its entirety:

TOP SECRET   Headquarters, BOMBER COMMAND,
                                          R.A.F. STATION, HIGH WYCOMBE, BUCKS.

PRIME MINISTER:
You asked me to let you have a note of the figures I used at Monday's
Conference. The following are some of the most significant:

Target for Strategic Bombing.
To destroy fifty of the most important industrial towns in Germany.

Results.
(a) Devastation caused (all but 3% in the last 14 months) is equivalent to the obliteration of half of the total built up areas of the 37 leading industrial cities in this country other

than London. These cities are: Birmingham, Glasgow, Liverpool, Manchester, Sheffield, Leeds, Edinburgh, Bristol, Hull, Bradford, Newcastle, Stoke, Nottingham, Portsmouth, Leicester, Cardiff, Plymouth, Sunderland, Bolton, Southampton, Swansea, Aberdeen, Coventry, Dundee, Derby, Gateshead, Huddersfield, Middlesborough, Norwich, Oldham, Preston, Rhondda, St. Helen's, South Shields, Stockport, Walsall and Wolverhampton.

(b) Loss inflicted on enemy production during the 10 months March-December 1943 represented the total loss of one month's work for every single factory worker in the whole of Greater Germany, or 4 months work out of 10 months for every worker in the attacked towns. The targets attacked housed predominately those engaged in the vital war industries and those who escaped were mostly those who contribute least to the German war effort. Since December 1943 the monthly rate of tonnage delivered to Germany has doubled, and is continually increasing.

Comparison of Results

Areas devastated: Central London 600 acres
Coventry 135 acres
Hamburg 6200 acres

Enemy's Defence.

At least 2,000,000 able-bodied Germans full time employed on direct defence, essential repairs, etc.

Mining.

Over 32,000 laid. Results, one known ship sunk or damaged for every 47 mines, (401 sunk, 287 damaged.) Some 40% of the total German naval personnel employed on anti-mine work of various descriptions.

Specific Pre-Invasion Targets.

29 out of 30 marshalling yards attacked are so destroyed as not to merit further attacks by heavy bombers.

17th May 1944.

A.T. Harris
Air Chief Marshal
Commanding-in-Chief
BOMBER COMMAND.[17]

The thinly-veiled desire to be released from the Overlord commitment at the earliest possible moment is readily apparent here. As we have repeatedly seen, Arthur Harris fretted about what he viewed as the multiplicity of diversions placed on his Command and its true purpose in his view—to lay waste to the German industrial cities and to force the Germans to sue for peace without the requirement for an invasion of the continent. Harris's exasperation was total,

> yet Portal was equally exasperated, for his subordinate's single-minded determination often seemed to ignore the dictates of the rest of the war. As John Terraine rightly reminds us, where else could the heavy, long-range aircraft needed to cover the Atlantic and in the Middle and Far East come from, if not from Bomber Command, and where else could the crews come from, if not from Bomber Command squadrons or OTUs? Ultimately, however, it all came down to the fact that in war resources are always limited; had Harris not pressed his case further than anyone else in his position would probably have done,

Bomber Command might well never have achieved as much as it did. (Along with the "panacea" targets, the U-Boat counter-offensives, the mining, the overseas deployments and clandestine operations in support of the Special Operations Executive) . . . Harris always knew at the end of the day that orders were orders, and in due course, as we shall see, he had to accept the biggest diversion of them all: direct support for the Normandy invasion.[18]

The Transportation Plan

And just how did the Transportation Plan come to pass? With the Casablanca Conference, whether Harris liked it or not, the strategic bombing campaign had been recognized as an essential *prerequisite* for the invasion of northwest Europe, and not a stand-alone war-winning effort. While by 13 January 1944, the AOC-in-C acknowledged that Overlord was now an "inescapable commitment,"[19] he warned of the limitations of his force to night operations, in suitable weather only, and only with the aid of embedded Pathfinders. He felt that specific targeting of his forces against gun emplacements was too specific, and that his bombers were unsuitable for cutting railway communications at pinpoint locations. Also, the large number of civilian casualties incurred on the transportation targets to this point of the war somewhat reinforced his argument. Harris additionally warned that providing the enemy with a respite from strategic area bombing would release many enemy resources for use elsewhere, and if this diversion lasted as long as six months, the enemy would also have time to make a marked industrial and defensive recovery. Thus, he argued for continued attacks on industry whenever possible.

As of late March 1944, just ten weeks prior to D-Day, it appeared that the aims of Pointblank still trumped those of Overlord. The targets, in order of priority, were:

1. The *Luftwaffe*
2. Transportation
3. Oil
4. The Cities

However, these priorities begged re-evaluation. At a joint, high-level meeting on 25 March involving General Eisenhower, his deputy, Air Chief Marshal Sir Arthur Tedder, Harris, Portal and General Carl Spaatz, the incumbent commander of the American Eighth Air Force, it was agreed that attacks on the *Luftwaffe* should be maintained, but did not need to be intensified. The recent free-ranging tactics of the Allied fighters, particularly the new P-51 Mustangs, were leaving a telling mark on German effectiveness. The attacks on the Reich's aircraft industry and related manufacturing were also scoring damaging blows. Furthermore, Harris soon prevailed upon Portal to release the night fighters with the most up-to-date AI radars for offensive/intruder operations over the continent. When used, not only within the bomber stream, but against the night fighter airfields, they had a devastating effect. The attacks against the transportation network were seen as an obvious Overlord priority. Oil was considered an important target in the medium term, but in the short term, Charles Portal did not feel it would be of particular benefit for the landings in France. As these senior commanders appeared to argue in circles, it became clear that the priorities of the air commanders were significantly different from those of Eisenhower and his staff. Harris remained strident in his view that the strategic bombing of Germany could still make a costly seaborne invasion unnecessary, and Spaatz vehemently echoed these viewpoints, as long as the focal point of the bombing was the enemy oil resources.[20] In the final analysis, however, Portal and the other senior commanders did not agree, and on 14 April 1944, Harris and his Command became answerable, through Sir Arthur Tedder, to Eisenhower. Here, it was conceded that Pointblank ultimately remained the highest priority, but "with Overlord the supreme operation for 1944, all possible support must be provided to the Allied Armies to assist them in establishing themselves in the lodgement area."[21] Prior to D-Day, the distilled priorities for the Allied air forces meant concentration on transportation and *Luftwaffe* targets. When circumstances permitted, and weather ruled out other higher priority targets, both forces were to attack the German cities, especially Berlin.[22] This caveat provided Harris with a considerable amount of discretional leeway in his selection of specific targets in the weeks and months to follow. Ultimately, part of the justification for this secondment of the strategic bombing forces was because six separate French marshalling yards had been attacked on a trial basis during the first three weeks of March, the results were highly successful, and it was evident that against such targets, Bomber Command could be much more effective than its helmsman had predicted.[23] Furthermore, a series of small-scale precision raids carried out by 5 Group Lancasters demonstrated great promise of being able to conduct operations with pin-point accuracy. Still, Harris resisted the eventual plan to target some seventy-four key rail centres in France and Belgium, as did Carl Spaatz. Harris maintained that the Overlord targets could be dealt with by the Halifax and Stirling squadrons, leaving the Lancasters free to attack the German cities. Spaatz also championed this position since he still wished to devote the bulk of his forces to daylight attacks against oil targets. Both commanders warned that, in spite of the success of the March trials, the risk of causing heavy collateral casualties among the local civilian populations was still considered great. The plan was then submitted to Churchill for approval, and partly because of his anxieties about civilian casualties, did not receive final approval until 15 April 1944. At this point, Bomber Command was allocated thirty-seven of the rail targets, the other half was assigned to the Americans, and the new directive for the strategic air forces was issued two days later by Tedder:

> This stated the overall mission as the progressive destruction and dislocation of the German military, industrial and economic system and (significantly) the destruction of vital elements of lines of communication. In the subsequent specific instructions to Bomber Command Harris's main aim was stated as the disorganising (sic) of German industry and his operations were to complement those of the Americans in reducing the *Luftwaffe* and disrupting rail communications. Thus, while the continued offensive against Germany retained pride of place within his terms of reference, he was also required to tackle communications targets in order to assist the Allied Armies in what was described as "the supreme operation for 1944."[24]

A Maturing Precision Attack Capability

Now that he had his orders, Arthur Harris threw himself into the task at hand. The first attack of this new campaign priority took place on the night of 18/19 April against the marshalling yards at Juvisy, for which "extraordinary measures (were) taken, including the special marking technique employed to ensure accuracy."[25] By ensuring accurate bombing, not only was maximum destruction of the target anticipated, every attempt was being made at the outset to minimize the number of collateral civilian casualties. Both the Prime Minister and the Defence Committee were greatly relieved to learn of the care that was being taken in this regard. The precision marking on

Juvisy was carried out by three *Oboe* Mosquitos from the Pathfinder Force, while the bombing itself was done by 202 Lancasters and four Mosquitos from 5 Group.[26] The parent unit of 617 Squadron, this formation was becoming increasingly recognized for its precision attack capability. On 6 April, Wing Commander Leonard Cheshire had led an extremely successful precision attack on an aircraft factory at Toulouse, which he marked from low level in a Mosquito. Shortly thereafter, Harris told the AOC of 5 Group, Air Vice-Marshal Ralph Cochrane, that increasingly henceforth, 5 Group would be employed as a separate force specializing in attacks by relatively small numbers of bombers against specific, precise targets. Accordingly, he ordered the transfer of three PFF squadrons to Cochrane's group, leaving the 8 Group commander, Air Vice-Marshal Donald Bennett, in protest.

> His monopoly of pathfinding itself was under threat and on 30 April he lodged his first protest . . . A fortnight later Cochrane reported to Harris on the great improvement in his Group's bombing resulting from the Mosquitos' low-level marking and attributed recent success largely to the three PFF squadrons. Harris's reply was suitably encouraging: no doubt the crews deserved much of the credit, he commented, but "an equal share in their success is due to those who, under your direction, have not been content with things as they are but have given a great deal of time and trouble to thinking out new ideas and new tactics."[27]

Soon, Bennett was complaining to Harris that the secondment of the three squadrons was having an adverse effect on morale in his group, and that Cochrane was not, at any rate, employing them correctly and to their fullest potential. Harris, however, needed both of these strong, ruthless commanders, now at loggerheads. He placated both and told Bennett there was still much gainful employment for the PFF. However, he also told Cochrane that he had no intention of returning the three 8 Group squadrons to the PFF in the immediate future, if at all. "The way was clear for Cochrane to continue his experiments on new techniques so that his 5 Group attacks could continue on the longer nights, and in due course Harris would also give (Air Vice-Marshal R.) Harrison's 3 Group a specialized role, this time on blind bombing with the use of *G-H*."[28] *G-H* represented a quantum leap in the development of navigation systems, since it combined levels of accuracy comparable to *Oboe* with the universal applicability of *Gee*. It had been introduced to service by 3 Group in October 1943, and it was eventually used to effect by other formations, including some from 6 Group. Around the same time, the K-band *H2S* Mark VI was also fielded, and this alleviated some system limitations over poorly defined or obscured targets. Of note, *H2S* became standard equipment for the Lancaster fleet in March 1944.

> Bomber Command coupled these new devices with revised tactics. Navigation was now so accurate that decoy fires and spoof raids could be used within a few miles of the actual route. The navigators and bomb-aimers were now sufficiently skilled to use an offset bombing point chosen for its visibility, and to aim their bombs at a given range and bearing from that point.[29]

Circumstances dictated that the various groups needed to exercise new, specialized equipment and skills, and since they would operate independently in smaller numbers with ever-increasing frequency, they each needed to develop their own precision marking and bombing techniques. In effect, Harris's Command was now finally pursuing the course of action he would have preferred prior to the formation of the elite PFF two years prior. In the last year of the war, these efforts bore significant fruit, with 617 Squadron leading the way as a true unit of highly-specialized experts.[30]

Experienced Canadians continued to serve proudly and with distinction on 617 Squadron throughout the remainder of the war. One such seasoned campaigner was Charles Lepine from Senneville, Quebec, a wireless operator who had earned a DFM during previous operations over the continent and in North Africa with 150 Squadron, RAF. Lepine recalls the inspirational presence of Leonard Cheshire as a commanding officer, as well as his most memorable operational flight, which was also his last. His near-clinical recollections of the emergence of mortal danger are particularly interesting, as are the details of exiting the stricken aircraft.

Group Captain Leonard Cheshire, VC, OM, DSO (2 Bars), DFC, at the age of 25, had been the youngest group captain in the RAF and had taken a voluntary drop in rank to take over the command of the squadron. It was my priviledge to have served under his command while at 617 Squadron. During his war years, he had gained the highest reputation among the crews of Bomber Command.

My most memorable operational experience was the Munich raid on 24 April 1944 with 617 Squadron on my second tour of operations. According to Wing Commander Cheshire's story, the most spectacular raid on Germany was the Munich raid by 200 bombers of 5 Group. With the exception of Berlin and the Ruhr, Munich was the most heavily-defended German target. It was later estimated that these 200 aircraft alone did more damage to Munich that night than all the previous raids on that city by Bomber Command and the USAAF. It was a quiet trip out. The routing and height strategy brought us to the Alps without incident. Standing in the astrodome during the flight across the Alps, I marvelled at the ease with which the Lancaster had risen to 20,000 feet to cross them. I recalled my Wellington days when the "Wimpys" laboured bravely, but barely cleared the peaks en route to our targets in northern Italy. However, the enemy defensive activities in the target area were much greater than had been forecast, and 617 Squadron was "first in" to get the aiming point well alight, mainly with incendiary bombs. We then made our bombing run without apparent harm and dropped our load near the markers laid down by the Squadron Mossies. Our Lancaster was then turned back on course to our home base. I was concerned that the *Monica* set, used over enemy territory for detecting approaching aircraft, had become unserviceable. The crew was advised of the problem and told to stay particularly alert. A short time thereafter, a loud explosion on the port side severely shook the aircraft. Leaping to the astrodome, I saw holes in the port wing, from which flames were already beginning to belch. My immediate reaction was that we had been hit by a fighter. The pressure build-up then blew holes in the top of the mainplane. Word to abandon the aircraft was immediately given by the skipper. When the bomb-aimer tried to open the front escape hatch cover, he found it jammed across the opening. While struggling, he caught the "D" release ring of his parachute pack on something and the white silk billowed into the bombing compartment. I immediately pressed the destruct buttons for the IFF set, removed my head set before clipping my 'chute pack on my chest, and started to move forward. However, appreciating the danger of delay, some of the crew, including myself, made our way to the rear fuselage side exit. While doing so, I noticed that the two gunners had already left the aircraft. I had misgivings about the *Monica* aerial mounted below the tailplane. Up until now, the captain had managed to hold the aircraft more-or-less straight and level. I then crouched momentarily and then launched myself into a steep dive out the door as best I could. I was then thankful that I had fallen clear of the protruding aerial, but did not escape entirely unscathed. The baseboard upon which the parachute was folded on my pack struck me on the side of the head when the 'chute emerged. The gash was not serious but produced enough blood to make me aware of a warm sensation on my neck as I descended. I then heard the explosion as our Lancaster hit the ground, and saw the glow of the ensuing fire. An initial worry was that I might have been hit by one of our aircraft, whose engines I could hear in the sky all around me. I didn't see any other 'chutes during my descent. Despite the fact that I was wearing no protective clothing over my battledress, I did not feel cold. I manipulated the shroud lines of my 'chute to control the swing which had developed, but I was unable to assess my height above the ground due to the darkness. Suddenly, I fell through the branches of a tree but the shroud lines and the 'chute above arrested my fall. However, they became entangled in the tree and presented an immediate problem for concealment once I got to the ground. I managed to tug and pull a lot of the parachute down, but had to climb back up the tree and burn some of the trapped lines free with a box of matches I carried. Finally, I had a great mass of parachute at my feet. I removed the battery and flotation flashlight from the Mae West and then searched for a hiding place for the rest of the stuff. However, the ground was hard and I had no digging tools. I also appreciated that I had to move out of the area very soon, as I had already been down for about two hours. I finally deposited the items in the centre of a large clump of bushes, covered it with what debris I could find, and stuffed my Mae West light and battery inside my battledress. I then oriented myself by the Polaris star and began to head westwards.[31]

However, the adventure was just beginning for Charles Lepine.

After a long and arduous escape attempt to reach France, I was finally caught trying to swim the Rhine River after crossing the Siegfried Line. I was then sent to *Stalag Luft III* at Sagan, the main air force officers camp in Germany. In February 1945, with the Russians close behind, we were made to walk 15-30 kilometers per day, always heading west and away from the Eastern Front. We slept in barns wherever and whenever the Germans could jam us prisoners in for the night. This second ordeal was not as bad as my first attempted escape to France. For one thing, I was not alone, and I also had a little barley and bread to eat as the Red Cross food ran out. We were finally entrained in boxcars en route to *Stalag IIIA* at Lukenwalde, situated 30 kilometers south of Berlin.[32]

The Costs of German Industrial Dispersal and the Retaliation Policy

Two significant diversions of Germany's national war effort that were directly brought about by the Allied bombing turned out to be particularly damaging to German industrial output. These were the decision to concentrate the production of war materials in underground factories, and Hitler's insistence on the production of a suite of *Vergeltung* (retaliation or revenge) weapons, designed to counter what the *Führer* termed the aerial terrorism of the bombing campaign.

The underground factory program was formulated during the autumn of 1943 once it became clear that Germany was going to be pummelled incessantly by progressively more robust, concentrated and accurate aerial bombardment. In the words of Richard Overy:

It was a vast plan. Hitler ordered the construction or conversion of over 93 million square feet of floor space. During 1944 work began on 71 million, but only 13 million were completed. The effort took half Germany's building workers, half a million men, and quantities of construction materials and machinery. Much of the completed underground plant was never occupied or utilized. The scheme was an economic fantasy; the reality was the diversion of valuable resources to a project of little strategic worth.[33]

Meanwhile, Hitler had become obsessed with striking directly back at England in retaliation for the night bombings. When efforts to rekindle the Blitz of 1940–41 with manned bombers failed, he focussed on an ambitious plan to drench the British Isles and the invasion ports with missiles, hoping to deter the Anglo-Americans from further bombing—or even to thwart the actual attempt at invasion through northwest Europe. To that end, several new weapons were ordered into production, most notably the Fieseler FZG 76 pilotless flying bomb, more commonly known as the V 1. Another was the first longer-range ballistic missile; the A 4 or V 2. These weapons programs did more good than harm to the Allied war effort since, along with being relatively ineffective overall, they limited the development and production of more promising conventional weapons such as the Messerschmitt Me 163 *Komet* rocket fighter, the Messerschmitt Me 262 *Schwalbe* jet fighter, and the *Wasserfall* and *Enzian* surface-to-air missiles.

Enter Tallboy

The emergence of this new suite of German secret V-weapons, coupled with the extensive reinforcement of the U-boat and E-boat pens, required some new weapon for the Allies with a sophisticated penetrating capability. The V-weapons were to be stored in massive, concrete bunkers, impermeable to Bomber Command's existing ordnance. Although by late 1943 the Command had the 12,000-pound high explosive bombs previously mentioned, these bombs had very thin casings and would shatter when dropped on solid concrete. However, the fertile mind of Barnes Neville Wallis had conceived and developed plans for a heavy, strong-cased and extremely streamlined bomb to be dropped accurately from great height on these hardened targets. With a terminal velocity in excess of the speed of sound, the bomb would impact with such energy that it would penetrate deeply underground prior to detonating, so that a series of sub-surface shock waves would collapse the heaviest structures from below. Known as Tallboy, this 12,000-pound weapon, fitted only to the Lancaster, was placed in serious production during the winter of 1943–44. The ultimate operational weapon in this category was the 22,000-pound Grand Slam. This massive, 25-foot 6-inch weapon, produced both in Britain and the United States, was delivered in limited numbers in February 1945, too late to see broad operational service. With a limited number of German targets still needing its attentions, 617 Squadron nonetheless managed to drop forty-one of the behemoths on various U-boat pens. The U-boat pens at Farge near Bremen had their twenty-three-foot solid reinforced concrete roofs successfully pierced by these awesome conventional weapons.[34]

Along with acceptance of their new weapons, 617 Squadron began to practice their precision weapons delivery skills in order to optimize delivery of these expensive weapons. They were assisted enormously by the new Stabilized Automatic Bomb Sight (SABS), which was not only gyro-stabilized but generated automatic aiming corrections to the bomb-aimer. Its drawback was that straight-and-level flight had to be maintained for the final twenty seconds of the bomb run, a restriction considered an unacceptable risk unless it could be performed in conjunction with special tactics, such as offset aim-points, devised and employed by highly skilled units such as 617 Squadron. Eventually, this "Squadron of Experts" could bomb at night using these weapons with such accuracy that three-quarters of the ordnance they released landed within a seventy-five-yard radius of the intended target.

Tallboy was first fully used on the night of 8/9 June 1944 by 617 Squadron in a raid on a railway tunnel near Saumur, some 125 miles south of the Normandy beachheads.

> The raid was prepared in great haste because a German Panzer unit was expected to move by train through the tunnel. The target area was illuminated with flares by 4 Lancasters of No. 83 Squadron and marked at low level by 3 Mosquitos. 25 Lancasters of No. 617 Squadron then dropped their Tallboys with great accuracy. The huge bombs exploded under the ground to create miniature "earthquakes'; one actually pierced the roof of the tunnel and brought down a huge quantity of rock and soil. The tunnel was blocked for a considerable period and the Panzer unit was badly delayed. No aircraft were lost from this raid.[35]

Soon, these weapons would also be used to telling effect against the hardened V-weapon launching sites, forcing the Germans to adopt a much less secure and more vulnerable policy of mobile launching.[36]

The transportation campaign continued, and by the eve of D-Day, some sixty separate attacks had put at least two-thirds of the thirty-seven assigned targets out of action for a minimum of a month. Furthermore the total cost in civilian collateral casualties had been kept well below the 10,000 total figure that both Churchill and Sir Charles Portal fervently hoped would not be exceeded.[37] So successful was the plan's implementation "that after the Allied landings had taken place scarcely any enemy reinforcements could be brought into action without lengthy detours or delays, a factor which proved crucial during the vital consolidation of the invasion beachheads."[38]

An Effective Synergy:
The Bombing and the Resistance Movement

This destruction of the French transportation network was without a doubt Bomber Command's foremost contribution to the success of Operation Overlord. In this campaign the two Special Operations squadrons based at Tempsford may well have been the most cost-effective units in all the Command. Teams of saboteurs supplied with high explosives by these units inflicted a lot of critical damage on both transport and the war industries. Often, a pound of plastic explosives placed at precisely the right spot and time could do a more effective job on key railway junctions, bridges, viaducts, and tunnels than an entire bombing force that might not even be able to find a specific target on a given night. Furthermore, this clandestine campaign had been successfully prosecuted for many months against the Germans prior to implementation of the formal Transportation Plan in April 1944. One of these Special Operations agents was a magnificent Canadian hero who never wore Air Force blue. His name was Major Gustave "Guy" Bieler from Montreal's Regiment de Maisonneuve. Born in France of Swiss parents, Bieler emigrated to Canada at an early age. A citizen-soldier in the prewar years with the Maisonneuves, he was also active as a school teacher and a translator for the Sun Life Assurance Company. Later he became one of the twenty-five uniformed Canadians of the Special Operations Executive (SOE) who were sent into Occupied Europe. Of those twenty-five agents, eight later died, most of them in horrible circumstances at the hands of their captors. On 28 November 1942, Bieler was parachuted into France to establish a sabotage network at St. Quentin, a city of approximately 60,000 people some eighty miles northeast of Paris.

The operation went awry from the start. Parachuting onto rocky ground, Bieler sustained a severe spinal injury and lay helpless for hours until he was taken to a safe house in Paris, where he hid for months in intense pain. His back was broken. By 7 April 1943, however, he found the strength to hobble to St. Quentin and shortly thereafter, went to work setting up his network. Singling out the French railway system for special attention, he was enormously successful. His group, in short order, destroyed an entire troop train, de-railed twenty others, damaged twenty more locomotives, wrecked an engine repair shop which included eleven locomotives and cut the Paris-to-Cologne rail line a total of thirteen times! He also deliberately asked London to leave the railways to his saboteurs, since in these days prior to the improved accuracy ultimately demonstrated during the implementation of the Transportation Plan, bombing was taking a significant toll of French civilians.

> On one occasion, to avoid loss of civilian lives, he refused to blow up an important munitions train on a siding near many houses. He made up for this by having another munitions convoy blown up in the uninhabited countryside.[39]

Guy Bieler was deeply loved and respected by the French with whom he worked, but he was still in intense pain from the injuries he had sustained parachuting into France. Overworked and exhausted, when a neighbouring agent in Lille was killed, Bieler took over his network as well. On 14 January 1944, fourteen months after his parachute jump, his luck ran out and he was picked up by the *Gestapo*. Under these conditions, the understood rule on capture was to hold out without talking, no matter what happened, for forty-eight hours, giving related agents and network members time to cover their tracks. According to witnesses in the sinister Fresnes prison where he was taken for questioning, Bieler held out for the next five months, enduring the most unspeakable of medieval agonies, particularly during the initial week of captivity, torments no-one should have to witness, let alone experience.

By mid-September 1944, he was incarcerated in the notorious Flossenburg concentration camp located in southern Germany, along with fourteen other British agents. While torture, compounded with his back injury, had decimated him physically, he had told his captors nothing throughout his long captivity. However, execution was inevitable for him.

> His courage and dignity had so impressed the Germans that when the gaunt little man limped his last painful steps and went fearlessly to his death, he did not go alone—he was accompanied by an SS guard of honour. They spared him gas or hanging. Guy Bieler stumbled to a wall in the prison courtyard and was shot . . . The day Guy Bieler died, aged 40, his old regiment, the Maisonneuves, having helped close the Falaise Gap, were fighting not far from St. Quentin.[40]

Shortly after the war, in Rideau Hall in Ottawa, Governor-General the Viscount Alexander pinned Bieler's Distinguished Service Order on his eleven-year-old son, Jean-Louis. Among his other awards were his appointment as a Member of the Order of the British Empire and the *Croix de Guerre avec Palme* from France.[41] According to a close friend, Bieler said he lived by a simple credo: "Either you serve or you don't. If you serve, give it all you've got."[42] Gustave Bieler certainly did that, in the fullest measure.

The Big Day and its Aftermath

Approaching D-Day, deceiving the enemy about the Allies' true intentions in Normandy was of paramount importance for Bomber Command. Widely diversified targets were bombed throughout

May. Then, on the nights of 2/3 June, 3/4 June and 4/5 June, deception raids were carried out on coastal gun positions in the Pas de Calais region. Only on the night prior to the invasion, 5/6 June, were the gun batteries along the Normandy coast pounded in an extensive and concentrated manner from the air.

5/6 June 1944

1012 aircraft—551 Lancasters, 412 Halifaxes, 49 Mosquitos—to bomb coastal batteries at Fontenay, Houlgate, La Pernelle, Longues, Maisy, Merville, Mont Fleury, Pointe du Hoc, Ouistreham and St. Martin Varreville. 946 aircraft carried out their bombing tasks. Three aircraft were lost—two Halifaxes of No 4 Group on the Mont Fleury raid and one Lancaster from No 6 Group on the Longues raid. Only two of the targets—La Pernelle and Ouistreham—were free of cloud; all other bombing was entirely based on *Oboe* marking. At least 5000 tons of bombs were dropped, the greatest tonnage in one night so far in the war.

110 aircraft of Nos 1 and 100 Groups carried out extensive bomber-support operations: 24 "Airborne Cigar" (ABC)–equipped Lancasters of No 101 Squadron patrolled all likely night-fighter approaches, so that their German-speaking operators could jam the German controllers' instructions; No 100 Group flew 34 RCM sorties and 27 *Serrate* and 25 Intruder Mosquito patrols. Two Intruders and one ABC Lancaster were lost.

58 aircraft of Nos 3 and 5 Groups carried out a variety of operations to conceal the true location of the invasion for as long as possible. Sixteen Lancasters of No 617 Squadron [led by Leonard Cheshire] and six *G-H* fitted Stirlings of No 218 Squadron dropped a dense screen of *Window*, which advanced slowly across the Channel, to simulate a large convoy of ships approaching the French coast between Boulogne and Le Havre, north of the real invasion coast. These flights required exact navigation; both squadrons had been practicing for this operation for more than a month. The second diversion was carried out by 36 Halifaxes and Stirlings of Nos 90, 138, 149 and 161 Squadrons. These aircraft dropped dummy parachutists and explosive devices to simulate airborne landings over areas not being invaded. Two Stirlings of No.149 Squadron were lost while carrying out this diversion . . .

Total Bomber Command effort for the night: 1211 sorties, eight aircraft (0.7 percent) lost. The number of sorties flown was a new record. British, American and Canadian divisions landed on five Normandy beaches early the next morning.[43]

The detailed Bomber Command Raid Report for the same night is very interesting, since it reflects the degree of coordination and sophistication which was now the norm on major Bomber Command efforts.

SECRET

NIGHT RAID REPORT NO. 625
COPY NO. 16

BOMBER COMMAND REPORT ON NIGHT OPERATIONS
5/6th JUNE 1944 (D-Day)
COASTAL BATTERIES, ETC.
COASTAL BATTERIES

PLANS OF ATTACK

3. <u>La Pernelle</u>. OBOE groundmarking and emergency visual marking. 5 OBOE Mosquitos were to drop red T.I. A flare force was to illuminate the target. If the OBOE aircraft

failed, 5 Group Mosquitos were to mark the A/P with red spot fires. In either case, 5 Group Lancasters (S.A.B.S.-Stabilized Automatic Bomb Sight—DB) were to back up with green T.I. If necessary, the Controller would transmit a false vector for bombing, having assessed the accuracy of the markers. H = 0335.

4. <u>St. Martin : Fontenay</u>. Controlled OBOE groundmarking. 5 OBOE Mosquitos were to drop red T.I. A Master Bomber was to direct each attack, dropping greens himself, if necessary. If the Main Force received no instructions, they were to aim at the centre of reds. H = 2350 at St. Martin; 2335 at Fontenay.

5. <u>Houlgate: Sallennelles: Ouistreham: Mont Fleury: Maisy: Longues</u>.
OBOE groundmarking with emergency H2S groundmarking. 5 Mosquitos were to mark each target with red T.I. Emergency blind markers either were to release on green T.I. on the intersection of an H2S flight line and a GEE lattuce line or might release on positive visual identification, if no T.I. were visible. But if T.I. were burning they were to hold their markers. Backers up were to aim green T.I. at the reds, the centre of greens, or the A/P itself if they could identify it visually. Main Force crews were to aim at the centre of reds or of greens. H = 0350 at Houlgate; 0030 at Sallennelles; 0505 at Ouistreham; 0435 at Mont Fleury; 0320 at Maisy; and 0420 at Longues. Mosquitos from H-3 to H-1. Emergency blind markers at H-1. Backers up at H+1 and H+2. Main Force from H to H+8.

6. <u>Pointe du Hoe</u>. OBOE groundmarking with emergency visual marking. 5 OBOE Mosquitos were to drop red T.I. 5 Group Mosquitos were to back up with green T.I., but if no OBOE markers had been dropped, these Mosquitos were to aim their greens visually at the A/P. The Controller was to assess the accuracy of the markers, and issue a false vector for bombing if necessary. Main Force crews were to aim the centre of their bombsticks at reds or the centre of greens, unless otherwise ordered. H = 0450.

NARRATIVE OF ATTACKS

9. <u>La Pernelle</u>. The first markers were scattered, but soon 2 reds and 2 greens were burning on the A/P, and the bombing was concentrated round them.

10. <u>Houlgate</u>. The early reds fell on the battery to the N.E. The greens were mostly 1,000 yards to the E., and one group landed on the cliffs over a mile to the N.E. Cloud increased during the attack, and the results could not be observed.

11. <u>Mont Fleury: Maisy: Sallennelles: Fontenay: St. Martin-de-Verrevilles: Longues</u>. Cloud was too dense over these targets for photographs to give any clear picture of the course of the attacks, but all were reported as fairly well concentrated.

12. <u>Ouistreham</u>. The first 4 groups of markers were scattered 500–2,500 yards to the E. of the A/P. At H+2, however, a tight cluster of 3 T.I. was burning immediately S. of the A/P, and these attracted some of the bombing.

13. <u>Pointe du Hoe</u>. Reds and greens were well packed around the A/P, and several sticks of bombs were seen to fall across it.

DAY RECONNAISSANCE

14. No reconnaissance reports were issued for these attacks.

ENEMY DEFENCES

15. Fighters were active over the Normandy coast throughout the night, although only in the later raids did they show much readiness to engage our bombers. It is significant

that no returning bomber sustained fighter damage. Flak was nowhere intense. One enemy aircraft was damaged off Sallennelles.

CASUALTIES

16. Only 6 aircraft were missing from these operations. One aircraft was shot down by flak at Mont Fleury and 2 were seen to go down in combat near Caen and Lisieux. None of the other losses were observed. One Halifax was wrecked in a taxying accident, and another crashed on landing.

MLM/MTA
BG/S.26342/2/ORS4
24th September 1944[44]

As important as the precursor bombing of German defensive positions was, it was probably the electronic deception initiatives that paid the most handsome dividends during Overlord. These were the three 100 Group squadrons that flew over the invasion fleet jamming German radio communications and radar, as well as the 111 highly skilled crews who flew those precise circuits over the Channel, dropping *Window* as they went in a timed pattern, creating an enormous "bogus" or "spoof" armada apparently destined for the Pas de Calais region. Murray Peden recalls his role in this historic event, tasked as one of five Fortresses from 214 Squadron to establish a patrol line approximately 80-90 miles to the northeast of the landing grounds, helping protect the assault forces from enemy aerial interference. After hours of timed patterns in Fortress "F-Fox" jamming enemy electronics and releasing chaff, not to mention a close encounter with a German night fighter, Peden and his crew were homebound. As they started their descent from their high-level operating perch, they experienced extremely heavy icing, but soon found themselves below the weather and in the clear. While many witnesses have commented about the massive conglomeration of Allied ships converging on the landing beaches that day, Peden offers a unique perspective on yet another type of armada that was about to become just as engaged.

> We left the French coast behind, continuing our descent, and headed back towards England. It was not yet daylight, but the darkness had begun to soften. Suddenly we saw a sight that brought a lump to my throat. A tremendous aerial armada was passing us in extended formation a mile or two on our left side. Not bombers, but C-47s: an airborne army. They were going in. We were coming out. For a long minute, I watched them sailing silently onward to their date with destiny. I thought of the men squatting nervously inside and felt like a slacker. After five or six hours in the air we were on our way home, heading back to a good breakfast and a clean bed. They were only a quarter of an hour away from going in by parachute or glider—to face what? We flew in silence for some time.[45]

Once the invasion forces were ashore, Bomber Command's task for the ensuing summer weeks would be to support the Allied armies by battering German strongholds, ammunition, oil and supply dumps, critical lines of communication targets, and anything which posed a threat to the Allied advance. Very soon after the landings particular attention was paid to the city of Caen in support of the Canadian 3rd Division's advance. The Bomber Command Report on Night Operations for 6/7 June 1944 elaborates, when Caen was one of nine rail and road centres under simultaneous attack:

3. Caen: Visual marking. A yellow T.I. was to be dropped 5 miles from the target on a bearing of 240 degrees True. 5 OBOE Mosquitos were to release yellows. The target was then to be illuminated by flares, in the light of which 2 red spot flares were to be dropped on the A/P. If these were accurate, they were to be backed up with 6 more red spot flares and 4 green T.I. Main Force crews were to aim the first bomb of each stick at the markers. A Master Bomber was to direct the attack. H = 0235. Bombing height: 1,700–2,700.

NARRATIVE OF ATTACKS

11. Caen. The target was accurately marked from low level, and bombing was concentrated, but cloud prevented photographic cover during the attack.

DAY RECONNAISSANCE

20. Caen. The central area of the town was in flames on the following day, and the area to the E. was heavily damaged. Fires were burning near the Bassin à Flot, where the lock gates leading to the River Orne, and those to the Nouveau Bassin, were destroyed. Dockside warehouses, etc., were badly damaged. The marshalling yards and 4 road bridges were blocked by craters, as were the roads leading from Caen to Falaise and Bayeux.

MJM/JT.

BC/S. 26342/3/ORS4,
25th. September, 1944:[46]

The bombing of Caen was intense that night, as recalled by mid-upper gunner Dick Bell of 434 Squadron:

We did a number of trips that summer over Caen. The night of D-Day, when we went in to bomb, the sky over the target was filled with planes. When we went in to bomb, it was all box bombing; that is, it was all very concentrated in a very small area, and the bombs were dropped on multiple attacks. We did three separate bomb runs that night. These tactics, although probably necessary and appropriate, seemed dangerous, as so many aircraft were going over the target at the same time and from different heights dropping our bombs. On one of our runs, a 500 lb. bomb went between the tail and the wing of our aircraft. The flak was also very thick. Looked like you could walk on it.[47]

Of the 123 aircraft that actually bombed Caen that night, six did not return, a 4.6 percent loss rate, high for the Overlord support operations. These losses represented half the twelve lost overall from the 1065 bombers (1.1 percent) despatched to all targets.[48]

Relentless Pressure

Bomber Command's activity during the immediate post-landing period concentrated heavily on road and rail centres in the battle area. The following night, Merrill Burnett had a bizarre experience while crossing the French coast inbound on a raid against a railway junction at Achères.

As we crossed a portion of the coast that Intelligence said was unfortified, we were coned by two searchlights and hit by flak, which knocked out our intercom. Pilot Officer Mann took evasive action by turning and diving out over the water and then levelled out. There was a full moon and I saw four parachutes go past the rear turret. Two landed on land and two in the water near the coast. As the aircraft was now flying level, I thought all had bailed out except me. I left the rear turret and moved forward and was then met by a blast of cold air from the front escape hatch, which was open. The mid-upper gunner, Sergeant Doug Harkness, was still in his turret and was unaware that anyone had bailed out. He remained in the turret while I went forward to notify our pilot of the bailouts. The mid-under gunner, Sergeant Hugh Galarneau, had come down from his turret and, as requested by Pilot Officer Mann, we checked the fuel supply. It appeared OK except for one tank, which was low. Our pilot then decided to fly back to England and in the bright moonlight, he found the airfield at Bradwell Bay in Sussex. I returned to my rear turret to prepare for landing. The airfield was blacked out and without communication and we landed downwind, ran off the end of the runway, through a fence and into a field. However, Mann was still able to turn the aircraft around, got it back onto the airfield, and parked it at the control tower. When the officials learned we had a full bomb load still on board, some of which were delayed action, they ordered us back into the aircraft and had it towed far away from all buildings. We were then interrogated separately by Station Intelligence as to why only part of the crew had bailed out. The final answer came in September 1944, when our original bomb-aimer, James White, showed up back in England and was interrogated. He had landed, hid his parachute, then hid out himself for a couple of days until he was able to contact the French Resistance. He spent the next few months with them while they disrupted the enemy in every possible way, until he was returned to Britain in September. It was later discovered that we had crossed the French coast fifteen miles port of track over a light flak and searchlight position.[49]

Merrill Burnett modestly downplays his role in getting his aircraft back to England that night, as he downplayed his part in the earlier mid-air collision with a 425 Squadron aircraft. However, his efforts were mentioned in a well-deserved DFM awarded to him in August:

As rear gunner this airman has participated in a number of attacks on various enemy targets and has displayed courage and determination of a high order. On one occasion, shortly after the target had been successfully attacked, his aircraft sustained very severe damage and went out of control. Before the captain could regain control, considerable height was lost. Although the order to leave by parachute had been given, Sergeant Burnett did everything possible to assist his captain and his services proved of immense value. His coolness, resolution and devotion to duty in the face of harassing circumstances set a very fine example.[50]

Canadian Air Gunners Shine

During Bomber Command's war, aircrew gunners measured up well to their primary responsibility, which was to keep a sharp look-out for other aircraft, both friendly and hostile. Many crews were saved, by a gunner's sharp eyes and timely warnings of an impending mid-air collision. And many more were saved by equally timely warnings of an approaching enemy fighter, allowing the pilot to take evasive action. However, few gunners scored air-to-air victories. The stealthy nature of the nocturnal bombing campaign permitted relatively few to bring their guns to bear on an enemy fighter, and once the daylight missions resumed in the closing months of the war, with notable exceptions, relatively few *Luftwaffe* targets remained. In addition, the larger calibre and more effective .5-inch weapons were not broadly available to the crews until the latter stages of the war, and even then, their employment was limited. The bulk of Bomber Command's war for the gunners was fought with .303-calibre weapons. In the succinct words of 405 Squadron mid-upper gunner Russ Hubley of Halifax, "They could shoot at us from 1000 yards or further while I had to wait until he was (just) 300 yards away."[51] Still, in the course of flying raids with 431 Squadron out of Croft, and many more with 8 Group's 405 Squadron out of Gransden Lodge, Hubley damaged at least three enemy fighters and was awarded the DFC for his stalwart actions.[52] Others were even more successful, and the very best of them appear to owe a portion of their success to the close relationships that formed between some rear gunners and mid-upper gunners. One such pair was mid-upper gunner Pilot Officer Clarence B. Sutherland from Truro, Nova Scotia, and Flying Officer Wallace McIntosh of the RAF. Both of these intrepid airmen were eventually credited with seven enemy aircraft destroyed, and they served together on 207 Squadron, flying out of RAF Station Spilsby in Lincolnshire. Clarence Sutherland completed thirty-five operations between 16 December 1943 and 5 August 1944, winning a DFC and Bar along the way. Summer operations were particularly hard on his squadron, which alone lost twenty crews— 140 men—between 20 June 1944 and 29 July 1944. While a number of his successes did not occur in conjunction with Wally McIntosh, many did, including his most memorable night of 7/8 June 1944 over France. Sutherland recalls:

7 Jun 1944. Balleroy, France

. . . Forêt de Cerisy is full of German tanks and it is about midnight. After leaving the target I see a fighter in the rear and both of us gunners open fire. The Ju 88 goes down in flames. About 10 seconds later, another Ju 88 is spotted. We fire and he blows up under our aircraft. The explosion lifts our aircraft up in the air. Twenty minutes later I spot a Me 410 and there are Lancasters with their lights on ahead of us. We hold and are ready, as we think he is going after another Lancaster, but he pulls up on our port side. We open fire and the Me 410 goes down in a glide, on fire, towards the coast of England. The next day Air Marshal Harris phones our station, talks to Group Captain Harris, our station commander, and asks, "Who the hell *are* those guys?" Flying Officer Wallace McIntosh and myself receive Distinguished Flying Crosses.[53]

Another sterling example of excellent Canadian gunnery crew coordination was the team of Flight Sergeant Peter Engbrecht, a Russian immigrant and blacksmith from Summerside, Prince Edward Island, and Flight Sergeant Gordon Gillanders from Fraser Hills, British Columbia. As mid-upper and rear gunners respectively, this skilled and effective pair from 424 Squadron operating out of Skipton-on-Swale successfully brought their guns to bear on four separate occasions. For their actions, Gillanders was awarded a Distinguished Flying Medal, while Pete Engbrecht received one of only twelve Conspicuous Gallantry Medals bestowed on Canadian airmen during the war. In all, Engbrecht tallied six confirmed aerial victories as well as two "probables," adding two confirmed that were shared with Gillanders after a torrid pace of solo and team scoring just prior to and shortly after the invasion. The CGM citation highlights these earlier actions, but it is important to bear in mind that Engbrecht continued to excel after he received his prestigious decoration:

As mid-upper gunner this airman has participated in several sorties and has proved himself to be an exceptionally cool and confident member of aircraft crew. On one occasion during a sortie his aircraft was subjected to fourteen separate attacks by fighters. In the ensuing flights, Sergeant Engbrecht defended his aircraft with great skill and two of the attackers fell to his guns. In June 1944 he took part in an attack on a target in northern France. On the return flight his aircraft was attacked on two occasions by fighters. Sergeant Engbrecht engaged the enemy aircraft with deadly effect each time and his brilliant shooting caused their destruction. His feats have been worthy of the greatest praise.[54]

However, while some Bomber Command gunners were remarkably successful, confirmed aerial victories tended to be few. Rudolph Thun offers the German viewpoint:

I think we had many more losses through weather, mechanical failures and British night fighters than through the return fire of bombers. I will never forget the crash in Greifswald due to engine failure shortly after lift-off, the roll-over on instruments at a pretty low altitude due to a sudden failure of the autopilot, the back flip during roll-out on a muddy airfield in fog, or the sneak attack of a British night fighter while flying on autopilot— fortunately, his use of tracer ammunition gave him away in time—or the many bomber and fighter attacks we had to endure on the ground. Still, in this war of individualists, the experienced pilots and crews had a fair chance to survive. The toll taken of the younger, inexperienced crews, on the other hand, was very heavy.[55]

The toll on even the most experienced night fighter crews for reasons other than combat was also heavy however. On 5 October 1944, the night fighter arm suffered an irreplaceable loss when *Oberst* Helmut Lent, *Kommodore* of *NJG 3*, holder of the Knight's Cross with Diamonds, victor of 110 aerial combats (102 at night), crashed on landing at Paderborn in his Ju 88C-6. Lent was severely injured, lingered for two days, then died. The rest of his crew and a war reporter accompanying them were also killed. Lent's loss dealt a grievous blow to the morale of the remaining night fighter crews.[56]

Bravest of the Brave

On the night of 12/13 June, Flying Officer Art De Breyne and his 419 Squadron crew, which included mid-upper gunner Pilot Officer Andrew Charles Mynarski, headed south out of their home base at Middleton St. George in Durham County towards Cambrai, France and a rendezvous with destiny. Their mount that night was a near-new Lancaster Mark X, KB 726, which this crew had flown operationally on the 5th, 6th and 7th of June. Since this was to be the De Breyne crew's thirteenth operation the mid-upper gunner, Andy Mynarski, found a four-leaf clover in the grass. He subsequently gave it to his good friend and "pub-crawling buddy," rear gunner Pat Brophy, for good luck. Brophy then put it in the headband of his service cap for safekeeping[57]. Mynarski, who had just been commissioned a pilot officer from non-commissioned rank prior to the Cambrai raid, used to joke about the rank differential between him and his pal Pat Brophy, who was already a flying officer. When they took leave of each other at day's end, Mynarski would habitually and playfully haul himself to attention, give Brophy an exaggerated salute and an enthusiastic "Good night, *Sir!*" in his soft Polish-Canadian accent.

KB 726, coded "A–Able," was one of a force of 671 aircraft, consisting of 348 Halifaxes, 285 Lancasters and 38 Mosquitos from 4, 5, 6 and 8 Groups, tasked with simultaneously attacking communications targets, mostly railway facilities, at Amiens, Arras, Caen, Cambrai, and Poitiers. The 419 Squadron crews were part of those assigned against the marshalling yard at Cambrai, and they were briefed to attack from relatively low level.[58] For the first time since D-Day, Bomber Command met significant night fighter opposition. During the first week after the landings, the *Luftwaffe* had been holding back the bulk of the night fighter arm for the defence of the Reich, but by 12 June 1944, they had moved many fighters forward to counter the Allied aerial attacks in the lodgement area. Weather conditions and the attack parameters chosen that night strongly favoured the defenders. They took a dreadful toll on the bombing force assigned against the French railway targets, felling twenty-three of the bombers, including three Lancasters from 419 Squadron.[59]

Crossing the French coast, KB 726 was almost immediately coned by searchlights, which pilot Art De Breyne successfully countered with an extremely steep, near-vertical dive. Roughly ten minutes later, now at low altitude but still not yet on the final bomb run into Cambrai, things got worse. De Breyne recalls:

> After being coned, we were picked up by a night fighter. Pat Brophy thought it was a twin that did not appear to be engaging us, but after initial contact, he lost track of it. So I said, "Where *is* he?", and Pat said, "I don't know. I've *lost* him." I guess he was working his way right underneath us then. Well, I wasn't going to just *sit* there, so I threw the Lancaster into a corkscrew. But as soon as I got the nose down, Pat said, "Oh *heck*, he's *underneath!*" Well . . . they had upward-firing guns, and I guess he had placed himself pretty well to follow us from underneath. The gunfire must have gone between the two gunners because they set us alight there, although I didn't know about that particular fire in the rear of the aircraft at that time. They also caught the port wing . . . two explosions there, two engines conked out and the gas tank in the wing between them was on fire. We also still had a full bomb load. Then, my instruments went black; no instruments at all, and the intercom *also* went dead. At that point, I knew we were not going to make it home. We must have now been down around 3000 feet at the bottom of the corkscrew, and with the battle damage, I had no choice but to *keep* it going down.
>
> I told Roy Vigars, the flight engineer, to get everybody up front out *fast*. I then flashed a "P" in Morse for "parachute" on the "P" switch, which gave a flashing red Morse repeater light at each of the relatively-isolated gunner's stations. Andy must have got it, because he acted upon it, but Brophy said he never saw it. My panel light lit up, so I knew we had at least one closed relay on board. Roy then moved out into the bomb-aimer's compartment in preparation for jumping, and when he did, he noticed the bomb-aimer, Jack Friday, lying face down on the floor. He had pulled up on the hatch cover and it hit him above the eye and knocked him out. He was just lucky he didn't fall through the hatch without his parachute, but the cover had wedged back in the hole sideways. [Roy Vigars then hooked the unconscious Friday to his 'chute, pulled the ripcord and quickly tossed him out of the aircraft before jumping himself.] However, I really didn't know what was going on down there. I had no communication with *anybody* anymore once I told Roy to get going! It was taking everything I could muster just to keep that aircraft in the air . . . In fact, if it hadn't been for one searchlight about ten miles off the port beam, I wouldn't have known what was up and what was down, but it gave me a reference point. After about two minutes of this, just going by the wind noise to judge my approximate airspeed, I knew I had to get out. Once I saw that everybody up front had jumped, I throttled back the starboard engines to keep the Lanc on a more-or-less even keel while I got out. I then dove through the forward hatch. At that point, I didn't know if I was twenty feet off the ground or a thousand feet, but I figured I was somewhere in between.[60]

Art De Breyne later recollected that he only got two or three good swings in his parachute before his feet hit the ground, and guessed that he had ultimately bailed out at between 500–700 feet. Pat Brophy now recalls what was going on further aft in KB 726.

The cannon bursts started a helluvva fire in the centre portion of the aircraft. There was hydraulic fluid all over the place when it started to burn, and with the descent Art had the aircraft in from the evasive action until he levelled it off later on, there was an awful roar through the fuselage. Up front, they had naturally opened the escape hatch and this, of course, generated even *more* wind and noise. Art had flashed us the "P" in Morse for "parachute." Andy may have seen it. I didn't because of the flames lighting everything up red. There was red, yellow, red, yellow, blue . . . every colour in the sky . . . I wouldn't have noticed it.[61]

Brophy left his turret and entered the rear portion of the Lancaster's fuselage to strap on his parachute in preparation for bailing out, and then, given the flames and smoke in the aircraft's interior, elected to return to the turret, rotate its doors aft, then bail out from the rear of KB 726. However, he had lost hydraulic power to the turret during the night fighter attack and therefore had to hand-crank his capsule to the aft bail-out position. Then, while the doors were in a completely intermediate position with neither access back to the rear fuselage door nor to the aft position, the hand-crank came apart in pieces in Brophy's hands.

Then I saw him. Andy had slid down from the mid-upper turret and made his way back to the rear escape hatch, about 15 feet from me, having received the "P" signal to bail out from the skipper. He opened the door and was just going to jump when he glanced around and spotted me through the plexiglass part of my turret. One look told him I was trapped.

Instantly, he turned away from the hatch—his doorway to safety—and started towards me. All this time the aircraft was lurching drunkenly as Art tried to keep it on an even keel without instruments. Andy had to climb over the Elsan chemical toilet and crawl over the tailplane spar, as there is no room at that part in the fuselage. These cramped conditions forced him to crawl on his hands and knees—straight through the blazing hydraulic oil. By the time he reached my position in the tail, his uniform and parachute were on fire. I shook my head; it was hopeless. "Don't try!" I shouted, and waved him away. Andy didn't seem to notice. Completely ignoring his own condition in the flames, he grabbed a fire axe and tried to smash the turret free. It gave slightly, but not enough. Wild with desperation and pain, he tore at the doors with his bare hands—to no avail. By now he was a mass of flames below his waist. Seeing him like that, I forgot everything else. Over the roar of the wind and the whine of our two remaining engines, I screamed, "Go back, Andy! Get out!"

Finally, with time running out, he realized he could do nothing to help me. When I waved him away again, he hung his head and nodded, as though he was ashamed to leave—ashamed that sheer heart and courage hadn't been enough. As there was no way to turn around in the confined quarters, Andy had to crawl backwards through the flaming hydraulic fluid fire again, never taking his eyes off me. On his face was a look of mute anguish. When Andy reached the escape hatch, he stood up. Slowly, as he'd often done before in happier times together, he came to attention. Standing there in his flaming clothes, a grimly magnificent figure, he saluted me! At the same time, just before he jumped, he said something. And even though I couldn't hear, I knew it was "Good night, *Sir*."[62]

I was very fortunate. The "Hail Marys" were coming very fast out of me, but Art had put the aircraft in a rather flat trajectory before he left. I saw the ground coming up, the starboard wing hit a tree about 18" in diameter, and this was just enough to give the fuselage a jerk that in turn gave the turret a jolt through about 45 degrees. I then popped out through the open doors and landed about 20-30 feet away up against a tree. I then felt myself all over. I could move everything, didn't have a scratch on me, not a drop of blood, *nothing*.[63]

The Victoria Cross was subsequently awarded to Pilot Officer Andrew Charles Mynarski, based largely on Pat Brophy's testimony, given after the rear gunner had returned to England that autumn. The citation for the award, which was presented to Mynarski's mother in Winnipeg after the war, reads as follows:

> Pilot Officer Mynarski was the mid-upper gunner of a Lancaster aircraft, detailed to attack a target at Cambrai in France, on the night of 12th June, 1944. The aircraft was attacked from below and astern by an enemy fighter and ultimately came down in flames.
>
> As an immediate result of the attack, both port engines failed. Fire broke out between the mid-upper turret and the rear turret, as well as in the port wing. The flames soon became fierce and the captain ordered the crew to abandon the aircraft.
>
> Pilot Officer Mynarski left his turret and went towards the escape hatch. He then saw that the rear gunner was still in his turret and apparently unable to leave it. The turret was, in fact, immovable, since the hydraulic gear had been put out of action when the port engines failed, and the manual gear had been broken by the gunner in his attempts to escape. Without hesitation, Pilot Officer Mynarski made his way through the flames in an endeavour to reach the rear turret and release the gunner. Whilst so doing, his parachute and his clothing up to the waist were set on fire. All his efforts to move the turret and free the rear gunner were in vain. Eventually the rear gunner clearly indicated to him that there was nothing more he could do and that he should try to save his own life. Pilot Officer Mynarski reluctantly went back through the flames to the escape hatch. There, as a last gesture to the trapped gunner, he turned towards him, stood to attention in his flaming clothing, and saluted, before he jumped out of the aircraft. Pilot Officer Mynarski's descent was seen by French people on the ground. Both his parachute and his clothing were on fire. He was found eventually by the French, but was so severely burnt that he died from his injuries. The rear gunner had a miraculous escape when the aircraft crashed. He subsequently testified that had Pilot Officer Mynarski not attempted to save his comrade's life, he could have left the aircraft in safety and would, doubtless, have escaped death.
>
> Pilot Officer Mynarski must have been fully aware that in trying to free the rear gunner he was almost certain to lose his own life. Despite this, with outstanding courage and complete disregard for his own safety, he went to the rescue. Willingly accepting the danger, Pilot Officer Mynarski lost his life by a most conspicuous act of heroism which called for valour of the highest order.[64]

Art De Breyne, Pat Brophy, Jim Kelly, the wireless operator, and Bob Bodie, the navigator, all successfully evaded capture and were eventually liberated by the advancing Allied armies in September, then subsequently returned to Britain. The flight engineer, Roy Vigars, and the bomb-aimer, Jack Friday, were captured and became unwilling guests of the Third Reich for the duration of the war.

Pat Brophy made a poignant observation about the isolation within which the bomber crews waged their war, and their legacy of undoubtedly many heroic deeds left unrecognized:

> There could have been cases in other aircraft as well where people just did not come back to tell the stories of heroism that occurred . . . I firmly believe that Roy Vigars, our flight engineer, should have gotten a commendation of some kind as well for saving Jack Friday's life by hooking up his parachute and throwing him out of the aircraft after he was knocked out by that hatch. But these stories, if someone didn't come back to tell them, would never be known, and how many stories could have been told *had* somebody come back?[65]

Many Bomber Command encounters with the German night fighters, although nerve-wracking and fraught with danger, were considerably more successful than the Mynarski experience. Jim Northrup elaborates from personal experiences garnered during the period. Again, his comments speak volumes about the strength and versatility of the frequently maligned later-model Halifaxes:

I had two other close encounters with enemy aircraft during my operational tour. When you had 1000 aircraft heading for the same aiming point, you were always ducking and weaving out of the way of some of them. And the "back-room boffins" had estimated at one time that there would be an average of two mid-air collisions for every 1000 aircraft launched.

My first encounter was with a Focke-Wulf 190. We had just bombed a target deep in the Ruhr Valley. I was at 23,000 feet and the area seemed to be full of fighters. I decided to get the hell out of there as quick as I could and slanted the aircraft downwards at 40 degrees and let her ramble. At 10,000 feet I was "right on the red line" indicating 320 mph and I was just about to start levelling out when I glanced out the starboard window. At that moment, the '190 went by like a bat out of hell. His port wing passed over my starboard wing within inches of each other. For a fraction of a second, the *Luftwaffe* pilot and I looked right at each other, and then he was gone. Mighty close . . .

The second time happened a few minutes after we had bombed Chemnitz . . . We had turned west and were on this course for half an hour when I got the scare of my life. A Halifax crossed over us at right angles to our course. This aircraft was so close that I could hear the roar of his engines, and my aircraft shuddered so violently that I was sure we had been hit and that my mid-upper gunner was dead. I screamed into the mike at him, "Sully, are you all right??" He gave a shaky "yes" and then said, "Where in the hell did *that* one come from?" Now I was so shaken up that I gave Sully hell and told him to keep his bloody eyes open and not to sleep on the job. Then, I immediately apologized to him, as no-one could have seen that particular aircraft coming at us.

Anyway, we were flying west at 25,000 feet and I am cold as my ground crew had not had time to install the plug-in for my electrically-heated flying suit. I am also still a little shaky from the near-collision. By now, I have developed the facility to feel other aircraft around me and I notice another Halifax at the same altitude and on the same course as myself, about 200 yards to my starboard. I am now looking in his direction about 60 percent of the time and am considering dropping a thousand feet to avoid him, when all of a sudden, I see the whole outline of his aircraft being hit by tracer fire. I say "Starboard!" to my gunners and they both direct their eyes accordingly. All of a sudden, there is a blinding flash as the Hally blows all to hell. The tracer pattern is so wide I figure that the fighter must have fired from around 1000 yards. He would have had both of us on his radar and probably figured he could get us both. Hence, the long shot, as this would give him time to swing his guns to bear on us. My rear gunner does not even get "Starboard, go!" out of his mouth before I am *gone*—45 degrees nose down and 80 degrees of bank. I see the tracers above us and I am pulling the control column right into my belly. I start to grey out but think that it is too soon to back off, so I glance at the airspeed indicator and see 300 mph; about 70 mph faster than I *should* be. My new aircraft, which has a high gloss finish, picks up speed in a dive faster than any aircraft I have ever flown. I tell the gunners that I cannot continue to go down when I reverse the corkscrew to port, so when I get to the "rolling level" part of the manoeuvre, they are to both give that fighter a good squirt and I will then pull our aircraft into a vertical climb. We go straight up like a cork out of a champagne bottle and lose the fighter, but my rear gunner has identified him as a Ju 88, the most deadly of the night fighters, and I'm sure he will pick us up on his radar again. Now we know this guy can shoot if he fires from straight and level, and no doubt he is very experienced, but

I also know he has never run into a Halifax as speedy as this one. This time, he comes in from the port side and "away we go," but this time I don't let the speed build up too much. As I reverse roll to starboard, the gunners give him a squirt when we are in the "no deflection" position and he breaks off his firing pass. Later, he attacks again and I have to use everything I have learned, including varying my airspeed from 140 miles per hour to 320 miles per hour, which seems to confuse him. I am now beginning to tire from throwing the aircraft around, as this waltz has been going on for a long time. However, I still have one trick left that I have never yet used—a negative "G" outside turn. I have done this in small aircraft but never in a Hally. I'm not sure if the aircraft will handle it but I do have confidence in the strength of this machine. I explain to the gunners what I am about to do and tell them that when they feel crushed up against the top of their turrets, to let go with everything they have. The man attacks again and I roll 90 degrees to starboard and ask the rear gunner to call out his range, because I have to have him within 600 yards if this is going to work. Guy (rear gunner) gives me the word and I then ram the control column forward as hard as I can. All four engines then quit under the negative "G" and the only sound comes from our guns. I hold this for about two *long* seconds, then roll level and go down. The gunners fire, claim they see hits on the fighter, and maybe they *did* damage him. By now I am soaked in sweat. I tell my navigator that we are descending to 4000 feet to get out of the strong head winds, and that I will now let the aircraft cruise at 235 mph. Eight hours and forty minutes after take-off, I set her down at East Moor. This gives us 21 hours of flying time out of the last forty hours and we are very tired. The navigator tells me that the battle lasted thirteen minutes; the longest time we had ever been under continuous attack.[66]

Shifting to Daylight Operations

Two days after Andrew Mynarski's Victoria Cross-winning experience, 221 Lancasters and thirteen Mosquitos carried out Bomber Command's first significant daylight raid since May 1943. Their targets were the fast German motor torpedo boats and other light naval forces harboured at le Havre that were threatening Allied shipping in the Normandy beachhead area. Again, the Tallboys were released by twenty-two Lancasters from 617 Squadron onto the reinforced E-boat pens in the port. This trial was successful, only one Lancaster was lost, and daylight operations thenceforth became a more common occurrence; Bomber Command's "heavies" were sortied with ever-increasing frequency and strength.[67] On 27 August, daylight operations went one step further, as the Official Command Campaign Diary explains:

> 243 aircraft–216 Halifaxes of No. 4 Group and 14 Mosquitos and 13 Lancasters of No. 8 Group–were dispatched on a historic raid to Homberg, the first major raid by Bomber Command to Germany in daylight since 12 August 1941, when 54 Blenheims had attacked power stations near Cologne for the loss of 10 aircraft. This raid was escorted by 9 squadrons of Spitfires on the outward flight and 7 squadrons on the withdrawal. One Me 110 was seen; the Spitfires drove it off. There was intense flak over the target but no bombers were lost. The (specific) target was the Rheinpreussen synthetic-oil factory at Meerbeck. The bombing was based on *Oboe* marking but 5-8/10ths cloud produced difficult conditions, though some accurate bombing was claimed through gaps in the clouds.[68]

A New Menace: The Crossbow Campaign

One week after the Normandy landings, the Germans had launched their first V 1 rocket attacks on London. The British had long been aware of the Reich's missile programs, and the Peenemünde raid of August 1943, along with subsequent raids directed against the rocket industries, had set these initiatives back significantly. When the V 1 attacks commenced on 12 June, they were too late to wreak havoc on the Channel ports. Furthermore, the first of the V 2s did not successfully attack Britain until 8 September 1944. As historian John Keegan has observed:

> By then the Luftwaffe's 155 Regiment had been driven back from the positions whence its V 1s could reach England; as a result, out of the 35,000 produced, only 9000 were fired against England and of these over 4000 were destroyed by anti-aircraft fire or fighter attack. The V 2s were never fired from their chosen launch sites in northern France; from Holland they could just reach London, on which 1300 impacted, and after October an equal number were directed at Antwerp, which by then was the Allied Liberation Armies' main logistic base.
>
> The V 2s killed 2500 Londoners between 8 September 1944 and 29 March 1945, when their launch positions were finally overrun by the 21st Army Group.[69]

Although the German flying bombs had little military impact on the Allied war effort, they caused enough casualties and civilian infrastructure destruction to merit a considerable portion of Bomber Command's assets being directed against the launching sites for the ensuing three months. The German flying bomb attacks were known as Crossbow, and the countermeasures to this onslaught consumed nearly half the energies of the Command and much of those of the 2nd Tactical Air Force as well. These taskings ultimately took the lives of some 3000 Allied aircrew during Crossbow, but General Eisenhower felt these targets deserved the highest priority. Also, it was considered vital to civilian morale at this late stage of the war to be seen to be actively taking steps to counter this new and intimidating threat.[70] Chester Hull, a distinguished late war commanding officer of 428 "Ghost" Squadron, recalls the counter-Crossbow campaign:

> When the flying bombs made their first appearance on the night of June 12th, a concerted defence by the air forces, the anti-aircraft and balloon commands marked the commencement of a campaign which lasted for eighty days. It was only brought to a close when the army overran the launching sites and forced the enemy to adopt other methods of launching the "doodlebugs" . . .
>
> To combat the new weapon and, perhaps of even more importance, to reassure the civilian population, the role of Bomber Command underwent a drastic change. Twenty-two of the 33 targets attacked by the Canadians during the period had direct connection with the robot bomb. Buzz bomb launching sites offered little that was really vulnerable to other than a direct hit, and even then, their vulnerability to anything but the largest bombs was questionable. Constructed as they were of reinforced concrete, the platforms showed little-or-no effect from a very near miss. With these facts in mind, it is easily understood why the site at Biennais was the objective for attack on three separate occasions.
>
> Then, as was to be expected, robot bomb installations were the objectives for raids in the latter part of the month, and included Forêt d'Eawy and Wizernes on the 27th of June. Forêt d'Eawy and Wizernes were twin attacks that were more than moderately successful. At Forêt d'Eawy, the weather was clear with some drifting cloud and the bombers got three fair patterns around the markers, which were dropped in a triangle.
>
> The attack on Wizernes, also completed without loss, was carried out in good weather and fair visibility. The markers were scattered at first but improved as the attack progressed, and fairly accurate bombing produced some good fires.[71]

Aircraft and crews from 6 Group had been part of a force of 405 aircraft which inaugurated the response to Crossbow on the night of 16/17 June with raids on four separate flying bomb launching sites in the Pas de Calais area. "All targets were accurately marked by *Oboe* Mosquitos and accurately bombed. No aircraft lost."[72] However, this cryptic entry in the official Bomber Command diary does not satisfactorily portray the drama of the event. According to the 425 "Alouette" Squadron Official History:

> [The Squadron] entered the buzz bomb battle by setting their bombsights on a V 1 supply depot at Sautrecourt. This was the occasion for plucky performances by Flying Officer E.L. Vawter and Sergeant C.A. Matthews, bomb-aimer and flight engineer respectively of Halifax "G-George." Three minutes after bombing time, tracer bullets pierced the fuselage in several places, one striking the pilot, Flying Officer H.M. Romuld. Vawter took over the controls while Matthews tended his wounded skipper. Vawter flew above the overcast until well over the English coast, descended through a break and headed for Woodbridge emergency field. With the engineer handling the throttles, flaps and undercarriage, the bomb-aimer managed to get "George" down on his third try. The captain had died of wounds some time before, but the others sustained no injuries during the landing and "George" was serviceable for operations the next day. Vawter and Matthews were "gonged" for showing bravery, resourcefulness and determination in bringing home safely six valuable aircrew and their aircraft.[73]

Indeed, Earl LeRoy Vawter from Allan, Saskatchewan, received a well-deserved Immediate DFC for his heroic and determined efforts that June night, and Sergeant Matthews, who was British, was later also decorated through his own chain of command.[74]

Another Case for Retribution?

The campaign against Crossbow, although ultimately successful, was not without its frustrations or costs to the Allies. In the month between 13 June and 15 July, 2579 V 1s reached England, of which 1280 impacted the Greater London area, causing significant damage and casualties as well as generating a lot of civilian despondency and alarm. Contrary to popular belief, and while Churchill later wrote in a dismissive, matter-of-fact manner about this menace, in early July he asked the War Cabinet to consider forms of retaliation against the German people. He at one point specifically "asked the Chiefs of Staff to examine the pros and cons of threatening to use poison gas ('principally mustard,' though only in a case of 'life or death,' or if it were certain to shorten the war by a year)."[75] Eisenhower later commented on this suggestion: "Let's, for God's sake, keep our eyes on the ball and use some sense."[76] Furthermore, War Cabinet correspondence on the subject from early July belies the *sang-froid* later exhibited by the Prime Minister in print. What follows are excerpts from a War Cabinet Minute dealing with the flying bombs, dated 3 July 1944, and an extensive follow-up note penned by the Air Staff shortly thereafter:

Extract from: W.M.(44) 85th CONCLUSIONS. MINUTE 4.
(3rd July, 1944–5.30 P.M.)

> (e) Counter-Measures. THE PRIME MINISTER suggested that it was necessary to consider whether counter measures should be used against Germany in view of the deliberate use of this weapon of an indiscriminate character.
>
> It was for consideration whether we should not publish a list of, say, 100 of the smaller

towns in Germany, where the defences are likely to be weak, and announce our intention of destroying them one by one by bombing attacks. It would, of course, be necessary to take account of the extent to which a policy of this kind would divert our air power from the support of our Allies in France and from targets, such as oil installations, factories, depots, flying bomb sites, attacks on which directly crippled the enemy's general war effort or his power to launch flying bomb attacks. There would also have to be some consultation with the U.S. and Soviet Governments before such a policy was adopted.

THE SECRETARY OF STATE FOR AIR pointed out that already 50 percent of our air strength was being used to counter the flying bomb attacks and that it would be extremely difficult to spare additional resources from the Battle of France. Again, the threats made by the enemy in connection with our attacks on Berlin showed that there was a grave risk that attacks of the kind indicated by the Prime Minister would lead to reprisals in the form of the shooting of any air crews who fell into German hands.

There was general agreement that the question raised by the Prime Minister should be considered.

The War Cabinet –

––––––––––––––

(11) Invited the Foreign Secretary and the Chiefs of Staff to consider and report on possible counter measures against Germany, in respect of the deliberate use of an indiscriminate form of attack.[77]

The response is a detailed note from the Air Staff, and its conclusions were eventually echoed back up the chain of command to the Prime Minister.

CROSSBOW—QUESTION OF RETALIATION

(Note by the Air Staff)

================

3. It is unlikely that any reaction on German policy could be observed before successful attacks had been made on 4 or 5 towns; it is possible that the success or failure of the policy of reprisals could not be assessed conclusively until perhaps 20 towns had been attacked.
4. If it were decided to make such attacks, it would be essential to make a public announcement that we were initiating a policy of reprisals, and to give full publicity to it in our propaganda to the German people.

Military Effort Involved:

For 20 towns the total required would be 12,000 tons to be delivered on the target. On the basis of past experience this would require either 4,500 R.A.F. heavy bomber sorties or 7,200 U.S. heavy bomber sorties, or some proportionate combination. This would amount to about 25 percent of one month's effort of the combined heavy bomber forces.

Results Likely to be Achieved:

8. The object of these attacks would be to influence the policy of the German High Command by their effect on the morale of the people and of the German armed forces . . . (Since the attacks would only directly affect about .5 percent of the German population), the immediate effects would, therefore, not be great, although news of their plight must

eventually circulate and there would be a long-term tendency to increase the anxiety of the inhabitants of all small communities in Germany and of their relatives at the Front. It is relevant to recall that the German "Baedeker" Raids on comparable raids in this country, which were clearly designated by the enemy as reprisals, had no influence whatever on our offensive policy at the time.

9. The effect of such attacks might be to increase rather than diminish German belief in the efficacy of *Crossbow*, in that they would amount to an admission on our part that we were suffering grave injury, and that we felt ourselves unable to combat the weapon by any other means. It is clear that one of the enemy's objects in the use of the weapon is to divert our efforts in this way from objectives directly relevant to the immediate prosecution of the war.

10. The conclusions to which these arguments point are:-

(a) There is no evidence that a policy of reprisals would produce the desired effects;

(b) It is, an any case, unlikely that such a policy would bear fruit in less than perhaps two months after its initiation;

(c) Its effect might well be to encourage rather than discourage German use of *Crossbow*;

(d) Once the policy was adopted, it would be difficult to withdraw from it should it prove unsuccessful.

Diversion of Effort Involved:

. . . reprisal attacks of the type contemplated would not be practicable, either for British or American bombers, except in conditions of good weather over Germany. Such opportunities are comparatively infrequent and our present policy is that advantage should be taken of every occasion which offers in order to attack targets of primary importance such as synthetic oil plants and refineries, aircraft factories and other objectives in Germany. These have been chosen on the ground that their destruction is likely to have the most immediate and decisive effects on the whole German effort. The weather provides so few opportunities for attacks on these primary targets that if we use them for reprisal attacks our bombing offensive against Germany will be seriously dislocated and its effects may be delayed for a considerable period.

General Considerations.

(a) The initiation of a policy of reprisals is in effect a proposal to the Germans that we will NOT bomb the threatened towns if the Germans abandon the use of the flying bomb. This is tantamount to opening negotiations with the enemy on the whole question of bombing policy—an admission of weakness which we did not make when our strategic situation as regards air attack was much less satisfactory than it is at present.

(b) The initiation of reprisals if it is not successful in turning the Germans from the use of the flying bomb, will almost certainly lead to a threat of counter-reprisals on their part. They are in a position to maintain with some reason that these long-range attacks on London, which is a military objective of importance, are not more indiscriminate or inhuman than our blind bombing attacks on area targets of military importance, such as Berlin. They will, therefore, be in a position to maintain that reprisals on our part are, in fact, the initiation of a new and more inhuman form of air warfare for which they can reasonably retaliate. The natural line of reprisal would be the murder of aircrews captured in the course of these operations, either by mock trial or by inciting the civilian population to take the law into its own hands.

The Germans are in a stronger position than ourselves if a policy of reprisals is initiated, as they are not limited by moral scruples or by public opinion. There is, therefore, little doubt that we should in the end be compelled to give way under pressure of this kind.

(c) *We have hitherto always maintained consistently in all public statements regarding our bombing policy that it is directed against military objectives and that any damage to civilians is incidental to our attack on the German war machine. This is a moral and legal point of great importance, both now and in the maintenance of our position after the war, and it would be greatly weakened should we now for the first time declare that we intended deliberate attacks on the civilian population as such.* [my italics]

<u>Conclusions.</u> 13. We are led by these considerations to recommend that a policy of reprisals should not be adopted.[78]

Inspirational Leadership Abounds

Throughout the summer of 1944, during this period of intense campaigning, inspirational leadership in the face of adversity would be displayed time after time, and it would come from the highest levels, as Chester Hull explains:

[After the highly-successful attack upon the Wizernes robot bomb installation on the 27th of June] . . . Air Commodore Ross, one of the 6 Group base commanders, was in the control tower at Tholthorpe watching his aircraft return from Forêt d'Eawy. When all but four had landed, he started for the post-op interrogations. Just as he was about to enter the debriefing room, there was a great yellow flash on the airfield. Running to the scene, Ross found that 425 Squadron's "A-Able," returning from the operation on three engines, had crashed into "U-Uncle," which was bombed up. By the time he arrived, both aircraft were burning fiercely with petrol tanks and bombs in imminent danger of exploding.

Ross immediately took charge, assisted by Flight Sergeant St. Germain, the bomb-aimer of "C-Charlie," which had just landed. Corporal Marquet, who was in charge of the night ground crew, and Leading Air Craftsmen McKenzie and Wolfe of the station crash tender. Ross and Marquet had just extricated the pilot when ten 500 pound bombs exploded and the rescuers were hurled to the ground. As the flying debris settled, a cry was heard from the rear turret of "A-Able" and the rescuers then turned their attention to the rear gunner, Sergeant Rochon. Undeterred by the flames which were rapidly approaching the tail, the air commodore, now assisted by St. Germain, McKenzie and Wolfe, hacked away at the perspex until a hole was made sufficiently large to pass an axe to Rochon. However, a hole large enough to allow Rochon to escape could not be made from the inside, and finally, St. Germain and Marquet had to break the steel supports of the turret to extricate the gunner.

Just then, another bomb explosion again threw the rescuers to the ground and St. Germain, rising quickly, hurled himself on one of the victims to protect him from flying debris. This blast caught the air commodore in the right arm between the wrist and the elbow, and virtually cut off his hand. Turning the further rescues over to his assistants, Ross walked calmly to the ambulance and was taken to the station sick quarters, where an emergency operation was performed and his right hand was amputated. As a result of this prompt action, the entire crew of "A-Able" was saved. I landed just ahead of "A-Able," and had heard the pilot notify the tower that he was on three engines. The first bomb exploded as I was turning off the runway. In addition to the other explosions mentioned above, ammunition was also "cooking off," so it was a bit of a wild scene as we taxied to our dispersal. We were not aware of the drama that was taking place behind us until after our debriefing.[79]

Air Commodore Ross was subsequently awarded a rare and prestigious George Cross, the citation for which noted that he "showed fine leadership and great heroism in an action which resulted in the saving of the lives of the pilot and the rear gunner."[80] Meanwhile Flight Sergeant J.R.M. St. Germain and Corporal M. Marquet both displayed courage of a high order, and Leading Air Craftsmen M.M. McKenzie and R.R. Wolfe both rendered very valuable assistance in circumstances of great danger. As a result of these actions the George Medal was awarded to St. Germain and Marquet, and the British Empire Medal to McKenzie and Wolfe. Furthermore, "before the year was out, St. Germain would move his GM ribbon to make room for that of a DFC."[81]

Arthur Dwight Ross, like "Black Mike" McEwen, had a reputation for leading by shining example, fearlessly and consistently from the front. Prior to winning his George Cross, he had been awarded a Mention-in-Despatches and a Gallantry category appointment as Officer of the Order of the British Empire for completing 72 sorties (385 operational hours) of war flying. Most of this operational flying had occurred in Canada as commander of an anti-submarine and convoy escort squadron. However, as a group captain in command of Middleton St. George, the OBE citation noted that "By his participation in sorties against Lorient, Hamburg and St. Nazaire, he has set a splendid example to all ranks."[82] He was also out of hospital and making motivational public appearances at Linton by early July, just two weeks after the amputation. Air Commodore Ross was subsequently elevated to the grade of Commander of the Order of the British Empire, in honour of his dynamic, selfless and courageous leadership, including service as commandant of the Royal Canadian Air Force Staff College in 1945.[83]

Helping With the Normandy Break-out: A Bitter Cost

Along with Crossbow operations during the summer of 1944, Bomber Command continued to be frequently tasked in support of the Allied land armies, whose advance had stagnated in Normandy. A month after the D-Day landings, a serious air assault was conducted on Caen to help break the land impasse. Chester Hull recalls:

> There were three direct attacks against German strong points, tanks, guns and armoured units holding up the (British) Second Army at Caen, which were outstandingly successful. By daylight on the 7th (of July), under perfect fighter cover, a large force gave an excellent demonstration of concentrated bombing on Bomber Command's first daylight operation in support of the ground troops. The bombing was directed by the Master Bomber who shifted the attack from time to time to give the effect of a creeping barrage. In appreciation of the air force's efforts, the Second Army sent the following signal: "Heavy bomber attack just taken place. A wonderfully impressive show and enormously appreciated by the Army."
>
> At dawn in the 18th, the air forces again came to the aid of the stalemated Army and devastated the Caen area with over 1000 "Heavies." As the van of the bombers arrived, many of the earliest were able to pinpoint their objectives, but five minutes after the first stick was dropped, the whole town lay under a thick bank of smoke and the Master Bomber took control. As in the earlier attack, the RCAF lost four crews. One of the kites missing was from the Leaside (432) Squadron, skippered by Flight Lieutenant J.H. Cooper, a veteran of 31 raids. Cooper and two other members of his crew were taken prisoner.

For the third time, a large force attacked the Caen area on the 30th (of July) when three of the well-chosen aiming points were well plastered. The Master Bomber directed his aircraft to go below the clouds and drop their bombs and, though some apparently did not hear his instructions, the majority of the RCAF crews came down before dropping their bombs. Aided by flares sent up by our own ground troops and the continued counselling of the Master Bomber, a very successful attack built up and the photographic aircraft brought back evidence of a severely pock-marked target. Fighter cover kept the Jerries at a respectful distance.[84]

Most, although not all, of the aerial bombing provided to the land forces that summer in Normandy was successful, although the land forces had great difficulty in advancing their vehicles through the extensive rubble fields created by the bombers in Caen. Still, inter-service cooperation was quite successful until mid-August—when fratricide entered the picture, as Sid Philp recalls:

On August 14 1944, Bomber Command was ordered to attack German troop positions facing the 3rd Canadian Division, which was advancing on Falaise. The initial bombing was accurate and effective but, half-way through the raid, a breakdown in communications led to grim results; the ground forces set off yellow identification flares—a colour that the Pathfinders were using to mark the target. Thereupon, about seventy aircraft (many of them Canadian) out of a total force of 805 planes started to bomb a large quarry in which a part of the Canadian Field Regiment was positioned. The Regiment took cover and most of the men went unscathed, but thirteen were killed and 53 injured. A large number of vehicles and guns were also destroyed.[85]

The Official Bomber Command Diary elaborates on this unfortunate event:

805 aircraft—411 Lancasters, 352 Halifaxes, 42 Mosquitos—to attack 7 German troop positions facing the 3rd Canadian Division, which was advancing on Falaise. Two Lancasters lost. A careful plan was prepared with Oboe and visual marking, and with a Master Bomber and a deputy at each of the 7 targets. Most of the bombing was accurate and effective but, about half-way through the raids, some aircraft started to bomb a large quarry in which parts of the 12th Canadian Field Regiment was positioned.

. . . Bomber Command crews claimed that the Canadians used the yellow flares before any bombs fell in the quarry; the history of the Canadian unit says the bombs fell first. The Master Bombers tried hard to stop further crews bombing in the wrong area but approximately 70 aircraft bombed the quarry and other nearby Allied positions over a 70-minute period . . . This is believed to have been the first occasion on which Bomber Command aircraft had hit friendly troops during the Battle of Normandy. The Canadian Artillery regiment was (also) machine-gunned by RAF Spitfires and USAAF Mustangs the following day!

Details of the Canadian side of the bombing come from *Into Action with the 12th Field* by Captain T.J. Bell (published privately in Canada) and from the personal reminiscences of former Lance-Corporal George R. Carter of the 12th Canadian Field Regiment.[86]

Flying Officer William Henry Johnston, a navigator and DFC winner from Ottawa, flew on this operation with 434 Squadron and has vivid recollections of what transpired in the target area.

Monday, 14 August 1944. This was to be my sixth out of seven raids with [him] as pilot. The attack was on the Normandy battle area in support of the 3rd Canadian Division, which was advancing on Falaise. The flight plan called for the bomb-aimer to identify the coast as the starting point and the navigator, using a stopwatch, to do a timed run on a fixed heading before bomb release. As we approached the target area at 1500 hours, the pilot said that aircraft around us had their bomb doors open and were dropping bombs and that he was going to turn around for another run. The bomb-aimer and I told him not to do this, that we hadn't completed the timed run. The bomb-aimer said he wouldn't drop the bombs until I said so. There followed a great argument and then the pilot decided to follow instructions.

. . . On return to base, interrogation was intense. We had a picture of the target and we escaped punishment, which consisted of substantial reductions in rank. That evening, [he] apologized to me for ever having questioned my competence. The crew, except for me, was screened (completed their tour) the next day after their raid on Soesterberg, a night fighter airfield in Holland.[87]

Ian Willoughby Bazalgette: The Other VC

Just prior to the Caen mishap, a Canadian airman won the nation's second air Victoria Cross of the war, although the Canadian linkage is somewhat tenuous. Squadron Leader Ian Willoughby Bazalgette was born in Calgary in 1918 of British parents, and went to school in Toronto. However, the family returned to England in 1927, settling in Surrey. Bazalgette initially joined the army in 1940, serving in the 51st (Anti-Aircraft) Regiment, but transferred to the Royal Air Force Volunteer Reserve (RAFVR) in 1941. After pilot training, he flew an exceptional first tour of bomber operations with 115 Squadron and was awarded a DFC in July 1943 for his combat accomplishments. An OTU instructional tour followed and he then joined 635 Squadron, a Pathfinder outfit based at Downham Market, for his second tour of operations. The mission on 4 August 1944 was a daylight raid conducted with a relatively small force against a V 1 site at Trossy St. Maxim. Contrary to the narrative of his subsequent VC, Bazalgette was not acting as the Master Bomber or even as the Deputy Master Bomber on the operation in question (although he had successfully performed these roles on earlier raids).[88] The Master Bomber was in fact employed at another major effort on a site in the Bois de Cassan and the Deputy Master Bomber had been lost in heavy anti-aircraft fire encountered during his marking run at Trossy. Success at Trossy was therefore contingent on the highly experienced Bazalgette "stepping into the breech," demonstrating initiative and assuming the marking duties. The Victoria Cross citation describes what happened next.

When nearing the target his Lancaster came under heavy anti-aircraft fire. Both starboard engines were put out of action and serious fires broke out in the fuselage and the starboard mainplane. The bomb-aimer was badly wounded. As the Deputy Master Bomber had already been shot down the success of the attack depended upon Squadron Leader Bazalgette, and this he knew. Despite the appalling conditions in his burning Lancaster he pressed on gallantly to the target, marking and bombing it accurately. That the attack was successful was due to his magnificent effort. After the bombs had been dropped the Lancaster dived practically out of control. By expert airmanship and great exertion Squadron Leader Bazalgette regained control, but the port inner engine then failed, and the whole of the starboard mainplane became a mass of flames. Squadron Leader Bazalgette fought bravely to bring his aircraft and crew to safety. The mid-upper gunner was overcome by fumes. Squadron Leader Bazalgette ordered those of his crew who were able to leave by parachute to do so. He remained at the controls and attempted the almost hopeless task of landing the crippled and blazing aircraft in a last effort to save the wounded bomb-aimer and helpless air gunner. With superb skill and taking great care to avoid a small French village nearby, he brought the aircraft down safely. Unfortunately it then exploded and this gallant officer and his two comrades perished. His heroic sacrifice marked the climax of a long career of operations against the enemy. He always chose the more dangerous and exacting roles. His courage and devotion to duty were beyond praise.[89]

Ian Willoughby Bazalgette and his two comrades were buried at Senantes, the village that he had spared no gallant effort to successfully avoid during his crash landing.

Many Bomber Command pilots struggled for control of their aircraft to give their fellow crew members a fighting chance to escape once the aircraft was doomed. However, as a measure of this event's uniqueness, historian Hugh Halliday believes that Bazalgette's "final valorous act was the culmination of a night of bravery—he had pressed on to the target after his Lancaster had been badly damaged, then accurately marked the target."[90]

Driving Hard Against the Axis

As the hot Norman summer dragged on, targets other than those in support of the land armies and the counter-Crossbow operations commanded the attention of Sir Arthur Harris and his planners. On the night of 25/26 August, a force of 412 Lancasters from 1, 3, 6 and 8 Groups attacked the Opel factory at Rüsselsheim in Germany. As it materialized, the Pathfinder marking was accurate and an official German report noted that the forge and gearbox assembly departments were immobilized for several weeks, although many other departments escaped significant damage. Fifteen Lancasters were lost on the raid, which constituted 3.6 percent of the attacking force.[91] Yet another Canadian airman distinguished himself on this raid in a summer punctuated by acts of uncommon valour by Canadian aircrew members of Bomber Command. Robert Burton Maxwell from Toronto, a Lancaster X pilot with 428 Squadron, won a rare Conspicuous Gallantry Medal that night.

> In August 1944 Flight Sergeant Maxwell was detailed to attack a target in Germany. When nearing the objective, his aircraft was struck by anti-aircraft fire, disabling an engine and damaging the electrical system. Despite loss of height and a wound in the leg, this airman pressed on to the target where the bombs had to be released manually. Flight Sergeant Maxwell then flew his aircraft back to England and effected a safe landing. His coolness, courage and determination to achieve success have been of a high order.[92]

Often, some of the better crews serving with the line bomber squadrons were syphoned off midway through their tours of operations for service with the elite Pathfinder Force. Bob Maxwell was of that number and, eventually commissioned and flying with 405 Squadron, he continued to excel, as noted in the subsequent award of a Distinguished Flying Cross:

> Since the award of the Conspicuous Gallantry Medal this officer has flown on a large number of operational sorties. He has taken part in attacks against heavily defended targets such as Kiel, Chemnitz, Merseburg and Berlin. Flying Officer Maxwell is an outstanding leader who has invariably displayed courage and devotion to duty of a high order.[93]

Throughout the summer and autumn of 1944, the war situation continued to evolve dramatically in favour of the Allies on all fronts. By September, when two elderly ladies were murdering lonely gentlemen callers in the Frank Capra film "Arsenic and Old Lace," and the first major

A 426 Squadron Halifax III on its hardstand at Linton. Note the Nissen hut in the foreground.
(DND PL-43473)

This particular Halifax
needs a lot of work.
(DND PL 42796).

Major Martin Drewes in front of his Messerschmitt Bf 110. (Author's Collection)

Opposite top: By 1944, the majority of Germany's major industrial centres were decidedly worse for wear. (DND PL52655)

Opposite bottom: This 431 'Iroquois" Squadron Halifax III is attacking a V-1 launch site in the French countryside close to a town, 25 June 1944. The scattered bomb craters speak to the efforts of earlier raids. (DND PL30780)

Heinkel's excellent He 219 night fighter. Another case of too little, too late. (Author's Collection)

In March, 419 "Moose" Squadron, flying out of Middleton St. George, became the first to equip with Lancaster Mk.Xs. Note the enlarged bomb-bay doors, designed to accommodate an 8000-pound bomb. Frontal guns had not yet been fitted. The aircraft in the foreground, KB711, the first Lancaster X lost on operations, went down on the night of 1-2 May 1944 during a raid on the railway yards at St. Ghislain in France. (DND PL29474)

Warrant Officer Bill Wade, the rear gunner, and Sergeant Doug Skingle, mid-upper gunner, exit this 408 Squadron Lancaster after completing their seventh operation, the day after D-Day. (DND PL29742)

Canadian gunners Pilot Officer DG Harkness and Pilot Officer MR Burnett, who both received DFMs and subsequent commissions for their gallant airmanship in August. (DND PL32309)

Flight Sergeant Peter Engbrecht (left), with an American colleague, was an outstanding Canadian gunner. (DND PL32774)

Peter Engbrecht receives his Conspicuous Gallantry Medal from King George VI at Leeming, 11 August 1944. (DND PL32404)

The exceptionally gallant Pilot Officer Andrew Charles Mynarski, VC.(DND PL38261)

The 12,000-pound Tallboy bomb, first used operationally by 617 "Dambuster" Squadron in Normandy on the night of 8/9 June 1944. (Author's Collection)

Sergeant Ormond Frank Brown (centre), a gunner with 433 "Porcupine" Squadron, who received a DFM for his bravery and tenacity when his Halifax III was hit hard by predicted flak while on a Crossbow operation in the Pas de Calais area, 4 August 1944. (DND PL 33108)

Detailed shot of a Halifax III dorsal turret. Note the open crew hatch in the foreground. (DND PL31715)

Two highly successful airfield raids.
Top: The results of a day attack on
the German night fighter base at
Deelen, Holland, on 15 August 1944.
(DND PL144254)

Bottom: Even more spectacular
results against the *Luftwaffe* base at
Volkel, Holland, 3 September 1944.
(DND PL32218)

Framed by the bomb dump, a Halifax III at rest. (DND PL42872)

La Presse Express, a 425 Squadron Halifax III. For each completed operation, a bomb symbol has been added to the flatcars behind the locomotive. (DND 30736)

Tail art was popular, as well as nose art. This appears to be a character drawn from the popular *Dogpatch* comic strip. It adorned a Halifax Mk. VII, which completed fifty-eight operations in service with both 420 and 426 Squadrons. (DND PL40133)

A number of 415 "Swordfish" Squadron members pose in front of a well-known veteran 432 "Leaside" Squadron Halifax VII, *Willie the Wolf*. Kneeling, fourth from the left, front row, is the extremely popular commanding officer of 415 Squadron, Wing Commander JHL "Joe" Lecompte. The nose art survived and is now on display at the new Canadian War Museum in Ottawa. (DND PL32876)

Wing Commander Wilbur P. Pleasance, DFC and Bar, inspects a Lancaster bomb-bay full of 1000-pound HE bombs during his tenure as CO of 419 "Moose" Squadron. The H2S dome can be seen in the background. (DND PL29078)

Opposite top: Looking somewhat weatherbeaten, 428 "Ghost" Squadron skipper Wing Commander Chester Hull's *Madam X*, with its likeness of Miss Lace from the Milton Caniff comic strip, *Male Call*. (DND PMR–71–551)

Opposite bottom: His Eminence Cardinal Villeneuve chats with ground crew from 425 "Alouette" Squadron during his overseas tour in October 1944. Note the tally board on the aircraft's fuselage indicates a preponderance of day operations over night operations at this late point in the European war. (DND PL33476)

Oscar from 424 "Tiger" Squadron, with its famous *Popeye* cartoon and its impressive operations tally, taxis for takeoff at Skipton-on-Swale, 13 November 1944. It eventually completed sixty-two operations before ending up in a British scrap yard during October 1946. (DND PL41055)

Another veteran Canadian Halifax with the proud crew that kept it flying and building up an impressive string of operations. (DND PL 42491)

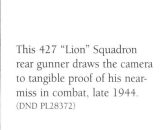

This 427 "Lion" Squadron rear gunner draws the camera to tangible proof of his near-miss in combat, late 1944. (DND PL28372)

television show, "The Gillette Cavalcade of Sports," was premiering on American television, the Allies had captured Rome and most of central Italy. On the Eastern Front, Soviet forces had steamrollered forward to the Vistula River in central Poland. Late in the month, however, General Montgomery's attempt to take Arnhem through the innovative but flawed Operation Market Garden had failed miserably, guaranteeing another winter for the European war and a lot of work for Bomber Command in the months to come.

The Oil Campaign

While the Transportation Plan, once adopted, was waged with at least polite compliance, loyalty and even some enthusiasm by Sir Arthur Harris from April until September 1944, the counter-oil campaign fared differently. By late September, once the land campaign had stagnated in northwest Europe and the strategic bomber forces had been returned to the fold of the Combined Chiefs of Staff of Bomber Command through the Air Staff and Sir Charles Portal, Harris sensed that an unrestricted return to his general area bombing campaign of the German industrial cities was in the wind. Accordingly, he had his staff prepare an updated list of sixty such targets, and he firmly believed that he could destroy the equivalent of two-and-a-half of these targets each month.[94] However, an Air Staff Directive of 25 September stated Bomber Command's new targeting priorities as follows:

> *First Priority*
> (i) Petroleum industry, with special emphasis on petrol (gasoline) including storage.
>
> *Second Priority*
> (i) The German rail and waterborne transportation systems.
> (ii) Tank production plants and depots, ordnance depots.
> (iii) Motorized Transport (MT) production plants and depots.[95]

For the immediate future, counter-air action had been assigned no particular priority, and the generalized city offensive was only to be undertaken when conditions were unfavourable to the new priorities. Obviously, the new priorities suited General Carl Spaatz, now the commander of the U.S. Strategic Air Forces in Europe. Oil had now been placed squarely in the highest position as the Air Staff, by the autumn of 1944, had warmed to the American point of view. Equipment, conditions and weapons were quite different from what had existed in 1941, and oil was now considered to be a " fundamental and potentially war-winning target system."[96] Furthermore, Sir Arthur Tedder told Portal the following month that the Oil Plan was not only sound, but it constituted a decisive threat to the German communications capability in the air and on land by breaking the enemy's control and power behind his lines. Additionally, Tedder believed that the plan should be broadened by synergistic linkage to attacks upon all the enemy's means of conveyance, "to attack *all* communications, railways, rivers and canals as well, thus strangling industry, governmental control, life itself. Concentrated on such an area as the Ruhr, and linked to a powerful ground offensive, Tedder was convinced that this would be decisive."[97] Portal, his staff and Tedder were in accord in this thinking, and it was once again Arthur Harris who was out of synchronization. To Harris, oil remained the hated "panacea" he had perceived it to be from the outset, in spite of the Soviet capture of Ploesti and the other Rumanian oil fields in August. According to Harris's biographer, Air Commodore Henry Probert:

He was still deeply suspicious of the prognostications of the Ministry of Economic Warfare; synthetic oil production was spread over many plants, often small, in different parts of Germany, and up-to-date intelligence about them was hard to obtain; the Germans under Speer were adept at dispersal and repair; and effective attack required a degree of accuracy which he was far from convinced his aircraft could achieve, especially against more distant targets.[98]

Spaatz and the Eighth Air Force, along with the Mediterranean Air Forces operating out of Italy, had already started to engage various oil targets in the run-up period to Operation Overlord. Rising to this cue, Air Vice-Marshal Bottomley, Portal's deputy, had asked Harris on 3 June 1944 to consider engaging ten synthetic oil plants in the Ruhr industrialized area as soon as practicable after the Normandy landings. However, an overall 11 percent loss rate of the 832 bombers despatched during three separate operations in June, which included a soul-destroying 27.8 percent loss rate on 21 June, a raid for which 6 Group was not called upon, had done nothing to convince "Bomber" Harris that these were either sensible or appropriate targets.

The first Bomber Command raid of the June trial series was an attack on the synthetic oil plant at Sterkrade/Holten on the northwestern outskirts of Essen by 321 aircraft—162 Halifaxes, 147 Lancasters and 12 Mosquitos of Numbers 1, 4, 6 and 8 Groups. It resulted in the loss of thirty-one of the attackers, including twenty-two of the Halifaxes, or 13.6 percent of those participating. The procedures and tactics employed on this operation reflected the tactical and technological sophistication now inherent within Bomber Command. Since thick cloud obscured the target, the marking was done by PFF Mosquitos using *Oboe*. A wide range of complicated electronic countermeasures was also being employed, including the first use of two new systems, *Mandrel Screen*, "in which *Mandrel*-fitted aircraft orbit positions 80 miles from the enemy coast to jam the early warning system, and *Fidget*, a ground jammer directed at those night fighter beacons used to transmit information to fighters."[99] However, not all the radio frequencies were successfully jammed this night, and since it would still be nearly a month until an intact Ju 88 was acquired by the Allies, complete with its *Naxos* and *Flensburg* electronic homing aids, *H2S*, *Mandrel*, *Piperack* and the tail-warning *Monica* radar were still being transmitted both enthusiastically and generously by some crews over enemy territory, in spite of Command warnings to exercise restraint. Their telltale electronic signatures made the defenders" task that much easier. *Window* was also deployed throughout the stream, but it did not totally frustrate the *Luftwaffe's* controllers this night. And while *Serrate*-equipped Mosquitos prowled in and around the bomber stream hunting German night fighters, "unfortunately, the route of the bomber stream passed near a German night fighter beacon at Bocholt, only 30 miles from Sterkrade. The German controller had chosen this beacon (code-named *Kürfurst*) as the holding point for his night fighters."[100] Two-thirds of the night's losses were later attributed to night fighters, although flak was also particularly intense and accurate in the target area, accounting for ten of the bombers. Number 6 Group dispatched 104 aircraft on this raid. Of these, four ground aborted for various reasons, six returned to base after getting airborne, eighty-two attacked the primary target, and twelve went missing: four each from 431 and 434 Squadrons, two from 429 Squadron and one each from 432 and 426 Squadrons.[101] Alan Sonderstrom, the nephew of one of the Canadian participants in this raid who did not return, poignantly narrates the last minutes of 434 Squadron's Halifax III, LK 801, coded WL-D. He told the story in such a gripping manner in a 2003 issue of *Airforce* magazine that it is recounted here in considerable depth.

At 0136 hours, rear gunner Cliff Wentworth detects an aircraft coming up from behind and immediately calls for Mike Laffin (pilot) to perform an evasive corkscrew manoeuver. LK 801 goes into a diving turn and the rattle of Browning machine guns can be heard throughout the Halifax. Seconds later the rear gunner speaks up: "Resume course," adding, "He sure is b——ing off in a hurry!", much to the relief of the crew. Laffin climbs the aircraft back up to an altitude of 16,000 feet, and Wentworth comments that it may have just been another Halifax.

At 0140 hours, the rear gunner detects two Ju 88s rapidly approaching from the rear. Through his intercom Cliff Wentworth instructs the pilot to perform another corkscrew. Both gunners are firing their weapons, damaging one fighter. Wentworth observes it falling to earth in flames. Another "bogey" approaches and LK 801 responds with a diving turn, but not quick enough. As the second fighter scores direct hits on the starboard wing as it roars by, the crew hears the thumping of striking bullets on the Halifax. The fighter is momentarily not a threat due to the corkscrew manoeuver, however, Clarence Sonderstrom [the mid-upper gunner] reports through his intercom that the starboard outer engine is on fire. Mike Laffin pushed the aircraft into a dive in hope of snuffing out the fire, then pulls up fast, but the engine continues to flame. Mike feathers the propellers and shuts down the burning engine; activating the Graviner switches to extinguish the fire is difficult. Mike Laffin then begins to transfer fuel from the right wing tank to the left to avoid an explosion. Clarence Sonderstrom announces that "the inner starboard engine is now on fire." Through his intercom, Mike Laffin inquires about injuries. Everyone reports back okay. Relieved, he orders the crew to bail out. No training resembles the situation the crew is in now; they are terrified, near panic, and prepare to bail out.

There are four avenues of escape in the Halifax, including a small hatch above the pilot's head. A second narrow escape hatch, a trap door, will lift out in the front lower section between the flight engineer's/navigator's area and the aircraft's nose. The third exit is the main door located behind the left wing underside. The bomb-aimer, navigator and wireless operator make sure all escape hatches are open on their levels. The rear gunner has the fourth exit, which is optional. He can climb out of his turret, strap on his parachute, re-enter the turret, rotate it 180 degrees, then fall clear of the aircraft. (Jim) Martin (navigator) is preparing to jump when someone suggests pressing on a little further. The pilot tells everyone to wait. Seconds pass. Clarence Sonderstrom reports from the upper turret, "The fire is getting worse. It's now engulfing the wing." Fearing a gasoline explosion and losing altitude, Laffin gives the final order to bail out. Searchlights occasionally illuminate the aircraft, but the breaking cloud is still preventing the anti-aircraft cannons from firing accurately. When the bail-out order is given, Martin jumps first, followed by (George) Chapman (the bomb-aimer). (Ken) Donaldson (the wireless operator/air gunner) has also jumped. Cliff Wentworth climbs out of his turret and heads for the main entrance.

Jack Druett (flight engineer) moves from his area, which is a level below the pilot, to the main hatch. Clarence Sonderstrom climbs down from the mid-upper turret and makes his way toward the main door. Jim Martin jumps at a considerably higher altitude than the rest of his crew. Looking up he sees his parachute has opened, but does not recall pulling his ripcord. Hearing the sound of other bombers above him, he fears that his parachute may snag an aircraft, or worse, get hit by a propeller, but he soon realizes the bomber stream is well above him. He cannot see the ground and is trying to figure out how far he has drifted with the wind.

Jack Druett jumps, followed by Cliff Wentworth. Mike Laffin hears Clarence telling him that everyone is out. Observing a night fighter approaching, he yells at Clarence,

"What are you waiting for? Get the hell out!" The Ju 88 lets loose a stream of bullets which rip through the Halifax, smashing the control column and injuring two of Mike's fingers. In the past fear-inspiring minutes, the escape hatch above his head has not been opened, LK 801's altitude has dropped well below 5000 feet, and he is sitting on his parachute. Through his intercom, Mike tries to make sure everyone is out. As there is no answer, he assumes he is the only one left. Making a crash landing crosses his mind but fate intervenes.

The right wing badly burned, the control column inoperable, the aircraft shaking, it rolls abruptly to the right, knocking Laffin off his seat. He falls to the main deck and struggles with his parachute. Suddenly, the nose of the aircraft dips and he rolls out the open [forward] escape hatch and deploys his parachute. Upon landing on the edge of a farmer's field, he also does not recall pulling his ripcord. He is feeling roughed up, knee aching, boots lost. He then hides his parachute and sets out walking west, hoping to avoid capture. LK 801 has crashed nearby on the southern outskirts of Ruurlo in Holland. Meanwhile, Jim Martin is descending, rubbing his numb, bare foot after losing a boot and a sock. Speculating where he is, he lands moments later in a wheat field and experiences a sharp pain in his ankle. The feeling has returned to his foot. Feeling safe for a moment, he cuts strips from his parachute and wraps his ankle. He will evade capture 'till the following evening. During interrogation, German troops then inform Jim that an airman had died in the crash.

Cliff Wentworth lands in a farmer's field and in attempting to hide his parachute, he tunnels into a haystack *and finds a hut hidden inside.* He sleeps there until the next evening. That night, a farmer and two other locals arrive, taking him to Jack Druett, who had also made it down successfully. Later, the pair met up with one more airman, a Flying Officer Kay. All will evade capture.

Upon hitting the ground, George Chapman sees LK 801 crash in flames. He is soon taken prisoner. A few days later, Mike Laffin is turned in by Nazi sympathizers. German officers stage a mock trial and convict him of murder. He is slated for execution but his sentence is later reduced and he is sent to a POW camp.

Clarence Sonderstrom is unable to escape the burning bomber. When the aircraft rolls to the right, the escape hatch on the left side is now facing up and the "G" forces prevent him from moving. German soldiers find his remains in the forward part of the wrecked aircraft. He is the only RCAF airman buried in the Ruurlo General Cemetery in the Netherlands.[102]

After the exploratory June oil raids, a second round of attacks the following month was less costly, and by August, the Air Ministry had largely been convinced that oil was a legitimate Number One priority.[103] However, Arthur Harris remained equally convinced, now that the immediate requirement for direct support of the land forces and the urgency of the counters to *Crossbow* had abated, that full-scale resumption of the area bombing offensive against Germany should be implemented. Again, he penned his opinions to his influential friend at Chequers, Winston Spencer Churchill. Harris responded on 30 September 1944 to a prime ministerial query about Germany's current prospects, which he based on his rare perusal of an intercepted *Ultra* signal. Harris felt certain that:

"the Boche would fight his damndest when driven back to his own frontiers" and noted the report's emphasis on the importance the Germans were attaching to retrieving the air supremacy which they had lacked in Normandy. They had recently been given considerable breathers from the bombing and full advantage must now be taken of the vast Allied air superiority to "knock Germany finally flat" and thus prepare the way for the armies in their "final and perhaps prolonged and desperate battles." Churchill responded immediately: "I agree with your very good letter, except that I do not think you did it all or can you do it all. I recognize however this is a becoming view for you to take. I am all for cracking everything in now on to Germany that can be spared from the battlefields."[104]

Harris took this encouragement as qualified approval for his own perceived bombing priorities, and it affected his conduct of the bombing offensive in the immediate future. As a consequence, and in spite of Air Ministry's direction otherwise, the month of October witnessed a much greater weight of effort devoted to area attacks than Bomber Command had conducted in the past. During the month, Bomber Command devoted only 6 percent of its bomb tonnage against oil targets, while the USAAF did little better, contributing only 10 percent of their monthly effort in kind. However, it was at precisely this time that intelligence reports indicated—and they were later proved to be correct—that Germany's oil situation was at its most desperate juncture.

> There were many factors affecting this imbalance, as would be highlighted in the subsequent debate between Harris and Portal, but the official historians judge that more could and ought to have been done. Such was the hitting power of the Anglo-American bomber force and so weakened were the enemy defences that it should have been possible, they contend, to deprive the Germans of virtually all their remaining oil production if the effort had been much more strongly concentrated upon it in the autumn months. On the other hand, as the BBSU Report states, the weather in this period was very poor, there were few occasions when oil targets could be visually bombed, and not many tactical opportunities for attacking them were in fact missed.[105]

Similar conclusions were reached by Australian historians of the period, as well as by the USAAF official history. In fact, the latter document states that by the end of November 1944, the weight of Bomber Command's efforts against oil targets was actually exceeding that of the Americans, and that they were proving to be both successful and effective. It goes on to say that the results obtained against the oil industry during the last months of 1944 were spectacular and were "more effective in terms of destruction than most Allied experts had dared to hope."[106] Furthermore, in spite of the qualified support forthcoming from the Prime Minister, as evidenced by the earlier Crossbow correspondence, Harris was also clearly at odds with the relative importance then being attached to the oil targets in the highest corridors of power to the oil targets.

The Evolution of a Hurricane

At the end of September Sir Arthur Harris was still unconvinced that attacks on the "panacea" targets of oil, transportation and the tank industry could damage the enemy's war making capability as much as broader, renewed attacks on the industrial cities. Accordingly, a compromise was struck by the Combined Chiefs which yielded Operation Hurricane I and Hurricane II. These raids were designed to demonstrate overwhelming Allied air superiority to the enemy in the northwestern European region of active land operations. The first was to be a series of concentrated attacks on the Ruhr area in an attempt to try to scuttle the enemy's war effort in a region directly facing the Allied land armies, while the second was to be a generalized reiteration of the campaign against transportation and oil. While Hurricane II has already been extensively covered, Hurricane I was a sub-set of a broader bombing phase informally known as the Third Battle of the Ruhr. It deserves special attention for its brief intensity and focus, and also for the significant role played in its prosecution by 6 Group.

A preliminary kick-off to Hurricane was made against Dortmund on the night of 6/7 October by 523 aircraft, "248 Halifaxes, 247 Lancasters, 28 Mosquitos—of Nos 3, 6, and 8 Groups. No.6 Group provided 293 aircraft—248 Halifaxes and 45 Lancasters, the greatest effort by the Canadian group during the war. Five aircraft were lost, less than 1 percent of the force raiding the Ruhr target on a clear night. The Pathfinder marking and the bombing were both accurate and severe damage was caused, particularly to the industrial and transportation areas of the city, although residential areas also suffered badly."[107] This bombing phase continued a week later when Hurricane I itself was launched in a combination of day and night attacks against Duisburg on 14/15 October. The day operation on 14 October combined 1013 Bomber Command "heavies" with 1251 B-17s and B-24s of the Eighth Air Force. That night, Bomber Command followed up with a further 1005 aircraft, attacking in two distinct blocks separated by two hours, a deliberate attempt to confuse the defenders and to overwhelm the emergency services of the enemy. Furthermore, enough Command assets were still available that night to mount a highly successful collateral attack on Brunswick with 233 Lancasters. In all, Duisburg was pounded with 9000 tons of bombs in less than forty-eight hours, producing significant damage, especially to the Thyssen and Duisburg-Hamborn mines and coke ovens. The total effort for the night produced 1572 sorties for a loss of ten aircraft, 0.6 percent of the attacking force. *"Total effort for the 24 hours: 2589 sorties, 24 aircraft (0.9 percent) lost. Total tonnage of bombs dropped in 24 hours: approximately 10,050 tons. These record totals would never be exceeded in the war."*[108]

On the night of 23/24 October, and again the following day, it was Essen's turn to be pounded. The night raid was mounted by 1055 aircraft, including 561 Lancasters, 463 Halifaxes and 31 Mosquitos.

> Unlike the thousand-bomber raids of 1942, this time no crews from training units had to be included in order to put so many machines in the air. Moreover, all those that partic- ipated were four-engined "heavies," so that a far greater weight of bombs was delivered. Bombing through cloud, the attackers caused 'extensive damage" to a complex of Krupp factories but lost only twelve crews—three (0.65 percent) of them from 6 Group. Thirty- six hours later a daylight raid brought 771 raiders back to the same target. Essen, like many other German cities, was now little more than a heap of rubble.[109]

This concentrated effort closed out the mini-campaign known as the Third Battle of the Ruhr. While parts of Essen's steel industry had already been moved to dispersed factories, "the Krupps steelworks were particularly hard hit by the two raids and there are references in the firm's archives to the 'almost complete breakdown of the electrical supply network' and to 'a complete paralysis.' The Borbeck pig-iron plant ceased work completely and there is no record of any fur- ther production from this important section of Krupps."[110]

Agreement to Differ

Sir Charles Portal soon attempted to force his subordinate Harris into even stricter compliance with the Combined Chiefs and Air Staff Directives with respect to oil. Many sharp exchanges took place between the two men in late 1944 and early 1945, and the details are well covered in Sir Charles Webster and Noble Frankland's official history, *The Strategic Bomber Offensive Against*

Germany 1939–1945.[111] By mid-November, Portal had become exceptionally annoyed over Harris's litany of excuses for non-compliance with the Oil Plan, which included weather and other tactical considerations—so much so that he wrote Harris that he (Portal) "at times wondered whether the magnetism of the remaining German cities has not in the past tended as much to deflect our bombers from their primary objectives as the tactical and weather difficulties which you describe so fully in your letter."[112] As November rolled inexorably onward into December, and the Chief of the Air Staff perceived no seeming improvement towards compliance by Bomber Command's chief, Portal, on 22 December 1944, angrily accused Harris of being unable to put his heart into the attack on oil. Harris had again reverted to labelling oil as one of the Ministry of Economic Warfare's (MEW) hated "panaceas," and advised Portal and his staff that prosecution of the Oil Plan to the degree of destruction mandated by the Air Staff would require 9000 sorties per month from his command, including 6400 at night against the central German targets alone, and the Eighth Air Force would have to pick up most of the long-range taskings. Harris was also very concerned that this campaign would lead to a return of the morale-eroding high casualty rates Bomber Command had endured so steadfastly and for so long. Portal was profoundly disappointed in Harris's attitude. He saw no reason why this task should be beyond the capabilities of both the strategic bombing forces, particularly if the attacks were concentrated against what he viewed as the most important remaining targets, the eleven synthetic oil plants in the central German Ruhr district. Portal was also no longer confident that Harris's staff at High Wycombe were devoting enough energy and thought in this direction, and offered that it would be a tragedy if, after so much effort to date invested against the oil targets, the task failed to be completed. He also concluded that losses as high as five-to-ten percent could be considered worthwhile against some targets, if necessary.[113] This prompted a stinging reply from Harris on 28 December 1944. Here, he again attacked the MEW and referred to oil as yet another "panacea," and also keynoted the attacks on the German aviation industry as a prime example of the futility of seeking panaceas.[114]

> "But you are quite wrong," he continued, "to say that if I hold that view I will be unable to put my heart into the attack on oil. It has always been my custom to leave no stone unturned to get my views across, but when the decision is made I carry it out to the utmost and to the best of my ability." Nor did he accept Portal's comments about his staff: "I do not give them views, I give them orders. They do and always have done exactly what I tell them to. I have told them to miss no opportunity of prosecuting the oil plan, and they have missed no worthwhile opportunity. As for losses, if 5–10% were to be regularly accepted the oil plan would be the only thing, and the last that Bomber Command would do."[115]

Thenceforth Bomber Command placed considerably more weight of effort behind the Oil Plan,[116] although it is an unanswerable question whether this would have occurred had not Portal taken Harris to task on the issue. Sharp exchanges continued between the two men into the new year.[117] And, although Harris ultimately complied with the Air Ministry directives in the bombing weight of effort tasked against oil, the two strong-willed commanders "agreed to disagree" on its importance. The Command was also doggedly supporting a host of other perceived diversions to the area attacks at the time, including continued support for the advancing land armies and operations against German naval forces. However, Harris also continued undeterred with the area bombing, right until the end. Furthermore, and in spite of these perceived differences between the two senior airmen, area bombing enjoyed Portal's support until the end of hostilities, as we shall see later.[118]

It has been suggested by some, including historian Max Hastings, that Portal should have dismissed Harris at this juncture of the war for his intransigence, which bordered on insubordination. But others, including John Terraine contend that Harris's popularity and prestige were such that the remedy would have been worse than the ailment in the ensuing backlash of public opinion.[119] In fact, Harris had volunteered to resign over the issue, but Portal refused to accept his subordinate's gesture, however frivolously it may have been tendered. As we have seen, Harris also had friends in the highest circles, and his dynamic leadership was an unquestioned asset to the war effort. Henry Probert in his book *Bomber Harris* sums up the issue with the following comments:

> As Harris himself later recognized, oil did prove more critical than he had judged at the time. Influenced by the views of Albert Speer, Hitler's Armament Minister, he wrote in 1947 that in the final weeks of the war all the German armed forces had been immobilized for lack of fuel, rendering the triumph of the oil offensive complete and indisputable. It was the one "panacea" that actually paid off.[120]

From the autumn of 1944 onwards, Bomber Command staged daylight raids with ever-increasing frequency until the end of the European war the following spring. This was somewhat ironic, since by this time, the Command had reached such a level of technological sophistication and tactical expertise that its aircrews were by and large as comfortable and as accurate at night against an obscured target as they were in daylight. The *Luftwaffe*, with a few notable exceptions, had by now been rendered largely impotent by the oil and transportation bombing campaigns; the relentless pounding of *Luftwaffe* stations and support facilities by the free-ranging tactical air forces; the dogged pursuit in the air, day and night, of the remaining German fighter forces by vastly more numerous hordes of Allied fighters; the takeover of enemy facilities by the advancing land armies; and, to a lesser extent, the bombing of the now largely decentralized aircraft industry. Still, the *Luftwaffe*, like a phoenix rising out of the ashes, did prove dangerous on occasion. Also, the Germans never appeared to run short of anti-aircraft artillery. The important targets remained stoutly defended with guns, and flak continued to claim many victims.

While the Command generally experienced much more acceptable loss rates from the spring of 1944 onward, there were certainly exceptions to the rule. Flight Lieutenant Lyle James from Sarnia, Ontario, was a later-war Lancaster pilot with 101 Squadron of 1 Group. In the short, operationally intense period from 12 September until 15 December, he and his crew completed a full thirty-two-raid tour of operations. However, 101 Squadron was a Special Duties unit tasked to perform *Airborne Cigar* (ABC) in concert with their regular Main Force bombing duties. As such, their special radio interception and jamming equipment, manned by German-speaking operators, was particularly susceptible to detection and homing when they were transmitting, which made their loss ratio among the highest in Bomber Command at the time. And while these Special Operators had direct links to RAF Intelligence personnel back in England, the tactical advice the home stations provided to the ABC crews in some evolving combat situations was not always considered the most appropriate. James's aircraft, coded "W2" or "William Squared," returned with battle damage on ten separate occasions, and three of this stalwart crew, including James, eventually received DFCs for their gallant work. Lyle James's diary provides an exciting snapshot of the operational tempo this crew experienced and the initiative they demonstrated during their tour of duty in the autumn of 1944.

23 Sep 1944 Neuse, Germany

Night, 4 hrs 40 minutes, 18,000 feet. It was on this trip that the virtuosity of Flying Officer "Gordie" Bullock (bomb-aimer) was put to the test. One of his many duties was to turn his bomb sight on approximately half an hour before the target. The bomb sight was driven by a "Pesco" pump, which spun at about 23,000 rpm, and the gyroscopic field that it set up at this speed stabilized the very delicate sight. However, about 15 minutes into the run, everything went dead! Later examination would show that a pin had sheared off. Now we had a fully loaded bomber rapidly approaching the target, and no way of aiming our load! However, Gordie, remembering some long-forgotten lecture given by an ex-bomb dropper, when we got to the proper height, had always made some dummy (practice) runs on features visible on the ground, and when the supposed target would appear in the cross-hairs, he would stick his wad of chewing gum on the perspex in front of him, and in theory, this became his new bomb sight. So when the original bomb sight toppled, Gordie carried on using nothing but some old Doublemint for a sight, and he got a very respectable bomb release picture for his efforts! He also got great praise from everyone from the commanding officer down. It was typical of the many ways in which Gordie contributed to our tour.

6 Oct 1944 Bremen, Germany

Night, 4 hrs 35 minutes, height 17,000 feet. Nearly had a head-on collision with a Dornier 217 night fighter over the target. He was flying against the stream, and at the same altitude as we were. Missed each other by 50 feet. Holes in both rear and mid-upper turrets. Mid-upper gunner, Bill Dean, had holes both in and out of the turret, narrowly missing his head. A piece of red-hot shrapnel fell into his flying boot, burning him. Hydraulic lines to the rear turret severed, rendering it inoperable. Intelligence ordered us to *climb* out of the target area (at 145 miles per hour), hoping to out-fox the German night fighters. I said to hell with this and *dove* out at my customary 220 mph. It was the only time that they ever used those particular (frontal) tactics, and the Jerry fighters took a very high toll of our boys that night.[121]

21 Nov 1944 Aschaffenburg, Germany

Night, 6 hrs 30 minutes, 12,000 feet. Attacked by two Ju 88s. The first fighter had just shot down a Lancaster about 100 yards off our starboard quarter. He then peeled off to his port and had us silhouetted against the flaming Lanc. Our mid-upper gunner, Bill Dean, gave me a running commentary on his actions, and when the German made his attack, Bill ordered "Corkscrew port, Go!" The corkscrew was a wild manoeuvre which we flew, and if it was successful, it caused the enemy fighter to miss. The Lanc was particularly suited to this manoeuvre and with the added incentive of that Jerry on my tail, with his four cannons and eight machine guns, old "Willie Squared" performed miracles! Tracer was flying both over and under our wings, but he didn't put a scratch on us! In the meantime, Bill was filling the Jerry with so much lead that he actually stalled and dove through the cloud. Fighter Number Two came on the scene about three minutes later and, of all things, he was chasing another Lancaster across our path. More wild corkscrewing and this time Bill hit him dead on his port engine. This fighter also broke off and we headed for home. For his efforts, Bill was credited with a "damaged" and a "probable" enemy aircraft, but more importantly, he saved our bacon that night![122]

A Force Multiplier: The Wooden Wonder

By the autumn of 1944 the "Wooden Wonder," Geoffrey de Havilland's and chief designer Roy Chadwick's outstanding Mosquito, had truly earned its place as a Main Force bomber in its own right. It could carry only one-third the bomb load of a Lancaster, but it could fly three times as many sorties as its four-engine cousin, and its loss rate per sortie was only a third that of the Lancaster. "It was capable of carrying the same payload to Berlin as the Flying Fortress, only so high and fast that it was seldom intercepted and regularly flew two long-range sorties a day with a change of crew. Many lives would have been saved if this had been recognized earlier, or even if the advanced night fighter version had been released sooner to escort the heavy bombers."[123] During the period from April to October 1944, at least 136 major raids by Mosquito formations were made on German industrial targets, including thirty-two separate raids on Berlin. These totals do not include almost nightly sorties in small "penny packets" against a host of other targets, as well as frequent, dedicated diversionary operations.[124] Mosquito operations provided exceptional value, conducted as they were with relatively light losses and doing much to wear down and confound the German night fighter resources and to lure them away from Main Force activities. Such was the diversification, technological sophistication, and flexibility being routinely demonstrated by Bomber Command during the last year of the war.

Many Canadians flew all variants of the wartime Mosquito operationally. One very distinguished crew was that of pilot Terry Godwin (see Chapter Two). Godwin flew two operational tours with Bomber Command and won both a DFM and a DFC. His navigator/bomb-aimer, Hugh Hay, also became a Bomber Command stalwart. During the war years Hay completed three operational tours and won both a DSO and a DFC . By the time he joined Terry Godwin in the right seat of a Mosquito, he had amassed sixty-three operational trips in Hampdens, Manchesters and Lancasters at a time when the loss rates were averaging 5 percent per operation. Godwin recalls wartime Mosquito operations flying on 692 Squadron out of Graveley with his distinguished companion, who appeared even more distinguished because he had been grey-haired since the age of sixteen:

> The target on our first Mossie trip was Brunswick in Germany. About eight more Mossies were flying that night from other squadrons as part of the relatively new light night striking force, all bombs and no guns. We got to our cruising altitude of 28,000 feet over the North Sea. There was no cloud at all and the full moon made it like daylight. Night bomber crews like Hugh and I were not comfortable in such clear air. Our *Gee* navigation system was still working but could only give us a fix to a point because it operated on VHF, which meant line-of-sight . . .
>
> Past the Dutch coast, cloud formed with tops to 10,000 feet, which made the moonlight even brighter. On every trip, Hugh had to do his navigation on a little clip board on his knee. Suddenly ahead of us I saw a condensation trail from one, then more of the other Mossies, which meant that we could be seen the same way. But, oh!! There ahead at two o'clock was a thin white vapour trail heading in towards the other Mossies. But then, the Jerry broke off to the left; 11 o'clock . . . 10 . . . then 9 as he turned back on a reciprocal track to ours. Our throttles were full open at this altitude. As Jerry went past the wingtip where he could judge our speed and turn-in to attack from the rear, I pushed the prop controls to the maximum continuous climb setting. Hugh called, "He's right behind us!!" I then pushed the RPMs right up to the absolute maximum position. The manifold pressure jumped because of the ram effect and the Mossie also jumped like a scared rabbit. I still

don't know how close the Jerry had been, or why he broke off—unless he had flown beyond his assigned control block.

After Brunswick we went to Düsseldorf and also Augsburg. March 1st shows we carried our first 4000 pound bomb in a modified Mark IV, but landed at Woodbridge—low fuel. March 13th brought us the Mark XVI Mossie with heavier engines, two-speed, two-stage superchargers, and built for the 4000 pounders. They were also pressurized to some extent. We were on leave for nine days but still managed to put in thirteen trips in March and fifteen in April. One trip was to Berlin [one of the longer hauls] with just the four 500 pounders.

. . . By May 1944, most people were expecting D-Day. On May 12 1944, we were told to do our night flying test and to dive in steps from 6000 feet and line up on one of the canals leading to the Wash—obviously to try to drop something into it. We were told nothing more at the time. At briefing the story unveiled. A naval officer explained that all the channels around the north end of Denmark had been filled with anti-shipping mines. The last one had just been laid so the channels were closed. The only connection from the Baltic was through the Kiel Canal. A large number of motor torpedo boats and other light ships had been held by Jerry "out of harm's way" in Baltic harbours and would be expected to proceed to the North Sea and the Channel when D-Day arrived. Logically, the Kiel Canal should be closed at just the right time. The level of water in the canal was right at its height and all other things made now that time.

"Gardening" was the code name for mine dropping; mines were "Vegetables," and were to be planted in their "Garden" at dawn on May 13 1944. They took up most of our over-sized bomb bays and they each weighed over 2000 pounds. The artillery officer showed us the gun emplacements along the canal. It seemed they were every 200 metres. There was one missing east of the railway high-level bridge halfway along the canal. "This is where you will drop, from 50 feet," he said. I pointed out to him afterwards that Jerry was too organized to have missed that spot. We got to the canal at dawn and approached the bridge from the northwest. We found a balloon on the south end of the bridge with a light machine gun that opened up on us. I veered away to the south then ran north across the canal and made the run from the west to the drop zone. Oh yes, that gun was there all right. My respect for the army co-op pilots who were looking down the throats of these things every day grew, because for each tracer actually seen, there were maybe six more in between.

Hugh was looking steadfastly forward through the bomb sight. In what seemed ages, other guns opened up, but it was likely only seconds. Bomb doors closed, we then headed for home at low-level, so no-one could find us.

Out of the thirteen aircraft we sent out, we lost one. Air Vice-Marshal Bennett allocated three Distinguished Service Orders and ten Distinguished Flying Crosses for the operation. Hugh Hay got one of the DSOs to add to his DFC. The citation accompanying the medal read: This officer has participated in a very large number of sorties, involving attacks on a wide variety of enemy targets. He has invariably displayed a high standard of courage and resolution. He has rendered much loyal and devoted service.[125]

Hugh now had credit for three tours of operations, as well as being an *Oboe* controller in between.[126]

International Cooperation at its Finest

American Eighth Air Force operations were very much in synergy with those of Bomber Command by the autumn of 1944. At this time, Clifford M. Black of Saint John, New Brunswick, and

Yarmouth, Nova Scotia, was a squadron leader and a flight commander flying Lancaster Mark Xs with 419 Squadron out of Middleton St. George. However, on a daylight raid during September, he and his squadron mates had an experience which gave a whole new dimension to the very spirit of Combined Operations.

> One day in September 1944, I was landing back at Middleton St. George, which was the most northern base in Yorkshire, from participation in a daylight raid. I was just turning off the runway and was headed to my dispersal point when I looked back to see if anything was on approach behind me. To my surprise, I saw a Fortress on finals, and the crew were firing off flares like crazy, presumably to draw the airfield controllers' attention to them. Anyway, they eventually landed and taxied over to park in front of the control tower.
>
> Later, when we were all being debriefed by the Intelligence Officers, it so happened that this American crew was sitting right behind us, and the Intelligence Officer was a young flying officer and an Irishman with quite a sense of humour. One of the first questions you normally got asked after a raid was, "Did you bomb the Primary Target?" So, I was listening to this American fellow right at my back when he said in this Texan drawl, "Weeeeellllll, ah've got kinda a sad story to tell ya. Ah got delayed on the take-off, and bah the tahme ah got airborne, ah couldn't fahnd ma formation." So he said, "Ah looked up and saw a bunch of Lancs goin' by, and I thought, 'Weeeelllll, they're goin' to a target. Ah might as well *join* 'em." So he *did* join and flew to the target, formatting on one of the other Lancs, I suppose . . . At any rate he then said, "Ah didn't know where we were goin' or anythin' else. Ah just watched what was goin' on. When the rest of the guys started throwin' out chaff, ah started throwin' out chaff. When they opened their bomb doors, ah opened mahne. When they dropped 'em, ah dropped 'em, and then ah followed these guys home. I dunno where we been or what we did or who we were bombin' or anythin' else."
>
> Then "Irish" the Intelligence Officer said, "What was your assessment of the flak?" Well, that particular day was completely overcast in the target area and we were using sky-marking, *Wanganui* marking. Using this technique, the Pathfinders would drop these things down and they would break open at the release point, then the bomb-aimer just "set everything at zero." We then rode in over the top of the markers on a certain heading and theoretically, we should have hit the target. These flares of ours came in different colours. We would start out with red and then they would be backed up with green or maybe blue . . . whatever . . . So anyway, the American *then* said, "Flak, weeeeelll now, ah've seen flak in my day, but ah've never seen *green* flak or *blue* flak or *red* flak, and the *funny* thing was, all these ol' boys were headin' right *for* it!" When our procedures were all explained to him, he thought it was a pretty good way to fight a war . . .
>
> When the debriefing was over, he said, "Bah the way, ah don't even know where ah *am*. What's the name of this here base?" So Irish told him, and he spent part of the next day with us before he went back to his unit. I bumped into Irish afterwards and I said, "You know, that young guy . . . Talk about *guts* . . . he didn't even know where we were going, he didn't know how tough the target was going to be, and yet he came along and flew the whole trip and followed us home." I talked to that American before he left the next day and he said he'd had a *great* time.[127]

Although there was mutual support and cooperation between Bomber Command and the Eighth Air Force in Britain, not every wartime eventuality could be codified, and aircrew innovation and cunning were occasionally called on in order to get a tricky job done. John Raymond Lyon from Stoney Creek, Ontario, was a rear gunner who completed a full tour of operations in February 1945, flying in late model Halifaxes with 420 Squadron:

On returning from a night operation to Stuttgart, we made an emergency landing at an American base. The next morning we discovered a 550 pound bomb in the partially-opened wing bomb bay, called the control tower, and asked for help. They immediately towed away all their B-17 Fortresses from around us. On calling again for help, they left us a jeep about 100 yards away. We drove it under the wing and the bomb-aimer pulled all the wires he could find away from the bomb. Then, the six other crew members stood on the jeep under the bomb, arms outstretched, and the bomb-aimer then opened the bomb doors and dropped the beast. We then gently lowered it into the jeep. After getting clearance for take-off and once we were well up in the air above the base, the pilot informed our American friends that we had left them a present in the jeep. That was the last we ever heard of it.[128]

A Strange Encounter

On the 15th of December on a night operation to Ludwigshafen, Cliff Black and his crew also had a bizarre encounter with a Fortress, only this event was far less innocuous than his September experience.

We were briefed on the Ludwigshafen target on December 15th 1944, and the target (difficulty) and flak were rated as being just "moderate." This assessment proved accurate. We had a pretty uneventful trip, really, until we were about halfway home. We were flying at between 16,000–18,000 feet when my engineer, who was then standing on my right, tapped me on the shoulder and said, "Look!" I then looked out at my left wingtip and there was a Fortress, just sitting there, about 100 yards off my wing. It was fairly dark, but you could clearly see the outline of the thing. I thought, "Gosh, that's peculiar." Anyway, I told my mid-upper gunner, "Larry, swing your guns on that fellow and just keep an eye on him until we sort him out." We went along like that for about two minutes, and then I said to myself, "You know, that's likely a 100 Group Fortress that's either lost or he's had his navigator incapacitated and he's looking to follow us home." Knowing how much faster the Lanc was than the Fortress, and thinking that if he tried to keep up with me he might run himself out of fuel, I thought I should slow down a bit to give him a break. So I slowly eased my power off . . . But he drifted on ahead of me, so I just kept backing the speed off until I got what I thought would be a good cruising speed for him, but he *still* ended up about 200 yards right in front of me. *Then*, to my great surprise, he cut right across in front of me and *opened fire*!! Luckily it was night and he was firing tracers. I saw the first of them and when I did, I just instinctively pulled up on the Lanc and rolled to the left, away from it, as I yelled to everybody, "Look *out*!!" Then, I peeled the Lanc off hard left. After a bit, I got her under more control and someone said, "My God, Mac (my bomb-aimer) has been hit." I could feel the shells hitting the aircraft, but I didn't know *where*. As I had pulled up, a shell had come through the nose of the aircraft and McKinnon (Mac) was at this moment standing right beside me. I didn't realize he was there, but I guess he had appeared right after I said to Larry, the mid-upper, to put his guns on that fellow. Mac obviously came out from behind the crew curtain because he habitually sat with the navigator on the way home, assisting in any way he could. At any rate, down he went. He fell almost back into the bomb-aimer compartment until someone got a hold on him. He had been hit right in the ball of his foot. You know, those shells were .5-inch, and the wound was pretty bad. They pulled him into the rest position, someone took his boot off and his foot was just a real *mess*! We carried shock pads, taped at intervals along the fuselage formers. The idea was, if you got wounded bad, to just reach for one of those things, which was full of sulfa or something, and wrap or tie it around the wound. That was pretty much the best you could do until the aircraft landed. Anyway, we looked after Mac as best we could. Those shells came through the nose of the aircraft, and this fellow was *really* accurate. When we looked closely afterwards, we estimated he had missed me by about four inches, then hit Mac. And there were three of us close side-by-side there at the time, because the engineer was always very close at hand, either standing or sitting in his little drop seat. Mac had kinda wedged in between him and me and unfortunately, he got hit.

On the way back, of course, I'm cursing this Fortress crew thinking, "My God, if *I* can recognize a Fortress, surely *they* can recognize a Lanc.' Mac was bleeding quite badly, so we went straight in to the emergency 'drome at Woodbridge, right on the coast. Almost as soon as we landed, the emergency crew was in the aircraft. They got Mac and rolled him up in a thing that looked like a Venetian blind, then passed him down and outside, just like a log. He was in the ambulance in a jiffy and then they were gone, even before I could get out of the aircraft. Their efficiency was really spectacular.

I checked on Mac in the morning and they had fixed him up pretty well, although they didn't then know if they were going to have to remove the rest of the foot or not. On the return trip, after the attack, that son-of-a-gun still wanted to sit with the navigator and help him out, which he did. At any rate, Mac eventually got the DFM for his efforts that night, and that was the last I ever saw of him. He was a good man with lots of guts . . .

When I got back to our base the next day, I naturally reported all of this. A day or two later, the Intelligence Officer told me an interesting story, and it was augmented years later by the release of information pertaining to a special group in the *Luftwaffe* that flew captured Fortresses. While the I.O. told his tale, I couldn't help thinking that if I hadn't told Larry to put his guns on that Fort, which made it a sort of "Mexican Standoff," they were probably waiting for us to pull our guns away from them. Then they would have opened up for sure and we would have "been goners," because they were just a hundred yards off our wingtip and they could have taken us out quite easily.[129]

The resolute McKinnon's DFM citation is interesting, for, no doubt because of the classified nature of the Fortress encounter at the time and their use as "Trojan Horses" by the enemy, the account merely suggests the adversary was an enemy fighter.

Flight Sergeant McKinnon has participated in many sorties against some of the most heavily defended targets in Germany. In December 1944 he was the air bomber in an aircraft detailed to attack Ludwigshafen. Shortly after the bombs had been released the aircraft was hit by bullets from a fighter. At the time, Flight Sergeant McKinnon was moving to a position from which he could continue his duties by assisting the navigator. He was then struck in the foot, which was badly injured. Although in considerable pain, Flight Sergeant McKinnon insisted on remaining at his post until assured that he could be of no further assistance. His example of courage and fortitude won great praise.[130]

The German ultra-secret special duties wing, *Kampfgeschwader 200* (*KG 200*), operated a limited number of captured American heavy bombers, including several B-17 Flying Fortresses, for clandestine operations behind enemy lines. Naturally, these aircraft held the advantage of being able to operate at night over enemy territory without arousing excessive suspicion. They were also pressed into service since Germany always had an acute shortage of long-range aircraft. *KG 200's* *Detachment Olga* was eventually tasked with parachuting agents into France, either individually or in specially constructed metal and plywood air-deployable containers holding up to three agents and their equipment. The *KG 200* crews also made routine supply runs to keep their covert charges in operation. By November 1944, the Fortresses had been used to develop long range night navigational procedures, and then flew subsequent operations to Greece, Italy, the Low Countries, Africa, Poland and the Soviet Union, as well as France. Always acting under the cloak of darkness while they dropped agents and supplies or acted as airborne listening posts, the *KG 200* aircrew felt they were relatively safe from attack. Contrary to popular postwar belief, the Fortresses were not used to deliberately penetrate the bomber stream or the American daylight formations and shoot down Allied aircraft. They were far too valuable a resource to be used in that manner. Also, for deliberate night-time combat use, they possessed neither the sophisticated *Schräge Musik* offensive firepower nor the specialized electronics and airborne radar of the night fighters. Rather, they operated in the tightest of security, and even many of the unit's ground personnel were unaware of its mission or the clandestine nature of its operations. The encounter with Cliff Black and his crew on the night of 15/16 December 1944 was undoubtedly a chance one, the attack more likely being an attempt to get rid of witnesses than anything else. Still, it is a fascinating story.[131] Cliff Black finished the war as a wing commander, the last wartime commanding officer of 426 "Thunderbird" Squadron, and was handsomely decorated for his "outstanding leadership and courage" with the DFC and the French *Croix de Guerre* with Silver Star.[132]

Sometimes, forced diversions into unexpected locations had amusing repercussions for the aircrews, as Reg Patterson recalls.

> On Christmas Eve of 1944, we were briefed for a raid on Cologne. I was flying as "Victor Two," as the call-sign went. My engineer was sick, so I was given a replacement. We took off around 5:30 in the afternoon and it was fully dark by the time we got over the Channel. We were about fifteen minutes back from the target when about eight bursts of flak came up, and they *all* hit us. Just a lucky burst fired up at the bomber stream in general . . . I slammed open the bomb doors and told the bomb-aimer to dump the load, which he did. Then, I very gingerly started easing the aircraft down, as there were aircraft all around us and below us. In this one multiple burst, we had lost three of the engines, one of the rudders, and there were numerous holes, some large enough to jump through, in the fuselage. When I thought I was below the stream, I turned to the west to get back over friendly territory. It was a bright, moonlit night, and I could see the ground. I asked the bomb-aimer what kind of territory was below us, and he said, heavily-treed hills. I didn't think much of bailing out into that . . . We were managing to descend very slowly, as the one remaining engine was at least giving us *some* flying ability. I asked the navigator to give us a course for an alternate airfield that we had a "flimsy" on, information I knew he had in his pocket. He muttered a lot of uncomplimentary words about pilots thinking that navigators knew everything, but he found the piece of paper. As all his instruments ran off the dead engines, he had to guess a lot of things, but he soon gave me a course to steer. By this time, we were down to about 3500 feet, the aircraft was starting to hold height on the one engine, and we were doing about 95 miles-per-hour. Unfortunately, I could smell gas and I knew we were losing fuel, and that the gas gauges were also out of commission. Finally, the navigator said, "That place is either one minute dead ahead, or I haven't the faintest idea where it is." We were all peering ahead and suddenly, there it was, right on the nose. It had crossed runways at 90 degrees, and one of the runways had fighters parked on it, but the other one was empty. I called "Hello, Darky," which was the normal RAF talk for trying to say hello to anybody, and it was the correct phraseology as prescribed "by the book," but I got no answer. I then told the crew

that I could see the runway in the moonlight, and that we were going in anyway. I then started around in a wide, right-hand turn into the good engine, which was the starboard outer, when a very British voice came on the radio and said, "Oh, hello, old chap. What's up?" I told him my plight, and he asked if I could do one more orbit while he got the flare pots lit. The Germans had earlier bombed out all the lights. Meanwhile, I had no idea of my remaining fuel state, but I said I would try to comply. By the time I got on the base leg again, the lights were all lit and I turned final, planning to keep it high until the last moment, then cut the engine and glide in. I told the crew to clear the turrets and to take up crash positions. As the rear gunner (Flight Lieutenant Bill Thoroldson, RCAF) was just out of the rear turret, he heard the mid-upper guns going off. He didn't know whether to climb back in his turret or to open the door and jump out! He finally reached the plug-in for his intercom and asked our mid-upper gunner what the hell was going on. It turned out that the mid-upper had caught his sleeve on the trigger as he was trying to get out of the turret.

I then called for the undercarriage and the right wheel came down, but the left one did not. In a "Lanc," you can see the wheels from the cockpit. We were now at the point of being in too close to the runway, so I had to go around *again*. We were still at circuit height, and I told the engineer to leave the wheels down. We then did a very tight circuit at around 90 knots, about one knot above the stall in that configuration. Then I turned on final, called for full flaps, and we got *nothing*. We ended up crossing the "button" of the runway, screaming along at about 155 knots. However, the wheels were now both showing "in the green," so I planted them on the asphalt and looked ahead to see a very short runway! I was just reaching over to dump the wheels up when we went over a rise in the runway, and there was another 3000 feet of asphalt ahead! We were soon met by some men of the RAF, who were there just to look after guys like us. As it turns out, they were putting together a Lancaster in their spare time from derelict parts received just this way, and they needed one more engine, so they were kind of glad to see us. Also, the following day was Christmas Day. Traditionally, the officers and the NCOs serve the men dinner, so these folks had just gained eight more officer waiters.[133]

As 1944 drew to a close, Mickey Rooney, twenty-four, and child star Elizabeth Taylor, twelve, appeared on the silver screen as two determined kids trying to get a horse to win the illustrious Grand National in the film "National Velvet," while ironically, horse racing was banned in December "for the duration." In the Pacific, a Japanese convoy was decimated off Leyte, and American aircraft pounded Iwo Jima in preparation for a major invasion early in the new year. On the Italian front, on 20 December 1944, advance elements of the Canadian 1st Division reached the Senio River, approximately thirty miles from Bologna. That same day, the last-ditch German counteroffensive in the Ardennes had advanced to Bastogne, the convergence point for five major road arteries. That threat would soon be contained and nullified, and on all fronts, the Axis forces were in full retreat. Global victory was just months away, but there was much work left to be done in those months of war that remained.

EIGHT

Götterdämmerung Over the Reich
The Final Acts: 1945

I want to go home, Mo.

—Mo Morrison's mid-upper gunner

Bomber Command ushered in 1945 as a combatant force light years removed from what it had been on the eve of war in September 1939. Sir Arthur Harris now had at his disposal a force of 1600 heavy bombers, dominated by a fleet of 1000 Lancasters available for operations at any given time. All these "heavies" were equipped with both *Gee* and *H2S*, and a substantial number also boasted *G-H*, for even greater navigational accuracy and flexibility. The Canadian Mark X Lancasters now carried twin .5-inch guns as standard armament in the mid-upper turret. Additionally, some of the rear turrets were being modified to accommodate .5-inch guns, augmented by *Village Inn* gunlaying radar. With this new system, the scanning dish antenna traversed and elevated in synchronization with the guns, and radar ranging information was projected on the gunner's sight. However, while the gunners could now engage targets beyond visual range, there remained the thorny problem of identification and discrimination between friend and foe. Eventually, this was overcome by the installation of the nose-mounted infra-red identification system previously mentioned (see chapter five), although it was fielded too late in the European war to see broad operational service.

During the four effective combat months of 1945, Bomber Command crews dropped over 181,000 tons of bombs, nearly 20 percent of the aggregate for the entire war. They also mounted 67,483 operational sorties from which 608 aircraft failed to return, an overall loss rate significantly less than 1 percent. However, this new-found ability to generate such a massive force routinely, repeatedly, and on demand masks the fact that significant losses still occurred on individual raids. Thus, while the odds of completing an operational tour increased dramatically during 1945, combat survival was far from guaranteed.

It is worthwhile to note just how this immense effort was divided up during the "twelfth hour" of the bombing offensive, January to April 1945:

Attacks on cities	66,482 tons	36.6 percent
Attacks on troops/defences	26,081 tons	14.4 percent
Attacks on transportation	28,102 tons	15.4 percent
Attacks on naval targets	11,140 tons	6.1 percent
Attacks on oil	47,510 tons	26.2 percent
Attacks on German Air Force	637 tons	0.4 percent
Attacks on specific industries	1236 tons	0.7 percent
Miscellaneous	552 tons	0.2 percent

These statistics certainly drive home the point that Sir Arthur Harris was still giving priority to attacks on the industrial cities. Indeed, twenty-nine of them, excluding Dresden, became targets of major area attacks during 1945. However, Harris also at long last made a major commitment against the enemy's oil assets, as well as paying close attention to a healthy number of other significant diversions, panaceas or not.[1]

Daylight Raids Predominate

By 1945, Bomber Command was flying regularly during the daylight hours, their flanks now covered throughout operations by hoardes of Allied fighters, especially Fighter Command Spitfires, Mustangs, and Tempests. However, the Command Halifaxes and Lancasters did not fly in the tight, disciplined and mutually supportive formations favoured by the B-17s and B-24s of the numbered American air forces. Rather, they flew in relatively loose "gaggles," still releasing their bombs by individual aiming on markers provided by the Pathfinders and other specialist forces. By 1945, marking techniques had reached new levels of maturity and sophistication, including the increasing use of offset tactics. Now, although the Main Force journeymen aimed for a single marking reference on a given target, different approach angles, combined with timed overshoots, provided a number of actual release points on every successful attack. The offset procedure reduced the predictability, and thus the vulnerability of the attacking bombers. Also, multiple streams consisting of simultaneous large-scale efforts on different targets were common by 1945, further confusing the defences and reducing predictability.

However, being able to see their fighting environment in daylight was a mixed blessing to Bomber Command's crews, who were so used to operating under the cloak of darkness for so many months. Geoff Marlow of 434 Squadron elaborates:

> The worst part of the daylight raids was seeing our buddies actually being hit by flak or shot down by fighters. At night, we did not seet hings in such detail. On an operation over Cologne, we saw at least two aircraft hit by flak, and observed many others, when attacked by fighters, spiral out of control, with some of the crew managing to jump out and float down in their parachutes to captivity. I also saw one of our bombers with an incendiary bomb lodged in his wing near the gasoline tank. It had been dropped from

above by one of our own aircraft, and I wondered what I would have done had I been its pilot—order the crew to jump for it immediately, or stay with the bomber until it reached friendly territory, never knowing when it might explode in a ball of flames. I never found out what happened—I was too busy juggling for position within the stream of bombers as we approached the aiming point, at the same time trying to follow the bomb-aimer's instructions.[2]

New Threats, New Challenges

It had become evident to Allied military planners that the defeat of Germany was now only a matter of time. However, the German Ardennes offensive at year's end, although unsuccessful, had caught the Allies unawares. A flood of new and innovative weaponry, ranging from the V 2s to the Me 262 and Me 163 jet and rocket fighters and the second-generation *schnorkelling* submarines, increased Allied wariness. The V 1 and V 2 rocket attacks had also generated a mood of general despair and war weariness among the British populace, and labour unrest was threatening to seriously impact the production output of the war industries. There was also concern at the highest levels that Germany, given the opportunity and any amount of respite from attack, would unleash biological, chemical, and even atomic weapons of mass destruction while in its death throes as a nation, either through desperation or in fanatical retaliation. A litany of such previous behavioural trends by the Nazi hierarchy gave credence to these fears. Furthermore, on 27 January, the dreadful bestiality of the Nazi regime was unequivocally revealed for the world to gaze on in horror and revulsion when advance troops of Soviet Marshal Konev's 60th Army overran the network of death camps around Auschwitz in Poland. Many more grim discoveries of this nature were in store for the advancing Allied armies on all the battle fronts.

Additionally, the Soviets had already lost massive numbers of their soldiers in combat, and the western Allies were also facing mounting casualties as they slogged relentlessly east towards the German heartland. Finally, the full might of the Allied coalition could not be brought to bear against the Japanese until the irrevocable defeat of Germany had been brought about. Therefore, every available means was now being sought to end the European war as expeditiously as possible.[3]

At the start of the year, due largely to abysmal winter flying weather which predominated over the British Isles and northwest Europe, bombing operations were clustered in relatively short periods of very intense activity during the first and third weeks of January. For the most part, the losses incurred were quite manageable,

> but a few old-style area raids provoked old-style responses. Thirty-one crews failed to return from Hannover on 5/6 January, 4.7 percent of the total, of which ten were from No. 6 Group and three from No. 425 Squadron, flying Halifax IIIs. At least one of the latter fell to *Schräge Musik*, to which there was still no effective counter if the enemy's approach was made correctly. "The whole trip went very smoothly," Sergeant E.J. Faulkner, a flight engineer on No. 425 squadron, recalled. "We were in sight of the target and preparing for the bombing run. Suddenly we were perforated with cannon shells from below." With their machine out of control and on fire, the crew bailed out. Five were taken prisoner, but the two gunners were killed. Eleven nights later, seventeen Halifax crews were lost at Magdeburg and a further ten Halifaxes at Zeitz, both deep penetrations. No. 6 Group was fortunate at Zeitz, as only one crew failed to return, but seven of the 136 sent to Magdeburg (5.1 percent) did not come back, including four from No. 420 Squadron.[4]

The emerging threats were also about to receive special attention:

Although the *Luftwaffe* and the German aircraft industry had been removed from November's directive, the Americans had become increasingly worried about the frequent appearance of jet aircraft and on 19 January jet fighter production, training and operational establishments again became a "primary objective for attack." "Certain objectives in the enemy's U-Boat organization" were also included in the new directive, although it was anticipated that these could be dealt with by a "marginal effort . . . incidental to other operations." Area targets could still be considered, and although a list of these (almost entirely in the Ruhr) "calculated to make the best contribution to our strategic aims" had been drawn up, the directive did not preclude Harris from selecting other cities when the towns on the preferred list could not be attacked.[5]

One costly raid of this period was made to Magdeburg on the night of 16/17 January. Joseph Lamarsh Hickson from Wheatley, Ontario, was a late-war air gunner flying in Halifax IIIs with the ill-fated 420 Squadron that night. Although he and his crew survived, Hickson recalls the raid in a very laconic manner, considering it is from the particularly harrowing position of a flyer who had almost completed his tour of operations.

Another trip among many I remember was flown on the 16th of January, 1945; the target, Magdeburg, Germany. After dropping our bombs, target ablaze, I started seeing fighters shot down in flames by night fighters. I counted many going down in flames—the adrenalin was running high as I kept a keen eye for many that might attack us. I even broke out in a sweat while flying at 18,000 feet in January, with the outside air temperature at about -50° F. I actually had to unplug my heated flying suit. Later, as things quieted down and we were crossing the enemy coast, headed back towards England, I noticed the cold settle over me and I had to plug the suit back in. Sure was nice to be back on the ground again. That was our 29th operational trip. Just one more to go.[6]

The Issue of Enemy Morale

All the Allied powers had acknowledged, as early as 1943, that strategic bombing would play a decisive role in bringing about the defeat of Germany, and by the time of the Octagon Conference at Quebec in September 1944, the British Chiefs of Staff had already given preliminary consideration to a plan conceived by Harris and his staff that summer. This basic concept postulated that

"it might become desirable in the immediate future to apply the whole strategic bomber effort to the direct attack of German morale." The Chiefs of Staff also agreed that attacks could usefully be undertaken in support of the Russian armies. These discussions culminated in the formation of a detailed plan called *Thunderclap*. The Chief of the Air Staff, Sir Charles Portal, presented this to his fellow Chiefs of Staff in August 1944. It envisaged a massive attack on Berlin about the time that the German Army had been defeated in the field. The strategic bomber force would then deliver the *coup de grâce* ending further resistance. By 1945, the Air Staff considered that *Thunderclap* might well appear to the Germans as an excellent example of close coordination with the Russians, thereby greatly increasing the morale effect. In January 1945, the Joint Intelligence Committee (JIC) played down the possibility of German resistance crumbling, but highlighted the scope for confusion in the movement of reinforcements and refugees if, by implication, critical towns in the infrastructure were attacked.

The JIC report coincided with preparations for the Allied discussions in Malta that were the precursor to the Yalta conference with the Soviets. In the meantime, Churchill had asked the Secretary of State for Air, Sir Archibald Sinclair, what plans he had for "basting the Germans in their retreat from Breslau."[7]

Sir Charles Portal then advised Sinclair that Thunderclap, as it had been conceived months earlier, would undoubtedly be both costly and indecisive, and instead recommended the continued absolute priority of oil targets, the submarine yards and the jet aircraft factories. However, Portal also endorsed the sentiments of the January JIC report and recommended specific attacks on Berlin, Chemnitz, Dresden, Leipzig, "or any other cities where a severe blitz will not only cause confusion in the evacuation from the East, but will also hamper the movement of troops from the West."[8] Sinclair then cautiously responded to the Prime Minister, leading with "You asked me last night whether we had any plans for harrying the German retreat from Breslau." He then said that oil should remain the paramount priority, but that secondary option attacks could be considered against East German cities when poor weather would not permit attacks against oil infrastructure. He reiterated specifically the cities mentioned by Portal, stating that not only were they the main administrative centres controlling military and civilian movements in the region, but they were also the main communications centres through which the bulk of all traffic moved. Sinclair then closed with, "To achieve results of real value, a series of heavy attacks would probably be required, and weather conditions at this time of year would certainly prevent these being delivered in quick succession. The possibility of these attacks being delivered on the scale necessary to have a critical effect on the situation in Eastern Germany is now under examination."[9] Churchill's particularly testy response to Sinclair is worth quoting in full:

Serial No M.115/5

SECRETARY OF STATE FOR AIR

I did not ask you last night about plans for harrying the German retreat from Breslau. On the contrary, I asked whether Berlin, and no doubt other large cities in East Germany, should not now be considered especially attractive targets. I am glad that this is "under examination." Pray report to me tomorrow what is going to be done.

W.S.C.
26/1/45[10]

The unequivocal tone of this correspondence generated the following immediate response from Sinclair to his Prime Minister:

TOP SECRET.

PRIME MINISTER.

Your Minute M.115/5. The Air Staff have now arranged that, subject to the overriding claims of attacks on enemy oil production and other approved target systems within the current directive, available effort should be directed against Berlin, Dresden, Chemnitz and Leipzig or against other cities where severe bombing would not only destroy communications vital to the evacuation from the East but would also hamper the movement of troops from the West.

The use of the night bomber force offers the best prospects of destroying these industrial cities without detracting from our offensive on oil targets, which is now in a critical phase. The Air Officer Commanding-in-Chief, Bomber Command, has undertaken to attempt this task as soon as the present moon has waned and favourable weather conditions allow. This is unlikely to be before about 4th February.

A.S.

27th January, 1945.[11]

Simultaneously, Portal's Deputy Chief of the Air Staff, Sir Norman Bottomley, formally instructed Harris to carry out the specified attacks. A series of meetings between Portal, Tedder, Bottomley and the American General Carl Spaatz reconfirmed oil as the number one bombing priority for strategic bombing forces based in Britain. This would, in turn, be followed by attacks on Berlin, Dresden, and Leipzig, which included the destruction of communications nodes servicing the respective fronts. Finally, there were the jet aircraft production plants. The Vice-Chiefs in London gave their blessings to these priorities and also added a demand for a more sustained effort against enemy tank production facilities. Thus, that portion of the bomber offensive known as Thunderclap was officially born within those other priorities, and, in concert with parallel daylight operations by the USAAF known as Clarion, it would consist of a series of punishing raids against the remaining industrialized German centres, designed primarily to disrupt enemy communications and transportation capabilities, but also to deal major blows to enemy morale.[12]

> The plot now moves to Yalta where the debate over who said what to whom becomes complex. Cold War Soviet propaganda has emphasized that the Russian delegation in the Crimea had no responsibility for the bombing of Dresden. The Allies were unequivocal in their inclusion of Dresden in the target list, in particular with its importance on the Berlin–Leipzig–Dresden railway. The Russian Deputy Chief of Staff, General Antonov, submitted a formal memorandum to the Allies requesting, *inter alia*, that air attacks against communications should be carried out "in particular to paralyse the centres: Berlin and Leipzig." The use of the wording "in particular" makes it, at best, disingenuous for the Russians subsequently to suggest that they had not requested action at Dresden. Although the documentary evidence from the Russian perspective is limited, it is highly improbable that informal or non-minuted discussions had left them in any doubt as to Allied intentions. It is worthy of note at this stage that Harris's role had been no more sinister than as a recipient of very high-level instructions.[13]

Dresden: Myths and Realities

British journalist and historian, Robin Neillands, maintains that the Soviet request to aid the Russian advance into Germany included specific mention of Dresden, a request that was sanctioned by the political leaders at Yalta a few days later. Furthermore, on 12 February, the day before the raid,

> a signal was sent from Spaatz's HQ to Major-General Edmund W. Hill, the senior USAAF officer with the US Military Mission in Moscow, asking him to inform the Soviet General Staff that the Eighth Air Force would attack "the marshalling yards" at Dresden "on the following day." This message tends to confirm that the Soviets knew about the proposed attacks on the eastern cities; the Western Allies did not normally keep the Soviets abreast of day-to-day bombing operations. The statement that the USAAF would attack Dresden "on the following day" is also interesting, for it tends to confirm the view that the Russians knew of the combined attack, if not the precise date. Had all gone to plan the USAAF

would indeed have attacked Dresden on 13 February, and been followed up that night by the RAF.

The declaration that only "marshalling yards" would be attacked enabled the Russians to deny later that they knew the city was to be destroyed and to imply that, had they known, they would not have approved—and this from a country that was allowing its soldiers to rape and murder at will as the Red Army advanced into Germany.[14]

Henry Probert, Harris's biographer commenting on this subject, mentions that while formal records from Yalta indicate that the only individual targets specified by General Antonov were Leipzig and Berlin, "the British Chiefs of Staff's own interpreter is certain that Dresden was also requested, not just by Antonov but also—strongly—by Stalin himself. In any case, when the Russians were subsequently told of the many operations being planned in their support, including attacks on Berlin, Leipzig, Dresden and Chemnitz, they raised no objections."[15]

Dresden. The very mention of the name has, for some, become synonymous with the wanton destruction of the beautiful, baroque capital of Saxony, the seventh-largest city in Germany at the time, whose normal population of 600,000 was in February 1945 swollen with refugees from bombings elsewhere and from the relentless advances of the Soviets. It has also, in the minds of some, embodied the deliberate slaughter of many human beings for no legitimate war purpose. Many recountings of the raids have tended to pillory the participating aircrews and, in particular, to demonize the Air Officer Commanding-in-Chief Bomber Command. But is this a fair, accurate, and objective assessment of what actually transpired?

We have already seen what led up to the decision to attack Dresden and the rationale for this action in the context of the war as it was being fought at the time. But why specifically Dresden? To answer, it is necessary to clarify a few myths that have become associated with the city.

Perhaps the first myth needing to be dispelled is that Dresden had been spared bombing until this point in the war, which therefore bred a false sense of security among residents and the German populace at large. In fact, Dresden had already been bombed by the USAAF on 7 October 1944 as a secondary target, while its oil refinery and marshalling yards became a primary target, again for the USAAF, on 16 January 1945. In all, over 800 of the city's residents had been killed in the previous two raids, and thus while Dresden had not been repeatedly savaged to the extent of Cologne, Mannheim, Kassel, Berlin, Hamburg, or Ludwigshaven, it was certainly not an unblemished target in February 1945, nor had residents any rationale for assuming the respite from aerial attack would continue indefinitely.[16] However, its relative distance from the United Kingdom, combined with more urgent bombing priorities and generally atrocious winter flying conditions had spared it the concentrated attentions of the Anglo-American bombing forces until this point in the war.

An eighteenth century hub of European culture, baroque Dresden boasted the discovery of the recipe for European porcelain, the legendary "White Gold" of Saxony. Home to many famous artists, particularly of the Rococo and Classicist styles, this "Florence of the North" was also at times the home of musical giants such as Carl Maria von Weber, Richard Wagner and Robert Schumann. Its famous Semper Opera House premiered no fewer than nine operas by Richard Strauss. However, Dresden was also a legitimate military target, and not just home to talcum powder, tooth paste and many of Germany's cigarette factories, as important as the latter items were to the morale of the German fighting forces.

The city was home to many long-standing and diversified industrial activities. In 1889, Fräulein

Christine Hardt invented the brassiere there. Dresden was also the first city in Europe to produce cigarettes, teabags, squeezable toothpaste, coffee filters, and the latex condom. It also became a major pre-war production centre for the typewriter and camera industries.[17] Dresden contained the Zeiss-Ikon optical factory, the Siemens glass plant, the Seidel & Naumann industrial complex and a Shell Oil refinery. Other facilities imbedded in the residential suburbs, as was the custom in Berlin and other major centres, were factories producing engines for Junkers aircraft, radar and other electronic components, fuses for anti-aircraft shells, gas masks, cockpit parts for Messerschmitt fighters, an arsenal and a poison gas factory. "These war factories employed somewhere in the region of 10,000 people—1500 of them in the shell-fuse factory alone—so it can hardly be maintained that Dresden made only a small contribution to the German war effort."[18]

The 1944 handbook to the German Army High Command's Weapon Office itemized 127 factories in the city of Dresden that were engaged in industrial war work, and an authority at the Dresden City Museum has recently categorized the list as being "very incomplete."[19] Many of Dresden's pre-war industrial activities were related to leisure and luxury goods, but by 1944, most of them had been converted to war work. Seidel and Naumann had largely switched from manufacturing sewing machines and typewriters to armaments; Richard Gäbel & Company, from marzipan and waffles to torpedo components; J.C. Müller Universelle-Werke, from cigarette making/packaging machines, to machine guns, aircraft parts, searchlights, torpedo parts and directional equipment made by 4000 workers, many of whom were foreigners from the occupied territories. They included 700 women, many of them Jewish, from Ravensbrück concentration camp. Bernsdorf & Company changed from manufacturing cigarettes to cartridges. The Deutsche Werkstätte at Hellerau in Dresden's northern reaches switched from building fine furniture to hosting an SS barracks and making wooden tail assemblies for combat aircraft. Radio-Mende switched from building commercial radio receivers to artillery observation devices, tens of thousands of electrical fuses for the *Luftwaffe*, specialized typewriters, field telephones, and two-way radios. In mid-1943 Radio-Mende alone employed approximately 2500 workers, many of them women, and over the next one and a half years, more women were brought in from forced labour sources, including 300 Russians and Poles from Flossenburg concentration camp and 600 from Bergen-Belsen. In the Albertstadt industrial area, Infesto-Works manufactured steering components for aircraft, U-boats and torpedos; Brückner, Kanis & Company served as a naval production and testing station for specialized turbines; and the Gläserkarrosserie GmbH Works III made parts for Messerschmitt fighters.[20] Furthermore, in the words of British historian Frederick Taylor, "The largest employer in Dresden by far . . . was Zeiss-Ikon. And it was a long time since that distinguished company had produced anything as innocent as a snapshot camera."[21] This firm made extensive use of Dresden's Jews, prior to their inevitable shipment eastwards for further "processing." Its specialities were precision optics and engineering—pivotal contributions to the German war effort.[22]

Nestled among the honeycombed rabbit warren of picturesque, baroque buildings in the city centre, or *Altstadt,* were the Central Telegraph Office, the Main Police Headquarters, a power station, one of the Siemens factories and a significant military transport headquarters and facility. Perhaps most importantly, Dresden was also a major rail hub and junction point, as well as a key nodal point in the German postal and telegraph network and, consequently, a critical location for the military with respect to transportation and communications. Three major rail stations and the

Friedrichstadt marshalling yards were all located a mile or less from the *Altstadt*, and both the north–south and east–west axes of the German state railway system ran directly through the city, which controlled rolling stock over in excess of 3000 miles of track. By late 1943 the Dresden railway directorate employed a total of 128,000 workers.[23] Furthermore, Dresden had not been declared an "open city" by the German government, one which possessed no military significance and should thus be spared from attack. "It was the hub connecting the two major rail lines between Berlin and Leipzig and accordingly was a troop concentration area. There was therefore no logical reason—other than its distance from Lincolnshire—for it to have been exempt from air attack."[24] It was, above all else, a legitimate transportation target, the kind that had been receiving priority attention from the Anglo-American bomber forces for many months.

It should also be reinforced that the purpose of Thunderclap had changed from its original form as proposed in 1944. The Thunderclap and Clarion mandates were now considerably broader than just attacks on enemy morale. Dresden was, in short, not a "twelfth-hour" target selected simply to terrorize the enemy population. And, although Dresden was a city of great beauty and cultural significance, it was also one of the most ardently pro-Nazi and zealously anti-Semitic cosmopolitan centres in the Third Reich, and it had enthusiastically embraced the German national socialism movement from its outset. *Gauleiter* Martin Mutschmann, the senior Nazi party official, provincial governor, and defence commissioner in Dresden, was particularly brutal and relentless in his persecution of local Jews and other "undesirables." A significant number of Dresden's citizens took their behavioral cues from the *Gauleiter*'s cruel example.[25]

Another important factor that made the Dresden raids viable in February 1945 was that, by this stage of the war, the city was very lightly defended.

> By early 1945, the German night fighter defences had become threadbare. The crews were tired and aviation spirit was at an absolute premium. Even though the area of the homeland and occupied territory that had to be defended had shrunk considerably under Allied and Soviet attack, the scale of air attacks was steadily increasing. The impact of the combined bomber offensive with its escorting long-range fighters had taken its toll on the *Luftwaffe*. Furthermore, the demand for heavy calibre artillery was huge; it has been estimated that even though over 20,000 artillery pieces were deployed for air defence purposes (and therefore not available for land warfare), there were still insufficient guns to protect everything. Dresden was comparitively low on the priority list, hence its earlier escape from air attack contributed to its eventual demise.[26]

Perhaps the most fundamental myth surrounding the bombing of Dresden is that the raids were conceived by Sir Arthur Harris and his command planners, and that the actual bombing was strictly an RAF operation. As we have seen, the genesis of the raids occurred much higher up the chain of command and was truly international in input from the beginning. The fact that both Allied air forces participated is conclusive evidence that the raids were sanctioned at a much higher level than Bomber Command. In the words of Robin Neillands:

> The accusation that Harris decided to destroy Dresden from sheer bloodlust would be too stupid to merit a reply were it not so widely believed by the public in Britain and several other countries. If the general public in Great Britain and elsewhere wish to blame someone for the destruction of Dresden, they will have to spread their net far wider than Air Chief Marshal Sir Arthur Harris and the men of RAF Bomber Command.[27]

Although there were initially profound misgivings at Bomber Command Headquarters in High Wycombe concerning the efficacy of bombing Dresden—it was a long way from home, little was known about the target area, the increased fuel requirement necessitated some reductions to bomb loads, winter weather could be problematic, and much could go wrong—once the die was cast, Harris put all his usual high-voltage energy into the task at hand.[28] The Combined Staff decided early that the Americans would lead the assault with a daylight attack against the transport system located at the city's outskirts, since attempting to bomb through the smoke of a preceding RAF night area attack in daylight by largely visual means would likely be difficult. For Bomber Command, the plan was to follow the Americans that same night, and it would play to its strengths and bomb targets in the city centre in two distinct waves in order to best exploit the confused conditions that would exist in Dresden after the initial American onslaught. According to Henry Probert:

> Those who contend that it was unnecessary, indeed wrong, to attack the city centre ignore the practicalities of trying to bomb with high precision at great distance and in conditions that were not only hard to predict but might conceivably lead to another Nuremburg. If the job was to be done at all it was essential to go for the city as a whole and in choosing a two-wave attack led by the specialized 5 Group, Harris sought to reduce the risks of failure to a minimum.[29]

The combined plan quickly deteriorated when weather forced a postponement of the American daylight portion of the attack. However, the weather cooperated to an extent with Bomber Command at Dresden. Attacking in the two waves separated by three hours, 1500 tons of high explosives and 1200 tons of incendiaries were unleashed on the city by 796 Lancasters and nine Mosquitos. The participating Canadians included ten Lancaster Pathfinder crews from 405 Squadron and sixty-seven 6 Group Lancasters, attacking in the second wave.[30]

> The first attack was carried out entirely by No. 5 Group using their own low-level marking methods. A band of cloud still remained in the area and this raid, in which 244 Lancasters dropped more than 800 tons of bombs, was only moderately successful. The second raid, hours later, was an all-Lancaster attack by aircraft of Nos. 1, 3, 6 and 8 Groups, with No. 8 Group providing standard Pathfinder marking. The weather was now clear and 529 Lancasters dropped more than 1800 tons of bombs with great accuracy. Much has been written about the fearful effects of the raid. Suffice it to say here that a firestorm, similar to the one experienced in Hamburg in July 1943 [and again at Kassel in October 1943] was created and large areas of the city were burnt out . . . Bomber Command casualties were 6 Lancasters lost, with 2 more crashed in France and 1 in England.
> 311 American B-17s dropped 771 tons of bombs on Dresden the next day, with the railway yards as their aiming point . . . The Americans bombed Dresden again on the 15th and on 2 March, but it is generally accepted that it was the RAF night raid that caused the most damage.[31]

Contrary to popular belief, the ensuing firestorm was not deliberately generated to maximize the number of casualties and the amount of property damage. Rather, like Hamburg in July 1943 and, to a lesser extent, Kassel in October 1943, the target structures, the attack conditions and the weather all combined to produce this effect. It is true, however, that Bomber Command planners sent the attacking forces in two distinct waves separated by several hours, somewhat similar to what had been done at Duisburg months earlier, as part of an attempt to confuse the enemy defences. Fires were also deliberately started by the initial attack force in an effort to overwhelm the emergency services, a long-practiced Bomber Command tactic. These fires were also intended to provide specific marking reference points for the main-wave bombing. For example, portions of the railway yards were able to be used as specific aiming points for the later attacking waves.[32]

According to the attack plan, markers would drop their Target Indicators (TIs) on a large, 500 foot-long sports stadium, the *Dresden-Friedrichstadt Sportsplatz*, located just south of the Elbe River at the northwestern edge of the ancient inner city, the *Altstadt*. The stadium, the middle of three spread across the breadth of the city, was chosen partially because of the distinctive radar return of a bend in the river nearby, should the need to bomb without visual reference to the ground prevail. Past maximum efforts had reinforced the need for large, distinct and unambiguous aiming and release points. The stadium and the *Altstadt* were singled out for these reasons, but also to exploit the inevitable phenomenon of bombing "creepback." This side-effect would optimize damage to the railway marshalling yards, the Seidel and Naumann factory, the Shell Oil plant, the train stations located in close proximity to the *Altstadt*, and the factories, which were imbedded within the residential suburbs.[33] Sir Arthur Harris was very concerned about his crews being able to find the target area and mark it properly. Therefore, the preliminary raid by 5 Group attacked from the northwest to southeast, fanning out on different headings in a series of timed procedural overshoots from the aim point to overfly and bomb the area between the Neustadt, Wettin and Central stations,[34] including portions of the *Altstadt*, at ranges of up to 2400 yards (1.5 miles) from the stadium. There was no shortage of legitimate targets imbedded within the *Altstadt* area. The larger and later main raid would attack from southwest to northeast, aiming off the fires started by the first raid and attacking other specific targets in the vicinity. Given the lack of concentration of results generally inherent in area bombing, which even in 1945 was still an inexact science,[35] a great amount of widespread damage was anticipated by concentrating on the *Altstadt* and its environs.

The RAF night raids and the USAAF day raids which followed[36] were to a large extent successful. Bomber Command's losses were very light on the night. Numbers vary, but only somewhere between eight and twenty-nine night fighters took off to intercept the preliminary force,[37] and the extremely confused ground controllers did not scramble intercepting forces at all against the main, second attack.[38] Approximately 70 percent of Dresden was destroyed by the ensuing firestorm with its hurricane-force winds, including much of the *Altstadt* with its beautiful baroque landmarks.[39] Many, many casualties ensued as a result of this raid. The blood cost has proven extremely contentious over time, fuelled in no small measure by later Soviet Cold War rhetoric issued as a means of demonizing the western Allies. Greatly and deliberately overstated at the outset by Joseph Goebbels and his propaganda ministry, the casualty count has generally been kept at misleading levels in the years that have followed.[40] While the losses were very high, they need to be placed in proper perspective. One reliable source bracketed the casualty estimates from 35,000 to 135,000 fatalities, "but when comparisons are made with other raids, including the 1943 firestorm raid on Hamburg and the recent USAAF daylight raid on refugee-crammed Berlin the previous month, something close to the lower figure—which is terrible enough—seems most probable."[41] In fact, the recent and critically acclaimed treatment of the raids by British historian Frederick Taylor estimates the actual death toll at between 25,000 and 40,000 fatalities and also reaffirms that Dresden was a "city of considerable military importance, both as a transportation hub and a major producer of armaments and military provisions."[42] The armament and war goods factories were reduced to about 20 percent of their previous operating capacity[43] but, although the rail network was extensively damaged, it was not totally ruined. However, as British historian Denis Richards points out, the city was devastated enough to be ruined as a potential main administrative and control node for the German land forces fighting not far to the east of Dresden.[44] Perhaps an even more significant result has been articulated by the German historian and wartime Dresden resident Götz Bergander, for while the raids were not intended to deliberately terrorize the Germans,

> It is right to say that the shockwave triggered by Dresden swept away what was left of the will to resist, as the Germans now feared that such a catastrophe could be repeated daily. Awareness of the inevitable defeat increased and the belief in miracles disappeared but, above all, there was the growing realization that it would be better if the end came soon . . . better to have a terrible end than endless terror.[45]

The official historians of Bomber Command's war, Sir Charles Webster and Noble Frankland, have suggested that Dresden became a turning point for the overall morale of the German people. They submit that the Nazi police state, specifically the *Gestapo*, had maintained an artificial and coercive form of morale until the scale of destruction in Dresden, the recent raid on Berlin, as well as a number of others, became common knowledge. The realization was soon pervasive that no piece of real estate in the Third Reich remained safe and secure from aerial bombardment.[46]

Freddy Fish, an RAF navigator, gives his impressions of the purposes stated for their bombing operations in general during this stage of the war and the Dresden raids in particular.

> I can assure you that at every briefing I attended—over thirty—we were *always* told that we were bombing a military target. My logbook shows references to "Industrial centre," "Armaments factory," "Oil plant," "Marshalling yards," "Industries," etc. . . . At all times, the aircrew I knew believed that we were bombing genuine, selected, military targets only; so to make out that we were some kind of slaughterers, deliberately, of innocent civilians is utter nonsense. At the time we did not know how many people were being killed and could only go on PRU (Photo-Reconnaissance Unit) assessed damage. We certainly did not think of ourselves as "terror flyers." We all thought we were hitting vital enemy targets and assisting our armies to win the war.[47]

Robert Geisel, a member of the RCAF who flew the raid while serving with 115 Squadron, recalls:

> This target (Dresden) was given to the crews as a main railhead supporting the German Eastern Front. Recent reports would indicate this was just a target to destroy, with no military value, but it was indicated to the crews that, with all the refugees jamming the roads and this being the closest railhead to the Eastern Front, the Russians had requested assistance and we complied with this request. It was to be many years before I heard of the destruction wrought on this raid, but I do recall that the fires were to be seen from a long distance after we left.[48]

The Propagandists Score Telling Blows

For those at High Wycombe and elsewhere who were involved in or responsible for the planning of Bomber Command's operations, the immediate aftermath of the Dresden raid generated considerable relief. After all, telling blows had been struck at minimal cost—a loss rate of less than 1 percent. However, some injudicious comments at a briefing given by a senior RAF press officer at SHAEF Headquarters in Paris on 17 February 1945,[49] followed almost immediately by an Associated Press (AP) despatch caused a public outcry. In his press conference, the RAF air commodore, perhaps defaulting to the earlier mandate associated with Thunderclap, later made statements and answered questions which were summarized incorrectly and embellished in the AP despatch, that the Allied air commanders had now made "the long awaited decision to adopt deliberate terror bombing of German population centres as a ruthless expedient to hastening Hitler's doom."[50] However, no one at the press conference, including the hapless air commodore, had used the expression "terror bombing" or anything that might imply the term. The AP reporter who drafted the despatch had taken liberties, and the SHAEF censors had imprudently approved the result. The AP bulletin was broadcast at the time in Paris and then widely published in the United States. It bolstered a deliberate attempt by Joesph Goebbels and his propaganda corps to discredit Allied bombing policy in the Allied nations. Wildly exaggerated casualty figures (by a factor of up to 1000 percent) and grisly photographs of the bombings were released through the neutral nations, particularly Sweden and Switzerland, for dissemination in the Allied camp.[51]

The despatch was greeted with broad dismay in America, where the public had hitherto had mostly reports that emphasized the precision and selectivity of American bombing. General George C. Marshall was quick to counter the despatch with a statement that Dresden had been bombed at the request of the Soviets, but this only partially alleviated the disquiet. In London, broad wartime censorship curtailed all but a brief preliminary exposure of the AP despatch. However, the issue was raised in Parliament on 6 March 1945 by a Member named Richard Stokes, one of the bombing campaign's most vocal and enduring critics. As Stokes rose to speak to the House,

> [Sir Archibald] Sinclair rose from his seat and pointedly left the Chamber. Stokes read out the AP despatch in full and then accused the government of hiding the true nature of the bombing campaign from the British public. Sinclair replied some hours later that the government was not wasting its time on purely terror tactics. Although criticism was relatively muted, the seeds had been sown for later outbursts of conscience.[52]

As Peter Gray has noted, all the draft international conventions of the 1930s against the bombing of civilian populations and the destruction of private property—and there were no binding resoultions agreed on at the time—were broken in due course by all the combatants.[53] When the Second World War entered its final year and the full obscenity of the Third Reich's behavior became broadly known, international legal nuances with respect to bombing became hardly worth considering. Ethical issues were similarly not broadly debated. The overriding concern was to win the war, by whatever means, as soon as possible. Peter Gray further notes that when looking at the entirety of Thunderclap and Clarion operations during the later months of the war, "The attacks on these cities were entirely consistent with Allied bombing policy of the time—on both sides of the Atlantic. Furthermore, the planning, execution and weapon selection were consistent with the standard procedures of the time."[54] The argument later voiced by some about the Dresden attacks, that it was unnecessary to bomb the city because the European war was already won, is patently absurd. As Canadian historian Terry Copp has observed, the raids took place a full month before any Allied soldier crossed the Rhine River into the German heartland, and three months prior to the eventual German capitulation.[55] In Feburary 1945 there were still many unanswered questions and combat variables obscuring the path to Allied victory.

Eyewitness accounts also dispute the notion that Dresden at the time had little or no direct military value, aside from the assets otherwise listed. A former USAAF colonel wrote:

> I was shot down over Austria on May 24, 1944, and four of my crew were killed. On or about 30 January 1945, we were evacuated from Stalag-Luft III in Silesia because of the advance of the Soviet Army, marched several days in sub-zero weather and then loaded onto German freight cars—60 men where 40 would have been crowded. The night before the RAF/USAAF raids on 13/14 February, we were shunted into the Dresden marshalling yard where for nearly 12 hours, German troops rolled in and out of Dresden. I saw with my own eyes that Dresden was an armed camp: thousands of German troops, tanks and artillery, and miles of freight cars loaded with supplies supporting and transporting German logistics toward the east to meet the Russians.[56]

The destruction of Dresden was an unfortunate act of war. Significant damage was caused, but with the hindsight of history, the great number of casualties incurred, as well as the massive amount of property damage levied appear disproportionate to the results obtained by the bombings. However,

> to the operational commanders, the formation commanders and the crews in their charge, the raids on Dresden and the other East German cities, were part of the complex tapestry that represented their part in waging war against the most odious regime then known to mankind. To them, it was just another raid.[57]

No Quarter, No Respite

Thunderclap targeting continued the following night when Bomber Command focussed on Chemnitz, located about forty miles southwest of Dresden. Known as the centre of Germany's hosiery and underwear manufacture, Chemnitz contained a number of important war industries and it was also an important Saxon rail hub. The Eighth Air Force had already visited the city four times; twice during 1944 and twice more—as recently as that very afternoon—as part of Thunderclap/Clarion. On the latest raid, the Americans had damaged a number of industrial plants in the southern suburbs. However, this first major Bomber Command raid on the city was not as successful. The raid took place in two waves separated by three hours, employing tactics similar to those used at Dresden. While an elaborate diversion plan to many other centres kept the Allied Chemnitz casualties down, the bombing was not very effective this night. Both waves found the target area blanketed by cloud, and only the relatively inaccurate form of skymarking could be employed. Post-operation reconnaissance revealed that, while many portions of the city were hit in a scattered manner, most of the bombs landed in open country. In all, 499 Lancasters and 218 Halifaxes from 1, 3, 4, 6 and 8 Groups participated in this raid. However, such was now the diverse capability of the Command that it was able to mount 1316 sorties on the night to such locations as Rositz near Leipzig, the Heligoland Bight, Berlin, Mainz, Dessau, Duisburg, Nuremburg and Frankfurt. In all, 23 aircraft, 1.7 percent of those despatched, were lost.[58] At Chemnitz, the 717 crews, which included 51 Lancasters and 64 Halifaxes from 6 Group,

> struggled to hit the railway yards whose destruction, they had been told, would be "of

great assistance to good old Stalin and his Marshal Zhukov, who are only a hundred miles away." Despite the scatter, some damage was done. "The firm of Auger und Söhn, manufacturing ammunition boxes, was completely destroyed . . . the bandage manufacturers Max Arnold suffered medium to heavy damage [and] drinking water was cut off." The Luftwaffe's response was better than at Dresden despite extensive jamming and spoofing, and thirteen machines were lost . . . of which three were from No 6 Group.[59]

During the weeks that followed Dresden, Canadian airmen, and those of Bomber Command generally, were flying operations all over the Third Reich, attacking transportation, rail and Thunderclap targets. They also returned time and again to the Ruhr, which was in the process of being surrounded and isolated by American land forces. However, Thunderclap targeting also took the Main Force further afield, including south to the periphery of the picturesque Black Forest region of Germany:

> Perhaps the most successful area raid in the region occurred on 23/24 February at Pforzheim, a jewellery and clock-making town on the Karlsruhe-Stuttgart main line. The marking, done from about 8000 feet, was accurate, and the crews . . . produced "destruction on a scale [and] as complete as at any target ever attacked. There was hardly a single building left intact throughout the whole area, and apart from the tremendous gutting by fires many . . . buildings were levelled to the ground. Damage to railway facilities was also heavy, the goods yard was completely burnt out, rolling stock destroyed, two of the river bridges had collapsed and the road over the rail bridge . . . was . . . hit and rendered unserviceable." Seven thousand were reported killed, and 45,000 left homeless. Although supported by *Mandrel, Window,* and raids on Darmstadt, Würms, Berlin, Frankfurt, Essen, and Oslo, the attackers nevertheless lost twelve crews, eleven from No 1 Group.[60]

Located at the junction of the Enz and Nagold rivers, roughly halfway between Stuttgart and Karlsruhe, this *Nordschwarzwald* city of 80,000 inhabitants presented an easy and distinct reference point on *H2S,* due to the confluence of the two rivers. Prior to this particular raid, the city had been hit eight times in daylight by the Eighth Air Force and a further five times by small RAF raids. Pforzheim was bombed because it was a significant transportation target, and also because of its specialized light industry in the manufacture of precision instruments. On the night of 23/24 February, 1825 tons of bombs were dropped on the city by 367 Lancasters and thirteen Mosquitos of Nos 1, 6, and 8 Groups in just twenty-two minutes, and 83 percent of the built-up area was levelled. The 6 Group contribution was fifty Lancasters. Overnight, Pforzheim had become the third-worst bombarded German urban area, surpassed in damage and destruction by only Hamburg and Dresden. Besides the massive road, rail and bridge damage, most of the identifiable factories were destroyed, including at least seven priority facilities. Thirteen Lancasters were brought down by fighters and flak, and although none were from 6 Group, four RCAF members were killed aboard the downed aircraft, and twelve more became late-war POWs. A number of others bailed out safely over Allied territory.[61]

Geoff Marlow was one of the 434 Squadron participants on this raid. He reflects on the Pforzheim mission in particular and on operational concerns in general for this period of the bombing campaign:

> The raid on Pforzheim, a centre for the manufacture of precision instruments, was conducted on a night with no protective cloud cover. German air controllers had no doubt

seen our bomber stream coming at them on their radar scopes and had scrambled the night fighters . . . As we entered German airspace the air controllers would have provided the night fighters with the direction, height and airspeed of our aircraft. Their pilots could tell when they entered the bomber stream because of the air turbulence churned out by the prop wash of our big, four-engined Lancasters and Halifaxes. Once inside the stream, the night fighters simply narrowed the gap on our unseen bombers they knew were somewhere out in front in the darkness. The night fighter's radio operator, sitting in the back seat, guided the pilot to the target. Their preferred angle of attack was from behind and below. We had no way of knowing whether the night fighters were stalking us until we suddenly saw one of our own bombers explode in flames. They attacked our bomber force continuously as we approached our objective, heavily laden with bombs. When loaded, it is difficult to take evasive action, so our bombers suffered heavy losses. Ahead of us, searchlights pierced the night sky. The master beams, pale blue shafts of light, were controlled by radar. Once they settled on one of our aircraft, several "slave" beams, which were brilliantly white, would converge on the master beam to saturate the captive aircraft in a cone of blinding light. It was a frightening experience to be caught in these beams; the pilot knew that, unless he could escape their grasp within moments, the enemy flak would concentrate on his aircraft and destroy it. On a previous night, I had been caught for a few seconds, but had managed to evade the cone by putting the plane through some particularly violent manoeuvres. In the distance I could see one of our Lancasters caught in this predicament. It was not long before it exploded in a ball of flame. Over the city of Pforzheim, flak filled the sky with its orange-coloured shell bursts, each one scattering its deadly fragments far and wide. Below us a fiery furnace raged. We were at 7500 feet, an unusually low altitude for a heavy bomber raid. The target area had already been identified by the Pathfinder Force ahead of us. They had dropped brilliant red, green and yellow flares throughout the area and the Master Bomber, [Captain Edwin "Tom" Swales, DFC, of the South African Air Force] in his 582 Squadron Lancaster, directed us where to drop our bombs in relation to the flares. On this raid he doggedly stayed over the target for half-an-hour and was awarded the Victoria Cross for his bravery under horrendous conditions, and for the accuracy of the attack.

As we returned home from the trip, we could see behind us the glow of the burning city against the night sky. We tried not to dwell too long on the fate of those who had plunged to earth in their flaming coffins. It was reassuring to see the English coastline gradually emerge ahead of us in the early morning mist. It would not be long now before we would be home, safe and sound for a few more hours, or perhaps a few more days.[62]

Unanticipated Personnel Shortfalls

During the last six months of the European war, although Bomber Command had evolved into a mature and reliable instrument, some practical problems continued to appear. Sir Arthur Harris was particularly concerned about the supply of munitions for his now-massive fleet. Late in 1944 he had registered disappointment on being informed that the production program for the ten-ton Tallboy Large bombs, later known as Grand Slam, along with "the (concomitant) modification of a full squadron of Lancasters was being heavily curtailed, and he was much relieved to hear that this was untrue since most of the bombs needed were to be produced in America." However, early in the new year, he wrote Portal about an increasing shortage with the mainstay 1000-pound General Purpose bombs, "which could well necessitate 'a partial and deliberate return to the area bombing of cities with incendiaries' and thus affect target selection."[63] Manpower issues also reared their heads. Since November 1944, the throughput of the BCATP had been drastically curtailed. Casualties following the Command's secondment to SHAEF in April had been lighter than expected, and a 40 percent drawdown of aircrew production had been initiated.[64] However, the training of replacement aircrew was now at an all-time high, thanks to the evolved efficiency of the Operational Training Units (OTUs) and the Heavy Conversion Units (HCUs), and crews were also finishing their operational tours in record time. This was leaving a dearth of operational experience on the bomber squadrons. Exacerbating the problem, many relatively senior officers, who had been "frozen" for the bulk of the war in instructional jobs with the BCATP and in other staff jobs in Canada, were now arriving in droves in an attempt to gain combat experience prior to war's end. They tended to be experienced aviators but they brought no battle experience with them, and were occasionally placed in air leadership positions in deference to their rank, when logic should have dictated otherwise. On top of all this, more crews were being assigned to the tactical air forces and to the other commands. Harris registered a specific concern on 30 January 1945 about the proposed plan to transfer approximately 100 recent OTU graduate crews for light bomber duties with 2 Group.[65] This was only a brief concern over operational experience, compared to the major concerns that had been registered in the summer of 1943, and these new issues were not unique to 6 Group. Air Commodore R.E. McBurney, Johnnie Fauquier's replacement at 6 Group Headquarters as Senior Operations Staff Officer (SOSO), in an echo of problems encountered in earlier times, was particularly concerned,

> about the frequency of bombing and navigation errors and he was even more upset by the number of so-called manipulation errors—failures to use electronic aids correctly—which, together with the "lack of offensive spirit' exhibited by a minority of crews, were causing an unacceptably high early return rate. He recommended that repeat offenders be dealt with quickly and firmly, adding that disciplinary action might be necessary. Although the idea of punishing crews by refusing to credit them with completion of an operational sortie when they were far off track did not win widespread approval among the squadron commanding officers, there was rarely any disagreement with the kind of treatment meted out to one navigator who, having knowingly bombed Hamburg 15 minutes early on 31 March 1945, was removed from operations and sent to the retraining centre at Sheffield for three weeks.
>
> There were cycles in 6 Group's history that were beyond anyone's control, however, and one of these—a marked falling off in the number of experienced crews available—was bothering Allerton Hall late in 1944. Once again, the loss rate was responsible, but in exactly the opposite way to 1943. With the tremendous decline in casualties after June 1944 and the sharp increase in the number of sorties flown, significantly more crews were completing their operational tours in significantly less time. Veterans were usually replaced by novices fresh from their Heavy Conversion Unit and, when such screenings came in bunches, as happened in late 1944, the overall level of expertise was bound to fall. It was not only that navigation and bomb-aiming suffered as a result—reason enough for Air Vice-Marshal McEwen's concern—but also, as we have seen, that artlessness in dealing with enemy fighters cost lives. Accordingly, there would be no let-up in the strict training regimen he had introduced nine months before.[66]

Further exacerbating the problem, most crews were "screened," or taken off operations, when their pilot flew his thirtieth raid, which meant that most of the aircrew in the other trades flew at least one or two operations fewer than their pilot, since the pilots were required to do those "second dickie trips" with seasoned crews at the outset of their tours in order to gain operational experience. Once screened, crews were broken up with some members posted to the OTUs or the HCUs as instructors, to other staff duties, or, as was frequently the case with the Canadians, they were posted home to Canada.[67] All these elements combined to gut the Command of aircrew experience on the operational squadrons. "So Bomber Command developed a point system that required crews on their first operational tour to complete about thirty-five sorties before being screened."[68]

In February Harris had decided to extend the first operational tour from thirty to approximately thirty-six sorties, based on that points system, a not unreasonable move given the experience shortfalls and the relatively few combat losses now being registered.[69] It affected relatively few crews, however, since by March, the number of OTU/HCU graduates effectively overwhelmed needs. Still, there were always some individuals affected, particularly if an individual group commander took an even more demanding interpretation of High Wycombe's new edict. Donald Bronson Daikens, a Canadian who flew his operational tour in Halifaxes with 76 Squadron in 4 Group out of Holme-on-Spalding-Moor, explains:

> We returned to our base to be screened after our 30th trip. When we got out of the kite we were like a bunch of kids. The pressure was off and we had lived through a tour. All the way into the Flights to be debriefed we were wrestling with one another and laughing and joking. Our Intelligence Officer, a "flight louie" [rank of flight lieutenant], checked us all on what we had to report.
>
> When we had finished, he said, "I hate to have to tell you chaps this but they have changed the point system and you people have *nine* more trips to go before you are screened." We then all turned pale and I felt like I had been kicked in the guts by a mule. I *knew* we would never live through! I was sure we would all die.
>
> We had to cancel our screening party at the pub. After our 39th trip, I was late getting to the party and had not yet eaten. I drank six double gin & tonics, one after the other, and passed out flat on my face while talking to our commanding officer and our pilot a half-hour later. Pure heroics.[70]

However, the points system was essentially deemed unnecessary before it could be fully implemented. Accordingly, on 15 April 1945, High Wycombe issued instructions that reduced the required number of first-tour operations back to thirty at month's end. "Even so, Bomber Command calculated that 29 RCAF aircrew had been killed or captured while flying first-tour sorties beyond the thirty limit."[71]

The Random Nature of Late War Combat

One of the features of these late war Bomber Command operations in February/March was that while the losses overall were generally low, various groups tended to suffer higher casualty rates at different times. Although it was 1 Group's turn at Pforzheim, in conjunction with 8 Group, they had eight crews fail to return from an attack on Bottrop in the Ruhr district on the night of 3/4 February. Also, 5 Group lost fourteen crews in bright, moonlit conditions over Karlsruhe on the night of 2/3 February (5.6 percent of those sortied), and thirteen more Lancasters (7.9 percent) attempting to breach the Mittelland Canal near Gravenhorst on 21/22 February.[72] Nor was 6 Group exempt from periods of intensified suffering, and it experienced four particularly bad raids during this time. The first came on the night of 21/22 February, that bad night for 5 Group as well, and a week after Dresden, when it lost six of 111 bombers despatched during a highly accurate area attack on Würms. The losses included three from 432 Squadron. Although an estimated 39 percent of the town's built-up area was demolished, "the enemy received 'unusually early warning by some means unknown' to High Wycombe at the time. Even single-engined fighters were in action over Holland."[73] Similar loss rates were incurred on 7/8 March, when five of 6 Group's 182 crews despatched to Dessau and Hemmingstedt failed to return. While the raid on the Deutsche Erdoel refinery at Hemmingstadt, about fifty miles west of Kiel, met with only limited success, the Dessau raid, a new target in the eastern region of the Reich, inflicted devastating damage. In all, 526 Lancasters and five Mosquitos of 1, 3, 6, and 8 Groups participated. Of this number, eighteen Lancasters were lost, 3.4 percent of the attacking force.[74] Mo Morrison recalls the Dessau raid from the perspective of a Canadian flying with 1 Group.

> First thought at briefing, "What a hell of a route." We went all over the north of Germany and as soon as we entered, we had flak and searchlights to contend with—all the way to target. We had predicted flak just past the Ruhr and got one small hole in starboard wing—quite proud of it! The target was very well marked and we bombed on skymarkers. Considerable flak over target but things quieted down on route home. Master Bomber was heard well. Very dark night and gunners well on their toes. Rear gunner (Harry Baker) very calm and collected at all times. Mid-upper (Chick Webb) quiet but efficient. Another long trip and "ropey" landing at end. Very tired. Papers say the joint is finished so I guess another Jerry town is fixed up. Total flying time [of operation]: 9:50.[75]

One of the bloodiest raids of the late war period was a major strike against Nuremburg on the night of 16/17 March. In fact, two major operations were mounted that night. In a dramatic and devastating blow by 5 Group, 225 Lancasters and eleven Mosquitos pounded the ancient cathedral city of Würzburg, inflicting extensive damage. While the raid was intended as a diversion away from the Nuremburg strike, Würzburg was also a legitimate transportation, communications, administrative and industrial target.[76] Meanwhile, 231 Lancasters from 1 Group and forty-six Lancasters and sixteen Mosquitos from 8 Group headed for Nuremburg. In a classic verification of the enemy's late war fighting capabilities, which could remain potent right until the end of hostilities, German night fighters found the bomber stream on its way to the target. While extensive damage was done to the city on this, Bomber Command's last heavy raid on Nuremburg of the war, twenty-four Lancasters, all from 1 Group, which represented 8.7 percent of the Lancaster force and 10.4 percent of the 1 Group effort, were lost.[77] Although this operation was not a 6 Group tasking, Canadians were certainly involved, as Mo Morrison recalls, first from his war diary, then from recollections made fifty years later:

> The idea kind of shook us as that place had been known as a "hot" target. Briefing was good and take-off on short runway OK. Nothing of interest on way across France and the flak over Stuttgart told us we were on track. Around the target there was bags of excitement, five dummy targets were lit, lots of fighter flares and as we were a little to port of track on (the target) run-up, we escaped most of the heavy flak. We could see the target and the PFF markers clearly. Master Bomber instructed us to overshoot the target, which we did. Things were quiet on route home and we landed fifth. 24 of the 200+ on the raid caught it. Dauphinee and Cooper from here. Dauphinee and crew were very good friends for a long time so it hurts. Hope they are POWs somewhere. Time, 8:35.[78]
>
> The Nuremburg trip was a bit of a downer, to say the least . . . Practically all the 24 shot

down, all from our Group and two from 100 Squadron, were nailed by night fighters. Of particular concern to our crew was the loss of George Dauphinee's plane. George and I had been best buddies through the training stream, as had his and our bomb-aimers and navigators, as well as those in the other Squadron loss, Cooper's crew . . .

This was the last great "hurrah" for the German night fighter force and they had a field day . . . or night . . . As we swung into our bombing run, the scene was right out of Dante's Inferno . . . The city was burning, bombers were going down, flak was coming up, fighter flares were turning night into day, and we were struggling to get along in old "Able Mabel," the most venerable of all our squadron aircraft with more than 120 "ops" painted on her nose . . . Now airplanes, like all of us, get weary as they get older . . . and in Lancaster years, I would reckon Able Mabel to be that night about the same age as some of us here tonight. At any rate, she was slow, and she wouldn't climb above 20,000-or-so feet, so we found ourselves under the second wave of bombers instead of leading the first wave . . . Now Chick Webb, our mid-upper gunner, [seventeen years old at the time] had the best view of all, particularly of the fighters and the bombers up above with their bomb doors open and about to drop their bombs—on us!! By that time, we were a fairly disciplined crew so there was very little chatter on the intercom, and besides, we were scared "witless" when an ephemeral voice floated over the intercom from the direction of the mid-upper turret—"I want to go home, Mo." This was just what we needed to bring us together to finish the job.[79]

The Jet and Rocket Fighters

While the last months of the European war were generally characterized by overwhelming Allied air superiority, there were a few disturbing anomalies, and they were portents of future air combat. The German jet and rocket fighters were introduced to the air combat arena far too late and in far too limited numbers to influence the outcome of the war. However, they produced a level of anxiety about their revolutionary capabilities all out of proportion to their actually modest combat effectiveness. Foreshadowed by the RAF's fielding of the twin-engine Gloster Meteor during the 1944 Crossbow campaign, this aircraft also saw limited operational service in the ground attack role in northwest Europe during February/March 1945. Nonetheless, in terms of diversification, the Germans were far ahead of the Allies in introducing these "cutting edge" technologies to battle. The twin-engine Messerschmitt Me 262 *Schwalbe* (Swallow) fighter and the *Sturmvogel* (Stormbird), a ground attack variant of the same aircraft, were the most prominent of the new jets. However, the Heinkel He 162 *Salamander*, the Arado Ar 234B *Blitz* and the Messerschmitt Me 163B *Komet* rocket fighter also numbered among this potential nest of vipers, and they were all operationally deployed prior to the cessation of hostilities. The disquiet they sowed among the Allies was largely a lack of intelligence about how many of these fighters the aircrews might expect to encounter. And since Bomber Command, too, was now operating increasingly in the daylight hours, the disquiet was not limited to American crews. But the single-engine He 162 *Salamander*, also known as the *Volksjäger* (People's Fighter), only became operational during the closing days of the war. Revolutionary in many ways, but particularly because it was manufactured largely from non-strategic materials and was supposedly simple enough for *Hitlerjugend* (Hitler Youth) boys with little more than glider training to operate, the *Volksjäger* actually proved difficult to fly, except in the hands of experienced pilots. By 4 May 1945 one Group of four squadrons, a total of fifty aircraft, had formed at Leck in Schleswig-Holstein, but British forces occupied the airfield on 8 May, VE-Day. Although only 116 He 162s were built, more than 800 were in various stages of production when hostilities ended.

The Arado Ar 234B Blitz twin-engine jet bomber made its operational début in July 1944. In all, 274 airframes were produced. But this aircraft was never designed as a fighter—it mirrored the Meteor's activities in attacking ground targets during late 1944 and early 1945—it never constituted a threat to the Allied bomber streams.[80]

The greatest concern was the Me 262. Contrary to popular opinion, British expert Dr. Alfred Price contends that the Messerschmitt jet was not significantly delayed in its combat access to the Anglo-American bomber streams by Hitler's 1944 demand that it be initially employed as a Blitz bomber against the Allied landings in France. While this decision, coupled with some bureaucratic ineptitude, resulted in a slight delay in fielding the fighter variant, Price contends the main reason was simply the teething troubles associated with producing sufficiently dependable jet engines to power the aircraft.[81] By the end of April 1945 more than 1200 Me 262s had been accepted by the *Luftwaffe*, but nearly 500 of them were destroyed on the ground during bombing attacks. The maximum number available at any time occurred on 9 April 1945, when approximately 180 Me 262s were on battle order. Walther Hagenah, an experienced fighter pilot who flew the aircraft operationally during the closing months of the war, recollects some of the problems associated with operating the revolutionary jet and provides an interesting point of view on the direct and indirect effects of the bombing on jet readiness:

> By the time I reached [the *Gruppe*] there were insufficient spare parts and insufficient spare engines; there were even occasional shortages of J-2 fuel. I am sure all of these existed and production was sufficient, but by that stage of the war the transport system was so chaotic that things often failed to arrive at front line units . . .
>
> In our unit, flying the Me 262, we had some pilots with only about a hundred hours total flying time. They were able to take-off and land the aircraft, but I had the definite impression that they were little use in combat. It was almost a crime to send them into action with so little training. These young men did their best, but they had to pay a heavy price for their lack of experience.[82]

In spite of their limitations, the presence of the jets was unsettling to the Allies. Their most successful day occurred on 31 March 1945, when the fighters generated fifty-eight sorties and felled sixteen Allied aircraft. The majority of the losses occurred when eleven bombers were brought down on a daylight raid against Hamburg. This was a maximum effort for 6 Group, which sortied 200 Lancasters and Halifaxes from fourteen different squadrons as part of an overall force of 469 attacking aircraft. Unfortunately, 6 Group also absorbed the most losses when a spirited and unexpected intervention by as many as thirty Me 262s, augmented by a few FW 190s, contributed to the downing of five Canadian Lancasters and three 6 Group Halifaxes.[83] Sandy Mutch, a late-war Lancaster pilot with 408 "Ghost" Squadron operating out of Middleton St. George, was captaining one of the 361 Lancasters sent to Hamburg to destroy the Blohm & Voss U-boat construction yards that fateful day. The early waves, well screened by an escorting force consisting of twelve squadrons of 134 Mustangs and 47 Spitfires, were unmolested by enemy fighters. Furthermore, the 100 6 Group Halifaxes also enjoyed good fighter cover and few of them saw much of the *Luftwaffe*. However, for the 100 Canadian Lancasters bringing up the rear of the stream, things were decidedly different. In the longest five minutes of their lives, this force was hotly engaged by the largest force of Me 262s ever committed to combat. In all, there were seventy-eight separate encounters recorded, and twenty-eight individual crews reported one or more engagements with the German jets. Even at that rate, 6 Group losses would probably have been higher had it not been for the timely arrival of a force of RAF Mustangs that had turned back to investigate the Canadian element, which was flying so far to the rear of the rest of the Main Force. Airborne at 6:15 am out of Middleton, Sandy Mutch elaborates on where and how things went wrong, and describes the ramifications of placing relatively inexperienced senior officers in combat leadership situations:

It was not until two hours later over the Netherlands when things began to go wrong. The leader appeared to become confused, made a dog-leg to lose time, and then signaled us to take over the lead.

Mac Day, our navigator, knew we had lost at least five minutes but we pressed on. Being the last gaggle in the raid, we knew we could be exposed to attack. Hearing the Master Bomber announcing that they were heading for home did not help our spirits. By the time we arrived at the target, about ten minutes late, the smoke markers dropped by the departed Pathfinders were both barely visible and too burned-out to be useful. So we bombed on the smoke cloud from the earlier attackers now billowing above the total cloud cover.

Then all hell broke loose. Vic Trueman, our tail gunner, began shouting that our gaggle was under attack by fighters and gave a running report of the battle and the aircraft being shot down around us . . .

Finally it was our turn and Vic screamed to "Corkscrew! Corkscrew!" I wasted no time going into this fancy manoeuvre but instead pressed the stick full forward into a negative-G bunt, a prohibited manoeuvre for Lancasters. The navigator, bomb-aimer and flight engineer all took wing and were pressed against the top of the canopy, while two Messerschmitt 262s in close formation cruised by above, like hungry sharks with white underbellies in a clear blue tropical sea. We had missed our rendezvous with death!

The boys behind saw our plunge and said, "There goes Mutch!" They were wrong. I pulled back the stick. The weightless crew members lost their wings and tumbled down into the bomb-aimer's front turret, nailed to the floor by the high-G forces. With our high speed, we bounced right back into the lead position. My tousled crew happily scrambled back to their positions, and our straggling became an American-like close gunnery defence formation . . .

Our debriefing went on for at least two hours where our multi-ringed brass subjected us to endless rehashing of the questions of "could have, should have, might have, I would have, etc., etc." Finally, I asked permission to pose a question, which was: "Why did you give the assignment of leading this formation, in which there were a half a dozen wing commanders and a dozen or more squadron leaders (many late arrivals from Training Command, low on battle experience), to a lowly crew of flying officers?" After a brief silence the meeting was terminated.

Reviewing the archival records of the day is enlightening. The navigation error by the three-man team (they were carrying an extra observer) was caused by the inability to harmonize a visual fix through broken clouds, with a *Gee* fix and a *H2S* fix. The review by Bomber Command concluded that this was a case of leadership failure and that in future, such raids should be led by a squadron commander (forgetting of course the fact that if the navigator team got confused, no driver in the front seat could come back to the rescue).

The damage done to the U-boat shipyard was minimal. Most of the bombs landed south of the target. (Bombing drifting smoke markers above 10,000 feet of cloud inherently was not very accurate.) On the ground, 75 people were killed.

The losses from the raid totalled eleven aircraft—eight Lancasters and three Halifaxes—eight of which were shot down by fighters, one by flak and two by collision. Fifteen aircraft returned with flak damage. Several returned home with cannon shell hits. Eight of the above losses, five Lancasters and three Halifaxes, were suffered by the gaggle we were leading which, as reported in the intelligence summary of the raid, was subjected to 47 individual attacks by at least as many as thirty Me 262 jet fighters and perhaps a few FW 190s. The casualties for the raid were 54 killed and 24 who safely parachuted to the ground to become prisoners of war. One of the Halifaxes shot down was that of the Blyth crew from 408 Squadron. All of the crew parachuted to safety. The losses were relatively low when compared to those in many of the earlier raids at the height of the bombing campaign . . . But there is a special sadness in that these losses occurred on a relatively-meaningless raid when the war was essentially won, and some of the individuals lost were on their second tour. Our claims totalled four Me 262s destroyed, three probables, and five damaged, and one Me163 damaged.[84]

The claim against the Me 163B *Komet* came from a 408 Squadron Halifax III crew flying out of Linton-on-Ouse. Harry L. Stilling of Edmonton, Alberta, was a late-war mid-upper gunner who logged twenty-five operations against German targets prior to VE-Day. Conrad Stewart, a friend, recalls the Hamburg trip as seen through Stilling's eyes, as well as an earlier memorable daylight raid to Cologne on 2 March 1945, the RAF's last visit to the cathedral city prior to its capture by American troops four days later.

Harry says that their crew experienced several unforgettable trips whereby they often had to use evasive action due to heavy flak from well defended targets. The closeness of the shell explosions and the sounds of ripping metal were frightening experiences. A particularly "shaky do" was their seventh operation, destination Cologne. Harry's aircraft, EQ-U, "Embraceable U," took several flak hits, but the pilot got it back to base at Linton. Unknown until touchdown was the fact that the port tire had been shot off and the "undercart" damaged severely. Upon contact with the runway, the gear collapsed, sending the port wing down to snag the ground and spin the aircraft around in circles. When the sparks and dust subsided, the fire crews arrived with axes to open hatches and pry open the tail gunner's turret. Luckily there were no serious injuries to the crew and no fire. Harry had a lot of respect for the Halifax aircraft.

On trip #17 to Hamburg, Harry's plane was attacked by the small German rocket aircraft, the Me 163 *Komet*. This small plane would zoom almost vertically to hit the bombers from the vulnerable belly position, their blind area. Harry saw his best friend, in aircraft EQ-S, flying slightly above and to the port side of his Halifax III. A second or so later, EQ-S took direct cannon fire and disintegrated "like so much confetti." The enemy jet levelled off at the peak of his climb and a mid-upper gunner making his first Op into enemy territory blasted it from the sky, part-payment for the loss of a Halifax and its seven-man crew.[85]

The Hamburg operation became the high-water mark of success for the Me 262 fighter forces, and their achievements this day would not be surpassed during the rest of the war. And in the words of Alfred Price, "Yet even on this most successful of days, the losses they inflicted amounted to less than one percent of the huge Allied forces over Germany. The effect was no more than a pinprick."[86]

Bomber Command was still very much a nocturnal force, however, and encounters, although infrequent, also occurred against the German jets at night. "John McQuiston, a pilot in No 415 Squadron, had seen his first (jet) at Düsseldorf in November. 'It travelled at terrific speed,' he recalled, 'and I caught a brief impression of bulbous, underslung engines.' Not knowing about jets, he 'wondered if my eyes or nerves were playing tricks. Nothing flew that fast.' "[87]

Those few Me 262s that served in the night fighter role were based at Burg near Magdeburg, and their task was to counter the previously immune Mosquitos that were making near-nightly attacks on Berlin. At first, single-seat variants were employed, and they were guided to their targets by searchlights, although one had been experimentally fitted with *Neptun* AI radar towards the end of 1944. This specialist unit was known as *Kommando Welter* after its commanding officer, *Oberleutnant* Kurt Welter, an eventual sixty-victory ace who was decorated with the Knight's Cross and Oak Leaves. *Kommando Welter* was soon re-designated as the 10th *Staffel* of *Nachtjagdgeschwader 11*. By 24 January 1945 Welter's personal night score in his jet mount stood at two four-engine bombers and two Mosquitos, thus proving the efficacy of the Me 262 for night operations. Within a week, a number of two-seat Me 262 trainers had arrived from Staaken airfield near Berlin and were fitted with FuG 218 *Neptun* radars and an operator's station kitted with a full suite of radio and communications equipment in the rear seat. While the fixed antennae in the nose cut the maximum speed of the Me 262 by approximately 40 mph, it still possessed an ample performance margin over the speedy Mosquitos. However, these aircraft conversions progressed slowly and the majority of Me 262 night operations were flown in single-seat variants without radar, assisted by the searchlights. It is believed that most if not all of the thirteen Mosquitos shot down at night over the German capital from January to March fell to the guns of Welter's Me 262s.[88] A proper night fighter variant of the two-seater, the Me 262B-2a, was flight-tested prior to the end of hostilities. It had a lengthened fuselage, which provided more space for additional fuel and a *Schräge Musik* installation, the *Neptun* radar, and a FuG 350 ZC *Naxos* apparatus. In a parallel development to Allied advances, one further prototype was fitted with a streamlined centimetric radar in a blunt-tipped nose section, but hostilities ceased before flight trials could be conducted.[89]

The other revolutionary fighter type encountered with some regularity during the closing months of the war was the diminutive Me 163B *Komet* rocket-propelled fighter, fastest of the "jets" with a top speed of nearly 600 mph. Over Osnabrück on the night of 6/7 December 1944, shortly after the first operational *Gruppe* had been established in northern Germany, at least two separate crews reported being attacked by, then claimed to have destroyed, a bright ball of light—one of the new Messerschmitts.[90] (Encounters with Jim Northrup and Harry Stilling's crews have already been mentioned, and other engagements with these nimble little fighters, nicknamed "Squirts" by Allied crews, are presented in pages to follow.) The aircraft's employment as a point target defence fighter severely hobbled its combat effectiveness. While it possessed superb top speed and climb performance, its exceptionally high rate of rocket fuel consumption limited it to approximately twenty-five miles of effective ranging from its home base. Production of the last of 364 machines ceased in February 1945, and the bombing of two key production factories, the perpetual shortage of rocket fuel and qualified pilots, the range limitations, the inherent instability of the rocket fuel mixture and indeed, the generalized chaos predominating in the Third Reich at this stage of the war all made it doubtful if, "after almost a year in service, the rocket fighter caused the destruction of more than sixteen enemy aircraft."[91]

On the night of 3/4 March, the Command sent 234 aircraft—201 Halifaxes from 4 Group and twenty-one Lancasters and twelve Mosquitos from 8 Group—to the synthetic oil refinery at Bergkamen. This raid was highly accurate. Not a single aircraft was lost over Germany and the damage meted out to the target was such that no further production of oil took place from this facility for the duration of the war. Another large and successful raid was mounted against the Dortmund–Ems Canal and a number of smaller diversionary sweeps were also conducted, although some losses were incurred during these attacks.

Operation Gisella

The *Luftwaffe* had a nasty and innovative surprise of its own in store for Bomber Command this night. In an audacious mass intruder attack against the British Isles, the Germans launched nearly 200 night fighters with orders to shadow the bombers back to their home bases and then generally commit mayhem in the Bomber Command traffic patterns when the big raiders were attempting to land. Operation Gisella, as the effort was code-named by the Germans, certainly caught the defences by surprise and the Germans managed to shoot down twenty bombers, "8 Halifaxes of No 4 Group, 2 Lancasters of No 5 Group, 3 Halifaxes, 1 Fortress and 1 Mosquito of No 100 Group and 3 Lancasters and 2 Halifaxes from the Heavy Conversion Units, which had been taking part in the diversionary sweep. Three of the German fighters crashed through flying too low; the German fighter which crashed near Elvington airfield was the last *Luftwaffe* aircraft to crash on English soil during the war."[92]

While this was indeed the *Luftwaffe*'s last determined and innovative counter-attack, those responsible for dispensing information on casualties feared the psychological impact of these incursions on a war-weary British public. It would appear that the government information services, particularly in light of the recent V-weapon attacks and the late war malaise then generally gripping the nation, were beginning to lose some of their vaunted transparency, even beyond normal wartime security needs. Paul Oleynik, a late-war RCAF pilot flying Halifax IIIs with 76 Squadron of 4 Group out of Holme-on-Spalding-Moor, Yorkshire, recalls the German attacks and their aftermath. For Oleynik and his crew, the raid on Bergkamen was their thirteenth war sortie:

> On the return as we were getting close to base about 2000 feet over the junction of the Humber and the Trent Rivers, I had my thumb on the mike button, ready to call in for landing instructions.
>
> The next thing I knew, there were white and blue flashes exploding over the nose of the aircraft. My first thought was that the wireless set had exploded and blown a hole out the port side of the aircraft. I then heard the rattle of bullets striking all along the aircraft. The attack came from the rear port quarter; there were bullet holes going from the rear of the port side windows through the cockpit and out through the front starboard windscreen. Normally, I lean slightly forward over the control column in preparation for landing, but for some strange reason, I had my head back and my arms straight out on the control column. Had I been in my normal position I would have had a couple of bullets go through the back of my head. We were raked from front to rear. I instinctively took evasive action by a quick corkscrew to port. After evading that attack, and since all the aerodrome lights were out, I took a quick course for the emergency aerodrome at Carnaby. During the time that we were raked, the wireless set had been hit. There was flying glass, sparking wires, and smoke all around the wireless equipment. The wireless air gunner, Bob

Freeman, had jumped out of his seat and was standing in the passage way. I tried to call the other crew members on the intercom but there was no reply from anyone. I realized that not only had we lost the intercom, but also our wireless and our radio. I finally got Bob's attention and had him come up into the cockpit. I had to yell into his ear to see if the navigator, Greg, was okay, and then have both of them go back to check on the gunners.

A few minutes later, Bob came back alone and said that Gil (rear gunner) was okay, but that "Junior" Maltby [from Kamloops, British Columbia], the mid-upper, was struck in the forehead and badly injured. They had lowered him out of the turret and had him at the crash position. I asked Bob to go back to help Greg try to make Junior as comfortable as possible, and to protect him as much as possible on the landing, because we did not know how much damage had been done to the aircraft.

En route to Carnaby, we encountered another attack, but this one was head-on. Although there were some strikes on the aircraft, we managed to evade that intruder and landed our badly-damaged Halifax at the Carnaby field. With the severe injury on board, I tried to make as smooth a landing as possible. However, on touchdown, the port tire collapsed. It was partly shot away and we started to ground loop to the left. This was taking us directly into the control tower. Since I could not straighten out the aircraft, I increased the radius of the ground loop in order to avoid colliding with the tower. I then crashed head-on into another Halifax and a steamroller that happened to be on the hard-standing, finally coming to a complete stop.

Just as we were evacuating the aircraft, the ambulance and the fire engines arrived. The ambulance attendants got Junior onto a stretcher and I accompanied them as they rushed to the hospital. A few minutes later, a doctor came over to me to say that they did everything they could to save Junior, but the head injury was so severe that it proved fatal . . .

The next morning, we went out to see our aircraft. There it was, up against another Halifax, with the nose almost pushed up to the cockpit windscreen. There were bullet holes all over the fuselage, and the perspex was shot out of the mid-upper turret. The bomb doors were hanging down with a number of bullet holes through them. How the aircraft remained airborne I will never know, but thank goodness for the strength of the Halifax. Unfortunately, due to the damage done to our aircraft and the one I crashed into, both were written off. After attending the funeral of our gunner at the military cemetery at Harrogate, Yorkshire, we returned to active duty with the Squadron.[93]

Oleynik later recalled that

The RAF put a news black-out on the night intruder attack so as to keep it secret. We survived because of the excellent flight training and because of the strength of the Halifax.[94]

Weather, the Constant Enemy

The worst late war raid by a significant margin for the Canadians was on the night of 5/6 March, two nights after the Luftwaffe's last attack over the British Isles, when 765 Command aircraft, including 185 from 6 Group, were sent as a Thunderclap operation to Chemnitz to finish the job they had started there three weeks earlier. It has been described in chapter five how nine 6 Group aircraft crashed soon after taking off in daylight from their Yorkshire bases in extremely icy conditions. No. 426 Squadron, flying out of Linton, was particularly hard hit this night, losing three of the fourteen Squadron Halifax IIIs participating in the operation because of the departure weather. Howie West, a rear gunner with the "Thunderbirds," recalls the Chemnitz raid, which was memorable for far more than the weather.

The Met Officer did not paint a very rosy picture for us, especially around the base and over the target area. Low clouds, light rain and the possibility of icing were forecast over the base, while the target was forecast to be covered in clouds. We would be bombing on flares and on instructions from the Master Bomber, and the Intelligence Officer reported that night fighters would be active along the route and over the target.

Later, as our first aircraft received his green signal from the control wagon, clearing him for take-off, he released brakes and started his roll down the runway. Soon, we heard a large explosion and realized he had "pranged." The next aircraft received the same treatment. The third Halifax managed to get airborne, but collided with yet another aircraft from a nearby base. The fourth aircraft got away okay, and then it was our turn. We started the take-off roll and halfway down the runway, I felt the tail rise and knew we would soon be airborne. Then, the large wheels lifted off and at about 500 feet, the flight engineer, Sergeant Ernie Haughton, warned the skipper that he should deploy the de-icers as there was ice forming on the wings. At this time, I felt the aircraft shudder and groan, but our pilot managed to keep it climbing and at about 9000 feet, everything seemed to steady out and we heaved a great collective sigh of relief.

A little less than 30 minutes short of target ETA, the mid-upper gunner, Flight Sergeant R.J. Murray, reported seeing two orange balls of fire approaching our aircraft from the port side and slightly above us. I swung the rear turret to the port side and waited for them to come into view, since the turret could only do a 180° traverse. Once I acquired them, I put my ring sight on those two orange balls. Soon, I noticed one of the fireballs getting larger, and they seemed to be getting further apart. It was then that I realized they were enemy rocket jets, Me 163s, and the leader was coming in on an attack curve of pursuit. I gave the order for the skipper to corkscrew down and to port and simultaneously opened fire with short bursts, keeping my ring sight in front of the attacker's flight path. Murray and I had discussed just this type of attack situation with Flight Sergeant W. Trotter, who had claimed two rocket fighters back in January. He had worked closely with his wireless operator, Flight Sergeant Burgess, who had tracked the attacking Me 163s on the *Fishpond* instrument. Murray and I felt the best way to handle the speed of the rockets would be to keep our aim well in front of them, using our tracers as a guide, and hope they would fly into a wall of fire. When our lead attacker broke off, I was able to see his underside and I noticed a smaller ball of fire in front of the larger ball of fire. I remember being very surprised that this aircraft was so small. Shortly after he broke off, we saw an explosion from his direction of flight and the sky lit up, showing a layer of thin clouds below us. Whether he blew up in the air or hit the ground is anyone's guess. Overall, I thought the encounter with the Me 163 had gone very smoothly, and we could keep track of him quite easily as the orange ball associated with the rocket propellant was very easy to see. However, it proved hard to really get a handle on his range, as we could not fit his wing span in our sights, the predominating orange fireball being larger than the wing span.[95]

Howie West more recently elaborated on the Chemnitz raid:

After resuming course for about ten minutes, the flight engineer notified the skipper that the oil pressure had dropped on the starboard inner engine, and he should shut it down and feather the propeller. The skipper attempted to do so, but there was no oil pressure remaining to make that happen. The prop then started to windmill. It was an awesome sight, watching the glowing red engine and the windmilling propeller. We could not do anything about it and we just hoped the propeller would fly off in a direction that would not cause any further structural damage, to our Halifax or to us! This was the worst part of the trip. Waiting for the prop to fly off seemed like an eternity, but it was probably only a few minutes. We were in luck. Eventually, it let go in a vertical direction, travelled in an arc, then descended towards the ground. By this time, the crew up front could see the target and we did our bomb run. After we bombed Chemnitz, the skipper put the nose down to clear the area as quickly as possible while we set course for home. We were doing well, but losing a little altitude as we went. Skipper then asked the navigator, Flight Sergeant Ted Gaffray, for a course to an emergency airfield near Paris.

In about 30 minutes, we ran into a searchlight battery and skipper descended quickly to avoid being coned. We dropped down to 13,000 feet and continued inbound to Paris at that height, since we could no longer climb. Approaching Paris, we made a quick calculation of our remaining fuel and decided to press on to Manston on the British coast near Dover, which had an operating *Fido* system. Nearing the coast, the crew in front saw those white cliffs of Dover and gave out a loud cry. After overshooting for another aircraft ahead of us, we were given a final clearance to land. After we hit the runway, all was going well until about three-quarters of the way down when the Halifax swerved violently to starboard, cutting through the pipes of the *Fido* system and finally coming to rest in the infield.

We were eventually picked up and taken to the Debriefing Room, where we were interrogated by a Polish officer. I don't think he understood us, I *know* we didn't understand *him*, but nevertheless, we were sure glad to be back on good old terra firma.[96]

Geoff Marlow of 434 Squadron, recently transitioned to new Lancaster Xs, recalls the Chemnitz operation from a different perspective. Marlow notes that the perils, like those for Howie West and his crew, were not restricted to just the departure phase that night. He also remarks on the selective release of casualty information to the public by the authorities at this late stage of the war.

On the 5th of March we were sent to Chemnitz, a large city in eastern Germany only twenty miles from the Czechoslovakian border. It was a filthy night, and we knew the trip would be long and arduous. Stratus clouds seemed to cover western Europe from 500 feet up to 20,000 feet. Moments after take-off, we entered stratus cloud and I began flying on instruments. We tried to climb above the clouds, but the heavily-laden Lancaster simply would not go any higher. During one of those attempts I took my eyes off the instruments briefly, and when I looked at them again, they told me that we were losing height at 1000 feet-per-minute and were in a 45° bank. As I got the aircraft back under control and back on course, I felt a little embarrassed, but when I looked at Frank Ferry (my flight engineer) sitting next to me, he seemed not to have noticed anything unusual, so I kept quiet and set about trying to regain the lost altitude . . .

As we neared the target and the cloud tops became lower, I could see the outlines of the other planes silhouetted against them. Passing to the south of Leipzig, and later, in the target area, we encountered heavy flak. Then, as we turned for home after dropping our bombs, we were attacked from the rear by a fighter. Crawf Dangerfield, in the rear turret, warned me of its approach and my blood quickened. Then, when it was at about 600 yards, he gave me the order to "Corkscrew port, go." I banked hard to the left and pushed the nose down violently, throwing all the loose objects in the bomber up to the roof. Then, after we had lost a little height, I pulled the Lancaster out of its dive and reversed the direction of the bank. We repeated this once more before resuming course, and it looked as though we had lost the fighter. Nevertheless, we kept the nose down a bit to gain speed and were almost glad to return to the sanctuary of the clouds. Suddenly, there was a drumming noise on the fuselage right under my cockpit that sounded like impacting bullets, but my imagination had misled me. The noise was caused by pieces of ice flying off the tips of the propellers. If we remained at this altitude, ice would build up on the wings and they would lose their lift. We had the choice of climbing into colder air above us and risking further attacks, or descending into warmer air within the clouds, knowing that our return routing took us close to mountainous countryside. I chose the higher route . . .

Perhaps more by good luck than anything else, we finally reached base, having been in the air almost ten hours, six of them spent in instrument flying. I was dead beat, but surprisingly, everyone was unusually pleased to see us when we landed. We soon found out why. Apparently, seven of our Canadian aircraft had flown into a thunder cloud soon after take-off and had disintegrated in the violent up-and-down air currents. In the winter skies over Europe, bad weather often proved worse than the enemy. The cumulo-nimbus clouds were the ones to avoid at all costs. In those days, radar capable of spotting them had not yet been developed. They rose to great heights and when visible to the naked eye, they could be distinguished by their dark, boiling, anvil-topped appearance. However, if they were buried in other clouds or hidden in the night sky, the first warning of their presence would be when the aircraft was suddenly pummelled as if by giant fists, and one would hear the inner structures of the plane groaning from the mistreatment to which it was being subjected. The pilot would have to change course quickly, hoping this would take him away from the danger and not further into it. On this occasion, seven pilots had unfortunately made the wrong decision and almost all the crew members died . . .

Over the target area that night, six more of our aircraft were destroyed, and my friend Johnny Kitchen was nearly another casualty when he collided with one of our aircraft as he manoeuvred to drop his bombs. Immediately afterwards, he was attacked by a fighter, but Johnny shook it off. Somehow or other, he made it back to a crash landing in England.

Another of our bombers was shot down by British anti-aircraft fire as it crossed the English coast near London—a very sensitive area. But that was not all. As some of our returning bombers groped their way home downward through the solid cloud mass that blanketed England, they passed through the zone in which the air temperature fell just below zero. Chilly droplets of moisture instantly froze onto the surfaces of their wings and propellers, gradually changing the shape of their airfoils. Four of our pilots failed to recognize the build-up of ice in time. Their planes tumbled out of the sky as so much dead weight, smashing into the English countryside below. If our aircraft had been equipped with the more sophisticated de-icing devices now available, these accidents could have been prevented.

None of the thirteen aircraft that crashed in England was reported to the public as missing or lost. Only those that went down over enemy territory were counted, so as not to dampen public morale or give solace to the enemy.[97]

Far East Bomber Operations

By 1945 Bomber Command possessed a truly global reach. Canadians served with pride and distinction in the Far East Air Force (FEAF) aboard Vickers Wellingtons, and later, Consolidated B-24 Liberators operating out of India against the Japanese in the Burmese/Malayan theatre, including Thailand. Operations took place both near the land battles, and to targets as far south as Rangoon, Bangkok and even Malaya, and out into the Indian Ocean.

> The bombers, of which the bulk were now Liberators which could reach the Malay peninsula with a round trip of 2800 miles (4500 km), were tasked with four main duties: to prevent enemy reinforcements from moving along the 5000 miles (8000 km) of railways in Burma (in particular, the infamous Bangkok-Moulmein line which had been built by Allied prisoners of war at a cost of 24,000 lives) with attacks on junctions and bridges; to attack reinforcements moving into Burma with attacks on the main ports as well as on the shipping itself; to destroy concentrations of enemy stores and munitions; and to saturate areas of the battlefield itself with bombs at the behest of the land forces. One squadron of Liberators was employed to lay mines in enemy waters.[98]

One Canadian aircrew member who distinguished himself in this theatre of operations was Pilot Officer John Anthony White, a Liberator navigator serving with 159 Squadron. He won a DFC for his actions in a bombing attack against an enemy-held railway bridge in Burma after suffering a serious chest wound. The citation for his award elaborates:

> In February 1945, this officer was the navigator of an aircraft detailed to attack an enemy bridge. In the run-in to the target the aircraft was met with intense and accurate anti-aircraft fire. The navigator's compartment was pierced and Pilot Officer White was wounded in the chest. Despite this, he remained at his post and played his part worthily in the attack on the target. Although in pain and suffering greatly from the loss of blood, Pilot Officer White insisted on fulfilling his duties. Although he fainted twice he recovered quickly and continued to navigate the aircraft home. After a flight of several hours duration, base was reached within a few minutes of the estimated time of arrival. This officer displayed outstanding courage, fortitude and determination.[99]

Naturally, there was also occasional levity aboard Liberators operating in the Far East Air Force, as one anonymous Canadian rear gunner recalls:

> We never carried waist gunners in our Liberators. If a gunner was needed, the wireless operator went back and manned a machine gun. Once we were headed for Bangkok, and the pilot told the wireless operator to go back and man the guns. I always flew in my rear turret with the doors open over the target to make sure I could make a swift exit. On this day, I happened to look back up the fuselage and there was the wireless operator lying flat on the floor. I jumped out of my turret and ran back to him. "Where are you hit?" I yelled.
>
> The wireless operator looked at me. "I'm not hit. But if you think I'm going to put my head out that window, you're fucking well crazy!"
>
> He never saw anything in his normal crew position up front and he wanted no part of looking at a target.
>
> It was on that trip, too, that the second pilot gave me a tip about putting my revolver between my legs before we started the bomb run. This, he said, was to protect your vital parts. Anyway, I did as he suggested but forgot to ask him if he took the bullets out of the gun before putting it between his legs. I found out later that he had never even thought about it.[100]

A Certain Duplicity

During the spring of 1945, the eddies of public disquiet generated by Dresden over Anglo-American bombing policy continued to swirl. Just six weeks after the February raids, Winston

Churchill, perhaps with an eye cast towards his legacy, penned a Minute to Lord Ismay, his military advisor to the Chiefs of Staff Committee and to the Chief of the Air Staff in particular, which Bomber Command's official historians considered "perhaps the least felicitous," well-expressed or appropriate of all Churchill's wartime correspondence.[101] The Minute appeared to endorse all the latest public criticism of Allied bombing policy, and it also seemed to shift the blame from the Prime Minister's shoulders to those of the air commanders responsible for implementing the policy. The implication was that Churchill had been misled and that his air leaders were conducting terror bombing on their own initiative, without his knowledge, but both these conditions were patently false.[102]

TOP SECRET.

SERIAL No D. 83/5

GENERAL ISMAY FOR C.O.S. COMMITTEE
C.A.S.

It seems to me that the moment has come when the question of bombing of German cities simply for the sake of increasing the terror, though under other pretexts, should be reviewed. Otherwise we shall come into control of an utterly ruined land. We shall not, for instance, be able to get housing materials out of Germany for our own needs because some temporary provision would have to be made for the Germans themselves. The destruction of Dresden remains a serious query against the conduct of the Allied bombing. I am of the opinion that military objectives must henceforward be more strictly studied in our own interests rather than that of the enemy.

The Foreign Secretary has spoken to me on this subject, and I feel the need for more precise concentration upon military objectives, such as oil and communications behind the immediate battle zone, rather than on mere acts of terror and wanton destruction, however impressive.

W.S.C.
28.3.45[103]

Sir Charles Portal immediately instructed his deputy, Air Marshal Sir Norman Bottomley, to solicit Sir Arthur Harris's comments. The Command helmsman's reply was prompt, as well as characteristically blunt and predictable. He pointed out

that the suggestion that the bomber offensive had been conducted for the "sake of increasing terror, though under other pretexts" was an insult both to the Air Ministry policy and to the crews that had carried it out. Harris went on to highlight the misperceptions over Dresden that would be obvious to any psychiatrist—"it is connected to German bands and Dresden shepherdesses." Rather, "Dresden was a mass of munition works, an intact government centre and a key transportation point to the East. It is now none of these things." He went on to discuss the policy underlying the bomber offensive, concluding with the warning that such scruples as the Prime Minister was considering would lengthen the war and increase the task facing the army both in Germany and against Japan.[104]

With equally characteristic flamboyance, Harris also observed that the bombing of the industrialized cities had fatally impaired the overall German war effort and was permitting the land forces to advance into Germany with fewer casualties than expected. He argued that it would be

A typical late-war Halifax crew, this one from 434 "Bluenose" Squadron. (Halifax Restoration Team, Trenton)

Part of the "Lost Legion," this Canadian trio serving with an RAF Lancaster squadron are, left to right, Flying Officers J.J. Leroux, L.G. Hahn and Doug Rose. Note the relative formality of their attire. (DND PL40448).

Piccadilly Princess, a Lancaster Mk.X from 424 "Tiger" Squadron. The nose art is a rendition of a Vargas girl drawn from *Esquire's* 1944 calendar. (DND PL44205)

Dresden target map, 1945. The racetrack aiming point is just above centre frame, slightly in from the left and south of the river. (Author's Collection)

The *Frauenkirche* in Dresden, prior to the bombing on 13 February 1945. (Author's Collection)

The *Frauenkirche* after the bombing. Although it was unscathed, the heat generated spontaneous combustion of the celluloid *Luftwaffe* files, stored for safekeeping in the basement. The resulting explosion left the church in ruins. (Author's Collection)

Group Captain Johnnie Fauquier, as commanding officer of 617 Squadron, posing beside an enormous 22,000-pound Grand Slam penetration bomb. (DND PL44700)

An Me 262A single-seat night fighter test variant, equipped with a *Lichtenstein* SN-2 radar. They were used to counter the speedy Mosquitos over Berlin. (Author's Collection)

Flight Lieutenant Jack Playford, a Canadian pilot serving with 100 Squadron flying out of Waltham in Lincolnshire, at the controls of *Able Mabel*. She finished the war with 132 operations successfully completed. Playford flew a full tour of thirty operations and was awarded the DFC. (Mo Morrison)

"Mo" Morrison's crew while serving with 100 Squadron, April 1945. Morrison is on the extreme left, while second from right is teenager Chick Webb. (Mo Morrison)

Hellzapoppin was a seasoned combat veteran, indicated by the impressive array of operational sorties accumulated, as well as a victory over an enemy fighter. This 426 Squadron Halifax has logged sixty-four operations, including eight Gardening sorties. (DND PL41622)

Squadron Leader B.D.C. Patterson from Calgary in animated discussion with ground crew in front of his late-war 426 Squadron Halifax VII, *Willie the Wolf from the West*. (DND PL32024)

The two Elizabeths visit 6 Group. Elizabeth the Queen Mother and a youthful Princess Elizabeth are accompanied by Air Vice-Marshal Clifford M. McEwen and Group Captain Sampson (left), the station commander, on an official tour of Middleton St. George late in the war. (DND PL32589)

X-Terminator from 419 Squadron eventually became the most combat experienced Lancaster Mk.X. It completed eighty-four operations and its gunners destroyed two enemy fighters during a long and distinguished wartime career. In this photograph, the engine access panels and the nose armament have been removed for servicing. (DND PL36866)

No. 6 Group attacks enemy installations on Wangerooge Island, 25 April 1945. Note the new, higher visibility roundel markings on the upper wing surfaces of the nearest Halifax. The extended wings and rounded wingtips of these later model Halifaxes show to good advantage here. (DND PL144281)

Opposite top: It's finally over. VE-Day in Piccadilly Circus, 8 May 1945. (Imperial War Museum)

Opposite bottom: Beer, songs, fireworks and high spirits made a grand and glorious first night of celebration, in this particular case, by personnel from 420 and 425 Squadrons at Tholthorpe. (DND PL44007)

It will soon be over for most of the aircraft of 6 Group as well. *Fearless Fox*, Lancaster Mk. X coded NA+F from 428 "Ghost" Squadron arrives back in Canada at Yarmouth, Nova Scotia in June 1945. (DND PMR 71-553)

A weatherbeaten *Passion Wagon* will also soon be recycled into pots and razor blades. (DND PMR 98-159)

a mistake to totally cease these attacks at the time unless it could be said with absolute certainty that eliminating city bombing would shorten the war and save the lives of Allied soldiers. Then, he made a somewhat rash remark, citing some words of Prussia's "Iron Chancellor," Otto von Bismarck: "I do not personally regard the whole of the remaining cities of Germany as worth the bones of one British grenadier."[105] Harris, in his no-nonsense and robust response when asked his opinions, probably never thought this correspondence, which had been marked at the time both "Personal" and "Top Secret," would one day be available for public scrutiny and subject to the endless parsings of armchair strategists and moralists. Furthermore, Harris's primary consideration, after getting the job done to the best of Bomber Command's abilities, was to minimize the risks incurred to his aircrews, who had already endured so much during this war.

Churchill also appears to have exercised a conveniently selective memory when he penned the offending Minute, choosing to ignore the various telephone conversations, memos and directives to Sir Archibald Sinclair in January, which had urged bombing attacks on the eastern cities.

> Churchill was well aware that the RAF was going to attack Dresden and the other eastern cities; the decision to do so had originated in Cabinet and had his full support. To deny it now did him no credit and was clearly an attempt to distance himself and his government from the political fallout among the neutral countries and in the USA—the comment that "The Foreign Secretary has spoken to me on this subject" is a pointer in this direction.[106]

Also, the Prime Minister's enthusiasm for using bombing as punishment had occasionally led him to excesses in rhetoric. These remarks occasionally required others, including Harris, to set Churchill's moral compass straight. The repeated considerations of reprisal raids in response to the German razing of Lidice, Czechoslovakia in 1942 and the Crossbow campaign in 1944 constitute ample proof of this trend.

At any rate, Portal enthusiastically endorsed Harris's views. And the Prime Minister's Minute had so shocked the Chiefs of Staff generally that Portal, backed wholeheartedly by Sir Archibald Sinclair, asked Churchill to withdraw it. Nonetheless, the Prime Minister was essentially a fair-minded man. He recognized the validity of the arguments and concerns of his Chiefs, and on 1 April 1945 he approved the substitution of a considerably more guarded and restrained note. What follows is the formal request for removal of the offending first Minute and the replacement correspondence.

<u>TOP SECRET</u>   D.89/5

OFFICE OF THE MINISTER OF DEFENCE

<u>PRIME MINISTER</u>.

After yesterday's Staff Conference, you said you would withdraw your "rough" minute, No.D.83/5 of 28th March, to the Chiefs of Staff Committee and C.A.S. about the bombing of German cities, and you instructed me to redraft the minute in less rough terms.

I. A redraft is submitted herewith for your consideration.
II. Meanwhile all copies of your previous minute are being withdrawn.

H.L. Ismay
<u>30th March, 1945</u>.[107]

PRIME MINISTER'S
PERSONAL MINUTE
Serial No. D.89/5

GENERAL ISMAY FOR C.O.S. COMMITTEE
C.A.S.

It seems to me that the moment has come when the question of the so called "area bomb-ing" of German cities should be reviewed from the point of view of our own interests. If we come into control of an entirely ruined land, there will be a great shortage of accomo-dation for ourselves and our Allies: and we shall be unable to get housing materials out of Germany for our own needs because some temporary provision would have to be made for the Germans themselves. We must see to it that our attacks do not do more harm to ourselves in the long run than they do to the enemy's immediate war effort. Pray let me have your views.

W.S.C.
1.4.45[108]

The revised Minute contained no refence to either "terror" attacks nor, specifically, the raid on Dresden. Nevertheless, the damage had already been done, and in spite of Lord Ismay's assur-ances to the contrary, the first Minute also remained on file, and the effects of public scrutiny and analysis of it in future would be far-reaching.[109]

Late War Operations

Throughout the spring of 1945 the aerial pummelling of the Reich continued relentlessly. On 23 March, a raid on Bremen was to be a precision strike against key bridges located there, highlighted by a significant number of Lancasters carrying the new 22,000-pound Grand Slam bomb.[110] In all, 117 Lancasters from 1 and 5 Groups were tasked with this operation, but for Reg Patterson and his seasoned crew from 101 Squadron, it would be a one-way trip:

> We were briefed for a daylight raid on Bremen. Various squadrons were taking turns leading daylight raids. This was our turn and specifically, it was "C" Flight's turn to lead, and I was in charge of "C" Flight . . . The RAF did not fly the tight, American-style defensive formation on daylight raids. Instead, they put a three-plane formation up front and then about 500 feet below them and a little bit behind were three others also in formation, and so it went for successive formations. The overall lead navigator was the only one navigating. The other three-plane leaders were carrying a route plot just in case the overall leader got shot down, and the rest just followed along somewhere in their 500-foot band. However, on this particular day, I was the guy on the "pointy end!" Just about everything went wrong. The Met winds, with which the navigator was working, were very wrong. We had tremendous headwinds; I was flogging my machine to hold to the timings that were briefed to us and my wingmen were hanging on, but a lot of the rest of them just could not keep up, so the formation was getting stretched out. Our route required us to fly past Bremen on the south side, then turn about and hit our specific targets on the way back. There were fifty aircraft from 5 Group carrying 22,000-pound *Grand Slam* bombs that were supposed to cut across just ahead of us and make a big noise down below. The winds were having an even greater effect on them. These huge bombs would not fit all the way into a Lanc, so they had to

take the bomb doors off and the *Grand Slams* stuck partially out the bottom of the fuselage, causing even more drag. To make matters worse, I lost an engine about a half-hour short of the target. The obvious answer was to lead the stream around in a 360° orbit to give the big boys time to get there, but my group was so far back and so spread out by now that this would have caused utter chaos. Anyway, we carried on as briefed and headed back across Bremen "out in front like a sore thumb," with everything in the town firing at us. We were supposed to take out a particular bridge with our load. Just after the bombs were dropped, we were hit square on the left wing root and the whole wing then fell off. Now, a Lanc may fly on one engine but it isn't worth a darn on one wing. The aircraft immediately started into a tight downward spin. The intercom was out because the flak hit had damaged everything on the control panel on my left side. The bomb-aimer was lying on the hatch in the nose, so he pulled it open and bailed out. I then helped the navigator get by my seat on the way to the nose, but I don't know what happened after that because he never got out. I was strapped into my seat with the parachute seat pack attached, as was normal for the pilot only. I looked up at the cockpit roof and saw that it had been shattered in a few places, so I reached up and broke some of the plexiglass free. Then, I undid my harness and rammed myself up through the hole in the roof. The wind outside the Lanc was indescribable even though I still had my helmet on. However, the wind quickly got under the flap on the helmet and I darn near choked to death before I managed to rip it free. I managed one more kick, and then I was falling free of the shattered Lanc, missing the tail by inches. I was still sailing "head-over-heels' when I pulled the rip-cord. When the 'chute opened, I had one leg tangled up in the shroud lines, so I was hanging upside down. I was pretty groggy from the initial blast of the flak. However, I soon realized that I was going to get a very nasty crack on the skull on landing if I didn't do some clever gyrations in a hurry. Anyway, I quickly grabbed the harness risers and pulled up on them, then landed on my shoulders in a pasture just behind a barn. The first thing I saw was a lady with a pitchfork heading right for me, but that is another story. As it turned out, my engineer didn't have a 'chute as it had shot off down the fuselage during the initial spin. The rest of the crew all had clip-on chest packs. Anyway, he braced himself against the fuselage wall and my seat and watched me get out, resigning himself to his fate. As he had no 'chute, he obviously saw no need to jump. Just then, of all things, a chest pack came whistling down the fuselage and he grabbed it, snapped it on and then dove head first through the hole that I had made. He pulled his 'chute and landed on his feet, and he was only at about 1200 feet above ground when he got out. We were at 22,000 feet when the whole thing started, and I got out at about 5000 feet. In the end, only the bomb-aimer, Flight Sergeant Morris Dillon, the engineer, Pilot Officer Ken Ward and myself survived. We all also subsequently survived the POW camp experience and returned home in due course.[111]

Flying Officer Stan Miller's operation on 8/9 April 1945 to Hamburg is representative of many ongoing dangers to the bomber crews . Miller and his 425 Squadron crew were relative newcomers to operations, this being only their third war sortie, but they became experienced combat veterans in short order on this particular night. This crew was part of a 440 aircraft force—263 Halifaxes, 160 Lancasters and 17 Mosquitos—from 4, 6, and 8 Groups tasked with attacking the Blohm & Voss submarine construction complex. This was also the last major Bomber Command visit of the war to Hamburg.[112] Partial cloud caused the raiders to become dispersed and while some damage was probably caused to the shipyards, the results were inconclusive. Some of the evasive manoeuvres attempted by Stan Miller this night would give new meaning to the term "buddy system."

After entering the briefing room at Tholthorpe, each aircraft captain confirmed their crew was in attendance. The route to the target and then home was reviewed. Then, the altitudes to be flown, the airspeeds, the take-off times, the altitudes to be maintained over the target, the call-signs, the colours-of-the-day, the expected opposition from anti-aircraft guns, searchlights and fighters were all detailed. The frequency of the Master Bomber and the colours he would use in target marking were noted with particular interest.

The weather briefing detailed the wind direction and speed for all segments of the trip. The timings at turning points were emphasized in order to make good the assigned arrival time over the target. There was forecast to be weather over the base for departure, but the target was supposed to be clear. The Wireless Air Gunner was given the Identification-Friend-or-Foe (IFF) codes and the appropriate identification colours for each hour of the flight. Then there was a briefing by the Intelligence Officer, and our squadron commander closed the session with a motivational pep-talk and extended his best wishes.

When the planning was completed, we were bussed to the awaiting Halifaxes. The time before engine start was spent stowing our equipment and giving our KW-E a final look-over. The last few minutes was dedicated to having a last cigarette, and then, the traditional "camouflaging" of the tail-wheel.

We departed on time. The first part of the trip was quiet, but as we approached the Danish coast, everyone was on full alert. There were occasional flashes of flak bursts and we also encountered the slipstreams of other aircraft from time to time. The searchlights also became more numerous as we reached our turning point toward the target.

Just after finishing that turn, we were trapped by a blue master searchlight, then coned as other searchlights rapidly converged on us. I immediately initiated a "corkscrew," and while we were in the lights, shells were bursting all around the aircraft. I continued with the corkscrew sequence as we worked our way southward, and I was working quite hard. Suddenly, the shell bursts stopped, which meant there were fighters about. Sure enough, we were soon attacked by a Focke-Wulf 190 and I had to start "corkscrewing" again. We were still being coned by the lights but on the fighter's second pass, the gunners reported hits as it broke away. Then, on my last evasive turn during this attack, I saw an aircraft to my left and below me, passing from left to right. I immediately did a sharp turn to the right to parallel that aircraft, hesitated a few moments, then did a sharp turn to the left, one part of me hoping for a transfer of the lights. As fate would have it, we were now in the dark, the searchlights behind us. I was very tired and very wet from perspiration after this whole drill. The time we were actually coned was somewhere around fifteen to twenty minutes, but it felt like a whole hour!

The target in the distance was now in sight, and it was well lit up with flares and searchlights. We made a turn to intercept the track to target and initiated a climb to get back to our assigned bombing altitude. Approaching the target, we heard the calm voice of the Master Bomber, who was at a much lower level and was giving changes to the aiming point. There was another ground area to the east that was well lit-up—it turned out to be a dummy site set up by the Germans. Once our bomb run was completed, it was a very keyed-up crew that headed for home.

After clearing the Dutch coast, a final bomb-bay check was made to ensure that we had no hung bombs. The wireless operator then picked up a message from Base—we were being diverted to Silverstone because of weather at Tholthorpe . . . After the debriefing, we had a well-deserved breakfast. Then, before turning in, I had a long shower and hung up my underwear to dry. Next day, we returned to Tholthorpe.[113]

The following day, Bomber Command was sent the furthest afield it would venture on a daylight raid during the war. This was a maximum effort of 230 aircraft—134 Lancasters, ninety Halifaxes and six Mosquitos—directed against the Engelsdorf and Mockau railway yards at Leipzig, another Thunderclap target. And, except for thirty Lancasters and the six Mosquitos from the Pathfinder Force, this raid was entirely a 6 Group effort. The weather was clear, the defending flak only moderate, the bombing accurate and the casualties were light, with only one Lancaster and one Halifax lost in action, a 415 Squadron Halifax from East Moor and a 433 Squadron Lancaster from Skipton.[114] However, the modest casualty statistics belie the high drama experienced by some crews on this operation. Geoff Marlow started early when he experienced something dreaded by every pilot in Bomber Command, a double engine failure on take-off from a short runway with a full load of fuel and bombs:

> On 10th of April we were briefed for a long daylight mission to Leipzig. We had a full petrol load and our bomb bay was filled with high-explosive bombs. At Croft we usually took off to the north, but on this occasion, due to a change in the wind direction, we headed south.
>
> Moments after lifting off from the runway, our port outer engine went dead and we started swinging to the left. A chill of fear settled in my bowels. I had always dreaded an engine failure on take-off, as I knew too well that it often resulted in a crash. In quick succession, I feathered the propeller, corrected for the swing and pulled a bright red lever in front of me that was for use only to obtain emergency power. When I did this, the port inner engine failed under the strain and lost half its power while the starboard engines worked at maximum boost. Under these conditions we were just able to maintain altitude at about 500 feet but could not fly straight. Even with full trim applied to the rudder, I was using all the strength of my right leg on the pedals to prevent us from going into a spiral dive to the left. If we had jettisoned our bombs, we would probably have blown ourselves up along with those below us. A forced landing would also have been fatal. Fortunately for us, the North Sea was only 30 miles to the east, exactly in the direction we were being forced to go by the pull of the starboard engines and, thankfully, there were no mountains in the way. If this had happened during a take-off to the north, we would have crashed into the Pennine Mountains, which rise above 2000 feet.
>
> The fifteen minutes it took us to reach the sea seemed interminable, but we finally passed over Scarborough and flew another twelve miles beyond the coast before Doc (bomb-aimer) released our bombs. Our Lancaster lifted 50 feet in the air as the six-ton load dropped away and splashed into the water below, exploding in a mass of spray. With the aircraft lightened of its heavy cargo, I gained better control. However, the only thing we could do now was return to base. The landing was a little tricky because as I cut back the power on the starboard engines, the plane swung violently to the right, and when we touched down and started to lose speed, I was unable to control the direction of the aircraft. We eventually came to a stop at the side of the runway where we awaited the arrival of our ground crew. When they drove up, they were very concerned about what had happened. We cadged a lift from them to go to "Flights" to remove our flying clothes, then headed towards the Mess to get a drink. However, we were called back to the briefing room to be interrogated on our reason for turning back from our mission. While we told our story, Headquarters rang up to say that we had dropped our bombs on a British naval minefield and that we should be severely reprimanded! However, when the squadron commander heard about it, he promptly congratulated us on having miraculously saved ourselves from a very close call. By coincidence, I received a promotion two days later to flight lieutenant.[115]

Laurence Motiuk provides an account of the rest of the attack:

> Meanwhile, the rest of the Main Force thundered onward towards the target. There was no cloud over Leipzig. Visibility was excellent and the crews were able to identify the target visually. Slight heavy flak, most of it accurately predicted, was bursting at 16,000 feet. A number of aircraft suffered flak damage. Crews saw several rocket-propelled Me 163s in the target area. Of three enemy aircraft shot down, one was an Me 163. Seventeen No 426 Squadron aircraft reached the target. From 1800 to 1808 hours, the crews completed their bombing runs. The bomb aimers in five (426 Squadron) aircraft conducted their attacks visually, and the rest sighted on the yellow Target Indicators as instructed by the Master Bomber. The bombing was accurate and concentrated, and as the crews left the target area, they could see black smoke rising up to 10,000 feet.[116]

Although the fighter opposition was limited on this operation, 6 Group registered a distinction on the day it could well have done without. The Germans fielded, apparently for the first and only time during the war, an innovative new weapon for their Me 163s, named *Jägerfaust* (Fighter Fist). This new system which demonstrated great promise, consisted of a salvo of ten vertically mounted 50mm mortar barrels mounted in the speedy rocket's wing roots, five on each side. Triggered by a photo-electric cell activated by the shadow of an enemy aircraft as it passed overhead, the system, was designed to allow even poorly trained pilots to make accurate attacks on enemy bombers. All the *Komet* pilot had to do was fly his aircraft, either head-on or tail-on, under the enemy bomber within 100 metres of its altitude and the triggering mechanism would do the rest.

On this particular day, prominent rocket pilot *Leutnant* Fritz Kelb of *JG 400* launched out of Brandis and caught what he thought was a lone B-17 separated from its parent formation near Leipzig. Kelb made a single, devastating high-speed attack with the *Jägerfaust* system and then reported the bomber as being shot down, shedding pieces.[117] However, there was no USAAF activity in the vicinity of Leipzig on 10 April 1945,[118] and a recent testimonial from a Canadian source strongly implies that Kelb's *Jägerfaust* victim was a 415 Squadron Halifax. Thus, the only Allied aircraft to be destroyed in combat by this new technology was in all probability Canadian.[119]

The small Me 163 defending force also impacted other Canadian flyers over Leipzig, and the ensuing actions earned veteran pilot Campbell Haliburton Mussells of Montreal, now flying a second tour of operations with 405 Squadron of the PFF, a Distinguished Service Order to add to his previously-awarded DFC:

> Just after making his first run over the target, the aircraft was attacked by an enemy fighter and sustained serious damage. The rear turret and the starboard rudder were shot away. The port rudder was smashed and both elevators were badly damaged. The aircraft dived out of control. As Squadron Leader Mussells fought to regain control he found that the trimming controls were useless. Nevertheless, he succeeded in levelling out after considerable height had been lost. To keep the nose of the aircraft up, the control column had to be lashed back. In circumstances of the greatest difficulty, Squadron Leader Mussells flew the crippled aircraft back to [Britain].
>
> After crossing the English coast, he ordered his crew to abandon the aircraft and, with the exception of the mid-upper gunner who was seriously wounded, they left by parachute. Squadron Leader Mussells flew on to the nearest airfield with his wounded comrade. With the control column still lashed back and without the aid of flaps, this officer showed superb skill in bringing the crippled aircraft down safely. Throughout a

most trying experience this officer displayed the highest qualities of leadership, skill and courage. His example was outstanding.[120]

The Kelb attack signalled the end of the Me 163's limited operational career. A host of problems had precluded it from being introduced into broader service. Given the sparkling performance of this little fighter, that undoubtedly boded well for many Allied aircrews.

With a View to the Future

As the spring of 1945 continued to unfold, the Prime Minister's newfound determination to put an end to the bombing of the German cities rapidly took effect. The fundamental guidance contained in the 1 April Minute (now purged of its offending portions) had promptly been acted on by the Air Staff. That same day, Sir Charles Portal recommended the termination of the area bombing offensive, other than that portion needed to support the land and sea campaigns. The Air Staff recommendations were subsequently approved up the chain of command and Sir Arthur Harris was so informed on 6 April.[121] However, before arriving at this recommendation, Portal very clearly articulated the purpose of, the justification *or*, and the caveats under *hich* area bombing could be continued, if necessary. Portal has been frequently cited, like Churchill, as having an eye to the historical record and to distancing himself from Harris and Bomber Command's campaign against the industrialized cities. However, in spite of the aforementioned difficulties with Harris over bombing priorities and degree of emphasis placed on the city attacks, Portal, staunchly defended Harris and made it very clear that area bombing still had its place. He remained convinced that it was useful under certain circumstances, even at that late stage of the war. He also made it very clear that the Command's precision attack capability was relatively newfound, and that, even with all the technological and tactical advances, it certainly had its limitations and was still not widely practiced by the bulk of the Main Force. Portal's document outlining these considerations is thus heavily excerpted here:

TOP SECRET

AREA BOMBING
Note by Chief of the Air Staff

2. It is only in recent months that the development of night fighting technique has enabled us successfully to undertake the night attack of particular industrial plants or relatively small objectives. By day, the successful bombing of these objectives requires clear skies over the target, conditions which occur on few occasions in the year. For these and other reasons, it has been an essential part of our policy, in order to extract from our bomber forces the maximum continuity and weight of attack of which they are capable, to attack important concentrations of German war industry by means of area attack.

3. The objects of attacking industrial areas have been:

(a) To destroy important industrial plants and to disorganise essential services and labour.
(b) To disrupt communications vital to the maintenance of order and the smooth and efficient working of the military supply organisation to the areas immediately behind the enemy's fighting fronts.
(c) To disorganise and disrupt the Nazi administration.

(d) To force the enemy to employ in defence, repair and rehabilitation measures, resources and manpower which would otherwise be used both in war production and in strengthening the offensive power of his armed forces.

4. In spite of recent advances in our ability to make precise attacks at night, the operational considerations which have in the past necessitated area attacks still exist. Nevertheless, it is recognised that at this advanced stage of the war no great or immediate additional advantage can be expected from the attack of the remaining industrial centres of Germany, because it is improbable that the full effects of further area attacks upon the enemy's war industries will have time to mature before hostilities cease. Moreover, the number of targets suitable for area bombing is now much reduced as a result of our past attacks and of the rapid advance of the Allied armies. For these reasons, and since Allied superiority in military resources is already overwhelming, the effort of the Strategical air forces is being directed primarily to secure the most immediate effect upon the enemy's ability to resist the Allies" advance into Germany. This is being achieved by disrupting communications vital to the armies as necessary.

5. There may still be occasions, however, when the disintegration of enemy resistance can best be brought about through the medium of area bombing. These may arise in the following circumstances.

(a) If resistance should stiffen on the Western Front or fail to disintegrate on the Eastern Front, attacks on built-up areas immediately behind the fronts holding reserves and maintenance organisations, and engaged in handling military supplies, may be as effective in the preparation for an assault as they have proved in the past. Such situations may occur when the Russians approach nearer Berlin and the industrial areas of Saxony, or when we advance into Central Germany from the West.

(b) It may become a military requirement to attack the communication systems of Central and Southern Germany, over which the enemy may attempt to move forces between the two fronts, or to withdraw to the redoubt in Southern Germany. The time factor may not always allow us to await precise bombing conditions and area bombing will then prove a necessity.

(c) There is strong evidence that the German High Command, its attendant staffs and Government Departments and the Party Organisation are to be established in a number of Thuringian towns for the purpose of directing continued resistance. The destruction of these towns by means of area attack may then become a military requirement.

(d) The German Navy has been forced by territorial losses to withdraw from the Eastern Baltic and to concentrate in the Western Baltic and North Sea ports, especially at Kiel. Here some eighty commissioned U-Boats and a large number of enemy naval vessels are congregated. The attack of this target which is already ordered may well involve widespread devastation in the town of Kiel with results which will approximate those of an area attack.

6. We appreciate the importance of refraining from the unnecessary destruction of towns and facilities which will be needed by our own troops or for Allied reconstruction purposes. If, however, we were to restrict our bomber forces to visual precision attack we should certainly reduce the contribution which they can make towards hastening the collapse of the enemy. It is considered that area attacks are still justified strategically, insofar as they are calculated to assist in the advance of the Allied armies into Germany or in shortening the period of the war. Any incidental further destruction of German cities

which is likely to be involved in the time remaining will certainly be small in comparison with that already accomplished.[122]

Accordingly, Washington was advised of the intended British change in direction of their strategic bombing policy, an initiative which the Americans soon fully endorsed.[123] However, in a sequel to this strategic sea-change, the city of Potsdam was heavily bombed on 15 April, which prompted the following testy Minute from Churchill:

PRIME MINISTER'S
PERSONAL MINUTE
SERIAL No. M/362/5.

SECRETARY OF STATE FOR AIR
C.A.S.

What was the point of going and blowing down Potsdam?

W.S.C.
19.4.45

Ref: Cabinet War Room Record No. 2051 for the 24 hours ending 0700, 15th April, 1945 —para. 8 (513 aircraft despatched to Potsdam).[124]

This, in turn, generated the following response from Portal. Clearly, the Air Staff were quite prepared to exercise their new limited mandate for area bombing when they felt the war situation clearly dictated it, even in Germany's "twelfth hour."

TOP SECRET

PRIME MINISTER

Your personal minute No. 362/5 of yesterday. The Joint Planning Staff and the J.I.C. (Joint Intelligence Committee) have drawn attention to the importance of Potsdam in an attack on the German Government machine.

2. The J.I.C. have pointed out that the control centre of the G.A.F. operational Headquarters has been evacuated to the Potsdam area as also have the O.K.L. (i.e., Air Ministry).

3. The object of the Bomber Command attack was the destruction of such control centres, of the communications leading West from Berlin through Potsdam, and of the barracks housing military and Nazi personnel.

4. The attack of this target was discussed and agreed at the Air Commanders' meeting at S.H.A.E.F. on the 12th April.

5. In accordance with your decision on the recommendation of the Chiefs of Staff, we have already issued instructions to Bomber Command that area bombing designed solely with the object of destroying industrial areas is to be discontinued. The attack of Potsdam, however, was calculated to hasten the disintegration of enemy resistance.

C.P.

20th April, 1945.   C.A.S.[125]

John Fauquier, Inspirational Leadership Personified

By now, the strategic air war over Europe was rapidly coming to a close. Significant targets worthy of Bomber Command's attentions were actually becoming more difficult to find, and operations against them were increasingly being conducted during the daylight hours by the Main Force. However, 617 Squadron continued to demonstrate excellence against a number of precision targets. The "Dambusters" were now under the command of John Emilius Fauquier, the unit's last wartime commander and the only non-Briton to lead the squadron.

Johnnie Fauquier was promoted to air commodore in January 1944 and appointed Senior Operations Staff Officer (SOSO) at 6 Group Headquarters after completing a second distinguished operational tour as commanding officer of 405 Squadron. In June, he was given command of 62 "Beaver" Base, consisting of RCAF Stations Linton-on-Ouse, East Moor and Tholthorpe. However, this inaction did not suit his aggressive spirit and in December 1944, he successfully persuaded Sir Ralph Cochrane to give him command of the Dambusters, contingent on his stepping back down in rank to group captain. That did not faze Fauquier, and 617 Squadron became his to lead for the balance of hostilities.

However, John Fauquier had big shoes to fill. The squadron members were, by this time, secure, even arrogant about their achievement of a number of spectacular precision bombing operations, spoiled in terms of outstanding leadership, and cynical that a Canadian outsider, in spite of his splendid operational record, could sustain their motivation and interest during the war's final hours. Their previous commanders had been legendary: Guy Gibson and Leonard Cheshire, both VCs, and then Willie Tait, Fauquier's predecessor, who had won two Distinguished Flying Crosses and a record *four* Distinguished Service Orders in an illustrious combat career. Cheshire and Tait had both flown over 100 operations. Tait had successfully led a mixed force of precision bombing specialists from 617 Squadron and 9 Squadron, thirty Lancasters in all, against the *Tirpitz,* which was then moored in Tromsö Fjord, Norway, just the month before. This Tallboy attack finished the giant warship off for good.

At his inaugural meeting with his new charges, one of them shouted at Fauquier, "Sing a song or take your pants off"—their elitist method of shattering the dignity of senior officers. Without batting an eyelash, Fauquier unhitched his trousers and was then cooled off from behind by a strategically aimed, and unfailingly accurate, half-pint of beer.[126]

However, Johnnie Fauquier would have the last word. In between operational sorties, he worked his crews incessantly and kept them occupied during a mid-winter period of inactivity in snow-storms with frosty PT drills, lectures on operational matters, and even parades mustered to shovel snow from the station runways. A driven perfectionist, he led operations fearlessly from the front, his unit running aground a German cruiser at year's end. Then, as Master Bomber, he conducted a successful Tallboy strike against U-boat pens in Bergen, Norway, in February 1945. On 13 March, 617 Squadron destroyed the Bielefeld viaduct, marking the operational début of the 22,000-pound Grand Slam bomb, which was supplemented by a number of Tallboys. Other railway point targets, extending all the way from the front lines to the Ruhr, were then systematically cut by Fauquier and his crews, including the Arnsberg, Arbergen and Nienburg bridges. Next on the squadron's "hit list" were the U-boat pens at Farge and Brest. At Farge, Grand Slams penetrated the twenty-three-foot thick reinforced concrete roofs of the pens, and, in conjunction with Tallboy hits, undermined and imploded the structures, rendering them useless.

Then, a reconnaissance sortie located the cruiser *Lützow* in the Baltic seaport of Swinemünde. Earlier, on the night of 9/10 April, a maximum effort directed against Kiel, had destroyed the pocket battleship *Admiral Scheer* and badly damaged the *Admiral Hipper* and the *Emden,* as well as dealing a major blow to the Deutsche Werke U-boat yard.[127] The *Schleisen* and the *Köln* were also taken out of action during this period by bombing.[128]

On 16 April, Fauquier led eighteen Lancasters to Swinemünde against the *Lützow*. Braving intense ground fire and suffering its last combat loss of the war, fifteen squadron aircraft bombed the capital ship with either Tallboys or 1000-pounders. All but two of the attacking Lancasters sustained flak damage, but three Tallboys had straddled the behemoth, one impacting between the dock and the ship's moored side. However, on examination of post-strike reconnaissance photos, 617 Squadron was disgusted to see the giant warship sitting, apparently untouched, exactly where she had been attacked. However, two days later, Intelligence confirmed that one of the Tallboys had ripped a giant hole in her hull, and that she had settled to the bottom at her moorings in less than fifty feet of water.[129]

Close to the end of hostilities, the Admiralty remained unconvinced that the bombing could have destroyed the massive U-boat pens at Hamburg, and so Sir Arthur Harris despatched Fauquier, another group captain, and an interpreter by jeep to investigate first-hand. The entire city was now supposed to be in Allied hands. On their arrival, they were astonished to find a work party of 200 German sailors labouring hard on the demolished pens. At that point, the German commander formally surrendered to Fauquier, then invited him and his party to lunch! Thus, it is believed that Johnnie Fauquier became the only RCAF officer to accept a formal surrender from an entire garrison of enemy forces.[130] His splendid leadership of 617 Squadron during the closing stanzas of the European war was recognized with the award of a second Bar to his Distinguished Service Order, the only such recognition accorded to an RCAF officer during the war.

> Since assuming command of the squadron in December 1944, this officer has taken part in almost all the sorties to which the formation has been committed. Early in February 1945, Group Captain Fauquier led the squadron in an attack on the U-Boat pens at Poortershaven. Photographs obtained showed that the bombing was accurate and concentrated. Since then, this officer has participated in a number of sorties during which the railway viaduct at Bielefeld, a railway bridge over the river Weser and a viaduct over a flooded meadow near Ardbergen bridge were all rendered unusable by the enemy. By his brilliant leadership, undoubted skill and iron determination, this officer played a good part in the successes obtained. He has rendered much loyal and valuable service.[131]

The Final Stretch

Meanwhile, the Main Force, that blunt instrument of Bomber Command, continued pummelling targets in the Third Reich. However, the increased frequency of daylight operations meant an increased need for relatively close attack formations and, unlike the Americans, formation flying was not a well-entrenched tactical activity for Bomber Command. On 18 April, nearly a thousand bombers—617 Lancasters, 332 Halifaxes and twenty Mosquitos—from all the groups, saturation-bombed the naval base at Heligoland as well as the adjacent island airfield at Düne. "The bombing was accurate and the target areas were turned almost into crater-pitted moonscapes."[132] Three Halifaxes were lost but, as always, high drama prevailed for even more crews. On this raid, 6 Group led the bombing effort with 112 Halifaxes in an attack on Düne airfield, in advance of the main attack on the neighbouring naval base. The weather over the target area was clear.

The first wave of the Main Force, made up of Halifaxes from No. 62 Base, hit the airfield. The Pathfinders' markers cascaded onto the airfield at 1228 hours, and a minute later Flying Officer R.B. Moase, piloting Halifax NP814/OW "U," and his crew flew the first Thunderbird (426 Squadron) aircraft over the objective. The bomb-aimer, Pilot Officer H. Rich, sighting on the red target indicators, bombed the intersection of the two runways. The remaining Thunderbird crews completed their runs within two minutes from 17,200 to 19,000 feet. Crews delivered a concentrated attack and could see several explosions and smoke rising to 6000 feet as they left the area. The Master Bomber was pleased with the progress of the raid, and in an emotional outburst called it, "Wizard bombing!"[133]

In Halifax PN226/OW "H," Pilot Officer J.A.H. Whipple and his crew had just completed their bomb run when the flight engineer alerted them that another Halifax was nearly directly above them with its bomb doors open and a full load of bombs still on board. The rear gunner, Flight Sergeant Howie West, recalls what happened next:

I looked up and told the skipper that he was fifty yards back and to the side and I felt that he could drop his bombs in a normal, sequenced manner and that they would miss us. However, as it happened, he jettisoned his bombs and they came tumbling down in one instantaneous load. Their aircraft started to move to the port of us and I watched a 500-pounder hit a 1000-pound "cookie." All I then saw was a large red flash and the concussion must have knocked the wind out of me. The skipper then did an intercom check and could not get an answer from me, so he sent the flight engineer back to the tail to see what was wrong. When he arrived at the turret, I was checking around to see where the shrapnel was as I had three holes in the plexiglas. I was surprised to see him there and he looked at my intercom connection and we saw that it was not pushed in tight. Somehow, the connection had come loose and I was unable to converse with the crew. Once this problem was corrected, the skipper had the crew check their areas and report back. At this point in time, the flight engineer was reporting every little hole and the skipper reminded everyone to report only serious problems which would jeopardize our safety . . . Some of the shrapnel from the explosion must have punctured the above-aircraft's petrol tanks because it exploded and crashed into the North Sea. Our only real concern was a large hole in the housing of the port undercarriage. The skipper took a direct course along the coast towards France while we continued our search for damage. It was then we decided we could make it across the North Sea . . .

When we arrived at our base, the skipper asked for an emergency landing. On the downwind leg of the circuit, he lowered the undercarriage and noticed that the port wheel was badly damaged. As we entered the "funnels," the tower notified us of our condition which, of course, we already knew. By this time, our skipper had made up his mind to land. As he had always told us, if he could get us down to within 100 feet of the ground, we would be all right. I had already turned my turret to starboard to position the doors for a hasty exit, and the skipper and Ernie, our flight engineer, put into plan what they had to do for the emergency landing. The idea was to land the aircraft on just the starboard wheel, keeping the port wheel off the ground as long as possible, preventing it from ground-looping. As we touched down on the runway, I felt a surge of power on the port side. As we slowed down, I heard skipper say "Not now," to us and we started to roll towards the control tower on the grass. He was cautioning us as to when it would be appropriate to step smartly out of the aircraft. Then, as we were coming to a full stop, I heard him say "Now," and everything went quiet and the port side went down and the Halifax settled with a little rocking in the grass. I exited the back of the aircraft and found all the crew out and looking at the damage. Skipper was soon awarded a DFC for his fine effort. Port and starboard main spars damaged, and there were 107 medium and large-size holes "from stem to stern," as the saying goes.[134]

This particular raid, a classic example of the accuracy now possible from Main Force crews when conditions permitted, effectively covered both islands with an extremely heavy concentration of craters. Most of the structures were destroyed and the remainder badly damaged. At Düne, the runways were effectively obliterated, most of the gun positions on both islands were neutralized and a huge underground oil storage facility was torched. Three Halifaxes were lost, all to flak.[135] Mo Morrison was part of the 1 Group effort on Heligoland, where he gained enormous respect for the actions of "Jock" Stewart, his Scottish wireless operator, when they developed a serious in-flight emergency. Morrison recalls the event, referring first to his wartime diary and then to a United Services Institute speech given fifty years later:

> A thousand aircraft setting off to bomb the small island of Heligoland and good neighbour Düne. The damned thing should be sunk by sheer weight of bombs alone. They put the wind up us at briefing by telling about all the defences. We had a small fire in the fuselage on last leg to target which lasted about twenty minutes. Funny thing, I wasn't as scared at the time as I should have been. The engineer and the wireless operator put it out finally and we stooged on. There was very little flak over the target and we went at about 120 knots behind some other character. Then, we buzzed off home swiftly and the raid was over. At Heligoland, it was a bright, sunny spring day. The war in Europe was obviously coming to an end but there was still work to do. We had a very heavy load of bombs—probably a record for us—and our route was, of course, over the North Sea. Just as we were beginning our run into Heligoland, Jock calls up on the intercom, "Skipper, we're ablaze!" After determining that the fire was somewhere in the main spar channel that ran through the fuselage and carried the fuel lines, I told Jock to try to put it out. He replied, "I canna, I've got a Group broadcast." He was our listening post for recalls or changes in plans of any sort and obviously thought that was more important than fighting a fire in a bomber, over the sea, with 14,000 pounds of high explosive on board! Now there's an example of training and discipline.[136]

On 25 April, 482 Bomber Command aircraft—308 Halifaxes, 158 Lancasters and sixteen Mosquitos of 4, 6 and 8 Groups—were launched against Wangerooge Island. The raid was intended to knock out the coastal batteries located on this Frisian island, since its guns controlled the approaches to the ports of Bremen and Wilhelmshaven. The weather was clear, the bombing accurate until dust and smoke obscured the target area as a result of these conditions. Six of the seven aircraft lost on this raid were downed by mid-air collisions en route and in the target area. In all, twenty-eight Canadian and thirteen British airmen were killed in these collisions, from which there was only one survivor.[137] Geoff Marlow recalls that the majority of these collisions actually took place prior to the target area:

> As we crossed the North Sea in daylight with the other heavy bombers in a loose gaggle, two aircraft from 431 Squadron, both with their crews on their first trip, started flying close formation some distance ahead of us. Because of their lack of experience, they didn't realize that the planes in front of them were churning up the air into horizontal vortices. In a matter of minutes, one of the aircraft rotated uncontrollably on its side and slid into the plane flying alongside. The collision broke the wing of one of them and the tailplane

of the other. They both spiralled out of control down to the sea below. Several crew members jumped by parachute, and we sadly watched them floating down to certain death in the ice-cold sea some 250 miles from the English coast. Unbelieveably, ten minutes later, two other aircraft with green crews did almost exactly the same thing. This time they were perhaps only 300 yards in front of us. As the aircraft collided, one of the engines must have been ruptured because we received a shower of thick oil all over the windshield, obscuring our forward vision completely. Out of my side window, I caught a glimpse of one plane breaking up. My gunners filled me in on the fate of them both as they spun down behind us to the sea. When an aircraft is severely damaged, it is very rare that the pilot can get out. He must try to keep the plane as steady as he can while the rest of the crew bail out, assuming none are injured. He then disconnects his oxygen and intercom, releases his safety harness, scrambles out of his seat, clips on his parachute pack, works his way down the spinning fuselage to the escape hatch some twelve feet ahead, and finally, throws himself out. Generally he is pinned down by centrifugal force and cannot go in the direction he wants. If he gets out in time, it is usually because he is thrown out, often unconscious. The bomb-aimer and flight engineer have the best chance because they are only a step or two from the hatch. The rear gunner, if he survives a fighter attack, need only (usually) rotate his turret and fall out. With my windshield blacked out, I continued to the target and flew back home on instruments, but I wondered how I would be able to land. Fortunately, I was again breaking in a new pilot, so with him beside me to fill me in on what he saw out his side window, we groped our way toward the ground and somehow managed to land on the runway. Our tour of thirty trips was over, and we thanked our lucky stars that we had made it through.[138]

That same day, Bomber Command flew what would be for many of the participating crews, the last daylight "heavy" combat operation of the war. It was hoped to catch the Führer in his Bavarian mountain retreat, but in fact, he never left Berlin.

> Berchtesgaden: 359 Lancasters and 16 Mosquitos of Nos 1, 5 and 8 Groups. Two Lancasters lost. This raid was against Hitler's "Eagle's Nest" chalet and the local SS guard barracks. Among the force were sixteen Lancasters from No 617 Squadron dropping their last *Tallboys*. Eight *Oboe* Mosquitos were also among the bombing force, to help with the marking, but mountains intervened between one of the ground stations transmitting the *Oboe* signals and the Mosquitos could not operate, even though they were flying at 39,000 feet! There was some mist and the presence of snow on the ground also made it difficult to identify targets, but the bombing appeared to be accurate and effective.[139]

The last significant nighttime combat use of Bomber Command's "heavies" took place later that night, when 107 Lancasters and twelve Mosquitos from 5 Group successfully attacked the oil refinery at Tonsberg in southern Norway. All intended offensive operations by Bomber Command ceased the following night, with the last Mosquito raids on Husum, Eggebek, Grossenbrode and Neumünster, all airfields in Schleswig-Holstein. However, a last-minute scare that the Germans were assembling ships at Kiel to transport troops to Norway to continue the fight from there generated airfield attacks around the city by another force of 8 Group and 100 Group Mosquitos on the night of 2/3 May. These raids were conducted without loss to the Mosquito force, but two 100 Group Halifaxes acting in support collided on the bomb run, killing thirteen of the sixteen crew members on board. These were the last Bomber Command operational casualties of the war, and they were all from the United Kingdom except for one free spirit from the Irish Republic.[140]

Shortly thereafter, Kiel was declared an open, undefended city. "As soon as this happened, all the military stores and some of the civilian ones containing rationed goods were thrown open to the public before Allied troops arrived 36 hours later."[141]

Sadly, it may well be that 6 Group's last wartime casualty was also its youngest. On 30 April 1945, Lancaster KB 879 from 428 Squadron was conducting a training flight over England when for some unexplained reason, it disintegrated in mid-air, killing all seven crew members. One of the gunners was Flight Sergeant Edward James Wright, who had been born in Montreal but grew up in Halifax. After graduating from bombing and gunnery courses, Wright embarked for overseas in July 1944, completed bomber OTUs and HCUs in Britain, then joined 428 Squadron on 22 April 1945. When he had enlisted in Winnipeg in late 1943 he was a slight young man who stood just 5' 6"in height and weighed 129 pounds, a "decidedly boyish-looking" young fellow who had undoubtedly falsely represented his age at the recruiting depot. After the war, when his mother claimed service death benefits, she testified that she had given birth to her son on 7 November 1928. Edward James Wright was just sixteen years of age when he gave his life for his country.[142]

Bombing with a Gentler Purpose

Meanwhile, Bomber Command had become involved in some particularly satisfying and unusual humanitarian flights. At the end of April, a large pocket of resistance in western Holland, deliberately bypassed and sealed off by the Allied land forces, was still under the control of the Germans. Many of the estimated three million Dutch citizens contained therein were close to starvation. For numbers of the elderly and the ill, it was already too late as their own meagre foodstuffs had been plundered by departing Germans prior to the area being sealed off by the Allies. While General Eisenhower and his staff at SHAEF acknowledged the need for an airborne relief mission, code-named Operation Manna, transport aircraft were still in very high demand for combat taskings. Conversely, the Anglo-American strategic bomber fleets now had very little to do, and thus it was decided that the supply drops would be made exclusively by Bomber Command and the Eighth Air Force. Soon, a truce was arranged with the local German occupation forces, who designated ten acceptable drop zones and also acknowledged the need for additional truck convoys carrying more supplies after the air drops. While this agreement was not actually signed until 2 May, the first air deliveries began on 29 April at the village of Waardenburg on the Waal River, situated a scant three miles behind the German front lines. Although the village was occupied by a paratroop detachment and the river bank bristled with flak emplacements, there was no enemy opposition, a situation which must have seemed particularly bizarre to crews who had been savaged by German guns just days earlier. At any rate, the guns would remain silent on this sunny, clear inaugural day of Operation Manna:

> Around ten o'clock in the morning there was a steady drone of many approaching bombers. When we looked up to the sky, we observed squadron after squadron of Lancasters and Liberators. They flew so low that the pilots were clearly visible. It was a unique moment. For five years, Allied planes had been watched with both hope and fear. This time they carried no bombs. But perhaps the most remarkable fact was that the German guns, which used to greet even single fighter or observation planes with their shells, remained silent. The gunners stood at their usual positions, but their orders were not to fire. Most

of them were pale and nervous, and one of them raised his fist to the sky and shouted: "Those damned things up there."[143]

During the period from 29 April to 7 May, Lancasters from 1, 3 and 8 Groups made 2835 relief sorties to the beleaguered area, delivering 6672 tons of food by air before the Germans surrendered, thus permitting ships and road transport to enter the pocket.[144] While 6 Group did not participate in the supply drops, 405 Squadron's Lancasters served as markers during missions flown on 30 April and on the 1, 2, 4 and 5 May to The Hague, and then again on 7 May to Rotterdam. Although spring rains and snow squalls with concomitant reduced visibilities sometimes caused scattered marking and overshot supply drops, much of the relief effort found its intended destinations. Perhaps fittingly, on the last day of Manna, things went exactly according to plan at Rotterdam. "In good weather and clear visibility, eight crews dropped their indicators from 350 feet 'just overshooting the White Cross . . . Early supplies seen dropping were well placed in the field around the White Cross.'"[145]

Naturally, hundreds of Canadians were crewmembers aboard these relief flights, which they flew under callsigns related to the products they were dropping, as Mo Morrison recalls:

> May 3: SPAM 1. Low-level supply dropping to the starving people of Holland. Target on outskirts of Rotterdam and we flew over at 500 feet and had a good look—then down onto the deck and over The Hague at roof-top height. Lots of fun. Time: 3:05. May 5: SPAM 2. Target a little further on—same business. Weather pretty bad all the way. It gives us a lot of satisfaction to do this. Time 3:15.[146]

Meanwhile, Bomber Command Lancasters had now started flying to Brussels and other continental airfields to collect and return to Britain prisoners of war recently released from the camps by the advancing Allied armies. Code-named Operation Exodus, 469 sorties were made by aircraft from 1,5, 6 and 8 Groups before the war ended, augmented by many more flights after the cessation of hostilities. Allied authorities were determined to repatriate the POWs as expeditiously as possible and not repeat the mistakes of the Great War, when some ex-prisoners were still not home for Christmas 1918, although the Armistice had been signed on 11 November. Nearly 75,000 prisoners were quickly brought home in this manner, and this time, the bombers were ably augmented by the Dakota transport squadrons.[147]

One frequently mentioned anecdote from this operation, too persistent, charming, and appropriate not to be true, centered around the late-war liberation of an air force officers' camp in northern Germany by advance units of a British armoured column. Supposedly, the column's commanding officer, a lieutenant-colonel, gathered all the former POWs in the camp's parade ground and tersely announced that plans were being made to fly them back very soon to England. At that point, one of the Canadian airmen, who had been an unwilling guest of the Third Reich for far too long, laconically replied, "Well, that would be a nice touch, colonel. After all, it was *flying* that got us here in the first place!"

Canadian airmen were extensively involved in these very satisfying humanitarian missions. Geoff Marlow of 434 Squadron and Mo Morrison of 100 Squadron recall these operations, which for them occurred just after VE-Day:

> On 10th May we flew to Juvencourt near Reims, France, to pick up some Commonwealth ex-prisoners of war. We flew quite low on a direct routing and landed on what had been

an advanced fighter airfield. There was no runway, only open wire mesh spread out in a strip over a rolling meadow. Hundreds of POWs were sitting around the field waiting their turn, and 24 were assigned to us. I don't know how they all fitted in, but every available bit of floor space was occupied. Many of them had been imprisoned for five years, but looked healthier than we did—quite a contrast to the pictures we had been seeing of the death camps in which millions of Jews had been exterminated. As we approached the English coastline, they took turns looking out of the astrodome trying to catch a glimpse of their motherland. It was a joy to see their faces light up. We landed them at Westcott, from which point they were sent on to their next destination in well organized fashion.[148]

Mo Morrison corroborates the feeling:

May 10: We flew directly to Brussels—the maddest aerodrome in the country—millions— well, a hell of a lot of aircraft around. Landed eventually and after an hour's wait we got our load—24 ex-POWs. Those boys were sure glad to get home and we were glad to get them there. We landed down by London, at Dunsfold, dropped them off then home again. Time: 3:50.[149]

Towards the very end of the bombing campaign in April, Sir Arthur Harris received a letter from a mentor, Lord Trenchard, which in the opinion of Henry Probert probably touched the bomber chief more than the host of accolades he would later receive.

Words are of little use but I would like to try. Your great task is over and by your relentless efforts you have succeeded. I know no man that could have been more determined to carry out what you did. I know no one who could have combined such determination with technical and operational knowledge. I give all credit to your staff and your wonderful aircrews and maintenance crews and all. But it was your leadership and knowledge that made Bomber Command the magnificent force it was. The world should thank you. Words I cannot find to say what I feel about the part the Royal Air Force has played in this war. Forgive an inadequate letter.[150]

The Curtain Falls

Very soon after the termination of combat operations by Bomber Command, it was all over in Europe. On 4 May 1945, German officers signed a blanket surrender document at Montgomery's 21 Army Group Headquarters on Lüneburg Heath for all the German forces in northwest Germany, Denmark and Holland, to be effective from the following day. On the 7th, General Eisenhower, with representatives from Britain, France and the Soviet Union, accepted the unconditional surrender of all German armed forces on all the fighting fronts, effective at 0001 hours on 9 May 1945. "Allied troops, fully supported by Bomber Command, had liberated the whole of western Europe in just eleven months of hard fighting. The British army lost nearly 40,000 men during the campaign. Bomber Command had lost 2128 aircraft during the same period, with approximately 10,000 airmen being killed."[151]

While the surrender was greeted with great joy and relief, the spool-down from operations during the preceding ten days had muted some of the anticipation of peace for some Bomber Command personnel. Both Mo Morrison as a Canadian airman on an RAF squadron and Laurence Motiuk as a Canadian airman within 6 Group recall the moment from their relative perspectives. In the words of Mo Morrison:

Paddy (my bomb-aimer) and I had been in the steel town of Scunthorpe, Lincolnshire at our (newly) favourite pub on May 7, 1945, when the news of the German surrender came. The pub was full of servicemen from several of the camps and airfields in the vicinity and local "popsies" out on the town. Music had just been re-introduced to the local pub scene and a well worn but very appreciated elderly couple were putting on skits from their music hall days of long ago. The skits were interspersed with songs while most of the pub patrons sang along.

All of a sudden a hush fell over the place as the "governor" (owner) stood up on his stool and began writing on the large blackboard at the back of the bar after shouting "Stop the music" in a voice usually reserved for "Time, gentlemen, please" at the end of the evening. He simply wrote "IT'S OVER" and that said it all. He remarked a few minutes later that he wanted to add "and we are out of beer" but didn't have the heart and went instead into the cellar where he had a keg in reserve for just this occasion. It was hardly needed as *The Crown* began singing, laughing, crying, dancing and shouting all at once in happy relief after five years of war.

Paddy and I had been working on an invitation to spend the night with some young women we had met previously and knew that two of them, sisters, were inclined to invite lonely airmen into their home after their widowed father had left for the graveyard shift at the steel mill. I think we would have made it too, had not some perverse sense of duty led us to believe that we should really be back with the squadron at this historic time.[152]

Laurence Motiuk recollects the celebration at Linton-on-Ouse:

On the morning of 8 May, Group Captain Donald Plesance [Station Commander] declared a general stand-down and informed all personnel that Prime Minister Churchill would announce VE-Day at 1500 hours. The station security plan went into effect, with guards at all strategic locations. After Mr. Churchill's speech, the station commander made a short Tannoy broadcast in which he thanked everyone for their hard work and cooperation, and gave all non-essential personnel two days off. The entertainment for the evening was then announced. Extra stocks of beer and spirits, which had been carefully hoarded for the occasion, were brought out and the festivities began. The NAAFI held a gala dance and merriment ran high in both the Sergeants' and the Officers' Messes. The celebrations continued until the early hours of the morning.

With little routine work to do, the holiday spirit prevailed on 9 May. The station's 3000 personnel all rejoiced and caroused, but for all their exuberence, never became rowdy or descended into hooliganism; damage was limited to two broken windows, apparently mistaken for doors.[153]

Peter S. Lennie, an RCAF Mosquito pilot, was in London for the VE-Day celebrations, and he recalls the festive mood of the occasion:

Never had I seen so many people all laughing with happy relief. I do not recall any signs of drunkenness—boisterous and raucous—of course—but pleasant and happy. The crowd walked and walked with no destination in mind, just a restless urge to keep moving.

To Buckingham Palace where we cheered the Royal Family when they appeared on the balcony. People waved as they clung to monuments, lampposts or each other. Then off to Whitehall to see and hear Winnie as he waved his cigar. No one could hear his words but one could almost feel the outpouring of gratitude for this great "man for his time."

Quite often open lorries would drive by, packed with men from all services. In some ESP manner the crowds became aware that these were POWs recently released and flown home. As each rolled by the cheering reached a crescendo.

Now we moved toward, through and around Piccadilly. It was here that we managed to purchase our one and only drink of the day—a Scotch that tasted a bit like gasoline. Someone in the crowd (I suspected a young lady) snatched my hat and disappeared. The replacement purchased the following day had a metal insignia rather than the fine cloth embroidery of the RCAF.

The crowd thinned as we made our way to Hyde Park where we gratefully applied our butts to the grass and leaned back on our elbows. It was here that a charming English lady approached us with an invitation to dine with her family. Since we had not eaten since early morning our acceptance was only delayed by politeness. A short ride on the tube—no recollection of the dinner courses—but we ate everything placed in front of us.

With good wishes all around and sincere thanks to our hostess and family, we proceeded to the station for the trip back to Oxford. At the time we did not realize the importance of the day but we had been observers at one of the greatest days in the history of the free world—VE-Day, 1945.[154]

The shooting in Europe was now over; Hitler's "Thousand Year Reich" had lasted but twelve, although it had left much of Europe and Eurasia in ruins and had generated enormous misery and suffering.

Epilogue

Always Another Dawn

They shall not grow old, as we that are left grow old:
Age shall not weary them, nor the years condemn,
At the going down of the sun and in the morning
We will remember them ...

As the stars that shall be bright when we are dust,
Moving in marches upon the heavenly plain;
As the stars that are starry in the time of our darkness,
To the end, to the end, they remain.

—Laurence W. Binyon[1]

Throughout the spring and summer of 1945, as plans solidified to send a Canadian fighting force to help close out the war in the Pacific, the western hemisphere spun increasingly towards a measure of post-war normality. The day following VE-Day, in Rome, Pope Pius XII made a radio appeal from the Vatican in which he thanked God for the end of hostilities in Europe, and then called for a speedy conclusion to the war in the Far East. The Number One song on the North American Hit Parade at that moment was "There! I've Said It Again" by Vaughn Monroe and his Orchestra, and John Hersey's "A Bell for Adano" would win the Pulitzer Prize for best new novel. On 21 May, actor Humphrey Bogart married actress Lauren Bacall in Mansfield, Ohio, in what would become one of Hollywood's most celebrated unions. That weekend, a three-year-old bay colt named Uttermost won the 86th running of the King's Plate, Canada's most prestigious horse racing event. Then, in early June, the pope, in a tone very different from the month before and using a rather unusual verb, publicly defended the Catholic Church's relationship with the Third Reich in 1933, saying that "nobody could accuse the Church of not exhibiting the true nature of the

National Socialist Movement."[2] On 21 June, future singing icon Anne Murray was born in the coal mining town of Springhill, Nova Scotia. Early in July, heralding a return to post-war economic normality, a civilian passenger car rolled off the Ford assembly line in Detroit for the first time since February 1942. Later that month, a Methodist Conference in Britain granted approval for unmarried women to become fully-ordained ministers of its church. Later in June, the new American President, Harry Truman, called for Japan to surrender unconditionally, or "face prompt and utter destruction" by Allied forces ready to "strike the final blows." And part of those forces included a significant Canadian military commitment to the Pacific theatre of operations.

Pacific Bound

In September 1944 the Canadian Cabinet War Committee had decided that, as a basis for planning, Canada would provide one army division and ancillaries of up to 30,000 troops drawn from the European theatre to fight with the Americans in an invasion of the Japanese home islands. This formation, the 6th Canadian Division, was to be led by Major-General Bert Hoffmeister, who had been a distinguished and successful divisional commander in Italy and northwest Europe. Service was entirely voluntary, and each volunteer would receive a fast ticket home to Canada and thirty days leave prior to embarkation for the Pacific.

The air element of this Canadian contribution consisted of participation in "Tiger Force," the name the RAF had given to its Very Long Range (VLR) Pacific bomber contingent, and detailed planning for this air component was being conducted by year's end.

> The RAF intended to deploy thirty-six heavy bomber squadrons equipped with Lancasters [and later re-equipped with Avro Lincolns] and would use air refuelling to bomb Japan from as yet undetermined locations in the Pacific. Eighteen fighter squadrons, initially Mustangs, eventually to be de Havilland Hornets [a derivative of the Mosquito], would escort the bombers, and the force would include four long-range transport, one air/sea rescue, and one photo-reconnaissance squadron.[3]

After much haggling with the Americans over basing on the island of Okinawa, Whitehall approached Ottawa with a firm request for assistance on 16 June 1945, "underlining the need for construction engineers, 2500 of whom it was earnestly desired would be Canadian, asking for two bomber squadrons for Tiger Force's first deployment, and holding out the hope that 'another six Canadian heavy bomber squadrons will be available for the second contingent of ten squadrons if and when this is approved.' "[4] Knowing this request was forthcoming, Prime Minister Mackenzie King's War Cabinet had already authorized the construction contingent, two bomber squadrons as well as transport squadrons, all of which were to be provided within a 23,000 manning ceiling. Consideration of the six additional bomber squadrons for the possible second deployment was deferred.[5] However, on 12 July, Cabinet gave its approval for those six additional squadrons, and London was so informed. Air Commodore Roy Slemon, then-SASO at 6 Group Headquarters, was to command the RCAF contingent.

> The advanced element of Tiger Force was to consist of one RAF Mosquito and nine Lancaster squadrons, five from the RAF, two from the RCAF, and one each from Australia and New Zealand. The follow-up element would be made up of one Lancaster-Catalina air/sea rescue squadron and eleven Lincoln squadrons [advanced derivative of Lancaster].

Two RCAF squadrons, numbers 419 and 428, were to be at their base and ready to operate by 1 January 1946. The force would ultimately consist of two operational groups, one Canadian and one British, and when the second contingent arrived in theatre, a Canadian group headquarters was planned. Tiger Force Headquarters itself would be integrated and 50 percent Canadian. The RCAF was making an effort, wherever possible, to have fully Canadian units in support of squadrons "on a basis commensurate with our front line effort." Consistent with the Prime Minister's policy announced on 4 April 1945, the RCAF was canvassed for volunteers—21.5 percent of the 103,402 men and women interviewed by 15 June had volunteered for service in the Pacific. The Tiger Force commander agreed to the participation of women, members of the Women's Division having volunteered at a much higher rate than men.

The British Chiefs of Staff assembled on 6 August to discuss the latest developments with Lloyd [Air Vice-Marshal Hugh Lloyd, commander-designate of Tiger Force], freshly returned from the United States, where he was still complaining about the uncertainty of a Canadian engineering contribution.[6]

In April, Headquarters RCAF Overseas had announced that "as soon as possible, No. 419 and No. 428 Squadrons at Middleton St. George and No. 431 and No. 434 Squadrons at Croft would be stood down from operations and returned to Canada for training. No. 405 Squadron at Gransden Lodge, No. 408 Squadron at Linton-on-Ouse, and No. 420 and No. 425 Squadrons at Tholthorpe would follow, and complete the (Canadian) bomber component of Tiger Force."[7]

However, on 6 August, the same day the British Chiefs of Staff were determining the way ahead for Tiger Force, the first atomic bomb used in warfare, code-named Little Boy, was dropped on the city of Hiroshima, destroying two-thirds of the city's 90,000 buildings and killing approximately 78,000 people. The following day, Rome announced that the use of an atomic weapon on Japan had "created an unfavourable impression on the Vatican." Two days later, the USSR declared war on Japan, the same day the United States became the first nation to sign the United Nations Charter. The following day, Soviet operations commenced against the Japanese in Manchuria and northern Korea, where their far more sophisticated mechanized forces dominated General Yamada's Kwantung Army. However, an even more cataclysmic event occurred the same day when the second atomic bomb, code-named Fat Man, was dropped on Nagasaki, killing another 74,000 Japanese citizens and city residents.[8] On 10 August 1945, Emperor Hirohito communicated to the Allies that Japan would accept the surrender terms, provided that surrender "does not compromise any demand that prejudices the prerogatives of the Emperor as Sovereign Ruler." Within four days, President Truman announced that Japan had surrendered unconditionally and that ceasefire orders were in effect. The need for Tiger Force, now reduced to being a mere "paper tiger," had been overtaken by events.

Back to the Dominion

Meanwhile the designated bomber squadrons for Tiger Force, their work done in Europe, had started to return to Canada. Geoff Marlow of 434 Squadron recalls his last days in Britain, which included a lot of partying, preparations for the upcoming Atlantic crossing, and providing impromptu flypasts for British citizens in general and old girlfriends in particular.

The flight across the Atlantic was to be via the Azores and Newfoundland, where our navigational radar could not be used. We therefore had to conduct several lengthly flights

Going home. Canadian Lancasters positioned for imminent departure to Canada, 1945. (DND PL44319)

Moving out. This 6 Group Lancaster named *Daisy* will soon be winging its way westward across the Atlantic. Nose guns have been removed. (DND PL44274)

Air Marshal Harris and Air Marshal McEwen give a wave and a thumbs-up farewell to one of the 15 408 "Goose" Squadron Lancasters that departed Middleton St. George for Canada, 31 May 1945. (DND PL44316)

No. 6 Group ground crew lined the runway to see the aircrew off and to wish them well. (DND PL44840)

Ken Underhill at rest on the fuselage of his Halifax, 1944. (Halifax Restoration Project, Trenton)

William Henry Johnston's crew in a happy wartime moment. (Halifax Restoration Project, Trenton)

over the North Sea to practice astro-navigation and new radio techniques. I spent a lot of hours in the Link trainer learning about Radio Range, a beam then used for Atlantic and North American flying. There was a big party in the Mess for those who were making this journey—most of the ground personnel and some new aircrew members were to be left behind. Doreen [a girlfriend] came over to join the fun. It was her first visit to our base and her first time to meet the officer component of my crew. The party was wild, as most Mess parties were at that time, but she said she had a good time.

Wally Rothenbush and I, being skippers of crews who had recently completed our tours of operations, went down to London on an overnight trip to collect from Canadian headquarters the silver "Operational Wings" for ourselves and our crews. These wings are additional to the regular flyers wings and can only be worn by those who have done thirty trips. I called Pam [another girlfriend] by phone and bid her farewell, the last time I would have an opportunity to talk to her for ten years. On returning to base, we had yet one more party, this time with our groundcrew. We went through the usual exchange of addresses, although in my case I had no idea where I was going. Finally, on 11th June, we left Croft for the last time and did a tremendous "shoot up" of the airfield as a parting shot to our friends there. But I also wanted to do the same to Doreen in Middlesborough. We came down to roof-top level and flew at top speed down the street where she lived. Suddenly I noticed everyone going into church and realized it was Sunday. I had not intended to disturb the peace at such a time, and I hope they did not hold it against me. I wrote a note to Doreen several months later to admit guilt but never had a reply.

We flew to St. Mawgan in Cornwall to refuel and to have a meal and a little nap. I called Di [yet *another* girlfriend] at her home in Wales to tell her I was on my way, and then, at 3 A.M., took off into the totally clouded black night sky enroute to the Azores, a six-and-a-half hour journey. The next leg was seven hours to Gander, Newfoundland, where we slept for awhile before proceeding to Dartmouth, Nova Scotia. Here, I think I made the worst landing of my career and, as it turned out, my last. I had flown a total of 802 hours since making my first flight three years previously.[9]

The crews of that most operationally senior of the repatriating bomber units, 405 Squadron, had left their 8 Group home at Gransden Lodge in late May, taking up temporary residence at Linton-on-Ouse. Then, on 16 June, they departed *en masse* for Canada. "The take-off of nineteen 'Lancs' . . . alternating running down port and starboard sides of the same runway, Number Two half-way down the runway as Number One was lifting off . . . forming up and doing a low-level fly past in 'Vics' of three . . . a magnificent show!"[10]

However, the departure of the last squadron Lancaster had been delayed. Its pilot, one of the squadron flight commanders and a unit stalwart, Wing Commander Donald J. "Tex" McQuoid,[11] had been tasked with directing the earlier *en masse* departure of the others from Linton. He would also be returning to Canada with the popular AOC of 6 Group, along with the air vice-marshal's "best friend." Squadron Leader John F. Roberts,[12] the navigator aboard this particular flight, recalls:

> The date was June 19, 1945. At 1100 hrs. I estimated our position as about halfway to the Azores from St. Mawgans, Cornwall. We cruised in brilliant sunshine at 8000 feet, just above a solid bank of clouds. "We" were the last crew of 405 Squadron, flying home from Linton-on-Ouse in a Canadian built Lancaster. With us were two passengers, Air Vice-Marshal C.M. McEwen, AOC 6 Group Bomber Command, and his Scottish Terrier, also known as "Black Mike." As I rose to stretch, the flight

engineer, Pilot Officer A.W. "Bill" Bishop (no relation to his namesake), his usual impish grin stretched from ear to ear, was pointing to our skipper, Wing Commander Don "Tex" McQuoid. The skipper was sitting with folded arms and half-closed eyes, relaxed while dependable "George" flew the "Lanc" steadily southward . . . Eventually, as we left the clouds behind us and rode the beam earthwards, the island of Terceira was a beautiful sight, ruby red in a sea of wrinkled green velvet under a deep blue sky. Our intended fuelling stop was extended, and after much delay, became an overnight stop. Gander was socked in, as it so often is! Like so many places and people you see and encounter in life, the jewel of the ocean, on closer examination, was not what it appeared to be. The rich, ruby red soil was volcanic dust, which rose in a cloud and hung in the still evening air as we trudged steadily downhill three miles to the nearest village. The five of us, who had exchanged our £ Sterling for Portugese *escudos*, endeared ourselves to the proprietor of the first pub we saw by each purchasing one or two bottles of good wine. The profit on these transactions put the publican in an expansive mood: drinks were on the house! While we sat on stools at the bar, the shot-glasses in front of us were repeatedly filled and emptied of many and various liquids. Finally, it was time to leave: we called a taxi. After a lengthy wait, during which the imbibing continued, the "taxi" arrived. Our conveyance was a two-wheel buckboard powered by a very small horse. "Bish" Bishop instinctively took the flight engineer's position to the right of the vehicle's pilot—a small man with half-shut eyes, who was wearing a huge straw sombrero and carrying a whip. The rest of us piled in the back, two pairs facing each other. At the crack of the whip the little horse started up the hill at a gallop, its dainty hooves churning up the volcanic dust, which rose in a crimson cloud from the rough road. We bounced about on the hard benches, one such bounce shifting all of us far enough back to lift the little horse clear off the road. While the tiny hooves pounded the air, the buckboard proceeded to roll down the hill. As we all shifted forward, the poor little horse also plunged forward with its heavy load. This manoeuvre, I regret to say, was repeated several times until "Bish," who had been unusually quiet, suddenly turned, tears streaming down his face, and exploded, "Stop! I can't stand it! All out!!" And out we went, without anyone having to ask why. We paid the driver his fare plus a handsome tip—in order to buy extra food for the over-worked horse—and completed our journey on foot. Bish turned to me. "Robbie," he said, "if, in the future, you're down on your luck and life is going wrong for you, just think of that poor bloody horse and things won't seem so bad!"[13]

Soon they would all be home, their very existence deemed superfluous by the capitulation of Japan, and by the perceived government need to downsize the bulk of the air force as expeditiously as possible.

What Now Remains

And whatever became of these Canadian warriors of the night, both the aircraft and the men who crewed them? The bombers, most of them good for nothing but war, have virtually disappeared, long since consigned to scrap heaps and smelters. Of the thousands of Bristol Blenheims built, only a handful exist worldwide, including one Canadian-built variant called the Bolingbroke. This aircraft, restored as a Blenheim, graces the Nanton Lancaster Society Air Museum in Nanton, Alberta. The world's only airworthy example of the type belongs to the Aircraft Restoration Company in Britain.[14] Of the operationally-disappointing Short Stirlings, the RAF ultimately accepted 2221 bomber variants and a further 160 transports. None have survived. The same holds true for the 209 dreadful Avro Manchesters produced during 1940 and 1941. Handley Page Hampdens fare a little better. Of 1430 "Flying Suitcases" built, 160 were manufactured in Canada by the Victory and Fleet aircraft companies. The Canadian Museum of Flight in Langley, British Columbia, has Hampden P5436, the last Fleet Aircraft-built variant. In the early 1990s, a second Hampden airframe in reasonable condition was recovered from a crash site in Russia, and the fuselage is being refurbished by the RAF Museum restoration facility at RAF Cosford.[15] The doughty Wellingtons, long a mainstay of Bomber Command, remained in service with the RAF until 1953. However, of the 11,461 produced, only one intact airframe exists, and that is on display at the RAF Museum in Hendon. The wreckage of another was recovered in 1985 from Loch Ness in Scotland, and it is being substantially restored for the Brooklands Museum at Weybridge in the United Kingdom.[16]

During the war, 7781 Mosquitos were built in Britain as well as in shadow factories in Canada and Australia. The Toronto de Havilland plant at Downsview churned out more than 1000 of them, commencing in September 1942. Almost all of those produced in Canada were bomber variants. At least four of them still exist in the country in various museums, including a B. Mark 20 in the Canadian Aviation Museum in Ottawa. A B. Mark 35 variant (CF-HML, formerly TA 717) is also under restoration to airworthy condition in Canada.[17]

Of the Command's true "heavy hitters," the Halifax and the Lancaster, little remains. A total of 6176 Halifaxes of all variants was produced, none of them in Canada. Only one intact specimen presently exists. It is a hybrid mix of a Mark II fuselage, Hastings wings, and parts from many other sources, and is displayed as a Mark III variant at the Yorkshire Air Museum in Elvington. In 1973, the RAF Sub-Aqua Expedition, aided by some dedicated civilians, successfully raised a Halifax Mark II, Series I variant, Serial No. W1048, from the bottom of Lake Hoklingen in Norway, where it had rested in ninety feet of water for thirty-one years. This aircraft has a distinct Canadian connection, as it was the one flown by the twenty-four-year-old Canadian friend of Reg Lane, Flying Officer Don McIntyre, against the *Tirpitz* on the night of 27/28 April 1942. The flight engineer, Sergeant V.C. Stevens, broke his foot in the ensuing crash landing and became a prisoner of war. The other five, including Don McIntyre, escaped to neutral Sweden and were eventually repatriated to Britain. The aircraft is now displayed in a preserved but unrestored condition at Hendon.[18]

However, a magnificent Canadian tribute to the Halifax is presently under restoration at the RCAF Museum in Trenton, Ontario. On the night of 23/24 April 1945, Halifax Mark VIIa, Serial No. NA 337 of 644 Squadron, was shot down by ground fire while on a Special Duties operation dropping supplies to the Norwegian Resistance. The aircraft then ditched in Lake Mjosa near the town of Hamar at about two o'clock in the morning. Unfortunately, all the crew except for the rear gunner, Flight Sergeant Weightman, perished from exposure in the lake's frigid waters before local Norwegians could rescue them later that morning. This Halifax lay undisturbed in its watery grave at a depth of some 750 feet for the next fifty years. Then, in the summer of 1995, a tenacious group of Canadians known as the Halifax Aircraft Association recovered the bomber for restoration and future display at the RCAF Memorial Museum. This determined and resourceful all-volunteer restoration team has already worked wonders. Once it is completed, estimated for 2006, and it is proudly displayed in its own purpose-built hangar, this pristine Mark VII will be the most authentic example of the type in existence. It is highly appropriate that the RCAF Museum display this particular variant, since 408, 415, 426 and 432 Squadrons all flew the Mark VII operationally for at least a limited period of time during the latter days of the European war.

The preservation of representative Lancasters has fared much better. This is due to a number of factors. First, unlike the Halifaxes, Lancasters enjoyed significant post-war employment in the air forces of several nations, including Canada. Second, as we have seen, the Lancaster has become the aircraft most closely identified with Bomber Command's wartime struggle. Considering the yeoman service provided by the "poor cousin Halifax," it is unfortunate that this Handley Page stalwart, particularly the later models, did not generate the same visceral appeal as the Lancaster. No particular urgency was generated during the early postwar period to save any examples of the "Lanc" for posterity. However, of the 7377 Lancasters produced, including 430 Mark Xs by Victory Aircraft in Malton, at least sixteen intact specimens are known to exist. This includes two on active flying status: B. Mark I PA 474 of the RAF's Battle of Britain Memorial Flight, based at RAF Coningsby, and B. Mark X FM 213, proud flagship of the Canadian Warplane Heritage Museum in Hamilton, Ontario. FM 213 was built in July 1945, too late to see wartime service. However, like many of its type, it was eventually modified to Maritime Reconnaissance/Maritime Patrol configuration, enjoyed a long trouble-free service life after some initial problems, and became one of the last Lancasters to be retired from active duty in early 1964. Today, it has been finished to represent 419 Squadron's KB 726, in an evocative tribute to the wartime exploits of Pilot Officer Andrew Charles Mynarski, VC.

At least seven additional Lancasters are on some form of static display in Canada. They include B. Mark X FM 159, pride of the Lancaster Society Museum at Nanton, Alberta. This aircraft honours the courage of Squadron Leader Ian Willoughby Bazelgette, VC, who originally hailed from nearby Calgary. Others include B. Mark X KB 839 at Canadian Forces Base Greenwood in Nova Scotia, and KB 882, which mutely guards the Trans Canada Highway at St. Jacques Airport on the outskirts of Edmonston, New Brunswick. This aircraft, with its weathered and benign appearance, has an interesting history in that it actually has a Second World War combat record. A veteran of late-war service with 428 Squadron, it flew operations against Hagen, Hamburg (twice), Merseberg, Leipzig, Kiel, and Wangerooge Island during the last six weeks of the bomber offensive. Flying Officer Kendall R. Fee, a DFC winner[19] and KB 882's wartime navigator, recalls the aircraft:

> In reference to Lancaster KB 882, now at Edmonston, I am very pleased to see old NA—R is being well looked after. We had the pleasure of bringing her back to Canada in 1945. We also put in seven operations in this machine and loved every rivet in her. The crew was as follows:
>
> > Pilot: Flight Lieutenant A.L. Ross, DFC, DFM
> > Navigator: Flying Officer K.R. Fee, DFC
> > Wireless Operator: Flight Lieutenant Aitken
> > Bomb-Aimer: Flying Officer E.K. Bergy
> > Flight Engineer: Flying Officer R. Loveday
> > Mid-Upper Gunner: Flying Officer D. Ferguson
> > Rear Gunner: Flying Officer W. Watson.[20]

And what of the men? Their graves and memorials are scattered across the length and breadth of Europe, North Africa and the Far East, from Berlin to Bournemouth, from Cairo to Calcutta. For the survivors, their post-war pursuits have been as diverse as the conditions and walks of life from which they entered the air force. Although post-war military service held neither appeal nor gainful employment for many, particularly in light of Canada's booming economy at the end of the Second World War, quite a few remained in the air force and carved out interesting and varied careers. Fred Sharp, a DFC winner and the last wartime commanding officer of 408 Squadron, rose to the rank of full general and was appointed Chief of the Defence Staff in September 1969. Roy Slemon and Larry Dunlap both became air marshals and air force icons. Both served as Deputy Commander-in-Chief, North American Air Defence Command (NORAD), and both were eventually appointed to the top "light blue" position, culminating their illustrious careers as Chiefs of the Air Staff. Chester Hull also held many senior service appointments and rose to the rank of lieutenant-general.

Reg Lane, that Pathfinder stalwart, also became a lieutenant-general and held many senior positions, including that of Deputy Commander-in-Chief NORAD, before retiring in December 1974 from a stellar and varied career that spanned thirty-five years of uniformed service to the nation. Subsequently, he became very active in civic organizations, and in 1978, he was elected National Chairman of the Federation of Military and United Services Institutes of Canada, the umbrella organization for twenty-six military institutes across the nation. Also, from 1983 until 1991, he was a member of the Consultative Group on Disarmament and Arms Control of the Department of External Affairs. In the fall of 1989, he was appointed by Order-in-Council to a three-year term as Director of the Canadian Institute for International Peace and Security, located in Ottawa.

"Mo" Morrison enjoyed a long and successful post-war career in the air force and eventually became a major-general. Cam Mussells, who had fought so valiantly against an Me 163 rocket fighter over Leipzig near war's end, eventually became a brigadier-general. Distinguishing himself yet again, he was appointed an Officer of the Most Excellent Order of the British Empire for his role in the Korean airlift as commanding officer of 426 (Transport) Squadron. Jack Watts also became a brigadier-general, as did Howard Morrison and Bill Newson. Morrison added an Air Force Cross to his DSO and DFC for exceptional service during the Korean War as a transport pilot. He retired as Vice Commander of the Central NORAD Region in 1968. Newson, the last wartime commanding officer of 405 Squadron, won a DSO and DFC and Bar for his exceptional service, and he participated in his squadron's last bombing sortie, the raid on Berchtesgaden, on 25 April 1945. After retirement from a long and successful post-war career, he served terms as President of the national Wartime Aircrew Association and Vice-President of Canada's Aviation Hall of Fame. Peter Engbrecht, who won his Conspicuous Gallantry Medal as a sharpshooting ace gunner with 424 Squadron, also remained in the air force after the war. During service with NORAD, he distinguished himself as a back-up crew chief, and he was also in charge of training at a long-range radar site in Colorado.[21]

Others followed many different paths. Bob Dale became President of the National Executive Committee of the Royal Canadian Air Force Association, Aide-de-Camp to the Lieutenant-Governor of Ontario, and excelled in business as Chairman and Chief Executive Officer of Maple Leaf Mills. Murray Peden became a securities lawyer and the first Chairman of the Manitoba Securities Commission in 1968. He also wrote the bestselling books, *Fall of an Arrow* and *A*

Thousand Shall Fall. Merv Fleming, who participated in that first night raid on Berlin on 25/26 August 1940, rose to wing commander rank during the war and won both the DSO and the DFC. Post-war, he had a long career with the Department of Transport, eventually becoming Controller of Civil Air Operations and Regulations. Others worked for government at various levels, and some ran for political office. No. 425 Squadron Wellington pilot Gilles Lamontagne was awarded a Mention-in-Despatches for his heroic actions over Essen one March night in 1943. Thirty-five years later, The Honourable J. Gilles Lamontagne of Quebec City was named Canada's Minister of National Defence, a post he held for four years. He later served as Lieutenant-Governor of Quebec and was made an Officer of the Order of Canada.

Still others became captains of industry and successful businessmen. Howard Ripstein of Montreal, after post-war service in the RCAF, excelled in the financial community and became a Professor Emeritus of Business at Concordia University. "Black Mike" McEwen had, in the opinion of Sir Arthur Harris, done such a magnificent job at the helm of 6 Group that Harris lobbied long and hard to get him a knighthood for his wartime contributions. However, Canadian regulations forbade the acceptance of such chivalric distinctions, and Harris's initiatives were for naught. Black Mike left the air force in 1946 to become a consultant to the aircraft manufacturing industry, and he subsequently became a Director of Trans Canada Airlines, the predecessor of Air Canada. Bob Turnbull of "The Flying Turnbulls" had a full post-war career in the air force, retiring in 1970. Unfortunately, he passed away just seven years later in Victoria, British Columbia. His brother John had chosen a very different path. He became the Executive Director of the Canadian Pharmaceutical Association and spent many years improving the standards of pharmacy, at home and abroad. These endeavours resulted in his appointment as a Member of the Order of Canada in June 1975.

And what of the irrepressible Johnnie Fauquier? At war's end, he was reinstated to his highest wartime rank of air commodore. Initially, he did some promotional work for the RCAF, but soon retired. He and his wife settled in Toronto, where he forged a very successful second career as the head of a large concrete construction firm. This is particularly ironic, since Fauquier had proved very adept at knocking down concrete structures during the war! He never touched the controls of an aircraft again, yet another irony from the man who had logged some 300,000 air miles as a commercial pilot prior to the commencement of hostilities.

But most of them just tried to live normal lives. Ken Underhill from Vancouver, a wartime bomb-aimer with 432 Squadron, speaks for so many in this respect:

> I prefer to comment on today's happenings. I feel I was very fortunate to survive 33 trips over enemy territory, seventeen to the Ruhr valley. I am now 77 years old—retired—I can still play tennis and golf. I have a wonderful wife, four children and ten grandchildren. You might say that we love family.
>
> Every year at the golf club we have a golf tournament on Armistice Day. At a recent one, I produced my best medal—my operational wing, which we received after being screened. The younger people were amazed when I told them that over 10,000 Canadian airmen from Bomber Command were killed during the Second World War. There seems to be less and less of us now.[22]

Many took advantage of Canada's excellent post-war veteran's benefits by returning to the classroom and becoming engineers and architects, building structures rather than destroying them. Many more became doctors and clergy, dedicating the rest of their lives to healing both bodies and souls. After the war, Hugh Hay, stalwart navigator, cross-trained as a service pilot, but he wanted more. Terry Goodwin explains:

> Hugh Hay got his pilot's course and his wings at age 29. After that I did not see much of him, but I did keep track of his whereabouts, and he agreed to be my best man when I married in 1948. After the war, he studied medicine and became the first fully qualified aircrew medical officer in the RCAF. A few years later, at the age of 35, he convinced the RCAF to check him out on Vampire jets. Later, as a wing commander, he was senior staff officer for medical affairs at Transport Command Headquarters in Trenton, Ontario. Still later, as a group captain, he commanded the Institute of Aviation Medicine in Toronto until he retired in 1966. He died in Ottawa on September 27, 1969, at the age of 53.
>
> Life out of the service had not been good to Hugh Hay. He had difficulty reconciling his Hippocratic Oath as a medical doctor with the death and destruction in which he had participated during the war. He was by no means the only aircrew member to have second thoughts, and to suffer depression as a result.[23]

Still others, mostly the pilots, became inexorably hooked on flying, and many carved out long, rewarding careers in commercial aviation, while others became flight instructors. William Corbett Vanexan of Smith's Falls, Ontario, was an early graduate of the BCATP. He flew the first of his two operational tours with the RAF's 57 Squadron during the dark days of 1941 and 1942, winning a DFC in the process. He returned for a second tour with 431 Squadron as a squadron leader in 1944, completing a wartime total of 61 sorties, and added a DSO to his honours. For all his exposure to dire combat perils, his aircraft was only hit once, resulting in just a slight injury to one crewman. Postwar, he joined Trans Canada Airlines and logged nearly 18,000 hours of commercial flying with TCA and later Air Canada, becoming a Regional Chief Pilot.[24]

On 17 August 2003, at the Oshawa Airport, Stan Miller celebrated the 60th anniversary of his first solo in a de Havilland Tiger Moth by flying his family and friends around in one! After twenty-three years of service in the post-war RCAF, Stan spent another eighteen years at Seneca College in Buttonville, Ontario, eventually becoming its Chief Flying Instructor and Chairman of Aviation and Flying Technology. Eighty years young in 2004, he currently flies Harvards—for which he still holds an aerobatic endorsement—Moths, Stearmans, and a Stinson V-77. Best of all, he shows no signs whatsoever of slowing down.[25]

In Closing

Many veterans carry the scars, both physical and mental, of their wartime experiences. None who lived through these events has remained untouched by them. While a number have such painful memories of the war that they refuse to talk about it, far more have said that, in spite of the grave dangers and the dreadful casualties incurred, they have never felt more alive than they did during that period of their lives. Some have felt remorse over their role in the war. Some have had great difficulty coping with post-war life, and for a few, the struggle has been too great. Far more have experienced anger and frustration. They have felt insulted and betrayed through the moralistic views of some post-war historical revisionists on the conduct of the bombing campaign. The veterans have, in many instances, had their contributions to the war effort maligned, or at best, marginalized. They have even been occasionally demonized through a combination of contrived Cold War rhetoric, the exhortations of peace activists, both the well-intended and the misinformed, and yet others with different and varied agendas.

While some veterans have been hobbled by what we recognize today as survivor's guilt, far more have treated their very survival for the great gift it has been. They have seized the essence of life and treated each day as a wonderful bonus, a great and golden opportunity to live life to the fullest. Most of them believed, and continue to believe, in the justness of their cause and in the part they played in the great struggle. The years have softened many of their horrors, but the excitement, and most importantly, the fellowships they forged during their wartime service have lasted lifetimes.

Of those who remain, most are now in their eighties, and their numbers wane dramatically and remorselessly with each passing year. When they get together, the hair is less and what there is of it is mostly white. Their bodies have changed with age, but their memories are quickly rekindled of events which took place long ago and far away, when they all wore younger men's clothes. Time has healed a lot of their pains, but the strong sense of comradeship, of shared dangers, and of lasting bonds forged in fire remain. Specific crews in particular, in the very essence of small-unit cohesion, have remained intensely close and loyal to each other over the years, celebrating successes and joys, and nurturing and providing succor to their brethren through the hard times. Howard Hewer, veteran Wellington wireless operator of service with 148 and 218 Squadrons, reflects on his wartime service while counting his blessings:

> Like other veterans, I have tried to make the most of the time given to me, and life has been bountiful. Not only did I have a long, rewarding air force career, and a second mini-career with the Ontario Government, I have been blessed with a loving partner, and with a son, Robert, and a daughter, Margaret . . .
>
> It is true that war brings out the best and the worst in man, but although we veterans of the air war celebrate the bonds that the challenges of operational flying created, we are deeply conscious of the horrors of war as we have seen it. As one writer observed, "The horror of war is absolute. The guilty, although deserving of it, are just as dead as the innocent." Survivors of Bomber Command, as proud as we are of the part we played, are humbled by words such as those of Marshal of the Royal Air Force Sir John Slessor, when he pondered the costly attacks that left such an indelible imprint on the horrors of the two world wars:
>
> "The compulsions of 1915 and 1940 produced two of the most unbelievable manifestations of human courage and endurance in the history of war—the infantry of 1914–1918 and the bomber crews of 1939–1945."
>
> I have never considered myself a brave man. But I was put into the company of brave men, and I could not very well have let them down.
>
> I don't believe I did.[26]

We, the citizens of present-day Canada, quite simply owe these men, as well as their fighting brothers in the other services, our rich todays as well as the promise of our tomorrows. They have been the guarantors of the bountiful, secure lives we now take so much for granted, paid for with their many sacrifices. For this great gift to the nation, they deserve both our profound gratitude and an objective attempt to place the bombing campaign in balance and in perspective.

It is perhaps most fitting that the words of Sir Arthur Harris, the helmsman of Bomber Command throughout its most arduous and successful years, should close this story:

There are no words with which I can do justice to the aircrew who fought under my command. There is no parallel in warfare to such courage and determination in the face of danger over so prolonged a period, of danger which at times was so great that scarcely one man in three could expect to survive his tour of thirty operations. . . It was, moreover, a clear and highly conscious courage, by which the risk was taken with calm forethought, for the aircrew were all highly skilled men, above the average in education, who had to understand every aspect and detail of their task. It was, furthermore, the courage of the small hours, of men virtually alone, for at his battle station the airman is virtually alone. It was the courage of men with long-drawn apprehensions of daily "going over the top." They were without exception volunteers, for no man was trained for aircrew with the RAF [and RCAF] who did not volunteer for this. Such devotion must never be forgotten.[27]

APPENDIX

The Balance Sheet:
The Costs and the Gains of the Bombing Campaign

Many survivors have paid a high price in lost health and happiness, made worse by the denigration of their efforts by critics ranging from the morally fastidious, through those who supported the campaign until they saw what it had done and then wished to distance themselves from it, to those with a political axe to grind. Like the firestorms that were its most dreadful expression, condemnation of the bombing campaign has fed upon itself until the flames of cant and the smoke of hypocrisy have obscured its many accomplishments, not least the saving of countless Allied soldiers' lives.

—Richard Holmes
Battlefields of the Second World War

Critics of the bomber offensive frequently argue that the materiel and human cost of the campaign far overshadowed the gains, and that the resources dedicated to it could have been more effectively utilized elsewhere. They have argued that the combat manpower could have been better used in the other fighting services, especially the army, and industry could have been used to produce more weapons for these fighting services. However, proponents of this line of thought assume that the weight of effort expended on the bombing campaign was inordinately high. Richard Overy maintains that it was actually rather modest. "Measured against the totals for the entire war effort (production and fighting), bombing absorbed 7 percent, rising to 12 percent in 1944–45. Since at least a proportion of bomber production went to other theatres of war, the aggregate figures for the direct bombing of Germany were certainly smaller than this. Seven percent of Britain's war effort can hardly be regarded as an unreasonable allocation of resources."[1] Further, although some significant infantry shortages were experienced in 1944, they never reached an extremely critical overall level and were eventually rectified. With respect to materiel, none of the services was conspicuously wanting for anything by 1943, and the British effort was thereafter bolstered by substantial North American war production.

The Down Side

Much of the criticism of the bombing campaign has focused on the human cost, the unquestionably heavy loss rates endured by Anglo-American aircrews, 81,000 of whom forfeited their lives aboard 18,000 aircraft lost from all causes.[2] However, these losses need to be placed in perspective, especially when compared to the twenty-to twenty-seven million war deaths suffered by the Soviet Union. Nonetheless, the human cost of the campaign was formidable. During the entire period of the Eighth Air Force's operations over Europe, which included Pointblank from 10 June 1943 until April 1944, roughly 26,000 American airmen of that numbered air force alone were killed, while another 20,000 became prisoners of war.[3] Bomber Command, in six years of war, lost 55,573 airmen, 47,268 on operations, and a further 8305 due to training, non-operational flying accidents and other causes.[4] Command aircraft losses from all causes totaled 12,330, of which 8655 went down over Germany, Italy and Occupied Europe.[5]

During the war, Bomber Command's 125,000 airmen[6] flew 364,514 sorties over Europe,[7] and the majority of the Command tonnage was dropped from the summer of 1944 until the cessation of hostilities. To put the total campaign in perspective, by VE-Day 955,044 tons of bombs had been dropped on Germany, Italy, enemy occupied territory and targets at sea. Approximately 74 percent of the total tonnage was delivered after 1 January 1944, and 70 percent of the total after 1 July 1944, from which time forward the Bomber Command loss rates were greatly reduced.[8] In round figures, 48,000 tons were dropped on European targets up until the end of January 1942, an additional 42,000 tons by year's end, another 158,000 tons in 1943 and the balance thereafter. Of the totals dropped on the European Axis powers during the war, 68.8 percent fell on the Reich itself, 30.19 percent on the enemy occupied territories, 0.94 percent on Italy and 0.07 percent on targets at sea.[9] "If the bombing of Germany had little effect on production prior to July 1944, it is not only because she had idle resources on which to draw, but because the major weight of the air offensive against her had not been brought to bear. After the air war against Germany was launched on its full scale, the effect was immediate."[10] Overall loss rates for the entire war averaged 2.58 percent per raid, which, ironically, would almost provide that "50-50 chance of survival" on which the operational tour lengths were codified in 1943,[11] but only for the first tour of operations. It did not include the accidental fatal casualties, 6.64 percent of the wartime force, nor did it include another 3 percent who were seriously injured in these mishaps. Reduced to round numbers for the entire duration of the war, of every 100 airmen who joined Bomber Command, 38 were killed on operations, eight became POWs, three were wounded, seven were killed in operational accidents or in training, and three were injured in training.[12] Therefore, only 41 out of 100 escaped unscathed from any of the aforementioned categories, although not necessarily unscathed by all manners of measurement. Only the *Kriegsmarine*'s U-boat arm suffered greater overall casualty percentages on a sustained basis.[13]

As a subset of the larger picture, the Canadian story is considerably more positive. Of the

91,166 RCAF aircrew who commenced training under the terms of the BCATP, 75,668 or 83 percent graduated in one of the aircrew trades. Of this number, and factoring in a trained surplus-to-needs of 10,500 Canadian aircrew late in the war, approximately 50,000 RCAF BCATP graduates eventually served overseas.[14] Bomber Command was far and away the majority employer of these graduates, and it is estimated that approximately 40,000 RCAF aircrew served either operationally or at an operational training unit with the Command at some time during the war.[15]

Here, one must note that both the total number of Canadian aircrew in Bomber Command service, as well as the total Canadian aircrew casualty figures, are surprisingly difficult to verify. In the absence of definitive overall figures, I have taken the liberty of making some reasonable assumptions, based on what is known. As we have seen, there were essentially three classes of Canadian aircrew in Bomber Command service:

> Canadians in indigenous RCAF Bomber Command squadrons, or in 6 Group;
> RCAF aircrew serving in RAF Bomber Command squadrons; and
> The CAN/RAF airmen, Canadians in the direct employ of the RAF.

However, the undisputed total number of RCAF aircrew fatalities in Bomber Command is 9919 of the 40,000 who served, of which 8240 (20.6 percent) were killed on operations. They included RCAF members serving in 6 Group, 405 (Pathfinder) Squadron of 8 Group, and RCAF members serving with RAF bomber squadrons. A further 673 (1.68 percent) were wounded in action, and 1647 (4.12 percent) were killed in operational accidents or training. Also, 1849 (4.62 percent) would become prisoners of war, while 659 (1.65 percent) were injured in operational accidents or training.[16] Compared to the overall war-long Bomber Command casualty rate, only 32.67 percent[17] (vice the 59 percent Command average) of all RCAF Bomber Command aircrew became statistical casualties, although this figure does not include an estimated 737 of at least 1106 CAN/RAF airmen, two-thirds of the total, who are believed to have served with Bomber Command in direct RAF service. Of the 1106 total, at least 778 are known to have been killed either operationally or accidentally,[18] and therefore a reasonable two-thirds extrapolation suggests a further 519 CAN/RAF Bomber Command fatal casualties can be added to the RCAF total, and subtracted from the British total. Similar cases can undoubtedly be made for other non-Britons on direct service in RAF units. Worthy of note, given the dynamic and wide-ranging nature of Bomber Command's war, many of its casualties are simply categorized as "Missing—presumed dead."[19] This is a poignant testimonial to the violent nature of their passing. For them, no burial plot or headstone to comfort loved ones and to mark their place of eternal rest. The skies over northwest Europe remain their cemetery. The Runnymede Memorial in Britain, dedicated in 1953, contains the names of 20,000 Commonwealth airmen of the Second World War who have no known graves. Included among them are the names of 3072 Canadians. Others are commemorated and/or buried in locations as diverse as Bournemouth and Berlin.[20]

There are a number of reasons for the significantly lower RCAF casualty rates. Although the CAN/RAF loss rate and that of RCAF aircrew serving in RAF squadrons essentially mirrored that of their British colleagues, Canadians were not present in large percentages during the very early days of Command operations when loss rates were relatively high. Nor did some aircraft fleets with the highest loss rates, such as the Manchester and the Stirling, ever equip RCAF bomber squadrons, although many Canadians crewed both types.

One should note that eleven RCAF Bomber Command squadrons had been formed prior to the official paper establishment of 6 Group in October 1942. However, the last six of those units were barely in existence prior to the group's official stand-up for operations in January 1943[21]. In all, there were 4203 known fatal 6 Group casualties during the 28 months of its operations.[22] If a Canadianization rate of 75 percent is applied to this number for the duration of the group's existence,[23] an estimated 3152 of 6 Group's 4203 fatalities were Canadian. Subtracting this number and the 1900 fatal RCAF Bomber Command casualties prior to 1 January 1943 from the 9919 total wartime figure, it is estimated that 4867 RCAF aircrew in RAF bombing squadrons forfeited their lives from 1 January 1943 until the cessation of all hostilities in August 1945. In the summer of 1944, there were approximately 10,200 RCAF aircrew in all RCAF squadrons overseas, and 16,000 RCAF aircrew in all RAF squadrons overseas[24]. These numbers represent 38.5 percent and 61.5 percent respectively of the totals of RCAF aircrew serving overseas, and the Bomber Command subset of these numbers would closely mirror this ratio. And the Canadian 6 Group losses of 3152 represent 39.2 percent of the known losses for the period, whereas the estimated 4867 RCAF aircrew fatalities in RAF units during the time-frame represent 60.8 percent of the estimated totals. Again, these numbers are logical when spanning a period when losses would be expected to be relatively equal throughout the Command.

The lowest loss rate in Bomber Command was 6 Group's overall 2 percent per operation, and this impressive statistic is yet another reason why Canadian bomber casualties fell significantly below the wartime Bomber Command average. However, 6 Group was not yet in existence during many of the darkest early days of the bombing campaign. While it did stumble at the outset relative to the performance of the other groups, its initial high loss rates were somewhat mitigated by the three Wellington squadrons syphoned off as 331 Wing to support the Allied landings in Sicily and Italy.[25] However, there is no doubt that the requirement to send experienced crews in support of Operation Torch degraded the overall experience level of the crews available for 6 Group's early operational challenges and adversely affected the loss rates for those then flying out of Yorkshire. Late in the bombing campaign, during the last year, the group's performance was second-to-none. In fact, its overall wartime loss rate of 1.8 percent for Halifaxes and Lancasters combined was the best in Bomber Command. These results are also a resounding endorsement of the very high calibre of leadership and the professionalism fostered within 6 Group, particularly after it was placed under the guidance of Air Vice-Marshal Clifford M. "Black Mike" McEwen.

If one adds the estimated 519 Bomber Command fatal CAN/RAF casualties to the known 9919 RCAF Bomber Command casualties, a reasonable estimate of overall fatal Canadian aircrew casualties during the campaign would be 10,438 out of 40,737 participants,[26] or roughly 25.6 percent of those who served.

However, there were periods of time when the odds against survival were particularly daunting. For example, with respect to 6 Group's Halifax II/V operations between March 1943 and February 1944, the average monthly loss rate was 6.05 percent per operation, producing a mere 16 percent survival rate.[27] Between August 1943 and March 1944, the group's Lancaster II loss rate averaged 5 percent per operation, producing a concomitant 21 percent survival rate.[28] During the group's first year of operations, for those flying Wellingtons between January and October 1943, the loss rate averaged 3.6 percent, producing a survival rate of 34 percent.[29] That said, the February 1944 decision by Harris to restrict the Merlin-powered Halifax II/V squadrons from operations over Germany due to service ceiling limitations during a period of brisk operational tempo undoubtedly saved Canadian lives. An earlier decision to relegate Bomber Command Wellington squadrons to mostly Gardening operations during the summer and early autumn of 1943 similarly eased the losses in that community.[30]

There is also no doubt that the particular time at which aircrew members commenced their operational tours significantly affected their chances of survival. Given a period of intense operational activity, it was not unusual for a crew to complete an operational tour within three calendar months, a common occurrence during the last year of the war. However, if, for example, those three months fell within the confines of the Second Battle of the Ruhr from March to July 1943, or the Berlin raids from November 1943 to March 1944, individual crew odds of survival were much less than, for example, those who commenced operations later in 1944. The later rates graphically illustrate how enormous the bombing weight of effort was during the final nine months of the war under increasingly favourable circumstances, and they somewhat mitigate the dreadful earlier statistics.

Accomplishments of the Bombing Campaign

So much for the losses . . . what of the gains? First, the gains were not only what was directly attributable to the bombing, such as the actual destruction of targets, but also constituted a host of indirect benefits brought on as adjuncts to the bombing. In Richard Overy's words:

> From Galbraith onwards the view has taken root that the only thing that Bomber Command did, or was ordered to do, was to attack German cities with indifferent accuracy. The Bombing Surveys devoted much of their effort to measuring the direct physical damage to war production through city bombing. This has produced since the war a narrow economic interpretation of the bombing offensive that distorts both the purposes and nature of Britain's bombing effort to an extraordinary degree.[31]

While part of the bombing effort was to be directed at Germany's home front military and economic structures if the nation first attacked civilian targets in an indiscriminate manner, very large portions of the overall effort were directed at many other targets for which the Command's aircraft were needed. Again, as Overy mentions, not even half the Command's total wartime dropped bomb tonnage was dedicated to the industrial cities.[32] Also, during the later stages of the campaign, even attacks against industrialized cities were frequently tactical rather than strategic, conducted as they were in support of the advancing Allied land armies. For much of the first four years of the war, support for the naval war comprised a significant portion of the Command's overall effort, while for much of 1944, it was extensively used in support of the invasion of northwest Europe. Additionally, Command aircraft were used for reconnaissance, for propaganda missions, for electronic warfare and deception operations, for support to Occupied Europe's resistance movements, and, as we have seen, for humanitarian aid and mercy missions towards the end of hostilities. Bomber Command was a true "Jack-of-all-trades," and it required the full resolution of its commanders not to become excessively and repeatedly diverted from its primary mandate by all the competing demands on its limited resources.[33] With the benefit of hindsight, while Arthur Harris was undoubtedly correct in his assessment of the need for a broad application of area bombing during the early innings of the campaign, his dogged rejection of the so-called "panacea targets" later on appears to have been somewhat myopic. Albert Speer and others dreaded timely follow-on efforts to the highly successful 1943 attacks on the Ruhr dams, Hamburg,[34] and the ball-bearing industry, and they believed that such a concentration of effort at the time would have been cataclysmic for the Reich. Similarly, an earlier and more dedicated application of effort against the enemy's oil resources, which pitted the Commander-in-Chief Bomber Command against the Chief of the Air Staff, might have brought the European war to an earlier conclusion. But such is the fog of war, and Arthur Harris sincerely believed he was following the correct course and was utilizing his Command to inflict the most damage under the circumstances presented to him. And the course he chose, the targets he elected to pursue, perhaps at the cost of others more viable, were certainly not without merit or justification. Again, the wisdom of hindsight needs to be tempered with the perceptions of the day. Besides, Harris was firmly convinced from an early stage of the bombing campaign that frequent, concentrated repeat visits to specific targets would bring prohibitive losses to his Command.

The bombing offensive was also seen as a way to avoid the carnage of trench warfare, exemplified by the abattoir that the Western Front had become during the Great War. "For Britain, with its small population and the lack of a large standing army, a small force of specialized volunteers was arguably a more effective way of mobilizing British manpower than the development of a large and inexperienced ground army."[35] Also, all the great early airpower theorists of the pre-Second World War period, including Guilio Douhet, William "Billy" Mitchell and Sir Hugh Trenchard, had espoused the primacy of offensive air operations, the relative invulnerability of the bomber and the comparative fragility of civilian morale. The bomber offensive was very much in lockstep with Britain's overall peripheral strategy, which meant a war of long-term economic attrition and opportunism against the Germans, as opposed to a directly confrontational war of mass and concentration. The bomber offensive was, in fact, the epitome of unconventional, guerrilla warfare, and thus in keeping with Britain's overall strategic plan.

Furthermore, the Command made possible a combat initiative that was deemed vital, not just for the damage it would cause the Third Reich, but for the galvanizing of both British and global support. It certainly affected American and Commonwealth opinion, as well as that of potential allies and enslaved nations, telegraphing British resolve to forcefully press home the fight against the tyranny of Nazism, alone if necessary. Its very prosecution assured Britain a pivotal say in the conduct of the war. It also did wonders for domestic morale, bolstering the British public in a time of great need for reassurance and hope. This evidence of commitment was never more important than after the German invasion of the Soviet Union during the summer of 1941. The bombing offensive constituted a second front, a significant source of relief to the beleaguered Soviets when no other offensive action was realistic or even possible. Later, bombing's contributions became a prerequisite to the successful invasion of northwest Europe; "an independent campaign to pave the way for a combined arms invasion of Hitler's Europe."[36] From April until September 1944, the majority of Bomber Command's activities were conducted in lockstep with the preparation, execution, and aftermath of the invasion through Normandy. And in the wake of this effort, the Command dealt decisive blows to the enemy's transportation and petroleum resources, effectively paralyzing the Third Reich in its final hours.

The total defeat of Germany's air force, through direct attacks on production facilities, airfield and support installations on the ground, and a highly successful war of attrition in the air, was a pivotal contribution to winning the war. Of the overall bombing offensive, Albert Speer, Hitler's Minister for Armaments and War Production, said: "As far as I can judge from the accounts I have read, no one has seen that this was the greatest lost battle on the Germans' side."[37]

And what of the specific direct and indirect effects of the bombing? The latter were in ways much more damaging to the Axis war effort, and while engineers speak of a Law of Unforeseen Advantages, many of these indirect benefits were anticipated, if not deliberately orchestrated. The direct damage was also highly significant however.

Once air superiority had been attained over the Third Reich by the spring of 1944, the Allied air forces exploited this turn of events in a series of concentrated and systematic attacks against the German synthetic oil industry and transportation systems. The attacks on both these resources contributed significantly to the final collapse of the Reich. For example, German domestic oil production plummeted from 673,000 tons in January 1944 to 265,000 tons in September, and aviation fuel was temporarily reduced to 5 percent of needs.[38] Since nothing was more germane to the collapse of the German armed forces than the irrevocable defeat of its airpower, the effective grounding of the *Luftwaffe* was a knockout punch. The campaign against the synthetic petroleum plants, the refineries, and the oil fields was the most effective means of rendering the *Luftwaffe* impotent. The overall shortage of aviation gasoline adversely affected flying training from as early as 1942, with a concomitant serious degradation in the quality of personnel. The specific output of aviation fuel actually fell from 195,000 tons in May 1944, to 35,000 tons by mid-summer, and to a paltry 7000 tons by September. Although stockpiled resources kept the *Luftwaffe* flying after a fashion throughout the summer, by autumn, shortages were acute. This had to be a bitter irony for Germany's air leaders, for it came at a time when the air industries achieved a new peak in fighter production, completing 3133 aircraft in September alone. Along with making this production increase in conventional-type aircraft of little military significance, the additional limited availability of low-grade fuels, which could only be used in high-performance turbojet aircraft, was one reason that a jet force could not be fielded in time to become a significant, widespread threat to the Allies. As a broader, over-arching result, the Eighth, Ninth and Fifteenth Air Forces, working in concert with Bomber Command, destroyed virtually all of Germany's coke, ferroalloy and synthetic rubber industries, 95 percent of its fuel, hard coal and rubber capacity, 90 percent of its steel capacity, 75 percent of its truck producing capacity and 70 percent of its tire production.[39] And while various contemporary sources, including German accounts, state that Bomber Command's area bombing contributed between 20 percent and 31 percent of the direct aircraft production losses, and between 35 percent[40] and 55 percent[41] of armoured vehicle production losses, many more losses were incurred while the Germans were attempting to distribute the finished products under near-continuous heavy air attacks. At any rate, the point is moot. Without fuel to convey the aircraft aloft or to get the tanks into battle, they were useless.[42]

> The loss of oil production was also felt in many other ways. In August 1944, the final run-in time for aircraft engines was cut from 2 hours to a half hour. For lack of fuel, pilot training, previously cut down, was further curtailed. Through the summer, the movement of German *Panzer* divisions in the field was hampered more and more seriously as a result of losses in combat and mounting transportation difficulties, together with the fall in fuel production. By December, according to Speer, the fuel shortage had reached catastrophic proportions. When the Germans launched their desperate counteroffensive on December

16, 1944, their reserves of fuel were far from sufficient to support the operation. They counted on capturing Allied stocks. Failing in this, many *Panzer* units were lost when they ran out of gasoline.[43]

At this juncture of the war, Arthur Harris may have exercised faulty judgement in not mounting a more enthusiastic and focused campaign against the oil resources, since he still put considerable emphasis on the bombing of the industrial cities. The counter-oil campaign was decisive, if arguably prolonged, by concentration on other interests. However, a number of industrial cities hit by Bomber Command during this phase included significant damage to oil and related targets. The results were on occasion significantly more successful than the USAAF's daylight bombing, thanks to a high degree of experience and accuracy with the blind-bombing aids *Oboe* and *H2S*, the Air Position Indicator (API), the Group Position Indicator (GPI) and the improved Mark XIV gyro stabilized automatic bombsight (SABS). The blow dealt was decisive; it just may have taken longer to deliver because of the conflicting priorities. Albert Speer concedes:

> The systematic air raids of the fall of 1944 once again throttled traffic and made transportation, this time for good, the greatest bottleneck in our war economy.[44]

Prior to the war, Germany possessed a world-class railway system that was very capable and well maintained, and it was complemented by an equally formidable inland waterway system for the movement of bulk material to and from the industrialized Ruhr. However, the railroad system became increasingly overburdened through the industrial dispersion necessitated by the bombing, and this dispersion required the construction of considerably more railroad infrastructure, which was highly susceptible to concentrated air attacks. While the German transportation system did not become a priority target until very late in the war, "the effects of the heavy air attacks beginning in September of 1944 were felt at once and were clearly apparent in the general traffic and operating statistics of the *Reichsbahn* . . . the heavy attacks of September and October produced a most serious disruption in railway operations over the whole of western Germany."[45] Concurrently, successful attacks on waterway targets devastated industrial traffic on the Rhine and the north German canals, causing the vital Ruhr district to suffer heavy declines in transport. For example, the Dortmund-Ems Canal, from October 1944 until March 1945, could average only 12 percent of the shipping attained during the previous year.[46] The supply of critical components to virtually all vital war production elements was severely impacted by the concentrated attacks of September and October, and reserves were virtually exhausted by November and early December. Most dramatic was the near-total curtailment of hard coal supplies to the Ruhr. "The consequences of the breakdown in the transportation system were probably greater than any other single factor in the final collapse of the German economy . . . most of the chaos which gripped the German economy was traceable directly or indirectly to the disaster which overtook the transportation system."[47] The loss of transportation infrastructure stymied the flow of basic raw materials, components and semi-finished products, and also severely limited the distribution of finished products.

It is true that large-scale priority attacks on the transportation system came too late in the war to seriously affect the German armed forces at the fighting fronts. "By the end of the war, however, it had so paralyzed the German industrial economy as to render all further war production virtually impossible. It had, moreover, removed the foundation of the civilian economy, suggesting the inevitability of eventual collapse under continued air attack."[48]

The Indirect Effects of the Bombing Campaign

Throughout Germany in 1944 alone, approximately 800,000 workers were engaged in essential repair work solely attributable to the bombing, especially to factories and to modes of communication. An additional 250,000 to 400,000 personnel were required to provide the necessary equipment, resources, and services to effect the repairs. Thus, a tremendous amount of the available manpower was diverted from other essential employment to the reconstruction effort.[49] Furthermore, industrial reconstruction itself was often subjected to push-pull meddling from the highest levels, breeding further manpower wastage. Albert Speer noted that Hitler himself was very shaken by the destruction of valuable historic buildings, particularly theatres. "Consequently, he was likely to demand that burned-out theaters be rebuilt immediately. Several times I tried to remind him of other strains on the construction industry."[50]

The bombing of the industrial cities forced a policy of decentralized production, or dispersal, and it placed additional burdens and vulnerability on the transportation and communication networks. As well, it diverted resources from new construction efforts. Dispersal was highly disruptive to industrial firms that had been centralized to operate at maximum efficiency. Dispersal also demanded a greater diffusion of and reliance on a very limited pool of skilled labour, and led to a sharp decline in the quality of weapons produced. Supervisory shortages also resulted in significantly more industrial sabotage from an increasingly unwilling, press-ganged and slave labour force. Decentralization denied the Germans the ability to operate a rational, efficient, highly centralized industrial war effort, which would have permitted much higher levels of output.[51] In the aircraft industry alone:

> Existing production schedules were disrupted and dilution of management supervision made itself felt. In the end, it increased the load on its overburdened transportation system and, when attack was concentrated on transportation, the final assembly plants lacked the necessary sub-assemblies and components. The policy of dispersal was then revised in favour of concentration underground, but it was too late.[52]

The frenzied production pace, aided by the bombing, led to significant decreases in quality control and greatly reduced worker productivity. Shortages of skilled labour and strategic materials, production interruptions, plant damage, slipshod construction, and even sabotage all led to declines in end-product quality. Nowhere was this more evident than in the aircraft engine industry, where the increasingly unreliable powerplants generated major problems in morale for the *Luftwaffe*, especially among the inexperienced fighter pilot cadre.

> Yet the night bombing campaign's greatest contribution to the winning of the war was precisely what Harris claimed and the conventional wisdom has so often discounted. The "area" bombing attacks did have a direct and palpable effect on the morale of the German population, and the German leadership, in response to that impact, seriously skewed Germany's strategy. Recent scholarship in the Federal Republic indicates that as early as the summer of 1942, the night bombing campaign was affecting German attitudes. In 1943, the heavy bombing caused a dramatic fall off in popular morale.[53]

As the foregoing words of American military historian Williamson Murray attest, the bombing's impact on enemy morale was significant. However, it was unrealistic to expect that in an extreme police state such as the Third Reich, a popular uprising and overthrow of the Nazi regime would ensue. Still, the cumulative effects of the bombing, especially the bombing by night, were intensely demoralizing. And once the Allies had designated the ruin of enemy morale, particularly that of the industrial work force, as an overt war aim, regular intelligence reports reinforced the views of senior Allied commanders that this war aim was being fulfilled. In fact, as early as the summer of 1940, British intelligence sources in neutral Switzerland reported the impact of the still-minimal bombing on enemy morale as follows: "A Swiss recently returned from Germany states there is some labour unrest in the Ruhr owing to the fact that workers are doing 12 hour shifts a day and fail to get a proper night's rest owing to aerial attacks."[54]

One of the most effective of an early series of Bomber Command raids, and one frequently underestimated in significance, was the bombing of Berlin on the night of 4/5 September 1940. While the damage was not extensive, the raids generated considerable public resentment. Adolf Hitler was goaded into switching his bombing priorities to a retaliatory campaign against London, just when the campaign against Fighter Command's airfields and command and control facilities was proving decisive. There is little doubt that this emotional decision by Hitler, soon echoed by Göring, ensured the survival of both Fighter Command and the British nation at their moment of greatest vulnerability. Furthermore, the following previously classified high-level British and Allied documents from 1942 provide substantiating evidence for continuing the bombing campaign against enemy morale. These observations were undoubtedly contributing factors to the evolution of the bombing policy. A letter from Paymaster General Lord Cherwell to Prime Minister Churchill of 30 March 1942 states:

> Investigation seems to show that having one's house demolished is most damaging to morale. People seem to mind it more than having their friends or relatives killed.[55]

Similar sentiments are expressed in these excerpts from Mr. Justice John E. Singleton's "Report to the War Cabinet on the Bombing of Germany," dated 20 May 1942:

> Another feature to which reference should be made is the recent German propaganda, which appears to show the anxiety felt in Germany on our air raids on that country . . . Now we expect to be able to deliver to Germany in the future a much greater weight of bombs than we received. If we can combine with this a greater measure of accuracy and intensified concentration, I feel it will have a very considerable effect, growing as the intensity of the bombing increases, and the more so if there does not appear to the German people any likelihood of their air force being able to deal with the forces of those opposed to them . . . Its effect on the German people will be much greater if the projected attack on Russia fails . . . It is right to say that among the things which are important from the point of view of morale of the people are housing, warmth, sleep and food . . . The first sign of the effect (of sustained bombing) may well appear in the German troops if they realize that those they have left at home cannot be protected from air attack, as was promised to them . . . I think there is every reason to hope for good results from a sustained bombing policy.[56]

And a missive a month later, on 22 June, from the US Consul General in Geneva through Bern to the US Secretary of State elaborates:

> There is reason to believe that high German military circles are fearful of the effect of a mass bombing designed to panic the civilian inhabitants of thickly populated districts into frenzied activity.[57]

The highly influential intelligence reports of late 1942 also appeared to validate the area bombing strategy against the industrial cities, just prior to the pivotal policy decisions that would be made at Casablanca early the following year. British Intelligence Report No. 346, 22 September 1942 notes:

<u>Unrest; Stories Spread by Evacuees</u>

Unrest in the bombed areas is great and in those districts to which the homeless and children from "air threatened regions" have been evacuated, a certain nervousness is already noticeable, because the evacuees naturally talk about their experiences.

<u>Destruction of Factories and Food Depots</u>

These big raids cause much destruction. In spite of the statements in the *Wehrmacht* reports, the destruction of war production facilities is fairly considerable. The loss caused by the destruction of food stores and depots is extraordinarily great, as the food cannot be replaced.[58]

The following is a British Intelligence "Report on Bombing's Effect on Housing and Division of Effort," from autumn 1942:

The loss of one's home and possessions has been found in this country (Germany) to be one of the most important points with regard to morale. Judging by the strict measures enforced on information of the results of our raids reaching the soldiers at the front, it would appear that the German authorities are aware of the effect it may also produce on the morale of the fighting services.[59]

And finally an excerpt from "An Estimate of the Effects of an Anglo-American Offensive Against Germany by the Chiefs of Staff Committee for the War Cabinet, 3 November 1942."

Conditions at Karlsruhe, as compared with Coventry and Lübeck, thus afford a striking illustration of the cumulative effects on organization and morale which have followed raiding, even on the relatively small scale we have achieved in the past few months. The change in outlook which has taken place is perhaps best shown by the pronouncements of Robert Wagner, the local *Gauleiter*. These emphasize that during air raids the individual must look after himself as best he can, and after that he must be prepared to do his own repairs without calling on the authorities to help him. Such instructions would be at least tolerable under a democratic system which expects the citizen in emergency to be capable of personal effort and initiative. They accord very badly with the accepted principles of Nazi centralized Government, and the admitted breakdown at this early stage of the State organization in which the Germans have been so carefully taught to place implicit faith is a significant indication of the effects which large-scale bombing may be expected to produce.[60]

The foregoing reports bolstered the wartime belief of the Allied commanders that the bombing campaign against enemy morale was viable and worthwhile. Therefore, although specific industrial and military targets were pin-pointed, it was broadly anticipated that not merely industrial materiel damage would occur, particularly because of the German propensity for embedding industrial facilities in residential areas. As historian Denis Richards has written: "With their homes, work places and neighbourhood amenities all destroyed, on top of all the privations they were thought to be suffering, the German people were expected to lose all their zeal, not only for production, but also for the Nazi regime."[61]

The Moral Issue

However, it must be clearly understood that no part of this policy deliberately mandated the slaughter of civilians, although heavy civilian casualties would be an inevitable result. Rather, the intention was to make it exceptionally difficult, if not impossible, for the enemy civilian work force to remain on the job. "It was hoped to break their will to do so by destroying their houses and all the comforts and necessities of a civilized urban life. If the civilians fled to the countryside, or the authorities managed to evacuate them from the major towns—as British mothers and children had been evacuated during the early days of the war—so much the better: the industrial desert (the primary goal) could be created with less loss of life."[62]

However, after the Battle of Britain, throughout that joyless winter of 1940–1941, the Germans adopted a broader night bombing campaign against the British industrial centres as a means of weakening resistance and disrupting the production and supply of war materials. In addition to London, Liverpool, Hull, Portsmouth, Coventry, and many other cities, including the east coast ports, were singled out for special attention. These were the so-called Baedeker Raids. From this point onwards, British authority no longer felt obliged to exercise due care and restraint with respect to minimizing collateral civilian casualties in the German industrial centres. Furthermore, this policy direction enjoyed widespread public support at the time.

Richard Overy believes the Allied bombing was severely disruptive to German society. Throughout the war, nearly nine million citizens were evacuated from the German cities, which not only dramatically reduced the potential work force, but also placed incredible strains on infrastructure to provide shelter, nourishment, and other essential consumer goods to all those displaced persons, further diverting resources from the war industries. Worker efficiency in areas directly threatened by the bombing suffered considerably; long, exhausting hours were spent in cramped air raid shelters or cellars. Absenteeism increased, and by 1944, it averaged almost four full working weeks per worker annually in the Reich. For example, at the Ford works in Cologne on any given day in 1944, at least one-quarter of the work force was absent. When the numbers documenting the unparalleled levels of productivity of German industry during 1944 are examined, one has to wonder what they would have been had the Germans not been faced with a near-constant threat of death from the air. Much of the production was generated by slave labourers who worked in atrocious conditions. This work force was never more than two-thirds as productive as free German workers, nor were they motivated to improvement beyond the spur of terror. Along with vast suffering, the bombing placed a definite ceiling on German productivity, even in a state of total war.

A significant amount of the increased late war industrial output is explained by the fact that Germany was deliberately working nowhere close to full war capacity for the first three years of the Second World War. When Albert Speer took the helm as Armaments and War Production Minister in February 1942, the nation was only producing three percent more of these products than in peacetime, and Adolf Hitler was adamant that the military endeavours of the Third Reich would not interfere with the consumer industries. Hitler expected a *Blitzkrieg* win in the Soviet Union, and he launched this precursor to what would eventually become total war on the foundation of a peacetime economic and industrial output. Until 1943, German industry was generally only working one ten-hour shift each day. Thereafter, policy changed to accommodate three shifts and a seven-day, twenty-four-hour operation, augmented by an involuntary work force of 2,500,000 prisoners and 1,500,000 workers press-ganged in from the occupied territories.[63]

As the bombing intensified, there were profound political ramifications to Speer's industrial policies. Hitler and his entourage lost confidence in Speer and began to blame him for all the nation's economic ills. Himmler became increasingly involved in economic matters and began running Speer's system at gunpoint, which in turn dissuaded many Germans.[64]

> Bombing appreciably affected the German will to resist. Its main psychological effects were defeatism, fear, hopelessness, fatalism and apathy. It did little to stiffen resistance through the arousing of aggressive emotions of hate and anger. War weariness, willingness to surrender, loss of hope in a German victory, distrust of leaders, feelings of disunity, and demoralizing fear were all more common among bombed than among un-bombed people . . . The disruption of public utilities in a community did much to lower the will to resist. Especially significant was the disruption of transportation service; it was the most critical public utility for the morale of the civilian population. Electricity was next in importance among the utilities, then water, then gas. A vital blow to the morale of a bombed community was the destruction of school and recreational facilities for children. This necessitated the evacuation of school children. Parents were doubly affected by such evacuation because they suffered not only the burden of family separation but also the possible loss of the moral guidance of their children to the Nazi Party.[65]

The Effect on German Morale

The highest German authorities were very concerned with home front morale throughout the bombing campaign. Albert Speer paraphrased Hitler on 8 March 1943 as follows: "Hitler repeatedly explained that if the bombings went on, not only would the cities be destroyed, but the morale of the people would crack irreparably."[66] To maintain a feel for the pulse of the nation's morale, German authorities fielded an extensive intelligence service, and the Official Morale Reports this service provided demonstrate that "in official German eyes the air war was of crucial importance in the struggle for popular support of the Nazi regime . . . These accounts consistently assert that air attacks were undermining morale and producing defeatism."[67]

Propaganda, a keystone of the Third Reich, was used as a means of stimulating morale and it permeated everything in German day-to-day life. However, "bombing had much to do with the final discrediting of propaganda, because it brought home to millions of Germans the tangible proof of Allied air power—indisputable proof completely at odds with the familiar Nazi propaganda." Surveys done after the war indicate that only 21 percent of the Reich's citizens regarded German information provided during the war as reliable, while 54 percent regarded it as being "completely unreliable."[68]

It is perhaps appropriate that Germany's pre-eminent conjuror of public opinion, Joseph Goebbels, should have the final word on the impact of the bombing on German morale. These brief excerpts from his "twelfth-hour" personal diaries belie the public vitriolic pronouncements on the bombing woven throughout the war by the German Propaganda Ministry:

12 March 1945

The air terror which wages uninterruptedly over German home territories make people thoroughly despondent. One feels so impotent against it that no-one can now see a way out of the dilemma. The total paralysis of transport in West Germany also contributes to the mood of increasing pessimism among the German people.

15 March 1945

Not only our military reverses but also the severe drop in the German people's morale, neither of which can now be overlooked, are primarily due to the unrestricted enemy air superiority.

31 March 1945

The political attitude of the people west of the Rhine was very bad. They had been demoralized by the continuous enemy air raids and are now throwing themselves into the arms of the Anglo-Americans, in some cases enthusiastically, in others at least without genuine resistance.[69]

This lack of resistance in the German urban areas at the end of hostilities undoubtedly hastened the German surrender, and, based on previous experiences, saved many late-war casualties on both sides by avoiding difficult and bitter house-to-house fighting.

> A real importance of the air war consisted in the fact that it opened a Second Front long before the invasion of Europe. That front was the skies over Germany. The unpredictability of the attacks made the front gigantic. Every square metre of territory we controlled was a kind of front line and because the attacks were both by day and night, it required a 24 hour state of continuous readiness.[70]

In recent years, a number of eminent German historians and political scientists have reversed a widespread and popular German stance that the area bombing was ineffective. Doctor Horst Borg, who was until relatively recently Chief Historian of the German Office of Military History, spoke at a Symposium on the Strategic Bomber Offensive, held at the RAF Staff College at Bracknell in the United Kingdom in March 1993, and undertook to dispel two persistent myths concerning area bombing and German civilian morale:

> He said: "Let me give you some recent views about the . . . bombing. The judgement that the British area attacks were ineffective can no longer be supported. For a proper assessment we have to look at indirect effects. Had there been no bomber offensive things in Russia might have developed differently." He also notes that over a million men were now on the AA guns. They would have served their country's war effort better in Russia, or in factories. Doctor Borg also dispels the myth of continued high morale under bombing. He defines morale as, "The will to continue to work for the war effort." But he makes the point that the people were prisoners of the Nazi regime. "Their political surveillance system meant doing what one was told and not shirking in the presence of others . . . morale was certainly weakened, as recent studies have revealed, and especially in cities suffering heavy attacks."[71]

German historian Götz Bergander has drawn a significant distinction between private morale and *war* morale in the Third Reich. Bergander maintains the former was never broken, because this constituted the will to live, "based on personal, family and vocational aspirations and generating inventiveness, stubbornness and the desire to assert oneself. The latter, reflected in people's ability to think about future prospects, was on the other hand severely damaged—much more than first thought."[72]

In reality, the air raids on cities and industry shook the foundations of the war morale of the German people. They permanently shattered their nerves, undermined their health and shook their belief in victory, thus altering their consciousness. They spread fear, dismay and hopelessness. This was an important and intentional result of the strategic air war, of this warfare revolution.[73]

Forced Diversions of Enemy Economic Effort

Very little credit has been given for the copious amounts of personnel and equipment that remained tied down in Germany in defence of the industrial cities, nor to those personnel required to repair the damage done by the bombing. Speer acknowledges that many new and promising battlefield technological improvements had to be shelved in order to produce additional anti-aircraft weaponry, and that half of the electronics industry was engaged in producing radar and communications equipment for the defence of the Reich. A third of the precision optics industry was required to produce gun sights for the flak batteries, which frequently left German field forces critically short of their own optical needs.[74] *Reichsmarschall* Hermann Göring positioned nearly nine thousand of the formidable and versatile 88 mm flak guns within the Fatherland, guns and operators which could have doubled the German defences against Soviet tanks on the *Ostfront*. By 1944, there were 14,489 heavy flak guns deployed in the west, while a further 41,937 light guns were similarly deployed to augment the heavier weapons.[75] Anti-aircraft shells consumed one-fifth of all ammunition produced. *Feldmarschall* Erhard Milch, the Quartermaster-General of the *Luftwaffe*, said that within the Reich, nearly 900,000 men, along with some women and children, were employed in the anti-aircraft forces alone by 1944.[76] In aircraft operations, from September 1942 until January 1943, the *Luftwaffe* was tasked to keep the beleaguered German garrison at Stalingrad supplied and to provide combat air support against a tightening Soviet noose. However, the need to honour the bomber offensive in the West, along with other *Luftwaffe* commitments and the renaissance of the Soviet Air Forces made this an impossible task. The resultant loss of the entire German 6th Army in February 1943 was therefore at least partially attributable to Bomber Command's efforts to that point of the war. By January 1944, 68 percent of the day and night fighter forces were dedicated to facing the Anglo-American bomber threat, leaving only 17 percent of these forces for the Eastern Front after other needs were accommodated. By October 1944, the percentage of fighter aircraft retained in the Reich would balloon to 81 percent.[77]

These formidable apportionments slowly but inexorably starved the German field armies of essential air support. By 1944, German bomber aircraft accounted for only one-fifth of all aircraft production, because of the overriding need for fighters at that stage of the war.[78] Thus, without the Allied bombing, German forces at the fighting fronts would have had much greater aerial support and protection, and Allied forces on all fronts would have been much more exposed to German aerial bombardment.

A significant number of unpredictable diversions of effort were produced by the bombing, although German war policy itself is as much to blame for the ultimate success of the bomber offensive. When *Generaloberst* Wever, the *Luftwaffe's* first Chief of Staff, died in 1936, Germany lost its most fervent advocate of the need for its own long-range strategic bomber fleet. Instead, the country geared its bomber production to medium and short-range types to be used in conjunction with land forces employing dynamic, short-term *Blitzkrieg* tactics. A truly strategic, independent bombing force would have made all the industrial targets within the United Kingdom accessible by air, as well as the vulnerable Soviet power stations and industrial complexes, the majority of which had been relocated to the east of the Ural Mountains by 1943. It would also have posed a significant long-range threat to Allied shipping convoys in the North Atlantic. However, lack of extended planning, underestimation of enemy capabilities, and conflicting war priorities brought about by different needs for different war theatres all played a part in delaying the development and production of a viable long-range strategic bomber until Allied bombing had forced fighter priorities on German aircraft production. Bureaucratic ineptitude, high-level bickering, sycophantic pandering to the frequently contradictory, meddlesome, unrealistic, and inappropriate war guidance of Adolf Hitler himself, as well as an extreme shortage of strategic materials, stymied this direction of effort.

From 1944 onwards, Germany was devoting the bulk of its aircraft production to day and night fighters, largely of obsolete models and technologies, for the defence of the Reich. The strategic and administrative decisions that were made in 1940 and 1941, and even earlier, with respect to bomber fleets and air tactics effectively sealed Germany's fate and guaranteed a permanent air inferiority for the rest of the Second World War. German air strategy, rather than being proactive and unpredictable, became reactive and almost totally predictable, in no small measure because of the Allied bombing.[79]

Approximately 70,000[80] aircrew members of the *Luftwaffe* were either killed or reported missing during the Second World War, and while they destroyed roughly 70,000 enemy aircraft on all fronts, they lost between 62,500 and 100,000 of their own machines in the process.[81] Many of the losses were fighter aircraft and fighter pilots, waging a hopeless battle of attrition, the majority of them in defence of the homeland. From the British camp, of the 8655 Bomber Command aircraft that went down over the Reich, Italy and Occupied Europe, approximately 6000 were attributable to air-to-air combat during the bombing offensive.[82] Nearly 1800[83] *Luftwaffe* night fighter aircrew, a very small portion of the larger *Luftwaffe* fatal casualty total, lost their lives during these predominately nocturnal engagements.[84]

Provocation of an Axis Response

One of the most significant effects of the bombing was that it goaded Hitler into striking back in a wasteful and inefficient retaliation campaign, embodied in the V-weapons program. This massive industrial diversion consumed the equivalent of 24,000 more fighter aircraft for the *Luftwaffe*, and neither weapon proved decisive. Also, the program squandered the nation's technical capacities, for it meant that much more promising technologies, such as the Me 262 jet fighter, the Type XXI and Type XXIII U-boats, new acoustic torpedoes and the surface-to-air *Wasserfall* missile had to be given much less priority in terms of both intellectual and material commitment.[85] In the words of Albert Speer, from the end of July 1943 onward, "our tremendous industrial capacity was diverted to the huge missile known as the V 2 . . . the whole notion was absurd."[86] Furthermore, the 1944 campaign against the V 1 launch sites, coupled with the earlier and costly Bomber Command raids on the rocket development centre at Peenemünde on 17/18 August 1943, and in October on the V 1 manufacturing site at Kassel, effectively blunted the limited impact of these weapons. Had they been available in quantity on D-Day, the effects of the bombs raining down on the embarkation ports and the massed invasion fleet could have been catastrophic for the Allies. The Me 262 could potentially have been a war-winner for the Germans. However, it was slightly delayed in its service debut by Hitler's insistence that it be produced as one of the retaliation weapons, namely as a *Blitz* bomber, before it was belatedly approved for production as a fighter during the winter of 1944. More serious was the delay, necessitated by the pursuit of other priorities at least partially generated by the bombings, in addressing the technological shortcomings of the jet's powerplants. Had the aircraft been mass produced as a fighter even six months earlier, its impact on Allied bomber formations could have been cataclysmic. In short, the bombing campaign generated unforeseen technological responses conducted at breakneck pace, and helped encourage the German executive branch towards desperate solutions forged by passionate aims of retribution, versus cold, methodical, and logical actions.

Some Sinister Threats Contained

Had Germany not been so diverted by the bombings and been free to mobilize its manpower and technological resources in a total war environment, chemical, biological and even atomic weapons might well have been in store for the Allies. And based on the Nazi track record, although the use of these weapons was certainly somewhat moderated by fear of reprisals in kind, there is considerable evidence to suggest that the German authorities had no scruples about employing them in acts of desperation, had they been widely available and deliverable. The Germans were not particularly focused on atomic weapons after the autumn of 1942, although their development remained a continuous worry for the Allies. As to whether Hitler would have had any moral reluctance to use them, Albert Speer's words are interesting: "I am sure that Hitler would not have hesitated for a moment to employ atom bombs against England."[87] And how, in Speer's opinion, did the bombing affect the pursuit of a focused German atomic program? "The increasing air raids had long since created an armaments emergency in Germany which ruled out any such ambitious enterprise. At best, with extreme concentration of all our resources, we could have had a German bomb by 1947."[88] Specifically, the wholesale evacuation of much of the Kaiser Wilhelm Institute for Physics research facility's infrastructure from the Dahlem suburb of Berlin to Haigerloch in the Black Forest, in response to intimidation generated by the Berlin air raids, undoubtedly forced considerable delays and confusion on the German atomic program and disrupted its focus.[89]

Furthermore, the curtailment of the V 2 program in the spring of 1945 was perhaps a more fortuitous event than is broadly realized for the Allies. Specifications were already under development for an advanced version of the rocket known as the A 10, which used the V 2 as a second stage booster, and it would have had a trans-Atlantic reach. Had Germany been able to put together an atomic weapon program to meld with this delivery capability, the results could have been cataclysmic. However, the bombings, the persecution of significant Jewish scientific talent, the widespread multiplicity of duplicating research programs, all of which were competing for Hitler's favour instead of working together, collectively conspired to stagnate German atomic weapons development. The Germans had failed to separate U 235, the essential fissile element, on a large scale by August 1944, even though they had by then succeeded in manufacturing uranium oxide, a core material for atomic weapons. Still, in the view of the Alsos Team of Allied atomic specialists that thoroughly ransacked Germany, both before and after VE Day, the Germans were years away from producing an atomic weapon at the same time the Allies were nearing successful completion of their own.[90]

With respect to biological warfare, recent research has determined that Germany was ready to deploy a foot-and-mouth virus against Britain during the final months of the war. Successful tests were conducted over Russian terrain against reindeer in 1943, but there was no guarantee that lagging German bomber and delivery system capabilities, hampered by the concentration on fighter development necessitated by the bombing, were able to accurately dispense the material.[91] The dispersal of chemical agents faced similar constraints. The deadliest nerve gas of the day, Tabun, was manufactured in quantity at Dyhernfurth on the Oder River late in the war. Considered ten times more lethal than Phosgene, which was, until then, rated the most lethal war gas, 15,000 tons of Tabun were produced before the Soviets overran the production facility in 1945. However, all the finished products had been fitted into different host munitions and removed from the production facility prior to Soviet occupation. At war's end, nearly a half-million artillery shells and more than 100,000 aircraft bombs filled with Tabun were found in German arsenals, but they became available too late to orchestrate a delivery campaign, and they were subsequently destroyed by the western Allies. Other German nerve gas agents were called Sarin and Soman. Sarin, far more lethal than Tabun, proved to be exceptionally difficult to manufacture. Competing priorities and technological problems associated with its delivery delayed the emergence of Sarin, although over 7000 tons of it had been stockpiled by the end of the war. However, had the time, the will, and the wherewithal remained to effectively field it, the Sarin stockpile would have been enough to kill all the occupants of at least thirty cities the size of Paris. Soman, an even more potent agent, was never developed beyond the laboratory.[92]

The Mining Campaign Pays Huge Dividends

Other Bomber Command "diversions"contributed significantly to the war effort. The mining campaign effectively denied the use of the western Baltic to the Germans for transit and training and curtailed trade in the region. Late in the war, the influence of *Grossadmiral* Karl Dönitz on Hitler was significant, particularly after Hermann Göring had fallen into disfavour. Bomber Command had been very successful in mining the shallow waters of the western Baltic, which then made retention of the eastern Baltic of paramount importance to the *Kriegsmarine*. However, the eastern Baltic was more difficult for bombers to reach and the deeper waters made mines less effective. In order to retain sea control of the region, Dönitz maintained that the Germans needed to hold the Courland Pocket in western Latvia, and also the Gulf of Danzig, Memel, and East Prussia. Hitler agreed completely with Dönitz's assessment and concurred that loss of the region would paralyze the *Kriegsmarine*, particularly its U-boat operations. In a late-war conference, however, *Generaloberst* Heinz Guderian proposed that the forces in Courland, Memel, and East Prussia be evacuated in order to provide troops to counter the impending Red Army spring offensive. Nonetheless, based on the influence of Dönitz, Hitler vetoed Guderian's proposal, and this effectively tied down forty German divisions, or a third of the forces available to fight the approaching Red Army. Furthermore, these tied-down forces contributed virtually nothing to the final defence of the German homeland, and protection of U-boat operations in the eastern Baltic was also by then a moot point. In the words of the Australian journalist and historian, Chester Wilmot:

> The history of the Second World War affords no more striking example of the interplay of naval, air and land power, or of the interrelation of the Eastern and Western Front or, for that matter, of the grotesque miscalculations and wild hopes that governed Hitler's strategy. Because the German Air Force was unable to protect the U-Boat bases and training waters in the western Baltic, the German Army was obliged to hold the eastern Baltic against the

Russians so that the German Navy might build up a new U-Boat fleet capable of inflicting a severe defeat on the Western Allies, and especially on the hated British, whose refusal to capitulate in 1940 had made inevitable that war on two fronts, which had already destroyed most of Hitler's empire and was in the process of destroying the Third Reich.[93]

No Respite for the U-boats

To demonstrate the direct effects of the bombing war against the *Kriegsmarine*, Harris pointed out that Bomber Command destroyed six German capital ships by either bombing or mining, in comparison to only four sunk during the entire war by the Royal Navy. Furthermore, Bomber Command's Official History recorded that the Command, working in conjunction with the American heavy bomber fleet, destroyed at least 207 German submarines during construction or in port after completion.[94] At the end of 1943, Dönitz held forth the promise of a reincarnated, invincible *Kriegsmarine*, spearheaded by a fleet of formidable new U-boats. These submarines, which incorporated many technological improvements to enhance survivability and combat effectiveness, were scheduled for initial delivery in the autumn of 1944. Ultra-high-speed radio transmitters, more sophisticated acoustic torpedoes, rubber coated hulls to complicate radar detection, as well as *schnorkel* underwater breathing devices and significant augmentation of the onboard batteries to allow the boats to remain submerged for protracted periods of time, were just some of the improvements incorporated into these formidable new weapons. However, other industrial diversions, brought on in no small measure by the bombings, had delayed production of the new boats. "First Brest, then Lorient saw the start of a long series of bombing raids which also greatly affected the civilian population, and the Germans soon realized the need to build shelters for personnel and equipment. To effectively protect the submarines themselves, it was necessary to produce solid bunkers . . . The accelerated construction of the U-boat pens at Hamburg was a direct result of the bombing of the sheltered U-boat bases in France."[95]

Partially as a result of this enormous diversion of economic effort, production of the new variants was not given a high priority until the spring of 1943, by which time the Battle of the Atlantic was effectively lost. The blue-water Type XXI and its much smaller coastal-operating cousin, the Type XXIII, could perhaps have made a difference had they been floated two years earlier. They were capable of formidable underwater ranges, and their performance characteristics were outstanding. They promised much better prospects for attacking Allied shipping and evading the escorts than did the conventional U-boats. Both required only a minimal daily time at *schnorkel* depth to keep their batteries charged, thus making detection extremely difficult. But the spectre of bombing vulnerability had perpetuated a decision in the summer of 1943 to build these submarines in inland factories in modules,[96] then transport them to coastal facilities for rapid final assembly. However, improper fitment between the modules created production delays, and transportation of the modules to the final assembly points was also affected by the bombing.

> The failure to achieve the objectives was mainly caused by organization troubles, faulty design and bad workmanship. It was particularly annoying when sections did not fit to each other because the specified tolerances were exceeded. All these took place mainly in the first half of 1944 and it was fixed in the second half of the year. At that time, however, the Allies realized the danger and started regular bombing raids, particularly on shipyards and water transport installations needed for transportation of massive Type XXI sections.[97]

Direct bombing delayed construction even further, such that only two Type XXIs and six Type XXIIIs were fully ready for combat by 1 May 1945, the date when 381 Type XXIs and 95 Type XXIIIs had been planned for delivery.[98] On top of the construction delays, the constant mining of the Baltic from the air inhibited the extensive training required on the new boats, delaying still further their introduction to service. Albert Speer elaborates on the effects of the bombing: "We would have been able to keep our promise of delivering forty boats a month by early in 1945, however badly the war was going otherwise, if air raids had not destroyed a third of the submarines at the dockyards."[99] For all the aforementioned reasons, hardly any of the new boats were operational at war's end, although their success in a few engagements trumpeted great promise. It was once again a case of "too little, too late."[100]

Paving the Way for Operation Overlord

The strategic bombing campaign made possible a direct invasion of northwest Europe in the summer of 1944. The lodgement in Normandy was a direct result of the generalized destruction of the German industrial and economic war machine, particularly the German Air Force, prior to the actual invasion. The secondment of Bomber Command and the Eighth Air Force from April until September 1944 to Supreme Headquarters Allied Expeditionary Forces under General Eisenhower resulted in a significant depletion, destruction and disorganization of the *Luftwaffe*, as well as the enemy's rail communications, prior to the invasion. In its immediate wake, these formations provided overwhelming direct tactical support for the land campaign. Bomber Command was particularly zealous in its pursuit of rail targets, attacking over one hundred of them prior to D-Day. Since much greater accuracy was possible in 1944, by June, most of the thirty-seven rail centres assigned to Bomber Command were either destroyed or heavily damaged. These efforts, coupled with the destruction of the Seine River bridges the week prior to the invasion, made effective German reinforcement virtually impossible. Air superiority then secured the flanks of the lodgement area after the landings, and concomitant attacks on oil production facilities further significantly handicapped both the German Army and Air Force.

Along with attacking other major military targets in France, Bomber Command dropped some 14,000 tons of high explosives on the Atlantic Wall fortifications during the prelude to the landings, including 5000 tons of explosives on the defending beaches themselves.[101] After the ground forces were ashore, the Command continued its attacks on rail and military targets, including successful efforts against the ports of Le Havre, Boulogne, Brest, Calais, St-Malo, and Cap Gris Nez. Most of France had been cleared of the enemy when Eisenhower handed control of Bomber Command back to the RAF on 16 September 1944. However, the Command continued to support the land armies in a tactical sense whenever called on to do so, including during the late-war push into Germany. The words of Joseph Goebbels bear testimony: " the enemy is afraid of severe casualties but, as soon as he meets resistance, he calls in his air force which then simply turns the area of resistance into a desert."[102]

The German Civilian Tragedy in Perspective

Collateral civilian casualties within the Greater German Reich are estimated by various sources to be approximately 410,000 civilian fatalities attributable to Allied bombing. However, to this number one must add 23,000 non-military police and civilians attached to the German armed forces, 32,000 foreigners and prisoners of war, and 128,000 displaced persons, which brings the total to approximately 593,000 persons. A further 60,000 Italians need to be added to this total within the context of the European Axis states. An additional 486,000 people were wounded or injured by the bombing within the Greater German Reich alone. While these are large numbers, they pale next to the genocide perpetrated on the peoples of Europe and Eurasia by the Germans and their allies. In the bombing war, in comparison, Great Britain lost roughly 65,000 civilians to aerial attack, approximately 43,000 of which occurred during the Blitz of 1940–41.[103] Total wartime losses in the German armed forces were approximately 3.8 million killed.[104] In pursuit of the stated Allied war aim of de-housing the civilian work force, 3,370,000 dwellings in the Reich were destroyed by the bombings, and 7,500,000 persons were made homeless.

The civilian loss of life from the bombing has, in Richard Overy's words, "occasioned the most bitter recriminations of all against the bombing strategy. It is something that Bomber Command survivors take seriously and have thought about deeply." Overy argues that the British Executive no longer felt obliged to act in restraint after the German bombing of Warsaw and Rotterdam during the war's opening stanzas, and that the tens of thousands of British deaths during the Blitz and the Baedeker Raids on British cities other than London "made redundant any further discussion about the rights and wrongs of bombing targets with the risk of civilian casualty."[105] Those who see fit to challenge the morality of the area bombing in particular should bear in mind that a far greater travesty would have been to allow the moral obscenity that was the Third Reich to prevail unchecked by whatever means were deemed necessary at the time.

Bombing conducted for the purpose of lowering enemy morale was not practiced exclusively by Bomber Command. We have covered the American attitudes and policies on area bombing, as practiced generally in Operation Thunderclap and Operation Clarion, and particularly at Dresden and Berlin. Major-General Frederick L. Anderson Jr. was the commanding general of the American Eighth Bomber Command for most of the Combined portion of the European air war. General Anderson noted that while the isolated, late war American bombing of mainly smaller urban centres was not expected in itself to shorten the war, "it is expected that the fact that Germany was struck all over will be passed on, from father to son, thence to grandson, (and) that a deterrent for the initiation of future wars will definitely result."[106] As the late-war evidence of Nazi atrocities mounted, best exemplified by the overrunning of the death camps and the institutionalized murder committed therein, there developed a significant Allied emotional hardening reflected in the partial tactical use of strategic bombers during the push through Germany in the closing weeks of the war. If a German urban area resisted and generated Anglo-American casualties, it was normally shelled and bombed into rubble. However, those centres that acquiesced peacefully were normally spared further destruction. For the most part, similar courtesies were not extended during the Soviet advance, and German citizens were quite aware of the distinction.[107] These actions reinforced the point that no citizen of the Third Reich was immune or exempt from the bombing, and that further armed resistance was futile. This deliberate demoralization of the enemy undoubtedly helped shatter the German will to resist, hastening the capitulation of German forces in the western urban centres, and thereby saving many lives, both Allied and Axis. In short, those running the war in the Allied camp believed that Nazism was an evil force let loose on the world, and it needed to be eradicated as quickly as possible and by whatever means necessary. The circumstances which prevailed during the war determined the bombing policy which was to follow, and this writer feels it is only appropriate to judge it in that context, rather than through the application of latter-day social and political values.

Allied Public Support for the Bombing

Public opinion surveys from the war confirm widespread Allied support for the bombing.[108] Neither politicians nor historians of the period challenged the policy at the time, and while British authorities staunchly maintained that civilian casualties were nothing but "an unfortunate by-product of attacks on industrial areas, there is little reason to believe that the general public would have complained had it been otherwise."[109] Further, there was very little questioning of the morality of the bombing during the war, and what little that did occur came primarily from isolated British religious leaders. In the spring of 1941, the Bishop of Chichester, George Bell, and Doctor Cosmo Lang, the Archbishop of Canterbury, both felt that the still-embryonic policy of bombing non-combatants should not be allowed to prevail. However, most British clerics supported the bomber offensive through its various stages of development. Dr. Cyril Garbett, the Archbishop of York believed that "often in life there is no clear choice between absolute right and wrong; frequently the choice has to be made of the lesser of two evils . . . and it is a lesser evil to bomb a war-loving Germany than to sacrifice the lives of thousands of our own fellow-countrymen . . . and to delay delivering millions now held in slavery."[110] Garbett then went on to argue compellingly in favour of Allied use of air power to bring the conflict to a swift, successful conclusion. These views were published in *The Times* on 25 June 1943, and they had the unequivocal approval of Lambeth Palace, home of the Archbishop of Canterbury.[111] Indeed, William Temple, who succeeded Cosmo Lang as the Archbishop of Canterbury, echoed Garbett's stance in favour of the bomber offensive, as Lang had also eventually done. Temple, reluctantly and yet with total conviction, concurred that the bombing was a necessary evil in a world far from perfect. In December 1942, he wrote opponents of the area bombing policy in part: "The worst of all things is to fight and do it ineffectively. Therefore, while I agree with you strategic consideration cannot stand alone, [the bombing] becomes very nearly decisive for our conduct."[112] Martin Middlebrook also offers the following opinion: "A country fighting for its very existence cannot afford to have strict boundaries of morality in the means by which it saves itself. It is sheer humbug to suggest that the use of bombers at this time was wrong when it was touch and go whether Britain survived at all."[113]

The Legality Issue

Even the German camp has long acknowledged that, moral issues aside, the area bombing policy as it was conducted during the Second World War was perfectly legal. During the war, Eberhard Spetzler was a legal staff officer in the *Luftwaffe*. Post-war, when he was a professor of law at the University of Göttingen, he opined that:

> Since there are separate rules for land and sea warfare and none was ever signed for aerial warfare, the Rules for Land Warfare cannot be applied to strategic bombing. Article 25 clearly states that it is meant to protect civilians during the physical conquest of their land. Bombers do not occupy enemy territory, they only destroy it. For a city to be protected by Article 25, it must not have any defenses. Fighters attacking bombers over their target must be considered [to be] defending the city.[114]

The area bombing of enemy cities has only been illegal since August 1948, when the Red Cross

It took a lot of personnel to make up a Second World War heavy bomber squadron. This is a late-war shot of 415 "Swordfish" Squadron. (Halifax Restoration Team, Trenton)

Not to be outdone, a Canadian Lancaster squadron strikes a similar pose. (DND PL42860)

Some of the inevitable casualties of war. At least these Canadian airmen, unlike so many of their colleagues, have identifiable graves. (DND PMR 93-293)

Others would suffer grievous wounds. Here, members of the RCAF Women's Division, Leading Airwoman C. Lavalee and Corporal Eileen Hassett, visit recovering "guinea pigs" in the plastic surgery facility at East Grinstead in January 1944. (DND PL26206)

Sow the wind and reap the whirlwind. Two views of the ruined city of Cologne, 1945. (DND PL42542, with ruined bridge, and DND PL42536)

Above: All too often, a violent momentary explosion in the sky was all that marked the passing of an entire bomber crew. A Lancaster blows up over Wesel on 19 February 1945 in a sky streaked with target markers. (DND PL144292)

Left: Sign in rubble-strewn streets of Mainz, Germany, close to the war's end. (Author's Collection)

The sign reads:

GEBT MIR FÜNF JAHRE
UND IHR WERDET
DEUTSCHLAND NICHT
WIEDER ERKENNEN
ADOLF HITLER

GIVE ME FIVE YEARS &
YOU WILL NOT
RECOGNIZE GERMANY
AGAIN

Convention on the Protection of Civilians in Wartime was signed in Stockholm.[115]

The widespread damage resulting from the fire raids on Rostock and Lübeck in March and April of 1942 was candidly and appreciatively reported to the British public at the time, and in far-away Ottawa, similar sentiments were recorded by none other than Prime Minister Mackenzie King. He noted in his diary that the Germans were the ones who had first embarked on an indiscriminate bombing policy.[116] While B.K. Sandwell, the liberalist editor of *Saturday Night* worried about the moral toll it would take on the crews themselves, in the end, he had to side with the policy:

> The defeat of Germany can only be brought about by killing Germans, and if the object of these raids is to kill Germans . . . it is a perfectly proper object. The blood of such innocent persons as these is not on us . . . The whole German people brought on themselves whatever calamities may issue for them out of this war, when they put themselves under the kind of government which was bound to make such a war ultimately inevitable. It is our unavoidable task to make Germany suffer.[117]

Other national papers echoed Sandwell's opinions:

> In its editorial of 31 May 1943, the *Toronto Telegram* declared that, while bombing undoubtedly meant "misery and death for the people of the Axis nations . . . it is better that they should be blotted out entirely than that the world should be subjected to the rulers they have tolerated so long, and there are many who hold that they must be made to know in full the horrors of war, if a new war is to be avoided." The *Winnipeg Free Press*, meanwhile, had already belittled the few who demanded limitations on bombing because they were asking "air crews still more to endanger their own lives so that they may perhaps save the lives of workers in industrial war facilities or living in the immediate neighbourhood of those targets."[118]

From a participant's standpoint, CAN/RAF pilot Kenneth McDonald recalls the manner in which he and his crew were received by factory workers on a motivational visit following his operational tour in 1943:

> I can testify to the hatred war breeds. When we finished our tour of operations in 1943, we were sent as a crew on a morale raising round of factories in London that were making Halifaxes. My job was to describe a typical op and to introduce the crew members. Each time I came to Tim McCoy, the rear gunner, and told the assembled workers that he could see the fires from fifty miles away on the trip home they burst into cheers. Those men and women had lived through the London Blitz, had lost homes and relatives, were still at risk from German bombs, and felt I'm sure that here in front of them was living proof not only that their work was worthwhile but that there was hope for an end to the war and their privations. They too had lived through the thirties when Hitler and his brownshirts took power, had witnessed on film and in newspapers the transformation of a country not unlike their own into an armed camp that threatened its neighbours while bullying or murdering any of its own citizens who dared to protest or who were judged to be racially or otherwise unpure.[119]

Area Bombing and the Japanese War

Not the least of the wartime contributions of the Allied bombing campaign in Europe was that its success inspired a similar late-war campaign against the industrial cities of the Japanese home islands. The strategic area bombing of Japan, conducted by the American 20th Air Force in 1944 and 1945, destroyed an area thirty times greater in size than did the two atomic weapon releases at Hiroshima and Nagasaki in August 1945. Ironically, when high-level daylight bombing with high explosives proved ineffective and costly early in the campaign, the Americans borrowed a page from Bomber Command by conducting a series of night raids at relatively low level using incendiaries. The success of this area bombing was a result of the unfettered use of those incendiary weapons against highly flammable targets that deliberately created firestorms. In reality the loss of 250,000 Japanese lives, the wounding or injuring of a further 500,000 and the destruction of 40 percent of the buildings in 66 industrialized cities had brought Japan to the brink of surrender prior to the atomic bomb drops on the 6th and 9th of August.[120] And yet, based on the fierce determination to resist an Allied invasion of the home islands, exemplified by the sacrifice of 2530 Japanese Navy aircrew members[121] and at least as many Army aircrew[122] on *Kamikaze* missions directed against Allied shipping (the last of which took place on the day of the cessation of hostilities, 15 August 1945), the Allied Executive was greatly concerned about the blood cost to *both* sides should an invasion of the Japanese home islands prove necessary. Winston Churchill elaborates:

> We had contemplated the desperate resistance of the Japanese fighting to the death with Samurai devotion, not only in pitched battles, but in every cave and dugout. I had in my mind the spectacle of Okinawa Island, where many thousands of Japanese, rather than surrender, had drawn up in line and destroyed themselves by hand grenades after their leaders had solemnly performed the rite of hara-kiri. To quell the Japanese resistance man by man and to conquer the country yard by yard might well require the loss of a million American lives and half that number of British—or more if we could get them there: for we were resolved to share the agony.[123]

Indeed, the Japanese War Cabinet, the military clique under the control of the Prime Minister, General Hideki Tojo, was determined to commit the Japanese people to mass suicide, calling "for the sacrifice of up to 100,000,000 Japanese lives, if necessary, to repel the Allied invasion of the home islands."[124] The area bombing of Japan had certainly dealt a debilitating blow to the Japanese war industries, and the remaining factories were on the verge of collapsing for want of component parts and damage to infrastructure. And yet, in July 1945, the Japanese aviation industry was still capable of producing over 1000 military aircraft per month, and many hundreds of warplanes were still available for home defence.[125] There was also no shortage of suicidally-inspired pilots available and willing to substitute courage for technological inadequacy and dive the aircraft into a massed Allied invasion force. Furthermore, "orders went out that every Japanese man between the ages of 15 and 60 and all women aged 17 to 40 would meet the invaders at beaches with sharpened bamboo poles. Allied peace feelers were rejected."[126]

Although it was a painful decision for the Allies, the two atomic drops, with the concomitant loss of an additional 150,000 Japanese citizens, combined with a rapidly worsening war situation, largely precipitated by the area bombing of the industrial cities, convinced the Japanese that further resistance was pointless. Defending against the massed fleets of formidable, heavily-protected B-29 Superfortresses was difficult enough, but the atomic drops on Hiroshima and Nagasaki convinced them that they were powerless to defend the entire nation from the high and fast-flying, singly-penetrating B-29s that could be bombing anywhere in the nation. This underscoring of the futility of further resistance spared the Japanese people from the obligation of being killed to the last available fighting man and woman. Therefore, strategic bombing undoubtedly ultimately prevented many casualties, both Allied and Japanese, by eliminating the need for an armed invasion of the Japanese mainland, the costs of which, measured by any yardstick, would have been horrific.

It is perhaps appropriate that the area bombing policy's most dedicated champion, Sir Arthur Harris, should have the last word on the moral justification of command policy. In one of his most famous newsreel speeches of the war, he reminded his audience that it was the Nazis who had "sown the wind," and that, in return, they would "reap the whirlwind."[127]

Bomber Command played an essential part as a guarantor of Allied victory during the Second World War. It provided an offensive tool that took the fight to the enemy when none other was available, and it gave the citizens of the Allied nations hope and pride while it did so. It provided Britain and the Commonwealth, through its very prosecution, a political dimension by which it could influence the conduct of the war. Its operations demanded a significant diversion of German resources away from the Eastern Front, thereby aiding the USSR in its part of the combined struggle. The Command struck substantial and unrelenting blows against enemy morale. It threw Germany's broader war strategy into disarray, and generated a loss of German air superiority, along with doing much significant damage to the Reich's war industrial base. Its actions made the way safer for an Allied re-entry into northwest Europe in 1944, and it effectively stymied German economic mobilization and technological development in many areas. While a great human price was paid for these accomplishments on both the combatant sides, in relative terms, the losses incurred to the Anglo-Americans were small when compared to those suffered elsewhere, such as in the USSR. And the overall cost was relatively low as a percentage of the total war effort, considering the gains that were realized. Canada's contribution to this campaign was highly significant, and the nation should be extremely grateful to those warriors of the night who held firm and proud from the right of the line in European skies so many years ago.

> Although the air war was only a part of an enormous conflict that swept over Europe, it did prove decisive in helping the Allies achieve victory, since it played an indispensable role, without which the Anglo-American lodgement on the continent and the final defeat of the Third Reich was inconceivable.[128]
>
> What bombing (in part) did—both area and precision—was to act as a constant source of attrition for most industrialists, interrupting transport flows, hitting small component factories, attacking gas, electricity and power supplies. Many of these were not critical but the important thing was their cumulative effect.[129]

∽∘∾

BRITISH PHONETIC ALPHABET
PRE-1943

A: Apple	N: Nuts
B: Beer	O: Orange
C: Charlie	P: Peter
D: Dog	Q: Queen
E: Edward	R: Roger/Robert
F: Freddy	S: Suga
G: George	T: Tommy
H: Harry	U: Uncle
I: In	V: Vic
J: Jug/Johnny	W: William
K: King	X: X-ray
L: Love	Y: Yoke/Yorker
M: Mother	Z: Zebra

BRITISH PHONETIC ALPHABET
1943–1945

A: Able	N: Nun
B: Baker	O: Oboe
C: Charlie	P: Peter
D: Dog	Q: Queen
E: Easy	R: Roger
F: Fox	S: Sugar
G: George	T: Tare
H: How	U: Uncle
I: Item	V: Victor
J: Jig	W: William
K: King	X: X-ray
L: Love	Y: Yoke
M: Mike	Z: Zebra

Notes

PROLOGUE

1. John Kenneth Galbraith, "A Life in Our Times: Memoirs, 1981," in Richard Overy, *Bomber Command 1939–1945—Reaping the Whirlwind* (London: HarperCollins, 1997), 184. As a member of the survey team, Galbraith endorsed the views that "Allied air power was decisive in the war in western Europe . . . on land, it helped turn the tide overwhelmingly in favour of the Allied ground forces. Its power and superiority made possible the success of the invasion. It brought the economy which sustained the enemy's armed forces to virtual collapse, although the full effects of this collapse had not reached the enemy's front lines when they were overrun by Allied forces . . . but with the impending collapse of the supporting economy, the indications are convincing that they would have to cease fighting—any effective fighting—within a few months. Germany was mortally wounded." Franklin D'Olier et al, *The US Strategic Bomb Survey—Overall Report—European War—September 30, 1945* (Washington: US Government Printing Office, 1945), 107.
2. British Directorate of Air Staff, Ministry of Defence, British Air Power Doctrine (AP 3000), Third Edition, (Norwich: Her Majesty's Stationery Office, 1999), 2.6.4.
3. Ibid.
4. Richard Overy, *Bomber Command*, 7.
5. Geoff Marlow, recollections of bombing missions over Germany, courtesy of Dick Wynne, letter to author, dated 15 November 2000.
6. Jost Dülffer, Jochen Thies, Josef Henke, *Hitler's Städte. Baupolitik im Dritten Reich*, quoted in Joachim Fest, *Speer—The Final Verdict* (London: Weidenfeld & Nicolson, 2001), 59, fn 31.

CHAPTER ONE

1. The German fixed-wing bombing raids against Britain during this conflict are often collectively referred to as the "Gotha raids." However, the *Gothaer Waggonfabrik AG*, which produced a series of these successful bombers, were not the only manufacturers of these types. Other successful heavy bombing aircraft were produced by the Zeppelin (the *Staaken* series) and Friedrichshafen firms. Nigel Smith & Peter Hart, *Tumult in the Clouds* (London: Hodder and Stoughton, 1997), 262–284.
2. Overy, *Bomber Command*, 13.
3. John Terraine, *The Right of the Line—The Royal Air Force in the European War 1939–1945* (London: Hodder and Stoughton, 1985), 11.
4. Brereton Greenhous, Stephen J. Harris, William C. Johnston, and William G.P. Rawling, *The Crucible of War 1939–1945—The Official History of the Royal Canadian Air Force*, vol 3 (Toronto: University of Toronto Press, 1994), 528.
5. David Ian Hall, "Arguments For and Against the Strategic Bomber Offensive: The Contrasting Views of Wing Commander T.D. (Harry) Weldon and RAF Chaplain L. John Collins," essay presented by Dr. Hall of Linacre College, University of Oxford, for the Bomber Harris Trust Essay Competition, 30 June 1997, 5.
6. Ibid.
7. Richard Holmes, *Battlefields of the Second World War* (London: BBC Worldwide, 2001), 179.
8. Overy, *Bomber Command*, 16.
9. Ibid, 24.
10. Ibid.
11. Ibid.
12. Even then, it would be two and a half years before a new crew specialist, the air bomber, would be established. It was also decided that only one pilot was necessary in medium and heavy bombers. The specialist observer, who both dropped bombs and navigated, would now be reclassified as strictly the navigator. Thus, the bomb-aimer and the navigator eventually became separate crew members. F.J. Hatch, *The Aerodrome of Democracy:*

Canada and the British Commonwealth Air Training Plan 1939–1945 (Ottawa: Ministry of Supply and Services, 1983), 108.

13. Terraine, *Right of the Line*, 83.

14. Overy, *Bomber Command*, 28.

15. Air Ministry, "Instructions Governing Naval and Air Bombardment," August 22, 1939 (PRO AIR 8/283) as quoted in Overy, *Bomber Command*, 30.

16. Brereton Greenhous and Hugh A. Halliday, *Canada's Air Forces 1914–1999* (Montreal: Art Global, 1999), 41.

17. Hugh A. Halliday, "The First of Many—Canadians in the Royal Air Force 1920–1945," paper given to the 6th Annual Air Force Historical Conference, Cornwall, Ontario, 21–23 June 2000, 3.

18. Ibid.

19. Ibid, 1.

20. To this date, Halliday has identified a wartime total of at least 1106 CAN/RAF aircrew, of which at least 698 are known to have enlisted prior to 1 January 1940. Halliday, "First of Many," 13.

CHAPTER TWO

1.   Jack Watts, "The RCAF Years," (video), RCAF Museum, Trenton, Ontario, 1994.

2.   Peter R. March, *Eagles—Eighty Aircraft that Made History with the RAF* (London: Wiedenfeld and Nicolson, 1998), 53.

3.   LGen (ret'd) Reg Lane, audiotape to author, 22 August 2001.

4.   Overy, *Bomber Command*, 36.

5.   Ibid, 50.

6.   Terry Goodwin, letter to editor, *Airforce* 25, 4 (Fall 2001), 47.

7.   Ibid, 48.

8.   Paul Nyznik, "A Canadian Hero in the Royal Air Force," *Airforce* 25, 1 (Spring 2001), 27.

9.   Ibid, 28.

10. The Story of Bomber Command, vol 4, "Strike Hard, Strike Sure" (Video) (Portland: Allegro, 2001).

11. Halliday, "First of Many," 9.

12. Dave Birrell, "Sergeant Pilot Albert Stanley Price: The First of the 10,000," *Airforce*, 23, 2 (Summer 1999), 53.

13. Henderson was awarded a Distinguished Flying Cross (DFC) early the following year for courage and determination under fire in helping press home attacks during the war's opening innings, but he was killed in action in July 1940.

14. Birrell, "Albert Stanley Price," 54.

15. Ibid.

16. At this point in the war and for some time to come, the Whitleys and the Wellingtons were still crewed with two pilots. Such was not the case with the Blenheims and the Hampdens, each with one pilot only. By early 1942, the second pilot as a regular crew member was considered an unnecessary luxury in all Bomber Command aircraft.

17. Halliday, "First of Many," 10.

18. Arthur Bishop, *Courage in the Air-Canada's Military Heritage* vol 1 (Toronto-Montreal: McGraw-Hill Ryerson, 1992), 129.

19. Greenhous et al, *Crucible of War*, 532.

20. Ibid, 533.

21. Ibid.

22. Ibid.

23. Ibid, 534.

24. Norman Shannon, "The Cattle Boat Brigade," *Airforce*, 20, 3 (Oct 1996), 10.

25. Ibid.

26. Greenhous et al, *Crucible of War*, 535.

27. Ibid.

28. Portal to Newall, ibid, 536.

29. "Warriors of the Night," pt 1 (video) a direct translation from the German), (Discovery Channel, 1999).

30. In August 1940, Kammhuber was appointed General der Nachtjagd, the head of the all-night fighter expanded XII Fliegerkorps. Greenhous et al, *Crucible of War*, 543.

31. "Warriors of the Night."

32. Greenhous et al, *Crucible of War*, 544.

33. Ibid.

34. Ibid.

35. Ibid.

36. Shannon, "Cattle Boat Brigade," 11.

37. As quoted in Greenhous et al, *Crucible of War*, 537.

38. DCAS to Bomber Command, 4 June 1940, PRO Air 9/131; quoted in Greenhous et al, *Crucible of War*, 538.

39. Intelligence Report from Grand to Lindemann, 19 July 1940, forwarded to PM under Lindemann's hand, in Public Records Office Premier 3/11/1, 25. Although this report, forwarded from Churchill's chief scientific advisor in the Cabinet appears rational and logical, not all initiatives from Lindemann (Lord Cherwell) were so. Frederick Lindemann was a scientist and academic who, as Lord Cherwell, was a true eminence grise as Winston Churchill's great friend, confidant, and senior scientific advisor to the Cabinet. However, his influence extended in great measure beyond his expertise, and he was not a military man. "Cherwell also used his position to promote particular strategies and tactics, even if it meant distorting the scientific evidence." David Zimmerman, *Britain's Shield—Radar and the Defeat of the Luftwaffe* (Stroud, United Kingdom: Sutton, 2001), 231. Not only did such incursions into military purviews place Cherwell at loggerheads with many senior uniformed members, his distortion of scientific and technological capabilities to suit his policy initiatives earned him the contempt of his scientific colleagues. However, his influence on Churchill was profound, and the Prime Minister would most often side with Cherwell on issues, whether they had merit or not. Ibid, 232.

40. Special Distribution and War Cabinet from Switzerland, Memo No. 529, 28 July 1940, in Public Record Office (PRO) Premier 3/11/1, 35.

41. Sir Charles Webster and Noble Frankland, *The Strategic Air Offensive Against Germany* vol 1 (London: Her Majesty's Stationary Office, 1961), 147.

42. Greenhous et al, *Crucible of War*, 538.

43. Webster and Frankland, *Strategic Air Offensive* vol 1, 233.

44. AHB (Air Historical Branch)/II/117/1(B), 122.

45. Floyd Williston, "Death of a Hero," in *The Halifax Herald*, Sunday, Sep 9 2001, [online] <http://www.Herald.ns.ca/stories/2001/09/09/f197.raw.>

46. Bishop, *Courage in the Air*, 129.

47. In January 1941 Fleming became the first Capital City airman of the war to be awarded a DFC. Clayton, a native of Victoria, was similarly decorated. Clayton added a Bar to his DFC and the Order of the British Empire (OBE) to his wartime laurels while subsequently commanding both 408 and 405 Squadrons during the dark days of 1942 and early 1943. Ibid, 129, 150.

48. Lord Portal, as quoted in Greenhous et al, *Crucible of War*, 539.

49. Sir Richard Peirse, VCAS, to Prime Minister Winston Churchill, 5 Sep 1940, in PRO Premier 3/11/11A, 549.

50. Greenhous et al, *Crucible of War*, 539.

51. Ibid.

52. Air Ministry guidance to Sir Richard Peirse, 25 Oct 1940, PRO Air 9/132, in Greenhous et al, *Crucible of War*, 540.

53. Secretary of State for Air, Air Ministry
    SECRET
    Whitehall, S.W.1
    7 October 1940
    Prime Minister
    About nine percent of our total bombing effort was directed against marshalling yards during the month of September. The proportion of the total number of primary targets to marshalling yards was about five to one, but of course they are a convenient last resort target when bad weather makes the location of primary and secondary targets difficult . . . the primary object of our bombing policy last month was to hinder the transport of supplies from Germany to France, and thus the German preparations for invasion. The Railway Research Service advised us that the best way to cause general dislocation of the railway communications to France was to bomb the marshalling yards in Germany because it is there that the trains are made up.

    To dislocate German railway communications is an object of high military and economic importance; but it is very difficult because damage to railway tracks is easily repaired. *Their most vulnerable point is marshalling yards because the Germans time all their trains from the marshalling yard and not from the railway terminus, as is the custom in England. Moreover, marshalling yards cannot work at night without lights and consequently work at them is easily brought to a standstill by occasional bombing during the hours of darkness.* (My italics)

Our object in bombing marshalling yards is therefore not primarily to cause material damage, but to force the railwaymen to dowse their lights and so make the marshalling of traffic impossible. Accordingly we send one or two aircraft to each yard night after night to create cumulative congestion and disorganization..

Intelligence reports indicate that the Germans have had considerable difficulty in transporting supplies from Germany to bases in Northern France and have been forced to supplement normal ground communication by the use of large numbers of transport aircraft.

(a) A highly placed neutral recently travelling from Holland was routed through Berlin, Munich and Constance. At the last moment this itinerary was changed and he could not travel either through Berlin or on the Rhine route. (Source: A.I.1.c.)

(b) Persons who travelled from Berlin and Cologne to Basle last week state that in each case they were compelled to change more than 12 times and even then there were delays for long periods outside some stations. (Source: A.A. Berne)

In addition, the Ministry of Economic Warfare report that the traffic in perishable foodstuffs from Holland has been practically at a standstill for considerable periods while damage is being repaired; that ships have been held up at Bremen and other ports through a shortage of coal; and that neutral travellers have taken three days for journeys that can normally be completed in a few hours.

Corroboration is given to these reports by our own experience under German bombardment. For example, the Ministry of Home Security report as follows:- "By the mass use of exploded and unexploded (delay action) bombs, severe dislocation of railway traffic was caused during the earlier part of September. This had the inevitable result of severe congestion in all marshalling and goods yards, thus presenting a set of first-class targets . . ."

I agree, however, that we must be very careful not to dissipate too high a proportion of our heavy bomber effort on purely harassing attacks.

(Signed)

Archibald Sinclair

Sinclair to Churchill, 7 Oct 1940, in PRO Premier 3/11/11A, 515.

54. Of interest, the Coventry raid was the *Luftwaffe's* first serious attempt at blind bombing. This was provided by releasing bombs on electronic cues provided by the *X-Gerät* or "Secret-X" system; a modified *Lorenz* radio navigation beam. It was devastatingly successful on this occasion.

55. Terraine, *Right of the Line,* 276.

56. Ibid.

57. Ibid.

58. Ministry of Aircraft Production Memo to Prime Minister, 30 Dec 1940, in PRO Premier 3/11/2, 55.

59. Memo Portal to Ismay, 25 Feb 1941, in PRO Premier 3/11/2, 48.

60. Terraine, *Right of the Line*, 277.

61. Ibid.

62. Greenhous et al, *Crucible of War*, 542.

63. Bob Dale at <http://www.torontoaircrew.com/Navigators/Dale_4/dale_4.html>, 1.

64. Hatch, *Aerodrome of Democracy*, 56.

65. Norman MacLennan, wartime letter (undated) to sister Flora as part of submission to author from Norma Kelkar (MacLennan's niece), 16 Nov 2001.

66. I.A. MacLennan, postcard to Mr. & Mrs. D.A.G. MacLennan, 15 Oct 1942.

67. Murray Peden, *A Thousand Shall Fall* (Toronto: Stoddart, 1979), 233.

68. Terraine, *Right of the Line*, 281.

69. Williston, "Death of a Hero."

70. Wilfrid John "Mike" Lewis, quoted in Overy, *Bomber Command*, 70. There were several reasons for the He 177's frequent and catastrophic engine fires. The common exhaust manifold on the two inner cylinder blocks would become very hot, and this in turn would cause any oil or grease that had accumulated at the bottom of the engine cowling to burst into flames. The fuel injection pumps also leaked and tended to pump more fuel than required under certain conditions. Also, the massive, coupled DB 610s did not have a firewall, which resulted in a tightly-squeezed confluence of fuel lines and electrical leads near the main wing spar, and this increased the likelihood of catastrophic destruction, should a fire occur. At altitude, the engine lubrication oil had a tendency to

foam. This resulted in a breakdown of lubrication, which would, in turn, disintegrate the connecting rod bearings which could then break through the engine crankcase, puncturing oil tanks and creating a fire. Alfred Price, "He 177 Greif—The Luftwaffe's Lighter," in *International Air Power Review*, 11, (Winter 2003–4), 158–173.

71. Wilfrid John "Mike" Lewis, quoted in William J. Wheeler (ed), *Flying Under Fire—Canadian Fliers Recall the Second World War* (Calgary: Fifth House, 2001), 27.

72. Lewis, quoted in Overy, *Bomber Command*, 70.

73. Mike Lewis had flown an earlier tour of 36 operations in Hampdens with 44 Squadron, which garnered him his DFC. The operation on which he was shot down and subsequently captured was his 61st raid. The RCAF eventually awarded him the two-tour operations badge. Lewis, quoted in Wheeler, *Flying Under Fire*, 28.

74. Werner Held and Holger Nauroth, *The Defense of the Reich—Hitler's Night Fighter Planes and Pilots* (New York: Arco, 1982), 71.

75. Bomber Command Diary, (online) at <http://www.raf.mod.uk/bombercommand/diary/diary 1941_1.html>,2.

76. Greenhous and Halliday, *Canada's Air Forces*, 44.

77. Ibid, 55.

78. Ibid, 85.

79. Hatch, *Aerodrome of Democracy*, 56.

80. Watts, "RCAF Years."

81. Ibid.

82. Allan D. English, *The Cream of the Crop—Canadian Aircrew 1939–1945* (Montreal & Kingston: McGill-Queen's University Press, 1996), 122.

83. Larry Milberry, *Sixty Years—The RCAF and Canadian Forces Air Command 1924–1984* (Toronto: CANAV Books, 1984), 98.

84. Greenhous et al, *Crucible of War*, 545.

85. Harold W. Holmes, "The First of Many," *Airforce* 18, 1 (Spring 1994), 6.

86. Ibid, 7.

87. Paul Nyznik, "A Canadian Hero," 28.

88. 408 *Squadron History* (Stittsville, Ontario: Aviation Bookshelf, 1984), 12.

89. Ibid, 13.

90. Greenhous et al, *Crucible of War*, 550.

91. Personal correspondence, Turnbull family papers, courtesy of Susan Turnbull Caton.

92. <http://www.airforce.ca/wwii/ALPHA-TU.html,> 16.

93. <http://www.torontoaircrew.com/Navigators/ Elliot_D_2elliot_d_2.html> 1.

94. LGen (ret'd) Reg Lane, audiotape to author, 22 Aug 2001.

95. Watts, "RCAF Years."

96. Greenhous et al, *Crucible of War*, 544.

97. Senior Air Staff Officer Bomber Command Memo to Groups, 3 July 1941, in PRO (Air) 14/232.

98. Various Bomber Command sources, as referenced by Greenhous et al, *Crucible of War*, 550.

99. Martin Middlebrook, "Bomber Command's War—The Turning Points," pt 2, *Flypast* No.206, (Sep 1988), 80.

100. Terraine, *Right of the Line*, 293.

101. Office of the Minister of Defence (MoD) Memo to Prime Minister on Bomber Command Operations, Oct 1941, PRO Premier 3/11/3, 91–93.

102. The reader should carefully note this principle of following up a successful attack. Its subsequent lack of application under another AOC will have significant ramifications in future.

103. C.R. Price, MoD Memo to Prime Minister, 25 Oct 1941, in PRO Premier 3/11/3, 96.

104. Bomber Command 1939–1945 Official Campaign Diary 1941, at <http://www.raf.mod.uk/bombercommand/diary/diary1941_3.html>2. Hereafter Bomber Command Diary.

105. Greenhous et al, *Crucible of War*, 559.

106. Bomber Command Diary, 2

107. Bottomley (DCAS) to Harris, 13 Nov 1941, at PRO Premier 3/11/3, 89.

108. Watts, "RCAF Years."

CHAPTER THREE

1. William Green, *Famous Bombers of the Second World War* (London: Hanover House, 1959), 131.

2. Overy, *Bomber Command*, 80.

3. Webster and Frankland, *Strategic Air Offensive*, vol 4, app 8, 144.

3a. Greenhous et al, *Crucible of War*, 576.

4. Overy, *Bomber Command*, 80.

5. Watts, "RCAF Years."

6. Middlebrook, "Bomber Command's War," pt 2, 82.

7. Greenhous et al, *Crucible of War*, 576.

8. When that happened, the British scientific community would quickly respond with anti-jamming devices of their own. In fact, *Gee* would remain in use throughout the entire European war. By the summer of 1944, there were no less than five separate chains of *Gee* signal transmitting stations radiating from Britain, and more were established on the continent after the invasion, since the closer the transmitter was located to the target, the better the accuracy it provided. Overy, *Bomber Command*, 105.

9. Greenhous et al, *Crucible of War*, 578.

10. Jerrold Morris, *Canadian Artists and Airmen 1940–1945* (Toronto: np, nd), 65–67.

11. Wilhelm Johnen, *Duel under the Stars* (London: William Kimber, 1969), 40.

12. Bomber Command Diary, Mar 1942, 5–6.

13. Morris, *Canadian Artists and Airmen*, 65–67.

14. Bomber Command Diary, Mar 1942, 6.

15. Ibid, Apr 1942, 4

16. Greenhous et al, *Crucible of War*, 582.

17. Ibid, 583.

18. Middlebrook, "Bomber Command's War," 83.

19. Ibid.

20. *Tirpitz* was attacked and sunk by Lancasters of 9 and 617 Squadrons, dropping 12,000-pound Tallboy bombs at Tromso Fjord on 12 November 1944, after earlier attacks in September by Bomber Command aircraft flying out of Russia, and attacking the ship in Alten Fjord. The leader of the ultimately decisive raid was the 617 Squadron commander, Wing Commander Willie Tait. In 1941, already an experienced Bomber Command pilot, he was the commanding officer of the Halifax Operational Conversion Unit when Jack Watts made the transition from Whitleys. By 1944, Tait was a Bomber Command legend with a record four DSOs and two DFCs nestled under his pilot wings.

21. Reg Lane said he nearly died of shock when, sometime later, Don McIntyre strolled into the Officers Mess at Abington and Lane thought he was looking at a ghost. McIntyre and his entire crew survived a spectacular crash landing of his blazing Halifax on a frozen lake. The airplane eventually burned itself through the ice. McIntyre walked his crew all the way to Sweden and he was eventually smuggled back to England in the belly of a BOAC Mosquito. In 1973, his aircraft was salvaged from the bed of the lake and, after partial restoration, was placed on public display at the RAF Museum at Hendon. Another of the lost Halifaxes that night was flown by Wing Commander D.C.T. Bennett, the Australian who would later form and command the Pathfinders. He would also have a spectacular escape via Sweden and would return to Britain five weeks after the raid. Lane, audiotape to author, 22 Aug 2001.

22. PRO Air 2/9598, 10 July 1942, at <http://www.airforce.ca/wwii/ALPHA-LA.LAR.html>

23. Watts, "RCAF Years."

24. AFRO 1413/42, 4 Sep 1942, at <http://www.airforce.ca/wwii/ALPHA-WA.TWO.html>

25. Watts, "RCAF Years."

26. AFRO 880-881/42, 12 June 1942, at <http://www.airforce.ca/wwii/ALPHA-GA.GE.html>

27. <http://www.torontoaircrew.com/Bomber_ Pilots/Gardiner_2/gardiner_2.html>

28. Turnbull family papers.

29. Hatch, *Aerodrome of Democracy*, 109.

30. Ibid, 175.

31. Greenhous et al, *Crucible of War*, 572.

32. Bishop, *Courage in the Air*, 153.

33. Greenhous et al, *Crucible of War*, 569.

34. Ibid, 570.

35. Lane, audiotape to author, 22 Aug 2001.

36. Stevenson, an Anglophile, felt Canadian airmen could best serve the war effort from RAF units, and thus ran afoul of the Canadian political executive. He significantly aided and abetted British "foot dragging" on the Canadianization issue. And many senior Canadian officials on the Home Front either inadvertently or deliberately

supported Stevenson in doing so by providing virtually no administrative direction or authority to Headquarters RCAF Overseas on policies regarding pay, promotions and medical/dental care to RCAF members posted to RAF units. To say the least, the span of control was enormous, tenuous at best, and ripe for abuse.

37. Greenhous et al, *Crucible of War*, 7.
38. Greenhous and Halliday, *Canada's Air Forces*, 86.
39. Greenhous et al, *Crucible of War*, 570.
40. Ibid.
41. Ibid.
42. Ibid., 571.
43. Ibid., 49.
44. Ibid., 83.
45. English, *Cream of the Crop*, 122.
46. Greenhous et al, *Crucible of War*, 50, 95.
47. English, *Cream of the Crop*, 122.
48. Ibid, 106.
49. Greenhous and Halliday, *Canada's Air Forces*, 52.
50. Terraine, *Right of the Line*, 464.
51. At the Allied Air Training Conference of May 1942, and in order to bolster their arguments against broader aircrew commissioning, the British claimed that the Americans were commissioning "80% of pilots, 100% of navigators, 50% of bombardiers, but no air gunners, radio operators or flight engineers." Hatch, *Aerodrome of Democracy*, 108. However, in relatively short order, the USAAF would commission virtually all of its pilots, navigators and bombardiers, but hardly any of its gunners, radio operators or flight engineers. Mark K. Wells, *Courage and Air Warfare—The Allied Aircrew Experience in the Second World War* (London: Frank Cass, 1995),123,133.
52. Leslie Roberts, *There Shall Be Wings* (Toronto: Clarke-Irwin, 1959), 156.
53. Greenhous and Halliday, *Canada's Air Forces*, 54.
54. Greenhous et al, *Crucible of War*, 94.
55. Greenhous and Halliday, *Canada's Air Forces*, 54.
56. Initially, Canada wished to form an indigenous group within Fighter Command. However, the decision was made that the group so designated would become part of Bomber Command, since Bomber Command groups possessed more organizational stability and would therefore be more practicable than a group within another command.
57. Greenhous et al, *Crucible of War*, 602.
58. Ibid, 593.
59. Terraine, *Right of the Line*, 486.
60. Bomber Command Diary, May 1942, 6.
61. Ibid. However, nine more accidental losses incurred on the return trip and landings brought the total to fifty, for a raid loss rate to all causes of 4.79 percent. Furthermore, twelve more of the returning aircraft were so badly damaged that they had to be written off, bringing the total raid cost to 62 aircraft, or 5.94 percent of the dispatched force. The total number of Allied aircrew killed from all causes on this raid was 291. Terraine, *Right of the Line*, 487.
62. Bomber Command news release, 31 May 1942, in PRO Premier 3/11/12, 685.
63. Telephone Message from B.B.C. Monitoring Service, from D.N.B., 1.46 p.m. on May 31, in PRO Premier 3/11/12, 686.
64. William L. Shirer, *The Rise and Fall of the Third Reich—A History of Nazi Germany* (New York: Simon and Schuster, 1960), 934.
65. Greenhous et al, *Crucible of War*, 594.
66. Wolfgang Falck, Warriors of the Night, prt 1 (video), (Discovery Channel, 1999) translation from the German.
67. Bomber Command Diary, May 1942, 6.
68. Letter and Minute in PRO Premier 3/11/12, 667.
69. Letter Benes to Churchill, 15 June 1942, in PRO Premier 3/11/12, 669.
70. Letter Harris to Churchill, 15 June 1942, in PRO Premier 3/11/12, 666.
71. Shirer, *Rise and Fall of the Third Reich*, 991.
72. W.M. (42) 43rd Conclusions, Minute 2, in PRO Premier 3/11/12, 665.
73. Bomber Command Diary, June 1942, 7.
74. Lord Cherwell, quoted in Holmes, *Battlefields of the Second World War*, 183.

75. Ibid.
76. John Singleton, "Report on the Bombing of Germany to Prime Minister Churchill," 20 May 1942, 10, in PRO Premier 3/11/4, 124.
77. Ibid, 125, 128, 133.
78. Overy, *Bomber Command*, 107.
79. Terraine, *Right of the Line*, 502.
80. Ibid, 503.
81. Middlebrook, "Bomber Command's War—The Turning Points," pt 3, Flypast, No.207 (Oct 1998), 48.
82. Indeed, by the end of 1944, 90 percent of the Main Force would use H2S-equipped aircraft. Gordon Musgrove, *Pathfinder Force—A History of 8 Group* (London: MacDonald and Jane's, 1976), 236.
83. It was acknowledged that H2S had a systemic error of roughly one-half the breadth of the target area. Thus, it tended to be used, especially by the PFF, as a back-up only when better marker fixes, either visual or *Oboe*, were not available. But *H2S* was effectively used in conjunction with *Gee* by Main Force navigators to get the pilot to the target area, where the air bomber could then direct the aircraft to the drop point marked by the PFF.
84. Musgrove, *Pathfinder Force*, 239.
85. Ibid, 13.
86. Kenneth McDonald, letter to author, 25 Aug 2000, from earlier letter to Michael LeBlanc, 13 June 1994.
87. Letter Harris to Linnell ATH/DO/5C, 16 Oct 1942.
88. Letter Harris to Sorley ATH/DO/4D, 18 Mar 1943.
   The only visible difference between the Mark III and the Mark VII Halifax was that the latter had its wingspan increased to 105 feet from 99 feet consistently, as opposed to on an ad hoc basis for the Mark IIIs. Again, the earlier Halifaxes had suffered the Stirling's fate of wingspan limitations based on prewar hangar door sizes!
90. Jim Northrup, letter to author, 18 Aug 2000.
91. Lane to author, 22 Aug 2001.
92. English, *Cream of the Crop*, 122.
93. For example, Wing Commander Ira Jones, a high-scoring First World War ace, noted that Major Keith "Grid" Caldwell, a distinguished and highly-decorated ace in his own right who commanded 74 Squadron during 1918, specifically referred to " the 'coloured troops' being the nickname which Grid gives to all Colonials." And Caldwell was a New Zealander. Ira Jones, *King of the Air Fighters* (London: Greenhill Books, 1989), 206.
94. Letter Harris to Churchill, 30 Sep 1944, in PRO Premier 3/12, 63B.
95. Greenhous et al, *Crucible of War*, 642.
96. Even here the logic of this aircraft holds water, since the later operational marks of the Halifax would share engine commonality with the Lancaster II.
97. Although in fairness, many of the squadron transitions to Lancasters from Halifaxes would not take place until close to the cessation of European hostilities. Ibid, 637.
98. Air Intelligence Result of Recent RAF Attacks Report to Prime Minister, 23 Sept 1942, in PRO Premier 3/11/12, 621.
99. Air Intelligence Report No. 346 to CAS, 22.9.42, in PRO Premier 3/11/12, 627–629.
100. Winston Churchill, policy note to War Cabinet, 16 Dec 1942, in PRO Premier 3/11/6, 179–182.

CHAPTER FOUR

1. In 1940, Churchill had urged Bomber Command "to cast a large number of bombs into Germany." Winston S. Churchill, *Their Finest Hour* (Boston: Houghton Mifflin, 1949), 604. Those tonnages would mount impressively in 1943/44. In March 1943, the figure reached 8000 tons; double that amount in July/August, and nearly 20,000 tons in March 1944. And this was just the beginning. In March 1945, the incessant pounding rose to an incredible peak of 67,500 tons for the month. Terraine, *Right of the Line, 537.*
2. Overy, *Bomber Command*, 110.
3. On 3 November 1942, Chief of the Air Staff Sir Charles Portal (with major input from Harris and his planners) presented the British Chiefs of Staff with a blueprint for a joint Anglo-American bombing offensive against Germany which assumed the aforementioned fleet size by 1944. It is particularly interesting, in that the German city numbers are exactly the same as those penned by Lord Cherwell in his earlier Memorandum on the bombing effects of The Blitz. His lasting influence on policy is undeniable. To paraphrase, 58 industrial towns and cities were specified, each of which could receive, in proportion to its size, roughly seventeen attacks of "Cologne" intensity. Or expressed differently, this scale of onslaught could force on every industrial centre in Germany with a population in excess of 50,000, in proportion to its size, ten attacks of "Cologne" intensity. It was believed

that a concentrated campaign of this nature would destroy at least one-third of all German industry and reduce at least six million residential dwellings to rubble, as well as a proportionate number of industrial buildings, transportation facilities, public utilities and power sources. It was also predicted to render 25 million Germans homeless, and since a substantial portion of German industry was required just to maintain the minimum subsistence of the German people, it was felt that the predicted industrial and domestic infrastructure losses would force on the Germans either the sacrifice of most of their war potential or the collapse of their internal economy. Sir Charles Portal, memorandum for the British Chiefs of Staff, 3 Nov 1942, in PRO Air 14/739A.

4. Chaz Bowyer, *History of the RAF* (London: Bison, 1988), 131.

5. The final formal step directed at Canadianization was the Balfour-Power Agreement, signed on 16 Feb 1944. It mandated that all RCAF personnel overseas were at the posting disposal of the RCAF Air Officer Commanding Overseas, until or unless placed at the disposal of the RAF for an operational or non-operational tour. It also formalized a new commissioning policy, where Canada could commission all qualified aircrew according to its own standards.

6. In fact, on 1 Jan 1943, a full 20 of the 47 male officers and 55 of 177 male other ranks at 6 Group Headquarters were on loan from the RAF. Greenhous et al, *Crucible of War*, 634.

7. Ibid, 635.

8. Harris papers, quoted in ibid, 636.

9. Group Capt (ret'd) W.H. Swetman, interview with author, 29 Aug 2000.

10 FLt J.T. "Jimmy" Sheridan, interview with author, 14 Oct 2002.

11. Greenhous et al, *Crucible of War*, 631.

12. J. Douglas Harvey, *The Tumbling Mirth—Remembering the Air Force* (Toronto: McClelland and Stewart, 1983), 36.

13. Ibid, 632.

14 Laurence Motiuk, *Thunderbirds at War—Diary of a Bomber Squadron* (Nepean, Ontario: Larmot, 1995), 48.

15. Greenhous et al, *Crucible of War*, 640.

16. This remark was probably made with respect to Air Vice-Marshal Brookes, since Harris wrote to both Portal and Sir Harold Balfour in January 1943 on the questionable first impressions Brookes's leadership style was generating. "A serious aspect of this matter is the very poor type of commanding officer which the Dominions seem to produce. Mostly hangovers from a prehistoric past. At the best they are completely inexperienced, and at the worst they are awful. I heard a comment the other day that the Canadian fighting crews were venting strong objection to being commanded by officers whose experience was limited to "six months flying training and 28 years political intrigue." Harris to Charles Portal (CAS) 10 Jan 1943, Portal Papers (copy DHist 87/89, Folder 10; Harris to Sir Harold Balfour 19 Jan 1943, PRO Air 20/3798. Harris was undoubtedly indulging in exaggeration to make his point, but his concern was not entirely unfounded. With such small pools of prewar regular officers to pick from, Dominion air forces, including the RCAF, were hard-pressed to provide individuals whose service backgrounds approached those of their British counterparts. Brookes, unwittingly, may have reinforced his AOC-in-C's suspicions. Ibid, 678. However, this writer has found nothing on record to indicate that Harris was generally or comparatively displeased with the calibre of the Canadian station and squadron commanders within his command. That said, it would appear that Johnnie Fauquier's command of the elite 617 "Dambuster" Squadron late in the war is the *only* occasion when an RCAF officer was appointed to command an RAF Bomber Command squadron during the war. This, on reflection, is unusual, considering the vast number of RCAF aircrew who served with RAF units.

17. Letter, Harris correspondence DO/3 Portal to Harris, 7 Feb 1943.

18. Webster and Frankland, *Strategic Air Offensive* vol 4 app 8, directive xxviii, 153–4.

19. Edward Jablonski, *America in the Air War* (Alexandria, Virginia: Time-Life Books, 1982), 65.

20. Wells, *Courage and Air Warfare*, 210.

21. Jablonski, *America in the Air War*, 142.

22. Combined Chiefs of Staff (Casablanca Directive), approved 21 Jan 1943, copy in DHist file 181.006 (D159), quoted in Greenhous et al, *Crucible of War*, 639.

23. Harris to Portal, as quoted in Robin Neillands, *The Bomber War—The Allied Offensive Against Nazi Germany* (New York: Overlook Press, 2001), 201, 202.

24. Overy, *Bomber Command*, 111.

25. Pointblank directive, 10 June 1943, in Webster and Frankland, *Strategic Air Offensive*, 158–160.

26. Musgrove, *Pathfinder Force*, app 2, 235.

27. Ibid.

28. Ibid, 245.

29. Ibid, 246.

30. Greenhous et al, *Crucible of War*, 712.

31. Philip J.R. Moyes, *Bomber Squadrons of the RAF and their Aircraft* (London: Macdonald, 1964), 307.

32. Musgrove, *Pathfinder Force*, 241.

33. Ibid, 247.

34. Ibid, 254–255.

35. Ibid, 249–251.

36. D.C.T. Bennett, *Pathfinder* (London: Mueller, 1958), quoted in Philip Kaplan, *Bombers—The Aircrew Experience* (London: Aurum, 2000), 226–227.

37. Terraine, *Right of the Line*, 518.

38. Lane, audiotape to author, 22 Aug 2001.

39. Terraine, *Right of the Line*, 519.

40. Ibid.

41. Shirer, *Rise and Fall of the Third Reich*, 1008.

42. Bomber Command Diary, 23/24 May 1943, 6.

43. *London Gazette*, 17 Sep 1943 and AFRO 2198/43, 29 Oct 1943, at <http://www.airforce.ca/wwii/ALPHA-BA.1.html>,6–7.

44. Ibid.

45. Reg Paterson, letter to author, 07 Nov 2001.

46. Holmes, *Battlefields of the Second World War*, 200.

47. Harris to Sir Archibald Sinclair, 30 Dec 1942, in PRO Air 14/3512 and PRO 19/354, in Greenhous et al, *Crucible of War*, 684.

48. Ibid.

49. During the height of the Berlin raids in Jan 1944, 6 Group Halifax losses peaked at a soul-destroying 9.8 percent per raid. Ibid, 680 (chart), 788.

50. Ibid, 686.

51. Ibid, 641.

52. Bomber Command Diary, 5/6 Mar 1943, 2.

53. Motiuk, *Thunderbirds at War*, 70.

54. Bruce Barrymore Halpenny, *Action Stations* (Cambridge: Patrick Stephens, 1981), 60.

55. Greenhous et al, *Crucible of War*, 616, and Greenhous and Halliday, *Canada's Air Forces*, 96.

56. Greenhous et al, *Crucible of War*, 678.

57. Ibid, 671.

58. The fifteenth and final heavy bomber squadron for 6 Group was acquired in July 1944,when 415 "Swordfish" Squadron, equipped with Halifax IIIs, was posted to the group from Coastal Command. While 405 Squadron would serve with 8 Group (PFF) from April 1943 until the end of hostilities, it would continue to be administered by 6 Group.

59. A specific example of this disruption is that five 6 Group squadrons changed their base location at least once during the height of the Ruhr campaign from April to June 1943. Ibid, 643.

60. Also, 405 Squadron in 8 Group would commence re-equipment with Lancaster Mark Is and IIIs in August. By war's end, twelve of fifteen squadrons of the group (including 405 Squadron) were equipped with Lancasters, including seven with the Canadian-built Lancaster Mark Xs. Admittedly, 408, 420 and 425 Squadrons did not convert to Lancaster Xs until just before VE Day. The others would operate a mix of Mark Is and Mark IIIs, both of which were superior to the Bristol Hercules-powered Mark IIs. Only three 6 Group units, namely 415, 426 and 432 Squadrons, were flying a mix of Halifax III/VII aircraft at VE Day. Christopher Shores, *History of the Royal Canadian Air Force* (Toronto: Bison, 1984), 59–60.

61. Later in 1944, all three of these airfields with their Heavy Conversion Units reverted to the centralized authority of the RAF Training Group.

62. Geoff Marlow, recollections of bombing missions over Germany, courtesy of Dick Wynne, letter to author, 15 Nov 2000.

63. Greenhous et al, *Crucible of War*, 644.

64. Ibid, 646.

65. Larry Dunlap, "The RCAF Years," (video) RCAF Museum, Trenton, Ontario, 1994.

66. Ibid. However, it should be noted that Air Marshal Dunlap's recollections of the air deployment to North Africa are somewhat at odds with the Official History and also the Operations Record Books (ORBs) of 420 and 425

Squadrons, and the Northwest African Air Force (NAAF) secret narrative of the period. They state that 420 Squadron aircraft were attacked in daylight over the Bay of Biscay by "several Junkers . . . in close formation;" that two of the 420 Squadron aircraft went missing and were presumed shot down, and that "one machine from No. 425 was also attacked and the crew eventually forced to bail out over Portugal, where they were interned." Nos. 420 and 425 Squadron ORBs, June 1943, DHist; AFHQ, NAAF secret narrative 4–5, DHist 74/452, in Greenhous et al, *Crucible of War*, 646.

67. Donald Marion (ed), *425 Alouette* (Ottawa: Dept of National Defence, 1978), 7.
68. Nora Bottomley, *424 Squadron History* (Stittsville: Hangar Bookshelf, 1985), 46.
69. Greenhous et al, *Crucible of War*, 649.
70. Ibid, 651.
71. P/O A.G. Grout, quoted in Bottomley, *424 Squadron History*, 43–44.
72. Ibid, 44.
73. Greenhous et al, *Crucible of War*, 652.
74. *London Gazette*, 21Apr 1944 and AFRO 1075/44, 19 May 1944, at
    <http://www.airforce.ca/wwii/ALPHA-GR.GW.html> .
75. Greenhous et al, *Crucible of War*, 654.
76. Portal to Edwards, 27 Sep 1943, PRO Air 8/782, in ibid.
77. Bottomley, *424 Squadron History*, 46.
78. Harvey, *The Tumbling Mirth*, 106.
79. Greenhous et al, *Crucible of War*, 654–55.
80. Overy, *Bomber Command*, 84.
81. Tom Coughlin, *The Dangerous Sky* (Toronto: Ryerson Press, 1968), 62.
82. Ibid.
83. Hugh A. Halliday, "The Mysteries of Gongs," *Airforce*, 27, 4 (Winter 2003–4), 41.
84. *London Gazette*, 24 Sep 1943 and AFRO 2386/43, 19 Nov 1943, at
    <http://www.airforce.ca/wwii/ALPHA-LA.LAR.html>.
    Only twelve CGMs were awarded to Canadian airmen during the Second World War, compared to 4017 DFCs and 515 DFMs. Larry Milberry, Canada's Air Force at War and Peace, vol 2 (Toronto, CANAV Books, 2000), 90. Considering that only two VCs were awarded during the period to members of the RCAF (and one to a Canadian in RAF service, Squadron Leader Ian Bazalgette), the CGM awards were rare, selective and prestigious.
85. Coughlin, *Dangerous Sky*, 63.
86. Greenhous et al, *Crucible of War*, 589.
87. Ibid, 590.
88. Ironic, since in Nov 1942, Kammhuber would reject the offer of a wooden, purpose-built night fighter, patterned on the de Havilland Mosquito, on the grounds that it would not show up distinctly on his GCI radars. Ibid, 609. It would eventually materialize later in the war as the Focke-Wulf Ta 154 Moskito, which was blindingly fast and demonstrated exceptional promise. However, it suffered from structural break-ups and there was not enough special adhesive available for mass production, once the primary supplier was bombed out of business, and the industry was not able to find a workable substitute prior to the cessation of hostilities. Held and Nauroth, *Defense of the Reich*, 199.
89. Various German sources, in Greenhous et al, *Crucible of War*, 591.
90. Towards the end of the war, the Germans successfully flew their own centimetric AI radar, the FuG 240 Berlin, the antenna of which was housed in a streamlined nose cone and fitted to the latest version of their Ju 88G night fighter, the Ju 88G7c. However, only 25 Berlin sets, developed from a captured H2S set, were produced, of which a mere ten were fitted to the Junkers Ju 88G7c. Once again, it was a case of "too little, too late." William Green, *Warplanes of the Third Reich* (London: Macdonald, 1970), 471.
91. Greenhous et al, *Crucible of War*, 661.
92. Albert Speer, quoted in Terraine, *Right of the Line*, 537.
93. Overy, *Bomber Command*, 197.
94. Raymond F. Tolliver and Trevor J. Constable, *Fighter Aces of the Luftwaffe* (Fallbrook, California: Aero, 1977), 399–400.
95. Ibid, 226. The left fin of Schnaufer's Bf 110G-4, with its 121 victory marks, is on permanent display in London's Imperial War Museum. Held and Nauroth, *Defense of the Reich*, 221.
96. Greenhous et al, *Crucible of War*, 662.
97. Ibid, 677.
98. Ibid, 678.

99. Combat stress and how the RAF and RCAF executives dealt with it shall be discussed in a later chapter. The 6 Group record was the *second* highest of the six groups, implying that others were faring worse.

100. Sqn Ldr P.T. Green, "Service History," DHist file 181.009 (D4254) and DHist Brookes biographical file and diary entry for 23 Apr 1943, in ibid, 679.

101. Various correspondence from the period, including Brookes/Slemon to 6 Group stations, 6 Group monthly summaries of operations and training activities in DHist file 181.003 (D296), PRO Air 14/485; and letters Harris–Brookes–Harris, 3–21 May 1943 in DHist file 181.009 (D1925), and No. 6 Group tactical report No. 6, June Operations, 4 July 1943, in DHist file 181.003 (D4472), all in Greenhous et al, *Crucible of War*, 679.

102. Surveyed in early June, less than half his crews had completed ten operational sorties, and nearly 75 percent were not halfway through their required tour of thirty operations, a situation due in no small measure to the need to send experienced crews to North Africa. Ibid, 680.

103. Ibid.

104. Several references, including Minute 13 to Saundby correspondence, 30 June 1943, in PRO Air 14/1794, and Saundby to Brookes, 17 July 1943, in DHist file 181.009 (D1925), all in ibid, 681.

105. Ibid, 682.

106. Ibid.

107. In visualizing the delivery concept, Wallis recalled an 18th Century sea battle tactic called "skip shot," whereby cannonballs were bounced across relatively placid waters at enemy vessels.

108. Sir Barnes Wallis, quoted in Frank C. Williams, "The Raid on the Dams—Part One: Preparation," *Airforce*, 9, 2 (July–Sep 1985), 28.

109. Various sources, including Christopher Shores and Clive Williams, *Aces High—A Tribute to the Most Notable Fighter Pilots of the British and Commonwealth Forces in WWII* (London: Grub Street, 1994), 657.

110. Aircrew interviews quoted in Secrets of the Dead, which examined Allied efforts to design a bomb that could destroy German dams, aired on PBS, 12 Feb 2003.

111. Max Hastings, *Bomber Command* (New York: Dial Press/James Wade, 1979), 216.

112. Williams, "Raid on the Dams" pt 1, 29.

113. Dave Birrell, "Dambuster Navigator," *Airforce*, 27, 1 (Spring 2003), 38.

114. Frank C. Williams, "The Raid on the Dams—Part Two: The Attack," *Airforce*, 9, 3 (Oct–Dec 1985), 17.

115. Ibid,18.

116. Ibid.

117. Two Canadians were flying with Hopgood that night. Ken Earnshaw, the navigator from Bashaw, Alberta, perished, but the bomb-aimer, John Fraser of Nanaimo, BC, survived to sit out the rest of the war as a prisoner. Frank C. Williams, "The Raid on the Dams—Part Three: Back Home," *Airforce*, 9, 4 (Jan–Mar 1986), 7.

118. Ibid, 36.

119. Ibid.

120. Ibid, 10.

121. Ibid.

122. Ibid, 37.

123. Ibid.

124. Neillands, *Bomber War*, 233.

125. Harlo Taerum, quoted in Dave Birrell, "Dambuster Navigator," 39.

126. Terraine, *Right of the Line*, 538–39.

127. Albert Speer, *Inside the Third Reich* (New York: Galahad, 1970), 281. As a matter of interest, the Sorpe was re-attacked later in the war with 12,000-pound high explosive penetrating Tallboy bombs, another Barnes Wallis innovation, and even with this much better ordnance, the dam was not breached.

128. Neillands, *Bomber War*, 233.

129. Speer, *Inside the Third Reich*, 281.

130. Ibid.

131. Fest, *Speer—The Final Verdict*, 165.

132. Neillands, *Bomber War*, 233.

133. Ibid, 234.

134. Sir Arthur Harris, quoted in Guy Gibson, *Enemy Coast Ahead* (London: Goodall, 1946), viii. Of interest, Peter O'Connor of 467 (RAAF) Squadron flew on Gibson's last operation, which was to München-Gladbach, and recalled: "It was a successful attack, controlled by Gibson as master bomber in his usual professional fashion. I vaguely remembered his last words over the radio: 'Good show chaps, you've got the bugger . . . now you can

piss off home,' but I cannot guarantee this. We had a routine trip back, and we couldn't believe it when we heard that Gibson had got the chop." Neillands, *Bomber War*, 234.

135. Sir Charles Portal, CAS Memo to Sec of State, 24 July 1943, in PRO Premier 3/11/8, 302–03.
136. Neillands, *Bomber War*, 235.
137. Tizard to Churchill, 22 July 1943, in PRO Premier 3/11/8, 309.
138. Ibid.
139. Churchill to Ismay, 23 July 1943, in PRO Premier 3/11/8, 306.
140. Portal to Sec of State, in PRO Premier 3/11/8, 303–04.
141. Roberts, *There Shall Be Wings*, 171.
142. Neillands, *Bomber War*, 235.
143. Greenhous et al, *Crucible of War*, 696.
144. Bomber Command Diary, 27/28 July 1943, 5.
145. AFHQ Secret Bomber Narrative, July 1943, DHist File 79/444.
146. Roberts, *There Shall Be Wings*, 171.
147. Holmes, *Battlefields of the Second World War*, 203.
148. Actually Herr Goebbels's statistical acumen was off the mark, as various sources have confirmed that Hamburg's population was approaching two million at the time of the raids. Joseph Goebbels, quoted in Shirer, *Rise and Fall of the Third Reich*, 1009.
149. Vanderkerckhove had been severely shot up while attacking Essen in March, but pressed on diligently and, partially for his conduct on that raid, was awarded a DFC in Aug. Roberts, *There Shall Be Wings*, 166, 172.
150. Speer, *Inside the Third Reich*, 284.
151. Greenhous et al, *Crucible of War*, 697.
152. Ibid, 698.

CHAPTER FIVE

1. Webster and Frankland, *Strategic Air Offensive*, 201–202.
2. Wells, *Courage and Air Warfare*, 2.
3. Bill Swetman, "The Avro Lancaster," in Jeffrey Ethell (ed.), *The Great Book of World War Two Airplanes* (New York: Bonanza Books, 1984), 399.
4. Wells, *Courage and Air Warfare*, 115.
5. Ibid, 161.
6. Hastings, *Bomber Command*, 214.
7. Wells, *Courage and Air Warfare*, 116.
8. J. Douglas Harvey, *Boys, Bombs and Brussels Sprouts* (Toronto: McClelland & Stewart, 1981), 6.
9. Ken Tout, *Tanks Advance* (London: Grafton Books, 1989), 4.
10. P/O David Oliver, a British Lancaster pilot, in Martin Middlebrook, *The Berlin Raids—R.A.F. Bomber Command Winter 1943-44* (London: Penguin, 1988), 318.
11. Ibid, 28, 210.
12. Holmes, *Battlefields of the Second World War*, 199.
13. Harvey, *Boys, Bombs and Brussels Sprouts*, 87.
14. Ibid.
15. Motiuk, *Thunderbirds at War*, 458.
16. James H. Waugh, at <http://www.airforce.ca/wwii/ALPHA-WA.Two.html>, 45–46.
17. Murray Peden, letter to author, 7 Feb 2001.
18. Halpenny, *Action Stations*, 109.
19. Wells, *Courage and Air Warfare*, 31.
20. Ibid, 115.
21. Peden, letter to author, 7 Feb 2001.
22. Bob Pratt in "Warriors of the Night."
23. "Airfields of Yorkshire," in *Flypast*, No. 207 (Oct 1998), 89. Further south at the Master Diversion Field RAF Woodbridge, another 1200 wartime recoveries were made utilizing FIDO. Peden, *A Thousand Shall Fall*, 408.
24. Terraine, *Right of the Line*, 33.
25. John Searby, *The Bomber Battle for Britain* (Shrewsbury: Airlife, 1991), 81.
26. Peden, *A Thousand Shall Fall*, 414.

27. Alan W. Mitchell, "Bomber Crews Were Men with a High Quality of Courage," in *Gaggle and Stream*, magazine of the Bomber Command Association of Canada (Aug 2002), 7.

28. Paul Nyznik, "Pathfinder!" *Airforce*, 21, 1 (Spring 1997), 8.

29. Russell Braddon, *Cheshire VC* (London: Evans Brothers, 1954), 115.

30. Bert Houle, in David L. Bashow, *All the Fine Young Eagles* (Toronto: Stoddart, 1996), 144.

31. "Able Mabel" completed 123 operational sorties, including six flown under the hands of "Mo" Morrison. The "senior surviving statesman" of all the Lancs is R5868, a Lancaster I coded PO-S, "S-Sugar," that flew 137 operational sorties with 83 and 467 Squadrons.

32. KB 732 was eventually flown back to Canada and placed into long-term storage in Calgary. It was struck off strength in May 1948. It was subsequently broken up for scrap. Dave Birrell, "VR-X Terminator—The Greatest of the Canadian Lancs," *Airforce*, 25, 4 (Winter 2002), 8–10. When contemplating these various amassed sortie counts, readers should bear in mind that the average life of an operational Lancaster was twenty-one war sorties.

33. Wayne Saunders, " 'G' for [G]inx—The Bizarre Tale of 425 Squadron's Cursed Aircraft," *Airforce*, 23, 3, (Autumn 1999), 16–20.

34. Martin Caidin, *Black Thursday* (New York: E.P. Dutton, 1960), 80.

35. Halpenny, *Action Stations*, 426.

36. Holmes, *Battlefields of the Second World War*, 197.

37. Some British aircraft, especially the Lancaster and the Stirling, had very small hatch doors. While the American B-17 Flying Fortress hatch doors were approximately 30" X 30", the Lancaster's was only 22" X 22", and was particularly difficult to find in the dark. "Operational research statistics showed that about 50 percent of Americans successfully bailed out of damaged aircraft. In contrast, only about one-quarter of British airmen made it safely out of Halifaxes and Stirlings." Wells, *Courage and Air Warfare*, 54. In the Lancaster, the only recommended egress point was the small nose hatch, particularly difficult to find in the dark. The main crew door on the right hand side of the Lancaster's aft fuselage was not considered viable as an emergency escape location, since it was located directly in front of the horizontal stabilizer, and there was too much risk of the crew member striking it on exiting the aircraft. However, negotiating the entire length of a stricken and frequently out-of-control Lancaster, including clambering over that formidable wing spar, was difficult at best. Just over one in ten Lancaster rear gunners survived if the aircraft was destroyed by enemy action. Bill Swetman, "The Avro Lancaster," in Ethell (ed) *Great Book of World War Two Airplanes*, 396.

38. Holmes, *Battlefields of the Second World War*, 197.

39. McDonald, letter to author, 25 Aug 2000. Ken McDonald remained in the RAF after the war, rising to the rank of group captain and adding an OBE to his DFC. On completion of service, he returned to Canada.

40. LGen (ret'd) Reg Lane, interview with author, 25 Jan 2002.

41. While the photographic proof of an individual crew's bombing was considered an essential part of post-operation analysis in order to determine the amount of destruction meted out to the target, it also served other purposes. First, it constituted proof that the crew had bombed the target area and had not "wavered" in pressing home their attack. Second, in a more upbeat vein, it allowed the authorities to recognize and acknowledge particularly accurate bombing with respect to the designated aim point(s). This was manifested in the awarding of Target Tokens, certificates signed by the appropriate group commander and presented to deserving crews, who had obtained particularly good aiming point photographs.

42. Holmes, *Battlefields of the Second World War*, 200.

43. Jimmy Sheridan, letter to author, 20 Sep 2000.

44. Pratt, "Warriors of the Night."

45. Peden, *A Thousand Shall Fall*, 412.

46. Overy, *Bomber Command*, 204.

47. Greenhous et al, *Crucible of War* vol 3 app A, "RCAF Casualties Overseas by Years of War," 912.

48. Overy, *Bomber Command*, 205.

49. Neillands, *Bomber War*), 368.

50. Ibid.

51. Violent crimes against the aircrew appeared to occur most frequently in the open countryside, predominantly committed by irate villagers or NSDAP (the Nazi Party) officials. In contrast, those apprehended by soldiers, particularly those of the *Luftwaffe*, were usually safeguarded, and most, although not all crews captured in the urban areas were not abused, which, considering that the cities were generally the primary targets of the bombing, seems rather curious. Ibid, 369.

52. When the news of the deaths was presented to the prisoners of Salag Luft III, and they asked how many of the

escaping prisoners had been merely wounded while bolting away, the German authorities were at a loss for an answer. Apparently, those responsible for the crimes did not consider that eventuality. Stalag Luft III, at <http://www.elsham.pwp.blueyonder.co.uk|gt_esc|>, 18, accessed 17 Feb 2004.

53. The bomber crewmen, all shot down between Jan and Oct 1942, were Gordon A. Kidder of 156 Squadron, Patrick W. Langford of 16 Operational Training Unit, George E. McGill of 103 Squadron, and James C. Wernham from 405 Squadron. All but Wernham were Wellington crewmembers, while the latter was aboard a Halifax II when downed. Rob Davis, Stalag Luft III—The Great Escape, at <wysiwyg://main.18/http://www.b24.net/pow/greatescape.htm>, 24, accessed 12 Feb 2004, and Stalag Luft III, at <http://www.elsham.pwp.blueyonder.co.uk/gt_esc|>, 23–29, accessed 17 Feb 2004.

54. In all, seventy-two Germans were placed on a wanted list for the murders. "Of the 72 on that list, 21 were eventually tried, found guilty, and executed. Nine more received prison terms ranging from ten years to life; ten had forestalled the investigation by committing suicide and a further ten were either acquitted or had charges against them dropped. Twenty-two could not be traced, were either found to have been killed in the last stages of the war or just disappeared; some of them, as was established, into Russian prison camps from which they never returned. Squadron Leader Jack Bushby, RAF, "After the Great Escape," reprinted in *Airforce*, 18, 2 (July 1994), 6.

55. Report of No. 1 Canadian War Crimes Investigation Unit on Miscellaneous War Crimes against Members of the Canadian Armed Forces (CAF) in the European Theatre of Operations, pt 2, 30 Mar 1946, Cases 67/Hagen/I and 67/Opladen/I, DHist 159.023 (DI), in Greenhous et al, *Crucible of War*, 859 and fn 96.(hereafter Rpt of No. 1 CWCIU)

56. E.W. Blenkinsop Biog. File, DHist, in Greenhous et al, *Crucible of War*, 801 and fn 19. Blenkinsop was awarded the DFC effective 11 Apr 1944 as per *London Gazette* of 21 Apr 1944 and AFRO 1186/44, 2 June 1944. He was also awarded the Belgian *Croix de Guerre avec Palme*, effective 17 July 1948 as per *Canada Gazette* of that date and AFRO 455/48, 23 July 1948, at <http://www.airforce.ca/wwii/ALPHA-BL.html>, 24.

57. Report of No. 1 CWCIU, 9 Sep 1939 to 8 May 1945, pt 2, Case 67/Dienst/I, DHist 159.95, in Greenhous et al, *Crucible of War*, 802 and fn 21.

58. Ibid, Cases 67/Kassel/I, and 67/Bourg Achard/I, DHist 159.95.023 (DI), 802 and fn 21.

59. Bomber Command Diary, Aug 1944, 7.

60. G.B. Lloyd, letter to Roy Carter's mother, 16 Apr 1946, at <http://www.airforce.ca/wwii/ALPHA-CA.html>, 67.

61. Award effective 13 June 1946 as per *London Gazette* of that date and AFRO 726/46, 26 July 1946, at <http://www.airforce.ca/wwii/ALPHA-CA.html>, 67.

62. Ed Carter-Edwards, "Canadians Who Served with the Halifax Bomber Recollections," Trenton, Ontario: Halifax Memorial, RCAF Museum. (Hereafter "Halifax Bomber Recollections")

63. "A History of the Air Force—World War II," at <http://www.achq.dnd.ca/handbook/hist2d.htm>, 9, accessed 1 June 1998.

64. Award effective 2 July 1946 as per *London Gazette* of that date and AFRO 781/46, 9 Aug 1946, at <http://www.airforce.ca/wwii/ALPHA-WA.TWO.html>, 16–17.

65. A.D. Dennis, "Halifax Bomber Recollections."

66. Greenhous et al, *Crucible of War*, 565.

67. Greenhous and Halliday, *Canada's Air Forces*, 100.

68. Ibid.

69. On 31 Dec 1943 there were 21,916 aircrew, 23,459 groundcrew and 895 members of the RCAF Women's Division within a total of 46,270 RCAF Personnel Overseas. One year later, on 31 Dec 1944, those numbers would reach the wartime high for the RCAF presence in Britain. The highest total for aircrew, 28,215, was actually recorded on 25 Sep 1944. Greenhous et al, *Crucible of War*, 48.

70. DFC awarded 1 Dec, as per *London Gazette*, 8 Dec 1944, and AFRO 337/45, 23 Feb 1945, at <http://www.airforce.ca/wwii/ALPHA-BO.html>.

71. John R. "Jack" Bower-Binns, "Halifax Bomber Recollections."

72. Merrill R. Burnett, letter to author, 7 Sep 2001.

73. Roger Coulombe, letter to author, 23 Oct 2000.

74. Hastings, *Bomber Command*, 215.

75. Readers should note that the author has been unable to verify Mr. Hastings's "notorious for indifference" categorical comment with any other reputable source, nor that 6 Group behavior was in any measurable way different from other Groups under the direction of a Master Bomber. Ibid, 163.

76. As quoted in ibid, 215.

77. Harvey, *Boys, Bombs, and Brussels Sprouts*, 39.

78. However, a significant number of senior RAF officers still did disparagingly refer to the men from the Dominions as "Colonials;" a term which had been out of vogue since British Prime Minister Joseph Chamberlain's Imperial Conference of 1897, marking the Diamond Jubilee of Queen Victoria's 60th year on the throne. At this conference, Chamberlain proposed the idea of a Commonwealth or Imperial Federation, with Britain at the helm of like-minded nations, who had now graduated from being "Colonials" to "Imperials."

79. Peden, letter to author, 25 Jan 2001.

80. Charles P. Symonds and Denis J. Williams, *Psychological Disorders in Flying Personnel of the Royal Air Force* (London: His Majesty's Stationery Office, 1947), 53.

81. MGen (ret'd) Lloyd C. Morrison, letter to author, 21 Feb 2001.

82. Sheridan, letter to author, 24 Oct 2000.

83. Northrup, letter to author, 18 Aug 2000.

84. Coulombe, letter to author, 23 Oct 2000.

85. Howard B. Ripstein, letter to author, 21 Nov 2000.

86. Northrup, letter to author, 18 Aug 2000.

87. Ron Cassels, *Ghost Squadron* (Winnipeg: Ardenlea Publications, 1991), 48.

88. More than 47,000 war brides of servicemen overseas, the vast majority of them from Britain, emigrated to Canada after the war. Jack Granatstein and Desmond Morton, *A Nation Forged in Fire* (Toronto: Lester & Orpen Dennys, 1989), 263.

89. Sid Philp, letter to author, 16 Aug 2000, previously sent to Mr. David Brown, 21 Jan 1994.

90. Halpenny, *Action Stations*, 3.

91. Greenhous et al, *Crucible of War*, 226.

92. J. Douglas Harvey, *The Tumbling Mirth—Remembering the Air Force* (Toronto: McClelland and Stewart, 1983), 68.

93. Ripstein, letter to author, 21 Nov 2000.

94. Coulombe, letter to author, 23 Oct 2000.

95. Philp, letter to author, 16 Aug 2000, previously sent to Mr. David Brown, 21 Jan 1994.

96. Paterson, letter to author, 7 Nov 2001.

97. Greenhous et al, *Crucible of War*, 526.

98. Wells, *Courage and Air Warfare*, 125.

99. Overy, *Bomber Command*, 149.

100. Terraine, *Right of the Line*, 522.

101. Ibid, 523.

102. As the war entered its closing months during the post-Overlord period, some adverse war news, as it affected Bomber Command, appears to have been deliberately withheld from the British public.

103. McDonald, letter to author, 25 Aug 2000, previously sent to Michael M. LeBlanc, 13 June 1994. M. Middlebrook and C. Everitt released *The Bomber Command War Diaries: An Operational Reference Book*, in London in 1985.

104. At the same time, the Pathfinders legislated a continuous tour of 45 sorties. Terraine, *Right of the Line*, 527. Since almost all PFF crews had previous operational experience, the number of sorties flown prior to joining 8 Group was supposed to have been applied to the required total. That said, this policy does not appear to have been applied with any degree of consistency. Of interest, it was generally felt that PFF faced the highest loss rates of all. However, that was not always the case. John Lewis, distinguished Canadian navigator veteran of PFF recalls: "Between 18 November 1943, my first op with 405 [Squadron], and 19 May 1944, my 24th, the squadron sent out 311 Lancs and lost 11, a rate of 3.53 percent. Bomber Command, during the same period, detailed 13,313 aircraft, lost 749, a rate of 5.62 percent." John Lewis quoted in Nyznik, "Pathfinder," 10.

105. A very important caveat to this policy was that the thirty-sortie first tour requirement could be waived by group and squadron commanders if they were satisfied that the individuals involved had carried out their duties satisfactorily and were in need of a rest from operations. Terraine, *Right of the Line*, 523.

106. In the words of one one combat veteran, a PFF group captain, "The battering we received over the North German Plain cost us more than a thousand aircraft and between seven and eight thousand lives. Berlin wasn't worth it." Greenhous et al, *Crucible of War*, 785. This is hyperbole, although only in a sense. In the course of the nineteen dedicated raids against "Whitebait", the Command code-name for Berlin, during the period 23 Aug 1943 to 31 March 1944, Bomber Command would lose 625 aircraft and crews, and at least a further 80 would crash in Britain with heavy loss of life. However, during the same period, the Command carried out 36 major raids against other important German industrial targets. In all, 1578 aircraft were posted missing from

the 55 cumulative raids of the period, for a loss rate of 5 percent, which was also the equivalent of *twice* the front line strength of Bomber Command at the time. Martin Middlebrook, "Bomber Command's War", pt 3 in *Flypast*, 207 (Oct 1998), 50–51.

107. Symonds and Williams, *Psychological Disorders*, 44, 45, 49.
108. D. Stafford-Clark, "Morale and Flying Experience", originally published in the *Journal of Mental Science*, reprinted in Alan W. Mitchell, "Bomber Crews Were Men with a High Quality of Courage", in *Gaggle and Stream* (Aug 2002), 8.
109. Don Charlwood, *No Moon Tonight* (Sydney: Goodall, 1990), 77.
110. Stafford-Clark, in Mitchell, "Bomber Crews," 7.
111. Halpenny, *Action Stations*, 49.
112. Wells, *Courage and Air Warfare*, 47.
113. Caidin, *Black Thursday*, 87.
114. Symonds and Williams, *Psychological Disorders.*,61.
115. Philp, letter to author, 29 Aug 2000.
116. Philp, letter to author, 16 Aug 2000.
117. Peden, letter to author, 7 Feb 2001.
118. Ibid.
119. Ibid.
120. The route illumination practice would re-appear later, in very distinctive and specialized formats, as the nightly operations assumed more and more complexity, including diversion or "spoof" raids. Also, specialty flares or markers were used to designate when to initiate or cease specialty operations, such as the use of *Window*.
121. Peden, letter to author, 7 Feb 2001.
122. Sutherland, "Warriors of the Night," pt 1.
123. Philp, letter to author, 16 Aug 2000.
124. Stafford-Clark, in Mitchell, "Bomber Crews," 7. This was certainly true for some peak periods of the bomber offensive. However, generally speaking, as we shall see, the crews would fare much better during the last calendar year of the war.
125. Wells, *Courage and Air Warfare*, 77.
126. Ibid.
127. English, *Cream of the Crop*, 81.
128. Quoted in ibid, 84.
129. Quoted in ibid, 88.
130. John Lewis, quoted in Nyznik, "Pathfinder!", 9.
131. Ripstein, letter to author, 21 Nov 2000.
132. Jim McInerney, quoted in Spencer Dunmore & William Carter, *Reap the Whirlwind* (Toronto: McClelland and Stewart, 1991), 256.
133. Coulombe, letter to author, 23 Oct 2000.
134. Sheridan, letter to author, 24 Oct 2000.
135. Dunmore and Carter, *Reap the Whirlwind*, 261.
136. Northrup, letter to author, 18 Aug 2000. Northrup's extremely rare night encounter with a German rocket fighter is unusual, in that the Me 163 Komet was armed with 30 mm cannons, not rockets. A battery of upwards-firing 50 mm mortar shells triggered by proximity to an enemy bomber through activation of photo-electric cells, the so-called *Jägerfaust* system, was experimentally fitted late in the war, but was only thought to have been used once in combat, and that was in daylight. All the *Komet* pilot had to do was fly his aircraft, either head-on or tail-on, under the enemy bomber within about 100 metres of its altitude. This approach technique does not match Northrup's description of the attack, with its forward-firing ordnance. It is possible that what Jim Northrup saw was tracer rounds from the Messerschmitt's 30 mm cannons, which were very slow firing weapons. It is also possible that he saw a night fighter version of the Me 262 *Schwalbe*, which was also experimentally fitted with various mortars and rockets, but this scenario is highly unlikely. Overall, the "tracer theory" is the most logical, given the known facts. There were certainly Me 163s stationed in the area of Germany Northrup would have been overflying on this operation according to Jeffrey Ethell & Alfred Price, *The German Jets in Combat* (London: Jane's, 1979), 134.
137. English, *Cream of the Crop*, 128.
138. Ibid.
139. Noel Ogilvie, "The RCAF Years," video interview at the RCAF Museum, Trenton, Ontario, 1985. Noel Ogilvie,

one of the tallest pilots in the RCAF at 6' 4" in height, was awarded a Mention-in-Despatches for his gallant efforts as a fighter pilot in the defence of Malta. Award effective 1 January 1943 as per *London Gazette* of that date and AFRO 232/43, dated 12 February 1943, at <http://www.airforce.ca/wwii/ALPHA-O.htm>, 18.

140. Peden, *A Thousand Shall Fall*, 416.
141. Greenhous et al, *Crucible of War*, 787.
142. Amazingly enough, several Canadian airmen would actually complete four operational tours in Bomber Command. Two known cases were Glenmore Ellwood, from Portage la Prairie, Manitoba, and James R. Dow, from Winnipeg. Both men attained the wartime rank of squadron leader and both were awarded the DSO as well as the DFC and Bar. Ellwood served as a Pathfinder with 405 Squadron where he flew on seven of the Berlin raids, then later became Johnnie Fauquier's navigator on 617 Squadron. He passed away in 1999. *Airforce*, 23, 2 (Summer 1999), 59. James Dow was, among other wartime postings, a bomb aimer with 635 Squadron, and he was in sustained action from late 1941 until late 1944. He passed away in 2000. <http//www.airforce.ca/wwii/ALPHA-DI.html>
143. A.R. Byers (ed.), *The Canadians at War 1939–1945* (Westmount: Reader's Digest Ass'n of Canada, 1986), 285.
144. Coulombe, letter to author, 23 Oct 2000.
145. Northrup, letter to author, 18 Aug 2000.
146. Byers (ed.), *Canadians at War*, 285. Although many 6 Group aircraft were lost after the first year of operations, the number of sorties generated was much greater thereafter, and the concomitant loss rate much less.
147. Ibid.
148. Navigation lights to this point had been normally turned on for take-off, then extinguished no later than crossing the English coast outbound and left extinguished until established for landing on recovery. Under McEwen's tenure, the requirement for "lights out" operations became significantly broader. Ripstein, letter to author, 21 Nov 2000.
149. Philip Ardery, *Bomber Pilot* (Lexington: University Press of Kentucky, 1978), 93.
150. Hastings, *Bomber Command*, 221.
151. Peden, *A Thousand Shall Fall*, 427.
152. Milberry, *Canada's Air Force*, 221.
153. Ibid, 90.
154. Overy, *Bomber Command*, 174.
155. Ibid.
156. Milberry, *Canada's Air Force*, 93–95.
157. Quoted in ibid, 225. Readers should note that the Immediate Awards were submitted for particularly striking or *singular* acts of heroism, whereas the Non-Immediate Awards were granted for *conspicuous gallantry*, which was interpreted to encompass longer-term, sustained courage or particularly evident devotion to duty in an operational sense. Ibid, 223.
158. Of note, a total of 9100 formal Commonwealth awards were presented to members of the RCAF during the Second World War, ranging from two Victoria Crosses (three, counting Ian Bazalgette as Canadian) and four George Crosses, to 2335 Mentions-in-Despatches and 302 Commendations. Halliday, "Mysteries of Gongs," 41.
159. At that time, there were 61,973 RCAF personnel overseas, numbering 25,678 aircrew, 34,825 groundcrew and 1470 members of the Women's Division. Greenhous et al, *Crucible of War*, Table 1, RCAF Personnel Overseas 1941–1945, 48.
160. Sir Arthur Harris, quoted in Milberry, *Canada's Air Force*, 125. In fairness, the vast majority of these accidental casualties, 8090 all told, were aircrew. Of this number, 1679 were RCAF. Of Bomber Command's ground staff, an additional 530 were killed, 759 wounded, and 1040 died from other causes. Of RCAF ground staff within the Command, 26 were killed, 25 wounded, and 35 died from other causes. Overy, *Bomber Command*, 204–205.
161. Russ Hubley, quoted in Buzz Bourdon, "The Survivors," *Airforce*, 26, 2 (Summer 2002), 46.
162. Air Commodore J.E. Fauquier, quoted in Breadner to Power, 7 July 1944, Power Papers, Queen's University, Box 64, File 1083, in Brereton Greenhous et al, *Crucible of War*, 765 and fn 15.
163. *London Gazette* citations, Jan 1945 and 8 June 1944, in Greenhous et al, *Crucible of War*, 765 and fns 16–17.

CHAPTER SIX

1. Searby, *Bomber Battle for Berlin*, 11.
2. Middlebrook, "Bomber Command," pt 3 *Flypast*, No. 207 (Oct 1998), 50.

3. Sir Arthur Harris, quoted in Webster and Frankland, *Strategic Bomber Offensive* vol 2, 190.

4. David Clay Large, *Berlin* (New York, Basic Books, 2000), 326.

5. The twenty-two cities specified in the Pointblank directive and the sub-set offensive specifically directed against the German aircraft industry, known as Argument, were Augsburg, Berlin, Bernberg, Bremen, Brunswick, Dessau, Eisenach, Frankfurt, Friedrichshafen, Gotha, Hamburg, Hannover, Kassel, Leipzig, Munich, Oschersleben, Paris, Regensburg, Schweinfurt, Stuttgart, Warnemünde and Wiener-Neustadt. All these cities either produced aircraft components, had aircraft assembly plants, or were centres for ball-bearing production. Greenhous et al, *Crucible of War*, 729.

6. Ibid, 711.

7. Large, *Berlin*, 344.

8. Coulombe, letter to author, 23 Oct 2000.

9. Similar bunkers were planned for Bremen, but they were never completed to match the grandeur of the others. Lesser structures in the same vein were also completed elsewhere, particularly in Atlantic Wall positions and also in some of the coastal fortresses. J.E. Kaufmann & H.W. Kaufmann, *Fortress Third Reich* (Cambridge, Massachusetts: Da Capo Press, 2003), 153–155.

10. Large, *Berlin*, 327.

11. Terraine, *Right of the Line*, 546.

12. Held and Nauroth, *Defense of the Reich*, 183.

13. Greenhous et al, *Crucible of War*, 703.

14. Bill Swetman, "The Avro Lancaster," in Ethell (ed.), *Great Book of World War II Airplanes*, 396.

15. Specialty units, known as *Beleuchtergruppen*, flying stripped and relatively fast Bf 110s, were formed to drop the flares into the target area and its approaches and exits. Held and Nauroth, *Defense of the Reich*, 39.

16. Tolliver and Constable, *Fighter Aces of the Luftwaffe,* 209.

17. Greenhous et al, *Crucible of War*, 705.

18. Held and Nauroth, *Defense of the Reich*, 191.

19. Rudolf Thun, Nachtjager–Oblt. Rudolf Thun, at <wysiwyg://30/http://www.geocities.com/Cape Canaveral/2072/thun.html>, 2.

20. Bob Braham, *Scramble* (London: Frederick Muller, 1961),176.

21. Christopher Shores and Clive Williams, *Aces High—A Tribute to the Most Notable Fighter Pilots of the British and Commonwealth Forces in WWII* (London: Grub Street, 1994), 146.

22. The FN 20, aside from its four .303-inch-gun unsatisfactory firepower, had practically no visibility, because of the exceptionally heavy turret framing. Harris, in his frustration, at one point observed that the only thing that could have been worse, particularly in a downward view, would have been to have built "the whole turret solid." Greenhous et al, *Crucible of War*, 684.

23. Ibid, 754.

24. Handley Page Halifax Armament, at <http://members.tripod.co.uk/ballance/tech/guns.htm> 5, and *The Gatefold Book of World War II Warplanes* (London: Brown/Orbis,1995), Item 14.

25. <http://members.tripod.co.uk/ballance/tech/guns.htm>, 4.

26. Greenhous et al, *Crucible of War*, 752–753.

27. <http://members.tripod.co.uk/ballance/tech/guns.htm>, 7.

28. Swetman, "Avro Lancaster," 396, and *Gatefold Book*, Item 1.

29. Greenhous et al, *Crucible of War*, 758.

30. Swetman, "Avro Lancaster," 409.

31. Dick Bell, letter to author, 22 Sep 2000.

32. Merrill Burnett, letter to author, 7 Sep 2001.

33. During the Magdeburg raid of 21/22 January, a damaged returning Lancaster from an RAF squadron provided the first definitive evidence that the Germans had equipped their night fighters with upward-firing weapons. Bomber Command Intelligence Report No. 13/44, 29 January 1944, in Greenhous et al, *Crucible of War*, 763.

34. Lloyd C. Morrison, interview with author, 8 March 2001.

35. Peter Spoden, "Warriors of the Night," pt 1.

36. *Oblt* (Dr.Ing.) Rudolf E. Thun, former *Staffelkapitan* (squadron commander) of 9/NJ6, in his description of an attack on a bomber in mid-1944 said, "Then a salvo from *Schräge Musik* into the left engines to give the crew a chance to get out—*Schräge Musik* shoots with pinpoint accuracy." <wysiwyg://30/http://www.geocities.com/CapeCanaveral/2072/thun.html>, 4

37. Rolland St. Jacques, letter to author, 23 Feb 2001.

38. Coulombe, letter to author, 23 Oct 2000.

39. Hastings, *Bomber Command*, 159.

40. Raymond Lee, *The London Observer*, quoted in Hastings, *Bomber Command*, 160.

41. St. Jacques, letter to author, 23 Feb 2001.

42. There was not universal applicability in the touchy subject of bodily functions during operations in the Halifax. As if life was not difficult enough "ex-Halifax crewmen relate how, when the pilot used his sanitary relief tube, poor aim or turbulence resulted in a shower of unwelcome fluid on their heads. If only the wireless operator was affected, the others laughed it off as 'local bad weather,' but when the radios fused, it was no joke." Harry Fraser-Mitchell, "Halifax Construction," in *Aeroplane* (May 2003), 60. Each aircraft type had a specific start sequence for its Four engines, and Geoff Warnes is referring to the Hercules engine-powered Halifax Mark III. The main reason was that most aircraft types had a master engine, or one which would power a majority of the aircraft's auxiliary systems, and that engine would normally be brought on line first. For example, the start sequence on Merlin engine-powered Lancasters was as follows: starboard inner, starboard outer, port inner, port outer. Geoff Marlow, recollections of bombing missions over Germany, courtesy of Dick Wynne, letter to author, 15 Nov 2000.

43. Greenhous et al, *Crucible of War*, 699.

44. SASO 6 Group to all bases and stations, 3 Aug 1943, in DHist File 181.005 (D70).

45. Bomber Command 1939–1945 Official Campaign Diary, 17/18 Aug 1943, at <http://www.raf.mod.uk/bombercommand/diary/aug43.html>, 4.

46. Spoden in "Warriors of the Night," pt 3.

47. Tolliver and Constable, *Fighter Aces of the Luftwaffe*, 411.

48. Friedrich-Karl Müller, quoted in Martin Middlebrook, *The Peenemünde Raid—The Night of 17–18 August 1943* (London: Penguin, 1982), 160.

49. Paul Zörner, quoted in Middlebrook, *Peenemünde Raid*, 164.

50. Ibid, 162.

51. Bomber Command Diary, 17/18 Aug 1943, 4.

52. Greenhous et al, *Crucible of War*, 701.

53. Martin Middlebrook and Chris Everett, *The Bomber Command War Diaries* (London: Viking, 1985), 422.

54. Motiuk, *Thunderbirds at War*, 122

55. The Ruhr Express would go on to compile a significant operational history, successfully completing 48 raids in service with 405 Squadron and later 419 Squadron. It was totally destroyed on its 49th operation, when it overshot the runway on landing. However, all members of its crew escaped safely.

56. Greenhous et al, *Crucible of War*, 642, 757–758.

57. Ibid, 705–706.

58. Middlebrook, *Berlin Raids*, 49–51. Rudolf Frank was eventually commissioned as a Leutnant and ended the war decorated with the Knights Cross and Oak Leaves, along with 45 confirmed victories. Tolliver and Constable, *Fighter Aces of the Luftwaffe*, 405.

59. Actually, the last Wellington raid of the war against a target in Germany was conducted by aircraft from 300 (Polish) and 432 (Canadian) Squadrons against Hannover on the night of 8/9 Oct 1943, as part of a larger force of 504 aircraft. All 26 participating "Wimpys" returned without loss. Bomber Command Diary, 8/9 Oct 1943, 2.

60. Greenhous et al, *Crucible of War*, 706, and Bomber Command Diary, 23/24 Aug 1943, 5.

61. Large, *Berlin*, 346.

62. Greenhous et al, *Crucible of War*, 708.

63. The Germans almost invariably tended to attack the aircraft in the lower levels of the bomber stream. In order to help provide a measure of mutual support to these unfortunates, which included both the Stirlings and the Halifax II/Vs, the abler Lancasters were occasionally ordered to transit and attack at the lower levels. However, once the fighter attacks began, the Lancasters would often climb to the relative sanctuary of the higher altitudes.

64. Bomber Command Diary, 31 Aug/1Sep 1943, 6; Greenhous et al, *Crucible of War*, 709. The designated *Aufnahmegaue* or evacuee receiving areas were in East Prussia, Mark Brandenburg, and the Wartheland. Over the period extending from the summer of 1943 until January 1945, the last time for which reliable records exist, the number of *registered* inhabitants in Berlin had dropped from approximately 3,665,000 to 2,846,000, with many more *unregistered* forced labourers, displaced persons, and souls in hiding. Also, many vital industries were transferred out of the metropolis, " including parts of the giant Siemens operation, which were

dispersed around the country. This proved to be the beginning of the end of Berlin's dominant place in German heavy manufacturing." Large, *Berlin*, 347. Naturally, all these relocations and dispersals created tremendous additional strains on already overtasked transportation, provisioning, communications and manpower segments of the economy.

65. Bomber Command Diary, 3/4 Sep 1943, 1.

66. Greenhous et al, *Crucible of War*, 710–711.

67. David S. Smart, " Halifax Bomber Recollections."

68. *London Gazette*, 15 Oct 1943, and AFRO 2610/43 17 Dec 1943, at <http://www.airforce.ca/wwii/ALPHA-SM.1.html>.

69. Robert E. Mackett recollections, at <http://www.torontoaircrew.com/Bomber_Pilots/Mackett_4/mackett_4.html>.

70. Peden, *A Thousand Shall Fall*, 317.

71. *London Gazette* 30 June 1944, and AFRO 1861/44 25 Aug 1944, at <http://www.airforce.ca/wwii/ALPHA-M.MAC.html>.

72. Middlebrook, "Bomber Command's War," 51.

73. Bomber Command Diary, 22/23 Oct 1943, 4.

74. CGM awarded to Cardy as per *London Gazette*, 9 Nov 1943 and AFRO 358/44, 18 Feb 1944, at <http://www.airforce.ca.wwii/ALPHA-CA.html>, 48.

75. Bomber Command Diary, 18/19 Nov 1943, 3.

76. Number 408 "Goose" Squadron also sent fifteen Lancaster IIs, to Berlin, making the total 6 Group participation on the raid 29 aircraft. Greenhous et al, *Crucible of War*, 735.

77. Motiuk, *Thunderbirds at War*, 154.

78. An eighth 6 Group Halifax ditched in the Channel on the return trip. Greenhous et al, *Crucible of War*, 735–736.

79. Ibid, 736.

80. Coulombe, letter to author, 23 Oct 2000.

81. Greenhous et al, *Crucible of War*, 736.

82. Ibid.

83. Middlebrook and Everitt, *Bomber Command War Diaries*, 446.

84. Bomber Command Diary, 22/23 Nov 1943, 4.

85. Left in its damaged state as a memorial to the war, the *Kaiser-Wilhelm Gedächtniskirche*, now half-ruined, half-restored, is a major Berlin tourist attraction. It has become an enduring symbol of the city. In 1959, a modern octagonal church was built in front of the ruined tower, as well as an imposing spire to its left. Berliners call the ruined tower the "rotten (hollow) tooth," and the new bell tower and octagonal church the "powder box and lipstick." Nearby is the 86-metre high office tower of the Europa Center, built on the bombed-out site of the old Romanisches Café, adorned with the famous Mercedes star. The whole complex was designed by architect Egon Eirmann to represent "the new rising from the old." The ruin and this modern structure are often photographed together. Large, *Berlin*, 470–471.

86. Bomber Command Diary, 22/23 Nov 1943, 4; Greenhous et al, *Crucible of War*, 737–738.

87. Greenhous et al, *Crucible of War*, 738.

88. Bomber Command Diary, 26/27 Nov 1943, 5.

89. Greenhous et al, *Crucible of War*, 745.

90. Coulombe, letter to author, 23 Oct 2000.

91. Motiuk, *Thunderbirds at War*, 160.

92. Greenhous et al, *Crucible of War*, 737–38, 745.

93. Granatstein and Morton, *A Nation Forged in Fire*, 164–185.

94. Large, *Berlin*, 330.

95. Ibid, 331.

96. For example, the *Flaksender* station at Deelen near Arnheim, the headquarters of *Jagddivision 3*, was known as *Primadonna*. The station would normally initiate their transmissions with a generic air raid warning for a large area or region, such as South Westphalia, and give a rough course for the bombers. More specific information, such as the believed intended target, would then follow. *Flaksender Domino*, the headquarters for *Flakdivision 22* at Dortmund, might transmit something like, "Achtung! Achtung! Viele Kuriere von Konrad-Richard 9 nach Ludwig-Paula 8." (Attention! Attention! Many bombers transiting from sector KR 9 to sector LP 8.") This information was followed by a course and other details as appropriate. From reference maps previously constructed,

citizens could individually plot the flight paths of the approaching bombers. Of interest, *Luftgefahr 15* was the wartime *Flaksender* code for the Berlin region—a code word that was being frequently heard around this time. After a fashion, this unique network provided the citizens of the Reich a certain peace of mind. Primadonna meldet . . . Luftwarndienst-Seite1, at <wysiwyg://22/http:expage.com/primadonnameldet>, 1–4.

97. During the early war years, the bunkers built in residential districts were often constructed to blend in with their surroundings, bomb-proof concrete slabs being covered with tile roofs and stone or brick veneers. This practice waned as the war progressed. By 1945, the American Strategic Bombing Survey concluded that enough shelters had been built in the German cities to adequately protect only about 15 percent of the population, and up to 75 percent, if the shelters were ridiculously overcrowded. Kaufmann & Kaufmann, *Fortress Third Reich*, 152.

98. Antony Beevor, *The Fall of Berlin 1945* (New York: Viking, 2002), 3.

99. Ibid, 2.

100. Ibid, 3.

101. Large, *Berlin*, 328.

102. Motiuk, *Thunderbirds at War*, 151.

103. Peden, *A Thousand Shall Fall*, 351.

104. Greenhous et al, *Crucible of War*, 637.

105. The maximum range, standard tankage, for the Lancaster Marks I and III was 2450 miles, while that of the Halifax Mark III with extended span wings was 1820 miles. Harry Fraser-Mitchell, "Second to None," in *Aeroplane* (May 2003), 68–9.

106. Bomber Command Headquarters, "An Examination of the Emergency Escape Arrangements from Bomber Command Operational Aircraft," 19 May 1945, DHist File 181.003 (D4598).

107. Fraser-Mitchell, "Second to None," 69.

108. Harry Fraser-Mitchell, "From Hell, Hull and Halifax, Good Lord deliver us.,"in *Aeroplane* (May 2003), 63.

109. Jim Northrup, letter to author, 12 Sep 2000.

110. Greenhous et al, *Crucible of War*, 749, and Bomber Command Diary, 16/17 Dec 1943, 3

111. Roger Coulombe, letter to author, 23 Oct 2000.

112. Other damage inflicted included significant results along the Wilhelmstrasse. Part of Hitler's Chancellery was burned out, and the Air Ministry, the Ministry of Justice, the Ministry of Food and Agriculture, the Foreign Office, the Treasury, the Ministry of Transport and buildings belonging to the Gestapo, among others, were all damaged, some extensively. In the Tiergarten, the diplomatic and ministerial complexes were very hard hit, including the War Office building. The particular portion of this installation that housed the secret service headquarters of the three armed services was completely gutted. AFHQ, Secret bomber narrative, Dec1943, 47–9, DHist 79/444; Bomber Command ASI, "Battle of Berlin, immediate assessment of results," Jan 1944, DHist 181.003 (D154); *The Berlin Diaries 1940–1945 of Marie "Missie" Vassiltchikov* (London: np, 1987), 127, in Greenhous et al, *Crucible of War*, 749–751.

113. Large, *Berlin*, 346–347.

114. 434 Squadron, in their Halifax II/Vs, were living up to their hard luck reputation, losing three of the nine 6 Group crews on the night, in spite of the fact that they should have fared rather well in their placement in the middle of the bomber stream, in the third of five waves. Greenhous et al, *Crucible of War*, 763.

115. Ibid, 770; Toliver and Constable, *Fighter Aces of the Luftwaffe*, 401–418.

116. Wolfgang Falck, quoted in Toliver and Constable, *Fighter Aces of the Luftwaffe*, 232.

117. Held and Nauroth, *Defense of the Reich*, 152.

118. Georg von Studnitz, *While Berlin Burns 1933–1945* (Englewood Cliffs, NJ: np, 1963), 145.

119. Rudolf Thun, at <wysiwyg://30/http://www.geocities.com/CapeCanaveral/2072/thun.html>, 3.

120. Bomber Command Diary, 21/22 Jan 1944, 4.

121. Middlebrook and Everitt, *Bomber Command War Diaries*, 447.

122. Jack E. Dickenson, "Halifax Bomber Recollections"

123. Henry Probert, *Bomber Harris—His Life and Times* (Toronto: Stoddart, 2001), 258.

124. Portal to Harris, 3 Jan 1944, Portal Papers, DHist 87/89, Folder 10B (1944), in Greenhous et al, *Crucible of War*, 766.

125. Portal to Harris, 14 Jan 1944, in PRO Air 2/4477.

126. Air Ministry OZ 332 20th Jan 1944 TOO 201700Z, an onward transmission from Chiefs of Staff No. COS (W) 1081stated to the CAS and others: "We are convinced the ultimate objective of the POINTBLANK plan should remain as stated in the Casablanca directive and that first priority should continue to be given to the attack on

the G.A.F. fighter forces and the industry on which they depend. The reduction in the German fighter strength is in fact an essential prerequisite to progress towards the ultimate objective of the POINTBLANK plan and is a vital requirement in creating the conditions necessary for OVERLORD." In PRO Premier 3/12, 114A.

127. Portal to Harris, 14, 27 and 28 Jan 1944, in PRO Air 2/4477; AHB Bomber Command Narrative, V, 134ff, DHist 86/286, in Greenhous et al, *Crucible of War*, 766.

128. Ibid, 767.

129. Extensive research has been unable to verify this team attack concept being used at night by the Germans at this time. Rolland St. Jacques, letters to author, 12 Jan and 23 Feb 2001.

130. There is an intriguing mystery associated with this shoot-down. The combat loss took place close to the issuance of the notorious *Kugel Erlass* (Bullet Decree) of 4 March 1944, which secretly authorized much more Draconian measures against captured or evading Allied airmen, and tensions and animosities towards these flyers were certainly high and rising at the time. What follows is a partial transcription of a recent letter from Rolland St. Jacques to the author 8 Dec 2004.

> I had requested and received, quite a few years ago, a copy of my military service from the National Archives in Ottawa. The portion of it relating to our aircraft being shot down had a copy of an "extract from German document K.E. 7579 & Death Card—Details of crash of a 4-engine aircraft of unknown type in KARCHA, RAUSSLITZ towards 21.00 hrs on 27.1.44." Said "extract" referred only to the names of the crew members and their fate—three survivors and four fatalities. Of the four fatalities, three bodies were reported near the crash site, and a fourth one at a place called Pinewitz, which, when I looked at it on a map, is about 100 miles or so from the crash site. This fact has aroused my curiosity, for it would appear that this crew member was attempting to evade capture and escape back to England. So what were the circumstances surrounding his demise?
>
> With this in mind, I wrote to the German Consulate in Montreal, looking at the possibility of obtaining a copy of the full document in question. My request was referred to the German Embassy in Ottawa, who sent it to the WASt Service in Berlin. All this correspondence was conducted in French, except for the answer from Berlin, which was in German. Fortunately, a good Dutch friend of mine translated the letter. It appears that the documentation drawn up by said WASt Service concerning former Canadian/British POWs (and presumably casualties) was seized and taken over by a committee of Allied officers in April 1945. According to their knowledge, these documents are now with the Ministry of Defence, Bourne Avenue, Hayes/Middlesex, UB3 1Rf, Great Britain. This last address advised me that they only deal with Army personnel and submitted possible avenues for inquiries, which obviously do not deal with the type of information I am seeking. They recommended I deal with the Canadian archives, but I did so long ago in reference to a note mentioning "photo attached," Only to be told that they supplied me at the time with all the information in their possession, and even if it contains a note to the effect "photo attached," said photo is not in the file. This would appear to be "the end of the line."

While it might be convenient to dismiss or trivialize these observations, attributing the 100 mile inconsistency to "the fog of war," to a reporting inaccuracy or to myriad other reasons attributable to the chaotic conditions existing in Germany at the time, a certain justification for a more sinister interpretation of these circumstances cannot be dismissed lightly. At any rate, a dollop of healthy skepticism regarding the fate of St. Jacques' fellow crew member at Pinewitz is certainly warranted. To this date, no further information has been made available to M. St. Jacques from the authorities.

131. Motiuk, *Thunderbirds at War*, 187.

132. After several operations on his leg in Britain and then later in Canada, Clint Seeley was eventually returned to the Manning Depot in Toronto, from where he was discharged on 16 June 1945. W.J. Clinton Seeley, letter to author, 21 Sep 2003.

133. CGM award effective 9 Feb 1944 as per *London Gazette*, 22 Feb 1944 and AFRO 644/44, at <http://www.airforce.ca/wwii/ALPHA-M.ME.html>,7.

134. Excerpt for recommendation to DFC, 1 Aug 1944 in PRO Air 2/8827, award effective 4 Nov 1944 as per *London Gazette*, 17 Nov 1944 and AFRO 239/45 9 Feb 1945, at <http://www.airforce.ca/wwii/ALPHA-M.ME.html>,8.

135. Motiuk, *Thunderbirds at War*, 190.

136. Bomber Command Diary, 15/16 Feb 1944, 3.

137. Air Ministry Policy Directive AMCS 171138A Feb 44, in PRO Premier 3/12, 102.

138. Greenhous et al, *Crucible of War*, 770.

139. Bomber Command Diary, 19/20 Feb 1944, 4.
140. Various references, including No 6 Group analysis of results, DHist 74/250, in Greenhous et al, *Crucible of War*, 771.
141. Ibid.
142. Bomber Command Diary, 24/25 Feb 1944, 5.
143. 405 Sqdn ORB, 24/25 Feb 1944, DHist, and AFHQ, Secret bomber narrative, Feb 1944, DHist 79/544, in Greenhous et al, *Crucible of War*, 773.
144. Speer, *Inside the Third Reich*, 286.
145. Fest, *Speer—The Final Verdict*, 166–167.
146. "Extract of Minutes of Defence Committee (Supply), 3 Jan 1944," Whitworth to Personal Sec to Sec of State, 24 Jan 1944, DBOps, "Note on operational value of the Halifax," 27 Jan 1944, "Extract Min Def Comm (Supply)
    27 Jan 1944," in PRO Air 19/352, in Greenhous et al, *Crucible of War*, 755.
147. Malcom R. "Mac" Smith, "Halifax Bomber Recollections."
148. Immediate DFM award to George Eric Hexter, effective 14 Apr 1944 as per *London Gazette* of that date and AFRO 1020/44, 12 May 1944, at <http://www.airforce.ca/wwii/ALPHA-HE.html>, 44.
149. Bomber Command Diary, 22/23 Mar 1944, 5.
150. Ibid, 6
151. Motiuk, *Thunderbirds at War*, 217.
152. Greenhous et al, *Crucible of War*, 780.
153. Bomber Command Diary, 26/27 Mar 1944, 7.
154. Coulombe, letter to author, 23 Oct 2000.
155. Ibid.
156. Martin Middlebrook, *The Nuremburg Raid* (London: Viking, 1986), 102.
157. Ibid, 155.
158. Greenhaus et al, *Crucible of War*, 782–783.
159. Bomber Command Diary, 30/31 Mar 1944, 7–8.
160. Harvey, *Boys, Bombs and Brussels Sprouts*, 187–8, 194.
161. Terraine, *Right of the Line*, 554.
162. Middlebrook and Everett, *Bomber Command War Diaries*, 446–447. A full seven 6 Group squadrons (Nos. 420, 424, 425, 429, 431, 432 and 433 Squadrons) would have converted to the Halifax III before the end of the Berlin raids, and all these units flew the new aircraft on at least some of the later operations to the Reich's capital. Middlebrook, *The Berlin Raids*, 364–366.
163. Middlebrook and Everett, *Bomber Command War Diaries*, 448–449.
164. Ibid, 450–451.
165. Middlebrook, *Berlin Raids*, 363–366.
166. Coulombe, letter to author, 23 Oct 2000.

CHAPTER SEVEN

1. H.P. Willmott, *The Second World War in the East* (London: Cassell, 1999), 155.
2. Greenhous and Halliday, *Canada's Air Forces*, 116.
3. While the effectiveness of the German night fighter force would be held down, it was never totally removed as a threat. In fact, right until the end, it was capable of delivering punishing blows on occasion. However, these isolated triumphs were the exception rather than the rule. Specifically, from January through March 1944, a bleak period for the Command, 760 aircraft had been shot down by night fighters alone on 19,573 sorties flown, a loss rate of 3.88 percent, with additional losses attributed to flak and to accidents. However, the improving trend is reflected in the follow-on statistics. From April through August 1944, 1171 Command aircraft would fall to the guns of the night fighters over 56,331 sorties (2.08 percent), while from September until year's end, 304 bombers would succumb on 27,449 sorties, for a loss rate of 1.1 percent. In 1945, from the New Year until the end of hostilities in Europe, 529 Command aircraft would fall to enemy fighters over 44,074 sorties (1.2 percent). Readers should again note, however, that the threat from flak never went away, and losses to this form of defence would occur right until the end. Readers should also note that the source being quoted here is German. A British source will be offered in the following chapter that provides an even better loss rate for 1945, since it credits the Command with flying significantly more overall sorties. Gerhard

Aders, *History of the German Night Fighter Force 1917–1945* (London: Jane's, 1979), 244.

4. Specifically, 72 percent. D'Olier et al, *US Strategic Bomb Survey*, 71.

5. Greenhous et al, *Crucible of War*, 831

6. Martin Middlebrook, "Bomber Command—The Turning Points," in *Flypast*, No. 209 (Dec 1998), 85. By April 1945, the total number of operational bombers available to the Command on a daily basis would be 1600, and by January 1945, Harris was quoting 230,000 personnel of all trades as serving in Bomber Command. Probert, *Bomber Harris*, 306.

7. Air Historical Branch, *The Rise and Fall of the German Air Force 1933–1945* (London: Army and Armour Press, 1983), 315.

8. Middlebrook, "The Turning Points," 85.

9. Aders, *German Night Fighter Force*, 166–167.

10. Sheridan, letter to author, 20 Sep 2000.

11. Northrup, letter to author, 18 Aug 2000.

12. Vic Johnson, "The Quest for 'M for Mike,' " *Airforce*, 21,4 (Winter 1998), 30.

13. John C. Turnbull, at <http://www.torontoaircrew.com/Bomber_Pilots/Turnbull_4/turnbull_4.html>, 1.

14. Burnett, letter to author, 7 Sep 2001.

15. Dick Bell, letter to author, 22 Sep 2000.

16. Peter van Geldern, Dutch historical expert on the Stirling, letter to author, 1 Dec 2000. Van Geldern also stated that the captured Mark I Stirling had a prominent nose section repair crudely accomplished with a form of foil material, and the aircraft's lower regions and underside were painted a bright yellow, conditions which should have been relatively obvious in the lighting conditions mentioned.

17. Letter Harris to Churchill, 17 May 1944, in PRO Premier 3/12, 94–95.

18. Probert, *Bomber Harris*, 259–260.

19. Ibid, 289.

20. Neillands, *Bomber War*, 315.

21. Ibid.

22. Ibid, 316.

23. The marshalling yards successfully attacked during the March trial were those in Trappes, Le Mans, Amiens, Aulnoye, Courtrai and Laon. Along with inflicting significant damage, the crew losses were minimal, as were the collateral civilian casualties in the target areas. Ibid, 290, and Bomber Command Diary, March 1944, 2–7.

24. Probert, *Bomber Harris*, 292.

25. Ibid.

26. Furthermore, only one Lancaster was lost on the Juvisy operation. That same night, 273 Lancasters and 16 Mosquitos from 1, 3 and 8 Groups conducted a concentrated attack without loss on the railway yards at Rouen, which resulted in much destruction. Such was a graphic example of Bomber Command's ever-increasing capability to mount more than one major effort per night to different targets simultaneously, which further threw the defences into disarray. Bomber Command Diary, April 1944, 3.

27. RAF Historical Branch Folders H57, 30 Apr 1944, and H59, 15 and 25 May 1944, in Probert, *Bomber Harris*, 294.

28. Ibid, 295.

29. Bill Swetman, "Avro Lancaster," in Ethell (ed.), *Great Book of World War II Airplanes*, 417–418.

30. A number of Bomber Command squadrons—617 Squadron flying specialized Lancasters, but also 9 Squadron, also flying Lancasters, and 106 Squadron equipped with Mosquitos—would become the Command's precision bombing force, "for use against small targets like the Anthéor Viaduct, the Dortmund-Ems Canal and the battleship *Tirpitz* as well as for target marking. Other groups, notably 1 Group, were developing their own target marking techniques, but Main Force operations were still led and marked by PFF squadrons, who would continue to take the lead until the end of the war." Neillands, *Bomber War*, 320.

31. Charles A, Lepine, letter to author, 14 Nov 2000. As previously mentioned, this was a much less preferred option to exiting through the forward hatch, because of the distance the forward crew members had to travel to the rear, and most importantly, the increased risk of accidental contact with the aircraft structure on the bailout, particularly the horizontal tailplane and avionics aerials. According to the Official Campaign Diary, the 244 Lancasters and 16 Mosquitos of 5 Group, including 10 Lancasters from 1 Group hit the target hard, although 9 Lancasters, 3.5 percent of the force, were lost. "The intense flak and searchlight defences did not prevent the low-flying Mosquito markers from carrying out their task properly." Leonard Cheshire was every-where over the target area in a Mosquito that night, acting both as chief marker and Master Bomber. In the

subsequent award of the VC presented to him, particular mention was made of the uncommon valour he displayed that night over Munich. The controlling he orchestrated was extremely effective, "and accurate bombing fell into the centre of the city." Bomber Command Diary, Apr 1944, 6. After a 6 July 1944 raid, during which Cheshire led 617 Squadron on the Mimoyecques V-weapon site, he was ordered out of combat by his Group Commander, Sir Ralph Cochrane. Cheshire had now completed four tours and flown 100 operations. His is the only known air VC awarded for *sustained* valour over the long, long haul, although particular mention was made of his skill and courage in pioneering and developing late war low-level target marking. He was an inspiration to so many with whom he served and commanded, including distinguished Canadian bomber airmen Reg Lane and Charles Lepine. Ibid, 3.

32. Charles A, Lepine, letter to author, 14 Nov 2000.
33. Overy, *Bomber Command*, 198–199.
34. Swetman, "Avro Lancaster," 413.
35. Bomber Command Diary, June 1944, 4.
36. Tallboy was also used to great effect on the 12 November 1944 against the battleship *Tirpitz*, once again anchored in a Norwegian fjord, but this time at Tromsö. A previous Tallboy attack against the behemoth, staged out of Russia by 617 Squadron in September when the ship was berthed in Altenfjord, only damaged it and it was subsequently repaired and moved to Tromso. Three direct Tallboy hits finished it off in November there. "The contrast between the *Tirpitz* attack and the early Bomber Command raids over the Schillig Roads and Wilhelmshaven was indescribable—they were a generation of weapons and a revolution in military electronics apart, but were separated by only five years." Swetman, "Avro Lancaster," 412.
37. Probert, *Bomber Harris*, 292. During the two months of the Transportation Plan's implementation, more than 42,000 tons were dropped by the Command on 33 of the 37 designated railway centres in France and Belgium. John D.R. Rawlings, *The History of the Royal Air Force* (Feltham,Middlesex: Temple Press, 1984), 146.
38. Ibid.
39. Byers, *Canadians at War*, 158.
40. Ibid, 163.
41. The citations for both the Distinguished Service Order and the *Croix de Guerre* are transcribed here in their entirety, courtesy of Hugh A. Halliday, 16 October 2003. Distinguished Service Order as per *Canada Gazette*, 1 Dec 1945 and CARO/6241, 3 Dec 1945. The recommendation for this award was prepared by Major-General C.M. Gubbins on 10 Sep 1945.

> This officer was parachuted into France on 28 November 1942, and was seriously injured in landing. Despite his injury he received a large number of parachute deliveries of arms and explosives and was decorated for his work up to February 1943. Throughout 1943, he undertook a large number of sabotage operations, including the destruction of an enemy troop train at Senlis in February 1943, twenty derailments between St. Quentin and Lille, damage to ten locomotives by means of abrasives in November 1943, and the destruction of eleven locomotives, an engine repair shop and other installations at Tourcoing in December. His D-Day sabotage organization was ready by the end of the year with teams equipped with explosives installed at twenty-five points on the railways in his area and groups equipped with sub-machine guns in position to attack road and rail convoys in the areas St. Quentin, Lon Guise, Bohin, Le Châtelet, Cambrai, Douai and Mauberge. He had also a group ready to cut the Paris-Lille telephone line. These groups carried out their work on or after D-Day with very great success. Major Bieler was arrested in February 1944. It has now been reported that despite the most barbarous torture by the enemy over a period extending over at least eight days, he refused resolutely to divulge the names of any of his associates, or the location of any arms dumps. Despite the intense pain he was suffering from the injury to his back, aggravated by atrocious torture designed expressly to exacerbate his injury, he faced the Gestapo with the utmost determination and courage and by his silence a British officer associated with him, his British radio operator and a considerable number of Frenchmen avoided arrest. Major Bieler was executed in the Flossenburg Camp in early September 1944.

The *Croix de Guerre avec Palme* (France), awarded as per CARO/6763, 23 Sep 1946:

> Major Bieler volunteered for missions in occupied territory, dropped by parachute in the Lille area 28 November 1942. Although severely wounded as a result of the drop performed his duties for a period of fifteen months despite suffering and in an area under the strict supervision of the Gestapo; contributed actively to the establishment of powerful gangs of saboteurs who performed numerous operations against railway and industrial installations in the area. Arrested by the Gestapo in

February 1944. Throughout his mission gave proof of the most splendid courage and perfect devotion in support of the triumph of the Allies cause and has correctly appreciated the support of the Resisting [sic] Forces.

42. Byers, *Canadians at War*, 164. St. Quentin and other French towns and villages have a "Rue du Commandant Guy" named after this great Canadian. Perhaps even more significantly, Bieler, who loved nature, now has a lake named after him on Baffin Island in the Arctic.
43. Bomber Command Diary, June 1944, 2–3.
44. Bomber Command Report on Night Operations, 5/6th June 1944. Night Raid Report No. 625, Copy No. 16 (Secret) in PRO Air. 14/3412, 13–14.
45. Peden, *A Thousand Shall Fall*, 383.
46. Bomber Command Rep on Night Ops, 6/7th June 1944. Night Raid Rep 626, Copy 16 (Secret) in PRO Air. 14/3412, 18–19.
47. Bell, letter to author, 22 Sep 2000.
48. Bomber Command Rep on Night Ops 6/7th June 1944, Night Raid Rep 626, Copy 16 (Secret) in PRO Air. 14/3412, 18.
49. Burnett, letter to author, 7 Sep 2001.
50. Award effective 22 Aug 1944 as per *London Gazette* of that date and AFRO 2274/44, 20 Oct 1944, at <http://www.airforce.ca/citations/wwii/BURNAND.htm>, 3–4. Sergeants Galarneau and Harkness also received the DFM for staying with the aircraft and their captain. The bomb-aimer, Flying Officer J.K. White, came down on land, avoided capture, and had many adventures with the French Maquis before being liberated and repatriated to Britain. The navigator, Warrant Officer D.S. Smith, also came down on land, but was quickly taken prisoner. The two men Burnett saw parachuting towards the water were the wireless operator, Warrant Officer W.G. McClelland, and the flight engineer, Sergeant S. Gilder. Gilder's body eventually washed ashore, but that of McClelland was never found. Motiuk, *Thunderbirds at War*, 269–270.
51. Russ Hubley, quoted in Bourdon, "The Survivors," 46.
52. In all, Russ Hubley completed 45 operational sorties between May 1944 and Feb 1945. Award of DFC effective 10 May 1945 as per *London Gazette*, 22 May 1945 and AFRO 1147/45, 13 July 1945, at <http://www.airforce.ca/wwii/ALPHA-HU.HY.html>.
53. Clarence B. Sutherland, "Air Gunner's Diary," *Airforce*, 22, 1 (Spring 1998), 22–24.
54. Award effective 4 Aug 1944 as per *London Gazette* of that date and AFRO 2101/44, 29 Sep 1944, at <http://www.airforce.ca/wwii/ALPHA-EM.html>, 7.
55. Rudolph Thun, at <wysiwyg://30http://www.geocities.com/CapeCanaveral/2072/thun.html>, 4.
56. Held and Nauroth, *Defense of the Reich*, 227.
57. Pat Brophy, "The RCAF Years—The Andy Mynarski Story," (video) RCAF Museum, Trenton, Ontario, 1992.
58. Bomber Command Diary, June 1944, 5.
59. In fact, Bomber Command's Night Raid Report for 12/13 June 1944 specifically noted, "The forces on both Amiens targets (Longeau and St. Roch), Cambrai and Arras all met stiff fighter opposition, mostly on the early part of the homeward routes. The Cambrai bombers, in particular, were heavily engaged from the target to Lille." However, luck ran out for the De Breyne crew even before they reached the target. Bomber Command Rep on Night Ops, 12/13th June, 1944. Night Raid Rep 632, Copy 16 (Secret) in PRO Air.14/3412, 36.
60. In the 1992 interview, Brophy stated he felt the attacking Ju 88 had not initially seen them, had probably been committed to attacking another bomber in the stream, and had probably only seen KB 726 once De Breyne commenced his precautionary corkscrew manoeuvre. Brophy, "Andy Mynarski Story; " Art De Breyne, "The RCAF Years—The Andy Mynarski Story," (video) RCAF Museum, Trenton, Ontario, 1992.
61. Brophy, "Andy Mynarski Story. "
62. Pat Brophy, quoted in Bette Page (ed.), *Mynarski's Lanc* (Erin, Ontario: Boston Mills, 1989), 57.
63. Brophy, "Andy Mynarski Story."
64. Awarded as per *London Gazette*, 11 Oct 1946, and AFRO 1042/46, 1 Nov 1946, at <http://www.airforce.ca/wwii/ALPHA-M.MU.html>, 42–43.
65. Brophy, "Andy Mynarski Story."
66. Northrup, letter to author, 29 Sep 2000.
67. Bomber Command Diary, June 1944, 6.
68. Ibid, Aug 1944, 12.
69. John Keegan, *The Second World War* (New York: Penguin, 1989), 582.
70. Terraine, *Right of the Line*, 653.

71. Reminiscences of LGen (ret'd) Chester Hull, interview at Royal Military College of Canada, Kingston, Ontario, 06 April 2001.
72. Bomber CommandDiary, June 1944, 8.
73. Marion, 425 *Alouette*, 21.
74. Award effective 22 Aug 1944 as per *London Gazette* of same date and AFRO 2274/44, 20 Oct 1944, at <http://www.airforce.ca.wwii/ALPHA-UV.html>.
75. Prime Minister's Minute No. D.217/4 to Cabinet Chiefs of Staff, dealing with gas only, and referenced at cover note to Chiefs of Staff Minute to Prime Minister, COS 1126/4, 5 July 1944, in PRO Premier 3/12, 81–83.
76. R.V. Jones, letter to *Daily Telegraph*, 11 June 1981, and Lord Tedder's Memoirs, 582, quoted in Terraine, *Right of the Line*, 652–653.
77. War Cabinet Conclusions, Minute 4, 3 July 1944, in PRO Premier 3/12, 92.
78. Note by Air Staff, "Crossbow—Consideration of Retaliation," in PRO Premier 3/12, 85–89.
79. Reminiscences of General Hull, 16 Apr 2001.
80. The Ross GC was one of only four ever awarded to Canadian servicemen, and the only one not done so posthumously. The remaining three were also awarded to members of the RCAF during the Second World War. Award effective 27 Oct 1944 as per *London Gazette* of that date and AFRO 293/45, 16 Feb 1945, at <http://www.airforce.ca.wwii/ALPHA-RO.2.html>, 25.
81. Marion, 425 *Alouette*, 21.
82. This gallantry OBE had been originally recommended as a Distinguished Service Order. Award effective 8 June 1944 as per *London Gazette* of that date and AFRO 1729/44, 11 Aug 1944, at <http://www.airfofce.ca.wwii/ALPHA-RO.2.html>, 25. According to Larry Milberry and Hugh Halliday, Ross was "a solid pre-war RCAF type who forged into hot action whenever the opportunity arose." Larry Milberry, *Canada's Air Force—At War and Peace*, vol 2 (Toronto: CANAV, 2000), 223.
83. Award effective 13 June 1946 as per *Canada Gazette* of that date and AFRO 660/46, 5 July 1946, at <http://www.airforce.ca.wwii/ALPHA-RO.2.html>, 26–27.
84. Reminiscences of General Hull, 16 Apr 2001.
85. Philp, letter to author, 16 Aug 2000.
86. Bomber Command Diary, Aug 1944, 7.
87. William Johnston, " Halifax Bomber Recollections."
88. Bomber Command Diary, Aug 1944, 2.
89. Award effective 17 Aug 1945 as per *London Gazette* of that date, at <http://www.airforce.ca/canraf/CANRAF.A-D.html>,23–24.
90. Milberry, *Canada's Air Force*, 93.
91. Bomber Command Diary, Aug 1944, 10–11.
92. Award effective 24 Oct 1944 as per *London Gazette* of that date and AFRO 239/45, 9 Feb 1945, at <http://www.airforce.ca/wwii/ALPHA-M.MAR.html>, 69.
93. Award effective 8 Sep 1945 as per *London Gazette*,25 Sep 1945 and AFRO 1768/45, 23 Nov 1945, at <http://www.airforce.ca/wwii/ALPHA-M.Mar.html>, 69.
94. Middlebrook, "Turning Points," 86.
95. Webster and Frankland, *Strategic Bomber Offensive* vol 4, 172, as quoted in Terraine, *Right of the Line*, 672.
96. Webster and Frankland, *Strategic Bomber Offensive* vol 3, 71, in ibid.
97. Terraine, *Right of the Line*, 673.
98. Probert, *Bomber Harris*, 306.
99. Bomber Command Rep on Night Ops, 16/17th June 1944, Night Raid Rep 636, Copy 16 (Secret) in PRO Air.14/3412, 51.
100. Bomber Command Diary, June 1944, 8.
101. Motiuk, *Thunderbirds at War*, 279.
102. *Oblt* Erich Lippert of 10/NJG 3 claimed he destroyed a four-engine aircraft at 0140 hours at the *Kürfurst* beacon at an interception altitude of 4700 meters or 15,420 feet. In all likelihood, his Ju 88 crew was the one responsible for the ultimate fate of LK 801 and Clarence Sonderstrom. Alan Sonderstrom, "Night Raid on Happy Valley," *Airforce*, 27,1 (Spring 2003), 42–46.
103. Ibid, 47.
104. Letters Harris to Churchill and Churchill to Harris, 30 Sep 1944, in PRO Premier 3/12, 63, as quoted in Probert, *Bomber Harris*, 305.
105. Ibid, 307.

106. Various official British and American sources, including W.F. Craven and J.L. Cate, *The Army Air Forces in World War II*, vol 3, 670, cited at ibid.

107. Bomber Command Diary, Oct 1944, 3.

108. Ibid, 7.

109. Greenhous and Halliday, *Canada's Air Forces*, 118.

110. Bomber Command Diary, Oct 1944, 11.

111. Webster and Frankland, *Strategic Bomber Offensive*, vol 3, 81–94.

112. Quoted in Middlebrook, "The Turning Points," 86.

113. Probert, *Bomber Harris*, 309.

114. There is no doubt that aircraft production had actually increased since the bombing of the aircraft industries had commenced, but this was due in no small measure to the German nation going on a "Total War" footing after Stalingrad, and to the forced dispersal and decentralization of the industry. This in turn expended or diverted a tremendous amount of industrial effort just to establish and run the new facilities, forced excessive reliance on a transportation system under constant attack, demanded even more usage of precious fuel reserves, and generated many quality control problems. Therefore, these indirect effects of the aircraft industry bombing certainly have to be factored into the ledger of results obtained against costs incurred.

115. Quoted in Probert, *Bomber Harris*, 310.

116. During the four effective months of European combat in 1945 Bomber Command would drop over 181,000 tons of bombs, which constituted nearly one-fifth of the aggregate for the entire war. Considering the multiplicity of "diversions" placed on the Command, even at this late stage of the war, and that 66,482 tons (36.6 percent of the effort) was devoted to attacks on the cities, it is commendable that a full 47,510 tons or 26.2 percent of the total effort for the period was devoted to oil targets. Terraine, *Right of the Line*, 678–679.

117. Late in January, the Paymaster General, Lord Cherwell, sent an alarming letter to the Prime Minister, which shortly thereafter reached the Chief of the Air Staff in Minute form. This was undoubtedly the catalyst for the final round of disagreements between Harris and Portal with respect to the Oil Plan. The letter follows:

> Postmaster General   Great George Street, S.W.1
> PRIME MINISTER
> THE BOMBING OF OIL TARGETS
>
> Since last April German supplies of all kinds of oil have been cut to about one-third. Petrol has been cut to about one-quarter or 150,000 tons a month for the whole of Germany—less than half of the monthly expenditure of S.H.A.E.F. The Germans naturally repair their plants rapidly, so that continuous bombing pressure is needed. Conversely any increase in our effort would reduce output pro tanto.
>
> During the last three months of 1944 the Allies dropped three times as great a weight of bombs on German communications as on oil targets. Attacks on bridges or supply lines just beyond the armies are, of course, entirely justifiable. I fear, however, that the plan for long-term attrition of German transport by bombing marshalling yards and locomotive depots, is still being allowed to divert a large part of the bombing effort from more useful targets. Even a part of the weight directed against railway yards would cause a notable fall in German oil supplies. In case you should feel disposed to send it, I have attached a draft minute to C.A.S. who would, I am sure, see that its purport reached Tedder.
> 26th January 1945 (Sgd) Cherwell

Letter Cherwell to Churchill, 26 Jan 1945, in PRO Premier 3/12, 30. Presumably, the Minute was meant to be principally directed against Sir Arthur Harris for action. Readers should also bear in mind that much of the wartime intelligence related to the enemy's real-time status with respect to oil holdings was acquired through Ultra sources, the interception and decryption of the German Enigma ciphers. While Portal was privy to this high-grade source of

intelligence, for security reasons, Harris was never extended the courtesy on a routine basis, nor is there any indication that arrangements were made to have him suitably briefed beyond very isolated exposure. This is surprising when one considers how determined Portal was to convince Harris in late 1944 and onwards of the need to vigorously pursue the Oil Plan. Harris was obviously aware of the existence of Ultra, but it did not constitute a day-to-day intelligence source for him, and he knew very little about its particulars. Probert, *Bomber Harris*, 313.

118. The tone of an end-Jan reply by Portal to Prime Ministerial correspondence leaves no doubt about the priority they both assigned to oil, but also to the presence of those diversions referenced.

PRIME MINISTER

Your Minute M.128/5 of the 28th January.

2. I entirely agree with you that oil targets should not be neglected in favour of the long-term attrition of German Communications. All the Air authorities, R.A.F. and American, are agreed that oil has top priority and that the bombing of communications is only justifiable at this time either to delay the departure of divisions for Russia, to turn the scale in a critical situation in the West, or when weather conditions prevent the attack of first priority targets.

3. I have had a long talk with General Spaatz this afternoon and we are in entire agreement on the above. We also intend, as you know, to apply as much bomber effort as we can to the cities of Eastern Germany, including Berlin; but oil comes first, and we must not miss a good opportunity to hit the submarine yards.

28th January, 1945   (Portal) C.A.S.

Minute Portal to Churchill (Air Bombing Policy), 28 Jan 1945, in PRO Premier 3/12,28.

119. Terraine, *Right of the Line*, 676–677.

120. Probert, *Bomber Harris*, 312.

121. Actually, James is mistaken about the blood toll levied this night. Of the 246 Lancasters and 7 Mosquitos despatched, only five Lancasters were lost (1.98%), and the operation was considered an outstanding success. Severe damage was caused to the two Focke-Wulf factories, the Siemens Schuckert electrical works, the AG Weser shipyard and other significant war industries. In fact, the raid effectively finished off Bremen and the planners felt that it need not be attacked by Bomber Command again, in a "maximum effort" sense, for the duration. Bomber Command Diary, Oct 1944, 3.

122. Lyle James, "A Bomber Pilot's Diary," *Airforce*, 19, 3 (Fall 1995), 19–22.

123. Lancasters would fly 156,192 wartime sorties for a loss of 3677 of their number (2.35 % per operation). Bomber Command's Mosquitos flew 39,795 wartime sorties and lost 310, for a loss rate of .78 percent per operation. The Lancaster also cost three times as much to build, carried seven to eight crew members as opposed to two, and utilized four Rolls Royce Merlin engines as opposed to the Mosquito's two. Incredibly flexible, the Mosquito would serve in many roles, including pathfinder, day and night fighter, main force and special duties precision attack bomber, intruder, coastal interdiction and reconnaissance platform. By war's end, 7780 of all types had been built, including more than 1000 by de Havilland's Downsview plant in Toronto from 1942 onwards. A total of 7377 Lancasters were built during the war years, including 430 Mark X variants in Canada by Victory Aircraft at Malton. Holmes, *Battlefields of the Second World War*, 186–187.

124. Bomber Command Diary, Apr–Oct 1944.

125. Award effective 29 Aug 1944 as per *London Gazette* of that date and AFRO 2274/44, 20 Oct 1944, at <http://www.airforce.ca/wwii/ALPHA-HA.03.html>.

126. Hugh Hay was not the only exceptionally distinguished Canadian Mosquito bomber navigator. Another was Robert G. Dale, who also earned a DSO and a DFC and flew three full operational tours. Dale later specialized in Mosquito operation on extremely hazardous duties with the Meteorological Flight, who flew unarmed all over Germany gathering meteorological data for Bomber Command's nightly sojourns. In this role, Dale's experience made him fundamentally irreplaceable. As Terry Godwin recalls, "When Dale completed his 50 trips the CO just called him in, told him he was indispensable and kept him for another 50 trips. That, plus his first tour on Wellingtons in 1 Group made three tours." H. Terry Godwin, "Hugh Hay, DSO, DFC—Top Navigator?", *Airforce*, 24,1 (Spring 2000), 36–39.

127. Clifford M. Black, audiotape to author, 24 Mar 2001.

128. John Raymond Lyon, "Halifax Bomber Recollections."

129. Black, audiotape to author, 24 Mar 2001.

130. Award effective 6 Apr 1945, as per *London Gazette* of that date and AFRO 765/45, 4 May 1945, at <http://www.airforce.ca/wwii/ALPHA-MC.H.html>,37.

131. The B-17s, designated Dornier Do-288s in *Luftwaffe* service, were very popular with their German crews, who praised both their rugged construction and their handling qualities. Fortresses known to have served with KG 200 as early as 1943 included a B-17F known as *Wulfhound* and given the German *Stammkennziechen* (registration) DL + XC; another B-17F coded SJ + KY; B-17F-85-BO (42-30048) named *Flak Dancer* and another named *Touch and Go*. Several other B-17s were later added to the unit's inventory in 1944, including a Lt. John Gossage's G-model coded XR O, captured at Schleswig on 3 March 1944; the Phillis Marie, a B-17F-115-BO (42-30713), captured at Werben on 8 March, and a B-17G-10-VE (42-39974) of the 452nd Bomb Group,

731st Squadron, forced down at Vaerlose airfield in Denmark on 9 April. Several of them were eventually lost on operations or due to accidents. At least one of the combat losses is thought to have occurred as late as 3 March 1945, shot down near Frankfurt by an RAF Mosquito while believed to have been engaged in supply dropping operations to the beleagured German garrison at Brest. Roger A. Freeman, *B-17 Fortress at War* (London: Ian Allan, 1977), 178–180; Keith Heitmann, "German Flying Forts—The Story of KG200," at <http://home.carolina.rr.com/bludden/csm/buzz/96/896.htm.> 8; Andrew J. Swanger, "KG 200 Took Part in many Covert Missions against the Allies and Became the Subject of Much Postwar Speculation," at <http://www.thehistorynet.com/WorldWarII/articles/1997/09973_text.htm>,2–3.

132. Distinguished Flying Cross award effective 18 May 1945 as per *London Gazette* of that date and AFRO 1085/45, 29 June 1945. *Croix de Guerre* with Silver Star award as per *Canada Gazette*, 20 Sep 1947 and AFRO 485/47, 12 Sep 1947, at <http://www.airforce.ca/wwii/ALPHA-BL.html>,1.

133. Paterson, letter to author, 7 Nov 2001.

CHAPTER EIGHT

1. Webster and Frankland, *Strategic Bomber Offensive*, vol 3 198, Fn 1, quoted in Terraine, *Right of the Line*, 678–679.

2. Marlow, letter to author, 15 Nov 2000.

3. Probert, *Bomber Harris*, 317.

4. DHist copy of Bomber Command Ops Record Book for Jan 1945. Also, No 6 Group analysis of results, DHist file 74/250; and Questionnaire for Returned Aircrew, DHist file 181.001 (D24), Folder 7.

5. Webster and Frankland, *Strategic Bomber Offensive*, vol 4, 179–183, quoted in Greenhous et al, *Crucible of War*, 854.

6. Joe Hickson, " Halifax Bomber Recollections."

7. Group Captain Peter W. Gray, "Dresden 1945—Just Another Raid?" *Royal Air Force Airpower Review*, 4, 1 (Spring 2001), 5. Considering the train of events which was to follow at Dresden, Churchill's choice of the word "basting" was imprudent, to say the least. While he undoubtedly meant it to mean "to thrash" or "to beat soundly," it unfortunately has another connotation associated with roasting. This may well have added to the emotional denouncement of the Dresden raids over time, as well as of those who sanctioned their prosecution.

8. Quoted in Webster and Frankland, *Strategic Bomber Offensive*, vol 3, 101.

9. Sinclair to Churchill (Top Secret), 26 Jan 1945, in PRO Premier 3/12, 37.

10. Prime Minister's Personal Minute to Sinclair, 26 Jan 1945, in PRO Premier 3/12, 34.

11. Sinclair to Churchill (Top Secret), 27 Jan 1945, in PRO Premier 3/12, 33.

12. Gray, "Dresden 1945," 6.

13. Ibid.

14. Neillands, *Bomber War*, 364.

15. Multiple references, cited in Probert, *Bomber Harris*, 319, Fn 28.

16. Neillands, *Bomber War*, 352.

17. Frederick Taylor, *Dresden—Tuesday February 13, 1945* (New York: HarperCollins, 2004), 33.

18. Neillands, *Bomber War*, 352.

19. Taylor, *Dresden*, 148.

20. Ibid, 149–153.

21. Ibid, 153.

22. Ibid, 155.

23. Ibid, 161.

24. Gray, "Dresden 1945", 7.

25. Taylor, *Dresden*, 62–75.

26. Figures supplied by the Air Historical Branch of the RAF, quoted in Ibid.

27. Neillands, *Bomber War*, 352.

28. However, Harris did fret about the efficacy of the attack, and, since Dresden was still considered second priority to Berlin, he asked his deputy, Sir Robert Saundby, to verify Dresden's validity as a target with the higher chain of command virtually at the "twelfth hour." On 3 Febr, 1200 B-17s accompanied by 900 escorting fighters had dropped nearly 2300 tons of bombs on the centre of Berlin, which was by now jam-packed with refugees fleeing from the rapidly-advancing Soviet forces. While an estimated 360 industrial facilities were destroyed in this raid and a built-up area one and a half miles square, which stretched across the southern half of the city centre

(*Stadtmitte*) was literally levelled, it was also was also popularly believed for years to have taken the lives of an estimated 25,000 inhabitants and itinerants. (That number of fatalities has since been much revised downwards). Theo Boiten and Martin Bowman, *Battles With the Luftwaffe—The Bomber Campaign Against Germany 1942–1945* (London: HarperCollins, 2001), 198. Thus, although Berlin still held the highest priority, it had been dealt a huge blow, and both Harris and Spaatz were now ordered to attack Dresden at the earliest opportunity. "Not until the 13th, when the right weather forecast at last arrived, did Harris seek formal agreement to the operation from SHAEF and order the attack. "With a heavy heart," Saundby said later, "I was forced to lay the massive air raid on"; and some of the Group Commanders recalled "the distinctly reserved note in Harris's voice when he confirmed the order, gaining the impression that he was dissatisfied with the whole affair." Confirmation by senior staff officers present, noted and quoted in Probert, *Bomber Harris*, 319.

29. Ibid, 320.
30. Greenhous and Halliday, *Canada's Air Forces*, 118.
31. Bomber Command Diary, Feb 1945, 677.
32. Greenhous et al, *Crucible of War*, 856.
33. Ironically, the Main Force bombing at Dresden was so concentrated that very little "creepback" actually occurred. This was one of the contributing factors to the creation of the firestorm.
34. Neillands, *Bomber War*, 366.
35. The transportation raids were, by their very nature, intended to block communications and sow confusion, the achievement of which would certainly involve the massive destruction of enemy city centres. To cite the American example, while the the USAAF was publicly opposed to this form of attack (in spite of what was done in practice), "Bombing 'blind' using radar, was known to be haphazard. On 26 January 1945 (General) Doolittle received a note from his bombing advisors informing him that the average bombing error using instruments was still about two miles and that to hit the target 'involved drenching an area with bombs to achieve any results.' " Neillands, *Bomber War*, 365.
36. The USAAF sent 311 B-17s against the city the following day, dropping 771 tons of bombs on the railway yards to the west of Wettin Station (one of three in the city, located a quarter to a half mile east of the Friedrichstadt Marshalling Yards), which were used as the primary aim point. Additional attacks by the Americans were completed on 15 Feb, then on 2 Mar, and finally, as late as 17 Apr. Gray, "Dresden 1945," 8.
37. Greenhous et al, *Crucible of War*, 857.
38. Neillands, *Bomber War*, 366, and John Keegan (ed.), *The Times Atlas of the Second World War* (New York: Harper & Row, 1989), 139.
39. Among the landmarks destroyed were the Semper Opera House, that beautiful baroque-domed "Stone Bell," otherwise known as the Frauenkirche Protestant Church, built between 1726 and 1743; and the magnificent, copper-domed Royal Palace. However, in a tribute to the indomitable spirit and resolve of the Dresdeners, all these artifacts will eventually be meticulously and painstakingly restored to their former glory. Most have now been completed or are in their final stages of reconstruction. In a powerful and hopefully lasting gesture of reconciliation, British volunteer funding in the form of the Dresden Trust made possible the delivery of the re-manufactured orb and cross for the Frauenkirche in Feb 2000. It will stand at the pinnacle of the rebuilt church, scheduled for completion in time to celebrate Dresden's 800th birthday in 2006.
40. Among those who, either knowingly or unwittingly, propagated the "top end" casualty rates was British journalist David Irving in his book, *The Destruction of Dresden* (London: Kimber, 1963). Mr. Irving, by his own admission, had no academic credentials in history. He was in fact a university drop-out. In the book, he electrified audiences worldwide by providing a "best estimate" of 135,000 fatal casualties, which he compared directly to 71,379 fatalities incurred at Hiroshima. The book, which included some very graphic photographs and these casualty figures, engendered broad-scale revulsion against the wartime Allied bombing policy. "and (it was) not extinguished when Mr. Irving himself candidly admitted his error in 1966 in a letter to The Times; in this, he quoted a report of the Dresden area police chief, of whose authenticity he said there was no doubt, giving a death toll of 25,000 dead, and 35,000 "missing." This is the best information that could be extracted from East Germany; it means that Dresden's ordeal was on roughly the same scale as Hamburg's—a similar tragedy. Mr. Irving, having "no interest in promoting or perpetuating false legends', hastened to publish this. Sharp and special criticism of the Dresden attack nevertheless continues, some of it far from temperate, and clearly fuelled by Nuclear Disarmament issues which have nothing to do with history." Terraine, *Right of the Line*, 678. Given Mr. Irving's later denial of the Holocaust, a judicious dollop of skepticism is in order when examining both his initial and his revised statistics, and his motives for advancing some forms of "evidence" in the first place. However, the fact that in recent years he has been roundly and broadly discredited is largely

irrelevant. Once his initial assessment, buttressed by other intemperate, non-objective evaluations of the raids had been advanced, the proverbial "genie was out of the bottle" and it still remains difficult to find objective treatments of the Dresden raids. However, that report unearthed much later by the Dresden police chief's office, mentioned by Irving, which was put together in early March 1945, assessed Dresden's death toll at approximately 25,000, with several thousand more fallen in all probability buried in the rubble. The additional figure of 35,000 "missing" quoted by Irving is extremely misleading, as this number was probably based on the chaotic displacement of citizens that prevailed in the wake of the Dresden raids. Taylor, *Dresden*, 351–352. Furthermore, as Peter Gray says, "The advent of the Cold War greatly exacerbated the temperature of the rhetoric. The annual tolling of bells throughout East Germany to correspond to the duration of (the) Bomber Command raid on Dresden is evidence of the propaganda effect sought and achieved—especially when it was mimicked in West Germany." Gray, "*Dresden 1945*", 12. However, as we shall see, a learned source from within Germany has recently revised the fatality estimates even further downward.

41. The quote implies the Berlin raid in question took place in January. Actually, it took place on 3 Feb, 1945. Neillands, *Bomber War*, 366. Taylor states, "The figure of twenty-five thousand victims of the Berlin raid of February 3, 1945—eight times what now appears to be the real number—still finds currency more than half a century later." Taylor, *Dresden*, 354. Peter Gray and Henry Probert cite casualty estimates for Dresden at the "top end" as ranging from 250,000 to 200,000, (Gray, 8, Probert, 320) but the German authority Götz Bergander, who has studied this matter carefully, believes the true figure rests between 35,000 and 40,000, but certainly not more than what occurred at Hamburg in July 1943. The broadly accepted casualty count for the Hamburg campaign is 45,000 fatalities, of whom 40,000 are believed to have perished the night of the firestorm alone. Probert, *Bomber Harris*, 320.

42. Frederick Taylor's research centred around access to British, American and German archives, including recently discovered documents not previously accessible because of Communist censorship. Taylor, *Dresden*, Editorial Review at <wysiwyg://17http://www.amazon.com/exec35347-2482549?v=glance&s=books&n=507846>, review accessed 23 Feb 2004, and Taylor, *Dresden*, 448.

43. Gray, "Dresden 1945," 8. Frederick Taylor contends that the Zeiss-Ikon complex alone employed almost 14,000 workers on war contracts by the time of the February 1945 raids. These figures augment even further Robin Neilland's numbers of those employed in the manufacturing sector in Dresden. Also, nearly 200 Dresden factories were damaged in the Feb raids; in 136 cases the damage was categorized as "serious." Many were considered important for military production, and the worst affected were the Zeiss-Ikon factories. Their Delta-Works was 100 percent destroyed, as were the Ica-Works, the Mü-Works, the Petzold & Aulhorn plant, and the Alpha-Works. Taylor, *Dresden*, 358–359.

44. Denis Richards, *The Hardest Victory* (London: Hodder & Stoughton, 1994), 274.

45. Götz Bergander, *Dresden im Luftkrieg* (Cologne: Böhlau Verlag, 1978), 349, quoted in Probert, *Bomber Harris*, 321.

46. Webster and Frankland, *Strategic Air Offensive*, vol 3, 224.

47. Quoted in Neillands, *Bomber War*, 394–395.

48. Quoted in Ibid, 354–355.

49. Mark A. Clodfelter, "Culmination Dresden: 1945", *Aerospace Historian* (Sep 1979), 135.

50. Quoted in Webster and Frankland, *Strategic Air Offensive*, vol 3, 113.

51. Taylor, *Dresden*, 360–372.

52. Gray, "Dresden 1945," 12.

53. Ibid, 11.

54. Ibid, 12.

55. Terry Copp, from paper to historical conference in Portage la Prairie, Manitoba, 1996, quoted in Neillands, *Bomber War*, 393.

56. Philp, letter to author, 16 Aug 2000.

57. Based on comments made by Marshal of the Royal Air Force Sir Michael Beetham, a distinguished veteran of Bomber Command, in *The Times*, 13 Feb 1995 (50th anniversary of the raid), and quoted in Gray, "Dresden 1945," 13.

58. Bomber Command Diary, Feb 1945, 7.

59. No 6 Group Analysis of Results, DHist 74/250, quoted in Greenhous et al, *Crucible of War*, 857–858.

60. Bomber Command Ops Record Book, Feb 1945, DHist, quoted in Greenhous et al, *Crucible of War*, 858, Fns. 86–88.

61. Milberry, *Canada's Air Force*, vol 2, 120. Bomber Command's total effort for the night was 666 sorties, with 17 aircraft (2.6 percent) lost. Bomber Command Diary, Feb 1945, 10.

62. Marlow, letter to author, 15 Nov 2000. This was the last Bomber Command VC of the war. Captain Swales had been attacked twice by a night fighter over the target area and had been badly shot-up in the process, but pressed home his marking and advisory runs with great determination and accuracy. While nursing his badly crippled Lancaster home, he encountered turbulent cloud which made the aircraft too difficult to control, and ordered his crew to bail out. This was accomplished successfully but Swales had no opportunity to get out and was killed in the crash. He had deliberately sacrificed his life to provide every last second of stability on the aircraft to give his crew every possible opportunity to jump. Swales is buried in the Leopold War Cemetery at Limburg in Belgium. His courageous and selfless behavior is reminiscent of that exhibited six months earlier by the Canadian Pathfinder hero, Ian Willoughby Bazelgette, VC. Bomber Command Diary, Feb 1945, 10.

63. Probert, *Bomber Harris*, 315.

64. Hatch, *Aerodrome of Democracy*, 187.

65. Probert, *Bomber Harris*, 315.

66. Greenhous et al, *Crucible of War*, 852.

67. Motiuk, *Thunderbirds at War*, 15.

68. Ibid.

69. Probert, *Bomber Harris*, 315.

70. Donald Daikens, "Halifax Bomber Recollections."

71. Greenhous et al, *Crucible of War*, 105.

72. Bomber Command Diary, Feb 1945, 9.

73. Ibid, and Greenhous et al, *Crucible of War*, 858. The ranking German night fighter ace of the war, Major Heinz-Wolfgang Schnaufer, was particularly destructive that night, shooting down two Lancasters in one sortie, then despatching seven more Lancs on a second mission later the same night. Few are the fighter pilots of any nationality who have been successful in broad daylight against nine different enemy aircraft on two separate missions. Schnaufer's score this night is unparalleled, and the odds are that some of his victims were Canadians. Toliver and Constable, *Fighter Aces of the Luftwaffe*, 225.

74. Bomber Command Diary 5, Mar 1945, 4.

75. MGen (ret'd) Lloyd C. Morrison, personal wartime diary, from letter to author, 21 Feb 2001.

76. Hermann Knell, *To Destroy a City* (Cambridge, Massachusetts: Da Capo Press, 2003), 19–21.

77. Bomber Command Diary, Mar 1945, 8.

78. Morrison, letter to author, 21 Feb 2001.

79. Morrison, excerpt from speech to United Services Institute, London, Ontario, Mar 1944, from letter to author, 21 Feb 2001.

80. Hartmut Feldmann, "From Heinkel to 'Stormbird'," *Flypast* (Aug 2003), No. 265, 39–40.

81. Specifically, the Junkers Jumo 004 powerplant needed high-temperature-resistant steel alloys to withstand the high tensile stresses and temperatures encountered in the turbine. However, the Allied economic blockade, exacerbated by the bombing, had left the Nazis in critically short supply of several essential metallic components, particularly nickel and chromium. Therefore, "the turbine blades for the Jumo 004 were manufactured from a steel-based alloy containing some nickel and chromium, though the material used was insufficiently resilient . . . The blades developed 'creep,' gradually deforming and increasing in length, and when this exceeded a laid-down limit, the engine had to be changed. The flame tubes of the Jumo 004 were formed from mild steel sheet, with an oven-baked spray coating of aluminum to prevent oxidation. This inelegant material did not survive long at the extreme temperatures generated in the hottest part of the 004, and as the engine ran the flame tubes slowly buckled out of shape. Limited by turbine blade 'creep,' flame tube buckling and other problems, the pre-production Jumo 004 engines rarely ran for more than ten hours. Then the Me 262 had to be grounded for new engines to be fitted." Production improvements eventually more than doubled the engine's life, but it remained the Achille's Heel of the jet. Alfred Price, "The Messerschmitt 262 Jet Fighter—Missed Opportunity or Impossible Dream?" *Royal Air Force Air Power Review*, 4, 2 (Summer 2001), 55.

82. Walther Hagenah, quoted in Ibid, 63.

83. Ibid, 14, and Sandy Mutch, "Retreat from Hamburg—Maximum Effort by RCAF 6 Group—31 March 1945," *Airforce*, 23, 4 (Winter 2000), 35.

84. Mutch, "Retreat from Hamburg," 34–37.

85. Conrad Stewart for Harry R. Stilling, "Halifax Bomber Recollections."

86. Price, "The Messerschmitt 262 Jet Fighter," 64.

87. John H. McQuiston, *Tannoy Calling: A Story of a Canadian Airman Flying against Nazi Germany* (New York, Praeger, 1990), 91.

88. While Kurt Welter was certainly leading by example and continued to mount an impressive score, others were also successful. Notable was *Feldwebel* (Sergeant) Karl-Heinz Becker, who destroyed five Mosquitos while flying a single-seater without radar between 21 March and 30 March 1945. Ethell and Price, *The German Jets in Combat*, 49.

89. William Green, *Famous Fighters of the Second World War* (Garden City, New York: Hanover House, 1960), 122–123.

90. No 6 Group Analysis of Results, DHist File 74/250, in Greenhous et al, *Crucible of War*, 849, and Motiuk, *Thunderbirds at War*, 407.

91. Ethell and Price, *German Jets in Combat*, 134.

92. Bomber Command Diary, Mar 1945, 2.

93. Paul Oleynik, "Memories of Scram," *Airforce*, 10, 2 (Summer 1986), 13–14.

94. Paul Oleynik, "Halifax Bomber Recollections."

95. Howie West later claimed this Me 163 as destroyed. Motiuk, *Thunderbirds at War*, 460. Given the prevailing weather conditions and the vagaries of the flight path geometry of the attacking force on Chemnitz, as well as the reported position at the time of the encounter, it appears the engagement took place around 20 miles northwest of Erfurt. This encounter was probably within the general flight envelope range of Me 163s based at Brandis (Polenz) airfield near Leipzig, the main Me 163 operating base for *Jagdgeschwader 400* at the time. The reported position would have placed the encounter at around 50 miles from Brandis, but given the aforementioned vagaries of the bomber's approach path, it could have actually taken place considerably closer to or even abeam Brandis. Ethell and Price, *German Jets in Combat*, 132, and Alfred Price, *The Last Year of the Luftwaffe* (Osceola, Wisconsin: Motorbooks, 1991), 35.

96. Howie West, letter to author, 4 Dec 2000.

97. Marlow, letter to author, 15 Nov 2000.

98. Rawlings, *History of the Royal Air Force*, 173.

99. Award effective as per *London Gazette*, 24 Apr 1945 and AFRO 918/45, 1 June 1945, at <http://www.airforce.ca/wwii/ALPHA-WH.html>, 25.

100. Harvey, *The Tumbling Mirth*, 109.

101. Quoted in Webster and Frankland, *Strategic Air Offensive*, vol 3 112.

102. Neillands, *Bomber War*, 373.

103. Minute (Top Secret) Churchill to Ismay et al, 28 Mar 1945, at PRO Premier 3/12, 25.

104. Gray, "Dresden 1945," 9.

105. Quoted in Probert, *Bomber Harris*, 322.

106. Neillands, *Bomber War*, 372.

107. Minute D. 89/5 (Top Secret) Ismay to Churchill, 30 Mar 1945, at PRO Premier 3/12, 23.

108. Attachment (Top Secret) to Minute D. 89/5 (Top Secret) Churchill to Ismay et al, 01 Apr 1945, at PRO Premier 3/12, 22.

109. Neillands, *Bomber War*, 373.

110. The first Grand Slam operation had been mounted by 617 Squadron as a feasibility demonstration on the Bielefed Viaduct just nine days earlier. Bomber Command Diary, Mar 1945, 6.

111. Reg Patterson, letter to author, 07 Nov 2001.

112. Bomber Command Diary, April–May 1945, 3.

113. Stan Miller, letter to author, 19 Sep 2003.

114. Bomber Command Diary, April–May 1945, 3.

115. Marlow, letter to author, 15 Nov 2000.

116. Motiuk, *Thunderbirds at War*, 476.

117. Ethell and Price, *German Jets in Combat*, 134.

118. The official USAAF combat chronology for 10 April 1945 states: "Eighth AF: 1224 HBs hit 8 A/Fs, 2 M/Ys, a factory A/F and repair hangars, an ordnance depot, and HQ buildings—all in northern Germany." Kit C. Carter and Robert Mueller (eds.), *The Army Air Forces in World War II—Combat Chronology 1941-1945* (Washington: US Government Printing Office, 1973), 623. The city of Leipzig is not considered to be in northern Germany. Furthermore, no other numbered USAAF Air Forces reported any activity in the Leipzig area. Also, the 433 Squadron Lancaster loss has been otherwise categorized. No. 6 Group Ops Record Book 10 Apr 1945, Martin Middlebrook and Chris Everett, *The Bomber Command War Diaries: An Operational Reference Book, 1939–1945* (London: Penguin, 1990), 694.

119. Stephen M. Fochuk from Canada recently declared: "On the 10th of April 1945, a rather large formation of No.

6 (RCAF) Group Lancasters and Halifaxes carried out a daylight raid on the railway centre and marshalling yards at Leipzig. Other than moderate flak being reported the only enemy opposition was in the form of 1 to 3 Me 163s. Several air gunners fired at the rocket interceptor(s) but no hits were confirmed. According to one witness a Me 163 destroyed a Halifax, which "blew up right in front of me." Komet Weapons: SG 500 *Jägerfaust* at <file:///C|/WINDOWS/Desktop/weapon01.htm>,3., accessed 2/9/04.

120. Award effective 17 July 1945 as per *London Gazette* of that date and AFRO 1478/45, 21 Sep 1945, at <http://www.airforce.ca/wwii/ALPHA-M.MU.html>, 35. The aircraft was later identified as an Me 163 fighter. Directorate of History and Heritage, *The RCAF Overseas—The Sixth Year* (Toronto: Oxford University Press, 1949), 163–164.

121. Probert, *Bomber Harris*, 325.

122. Note (Top Secret), (undated) by Sir Charles Portal at PRO Premier 3/12, 18–21.

123. Additional correspondence contained at PRO Premier 3/12, 7–17.

124. Churchill to Sinclair and Portal, 19 Apr 1945, at PRO Premier 3/12, 3.

125. Portal to Churchill, 20 Apr 1945, at PRO Premier 3/12, 2.

126. Paul Brickhill, *Dam Busters* (London: Evans Brothers, 1951), 201.

127. Bomber Command Diary, April–May 1945, 3.

128. Overy, *Bomber Command*, 85.

129. Bomber Command Diary, April–May 1945, 5.

130. Brickhill, *Dam Busters*, 205.

131. Award effective 1 June 1945 as per *London Gazette* of that date and AFRO 1147/45, 13 July 1945. Fauquier would later be made a *Chevalier* of the *Legion d'Honneur* and also awarded the *Croix de Guerre avec Palme* by France. *Canada Gazette*, 20 Sep 1947, and AFRO 485/47, 12 Sep 1947, all at <http://www.airforce.ca/wwii/ALPHA-FA.html>, 20.

132. Bomber Command Diary, April–May 1945, 5.

133. Motiuk, *Thunderbirds at War*, 479.

134. West, letter to author, 21 Sep 2000.

135. Motiuk, *Thunderbirds at War*, 480.

136. Morrison, letter to author, 21 Feb 2001.

137. Bomber Command Diary, April–May 1945, 7.

138. Marlow, letter to author, 15 Nov 2000.

139. Bomber Command Diary, April–May 1945, 8.

140. Ibid, 10.

141. Ibid, 8–9.

142. Milberry, *Canada's Air Force* vol 2, 127.

143. Walter B. Maas, *The Netherlands at War* (London: np, 1979), 239, quoted in Greenhous et al, *Crucible of War*, 887.

144. Bomber Command Diary, April–May 1945, 9.

145. No 405 Squadron Ops Record Book, 7 May 1945, DHist, quoted in Greenhous et al, *Crucible of War*, 888.

146. Morrison, letter to author, 21 Feb 2001.

147. Bomber Command Diary, April–May 1945, 8, and Greenhous et al, *Crucible of War*, 888–889.

148. Marlow, letter to author, 15 Nov 2000.

149. Morrison, letter to author, 21 Feb 2001.

150. Lord Trenchard to Sir Arthur Harris, 29 Apr 1945, Harris family papers quoted in Probert, *Bomber Harris*, 326.

151. Bomber Command Diary, April–May 1945, 10.

152. Lloyd C. "Mo" Morrison, "Our War Just Ran Out," *Airforce*,19, 2 (Summer 1995), 13–14, and letter to author, 21 Feb 2001.

153. Motiuk, *Thunderbirds at War*, 491.

154. Peter S. Lennie, "As I Remember the Day," *Airforce*, 19, 2 (Summer 1995), 14.

EPILOGUE

1. The fourth and seventh stanzas of British poet and art critic Laurence Binyon's famous *For the Fallen*, an evocative tribute to the dead of the British Expeditionary Force killed in 1914 and written the same year. The fourth stanza in particular has developed a life of its own over the years as *The Ode*. It is frequently recited at Remembrance Day ceremonies throughout the Commonwealth, particularly in Canada and Australia.

2. On 20 July 1933 the future Pope Pius XII, then Cardinal Secretary of State of the Holy See Eugenio Pacelli, presided over the signing in Rome of the Reich Concordat between the Vatican and National Socialist Germany . . . Pacelli effectively "shook hands with the devil" by entering into this agreement with Hitler and the Nazis. He envisioned an authoritarian state (the Third Reich) and an authoritarian Church under the exclusive direction of the Vatican bureaucracy in an eternal league, protecting the German Church from what Pacelli perceived was the far greater menace of Bolshevism. In return for Nazi acceptance of the Code of Canon Law (the tenets of which they would routinely violate in future months and years), which supposedly guaranteed many rights and freedoms to the German Catholic Church, the Nazis eliminated all organized Catholic political opposition through the disbandment of the Catholic Center Party, the last significant bastion of resistance to Nazi obtainment of absolute power in Germany at the time. The Concordat effectively integrated the Catholic Church into fascist Germany, just as the similar Lateran Treaty had integrated the Church into fascist Italy, all in the name of more authoritarian, centralist Vatican control for the Church. It also provided the Nazis with a tremendous propaganda coup, since it trumpeted to the world that, according to the Vatican, German nationalism was justifiable to the religiously faithful and fully compatible with the Catholic faith. This abrogation of moral responsibility would help pave the way for the myriad excesses of the Nazi regime. Thenceforth, and with only relatively-minor exceptions, which were "too little, too vague and too late," the Vatican maintained a stony silence with respect to Nazi atrocities in Italy as well as in Occupied Europe and Eurasia. For excellent recent scholarship on the subject, see John Cornwell, *Hitler's Pope—The Secret History of Pius XII* (New York: Penguin, 1999), and Peter Godman, *Hitler and the Vatican—Inside the Secret Archives that Reveal the New Story of the Nazis and the Church* (New York: The Free Press, 2004).

3. "Operation Mould: Outline Administrative Plan," 23 Nov 1944, in DHist File 181.003 (D5092), quoted in Greenhous et al, *Crucible of War*, 117 and fn 41.

4. Ibid, 123.

5. Ibid.

6. T.W. Melnyk, RCAF Planning for Tiger Force, unpublished DHist narrative, May 1978, 80–84, and other references, quoted at Ibid., 124 and fn 64.

7. Motiuk, *Thunderbirds at War*, 490.

8. Keegan, *Second World War*, 584.

9. Marlow letter to author, 15 Nov 2000. Flight Lieutenant Jack Warren Rothenbush of Vancouver was awarded the DFC effective 8 Sep 1945 as per *London Gazette*, 21 Sep 1945 and AFRO 1704/45, at <http://www.airforce.ca/wwii/ALPHA-RO.2.html>, 24.

10. John F. Roberts, "Memories of 405 Pathfinder Squadron and the Last Flight Home," *Gaggle and Stream*, Journal of the Bomber Command Association of Canada, 4 (Winter 2003–4), 3.

11. Donald James McQuoid of Summerberry, Saskatchewan, had amassed an outstanding war record during his service overseas. He participated in many challenging operations while flying with 58 Squadron and later with 405 Squadron, serving with distinction in the roles of Master Bomber and Deputy Master Bomber and picking up a DSO as well as a DFC and Bar along the way. Citations and details at <http://www.airforce.ca/wwii/ALPHA-MC.L.html> 39–40.

12. John Fulton Roberts of Toronto was awarded the DFC effective 18 May 1945 as per *London Gazette* of that date and AFRO 1085/45, 29 June 1945, at <http://www.airforce.ca/wwii/ALPHA-RO.1.html>, 17.

13. Roberts, "Memories of 405 Pathfinder Squadron," 8.

14. Mark Nicholls, "Bomber Survivors," *Bomber Command Flypast Special*, Classic Series No. 13, 22.

15. Harold Skaarup, *Canadian Warbird Survivors 2002* (San Jose, California: Writers Club Press, 2001), 260–261.

16. Ibid, 340.

17. Nicholls, "Bomber Survivors," 23.

18. Halifax W1048, at <http://www.halibag.com/hendon.htm>, 1.

19. Citation for DFC undoubtedly earned partially in KB 882, effective 8 Sep 1945 as per London Gazette, 21 Sep 1945 and AFRO 1704/45, 9 Nov 1945 reads: "This officer has displayed great courage and determination coupled with exceptional skill and ability as a navigator. His tenacity of purpose and ability to concentrate on a particular problem under any circumstance with no regard to personal comfort or well-being has made him invaluable to his pilot. His ability and unselfish devotion to duty have been an inspiration to all." <http://www.airforce.ca/wwii/ALPHA-FE.html>, 1.

20. Letter K.R. Fee to Edmunston Municipal Airport, 1 Dec 1985.

21. Bishop, *Courage in the Air*, 144.

22. Ken W. Underhill, " Halifax Bomber Recollections."

23.   Goodwin, "Hugh Hay, DSO, DFC—Top Navigator?" 39.

24.   DSO and DFC citations, along with particulars of wartime service, at
       <http://www.airforce.ca/wwii/ALPHA-UV.html>, 17–18, and Dr. Steve Lukits, letter to author, 16 Mar 2004.

25.   Eric Dumigan, "Celebrating 60 Years of Flying," *Airforce*, 27, 4 (Winter 2003–4), 47.

26.   Howard Hewer, *In for a Penny, In for a Pound—The Adventures and Misadventures of a Wireless Operator in
       Bomber Command* (Toronto: Stoddart, 2000), 255.

27.   Arthur Harris, *Bomber Offensive* (London: Collins, 1947), 267.

APPENDIX

1.   Overy, *Bomber Command*, 200.

2.   Wells, *Courage and Air Warfare*, 2.

3.   Ibid, 16.

4.   Overy, *Bomber Command*, 204. For the record, 1479 men and 91 women in ground crew duties, often
       hazardous, were also killed during the war. Holmes, *Battlefields of the Second World War*, 180.

5.   Milberry, *Canada's Air Force*, vol 2, 127.

6.   Of note, Robin Neillands appears to be the only reputable author who cites 110,000 versus 125,000 as the
       total number cof aircrew who flew with Bomber Command during the war years, nor does Neillands cite his
       source. Sir Arthur Harris and a host of other distinguished sources, including Richard Holmes, all use the
       125,000 figure. Further, if the Neillands total number is correct, then the overall fatal loss rate climbs from 45
       percent to 51 percent. Neillands, *Bomber War*, 379.

7.   Harris, *Bomber Offensive* , 267, and Overy, *Bomber Command*, 202.

8.   Ibid, 209; Terraine, *Right of the Line*, 537.

9.   Overy, *Bomber Command*, 209.

10.   D'Olier et al, *US Strategic Bomb Survey*, 71.

11.   <http::/www.nucleus.com/~ltwright/bc-stats,html>

12.   The earlier years were proportionately much more dangerous. For example, in 1942, the average loss rate per
       operation was 4.1 percent. By 1944, this had diminished to 1.7 percent and by 1945, to 0.9 percent; the latter
       two years represented nearly two-thirds of the Command's wartime sortie total. Overy, *Bomber Command*, 204.

13.   Of the 1113 U-boats commissioned after the start of hostilities , plus the 56 available at war's commencement
       , 821 or 70.23 percent would be lost due to enemy action or marine accidents, and of the 41,000 personnel
       attached to the wartime U-boat arm, more than 27,000 or 66 percent would forfeit their lives. Roger Sarty,
       Canada and the Battle of the Atlantic (Montreal: Art Global, 1998), 160; V.E. Tarrant, *The U-Boat Offensive
       1914–1945* (London: Cassell, 1989), 169. Specifically, out of 859 boats sent out on war patrols, 648 (75 per-
       cent) were lost and a full 429 of these yielded no survivors. Clay Blair, *Hitler's U-Boat War—The Hunted
       1942–1945* (New York: Modern Library, 2000), 705.

14.   English, *Cream of the Crop*, 137, 140–141.

15.   The Bomber Harris Trust, *A Battle for Truth*, (Agincourt: Ramsey, 1994), 25. The 40,000 RCAF Bomber
       Command airmen were but a fraction of the total 93,844 "all trades" RCAF personnel who served overseas.
       Greenhous et al, *Crucible of War*, xxiii.

16.   Ibid.

17.   These statistics provide a chilling counterpoint to the casualties sustained by the Canadian Expeditionary Force
       during the Great War. Of the 619,636 men who were enlisted, 9.6 percent became fatal casualties, while a fur-
       ther 27.9 percent were non-fatally wounded, producing a total casualty rate of 37.5 percent. At first glance, the
       overall Second World War RCAF bomber aircrew casualty rate of 32.67 percent compares favourably, but the
       total *fatal* casualty rate at nearly 25 percent is much higher. However, readers should bear in mind that a signif-
       icant number of the non-fatal casualties would later prematurely succumb during peacetime as a result of their
       war wounds and inadequate follow-on treatment. Extrapolated from Desmond Morton and J.L. Granatstein,
       Marching to Armageddon— Canadians and the Great War 1914–1919 (Toronto: Lester & Orpen Dennys, 1989),
       Appendix B, 279.

18.   Milberry, *Canada's Air Force*, 41.

19.   Overy, *Bomber Command*, 205.

20.   Milberry, *Canada's Air Force*, 93, 127.

21.   <http://www.nucleus.com/~/twright/bc-stats/html>

22.   Greenhous et al, *Crucible of War*, 864.

23. The range over the period was 65–87 percent, but it is felt that the 75 percent weighting counterbalances the period of maximum effort and participation, the latter months of the group's existence, with the significantly higher loss rates of the first year of operations. Ibid, 55.

24. Ibid, 15.

25. In January 1944, sixteen Bomber Command squadrons, none of which were Canadian, were flying operations in the Mediterranean theatre, while another ten squadrons were doing so in the Far East out of India and Ceylon. All these units had very low operational loss rates compared to their UK-based counterparts. Overy, *Bomber Command*, 84–85.

26. Participants are considered to be the estimated 40,000 RCAF aircrew who served, plus two-thirds of the 1106 CAN/RAF aircrew known to have served directly in the RAF.

27. Embedded within this statistic are even more chilling ones. For example, between 11–13 May 1943 and 21–25 Jun 1943, 6 Group's missing rate rose to 11.5 percent, and on the night of 12/13 May, on a raid to Duisburg, to 13.3 percent. Also, Halifax losses from mid-Dec 1943 to mid-Jan 1944 averaged 9.8 percent. Greenhous et al, *Crucible of War*, 671, 681.

28. Ibid, 681.

29. Ibid, 683.

30. During the (generalized) period of the Battle of Berlin, "1081 crews failed to return from 24,754 night bombing sorties (4.36 percent), mining cost just twenty-one of 2078 sorties (1.01 percent). No. 6 Group contributed 395 of the latter, losing four crews, or exactly the overall percentage rate." No. 6 Group Analysis of Results, DHist 74/250, in Ibid, 788.

31. Overy, *Bomber Command*, 183.

32. To be precise, it was 430,747 tons dropped out of 955,044 total, or 45.1 percent.
    <http:/www.nucleus.com/twright/bc-stats/html>

33. Overy, *Bomber Command*, 184.

34. They also dreaded surges of effort similar to the Hamburg raids of Jul–Aug 1943 on other industrial centres.

35. Overy, *Bomber Command*, 185.

36. Ibid, 191.

37. Albert Speer, "Spandau: The Secret Diaries," in Bomber Harris Trust, *A Battle for Truth*, 64.

38. Overy, *Bomber Command*, 191.

39. Edward Jablonski, *America in the Air War* (Alexandria, Virginia: Time-Life Books, 1982), 142.

40. Overy, *Bomber Command*, 191.

41. Jablonski, *America in the Air War*, 142.

42. E.L. Homze & H. Boog, *The Luftwaffe* (Alexandria, Virginia: Time-Life Books, 1982), 161.

43. D'Olier et al, *US Strategic Bomb Survey*, 39.

44. Speer, *Inside the Third*, 224.

45. D'Olier et al, *US Strategic Bomb Survey*, 60.

46. Ibid, 61.

47. Ibid, 62.

48. Ibid, 65.

49. Overy, *Bomber Command*, 192.

50. Speer, *Inside the Third Reich*, 299.

51. Overy, *Bomber Command*, 197.

52. D'Olier et al, *US Strategic Bomb Survey*, 19.

53. Williamson Murray, *The Luftwaffe—Strategy for Defeat* (Secaucus, New Jersy: Chartwell, 1986), 223.

54. Memo No.529 (Special Distribution and War Cabinet from Switzerland), 28 Jul 1940, in PRO Premier 3/11/1, 35.

55. Churchill at War, The Prime Minister's Office Papers 1940–45, Unit 1, in PRO Premier 3/11/4, 144.

56. Ibid, 112, 116.

57. PRO Premier 3/11/12, 661.

58. Ibid, 627.

59. Ibid, 622.

60. PRO Premier 3/11/7, 290.

61. Denis Richards, *The Hardest Victory*, (New York: Norton, 1995), 112.

62. Ibid, 86.

63. Dudley Saward, *Bomber Harris—The Authorized Biography* (London: Cassell, 1984), 162–163.

64. Overy, *Bomber Command*, 197; Richard Overy, "A Presentation to the Symposium on the Strategic Bomber Offensive, 1939–1945," RAF Staff College Bracknell, 26 March 1993.
65. D'Olier et al, *US Strategic Bomb Survey*, 96–97.
66. Speer, *Inside the Third Reich*, 262.
67. D'Olier et al, *US Strategic Bomb Survey*, 97.
68. Ibid, 98
69. Joseph Goebbels, *Final Entries 1945* (New York, Putnam's,1978), 117, 149, 299.
70. Speer, " Spandau: The Secret Diaries," 64.
71. Burke Cahill, member, Canadian Committee for the Study of World War II, letter to Director General History, NDHQ, circa 2000, at <http://www.blvl.igs.net/~jlynch/bharis60.htm> 4.
72. Probert, *Bomber Harris*, 337.
73. Götz Bergander, quoted in Ibid, 338.
74. Speer, *Inside the Third Reich*, 278–279.
75. Overy, *Bomber Command*, 197.
76. Bomber Harris Trust, *Battle for Truth*, 65; Overy, *Bomber Command*, 213.
77. Overy, *Bomber Command*, 197, 214.
78. In fact, even *Luftwaffe* bomber commanders had long argued for a concentration on fighter production, far earlier than it was actually done.
79. Murray, *Luftwaffe—Strategy for Defeat,* 225.
80. Matthew Cooper, *The German Air Force 1933–1945* (London: Jane's, 1981), 377. Also, between 1 Sep 1939 and 28 Feb 1945, the last date for which reliable figures exist, *Luftwaffe* fatalities included 44,065 aircrew killed and another 27,610 missing or captured. Alfred Price, *A Pictorial History of the Luftwaffe 1933–1945* (London, Ian Allan, 1969), 59.
81. Homze and. Boog, *Luftwaffe,* 170.
82. Most of the remaining losses were attributed to flak.
83. Cajus Bekker, *The Luftwaffe War Diaries* (London: MacDonald,1967), 380.
84. Specifically, the German night fighter arm accumulated a wartime total of 6048 air-to-air victories, 215 during day operations and 5833 at night. Of the latter total, only 1041, or one-sixth, were gained over the Eastern Front. Aders, *History of the German Night Fighter*, 239. *Nachtjagdgeschwader I* alone accounted for 2318 victories, measured against 676 fatal aircrew casualties. Held and Nauroth, *The Defense of the Reich*, 219.
85. Overy, *Bomber Command*, 201.
86. Speer, *Inside the Third Reich*, 365.
87. Ibid, 227.
88. Ibid, 229.
89. Beevor, *Fall of Berlin 1945*, 139. On 24 April 1945, Soviet troops reached Dahlem, and the Kaiser Wilhelm Institute for Physics the following day. Along with various pieces of useful equipment, NKVD troops found "250 kilograms of metallic uranium; three tons of uranium oxide; twenty litres of heavy water." Ibid, 324–325. Furthermore, related work was being conducted at a plant in Stassfurt in northern Germany, where an Allied team led by John Lansdale, head of security for the Manhatten Project, found a cache of bomb materials on 17 Apr 1945. Specifically, the team discovered about 1100 tons of ore, some in the form of uranium oxide. This team, the one known as the Alsos Mission, additionally rounded up several prominent German atomic scientists in the region within a week, including Werner Heisenberg and Otto Hahn. Anahad O'Connor, "John Lonsdale," *The Scotsman*, Mon, 8 Sep 2003, at <wysiwyg://14/http://www.news.scotsman.com/obituaries.cfm?id=989462003>
90. Keegan, *Second World*, 582.
91. "Nazis Planned to Use Virus Against Britain," in *The Times*, Mon 12 Mar 2001, at <wysiwyg://3http://www.the.times.co.uk/article02-97518,00.html>
92. Brian J. Ford, *German Secret Weapons: Blueprint for Mars* (New York: Ballentine's, 1969), 106–110; *Forgotten Battles: The Weapons: Tabun Nerve Gas*, at <wysiwyg://19/http://www.geocities.com/pentagon/bunker/335/germweps/tabun.html>
93. Chester Wilmot, *The Struggle for Europe* (London: Wordsworth, 1998), 620.
94. Noted in Middlebrook, *Nuremberg Raid*, 312.
95. Jan Heitmann, "Destroying the Hamburg U-Boat Pens," in *After the Battle*, vol 3 (London: Battle of Britain International, 2001), 30–31.
96. Speer, *Inside the Third Reich*, 273.

97. *U-Boat—The Elektroboats—Getting Ready,* at <http://uboat.net/technical/electroboats> 3.htm
98. Ibid.
99. Speer, *Inside the Third Reich,* 274. On the night of 8/9 Mar 1945, 312 Bomber Command aircraft dropped 983 tons of bombs on Hamburg, inflicting heavy damage on the Blohm & Voss shipyard and also destroying boats at the Howaldswerke yard. On 31 Mar, 469 aircraft dropped 2217 tons, inflicting more severe damage on the Howaldswerke facility. Again on 9 Apr, 17 specialty Lancasters bombed Hamburg's Fink II pens with fifteen five-ton Tallboys and two ten-ton Grand Slams, causing serious damage to the pens themselves, as well as the neighbouring barracks, boiler houses, storage houses and workshops. The night prior to this impressive day raid, 440 Main Force bombers had dropped 1481 tons on the Hamburg port facilities. Heitmann, "Destroying the Hamburg U-Boat Pens," 34–35.
100. Only Type XXIIs *U 2511* and *U 3008* were operational by the end of hostilities. Robert Hutchinson, *War Beneath the Waves* (London: HarperCollins, 2003), 104.
101. Overy, *Bomber Command,* 88.
102. Goebbels, *Final Entries 1945,* 298.
103. Holmes, *Battlefields of the Second World War,* 215.
104. Overy, *Bomber Command,* 202; Bekker, *Luftwaffe War Diaries,* 386.
105. Overy, *Bomber Command,* 202.
106. PRO documents as quoted in Richard Norton-Taylor's "Allied Bombers Chose 'Easy' German Targets," in *The Guardian,* Thurs Aug 23, 2001.
107. In spite of all their pious, post-war posturing, particularly with respect to Dresden, the Soviets made no attempt whatsoever to spare the Reich's civilians from bombing or shelling. In fact, quite the opposite occurred.
108. Wartime polling on the bombing was frequent. Some representative examples follow:
Canada, 11 Nov 1942– "Do you approve or disapprove of bombing Germany's civilian population? Of Italy's? Of Japan's?" (CIPO)

	National Total Germany's	Italy's	Japan's
Approve	57%	51%	62%
Disapprove	38%	44%	34%
Undecided	5%	5%	4%

Great Britain, Dec 1943– "How do you feel about the bombing?" (Only one answer per respondent allowed) (BIPO)

Satisfaction, getting some of their own medicine, keep it up...........47%
We are justified in doing it. It is a necessity.....................................17%
Dislike bombing but necessary under present circumstances..........16%
Sorry for the kids and old people but it's necessary...........................3%
They should bomb only industrial plants and communications........2%
I am against bombing..7%
Miscellaneous..6%
No answer; don't know...2%

Great Britain, Dec 1943– "What do you think are likely to be the effects of the bombing of the German cities?" (Only one answer per respondent allowed) (BIPO)

Upsets German morale..40%
It will shorten the war..24%
Smash war industries..10%
Bombing will win the war..3%
Bombing alone will not win the war...3%
Germans will retaliate..2%
Miscellaneous...9%
Don't know...5%

Hadley Cantril (ed), *Public Opinion 1935–1946* (Princeton: Princeton University Press, 1951), 1068, 1069.
109. Greenhous et al, *Crucible of War,* 726.
110. David Ian Hall, "Arguments For and Against the Strategic Bomber Offensive: The Contrasting Views of Wing

Commander T.D. (Harry) Weldon and RAF Chaplain L. John Collins," essay by Dr Hall, U. of Oxford, for the Bomber Harris Trust Essay Competition, 30 June 1997, 10.

111. Ibid.
112. Ibid.
113. Middlebrook, *Nuremberg Raid*, 314.
114. Eberhard Spetzler, *Luftkrieg und Menschlichkeit* (Göttingen,1956), quoted in Hermann Knell, *To Destroy a City* (Cambridge, Massachusetts: Da Capo Press, 2003), 326–327.
115. Ibid, 329.
116. Greenhous et al, *Crucible of War*, 727.
117. B.K. Sandwell, *Saturday Night*, Editorial, 13 June 1942, 13.
118. "Few Will Object to Continuance of Allied Raids," in *Toronto Telegram*, 31 May 1943; "Bombing Civilians," in *Winnipeg Free Press*, 27 Apr 1943, quoted in Greenhous et al, *Crucible of War,* 728.
119. Kenneth McDonald, letter to author, 25 Aug 2000, from letter to Thomas Fleming, 22 July 1997.
120. Hew Strachan, *European Armies and the Conduct of War* (London: Routledge, 2001), 188.
121. Statistic from Japanese Navy *Kamikaze* memorial, naval museum, Japanese Maritime Self-Defence Force Officer Candidate School, Etajima Japan, 16 July 2002.
122. Masatake Okumiya, Jiro Horikoshi and Martin Caidin, *Zero* (New York: ibooks, 1956, 2002), 354.
123. Winston Churchill, *The Second World War*, vol 2 (New York: Time-Life Books, 1959), 561.
124. Statistic from the Hiroshima Peace Museum, Hiroshima, Japan, 15 July 2002. The War Cabinet was apparently figuratively calling for the sacrifice of every Japanese man, woman and child, if necessary, since the total population of Japan as late as Apr 1947 was just over 73 million.
125. Okumiya et al, *Zero*, 362, 378.
126. Edward Jablonski, *America in the Air War* (Alexandria, Virginia: Time-Life Books, 1982), 169; Peter Jennings and Todd Brewster, *The Century* (New York: Doubleday, 1998), 276.
127. Quoted in Overy, *Bomber Command*, 202.
128. Williamson Murray, *Strategy for Defeat,* 234.
129. Overy, "Presentation to the Symposium," 19.

Glossary and Abbreviations

AASF—Advanced Air Striking Force

ABC—*Airborne Cigar*, the jamming of German fighter VHF radio communications

Abigail—bombing campaign against selected German towns, autumn 1940

AFC—Air Force Cross

AFDU—Air Fighting Development Unit

AFS—Advanced Flying School

AFTS—Advanced Flying Training School

AGLT—Automatic Gun-Laying Turret

AI—Airborne Intercept

Aldis Lamp—British signal lamp manufactured by the Aldis Company

Amatol—high explosive used in blast bombs

AOC—Air Officer Commanding

AOC-in-C—Air Officer Commanding-in-Chief

API—Air Position Indicator

Apron—a hangar's paved surrounding area

Argument—concentrated attack by RAF and USAAF on German aircraft production, Feb 1944

Barbarossa—German attack on the USSR, June 1941.

BCATP—British Commonwealth Air Training Plan

BCDU—Bomber Command Development Unit

BEM—British Empire Medal

Benito—German night fighter control system

Berlin—Airborne Intercept radar

Berlin Method—policy of dropping both skymarkers and groundmarkers regardless of cloud conditions over the target

Big City—Berlin

Blood Wagon or Meat Wagon—Ambulance

Boozer—warning device to Bomber Command crews of enemy radar tracking them. A yellow light illuminated if the bomber was being held in an AI beam and a red light if it was being held by a *Würzburg* radar

Briar—device to disrupt *Egon*

Bumerang—German device used to detect *Oboe* transmissions

Carpet—device to jam *Würzburg* GCI radar

CAS—Chief of the Air Staff

Caterpillar Club—membership required an emergency parachute descent from an imperilled aircraft.

CB—Companion of the Order of the Bath

CBE—Companion of the Order of the British Empire

CBO—Combined Bomber Offensive

CGM—Conspicuous Gallantry Medal

Chastise—air attack on German dams, May 1943

Chop Rate—RAF slang for loss rate of aircraft on operations.

Clarion—American operation to disrupt German communications and morale by widespread bombing and fighter attacks, Feb 1945

Collect a gong—be awarded a decoration

Coned—being caught and held by enemy searchlights

Cookies—4000-pound high-capacity blast bombs

Corkscrew—manoeuvre for evading enemy air attack in a bomber

Corona—counterfeit orders or commands transmitted by radio to German night fighters

Creepback—bomb impact drift back along the line of approach to the target

Crossbow—bombing campaign associated with attacks on V-weapon launch sites

Darky—RAF radio frequency for emergency calls from returning aircraft

Dartboard—jamming measure used against German fighter communications

D-Day—6 June 1944, beginning of Operation Overlord

DFC—Distinguished Flying Cross

DFM—Distinguished Flying Medal

Ditching—forced landing of an aircraft on water

Donnerkell—device for detecting *Oboe*-equipped aircraft

Dragoon—invasion of southern France, summer 1944

Drem Lighting—system of outer markers and approach lights at many British airfields early war

Drumstick—jamming of German fighter radio control channels

DSO—Distinguished Service Order

Dudelsack (Bagpipes)—device for jamming British radio and wireless transmissions

Düppel—strips of metallic foil air-dropped to confuse enemy radar, *Window* to Allied forces

Eclipse—contingency plans for early German surrender. Not executed

Egon—German radio navigation aid for night fighters

Exodus—repatriation operation by air of Allied ex-POWs

FIDO—Fog Investigation and Dispersal Operation. Fog dispersal for runways by using a double row of gasoline- fed burners

Fishpond—airborne radar for warning Bomber Command crews of nearby enemy aircraft

Flak—German *Fleigerabwehrkanonen*, or anti-aircraft artillery

Flamme—German device for homing on IFF and *Mandrel* transmissions

Flensburg—German electronic device to direct night fighters to *Monica*, *Mandrel* and *Piperack* transmissions

Flight Louie—RAF slang for the rank of flight lieutenant

Flimsy—list of "friendly" airfields in the war theatre with names, locations, signal letters and secret radio call signs changed every day. Written on rice paper, to be eaten by navigator rather than fall into enemy hands

Flip—a short flight in an aircraft

Freya—German early warning radar

Freya-Halbe—device to negate the effect of *Mandrel* on *Freya*

Gardening—Mine laying operations in enemy waters

Gee—British radio aid to navigation using 3 ground transmitting stations

George—automatic pilot. "Let George do it"

Gerhard—German device for detecting *Monica* transmissions

Geschwader—*Luftwaffe* organizational formation, roughly equivalent to an RAF group, usually composed of three *Gruppen*, or wings, usually made up of three *Staffeln* or squadrons

GC—George Cross

GM—George Medal

GP—General Purpose bombs, manufactured in 250, 500, 1000 and 4000 pound sizes

G-H—Allied blind bombing device. *Oboe* in reverse

Giant Würzburg—German early warning radar permitting fighter controllers to track night fighters and their targets

Gisella—German attack on Bomber Command airfields, March 1945

Gomorrah—concentrated incendiary operations against Hamburg, Jul-Aug 1943

Goodwood—attack by Second British Army southeast of Caen, Jul 1944

Grand Slam—22,000-pound high-velocity deep penetration bomb

Grocer—another RAF device for jamming German AI radars

H2S—airborne ground-mapping radar aid to navigation and target identification

H2X—American version of *H2S*

Halibag—Slang for Handley Page Halifax bomber

Happy Valley—Ruhr Valley

HC—High capacity blast effect bombs, manufactured in 2000, 4000, 8000 and 12,000 pound sizes

HCU—Heavy Conversion Unit

HE—High Explosive bomb

Heinrich—German device for jamming *Gee* transmissions

Helle Nachtjagd—German air defence system of searchlights to highlight enemy bombers for flak and night fighters

HF—High Frequency radio

HF/DF—High Frequency Direction Finding

Himmelbett—"Bedspring in the Heavens," German air defence system extending from Denmark to middle of France. It used radio communications to integrate early-warning and interception radar facilities, searchlight and flak batteries, fighter control stations and fighter squadrons. Also known as the *Kammhüber Line*, after its founder

Husky—Allied invasion of Sicily, Jul 1943

Hydra—Bomber Command attack on Peenemünde, Aug 1943

IFF—Identification Friend or Foe. Allied electronic target discrimination device

Incendiary—bomb designed to start and to sustain fires. Manufactured by Allies in 4 pound size (Mk. IV Thermite; Type E and Type X), and 30 pound size (Jet J and phosphorus)

Jagdschloss—Another German early warning radar

Jostle—device to jam German radar transmissions, particularly AA barrage fire

Jubilee—amphibious raid on Dieppe, 19 Aug 1942

Kiel—German infra-red detection device

Knickebein—German navigation and bombing aid

Korfu—radar homing device used against *H2S*

Lanc—slang for Avro Lancaster bomber

Laubfrosch—German device for detecting *H2S* emissions

Lichtenstein—German Airborne Intercept radar

LMF—Lack of Moral Fibre

Mae West—life-saving waistcoat for sea survival, named after famous American actress

Mammut—German early warning radar

Mandrel—radio jamming saturation of German early-warning system

Manna—air operation to supply starving Dutch, Apr-May 1945

MBE—Member of the Order of the British Empire

MC—Medium-capacity blast effect bomb. Manufactured in 250, 500, 1000, 4000, 12,000 and 22,000 pound sizes

Met—weather report - meteorological conditions

MEW—Ministry of Economic Warfare

MiD—Mention in Despatches

Millennium—first 1000-bomber raid, conducted against Cologne, May 1942

Monica—British electronic device for warning bomber crews of approaching enemy night fighters

Musical—Prefix added to marking techniques when Oboe Mosquitos did primary marking

NAAFI—Navy, Army and Air Force Institute. Provided services to members of the British and Allied armed forces

Naxburg—German ground-based radar used for tracking H2S emissions

Naxos—German airborne radar for tracking H2S

Neptun—another German AI radar, used later in the air war

Newhaven—technique for ground marking targets with flares or target markers, blind-dropped by H2S or Oboe, and confirmed by visual identification of target. Termed "H2S Newhaven" or "Musical Newhaven," depending on target-finding aid used

Nickeling—propaganda leaflet raids

Noball—code name for a V1/V2 site

OBE—Officer of the Order of the British Empire

Oboe—British electronic blind bombing device, used by Pathfinders for target marking

Obviate—Lancaster operation against Tirpitz, Oct 1944

Occult—system of beacons positioned along British coast, with a secondary belt further inland, that flashed Morse code signals to approaching aircraft to help them fix their location

OKL—Oberkommando der Luftwaffe—Luftwaffe headquarters

OKW—Oberkommando der Wehrmacht—Armed Forces headquarters

Operational—RAF slang for anything that works

ORB—Operations Record Book

ORS—Operational Research Section

OCU—Operational Conversion Unit

Ops—combat operations or missions

OTU—Operational Training Unit

Pancake—slang for crash-landing aircraft with landing gear retracted

Parametta—technique for ground marking targets with coloured Target Indicators (Tis) blind-dropped by H2S or Oboe. Called "H2S Parametta" or "Musical Parametta," depending on target-finding aid used

Perfectos—British electronic device that triggered German IFF equipment

PFF—Pathfinder Force, No. 8 Group, Bomber Command

Photoflash—19 pound or 40 pound 4.5 inch bomb produced a photographic flash when bomb was released, so camera on aircraft could photograph bomb release point

Pickwick—codename for instruction to Main Force from Pathfinders to bomb upwind edge of target smoke

Pink Pansy—2700 pound red target marker

Piperack—British airborne device for jamming German AI radars

Plunder—British 21st Army Group crossing of Rhine R., Mar 1945

Pointblank—bombing directive by Joint Chiefs of Staff for bombing priorities of Combined Bomber Offensive, June 1943

POW—Prisoner of War

PPI—Planned Position Indicator

Prang—slang for crash, destroy or damage an aircraft severely

Pundit—technique to identify friendly airfields to aircrews by flashing Morse signals

Ramrod/Circuses—codenames for1941 Fighter Command effort to lure Luftwaffe into battle by selective bombing of ground targets with a few heavily-escorted bombers

Red Blob—250 pound red target marker

Sägebock—German electronic device for detecting IFF emissions from Allied aircraft

SASO—Senior Air Staff Officer

Scarecrow—mythical German pyrotechnics designed to simulate destruction of a bomber in flight. In fact, all alleged *Scarecrows* were genuine mid-air explosions

Schräge Musik—"Hot or slanted" jazz music. German term for upward-firing cannons mounted on night fighters

Scrubbed—RAF slang for operation cancelled

Second Dickey—RAF slang for a second pilot or a new aircraft captain flying with an operationally-seasoned crew to gain experience prior to taking his own assigned crew out on their first operation

Serrate—British electronic device used for homing on radar emissions from German aircraft

SHAEF—Supreme Headquarters Allied Expeditionary Force

Shaker—1942 target identification technique employing incendiary bombs dropped by *Gee*-equipped marking aircraft

Shiver—jamming device used against *Würzburg* GCI radars

Shooting a line—slang for exaggerating one's accomplishments. In the RAF, "shooting a line" was considered bad form

Sledgehammer—plan (instigated by Americans) for limited invasion of France 1942

Smoke Puff—sky marker for day/night blind bombing, filled with red, green, blue or yellow pigment, that left a persistent smoke stain in target area

SN 2—German AI radar

SOE—Special Operations Executive

SOSO—Senior Operations Staff Officer

Sky Marker Floater—250 pound cluster projectile with 27 coloured parachute flares

Spanner—early German infra-red airborne target detection device

Spoof—subsidiary attack to draw enemy night fighters away from Main Force

Sprog—slang for inexperienced aircrew, or newcomers to operations

Spot Fire—250 pound red, green or yellow target marker

Steinbock—German air attacks on London, 1940

Tail-end Charlie—slang for rear gunner in a bomber, or pilot of rear aircraft in formation

Take to the silk—slang for bail out of an aircraft

Tallboy—12,000 pound high-velocity deep penetration bomb

Thunderclap—originally planned as a massive air attack on Berlin to hasten German surrender. First proposed Aug 1944 for spring 1945, but not executed in its planned form

TI—Target Indicator. A 250 pound bomb case packed with 60 9-inch green, red or yellow candles, or a 1000 pound bomb case packed with 200 candles

Tiger Force—RAF (and Dominion) component tasked to assist Americans in strategic bombing of Japan

Tinsel—jamming of German fighter radio communications and control channels

Torch—Allied invasion of northwest Africa, Nov 1942

Totalize—First Canadian Army attack toward Falaise, Aug 1944

Tractable—follow-up First Canadian Army attack to close Falaise Gap, Aug 1944

Ultra—signals intelligence derived from penetration of German *Enigma* cypher machines

USAAF—United States Army Air Force

Varsity—airborne operation to establish a bridgehead on east bank of Rhine R., Mar 1945

VC—Victoria Cross

VCAS—Vice-Chief of the Air Staff

VE-Day—Victory in Europe Day, 8 May 1945

Vegetable—air-dropped sea mine

Veritable—First Canadian Army attack on Rhineland, Feb-Mar 1945

VHF—Very High Frequency (radio)

Village Inn—British tail-mounted, rear-looking warning radar

VJ-Day—Victory over Japan Day, 15 Aug 1945

WAAF—Women's Auxiliary Air Force

Wanganui—sky-marking targets with coloured flares and markers blind-dropped by *H2S* or *Oboe*

Wasserman—German early-warning radar

Whitebait—codename for summer 1943 Bomber Command raids on Berlin

Wilde Sau—"Wild Boar," German "freelance" night fighter

Wimpy—slang for Vickers Wellington bomber

Window—strips of metallic foil precisely cut to wavelength of enemy radar, air-dropped in bundles to confuse those radars with a saturation of false echoes. Also called "chaff"

Wingco—slang for wing commander rank

Wizard—slang for first-class, or deserving of highest praise

Würzburg—German ground-controlled interception radar

"**Y**" **Aircraft**—Bomber Command aircraft equipped with *H2S*

Ypsilon—German night fighter control system

Zahme Sau—"Tame Boar," German ground controlled night fighter

Zephyrs—averaged winds aloft provided by selected crews and broadcast to all participating bombers on a raid

Select Bibliography

405 Squadron Operations Record Book, 7 May 1945. Dept of History & Heritage, Dept of National Defence, Ottawa, nd.

408 Squadron History. Stittsville, Ontario: Aviation Bookshelf, 1984.

424 Squadron History. Bottomley, Nora. Stittsville: Hangar Bookshelf, 1985.

Aders, Gerhard. *History of the German Night Fighter Force 1917–1945*. London: Jane's, 1979.

Ardery, Philip. *Bomber Pilot*. Lexington: University Press of Kentucky, 1978.

Bashow, David L. All the Fine Young Eagles. Toronto: Stoddart, 1996.

Beevor, Antony. *The Fall of Berlin 1945*. New York: Viking, 2002.

Bekker, Cajus. *The Luftwaffe War Diaries*. London: MacDonald, 1967.

Bennett, D.C.T. *Pathfinder*. London: Mueller, 1958.

Bergander, Götz. *Dresden im Luftkrieg*. Cologne: Böhlau Verlag, 1978.

Bishop, Arthur. *Courage in the Air - Canada's Military Heritage*. Vol 1. Toronto-Montreal: McGraw-Hill Ryerson, 1992.

Blair, Clay *Hitler's U-Boat War—The Hunted 1942-1945.* New York: Modern Library, 2000. 705.

Boiten Theo, and Martin Bowman, *Battles With the Luftwaffe—The Bomber Campaign Against Germany 1942–1945*. London: HarperCollins, 2001.

Bomber Harris Trust. *A Battle for Truth*. Agincourt: Ramsey, 1994.

Bowyer, Chaz. *History of the RAF.* London: Bison, 1988.

Braddon, Russell. *Cheshire VC*. London: Evans Brothers, 1954.

Braham, Bob. *Scramble*. London: Frederick Muller, 1961.

Brickhill, Paul. *Dam Busters*. London: Evans Brothers, 1951

Britain. Air Historical Branch. *The Rise and Fall of the German Air Force 1933–1945*. London: Army and Armour Press, 1983.

British Directorate of Air Staff, Ministry of Defence. *British Air Power Doctrine*. AP 3000. 3rd Edition. Norwich: Her Majesty's Stationery Office, 1999.

Brophy, Pat, Art De Breyne et al. "The RCAF Years—The Andy Mynarski Story." RCAF Museum, Trenton. Video.

Byers A.R., ed. *The Canadians at War 1939–1945*. Westmount, Quebec: The Reader's Digest Ass'n of Canada, 1986.

Caidin, Martin. *Black Thursday*. New York: E.P. Dutton, 1960.

Cantril, Hadley, ed. *Public Opinion 1935–1946*. Princeton: Princeton University Press, 1951.

Carter Kit C., and Robert Mueller, eds. *The Army Air Forces in World War II—Combat Chronology 1941–1945*. Washington: US Government Printing Office, 1973.

Cassels, Ron. *Ghost Squadron*. Winnipeg: Ardenlea Publications, 1991.

Charlwood, Don. *No Moon Tonight*. Sydney: Goodall, 1990.

Churchill, Winston S. *Their Finest Hour* Boston: Houghton Mifflin, 1949.

Churchill, Winston. *The Second World War.* Vol 2. New York: Time-Life Books, 1959.

Cooper, Matthew. *The German Air Force 1933-1945*. London: Jane's, 1981.

Cornwell, John. *Hitler's Pope—The Secret History of Pius XII*. New York: Penguin, 1999.

Coughlin, Tom. *The Dangerous Sky*. Toronto: Ryerson Press, 1968.

Craven, W.F. and J.L. Cate. *The Army Air Forces in World War II*. Vol 3. Chicago: University of Chicago Press, 1951.

D'Olier, Franklin et al. *The US Strategic Bomb Survey—Overall Report—European War—Sep 30, 1945*. Washington: US Government Printing Office, 1945.

Directorate of History and Heritage. *The RCAF Overseas—The Sixth Year*. Toronto: Oxford University Press, 1949.

Dunmore, Spencer & William Carter. *Reap the Whirlwind*. Toronto: McClelland and Stewart, 1991.

English, Allan D. *The Cream of the Crop–Canadian Aircrew 1939–1945*. Montreal & Kingston: McGill-Queen's University Press, 1996

Ethell, Jeffrey and Alfred Price. *The German Jets in Combat*. London: Jane's, 1979.

Fest, Joachim. *Speer—The Final Verdict*. London: Weidenfeld & Nicolson, 2001.

Ford, Brian J. *German Secret Weapons: Blueprint for Mars*. New York: Ballantine's, 1969.

Freeman, Roger A. *B-17 Fortress at War*. London: Ian Allan, 1977.

Gatefold Book of World War II Warplanes. London: Brown/Orbis, 1995.

Gibson, Guy. *Enemy Coast Ahead*. London: Goodall, 1946.

Godman, Peter. *Hitler and the Vatican—Inside the Secret Archives that Reveal the New Story of the Nazis and the Church*. New York: The Free Press, 2004.

Goebbels, Joseph. *Final Entries 1945*. New York, Putnam's, 1978.

Granatstein J.L. and Desmond Morton. *A Nation Forged in Fire–Canadians and the Second World War 1939–1945*. Toronto: Lester & Orpen Dennys, 1989.

Green, William. *Famous Bombers of the Second World War*. London: Hanover House, 1959.

———. *Famous Fighters of the Second World War*. Garden City, New York: Hanover House, 1960.

———. *Warplanes of the Third Reich*. London: Macdonald, 1970.

Greenhous, Brereton, and Hugh A. Halliday. *Canada's Air Forces 1914–1999*. Montreal: Art Global, 1999

Greenhous, Brereton, Stephen J. Harris, William C. Johnston, and William G.P. Rawling. *The Crucible of War 1939–1945: The Official History of the Royal Canadian Air Force*. Vol 3. Toronto: University of Toronto Press, 1994.

Halliday, Hugh A. "The First of Many–Canadians in the Royal Air Force 1920–1945." Paper given to the 6th Annual Air Force Historical Conference, Cornwall, Ontario, 21–23 June 2000.

Halpenny, Bruce Barrymore. *Action Stations—Military Airfields of Yorkshire*. Cambridge: Patrick Stephens, 1981.

Harris, Arthur *Bomber Offensive* London: Collins, 1947.

Harvey, J. Douglas. *Boys, Bombs and Brussels Sprouts*. Toronto: McClelland & Stewart, 1981.

Harvey, J. Douglas. *The Tumbling Mirth—Remembering the Air Force*. Toronto: McClelland and Stewart, 1983.

Hastings, Max. *Bomber Command*. New York: Dial Press/James Wade, 1979.

Hatch, F.J. *The Aerodrome of Democracy: Canada and the British Commonwealth Air Training Plan 1939–1945*. Ottawa: Ministry of Supply and Services, 1983.

Heitmann, Jan. "Destroying the Hamburg U-Boat Pens." in *After the Battle*. Vol 3. London: Battle of Britain International, 2001.

Held, Werner, and Holger Nauroth. *The Defense of the Reich–Hitler's Night Fighter Planes and Pilots*. New York: Arco, 1982.

Hewer, Howard. *In for a Penny, In for a Pound—The Adventures and Misadventures of a Wireless Operator in Bomber Command*. Toronto: Stoddart, 2000.

Holmes, Richard. *Battlefields of the Second World War*. London: BBC Worldwide, 2001.

Homze, E.L., and H. Boog. *The Luftwaffe*. Alexandria, Virginia: Time-Life Books, 1982.

Hutchinson, Robert. *War Beneath the Waves*. London: HarperCollins, 2003.

Irving, David. *The Destruction of Dresden*. London: Kimber, 1963.

Jablonski, Edward. *America in the Air War*. Alexandria, Virginia: Time-Life Books, 1982.

Jennings, Peter, and Todd Brewster. *The Century*. New York: Doubleday, 1998.

Johnen, Wilhelm. *Duel under the Stars*. London: William Kimber, 1969.

Jones, Ira. *King of the Air Fighters*. London: Greenhill Books, 1989.

Kaplan, Philip. *Bombers—The Aircrew Experience*. London: Aurum, 2000.

Kaufmann J.E., & H.W. Kaufmann. *Fortress Third Reich*. Cambridge, Massachusetts: Da Capo Press, 2003.

Keegan, John. *The Second World War*. London: Penguin, 1989.

Keegan, John ed., *The Times Atlas of the Second World War*. New York: Harper & Row, 1989.

Knell, Hermann. *To Destroy a City*. Cambridge, Massachusetts: Da Capo Press, 2003.

Large, David Clay. *Berlin*. New York, Basic Books, 2000.

Maas, Walter B. *The Netherlands at War*. London: np, 1979.

March, Peter R. *Eagles—Eighty Aircraft that Made History with the RAF*. London: Wiedenfeld and Nicolson, 1998.

Marion Donald, ed., *425 Alouette*. Ottawa: Dept of National Defence, 1978.

McQuiston, John H. *Tannoy Calling: A Story of a Canadian Airman Flying against Nazi Germany*. New York, Praeger, 1990.

Middlebrook, Martin, and Chris Everett. *The Bomber Command War Diaries: An Operational Reference Book, 1939–1945*. London: Penguin, 1990.

———. *The Berlin Raids–R.A.F. Bomber Command Winter 1943–44*. London: Viking, 1988.

———. *The Nuremburg Raid*. London: Viking, 1986.

———. *The Peenemünde Raid—The Night of 17/18 August 1943*. London: Penguin, 1982.

Milberry, Larry *Canada's Air Force—At War and Peace*, vol 2 Toronto: CANAV, 2000.

———. *Sixty Years—The RCAF and Canadian Forces Air Command 1924–1984*. Toronto: CANAV Books, 1984.

Morris, Jerrold. *Canadian Artists and Airmen 1940–1945*. Toronto: np, nd.

Morton, Desmond, and J.L. Granatstein. *Marching to Armageddon—Canadians and the Great War 1914-1919*. Toronto: Lester & Orpen Dennys, 1989.

Motiuk, Laurence. *Thunderbirds at War—Diary of a Bomber Squadron*. Nepean, Ontario: Larmot, 1995.

Moyes, Philip J.R. *Bomber Squadrons of the RAF and their Aircraft*. London: Macdonald, 1964.

Murray, Williamson. *The Luftwaffe—Strategy for Defeat* Secaucus, New Jersy: Chartwell, 1986.

Musgrove, Gordon. *Pathfinder Force—A History of 8 Group*. London: MacDonald and Jane's, 1976.

Neillands, Robin. *The Bomber War—The Allied Air Offensive Against Nazi Germany*. Woodstock, New York: Overlook Press, 2001.

Okumiya, Masatake, Jiro Horikoshi and Martin Caidin. *Zero*. New York: ibooks, 1956, 2002.

Overy, Richard. *Bomber Command 1939–1945—Reaping the Whirlwind*. London: HarperCollins, 1997.

———. "A Presentation to the Symposium on the Strategic Bomber Offensive, 1939–1945." RAF Staff College Bracknell, 26 March 1993

Page, Bette ed. *Mynarski's Lanc*. Erin, Ontario: Boston Mills, 1989.

Peden, Murray. *A Thousand Shall Fall*. Toronto: Stoddart, 1979.

Price, Alfred. *The Last Year of the Luftwaffe*. Osceola, Wisconsin: Motorbooks, 1991.

———. *A Pictorial History of the Luftwaffe 1933–1945*. London, Ian Allan, 1969.

Probert, Henry. *Bomber Harris–His Life and Times*. Toronto: Stoddart, 2001.

Rawlings, John D.R. *The History of the Royal Air Force*. London: Aerospace/Temple Press, 1984.

"RCAF Years, The." RCAF Museum, Trenton, Ontario, 1994. Video interviews, various contributors.

Richards, Denis. *The Hardest Victory,* New York: Norton, 1995.

Roberts, Leslie. *There Shall Be Wings—A History of the Royal Canadian Air Force*. Toronto: Clarke-Irwin, 1959.

Saward, Dudley. *Bomber Harris—The Authorized Biography*. London: Cassell, 1984.

Searby, John. *The Bomber Battle for Berlin*. Shrewsbury: Airlife, 1991.

Shirer, William L. *The Rise and Fall of the Third Reich—A History of Nazi Germany*. New York: Simon and Schuster, 1960.

Shores, Christopher, and Clive Williams. *Aces High—A Tribute to the Most Notable Fighter Pilots of the British and Commonwealth Forces in WWII*. London: Grub Street, 1994.

Shores, Christopher. *History of the Royal Canadian Air Force*. Toronto: Bison, 1984.

Skaarup, Harold. *Canadian Warbird Survivors 2002*. San Jose, California: Writers Club Press, 2001.

Smith, Nigel, & Peter Hart. *Tumult in the Clouds*. London: Hodder and Stoughton, 1997.

Speer, Albert. *Inside the Third Reich*. New York: Galahad, 1970.

Spetzler, Eberhard. *Luftkrieg und Menschlichkeit*. Göttingen, *Warriors of the Night*. pt 1. np, 1956.

Strachan, Hew. *European Armies and the Conduct of War*. London: Routledge, 2001.

Strike Hard, Strike Sure, The Story of Bomber Command. Vol 4. Portland: Allegro, 2001. Video.

Swetman, Bill. "The Avro Lancaster," in Jeffrey Ethell, ed. *The Great Book of World War Two Airplanes*. New York: Bonanza Books, 1984.

Symonds, Charles P., and Denis J. Williams. *Psychological Disorders in Flying Personnel of the Royal Air Force*. London: His Majesty's Stationery Office, 1947.

Tarrant, V.E. *The U-Boat Offensive 1914-1945*. London: Cassell, 1989.

Taylor, Frederick. *Dresden—Tuesday February 13, 1945*. New York: HarperCollins, 2004.

Terraine, John. *The Right of the Line—The Royal Air Force in the European War 1939–1945*. London: Hodder and Stoughton, 1985.

The Gatefold Book of World War II Warplanes. London: Brown/Orbis, 1995.

Tolliver, Raymond F., and Trevor J. Constable. *Fighter Aces of the Luftwaffe*. Fallbrook, California: Aero, 1977.

Tout, Ken. *Tanks Advance*. London: Grafton Books, 1989.

von Studnitz, Georg. *While Berlin Burns 1933–1945*. Englewood Cliffs, NJ: np, 1963.

Warriors of the Night. pt 1. Discovery Channel, 1999. Video.

Webster, Charles, and Noble Frankland. *The Strategic Air Offensive Against Germany*. Vol 1. London: Her Majesty's Stationery Office, 1961

Wells, Mark K. *Courage and Air Warfare—The Allied Aircrew Experience in the Second World War*. London: Frank Cass, 1995.

Wheeler William J., ed. *Flying Under Fire—Canadian Fliers Recall the Second World War*. Calgary: Fifth House, 2001.

Willmott, H.P. *The Second World War in the East*. London: Cassell, 1999.

Wilmot, Chester. *The Struggle for Europe*. London: Wordsworth, 1998.

Zimmerman, David. *Britain's Shield—Radar and the Defeat of the Luftwaffe*. Stroud, United Kingdom: Sutton, 2001.

ARTICLES AND PAPERS

"Airfields of Yorkshire." *Flypast* No. 207 (Oct 1998).

Birrell, Dave. "Dambuster Navigator." *Airforce* 27, 1 (2003).

——. "Sergeant Pilot Albert Stanley Price: The First of the 10,000." *Airforce* 23, 2 (1999).

——. "VR-X Terminator, The Greatest of the Canadian Lancs." *Airforce* 25, 4 (2002).

Bourdon, Buzz. "The Survivors." *Airforce* 26, 2 (2002).

Bushby, Jack, RAF. "After the Great Escape." Reprinted in *Airforce* 18, 2 (1994).

"Canadians Who Served with the Halifax Bomber Recollections." Trenton, Ontario: Halifax Memorial, RCAF Museum. Various contributors.

Clodfelter, Mark A. "Culmination Dresden: 1945." *Aerospace Historian* (Sep 1979).

Dumigan, Eric. "Celebrating 60 Years of Flying." *Airforce* 27, 4 (2003–4).

Feldmann, Hartmut. "From Heinkel to 'Stormbird'." *Flypast* No. 265 (2003).

Fraser-Mitchell, Harry. "From Hell, Hull and Halifax, Good Lord Deliver Us." *Aeroplane* (May 2003).

——. "Halifax Construction." *Aeroplane* (May 2003).

——. "Second to None."*Aeroplane* (May 2003).

Goodwin, H. Terry "Hugh Hay, DSO, DFC—Top Navigator?" *Airforce* 24, 1 (2000).

——. letter to editor, *Airforce* 25, 4 (2001).

Gray, Peter W. "Dresden 1945—Just Another Raid?" *Royal Air Force Airpower Review* 4, 1 (2001).

Halliday, Hugh A. "The Mysteries of Gongs." *Airforce* 27, 4 (2003–4).

Holmes, Harold W. "The First of Many." *Airforce* 18, 1 (1994).

James, Lyle. "A Bomber Pilot's Diary." *Airforce* 19, 3 (1995).

Johnson, Vic "The Quest for 'M for Mike.' " *Airforce* 21, 4 (1998).

Lennie, Peter S. "As I Remember the Day." *Airforce* 19, 2 (1995).

Middlebrook, Martin. "Bomber Command's War—The Turning Points." Pt 2. *Flypast* 206 (1988).

ææ, Martin "Bomber Command's War—The Turning Points." Pt 3. *Flypast* 207 (1998).

Mitchell, Alan W. "Bomber Crews Were Men with a High Quality of Courage." *Gaggle and Stream*, journal of the Bomber Command Association of Canada (Aug 2002).

Morrison, Lloyd C. "Mo." "Our War Just Ran Out." *Airforce* 19, 2 (1995).

Mutch, Sandy. "Retreat from Hamburg—Maximum Effort by RCAF 6 Group, 31 March 1945." *Airforce* 23, 4 (2000).

Nicholls, Mark. "Bomber Survivors." Bomber Command *Flypast* Special, Classic Series No. 13.

Nyznik, Paul. "A Canadian Hero in the Royal Air Force." *Airforce* 25, 1 (2001).

——. "Pathfinder!" *Airforce* 21, 1 (1997).

Oleynik, Paul "Memories of Scram." *Airforce* 10, 2 (1986).

Price, Alfred. "He 177 Greif—The Luftwaffe's Lighter." *International Air Power Review*, 11 (2003–4).

——. "The Messerschmitt 262 Jet Fighter—Missed Opportunity or Impossible Dream?" *Royal Air Force Air Power Review* 4, 2 (2001).

Roberts, John F. "Memories of 405 Pathfinder Squadron and the Last Flight Home." *Gaggle and Stream* 4 (2003–4).

Saunders, Wayne. " 'G' for [G]inx—The Bizarre Tale of 425 Squadron's Cursed Aircraft." *Airforce* 23, 3 (1999).

Shannon, Norman. "The Cattle Boat Brigade." *Airforce* 20, 3 (1996).

Sonderstrom, Alan. "Night Raid on Happy Valley." *Airforce* 27, 1 (2003).

Stafford-Clark, D. "Morale and Flying Experience." Reprinted in Alan W. Mitchell, "Bomber Crews Were Men with a High Quality of Courage." *Gaggle and Stream* (Aug 2002).

Sutherland, Clarence B. "Air Gunner's Diary." *Airforce* 22, 1 (1998).

Williams, Frank C. "The Raid on the Dams—Part One: Preparation." *Airforce* 9, 2 (1985).

———. "The Raid on the Dams—Part Two: The Attack." *Airforce* 9, 3 (1985).

———. "The Raid on the Dams—Part Three: Back Home." *Airforce* 9, 4 (1986).

Index

Page numbers for illustrations are in **boldface**.